LEWIS THOMPSON

JOURNALS OF AN INTEGRAL POET

Volume One — 1932 to 1944

LEWIS THOMPSON

JOURNALS OF AN INTEGRAL POET

Volume One — 1932 to 1944

Edited with Introduction and Commentary
by
Richard Lannoy

First Edition

Fourth Lloyd Productions, Burgess, Virginia.

The complete papers of Lewis Thompson are held in trust at
Washington State University, Pullman, Washington, USA.
The editor and publisher greatly appreciate
the University's permission and access
to these materials.

Fourth Lloyd Productions
512 Old Glebe Point Road
Burgess, VA 22432
e-mail: stodart@kaballero.com
www.richardstodart.com

Printed in the USA by Lightning Source Inc.
ISBN 0-9 717806-1-7 paperback
Library of Congress Control Number: 2006937707
Edited by Richard Lannoy

Book and cover design by Richard Stodart
Composition by Richard and Nancy Stodart

Cover photograph of Lewis Levien Thompson,
Trivandrum, India, 1941

I certainly do not know 'where I am': one will never know and Reality has no 'where'. One's individuality is pure paradox—resolutely nowhere in all directions. Yes, perhaps it is true that this must be cancelled by one's becoming resolutely everywhere in all directions so that one may consciously reach the Unnameable prior to both—but what a bore! How can passion harness itself to such a sickening programme? For passion is direct and simple, intransigent. Well, of course I cannot penetrate to what I really want to say....

Letter to Ella Maillart, 7.IX.1941

CONTENTS

ACKNOWLEDGEMENTS

I wish to thank Washington State University, Pullman, WA, for granting me access to the Lewis Thompson Archive, and for permission to publish this generous selection from Lewis Thompson's journals, of which they hold the Worldwide copyright.

I would also like to express my deep gratitude to the family of Lewis Thompson for the trust they placed in me to conduct my research in complete freedom since the 1950's.

Although I never met Lewis Thompson—he died four years before I reached India—I have had the good fortune to meet virtually all his friends in India. His last living colleague, Raja Rao, the renowned metaphysical novelist, died in July 2006 at the age of ninety-eight. Among those I met who knew Thompson well and with whom I became close friends, I would particularly like to acknowledge Blanca Schlamm (Atmananda)—who discussed at length Thompson the man, his wide-ranging vision of life, the nature of his thought, spiritual endeavours and his prodigiously voluminous writings; Ella Maillart, the Swiss explorer and author; and Deben Bhattacharya.

Among others, Earl Brewster, the Buddhist painter and Thompson's American host in the Himalayan foothills; Dr. S.R. Ranganathan, the eminent library scientist with whom Thompson had discussions for many years on spiritual matters; and Dr. Alice Boner, a versatile Swiss Indologist—all helped me to form a picture of this elusive and extremely subtle man. To more than a dozen others who figure in these pages I owe a debt for much interesting information on Thompson.

Apart from Sri Aurobindo, Ramana Maharshi and Sri Krishna Menon, the only two individuals of importance in Thompson's peripatetic life I have not met are a Trivandrum friend, Ure, who looked after his musical scores, and Alan Chadwick at Ramana Maharshi's ashram, who provided him with financial support in South India.

I would also like to mention the help I received from Pupul Jayakar, Momin Latif, Dalu Jones, Raimonda Buitoni and Count Nicolo Sella di Monteluce in connection with the publication of *Mirror to the Light*, by Ian Fenton at Coventure, which includes a selection I edited of more than 500 of Thompson's aphorisms—from a total of over 7000—the philosophical backbone of the Archive.

I also acknowledge Stephen Spender and Elias Canetti, for their significant professional help; Andrew Harvey, who brought the appreciation of a poet's sensitivity to *Black Sun: The Collected Poems of Lewis Thompson*; Professor Fritz Blackwell, Head of the Asian Department at Washington State University, who provided abundant friendly support; Joseph Geraci, for his unfailing help and editorial acumen.

I would finally like to thank my publishers at Fourth Lloyd Productions, Richard and Nancy Stodart, for their dedication to the task of bringing Lewis Thompson's integral vision of Reality to as many readers as possible, and Stuart Bradford and Steve Haines for their generous financial contributions to this project.

This account of all the people to whom I am grateful would not be complete without the many schoolchildren, Thompson's pupils at Rajghat, who, in our chats together when they had already reached adolescence, impulsively expressed their admiration for their former teacher.

by his father, but this lasted only for a short time until the latter's death in 1928. However, there is no reference to this episode in the poignant notes on his early life which he thought worthy to record, and no more than a passing reference to the period when he worked at a City bank on Gracechurch Street. His sisters have a genuine, almost total forgetfulness about their early years, while Lewis, on the other hand, remembered much but had no great desire to leave any permanent record of daily events unconnected with the spiritual life. He kept a journal from 1937 to the end of his life but confined his account to inner events, or to experiences where the inner and outer fused into an inseparable whole. In this respect he was scrupulously attentive to detail and wrote profusely and concretely, with utmost regard for factual accuracy and sensuous imagery.

At the age of fourteen, Thompson was befriended by a Woodford draper called Harding who was a Buddhist and he began to read earnestly in the spiritual literature of the East. He caused some consternation at home when he was found burning incense in his room. From then on there was an appreciable distancing from his family. The inheritance of a small legacy from his aunt in West Molesey gave him financial independence for some years.

Lewis was set apart from family and friends less through any conspicuous artistic talent (with the exception of a beautiful voice as a member of the school choir) than through singleness of focus and the consistency with which he concealed the true direction of his interests as long as he remained in Europe. Apart from wide reading in adolescence of English, French and German literature, his focus was exclusively on the religious experience, the cultural and psychological refinement of which we speak of as spirituality. He appears to have early on developed a gracious but formal mask of correct and considerate behaviour, pronounced by his need to protect his hypersensitivity. This is consistent with the formal elegance of his early prose style and his conviction that the deepest spiritual realism is always impersonal. But his courtesy springs from a source other than the mere need for a mask. 'If I remember', he writes in 1940, 'the old courtesy that E.C. admired: it was simple and beautiful because really genuine, it expressed the only perfect aristocracy, that of the psychic being.'

With greater maturity he was to develop a talent for highly communicative personal relationship, resourceful consideration for others and a refined tenderness of sensibility which could at once be breathtakingly intimate, warm-hearted, unegoistic and impersonal. There would always remain an essential part of him which was detached, even at moments of fieriest passion. As a young man who left home to live in rented London accommodation, he startled all whom he came to know well with his reckless indifference to earning money and building a career. As Yeats says, 'a gentleman is a man whose principal ideas are not connected with his personal needs and his personal success'. Thompson transformed the traditional qualities of the gentleman into a supple, searching and refined sophistication—with the feeling for style of the Continental *litterateur*, muted by English indifference. This un-English component should not be underestimated, although there is little or nothing in his background to account for his almost Rilkean subtlety, unsupported as it was by affluence or extended exposure to life on the Continent. One unusual detail: he experimented with the Mexican hallucinogen Peyote in 1932; few Englishmen would have ventured to do so at that date even had they had the ingenuity to track it down. An extremely agile mind and passionate critical spirit misled some to believe him the pure intellectual type, whereas he was essentially a man of imagination, a poet rather than a scholar or mystic. There is no doubt whatever that he displayed an astonishingly clear and penetrating intellect, and that he made a strong impression on the likes of Sir Edward Denison Ross, then Director of the School of Oriental Studies at London University. Ross befriended the intensely studious young man and gave him free rein to use the School's library. What he almost certainly did not realise, for it was a category of mental ability that had no name in the Anglo-Saxon academic world in those days—nor indeed is commonly recognised nowadays either: that Thompson was that rare being, a man of *spiritual intellect*, a conjunction which many would vulgarly believe to be a contradiction.

Nevertheless Denison Ross was an important enough figure in Thompson's life to have one of the sections in the latter's Collected Poems, as drafted in 1949 in Benares, dedicated to him. Ross opened up to him the whole grand vista into Oriental Culture, as it was then called, such as few men in the 1920's could have done. The year Thompson was born, 1909, Aurel Stein returned from his first three spectacularly successful expeditions to the Silk Road with the most extensive collection of priceless manuscripts ever to be gathered from that vast Central Asian region, most of it Buddhist in origin—treasure comparable in richness to the discovery of Tutankhamun's Tomb. Ross, who started life as Principal of the high-grade Calcutta Madrasa of Islamic Studies, was put in charge of compiling the initial inventory of tens of thousands of Stein's finds deposited at the British Museum. So it was through Ross that Thompson obtained a notion of the depth, extent and complexity, of the Central, Southern and East Asian Buddhist heritage, when most English enthusiasts, mystics, occultists had little notion of this huge body of tradition. Among his few friends who dabbled in this heritage, or who had connections with the Theosophists, their acquaintance with Buddhism was confined to, say, a handful of Hinayana texts translated from Pali, and a similar level of reading in Mahayana Buddhism. The Pan-Asian purview of Ross, which Thompson took on board, was to have a lasting effect on how he viewed Asian culture and India's seminal role in the spread of Buddhism. He also picked up from Ross some knowledge and high respect for Islamic culture, particularly Sufism.

In considering Thompson's formative years, we should bear in mind this much less familiar and undervalued path into Modernism—literary, aesthetic and spiritual—which he chose to follow, in the steps of literary figures such as Yeats, Ezra Pound, Arthur Waley and Count Herman Keyserling. Of cardinal importance to this alternative approach was its insistence on the substantiality of mental process. This was as true of occultism—hugely attractive to the intelligentsia at that time—as of psychoanalysis and of mysticism, together with a concentration on symbols as a key to insight important to a young poet.

The Influence of W.B.Yeats

Esoteric symbolism, which did have authentic ancient roots, however synthetic and sentimentalised it may have become in the hands of late 19th century occultists, is what Yeats found so satisfying, and so useful in his poetry, through association with the Order of the Golden Dawn. Yeats' input into the mystical sphere became a central influence on early twentieth century literature. Occult practice and growing acquaintance amongst the intelligentsia with the world's greatest mystics in a new global context, were founded on the disciplined and examined consciousness, and in that respect were related to the psychological and psychoanalytical sciences of the time. Like scientists—indeed, some were scientists—they were enlarging the boundaries of the natural, so that spiritual experience could be assimilated into the newly secularised mind.

With the astonishingly absorptive capacity of a still uncertainly secular young mind, Thompson tapped into this rich vein of speculative and spiritual thought, as can be seen by scanning his check list of cultural events with which he had some contact in the 1920's. For example, he made an exhaustive study of all the latest scholarly publications on William Blake, a central influence throughout his life; the explosion of Rimbaud's *Les Illuminations* and *Un Saison en Enfer* into the consciousness of Continental Europeans had a particularly incandescent effect upon the young Englishman's imagination; and he attended Keyserling's lectures on Asian spirituality at the Trocadero in Paris, at which for the first time in Western history a major literary personality presented a convincing and respectful picture of Eastern religion on equal terms with that of Europe. No doubt Lewis was an impressionable young man who had yet to view all these riches with anything like ordered clarity. But one thing stands out at this early point in Thompson's life: his brilliant, diamond-like spiritual purity and acuteness of mind. He was so ablaze with inner light that nobody quite knew how to handle him; the numerous misunderstandings to which this lead, of course, were extremely painful to an exceptionally shy and hypersensitive young man. Socially and academically a complete nobody, a stranger to privileged circles, nevertheless Thompson had an unerring eye for spiritual authenticity. This would always be his greatest strength and get him out of trouble when isolation would have immobilised any individual less sure in judgement. A lone figure, he would always inhabit a Gobi Desert of solitude. Yet—with a genius that baffles—he would never diverge from the centrality of the Great Tradition—as the universal spiritual culture has been valued for three millennia. Thompson may have looked like a rank outsider. He was not: he was at the heart of things from start to finish.

Yeats was certainly a prime influence, and no more so than in Thompson's efforts to come to terms with his own unusually distinctive and puzzling identity. To this end, he studied closely the complex schema of human types presented in *A Vision* devised by Yeats and, though unacknowledged, also by George Yeats, William's wife. She too was a highly gifted interpreter of occult vision in her own right. Whatever we may think of that extraordinary book and its mediumistic transmission to Yeats by his long-suffering young bride, most conveniently it provides us with a ready-made character-study of Thompson. For he selected with Thompsonian precision from its twenty-eight human types which comprise the psychic 'clock' of spiritual development—Phase 17—as the sole model template to which his own personality most closely corresponded. In his terms, it fitted him perfectly. It certainly left a deep imprint on his self-perception and he was consciously guided by it in the mode of his relations to other people. The highly intricate diagram, which he copies out with such care, of the workings of that 'clock' indicates the importance which he attached to the Yeatsian system. But it is not easy to follow in a brief summation.

Yeats describes the 'true' Phase 17 type in the life cycle as chiefly concerned with expressing the creative imagination through *antithetical emotion*, certainly and without doubt a biographical constant that was omnipresent throughout Thompson's life. On the other hand, those who try to resist their true nature according to type are impelled towards enforced self-realisation, something that dogged Thompson throughout his sixteen years' residence in India and which he vigorously strove (and went on record for doing so) to avoid.

Yeats calls Phase 17 'the Daimonic Man (*Dai*monic, not *de*monic)...The Will is falling asunder...The separated fragments seek images rather than ideas' (very pertinent with regard to the imagery of his poems), and these the imagination 'must synthesise in vain, drawing with (imagination's) compass-point a line that shall represent the outline of a *bursting pod*.' It would be exactly the image of a *bursting pod* that the great Indian sage, Anandamayi, a Bengali woman, would apply to a person with Thompson's kind of problem: 'When one's problems are made more acute one feels disturbed and thereby one's Search will be intensified. Before thread can be spun and woven into cloth the pod in which the cotton was enclosed has first to burst open and be entirely destroyed. To prepare oneself really means to uproot completely the sense of "I".'

To continue with Phase 17: 'The being (in this phase) has for its supreme aim...to hide from itself and others this separation and disorder' (seeking images rather than ideas). It conceals them under the emotional Image derived from another phase (each Phase has its opposite, with which it is in tension): 'Seen by lyrical poets, of whom so many have belonged to the fantastic Phase 17, the man of this Phase becomes *an Image where simplicity and intensity are united*'—my italics for obvious reasons—'he seems to move among yellowing corn or under overhanging grapes.' This marvelously Blakean touch is utterly appropriate as a metaphor for Thompson's personal myth. If 'true to phase, the man of this type must turn all the synthetic power of the imagination to that task. He finds...a Mask of simplicity that is also intensity...The Will, when true to phase, assumes, in assuming the Mask, an intensity which is never dramatic but always lyrical and personal, and this intensity, though always a deliberate assumption, is to others but the charm of their being'.

Although somewhat obscure, the psycho-dynamics of Phase 17, such as the antithesis at its roots between simplification through intensity, do assist elucidation of the complex nature of our particular young poet. The man of Phase 17 selects some object of desire, but Fate snatches it away and he suffers a sense of loss (Thompson loses his spiritual master in India). Until the desired 'unity of being' is attained—and in this Phase 17 is prophetic—the imagination will be employed to isolate the desired image as *a conception in the mind*, a concern which, as we shall see, would very greatly exercise Thompson's attention to the end of his days.

'Perhaps all those who belong to Phase 17, at some time or other, in moments of fatigue, give themselves up to fantastic, constructed images (this is particularly evident in Thompson's later verse) or to an almost mechanical laughter.' I would guess that it was through the persistent fatigue from whichThompson would suffer, that he turned the 'mechanical laughter' in upon himself by writing endless dry and mechanistic sophistries in his journal because he was too exhausted to know when to stop. Yeats called this 'automatism', and Thompson adopted the word to describe these states when he switched to autopilot. To the dismay of those close to him, Yeats (who saw a lot of himself at Phase 17) would say that in those circumstances the Mask of simplification wears a smile of detachment. From Blanca Schlamm's frequent descriptions of Thompson five years before he died, when her memory of him was still fresh, I got the impression that, without knowing what Yeats characterised as the 'Mask of simplification', this was, she told me, precisely what happened to Thompson's facial expression: he called it his 'cardboard look'! Blanca was a close friend of his—they met daily—during the five years when Thompson was 'resident poet' at Jiddu Krishnamurti's school at Rajghat in Benares.

Again and again, Thompson's written self-portraiture in his journal mirrors the Yeats characterisation, especially the antithesis of simplicity and the honeycombed intricacy of what he frequently calls 'perversity' or, occasionally, 'automatism' which can run and run in an effort to escape from self-hatred. Thompson paid a terrible spiritual and psychological price to write about his inner struggle so accurately, truthfully—with 'the exactitude of a rose'.

The high-flown metaphors Yeats uses, the arcane symbols, the pedantic schemata of the 28 'incarnations' on the wheel of *A Vision*, do nevertheless possess psychological consistency and cogency, at least at Phase 17, which appears to apply to Yeats himself. The axial position of antithetical emotion is more than a characterological nicety. In later years, when things were getting really tough for Thompson, he worked with his contrary emotions in his poetry by making them the explicit basis for an entirely positive esemplastic enterprise with which to achieve 'unity of being' in an exemplary fashion.

His recklessness never waned. On the contrary, it increased with time. The change from the genial, mop-haired young Irish 'red-beard' to the astringent thinker, whose physical appearance is pared down equally by the Indian climate, is ample testimony to this. The situation of the man can be looked at in another way too—as an extraordinarily fruitful interplay between the Western will towards intellectual mastery and the sinuous flexibility of Eastern wisdom. Such was his fiery temperament that he de-

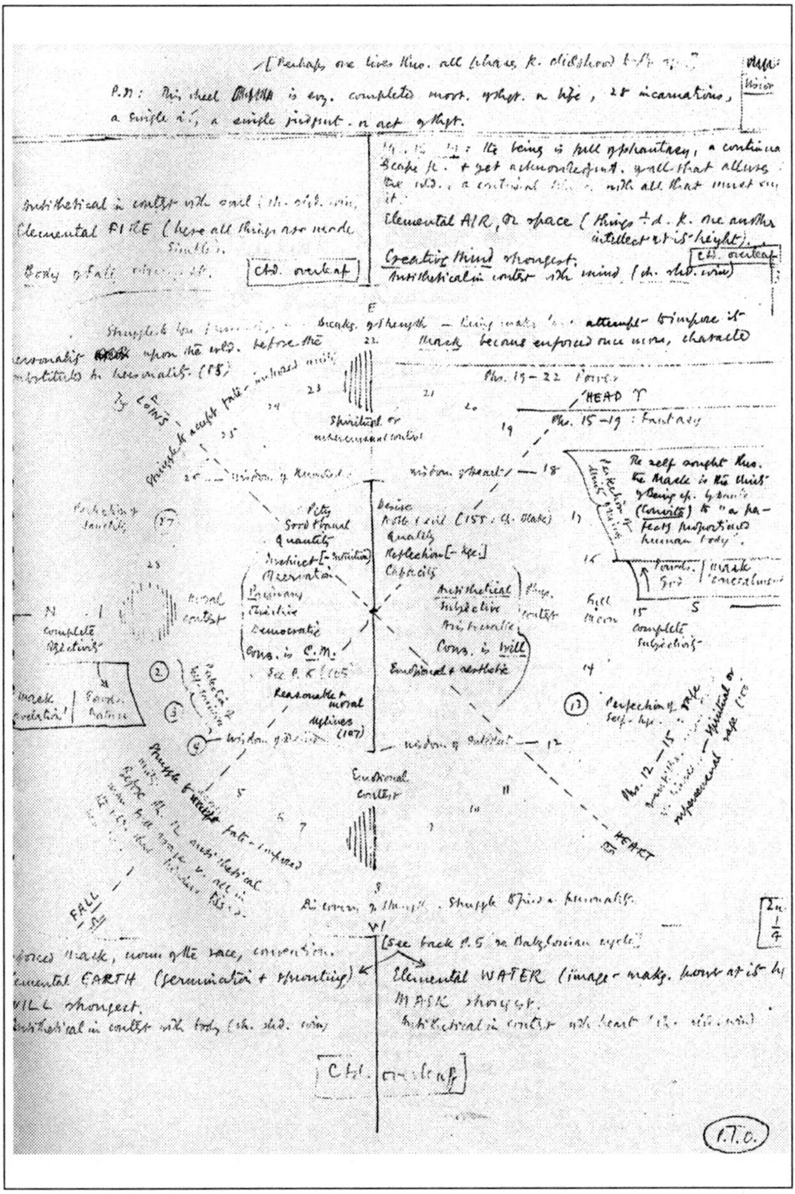

Fig. 4. Three pages of notes and extracts from W.B.Yeats, *A Vision*. The diagram is a faithful copy from the book. Thompson believed that Yeats's Phase 17 was an exact description of his own psychic nature.

liberately allowed others to think him ruthless and uncaring, even diabolical. If he found that others less strong-willed became disconcerted by the vehemence of his argumentation, he would accentuate it—to a fault—and thus provide them with an excuse to end the association with a free conscience!

Thompson came from a voluble family with Irish temper to match. In my interactions with them I never saw any reticence in their willingness to do battle for any cause about which they felt passionately. But when it came to talking about their mysteriously unremembered, but idolised son, brother or uncle, the Daimonic Man wore the Mask of simplification like a Cap of invisibility. Over many years of impecunious existence, especially in the punishing Gangetic climate, he had less of the necessary vital energy to sustain his charming extravagance of manner, his ravishing impulsiveness, humour and especially his radiant lyricism in the company of children amongst the fishermen's shacks on the beach at Madras. He also had a winning conversational generosity and beautifully clear expression of thought, particularly towards women, for whom he showed sympathetic interest and immense curiosity. Close friends—we see him here in correspondence with Ella Maillart and Ethel Merston, both of them highly intelligent observers—could plainly see the contrary pulls of his antithetical nature while still granting him his ability to resolve the duality by the act of writing. He was right to look upon his writing of a journal as yoga, and he particularly favoured the charming Picasso Rose Period 'saltimbanque' (from the same little band as Rilke writes about in his Fifth Duino Elegy) balancing acrobatically on a spinning ball, an archetype of perfect equilibrium maintained amidst life's unceasing contraries. As Blake would say, 'Without contraries is no progression'. And Thompson would say, 'We are never the same for two minutes at a time'.

Discovering Arthur Rimbaud

Long before Lewis left for India his move to independent lodgings was the decisive break from the security of his family home. It coincided with the first onset of profound inner unhappiness antithetical to moments of purest youthful joy. From the age of seventeen, throughout the remaining five years of his residence in Europe, he experienced almost unbearable anguish in the European environment. This was especially notable during the time he worked in a City bank. It was not so much that he found nothing which appealed to him in either the past or the present European life and culture. On the contrary, there is enough to deduce from his lists of cultural events and book-titles to indicate how varied were his enthusiasms. It was more a question of his own deep inner alienation, about which he writes graphically in our first chapter. Most immediately, his agony sprang from a feeling of helpless incapacity to communicate to close friends how deeply he experienced the molten intensity of his own fugitive moods of mystical elation and his abysmal plunges into despair. Above all, he realised, at eighteen, the impossibility of finding words to express, at the level of rational consciousness, states which went beyond reasoning and accidents of personality.

This anguish coincided with his early discovery of the poet Rimbaud (1854–91), who had abandoned at the age of twenty-two one of the most lyrically radiant outpourings of verse in all French literature. There is no doubt that Rimbaud inspired the making of Thompson as writer and spiritual pilgrim. Yet there is paradox here too, as he clearly indicates: 'It is perhaps because Rimbaud saw with terror, delight and despair the superior reality of certain states he entered that the 'sophisme magique' of words necessary to suggest his experiences as if for the sake of the rational consciousness seemed to him a lie, hopeless because unnecessary.' If Thompson was to write at all it could only be after having taken stock of his motives and of his experiences in the light of Rimbaud's rigour and searing truthfulness, his insistence on discarding the whole bourgeois way of life, bag and baggage. For the man with the *Mask of simplicity* writing itself is a kind of deceit, a necessary hypocrisy: 'The truth can not be told'. Inspired by Rimbaud, Thompson devotes his life to the conversion of this hypocrisy into an athletic instrument of truthfulness: here is born that peculiar tension which runs throughout everything he wrote. It is the dilemma of Chuang-Tzu: 'Tao cannot be defined. The one who knows does not speak. And the one who speaks does not know. Therefore, the Sage preaches the doctrine without words.' And still, Chuang-Tzu speaks...

Rimbaud is out to change man through poetry: 'the alchemy of the word'.* All revolutionary endeavour aims at the recuperation of alienated consciousness: the end of alienation is the end of language. This return to the original unity Chuang-Tzu calls 'entering the bird cage without making the birds sing', the Chinese for 'cage' being the same as 'return', 'song' the same as 'names'. In other words, 'returning to the place where names have no meaning', where the poetic image alone can express the inexpressible.

---

* 'L'alchimie du verbe'—this was to be the starting point of Thompson's entire enterprise. It is what he calls Transformation, his Yoga, the poet's path of transubstantiation, his counter-reformation. And it echoes the project of Rilke too: the transformation of everything *within*, of transforming the terrestrial into the 'invisible'.

During the first three decades of the twentieth century Rimbaud was widely respected as the archetype of modern anguish, the man of genius driven by extreme alienation to take up a life of wandering and reckless endeavour. His abrupt renunciation of poetry was seen as an eloquent comment on the crisis in literature and spirituality of the West. For Thompson, the crucial element in Rimbaud's life was the fact that a poet of genius had renounced literature out of an unbearable sense of spiritual failure. He saw in the 18-year-old Rimbaud an intensified mirror-image of his own strenuous aspiration, his disillusionment with organised religion and with a profession of letters on the verge of spiritual bankruptcy. Rimbaud was that rare being, a writer who had the courage to carry his protest against the lie of Western materialism to its extreme conclusion, to take upon himself the scandalous Way of the Cross, and live out the uncompromising agony of his desolation to an inglorious, silent end. Many writers have since been fired by the extravagant delinquency and rage of Rimbaud's denunciations. Thompson is not unique in the extent to which his life was transformed by this perilous example. What is remarkable is that he fuses the ambiguous inspiration which Rimbaud's example ignited in him with the seemingly incompatible discipline of Indian spirituality. The stubborn Rimbaud put himself beyond the reach of rescue in self-chosen exile at remote Harar in Ethiopia, trading arms in the mountains. Thompson's Harar is an ashram; for the penance of Rimbaud's silence he substitutes the burning-ground of the word: poetic aphorism.

This fascination with Rimbaud at a crucial period in Thompson's formative years rests on an interesting psychological affinity between the two men. Professor C.A. Hackett, a distinguished Rimbaud scholar points out: 'At every period in his life, Rimbaud was an absolutist. As a child he was either the outstanding pupil or the out-and-out rebel. As an adolescent he was a poet in an absolute sense because he demanded everything of poetry. The same sin of pride explains his absolutism as a trader, a way of life into which he converted all his power, all the strong determination which had once made him a prize pupil, a rebel, a poet.' In his recollection of his early years in Europe, Thompson describes himself in remarkably similar terms, though he refuses to call his fault pride, but rather 'will to the Absolute'. In a poem he says, 'It is not pride and not despair, but love.'

In one other respect Thompson reveals how close were his objectives to those of Rimbaud. Hackett speaks of 'a single imperious force by which, in different and apparently opposed ways, Rimbaud sought to reach one and the same end: his independence and maturity. They show quite clearly and unambiguously what was implicit in the whole of the poetic work, namely, that writing for Rimbaud was never a mere literary exercise but a continuous striving towards personal fulfilment.'

In terms of all Rimbaud's literary remains Thompson knew as much as anybody about his work and his life as had been published. He would therefore be well informed about the very difficult relationship which Arthur had with his exceedingly authoritarian, domineering and cantankerous mother. It was all recorded in his own writings and correspondence, and in the various first-hand accounts by members of the Rimbaud family and Arthur's friends and teachers who were close to him before he left Charleville, or later France. There is at least fifty times more material on Rimbaud's background and family than there is on Thompson's, even today when his nieces and nephew are still alive and can tell me no more than the little which they could. Since Thompson chose to view Rimbaud as his hero, exemplar, literary, and to some extent even his spiritual model, it was bound to cross his mind that the relationship between mother and son was at least psychologically closely similar to his own, despite enormous differences between the personalities of the two mothers, their personal circumstances, and the fact that Rimbaud did see his mother from time to time after he left for Paris, gave up writing poetry and travelled abroad. The truly appalling coldness with which Madame Rimbaud treated her son during the period of excruciating pain that he suffered in the last three months of his life following his amputation (his mother was at his bedside in Marseilles for that, and then left his sister with him and returned to run her farm in Roche), and her unrelentingly grim antagonism towards him right up to the moment of his death, would have been to Mrs. Thompson inconceivably unmotherly. Mrs. Thompson's African whip story is mild compared with Madame Rimbaud's grotesque treatment of Arthur and everyone else. There is, however, one trait that is shared in common by both women: their self-pity at having been 'deserted' by their sons, and their constant complaints to Arthur and Lewis of this supposedly unfeeling, even callous filial indifference. While both women were overbearing in their possessive attachment to their sons, they both treated their two respective daughters in a more balanced maternal fashion. In general, therefore, I am not inclined to be hard on Mrs. Thompson, except in one particular respect, her petty and dismissively casual, indeed thoughtless decision to have all Lewis's beautifully penned letters (save half a dozen that she mislaid) pulped for the wartime Salvage Campaign. For it was to his mother that Thompson sent detailed descriptions of his life abroad throughout his adult life once he left home. Disastrously, this leaves a gap in the rich literary archive which he left behind.

He himself raised 'description' to the small 'Vocabulary' of archetypal terms with which he structured his thought, particularly in his aphorisms. In what he wrote about his approach as a writer of a journal, Description is a key archetype. In his view it is the 'dross' which expresses only the individual's ego. By writing in this fashion to his mother he was 'exhausting' whatever might possibly obscure true vision. He knew from long experience, as Rimbaud did, that there was no way that he could relate to or be accepted by his mother in any other way than at the level of the ego. It is my feeling that Mrs. Thompson understood this, that despite their surface charm, Lewis was 'second-besting' her in those letters.

My knowledge of Mrs. Thompson, whom I never met, mostly comes from Deben Bhattacharya, the writer-collaborator with Thompson in the translation of the devotional poetry of the great Vaishnava Sahajin, Chandidas. Following Lewis's sudden death, Deben, whom I knew closely for forty five years until his recent death, having sent the celebrated English poet Edith Sitwell a copy which Thompson had only just finished typing, of his Collected Poems, gave up everything in India, leaving his wife and children with his family in Benares, and went to London to find a publisher for them. Despite help from Edith Sitwell, Stephen Spender, and introductions to distinguished English writers, like Arthur Waley and Sir Mortimer Wheeler, no publisher was interested in a recently deceased unknown English mystical poet. Meanwhile, Deben, with a heavy heart and full of presentiment that he would have to face an emotional and complex response, went off to Epsom to meet Mrs. Thompson and her grieving family. This was the first time that Deben had left India; it was the first time that the widow of an English soldier who had served in India had ever received a visit in her own home by an Indian. For Deben, a high-caste Brahmin (as penniless as Lewis had been in India), to enter the home of non-vegetarian English people who had a background of British army life in which, in a brief bizarre interlude, Deben himself had also served—and heartily detested—was comparable with Thompson's entry into the orthodox brahmin household of Dr. Ranganathan! Such are the complexities which follow the end of an imperial era.

Deben told me that Mrs. Thompson was inconsolable, but paradoxically keen all of a sudden, to see her son taken to the bosom of the British public as the golden boy poet—like Rupert Brooke, say—a sort of post-Rudyard Kipling Imperial bard, whose verse might go down well with readers of *The Daily Mail* who knew the latter's poem, *If*, by heart. It was almost impossible, unless he were to be cruelly plain-spoken, to disabuse Mrs. Thompson of her delusion. She besought Deben to come on frequent visits, and to stay in Lewis's old room, particularly as her grandchildren adored their legendary uncle's Indian friend. He did visit her as often as circumstances permitted, but with a sinking heart realised that Mrs. Thompson was transferring her affection for Lewis onto himself. He thought it would be in everybody's interests if he extricated himself from this situation, especially since he had no success whatever in finding a publisher.

Lewis's independent ways were a great trial to his mother's deep affection and concern, brought up as she was according to the strict code of conduct in Anglo-Irish Protestant families. In spite of his abrupt departure for India without prior warning, or even a hint as to his intention, nevertheless Lewis was always as considerate to her as long-distance correspondence would permit. He took pains to write her graphic letters from time to time in which he went out of his way to explain in simple language something of the depth and complexity, the seriousness and discipline involved in trying to fulfil his spiritual aspirations and extremely unusual way of life—the latter, of course, being the real sticking-point at which his mother lost all comprehension of what he was trying to do.

Although in their correspondence there was protestation of great affection on both sides, the thought of his mother's unyielding attitude towards the sense of his endeavours was the cause of much heart-searching by Lewis. He reflected on the problem in his journal and took into account the predictions of several detailed horoscopes he had cast for him that he might determine when it would be appropriate to pay his mother one last visit before she died. It transpired that his own death preceded hers. Meanwhile, he would write to her from Madras that he was treated as a member of the Ranganathan family, and hence there was no occasion for her to feel alarm. His oldest friend in India, P.K. Rajgopal, knew how deep was his distress on her behalf, so he would himself write Mrs. Thompson letters which depicted her son in glowing colours.

The ambivalence of family feeling towards him was expressed by persistent demands to know if he was *happy*, as if that alone would justify his long absence, without regard for what he might be trying to do by way of achievement. This was in spite of his repeated assertion in letters home (modestly free of pretentiousness or pomposity), that he cared nought for personal happiness and that happiness was irrelevant when striving towards discovery of the true nature of the Self and its relation to Ultimate Reality. Occasionally, he would confide to his journal that his life had been, ever since adolescence, one of isolation, loneliness and frustration, even though he had brought it all on himself by his own folly. Yet he would qualify this with a poignant reminder that his suffering was of the surface ego alone, while there persisted beneath all his tribulations a changeless and unshaken feeling of serenity and joy.

Thompson's 'Rimbaud'

I have beside me on my desk as I write one of Thompson's most important possessions, which travelled with him wherever he went: his *Collected Poems of Arthur Rimbaud*. This particular copy of the standard *Oeuvres Complétes* in the 1920s edition is unique, and an extraordinary object. Somewhere around 1939, Thompson had it rebound in order to incorporate a whole sheaf of additional pages. The job went to one of Dr. Ranganathan's most expert binders at the Library who, amongst other things, preserved the original rounded French corners on the pages that had to be added. Thompson chose the cloth for the binding with his usual care: a brilliant cerise silk which retains its intense hue even after it had travelled on Indian Railways and buses for ten years, and no doubt on occasion lay in the full Indian sun. But the book was very heavily used by its proud owner, so that when Blanca Schlamm passed it on to Ella Maillart after Lewis died it had to have the spine reinforced by Ella, using a durable Swiss adhesive tape—cadmium red, with lemon yellow label; so it has lost a little of its original Tantrik effect. Even so, it is a wonderfully charismatic object. Just to hold it and leaf through its browning pages, and feel the soft trimmed edges of its pages—enlarged so that it is now one and three-quarters inches thick—and the texture of its battered binding is, however faintly, to travel with it into the inscrutable depths of these vast lands through which it used to pass so frequently. The book is eight inches high by five inches wide, so that it fitted easily into the shoulder bag which travelled everywhere with Thompson, along with the black wallet which held strips of paper on which to write aphorisms or notes.

The book is a kind of modern Book of Hours, 'illuminated' by Thompson's annotations, pencilled-in English translations of Rimbaud's unusually rich and very special vocabulary. It also contains no less than one hundred and forty three pages of extremely densely written Thompson transcriptions of newly discovered Rimbaud manuscripts, lengthy quotations from the burgeoning literature on Rimbaud, handwritten copies of poems that had not yet been incorporated into this edition of the *Ouevres Complétes*, copies of newly unearthed correspondence, material relating to his years in Ethiopia, Egypt and Cyprus, and thirty pages, diligently transcribed, which describe the appalling details of Rimbaud's agonising last few months—the atrocious nineteen-day trek in a litter, in pouring rain from Harar to a ship in Aden when he was mortally ill with cancer, his amputation of a leg in Marseille, his return home to the monstrously cold and petulant Madame Rimbaud in the Ardennes, and his shattering death back in Marseille. One gets the impression that this latter task by Thompson provided a gauge for his own suffering: 'If I think I've got troubles just remember Rimbaud'.

This treasured book is not a sign of morbidity; on the contrary, most of its four hundred odd pages are a veritable touchstone of fiery inspiration. Of particular interest to me is the section with the seventeen-year-old schoolboy Rimbaud's reading list; eight books on alchemy and esotericism, *in their original editions*—from the provincial Charleville Municipal Library—that date between 1571 and 1732. Yet there are still people for whom Rimbaud was a snotty delinquent who was turned into a cult figure by a bunch of Parisian aesthetes and pederasts, when actually he was the first true 'adolescent' in the history of Europe, who also happened, when aged seventeen, to have 'written poetry unique not only in colour, force and imagination, but also in sureness of touch and technical perfection...' (Geoffrey Brereton, 1937). I also think that Thompson's *Rimbaud* is vivid evidence that Rimbaud was not an English eccentric who became a Primitivist in an exotic Eastern land out of a sense of Western cultural failure, but a creative and supremely French writer who gave equal weight to the great spiritual achievements of both the Eastern and Western worlds. Rimbaud's *Oeuvres Complétes* reveal his profound grasp of both heritages and is certainly the product of an incandescent poetic imagination, not of academic scholarship.

Plain Facts

The conditions and circumstances of Thompson's life in India are difficult to visualise half a century after his death, even by those familiar with his particular environment. Indeed, it might well be the case that recent visitors to India are likely to be under some misapprehension as to the material, physical and logistical conditions with which Thompson had to contend. For one thing, the new material affluence of the educated urban middle class has fallen like a dense screen between the Western observer and the India which was Thompson's daily environment. Even the religious climate of Hinduism has radically changed and has become increasingly materialistic. But of course the greatest change of all in terms of social relations between Indians and foreigners is that India was a part of the British Empire in Thompson's day, and for much of his residence a world war raged in the background.

Thompson was unusual in his principal charisma: a very un-English spiritual intellect. In a social context, therefore, he stuck out like a sore thumb. There was no cushioning class privilege, and the fact that he was British acted as a kind of social stigma amongst spiritually minded Indians, unless and until they got the measure of his insight.

What would have been the whites' attitude towards an Englishman of Thompson's inclinations in the India and Ceylon of the British Raj? Openly hostile. To virtually every person of white skin the soft-spoken, penurious Englishman would have been a total anathema, contemptible, a pariah, a traitor to his race, or perhaps a harmless, certainly a misguided, eccentric. Most Indians, on the other hand, would have a more ambiguous response, more courteous, more open-minded. But in South India, where Thompson lived for eleven years—he never returned to England—orthodox Brahmins would have nothing to do with him socially until they knew him well. In any case, the orthodox would never eat in the same room with a Britisher. There was a tremendous hullaballoo in the Ranganathan household when the great librarian invited him home, even though Thompson acted as a kind of 'unofficial guru' to Ranganathan, calling him back to his religious customs and beliefs following a Western education. In fact, Ranganathan told me that in spiritual matters he deferred to Thompson with complete absence of self-consciousness—one of the most remarkable admissions I've ever heard from the lips of an Indian, especially an eminent elderly scholar with an immaculately painted Ramaujan brow-mark of the highest Brahmin caste.

Certainly, to Indian Anglophiles, pro-British civil servants, officials, businessmen and professionals, Thompson would have been completely baffling. As the years went by and the class of Westernised, English-speaking urban people he encountered socially—a word I hesitate to use, for Thompson did not have a social life in the sense of drinks, dinner parties and whatnot—became much more numerous, Thompson would have seemed a very odd fish. Any Westerner who took a serious interest in Indian spiritual matters was so rare and usually so ill-informed, that he or she was approached by Indians with a certain amount of suspicion and a great deal of caution. Those Hindus vested with a degree of spiritual authority, such as priests, monks, university scholars, ashram inmates and disciples of well-known gurus, were accustomed to the crass ignorance of Westerners, or their naive credulity, were thus inclined to adopt an unbearably patronising manner or cold and remote grandeur befitting any contact with 'untouchable' barbarians (mlecchas). But Thompson did not fit any known category or type, not even that of the Western ashram devotee. But then even today, Thompson's style of writing on spiritual matters does not commend itself to Indian readers: it is 'too Western' for Indians, 'too Indian' for most Westerners with a conventional view of Indian spirituality! And of course

Thompson himself got on best either with open and unpretentious folk, or with those secure in their own culture, of which there used to be plenty in every class and most walks of life in those days, if many fewer now.

The fact that Thompson was impecunious is very important to our understanding of his situation in India. For a man who found the Indian climate more difficult to bear the longer he lived there (not uncommon amongst foreigners long resident), he literally could not afford to have a balanced and nutritious diet, nor obtain good medical attention during his serious bouts of illness, nor live in salubrious surroundings or decent accommodation for most, but not for all his seventeen years residence. There were occasions, such as his return to Ceylon, which is described in unusual detail in his journal here, when he was entirely comfortable, but usually these were welcome respites from poor conditions elsewhere, when he was recuperating from overwork and very debilitating living conditions. Ella Maillart described his low energy and incredibly listless bodily movements and style of lethargic walking with a note of despair and impatience. After her trek through the wastes of the Tibetan plateau with so very different and so much fitter an Englishman—Peter Fleming—Thompson's physical condition must have been exasperating for the oaken vigour of the Swiss Olympic skier!

To be as impecunious and dependent on the generosity of others (save for five years on a peon's miniscule wages at Rajghat School in Benares), made life exceedingly difficult for Thompson. There were no anti-biotics, malaria was endemic, typhoid fever frequent. Six foot two inches tall, he was visibly under weight. His temperament and zeal for work were such that he severely neglected himself, forgot to eat and suffered from debilitating disorders of the common sort. He often worked stupefyingly long hours in stifling libraries, the sweat pouring off him, engaged in exhausting intellectual effort and without anyone to look after him in a home that he could call his own. But he would have fought to the death had anyone challenged his right to live the way he chose.

The Indian Background

In a letter to his sister, Thompson says that, had he known when he left England exactly why he went to India, he probably would never have needed to go. But he certainly did not go to acquire scholarly knowledge of Indian culture. He thought that Europe had lost the continuity of its tradition of spiritual enquiry and direct manifestation of that tradition in living exponents or masters. At least in India he could meet those few exceptional men and women who still represented and manifested their traditions of unbroken spiritual gnosis. He knew that the interests of the Indian population now lay elsewhere—particularly in the struggle to achieve independence from the rule of his fellow countrymen. He neither studied the culture for its own sake nor concerned himself with the independence movement even though he was in full sympathy with its objectives.

As he himself indicated to a friend in a letter which provides the superscription to this book, there is no short and easy definition of the goal he set out to reach. In retrospect, without doing too much violence to his way of seeing things, it is possible to describe his journey of self-discovery within the universal framework of the *Philosophia Perennis*, of which Aldous Huxley writes: 'the phrase was coined by Leibniz; but the thing—the metaphysic that recognised a divine Reality substantial to the world of things and lives and minds; the psychology that finds in the soul something similar to, or even identical with, divine Reality; the ethic that places man's final end in the knowledge of the immanent and transcendent Ground of all being—the thing is immemorial and universal.' (Aldous Huxley, *The Perennial Philosophy.*)

Thompson had read widely and attentively in the literature of this universal tradition. He was steeped in the metaphorical language of William Blake, and he was a keen reader of Yeats. The sobriety of the Christian mystics—Meister Eckhart, Jacob Boehme, St. Theresa of Avila, St. John of the Cross, made a lasting impression. But a European context in which contemplative Christian spirituality could be lived, not merely studied and thought about, was beyond his reach.

He was also well acquainted with Buddhist literature. However, he lived at a time of bookish and intellectual bias; the very small minority who interested themselves in such matters preferred the armchair academic safety of studying 'Indian philosophy' to the more challenging course charted by India's spiritual masters and their implicit call of face-to-face encounter. In their seclusion, most such Europeans declined, in any active sense, to face the fundamental imperative of all Eastern aspirants: direct perception of divine Reality through the adoption of various contemplative techniques. According to this tradition, truths have to be lived rather than merely delved into or studied by the mind, however perceptive, subtle or penetrating its range. Intrinsic to such endeavour is the recognition in every Eastern tradition that it is advantageous, if not essential, for the seeker not only to submit himself to discipline and individual tutelage of a master who is at one with the divine Reality, but to develop a relationship deeper than one of learning, and which is nurtured and irradiated by love. Whether the seeker establishes such a bond, or finds what Indian tradition calls 'the guru within', the nature of this Reality is such that it can only be directly and immediately apprehended by one who is loving, pure in heart, and poor in spirit. It should also be pointed out that whereas recourse to Oriental cults has now become popular, even fashionable, in those days it was a daunting challenge to seek out a living master; any genuine seeker was bound to generate hostility among fellow Europeans and would have to endure great loneliness if in need of European company;Thompson had no such need.

The upshot of Thompson's study in Europe was a determination to go beyond it to direct spiritual knowledge without the mediation of books. Of his sincere devotion to such a search there is no doubt; but, as we shall see, he adopted a highly idiosyncratic approach which departed in a number of ways from the classic pattern. The prime tools in India are meditation and yoga; although Thompson intermittently practised both at prescribed times, in a novel way he chose to make the act of writing their equivalent, developing a continuously flowing stream of concentration.

It is the nature of direct spiritual knowledge that there will be a change in the being of the knower. However, our everyday surface existence makes it almost impossible for us to appreciate how profound a change that might be. And what are we to make of a man who claims to have discovered within his nature a subtle constituent resembling, or even identical with, the Reality substantial to the world? The very terminology seems alien and the kind of knowledge to which Thompson aspired cannot in its nature be understood in academic terms or solely by intellectual effort.

Thompson was unusual to the degree that he retained his interest in things Western while deeply absorbed in his Indian quest. His first loyalties were to Eckhart, Pascal, Blake, Dostoievski, Kierkegaard, Nietzsche; to Rimbaud and Yeats he owed much as poet, belonging to the generation of Arthur Waley, Dylan Thomas, Stephen Spender, George Barker—as his style reveals; as aphorist he bears out the dictum of Elias Canetti: 'The great writers of aphorisms read as if they had all known each other well.' Nevertheless, he belongs within a larger domain under the twin aegis of two supreme world teachers, the Christ and the Buddha. Among living spiritual masters, whom he personally met and deeply admired over a long period of close association, were Sri Ramana Maharshi of Arunachala, Sri Aurobindo of Pondicherry, Jiddhu Krishnamurti, and the Bengali woman sage, Sri Anandamayi. For seven years he maintained the closest association with Sri Krishna Menon, a 'man of realisation' whom, in the tradition of not referring to one's master directly by name, he called the Jnani. He refused all connection with doctrinal religion and saw the quest for self-discovery as the most fundamental activity, ultimately the sole responsibility for any human being. Religion and mysticism he regarded as avenues of escape from his essential task; he was not a convert, never renounced anything, was against asceticism but not against the prime discipline of *tapas*—a Sanskrit term equivalent to Alchemy's *annealing fire*—without which he sees all effort as demonic.

There are few Indian technical terms with which we need concern ourselves here. Thompson recognised in himself all the root tendencies which give gradations of focus to a Hindu *sadhana*, or plethora of techniques with which to attain enlightenment. Thus a *jnani* is one who employs discriminatory insight and non-discursive knowledge; a *bhakta* approaches a personal deity with intense spiritual devotion; a *yogin* is one who develops perfect command over the body and all levels of consciousness to achieve ultimate union; a *tantrika* harnesses the imperfections of the demonic and instinctual forces to serve his ends in a less-than-perfect world; an *advaitin* is a *jnani* who adopts the astringent path of absolute non-dualism. One who adopts spiritual discipline of this kind is called a *sadhaka*. Thompson objected to being called a sadhaka but favoured a synthesis of ideas culled from all these approaches. This synthesis probably accounts for the name, Chililananda—a compound of chit (knowledge), lila (devotion) and ananda (bliss), which was given to him for a time by the Jnani.

Thompson's attitude towards sadhana was highly ambiguous; nevertheless, the important consequence of his outlook was that he so deeply assimilated Hindu, Buddhist and Sufi tradition that they became a totally unostentatious part of his very being. At all times meticulous in his choice of words and restrained in the use of Sanskrit technical terms (though he knew them to be unrivalled in precision), in his writing he preferred a completely nontechnical vocabulary, as simple as he could make it, universal in application, but also precise in its own way. He expended much effort in perfecting this vocabulary, which is best judged by reading his collected aphorisms, *Mirror to the Light*. This vocabulary was certainly consistent with his reluctance to set the terms of his own search within a specifically Hindu frame of reference. 'My sadhana is that I have no sadhana', he used to say, for the simple reason that any sadhana is a *language* and he was modest enough to disclaim any proficiency in it. When pushed, he would sometimes admit that of all Indian paths the most attractive to him personally was that of *sahaja*—perfect spontaneity and effortless being, a state of constant Presence. But he would use the word 'Presence' rather than reduce himself to a ventriloquist's doll opening and closing its mouth to the bidding of someone or something else. He would get into long debates with friends and teachers in defence of this position. The goal of perfect Presence alone was congenial to him in so far as, ultimately, he was more poet than sadhaka. On one occasion, in reply to a point Thompson had made on these lines, his friend and benefactor, Alan Chadwick, for many years a resident sadhaka in the ashram of Sri Ramana Maharshi, had this to say: 'Yes, to be without effort; but as the Maharshi repeatedly says, one is unable to be without effort now and effort will be impossible then. One must make an effort to be without effort. One may bluff oneself that one is being without effort, but it does need an effort to maintain that state.' In so far as he knew that he did not *know*, Thompson 'knew' this perfectly well; in fact, he was assiduous in his effort to be without effort!

From time to time he would experiment with various aspects of sadhana, including the recitation of a *mantra*—sacred invocation, somewhat similar to the Christian Prayer of the Heart. But he arrived at his own conclusions about the usefulness to himself of such practices, and these were for the most part negative. Apart from his involvement, often for many consecutive months, in the discussion which centered round some spiritual master, he spent much time reading—not as a substitute for 'direct perception' and experiential learning, but to supplement it. The most important activity to which he contributed subtlety and occasional provocation was *satsang*—an inclusive term not only for discussion but also the living enactment of association together of spiritually like-minded people, usually in the company of the teacher. Thompson enjoyed this association and if writing to such associates may be counted as an extension of satsang, then he was indefatigable in the clarity and care he brought to such an activity. He exercised great patience in helping others to reach a sharper focus in their own sadhana. His influence on friends through satsang and correspondence rested on sheer mental agility combined with considerable intuitive insight—the more effective in an area where communication through words is notoriously confusing.

But it would be a mistake to stereotype Thompson as just a 'brain' amidst the obscure thickets of mystical speculation: his passionate integrity in human relationships became as intense as were his intellectual powers, transforming these discussions into the occasion for substantive spiritual development. No recluse, he was constantly in the company of others and threw himself into relationship with loyalty and concern, regardless of the strain which this imposed on his poor health. It was also a great temptation for him to make long detours of reflective study rather than take the final leap into full Presence. His journal is full of references to these delays, which usually resulted from his impetuous embroilments with friends and acquaintances. One of his closest friends, the travel writer Ella Maillart, says he constantly fought a losing battle with dwindling energy; too often he frittered it away on the effort to elucidate a point or a controversy. Some error or confusion detected in another's thought would arouse all his passion, and often ended in definition of shades in the meaning of an argument so fine that everyone else retired in bafflement. However, he could be disarmingly direct, simple and serious with an interlocutor whose sincerity he could trust; on such occasions, his measured advice and clarity were such as to leave an indelible impression of integrity and piercing insight. He could also be humorous and playful, especially with children, whom he treated with robust kindred feeling and exquisite tact, once again lavish in expenditure of time and effort. The headmistress of the school where he worked for four years was initially put off by his sharp intelligence, until she began to discuss with him the problems of the children, only to find him resourceful, perceptive and uncommonly able to see the matter from the child's point of view, realistically. Another trait was his readiness to moderate his personality according to the varied nature of his acquaintances. Thus the range of his attention, in itself a cardinal feature of his sadhana-less sadhana, was quite wide, embracing everyone from the most austere and impersonal to the most intimate human exchanges. This was his 'integral yoga': the challenge was, at all times, to transform the colourful spectrum of his concerns into the white light of *sahaja*. Taken to its logical conclusion, the perfect spontaneity of sahaja can lead to a quality of relatedness which is, simply, pure spiritual love.

But he did have help. There were generous hosts, like Ranganathan, P.K.R. and Ure, all of whom would slip him rupees when he needed them for food or travel. This too was obviously an unsatisfactorily precarious situation. Then there was Alan Chadwick, an English devotee of Ramana Maharshi and a long-term resident at the Arunachala Ashram, who provided Thompson with a small regular sum of money just enough to keep the wolf from the door. Thompson was frugal to the point of self-torture, giving away the few rupees he had to worthy sadhus and children, or whoever he thought deserving. Friends would give him expensive shawls and coverlets, but these he hardly ever kept for long before they would find their way on to the shoulders or the cots of elderly holy folk and the like. When ten-rupee notes (sufficient for at least five dinners) fluttered off his desk in the fan and out of the window he chuckled to Blanca Schlamm with delight: 'money is for circulation—it must be kept moving!', Thompson was, in fact, deadly serious in his indifference to money, just as he was deadly serious in his grief and pain that the lack of it left him depleted of energy for want of a square meal, and deprived him of the books and the 'things' for which his aesthetic spirit desperately craved and which were inherently costly. The stark, anti-aesthetic and meager furnishings which were prevalent in Indian interiors were dispiriting for a man with hyper-sensuous tastes and a zestful capacity to relish creaturely comforts. He also felt starved of psychically vibrant companionship, particularly of the 'Continental' variety, which explains his willingness to spend so much time with Ella Maillart, and even share a house with her. Ella was a woman of great integrity and strength of character, but in those days, compared to Thompson she was a spiritual novice; sometimes he would rage against what he cheerfully called to her face, her 'Khirgiz barbarism'! He spent much time in the mid-1940s editing her books, *The Cruel Way* proving to be the most intractable by his extremely demanding standards.

The fact of the matter was that Thompson had spent so much of his time by then in the far reaches of consciousness, and exploring matters beyond the boundaries of the familiar that he had become almost incomprehensible to the strange medley of people with whom he mixed. In some regards he was ahead of his time; for instance, as I have briefly mentioned, he anticipated a mode of 'Gestalt' perception long before it was adopted by many psychotherapists; but his mode of 'resisting' the effects of psychotropic drugs, which is an ancient yogic practice, does not appear to have been picked up by even the latest research in the twenty-first century; Thompson's understanding of multiple levels of consciousness does seem to be gaining ground (viz. the 'perconscious' proposed by L.L.Whyte). It is perhaps our more precarious individual toe-hold on sanity now in an increasingly insane world, the narrower cultural front and, as a counterblast, the further expansion of spiritual insight by 'devout sceptics', which circumvents adoption of any religious affiliation in areas and on levels where Thompson had been among the early explorers, that now permit us to see more clearly than did his friends the acuteness of his vision. What once looked like a strangely unreal life, a phantasmagoria of remote sensibility and arcane psychic subtlety, can now be seen to have reached a richly serious and penetrating depth, a wide tolerance, when so much has become shallow, petty and frightened.

A Poet's Autobiography

Thompson sets out to chart his course through his *vie intérieure* on a journey from the ego to the Self. When he writes of an event, a person, a self-discovery or revelation, the whole enterprise is geared for movement in a direction diametrically the opposite of factual recollection, wherein the descriptive, historical or autobiographical writer *recreates the past.* This does not mean that we are given no factual information, but what is selected must be of such a nature that it meets the needs of 'the man delivered from the order of time'. In other words, it is not enough that facts recall events: they must also effect transformation of events in time into the dimension of the unchanging: 'Memory—transformation of the past—horoscope', is the way he sums up.

A *pilgrimage* is a long and hazardous journey toward a distant goal. The perfect and completed pattern of such a spiritual quest is the discovery of the Self, Realisation, or a Revelation of the Divine. This is followed by a *return* journey home, often of an equally perilous nature. In the case of Thompson, who died at the age of forty, he is suddenly struck down by the sun in the sacred city of Benares—traditionally the most auspicious city in which to die. It might be assumed that the pilgrim never reaches his goal if he dies prematurely. Another interpretation can be put upon this particular pilgrimage: Thompson sets out and makes his way towards his goal, reaches a climax in the mid-nineteen forties with the attainment of what in India are called states of *nirvikalpa samadhi*, is dismissed by his teacher, and then begins the task—'everything is yet to be done', as he puts it—of reaching home by way of a perilous descent from the visionary heights. The last three days of his life, when he is in a coma, constitute the classic psychic transportation at the completion of his pilgrimage—that 'completion' he often refers to, as when Rimbaud's abandonment of literature leads towards 'completion': the pilgrim's *arrival* home.

At every point on his journey we feel as if he is about to be granted the epiphany. Inconclusive or partial illumination unassumingly passes by as too fugitive to be worthy of record—or it is ineffable, both beyond words and life in time, axiomatic. The goal of self-realisation is itself pure paradox: it *is.* Outside time, subsisting beneath the veil of experience, the tricks of the mind, the dramatisation of the ego, Realisation is, in a sense, constant, always existent. The objective of the pilgrim is likewise ever outside events in history and egoic experience. It is the poet's vision which articulates through the symbolic potency of word-images that which is ever-present and yet inexpressible: *home*, *goal*, *return*—landmarks in a dream; the conclusion of pilgrimage an Awakening which passes beyond history. The discontinuous form of Thompson's journal opens upon this dimension of the Potential *between entries.*

Thompson is an integral poet, even though his most important poetry was written in the form of the aphorism.* His journal prose is charged with poetry, for metre and verse are not indispensable in poetry. His writing is at one with the pursuit of his spiritual objectives. He constantly refines those objectives by proposing definitions through succinct metaphor, the aphorism his minimal starting-point. 'A poetic mind', Gaston Bachelard reminds us, 'is purely and simply a syntax of metaphors'. To balance the extreme contraction of the aphorism he eventually opts for the journal as an additional means of expression. He does not fully commit himself to writing verse until his poetic gifts have been developed by years of work within the syntactical rigour of the aphorism and short lapidary excursions of the journal.

He began to refine his distinctive use of language as early as 1929, based on no more than two or three dozen key words. During his last years in Europe and earliest Indian years, he used this simple vocabulary within a carefully organised, long cogitated, but spare structure of thought. The whole ground plan was outlined in those years on less that fifty sheets of foolscap—root aphorisms from which the whole of *Mirror to the Light* stems.* For the rest of his life all his thought and writing is contained within that basic modal structure: it expands but is never radically modified. Like a classical Indian *raga*, he extemporises endless variations within a quite simple and restricted set of modal notes, or 'vocabulary'. He considered this modal component to be rooted in the timeless concepts of classical Western thought; only in his subtle variations does he take liberties with traditional melody and display his personal idiosyncrasies, a free spirit ever seeking to recover that pristine classicism from moribund convention. He strives to go beyond his European roots, beyond humanism, beyond philosophy, beyond morality, eventually even beyond mind and the delusions of the retarding, ever-obtrusive ego.

In his journal Thompson slowly sheds the necessarily impersonal tone of the aphorisms and begins to record his daily progress in transit from youthful naivety to a genial and sophisticated subtlety. En route he discards the excess baggage of humanism along with the rectitude of the solemn young man, and becomes more accessible, more the poet, more eloquent. But

---

**Mirror to the Light*, his collected aphorisms, is what Bachelard would call a 'poetic analysis of man'. It seems that Thompson believed in the rocket-like power of poetry to soar momentarily into the heaven of high inspiration. At that instant the poet regains the prior and constant state of Realisation underlying the whole exuberant tragi-comedy which is the Ego. It is the fate of the writer-poet ever to fall back, like a spent rocket, into the impotence of egoic existence. Thompson's archetype Poet transcends the limitations of literary poetry and the limitations of occasional brief inspiration (and therefore the self-justifying need to *write*). At the level of Pure Poetry all life and action expands in Effortless Being, or Sahaja: 'One must become Poetry'.

he mistrusts this eloquence and resorts to the resistant discipline of verse and metre as a better means to create not description but *symbol.* As a writer, the journal offers greater freedom of play with language compared to the stark austerity of the aphorism: luxuriant vocabulary, density of texture, ambient sentences of reflective comment interspersed with the pellucid phrasing of a *diarium spirituale*, the otherness of dream, ardent self-exhortation, scorching self-criticism.

But this is to speak in purely literary terms: it is not the whole story. To understand precisely what the journal offers as a means of expression for Thompson—and it is a most unusual re-casting of the form which he undertakes—it is helpful to compare this unique example of a poet's journal with those of other modern poets, including that veritable archetype of the genre and one which Thompson had read with enormous interest: Baudelaire's *My Heart Laid Bare*. Susan Sontag gets to the nub of the matter:

> Poet's prose not only has a particular fervour, density, velocity, fibre. It has a distinctive subject: the growth of the poet's vocation.... Poet's prose is mostly about being a poet. And to write such autobiography, as to be a poet, requires a mythology of the self. The self described is the poet self, to which the daily self (and others) are often ruthlessly sacrificed. The poet self is the real self, the other one is the carrier; and when the poet self dies, the person dies. (To have two selves is the definition of a pathetic fate.) Much of poet's prose—particularly in the memoiristic form—is devoted to chronicling the triumphant emergences of the poet self. (In the journal or diary, the other major genre of poet's prose, the focus is on the gap between the poet and the daily self, and the often untriumphant transactions between the two. Poet's diaries—for example, Baudelaire's or Blok's—abound with rules for protecting the poet self; desperate maxims of encouragement; accounts of dangers, disappointments and defeats.)
>
> Susan Sontag, *A Captive Spirit*: Selected Poems, by Marina Tsvetaeva, London, 1983

The context of poet's prose, as outlined here by Sontag, fits the case of Thompson quite closely, but only in the narrower, literary sense, not (within the compass of this brief quotation) of the larger spiritual issues which are Thompson's overriding concern.

The most important section in this whole book to help us understand his precise objective as writer of a journal is that in which he himself, with characteristically succinct clarity, tells us exactly what he is up to: Journal about Journal. In the present book it will precede his commencement of a journal in 1937; it can also be read with profit in conjunction with the above quotation from Sontag.

The essential points we need to know here are expressed with aphoristic brevity:

> A journal can be sustained only for the sake of, or in tension with, the ego.
> Otherwise, there is transformation.
>
> Except as Hypocrisy which must finally make it irrelevant, a journal is description, delay and self-circling in the mind. Real action, promptitude, results and continuity are in another dimension.
>
> This journal can perhaps record nothing, essentially, but lapses and vacillations from Normality—the perfect economy sensual, mental, active which is its own satisfaction—or rather, the satisfaction of the most organically direct and continuous will to growth towards the fullness of Reality.
>
> The ever-inconclusive dynamic force of a journal is tension with the ever-changing ego....
>
> Intelligence is complete only in freedom from the ego. Otherwise the ego is always observing, judging, and critically arranging all one's thought, experience and expression from the point of view of self-defensive standards of poise, sanity, scepticism, grace.
> The first quality of intelligence is complete disinterested daring.
> All need and occasion of expression to oneself depends upon division in consciousness. Economy lies in at least sustaining the level where division is that between one's fully organised self and a greater potential Whole. Then all self-expression becomes yoga.
> The relation of an unorganised present self to a greater potentiality produces romantic expression, revelatory perhaps but inconclusive and technically inconsistent, ineffective.
>
> A journal can be free of egoism or sentimentality only if it tests and extricates the Potential, the new, the unknown.
>
> Nor can a journal contain the silent thoughts that are acts, that are both the past and the future.

Thompson's journal is yoga, the poem is yoga, the aphorism is yoga—but only in so far as the real action is writing which proceeds from 'one fully organised self' (Sontag's 'triumphant emergences of the poet self'). The whole drama of Thompson's journal, indeed the only drama, is that it is written throughout in *tension with the ego*. At once we can see his departure from Sontag's typology of the poet self and the daily self. In his terms, *both* are egoic. In other words, he posits another tier of meaning altogether. He aims at a form of journal which dispenses with records of most instances when he is in a state of what he calls Normality. That is to say, those innumerable instances when all is well, the daily occurrence of events which are their own satisfaction. He strives to attain the almost impossible level—a writing (or action) that he calls 'true Poetry—a moment of such complete Presence that all writing, even poetry, is irrelevant. These moments he had often, but they too cannot be the subject of his journal, only an implicit and wordless *contredanse*.

There is no doubt that, to read this journal with full attention calls for a somewhat unusual ability. The spaces between entries are full of those 'silent thoughts that are acts'. These spaces also record the passage of time. Because we read fast, impatiently, we cannot register the import of time's passage as our eyes flick from one day's entry to the next, a month, sometimes even years rich with event, that may be implied by those little insignificant spaces between the entries. And who, other than one who is privileged to turn the little slips of handwritten paper on which the journal was written through most of Volume I (the tabloid form of the bound quarto and foolscap volumes is a dazzling innovation which only starts with the move to Benares at the end of 1943, mainly in Volume II), can register the sheer potency and enigma of a single, dated slip which bears only the pregnant question: '*For whom* is this journal written?'

Everything, then, depends upon what Thompson means by *transformation*.* For this alone justifies his writing a journal.

> The only integral science of consciousness is yoga. Yogic psychology considers the dynamics of consciousness as something to be integrally fulfilled and transformed.
>
> By yoga I mean what is entirely non-religious, non-metaphysical and non-mystical—what is rather the completion of art as creation beyond the human limits. Yoga is 'spiritual' only as will to the complete actuality of the Spirit. As a process yoga is Transformation into the Divine and of the Divine into everything.
>
> What the intellect fears above all is transformation: for this

*It may now be more easily inferred that Thompson's use of the word Transformation as the poet's proper function, is synonymous with Rimbaud's central project: the alchemy of the word.

> experience there are neither objects nor human beings, but the spiritual world in which all possible relations are immediate. For the senses and the intellect and the ego this is an intense blindness.

From his standpoint, words are 'provisional', the merest sketch, 'literary definition'. 'Presence is known only in terms of absence.' True vision can be attained, perfect Presence *is* possible; yet he maintains truthfulness though faced with the human precariousness of vision. There is no descent into human pathos here, no resort to egoic Humanistic self-pity. He does not permit himself to be lulled into a sentimental delusion of enlightenment attained while momentarily absorbed in a fleeting state of being which he calls Poetry, pure action. He is aware that he constantly lapses from Presence; yet the precision with which he pinpoints each source of failure is the substance of many entries in his journal. Recognising that he cannot realise his vision, he has a vision of what he has not had: this is twentieth century Modernism! The corollary of such realism is honest depiction of the very thing which is the opposite of vision. Modernist art tends to memorialise experience at the furthest remove from vision. Thompson employs paradox as the Modernist painter uses error, failure and incompletion—to obtain a closer approximation of true vision, its spontaneity. Effortless Being.

> Whoever is truthful discovers his real situation. Discovering what is contemporary for him he begins to move towards Presence. *Employing the ego* he continually exhausts it and is free of it. He employs all apparatus: his action is enjoyment. He has always discovered the real situation.
>
> *Mirror to the Light*

This kind of Gestalt therapy *avant la lettre* dismayed his Indian teachers as no more that the usual Western insistence on the ultimate reality of the ego. Thompson's tendency to express the dark side of experience when it indubitably was dark, in the interests of truthfulness, was regarded as counter to spiritual sadhana, even as demonic. More than in any other respect, it is in his vision of Evil, and truthful admission of personal torment that Thompson reveals his deeply occidental temperament, his prior allegiance to Western Modernist modalities. Here Sontag's 'pathetic fate' does have some relevance, but it is lightened, losing disproportionate Modernist emphasis by his resort to the more ancient traditions of genial Eastern thought, particularly the Buddhist attitude towards Shunya, the East's answer to modern Western Nihilism.

Thompson's individual sense of tragedy (he sees Dostoievsky, Nietzsche, Beethoven as kindred spirits in this regard) leads him to mourn the lost Eden of Western civilisation's spiritual wholeness. Here he adopts an adversarial role in his critique of Western norms and pretensions. Following on from Nietzsche, he opposes the false humanism, sentimentality and abstract materialism of the West with a species of trans-humanistic realism tempered by the diamond-hard clarity which can only come through a perception of the transcendent as man's *first* priority. Here he is adamant.

His journal is indeed concerned with the poet's vocation, yet few Western poets today are ready to risk pretentiousness, as he does, by attempting to restore the poet's function as *seer*. The last to try were Blake, Nietzsche and Rimbaud. We no longer have a Western cultural context in which this would seem remotely feasible for a poet. At least the archetype of the seer is still alive in the Indian psyche, even if this is no longer a relevant issue for contemporary Indian poets. Thompson was in India to test the living tradition and see what it could offer him in a personal situation of crisis. Here lies his deep sense of homelessness: 'I wander tombless, with no authentic name'.

His solution—and he saw himself as dogged by many disappointments in regard to it—is discomforting to the Western liberal humanist. This is nothing to do with his sense of tragedy but because of rigorous truthfulness to what he places in opposition to tragedy: self-transcendence through egolessness. To the liberal humanist, or the man of letters, the artist, the expensively educated, this would seem not only bleak but misguided, even threatening. Nowadays, most people in the West refuse to consider such a prospect. Indeed, it is often forgotten that the attractive ideal of Eastern tranquillity is only attainable other than by a 'dying to self'—the root of all spiritual endeavour, including that of the West. In a secular age it is the ego itself which alone seems to offer us an ultimate redoubt of certain identity.

Thompson's special value in this regard lies in the exhilarating vividness with which he tries to convince us otherwise: that the transcendence of the ego can be accomplished, in the fullness of time, not by dismal suppression, or ascetic, moralistic 'self-denial', but by a vibrant, genial, acrobatic, intelligent, imaginative promptitude and passionate truthfulness. Though he appreciates how formidable the difficulties would always be, and experiences the anguish of failure through his own obstinate perversity, he never falters in his conviction. He depicts in imagery of great beauty and luminosity the universal human capacity to mobilise *all the faculties* for attainment of spontaneity and effortless being. The inner propellant of his thought here is a tension between expansive affirmation of the Blakean Whole Man and the pull towards extreme contraction at the zero point of 'verticality'—which Yeats viewed as creative nullity. Thompson sought to overcome this problem tirelessly, not so much trying to square the circle as picturing himself on the 'holdless precipice' immediately below the summit of vertical vision. He devotes himself, as he has written, with the concentration his chosen Indian ambience instills, to '...those strong and secret things and thoughts which others fear and know not'.

Childhood solitudes leave indelible marks on certain souls. One of the key passages in Thompson's reminiscences of his early years is that in which he recalls the idyllic summers he spent at the Priory; his being takes comfort from it, he returns to this durable, permanent, immobile world of the old house in dreams and reveries. His maturity is constantly renewed by the freshness of childhood which never stops growing within him, abetted by the company of children, with whom he loved to play in India. His journal reflections are enriched by this most living of treasures when his being is touched by the glory of living. The great archetype of life beginning remained within him as a principle of unconditioned spontaneity and immediacy throughout his life, restoring to him the kindling sense of possibilities and new beginnings, lightening that knowledge of 'strong and secret things' which is captured by the camera in the smile of the eleven-year-old Lewis. The very fact that all his writing consists of short pieces in series, time arrested in the brilliant light of a moment's vision, reflects this cardinal importance to him of childhood's timeless season. Philosophy continues: the aphorist starts all over again.

> In opposition to historical time, successive and infinite, modern poetry since Blake has affirmed the time of origin, the moment of beginning. The time of origin is not a before, it is a now. It is a reconciliation of the beginning and the end; every now is a beginning and every now is an end. The return to the beginning is a return to the present.
>
> Ocatavio Paz, Children of the Mire,
> Cambridge, Mass., & London, 1974, p.157

The uneventfulness of a life where solitude could never entirely evaporate even amidst friends, laid Thompson open to the risk that each and every event, such as it was, would become either an ecstasy or a trauma.

To my knowledge, no Westerner has ever attempted to achieve, in India, anything like Thompson's unique fusion of literary, poetic and spiritual quest in one long, sustained stream of self-scrutiny. Nobody else seems to have possessed the peculiar combination of talents to lift that self-scrutiny above the limitations of an almost grotesquely private and specialised routine so that the resulting message is free of morbidity and self-engrossment.

Portable Manuscripts

What began for the eighteen-year-old Thompson as an inner spiritual adventure, was forged into a mature spiritual and poetic gnosis under the influence of India's ancient traditions. The story of that slow process is the substance of this journal. It is a tale of risk, conducted on the brink of disaster with intelligence and a rare conviction. It is the accomplishment of an unusual singleness which at every moment threatens to fail. To all outward appearances his activities seem random, inconsequential, as if he were wasting his life with profitless and unceasing self-scrutiny, caught in the vicious circle of inner rambling. But as he observes, 'Only he who is bound by time thinks he can 'waste time"'. We should view the unsatisfactoriness of Thompson's daily life, its failures, delays and detours, with the contrasting wealth of reflective writing distilled from it, where he pursues what he calls 'the rarity of complete risk'.

For a person who spent his working life in constant travel, the papers are in almost miraculously well-ordered preservation. Practically everything he ever wrote bears the date of its composition, and most of it was filed in a most efficient index system or in a carefully paginated and bound *mise-en-page*. His papers had to be portable, functional and, as far as possible, proof against climate and pests: accurate indexing made for instant accessibility among the tens of thousands of individual items. The tin trunk containing them—virtually his entire belongings save a few books and a spare set of clothes—served as his filing cabinet. Even thirty-five years after his death, insecticide powder against white ants still came out of the original manuscript boxes. For a singularly precarious existence, where the very nature of experience is vertiginous, fugitive, the organisation of such intricate material is a feat in itself, like the log of a careful navigator on a long sea voyage.

What has disappeared in cold print is the emotional vivacity of the expressive handwriting, which exactly conveys the variations in mood, the patience or the hurried urgency with which the entries are so variously penned. Thompson's handwriting, usually very neat if at all times very small or scrawled at speed in the middle of the night and extremely hard to read, varied enormously from year to year, even from day to day. It registers mood like a seismograph. Meticulous observation, mental concentration, elation, sensuous enjoyment, psychic vitality or fatigue, self-criticism, analytical melancholy, delirium, visionary ecstasy—all have their exact calligraphic correspondence. If Thompson's activities and daily fluctuations in inner vitality are hardly momentous taken piecemeal, his sustained attentiveness is of an order which commands utmost respect, especially when he maintains the distinction of his style even under trying conditions of noisy interruption—in crowded hostels and railway compartments.

The manuscripts of most entries culled for this book bear the signs of their greater personal significance and difficulty in the writing—excitement, passion or stress, erratic handwriting, second thoughts, corrections, interpolations. Careful handwriting is usually maintained in passages which he intends to read frequently—entries which read like prayers; again and again, he uses such occasions to reformulate his goals and clarify his sense of purpose. It is as if the long portions of the journal which have been excluded from this selection were no more than the equivalent of yogic exercises, and some read like Stream-of-Consciousness. He often concludes an entry with a summary passage like an incantation; these come as an anti-climax, as if he is straining after the echoes and correspondences of a poem in a medium which cannot contain them. If prose is a line—straight, crooked or spiral—that moves forward purposefully towards a specific goal, then many passages here must be accounted failures. The poem, on the contrary, is a self-sufficient circle, an echo-chamber. But the journal also has as its mission the transformation of consciousness. From time to time, Thompson strives to convert the short passages of prose into a circle and make of it a mnemonic device for effecting inner change: memoranda into prayers, verbal amulets into jingling mantras—an *alchemy of the word.*

On a slip he notes, cryptically, but with precision, the function of his journal:

Memory—transformation of the past—horoscope.

To concentrate, as few writers do, so single-mindedly on the inner life, necessarily means the weeding out of incident and action, description and contextual explanation. We have to rely solely on his brief notes for the facts of his early life. For the early years in India there is no more than a fragmentary record, and a highly selective one at that. We must also surmount the initial problem of unfamiliarity in the West with the solid depths, as distinct form the facile shallows, of India's vast and complex spiritual culture. Nevertheless, the wealth of material from 1937 onwards amply compensates for the fragmentary nature of the early record. Thompson intended to publish substantial extracts from his journal and had already begun to index these in the last year of his life, and to type the beginning. No doubt he would have added explanatory material on the Indian context had he lived to complete his task. But he was far too spontaneous a man to settle into the pedant task of assembling what came from his pen in a steady outpour of reflections and anecdotes, too fleeting for deliberate, willed, formal work. As it is, this has had to be done posthumously, with the addition of explanatory editorial interventions.

His singularly persistent refusal to participate in the world of money frees him from any preoccupation with selling his work. Instead, he freely and courageously devotes himself to mystery, recovering from its depths insights far beyond what the ego on its own could ever achieve. What has been received in these depths is essentially gratuitous—it is freed and passed along, to liberate us in turn. One has only to scrutinise the choice of imagery he favours to notice how he rejoices in a simple repertoire of images expressive of this plenitude. He so often concludes an intricate train of thought by dropping in our lap the gift of fruitful harvest among what Yeats, in *Vision*, called 'the yellowing corn or under overhanging grapes'.

Thompson makes us spectators to the continual tug-of-war between typical Western solipsism and Eastern self-transcendence. There is no attempt to disguise the sheer complexity and obtrusiveness of the modern Western ego-structure in the face of a considerably more supple and suave Eastern disdain for individualities. And he is prepared to risk contradicting himself by a self-observation which defeats the ultimate goal of self-realisation. Such insight as he gains through the rocketing intensity of the aphorism has the rough temerity of one who knows that anything he states will be provisional, no matter how scrupulous his use of language. It is, therefore, the opposite of the crystal certitude of the Eastern *sutra*, or 'thread'—an aphorism long honed and polished, as if by the collective effort of numberless generations. In contrast with the sublime, impersonal distillation of the sutra, Thompson's method achieves a disturbing urgency, immediacy and directness that is in every way completely of his time and unique in its force of conviction.

His literary craftsmanship as writer of a journal rescues him from the brink of failure through his persistent counterpoint of the leisured meander with the throw-away concision of the urgent telegrammatic memorandum. This calls for a quality of concentration and literary technique so perfectly fused that, through a kind of automatism of mind and pen, they assume the character of a perfectly executed (and therefore unwilled) series of yogic *asanas*. He waged a constant battle against dwindling energy, ill-health and their mental consequence—perverse dust-storms of destructive self-criticism. He so ardently sought a free-flowing spontaneity that he exhausted himself in the process, the resulting sickness trapping him in long fallow periods when he felt himself to be merely going through the motions of the contemplative life without the necessary vital energy for the real thing.

That he was a bundle of contradictions and a man divided he was the first to admit. But that fatal division is our gain, for otherwise how could he record such endeavours? As it turned out, he delayed the attainment of his goal through the effort demanded in its recording.

The nub of the matter is plainly put: it is on our individual selves that the work has to be done. Not the West, not the East, not even India can relieve us of that responsibility. If Thompson could have pursued his quest other than by following a way of life such as his anywhere else but India—at that time—is an open question. Certainly, it is so singular in its focus and its restrictions, so 'cabin'd', 'cribb'd', 'confin'd', that only an exceptionally strong individual prepared to work within those limitations could make anything of it creatively. No doubt the impression we have of him as in some ways privileged and protected is partly due to the fact that he had no interest in recording the details of the mundane circumstances in which he lived from day to day, and lavished all his care on recording experiences which, by definition, pull away from those circumstances. It should be remembered that for the greater part of the time he lived in the most meagre accommodation—in the backstreets of Madras and Trivandrum—with poor labourers, students, pilgrims and dossers, usually in noisy and overcrowded communal lodgings. As editor of his manuscripts, I have often been pulled up short, after reading a particularly delicate or subtle train of thought, with its luminous imagery and refinement of nuance, by the fact that it was written on the back of his meal ticket in a cheap worker's cafe, or that he had been interrupted, in the surrounding clamour, by the importunate curiosity of all and sundry. The fact that he so seldom refers to his immediate surroundings makes his sudden shift of location from ashram to military barracks appear an almost ludicrous contrast. This was not so: the contrast is that, for once, he describes his immediate surroundings and associates—neither more nor less imcompatible than they really were. Similarly, we would have no idea, from the lush and idyllic descriptions of the landscape in Ceylon* during his six-month stay there in the mountains, and his record of correspondingly expansive inner reveries, that he was constantly interrupted by talkative fellow-guests interested only in the most banal of day-to-day concerns. Whether it be considered a curse or a gift, his deep solitude was a purely inner state.

We would be wrong to project on this wandering Englishman the image of a privileged eccentric whose sole associates were the sensitive and spirtually inclined, their austerity relieved by frequent retreat to the comfort-

---

* The old name for Sri Lanka has been retained throughout.

able bundalows of the British Raj. Quite apart from his distaste for such a recourse, he led such an impecunious existence that the few occasions when he did avail himself of affluent hospitality were brief interludes of recuperation from illness or exhaustion brought on by prolonged exposure to life on the borderline of survival. He drew no distinction between the 'worldly' and the 'unworldly' because he found both equally prone to their own passions and pettiness, equally prey to misfortune and mundane preoccupations. He was by no means insensitive to, or unaware of, the harsh realities of daily existence among the poor. Occasionally he lodged, for example, for months at a time with fisherfolk who lived in shacks on the beach at Madras, tutoring a number of shool-children whose parents were too poor to pay him. At the start and end of his Indian years he lived for years at a stretch without the benefit of affluent hospitality. In fact, the severe restrictions were less of a social or financial nature, more a matter of mental disposition, entirely self-imposed—as consciously contrived as any *sadhana*—as if he lived in an imaginary ashram without walls. This was both his strength and his weakness: it permitted him to filter experience with a discriminating, but selective, eye, yet protect himself from the normal inconveniences, frictions and despair which most who earn a living must endure. At least he knew this and never entirely lost the good grace to reckon himself comparatively fortunate; for one thing, he possessed the writer's knack of putting himself in the shoes of others and was astutely observant of his fellow men and the true nature of their lot. He may have lacked the common touch but not the salty realism and compassion on which it rests.

Nevertheless, I have often, quite understandably, been asked whether it is realistic to expect that anyone could really live as Thompson enjoins—and that, even were this possible, then it could only be in conditions so contrived as to be at least as confined, specialised and protected as Thompson's own life in India. The irony, of course, is that as time went by (Volume II of his journal makes this plain), Thompson found them increasingly exhausting to endure. Whatever follies he committed in the way he lived—and God knows, he recognised them as such and paid dearly—what he enjoins, though coloured by his own circumstances, is too uncomfortably close to classic teachings universally propounded by all the great traditions of the world's widsom to be lightly cast aside as the mere idealism of the eccentric.

The problem is a familiar one: wherever one finds a proposal to achieve astringent and extreme reduction of content to minimalist simplicity and watchful awareness, the objection is raised that no more than a few rare souls will ever have the will for it. The answer of Christian, Buddhist, Hindu and Sufi tradition to the question of their seemingly unattainable standards is beautifully echoed in these words of Yeats:

> Nations, races, and individual men are unified by an image, or bundle of related images, symbolic or evocative of the state of mind which is, of all states of mind not impossible, the most difficult to that man, race, or nation: because only the greatest obstacle that can be contemplated without despair rouses the will to full intensity.

It was, I believe, Thompson's determination to make his ideas work in the larger world that gave him the drive to keep open the lines of communication even when they were stretched to the very limit. This gave him a feeling of urgency, as if at the end of a long-distance telephone line. He devoted the most scrupulous attention to devising an appropriate language in which to couch his discoveries, so that his exact and exacting message would have the utmost directness, universality and cogency:

> Exactitude is complete and justified only for the sake of the new, the Unique: it is always organic, poetical—the exactitude of the rose.

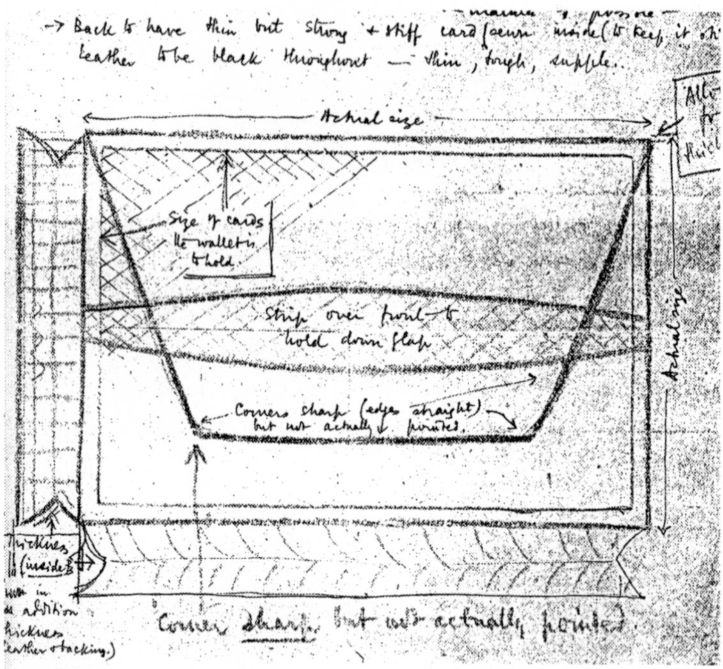

Fig. 5. Thompson's design for the black leather wallet he carried on his person at all times in which to keep uniforn postcard-size slips of paper on which to write his aphorisms and, until 1943, his journal. The actual wallet is in the Lewis Thompson archive at Washington State University.

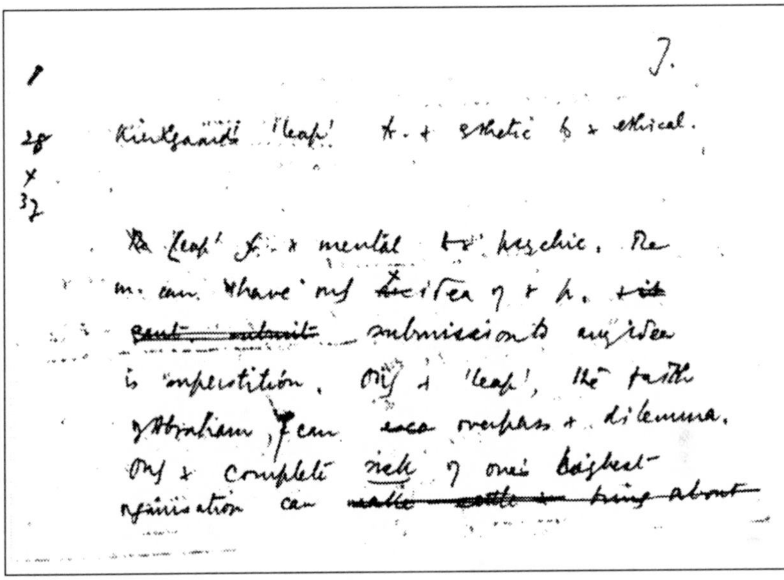

Fig. 6. A relatively easy instance of deciphering Thompson's high-speed abbreviation:

28.X.37.
Kierkegaard's 'leap' from the aesthetic to the ethical.

'Leap' from the mental to the psychic. The
mental can have only the idea of the psychic and
submission to any idea
is superstition. Only the 'leap', the faith
of Abraham, can overpass the dilemma.
Only the complete *risk* of one's highest
organisation can....

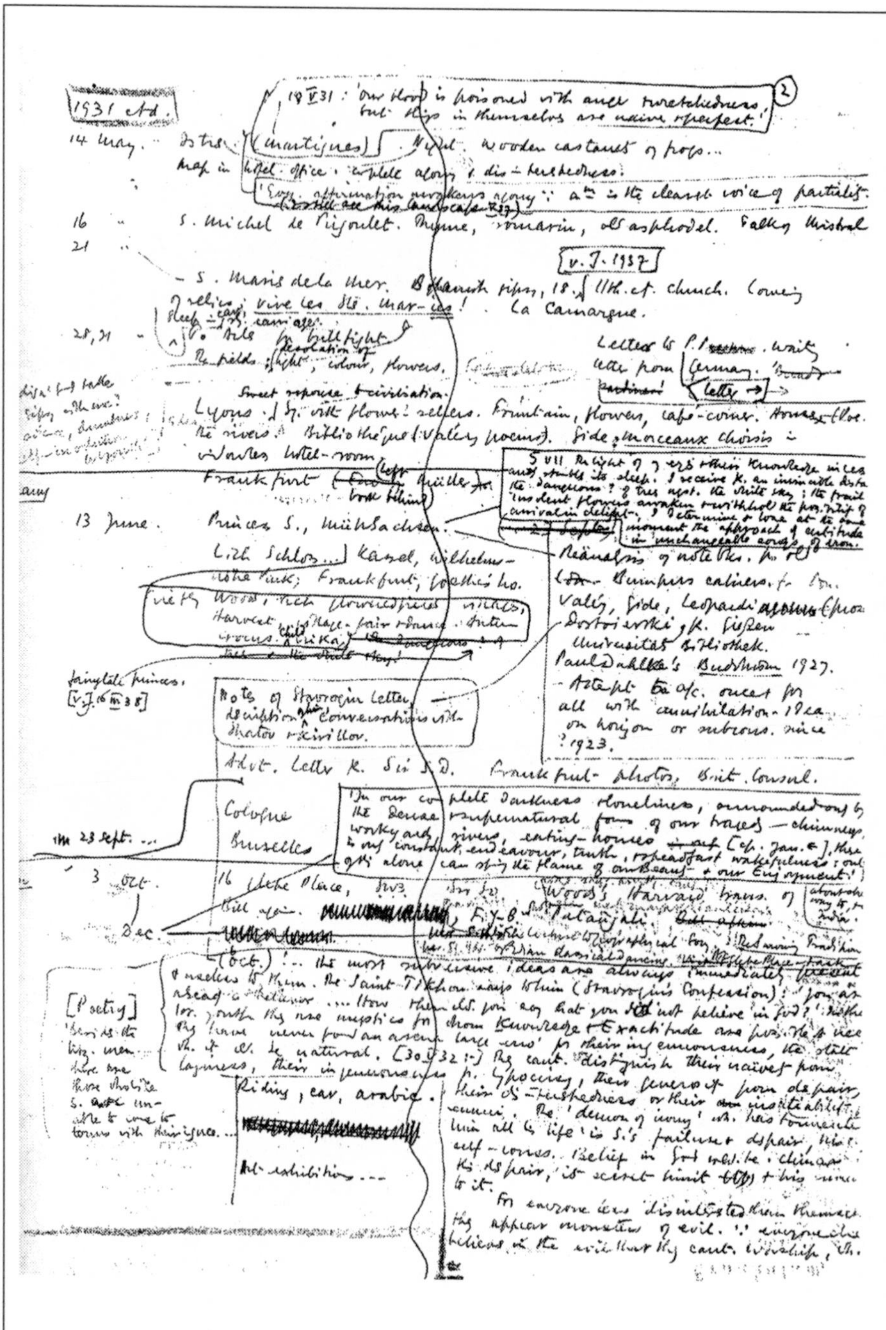

Fig. 7. Thompson's checklist of early itinerary—both samples (figs. 7. and 8.) are the sole record of his whereabouts prior to his departure for India.

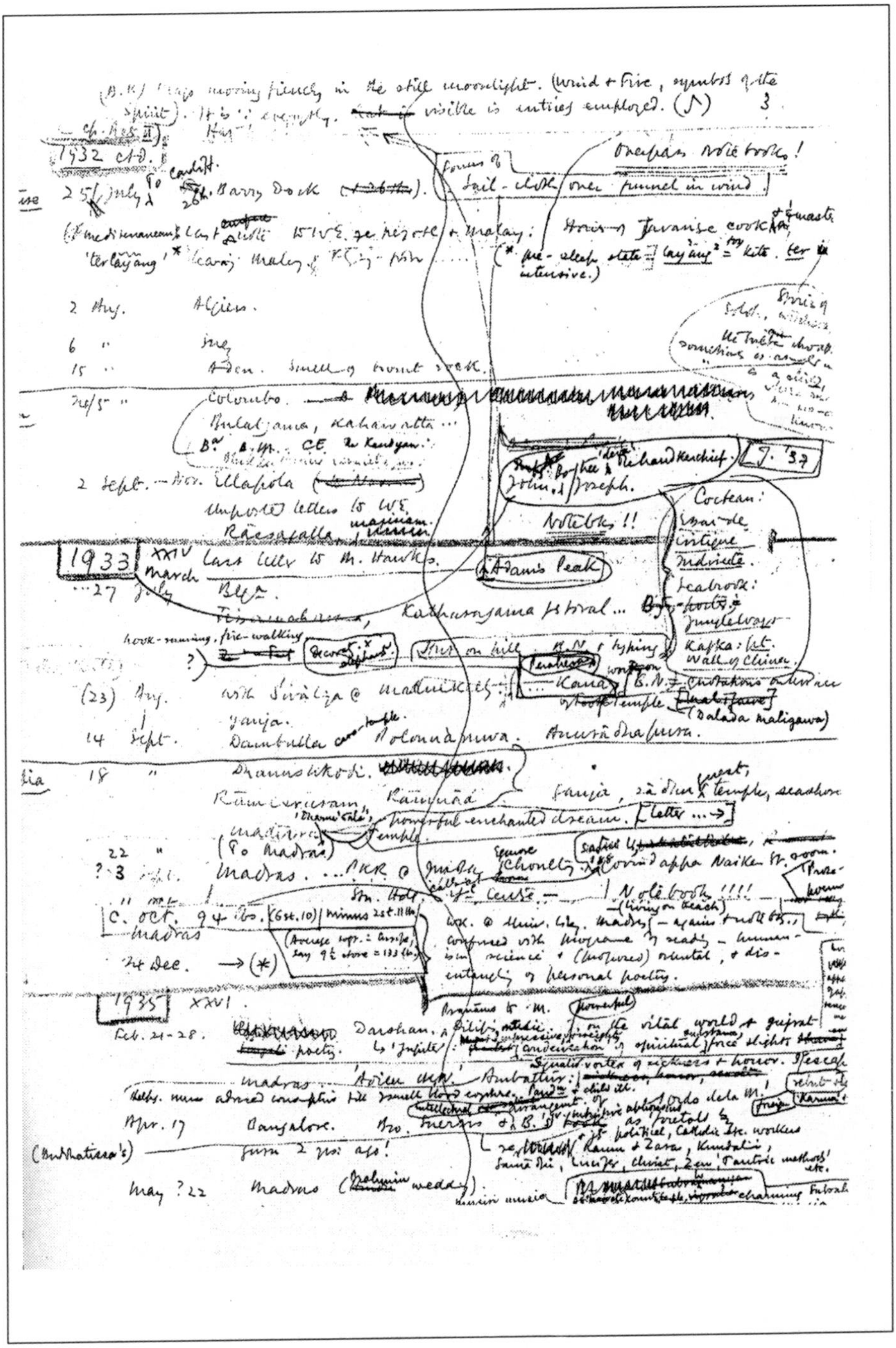

Figure 8.

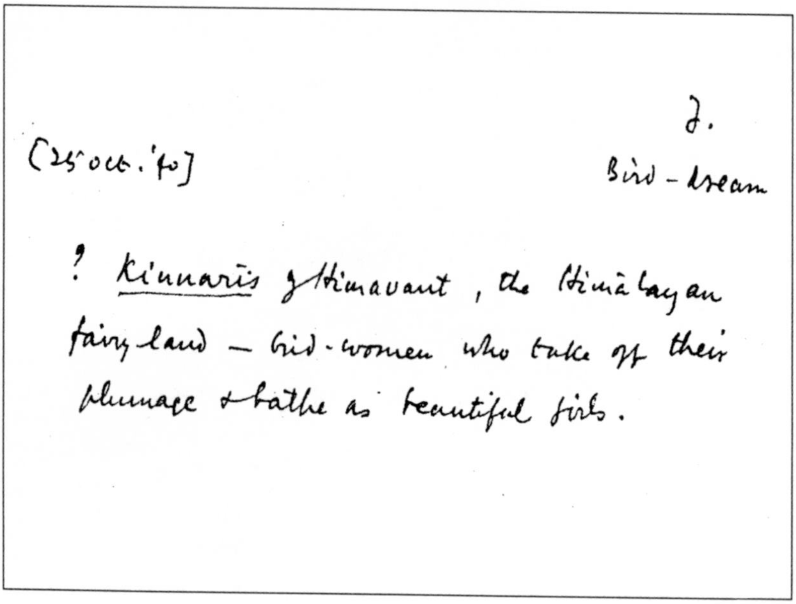

[25 Oct. '40] J.
Bird-dream

? Kinnaris of Himavant, the Himalayan fairy-land — bird-women who take off their plumage & bathe as beautiful girls.

Fig. 9. Journal slip

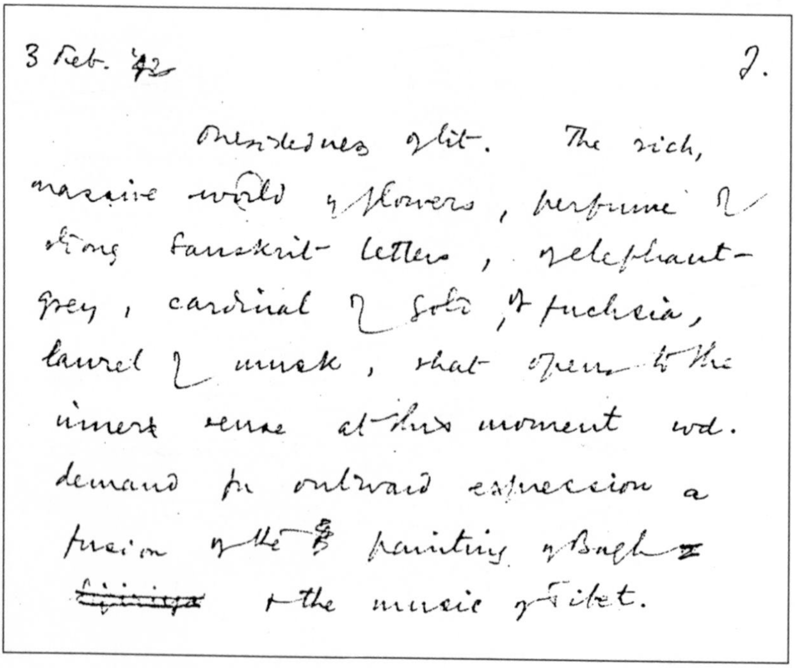

3 Feb. '42 J.

Onesidedness of lit. The rich, massive world of flowers, perfume & strong Sanskrit letters, of elephant-grey, cardinal & gold, of fuchsia, laurel & musk, that opens to the inmost sense at this moment wd. demand for outward expression a fusion of the ~~B~~ painting of Bagh ~~&~~ ~~[illegible]~~ & the music of Tibet.

Fig. 10. Journal slip

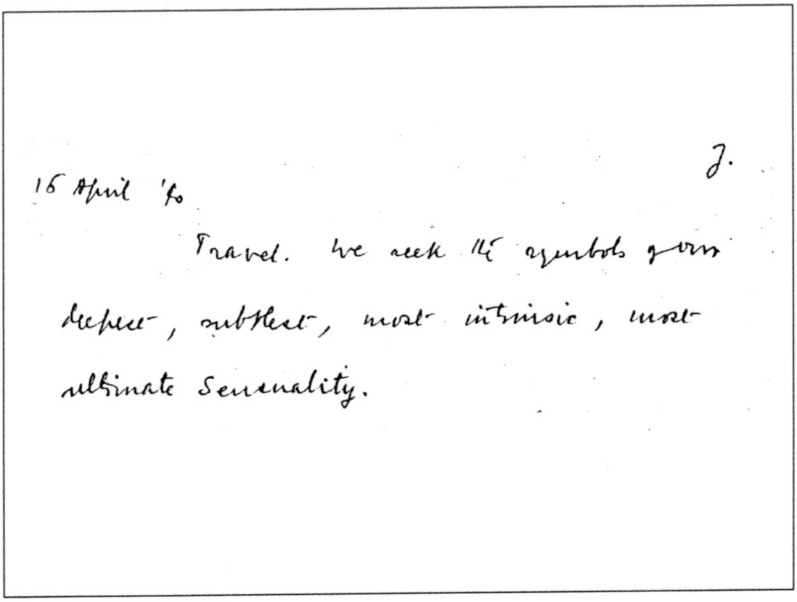

16 April '40

J.

Travel. We seek the symbols of our deepest, subtlest, most intrinsic, most ultimate sensuality.

Fig. 11. Journal slip

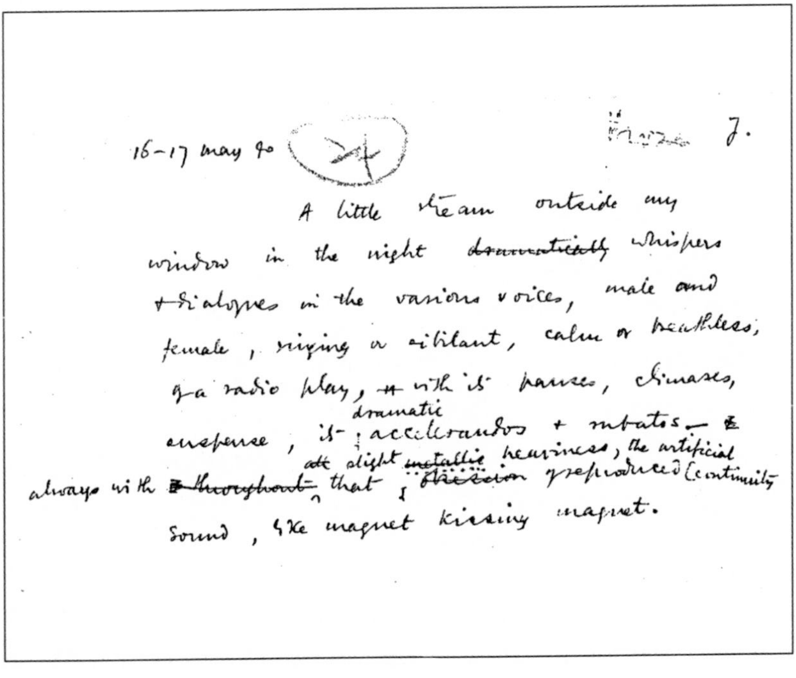

16-17 May 40

J.

A little stream outside my window in the night ~~dramatically~~ whispers & dialogues in the various voices, male and female, singing or sibilant, calm or breathless, of a radio play, with its pauses, climaxes, suspense, its dramatic accelerandos & rubatos — always with ~~throughout~~ that slight ~~metallic~~ heaviness, the artificial [illegible] reproduced continuity sound, like magnet kissing magnet.

Fig. 12. Journal slip

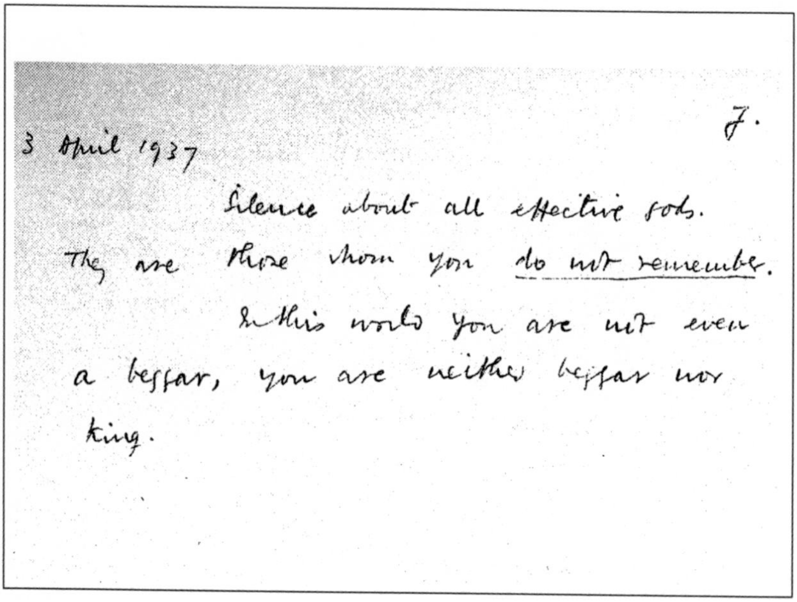

3 April 1937 7.

Silence about all effective gods.
They are those whom you do not remember.
In this world you are not even
a beggar, you are neither beggar nor
king.

Fig. 13. Journal slip.

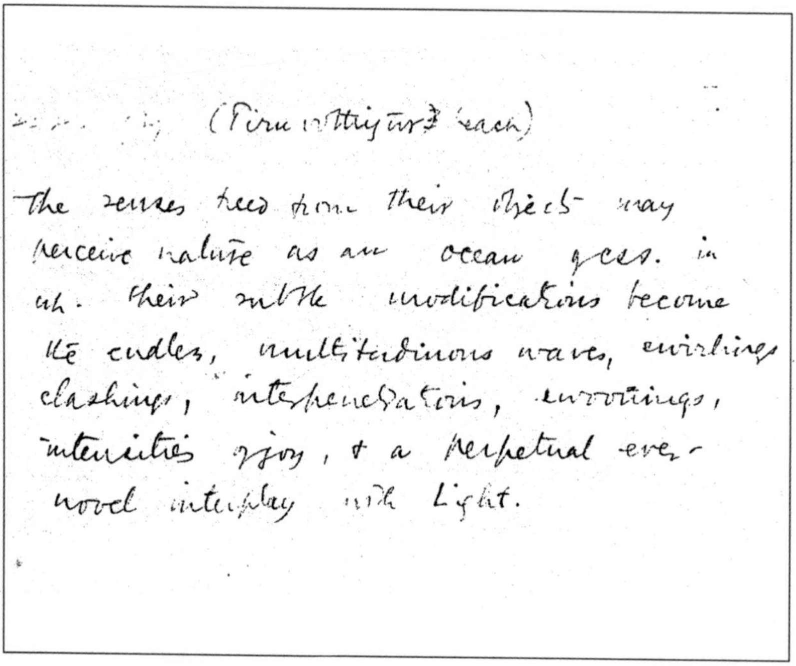

(Tiruvottiyur beach)

The senses freed from their objects may
perceive nature as an ocean of ess. in
ah. their subtle modifications become
the endless, multitudinous waves, swirlings,
clashings, interpenetrations, surroundings,
intensities of joy, & a perpetual ever-
novel interplay with Light.

Fig. 14. Journal slip.

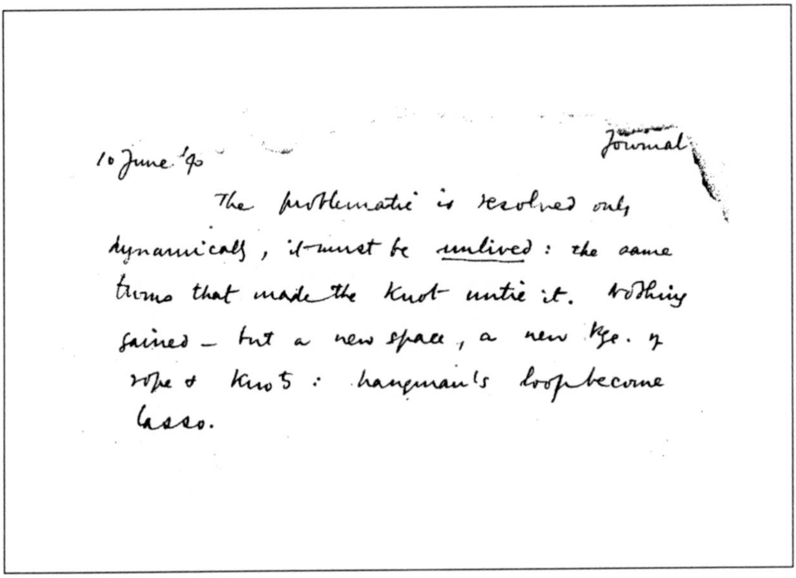

10 June '40 Journal

The problematic is resolved only dynamically, it must be unlived: the same turns that made the knot untie it. Nothing gained – but a new space, a new use of rope & knots: hangman's loop become lasso.

Fig. 15. Journal slip.

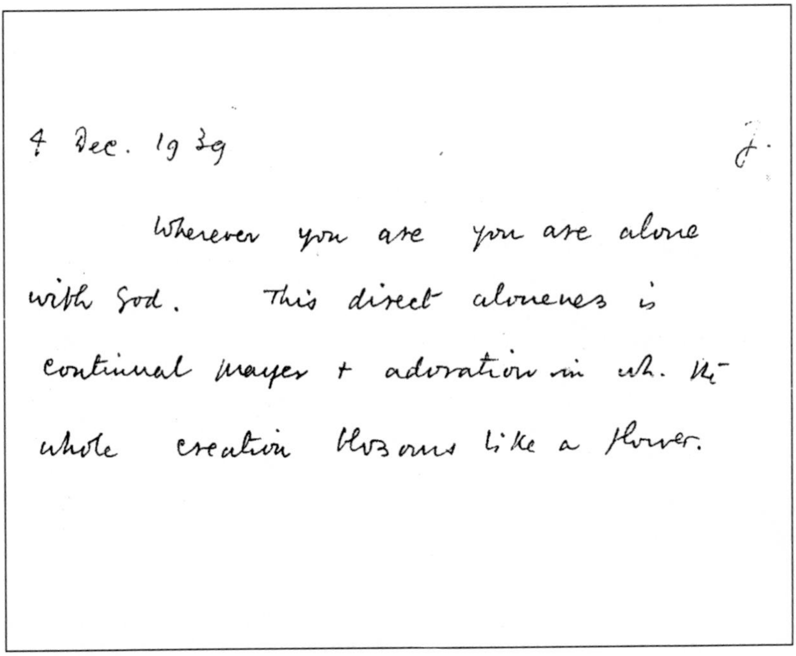

4 Dec. 1939 J.

Wherever you are you are alone with God. This direct aloneness is continual prayer + adoration in wh. the whole creation blossoms like a flower.

Fig. 16. Journal slip.

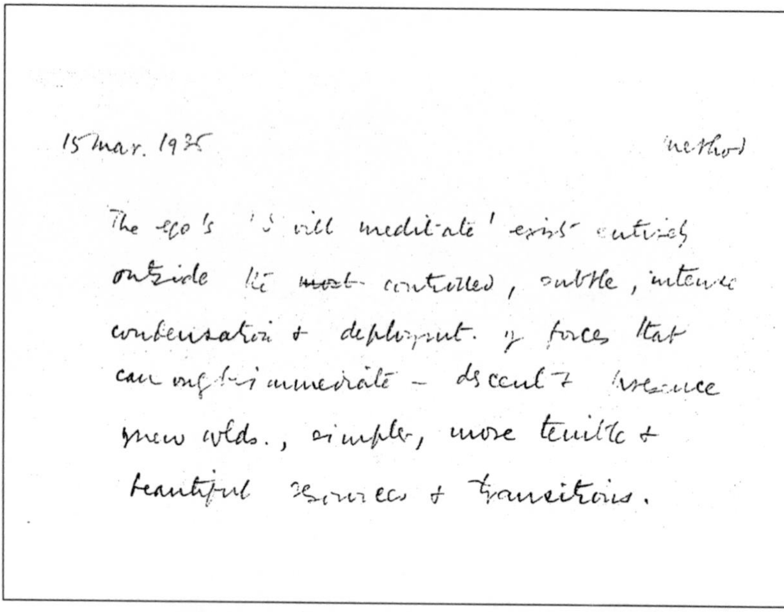
15 Mar. 1935 Method

The ego's 'I will meditate' exists entirely outside the ~~most~~ controlled, subtle, intense condensation & deployment of forces that can only be immediate – descent & presence of new wlds., simpler, more terrible & beautiful resources & transitions.

Fig. 17. Journal slip of a key statement in which he opposes Method to ego-willed *sadhana*. Essential basis for all subsequent discord with the Jnani, Sri Krishna Menon:

15 May, 1935 Method

The ego's 'I will meditate' exists entirely
outside the most controlled, subtle, intense
condensation and deployment of forces that
can only be immediate—descent and presence
of new worlds,simpler, more terrible and
beautiful resources and transitions.

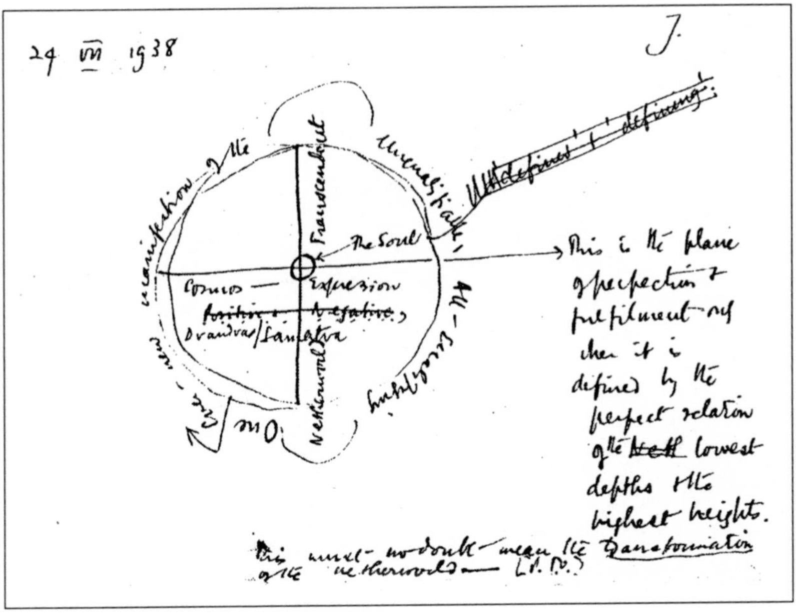

Fig. 18. Journal slip.

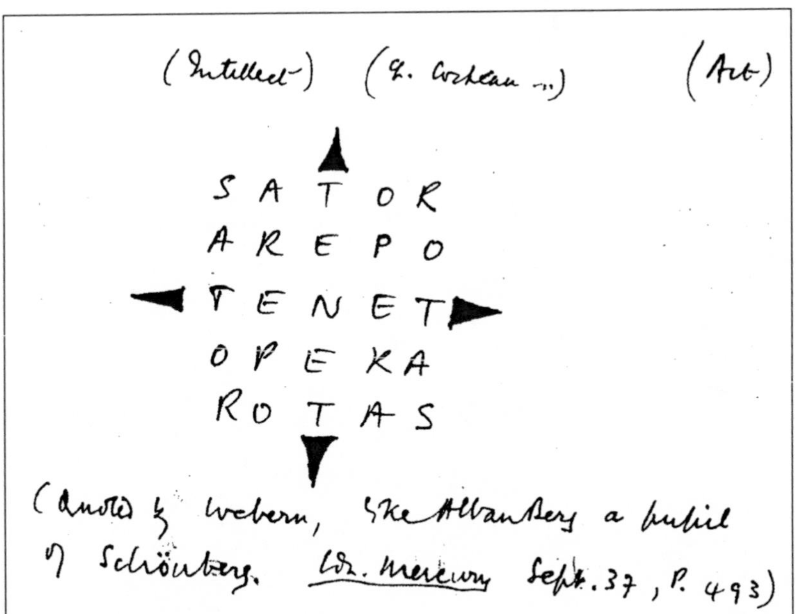

Fig. 19. Journal slip.

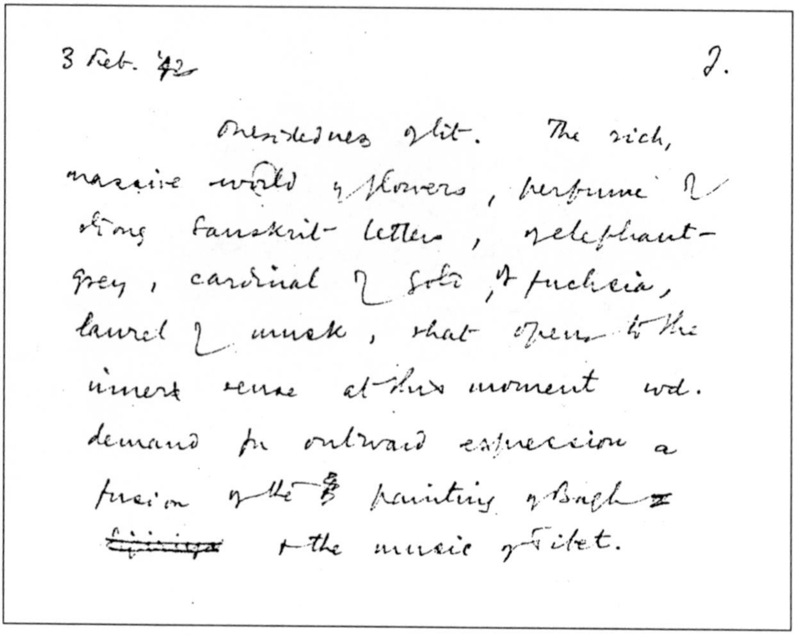
3 Feb. '42 J.

Onesidedness of lit. The rich, massive world of flowers, perfume & strong Sanskrit letters, of elephant-grey, cardinal & gold, of fuchsia, laurel & musk, that opens to the inmost sense at this moment wd. demand for outward expression a fusion of the painting of Bach & the music of Tibet.

Fig. 20. Journal slip.

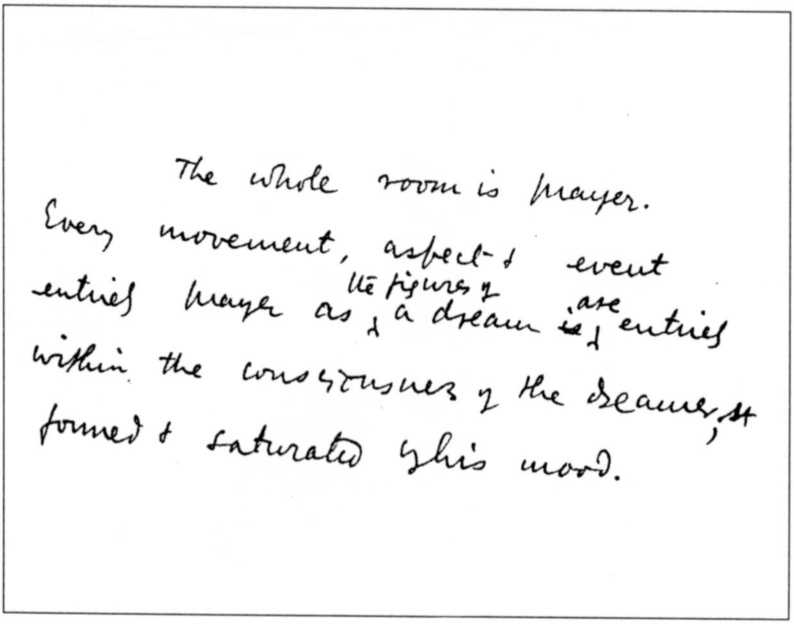
The whole room is prayer. Every movement, aspect & event entirely prayer as the figures of a dream are entirely within the consciousness of the dreamer, formed & saturated by his mood.

Fig. 21. Journal slip, written at Ramana Maharishi Ashram.

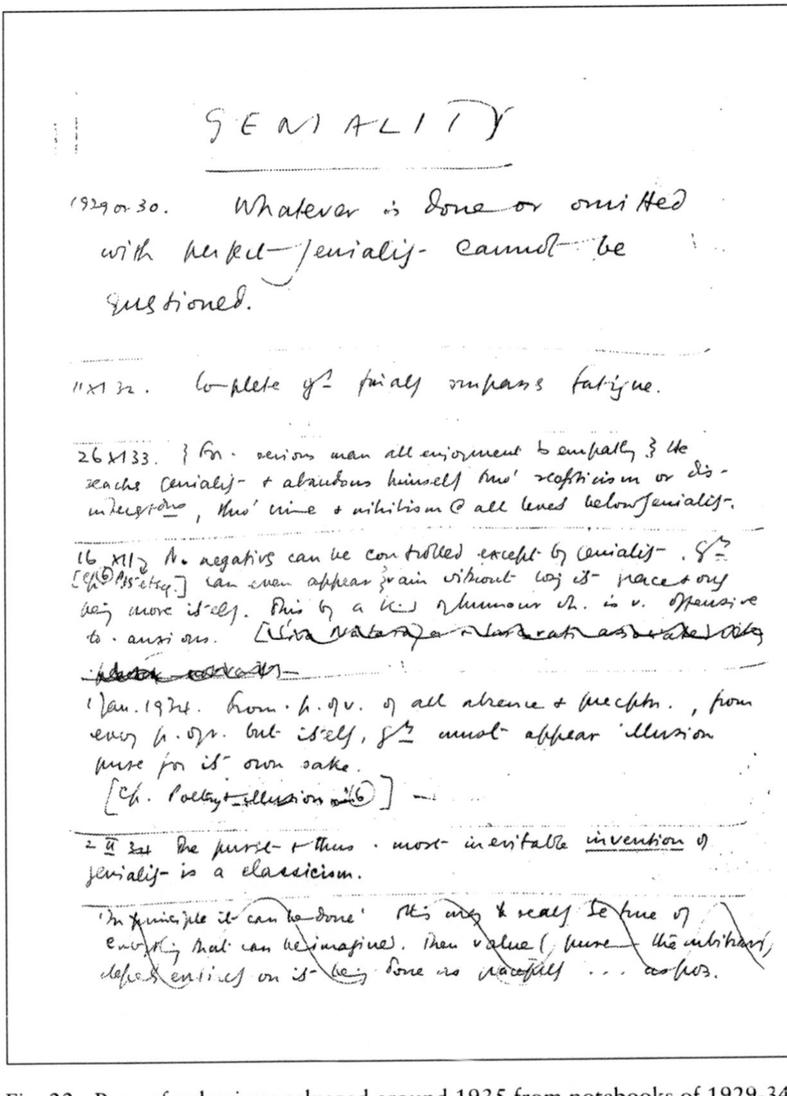
GENIALITY

1929 or 30. Whatever is done or omitted with perfect geniality cannot be questioned.

2 II 34 The purest + thus most inevitable invention of geniality is a classicism.

Fig. 22. Page of aphorisms salvaged around 1935 from notebooks of 1929-34 which were then destroyed. All aphorisms were filed under subject until this project was completed in 1943. Use of uniform-sized slips begun in 1936.

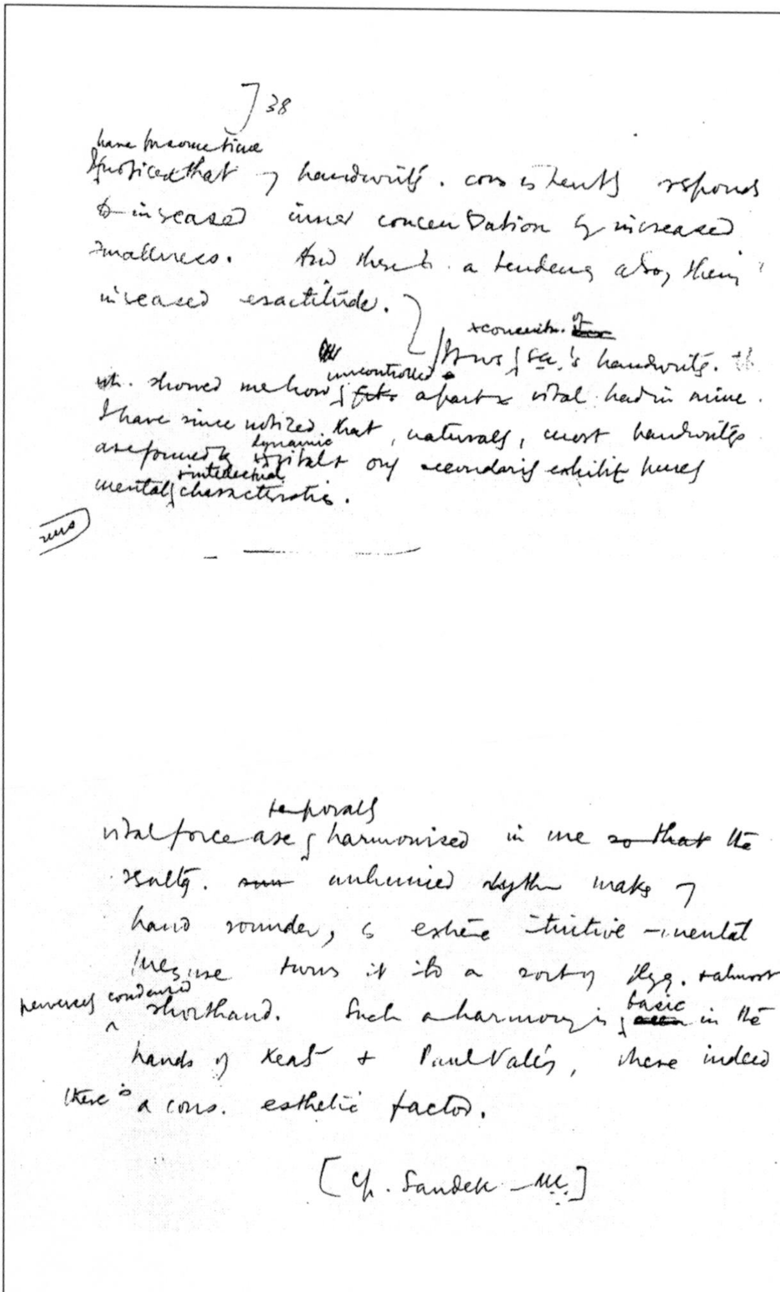

Fig. 23. Journal reflections on his own handwriting, 1938, with references to the handwriting of Sri Aurobindo, Keats and Paul Valery.

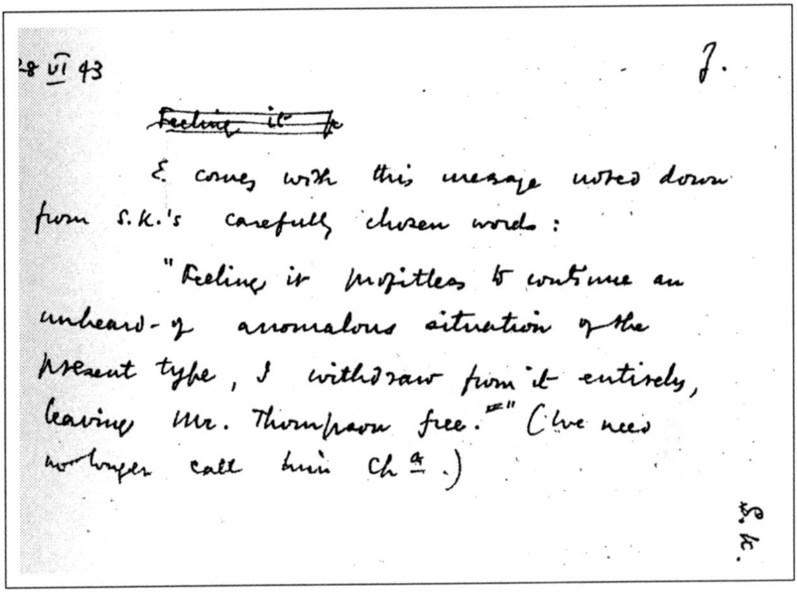

28 VI 43 J.

~~Feeling it~~

E. comes with this message noted down from S.K.'s carefully chosen words:

"Feeling it profitless to continue an unheard-of anomalous situation of the present type, I withdraw from it entirely, leaving Mr. Thompson free." (We need no longer call him Chª.)

S.K.

Fig. 24. Journal slip. The sole reference to the mode by which the Jnani chose to terminate their relationship.

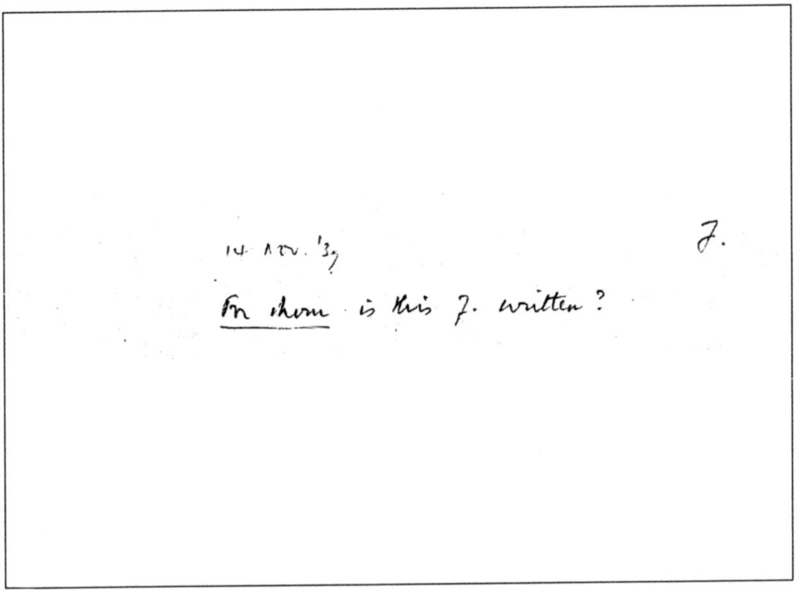

14 Nov. '37 J.

For whom is this J. written?

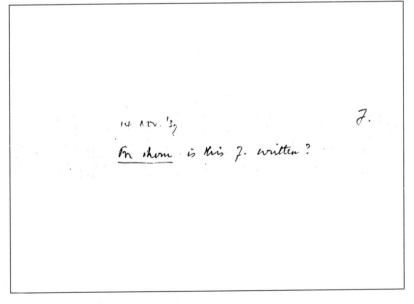

Fig. 25. Journal about journal slip.

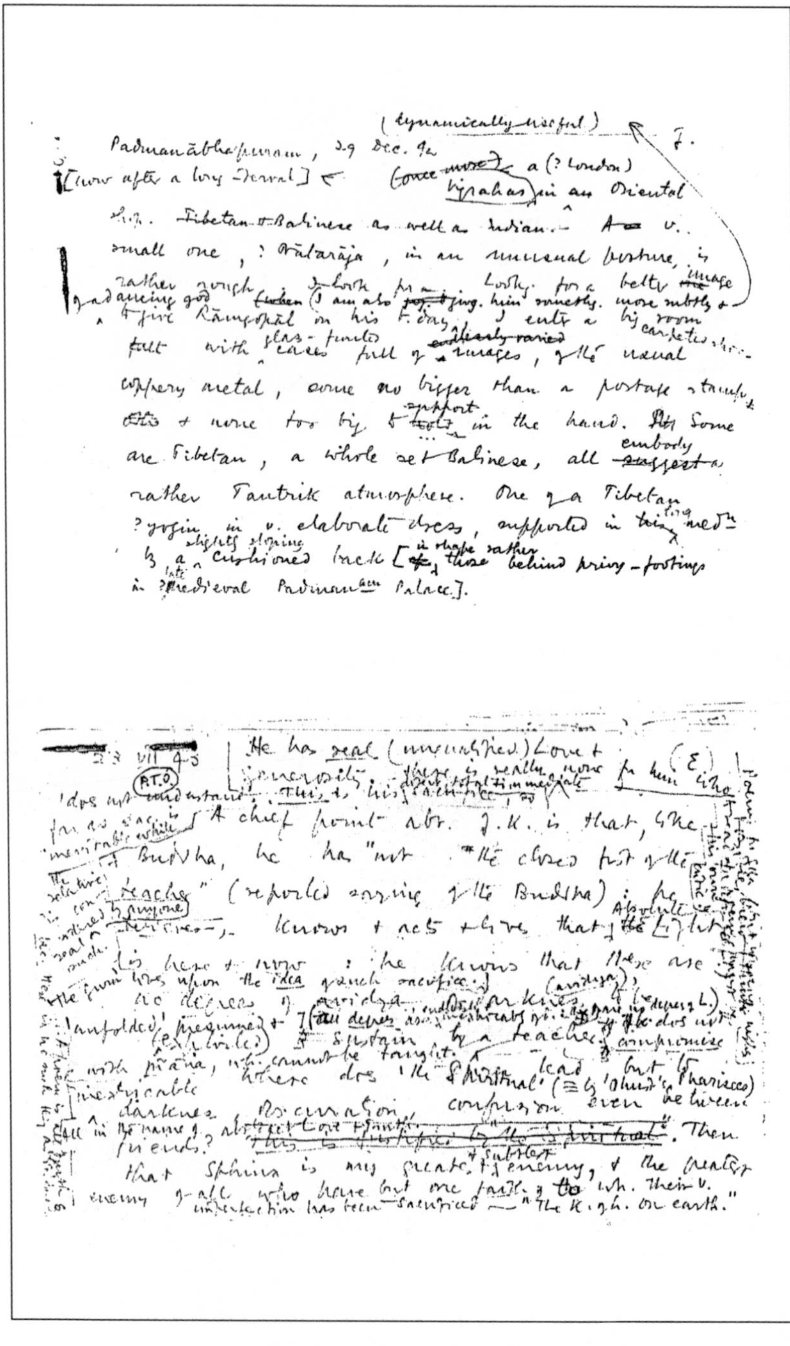

Fig. 26. Two specimens of Thompson's handwriting at its smallest.

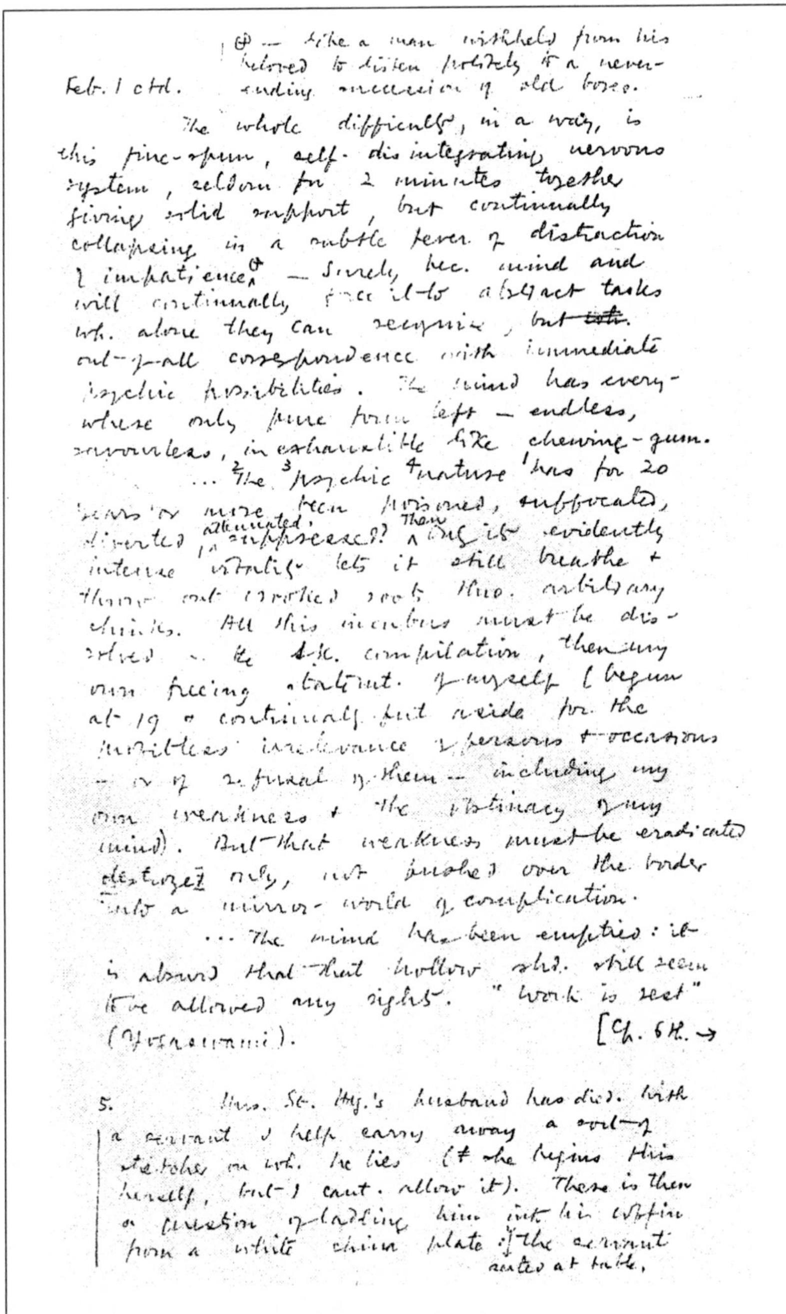
(✝) — like a man withheld from his beloved to listen politely to a never-ending succession of old bores.

Feb. 1 cont'd.

The whole difficulty, in a way, is this fine-spun, self-disintegrating nervous system, seldom for 2 minutes together giving solid support, but continually collapsing in a subtle fever of distraction & impatience(✝) — Surely, bec. mind and will continually force it to abstract tasks wh. alone they can recognize, but ~~with~~ out-of-all correspondence with immediate psychic possibilities. The mind has everywhere only pure form left — endless, savourless, inexhaustible like chewing-gum.

... The psychic nature has for 20 years or more been poisoned, suffocated, diverted, attenuated, suppressed?? Then only its evidently intense vitality lets it still breathe & throw out crooked roots thro. arbitrary chinks. All this incubus must be dissolved ... the S.K. compilation, then my own freeing statement of myself (begun at 19 & continually put aside for the worthless irrelevance of persons & occasions — or of refusal of them — including my own weakness & the obstinacy of my mind). But that weakness must be eradicated destroyed only, not pushed over the border into a mirror-world of complication.

... The mind has been emptied: it is absurd that that hollow shd. still seem to be allowed any rights. "Work is rest" (Vivekananda). [Cf. 6th. →

5. Mrs. St. Hy.'s husband has died. With a servant I help carry away a sort of stretcher on wh. he lies (& she begins this herself, but I can't allow it). There is then a question of ladling him into his coffin from a white china plate of the servant eaten at table.

Fig. 27. Page of scrupulously neat handwriting in a notebook of 1943, a period notable for stability and intense concentration.

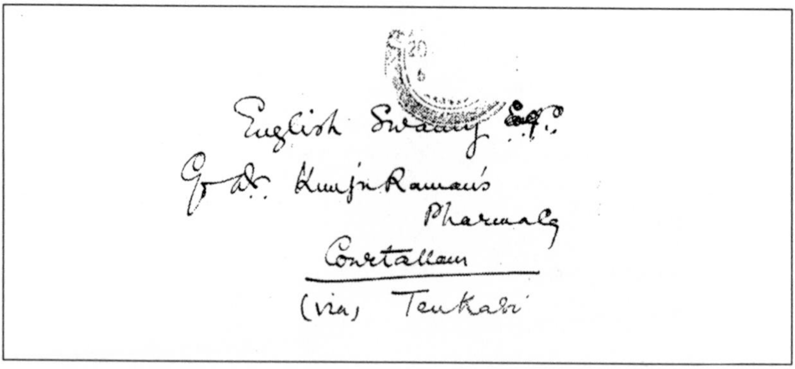
English Swamy Esq.
C/o Dr. Kunju Raman's
Pharmacy
Courtallam
(via) Tenkasi

Fig. 28. Envelope addressed to Thompson, carefully cut to be used as journal slip on reverse.

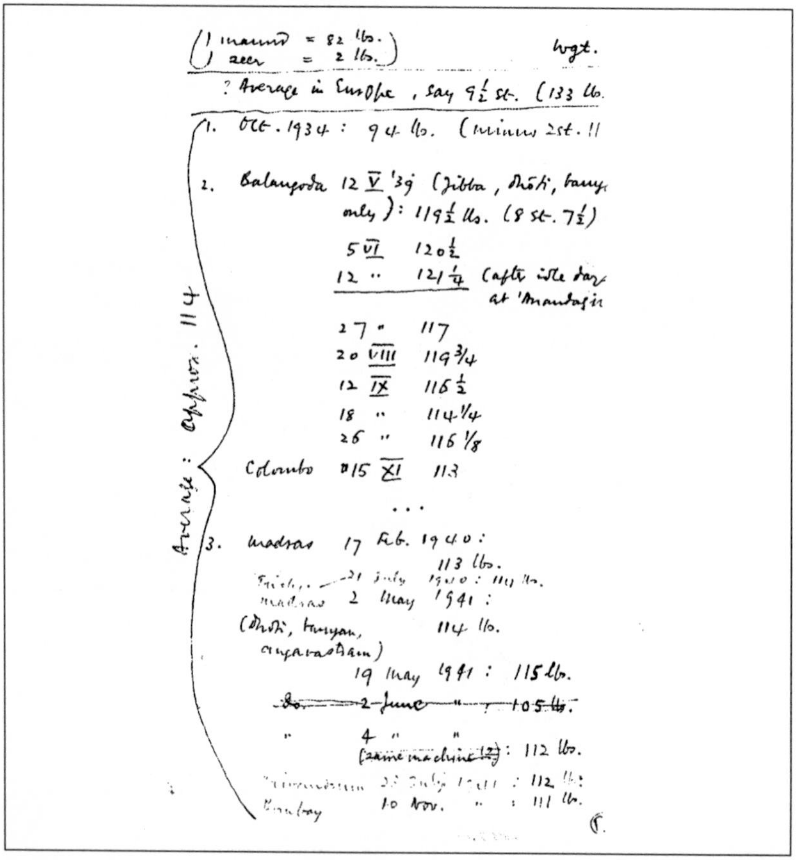
(1 maund = 82 lbs.)
(1 seer = 2 lbs.)
wgt.
? Average in Europe, say 9½ st. (133 lbs.
1. Oct. 1934: 94 lbs. (minus 2 st. !!
2. Balangoda 12 V '39 (Jibba, Dhoti, banyan only): 119½ lbs. (8 st. 7½)
5 VI 120½
12 " 121¼ (after idle day at 'Anandagiri
27 " 117
20 VIII 119¾
12 IX 116½
18 " 114¼
26 " 116⅛
Colombo 15 XI 113
. . .
3. Madras 17 Feb. 1940: 113 lbs.
2 May 1941:
(Dhoti, banyan, angavastram) 114 lbs.
19 May 1941: 115 lbs.
~~do. 2 June " : 105 lbs.~~
" 4 " " (same machine !?): 112 lbs.
Bombay 10 Nov. " : 111 lbs.
Average: approx. 114

Fig. 29. Thompson's weight chart, which he kept throughout his life in India, providing clues to his varying state of health additional to his regular notes which he made weekly, sometimes daily.

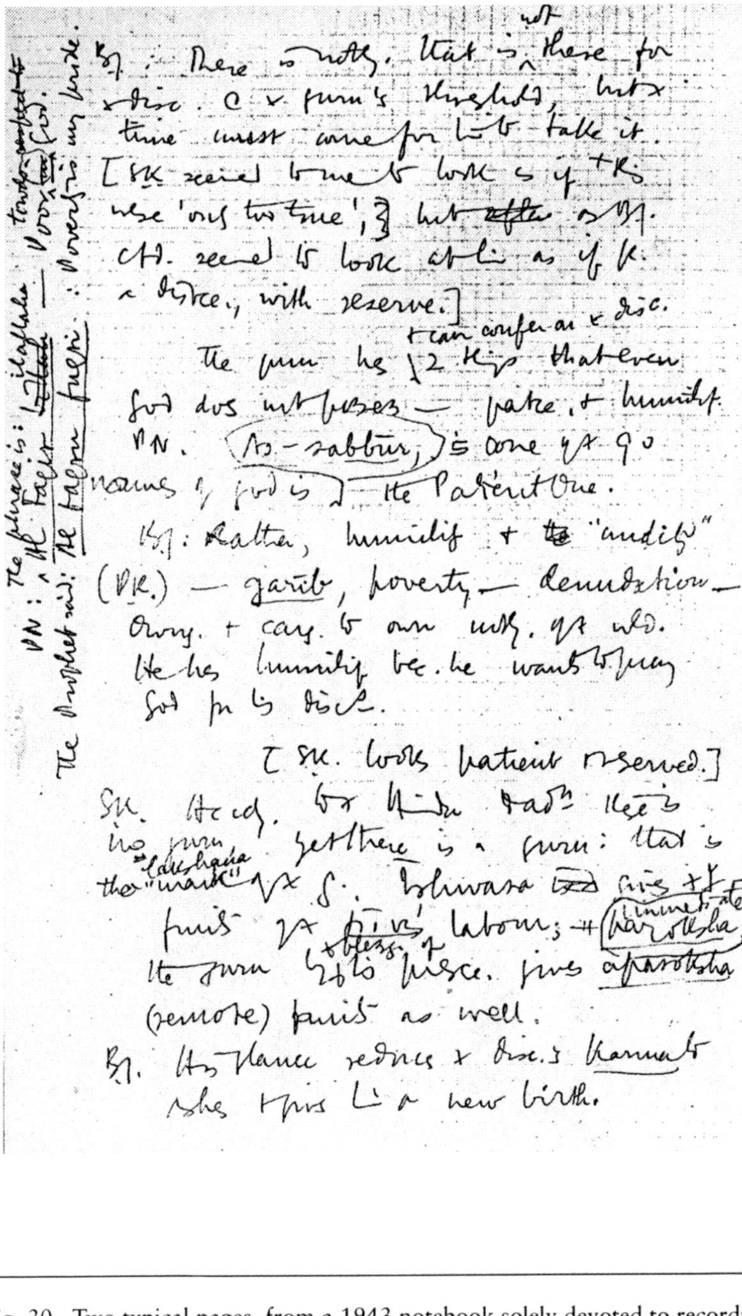

Fig. 30. Two typical pages from a 1943 notebook solely devoted to recording talks with the Jnani.

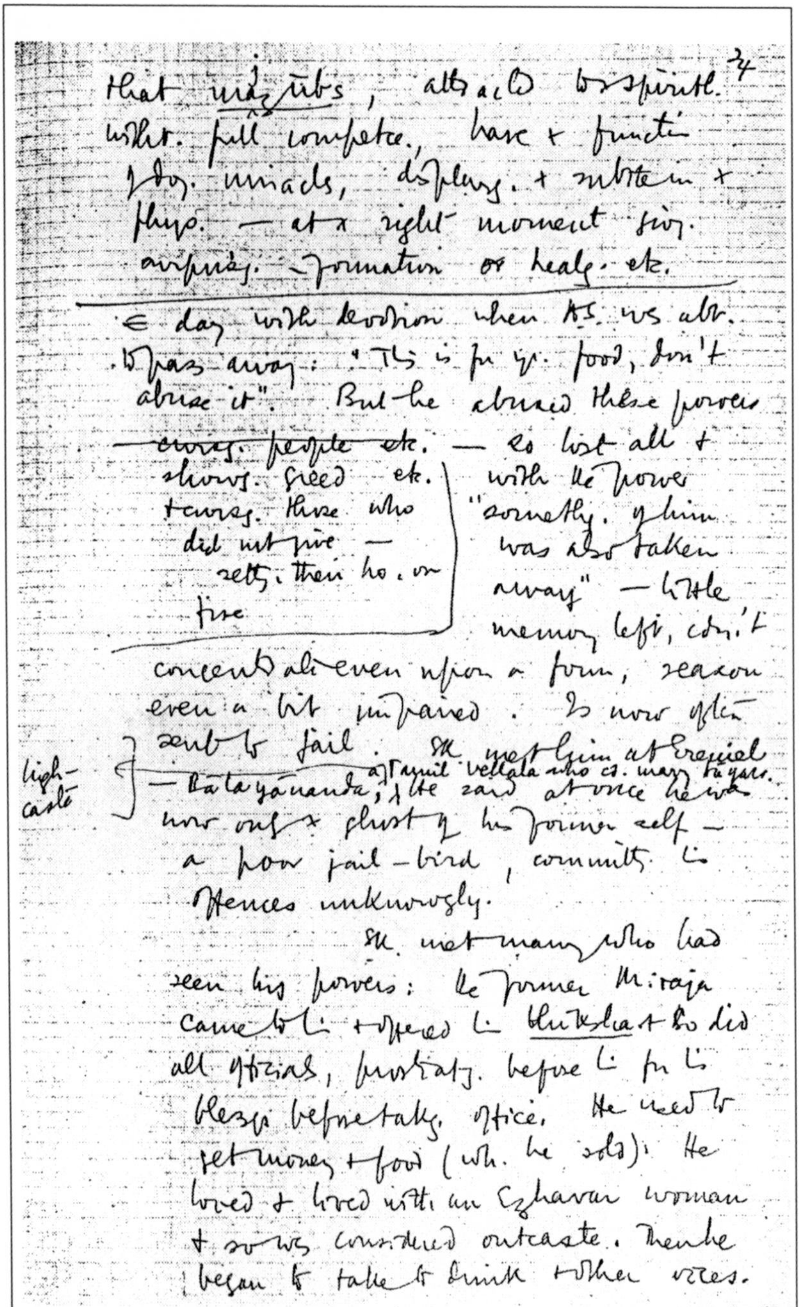
that mazūbs, attracted to spirit. 24
without full competence, have + function
of dog. miracles, displays + subtle in +
phys. — at a right moment give
anything — formation or healing etc.

One day with devotion when A.S. was about
to pass away: "This is for your food, don't
abuse it". But he abused these powers
~~curing people etc.~~ — so lost all +
showing greed etc. tearing those who did not give — setting their house on fire
with the power "something of him was also taken away" — little memory left, can't
concentrate even upon a form, reason
even a bit impaired. Is now often
sent to jail. SK met him at [illegible]
high-caste — Balayananda, after Tamil Vellala who [illegible] many years. He said at once he was
now only a ghost of his former self —
a poor jail-bird, committing
offences unknowingly.
SK. met many who had
seen his powers: the former Maharaja
came to him + offered him bhutkshast. So did
all officials, prostrating before him for his
blessing before taking office. He used to
get money + food (which he sold). He
loved + lived with an Ezhavan woman
+ so was considered outcaste. Then he
began to take to drink + other vices.

Fig. 31.

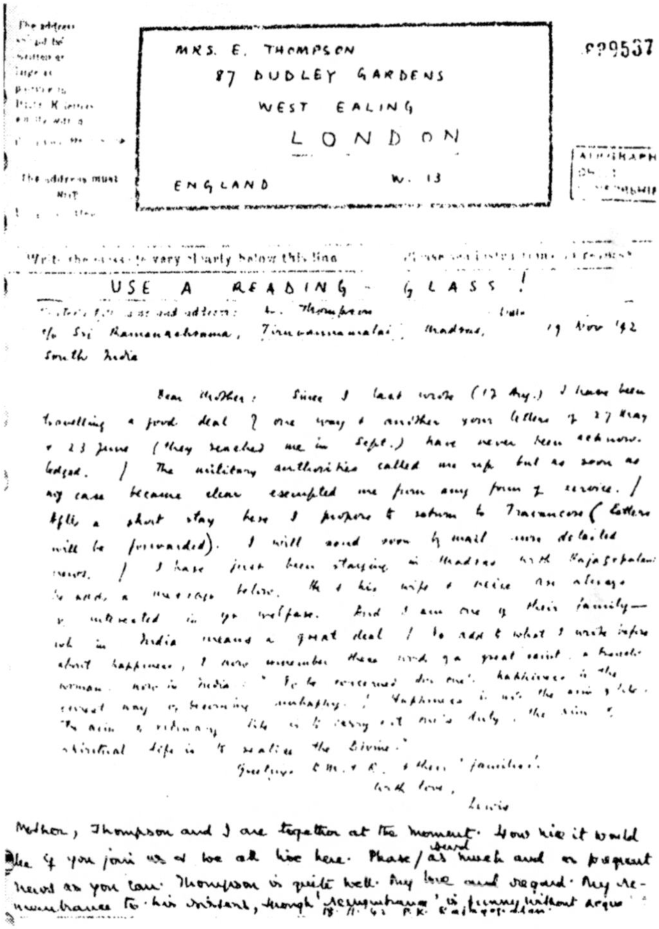

MRS. E. THOMPSON
87 DUDLEY GARDENS
WEST EALING
LONDON
ENGLAND W. 13

USE A READING - GLASS!

L. Thompson
c/o Sri Ramanasramam, Tiruvannamalai, Madras, South India
19 Nov '42

Dear Mother: Since I last wrote (17 Aug.) I have been travelling a good deal. [illegible] your letters of 27 May & 23 June (they reached me in Sept.) have never been acknowledged. / The military authorities called me up but as soon as my case became clear exempted me from any form of service. / After a short stay here I propose to return to Travancore (letters will be forwarded). I will send soon by mail more detailed news. / I have just been staying in Madras with Rajagopalan [illegible] below. He & his wife & [illegible] are always [illegible] interested in yr welfare. And I am one of their family [illegible] in India means a great deal / To add to what I write before about happiness, I now remember these words of a great saint, a [illegible] woman now in India: "To be concerned [illegible] happiness is the [illegible] unhappy. Happiness is not the aim of life. [illegible] The aim of ordinary life is to carry out one's duty, the aim of spiritual life is to realise the Divine."

Greetings to M. & R. & their families.

With love,

Lewis

Mother, Thompson and I are together at the moment. How nice it would be if you join us & we all live here. Please send as much and as frequent news as you can. Thompson is quite well. My love and regard. My remembrance to his [illegible], though 'acquaintance' is funny without acqu[illegible]

18. 11. 42 P.K. Rajagopalan

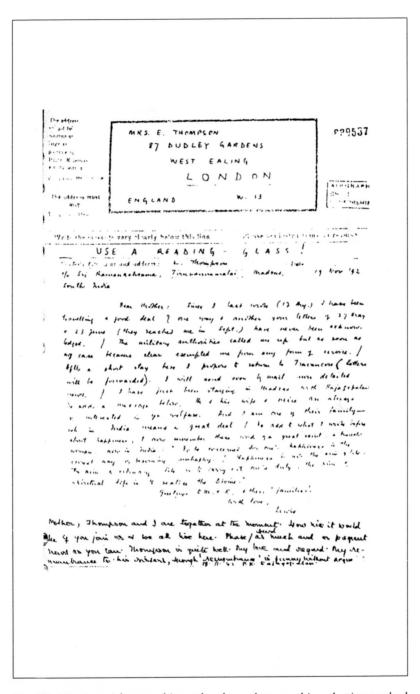

Fig. 32. Wartime airletter to his mother, by a photographic reduction method introduced for handling overseas mail. Message appended by P.K.R. at bottom.

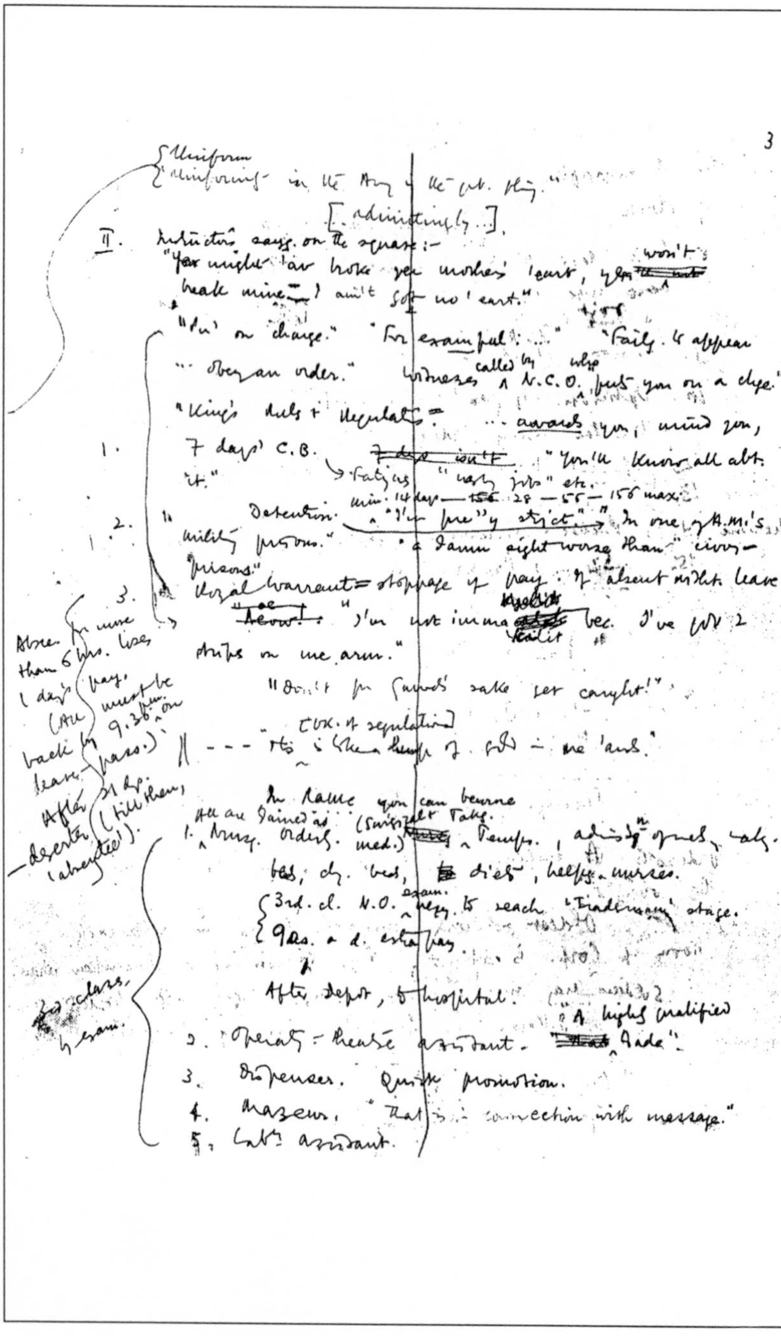
3

[illegible] in the Army [illegible]

[admittingly..]

II. Instructor says on the square:— "You might 'av broke yer mother's 'eart, you won't break mine — I ain't got no 'eart."

"Put on charge." "For exampul: ..." "Fails to appear ... obey an order." Witnesses called by N.C.O. who puts you on a chge."

"King's Rules & Regulations = ... awards you, [illegible] you,

1. 7 days' C.B. ... "You'll know all abt. it." → fatigues "nasty jobs" etc.

2. " Detention min. 14 days — 28 — 56 — 156 max. "Pre'y strict." In one of H.M.'s military prisons." "A damn sight worse than civvy prisons."

3. Royal warrant = stoppage of pay. If absent without leave.

"I'm not immune bec. I've got 2 stripes on me arm."

"Don't for God's sake get caught!"

[OK. of regulation] --- "It's like a lump of soft in me 'and."

In Ramc you can become ... All are trained as (Surgical Tech.)

1. Nursg. Orderly. med.) Temps., admin of meds, [illegible] beds, chg. beds, diets, helping nurses.

3rd cl. N.O. exam. necy. to reach 'Tradesman' stage.
9as. a d. extra pay.

After depot, to hospital. "A highly qualified Aide"

2. Operating-theatre assistant.

3. Dispenser. Quick promotion.

4. Masseur. "That is in connection with massage."

5. Lab. assistant.

Absent for more than 6 hrs. loses 1 day's pay. (All must be back by 9.30 p.m. on leave pass.) After 21 days — deserter (till then 'absentee').

3rd class, by exam.

Fig. 33. Page from Devlali Barracks journal. Vertical line means that he has rejected it as more description, and I have followed suit.

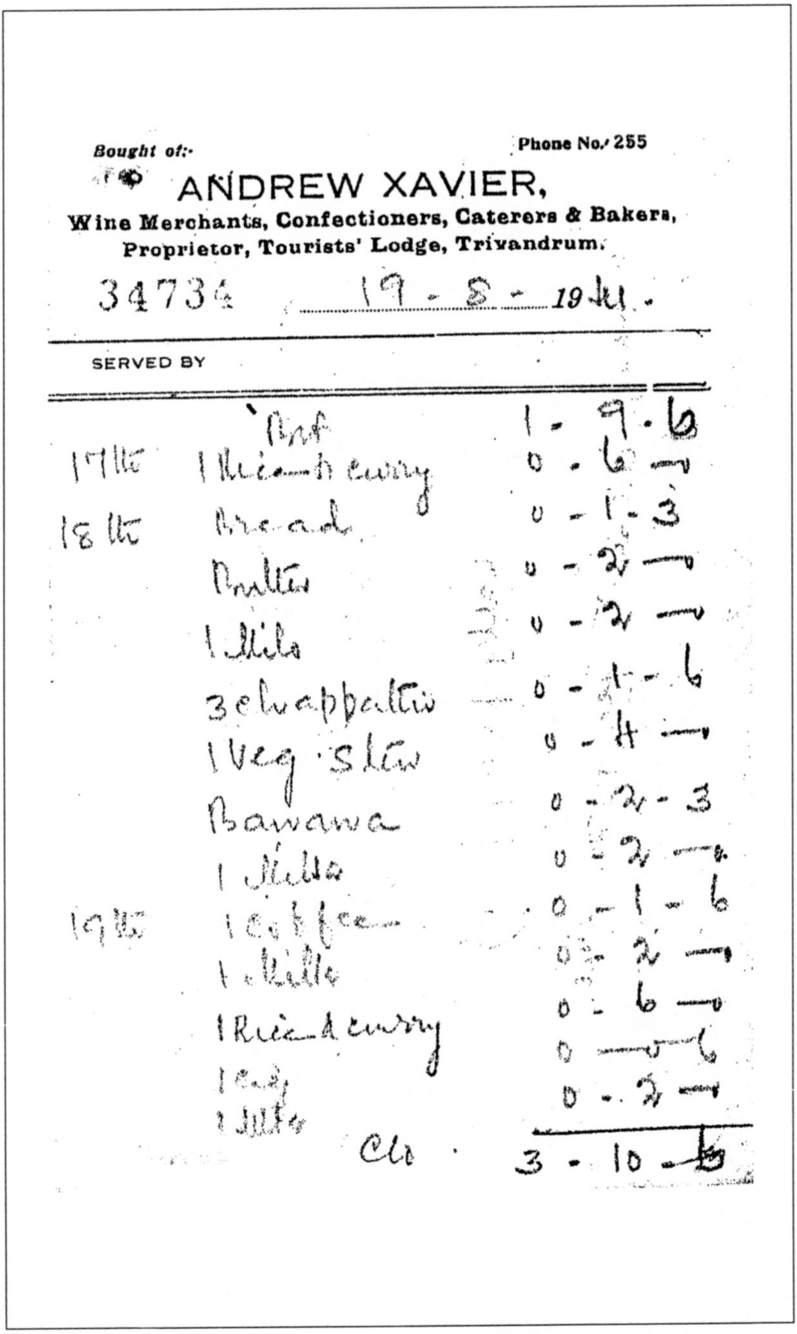
Bought of:- Phone No. 255

ANDREW XAVIER,

Wine Merchants, Confectioners, Caterers & Bakers,

Proprietor, Tourists' Lodge, Trivandrum.

34734 19-8-1941.

SERVED BY

	Bref	1-9-6
17th	1 Rice & curry	0-6-0
18th	Bread	0-1-3
	Butter	0-2-0
	1 Milk	0-2-0
	3 chappathi	0-1-6
	1 Veg. stew	0-4-0
	Banana	0-2-3
	1 Milk	0-2-0
19th	1 coffee	0-1-6
	1 Milk	0-2-0
	1 Rice & curry	0-6-0
	1 egg	0-0-6
	1 Milk	0-2-0
	Cts	3-10-6

Fig. 34. Lodging house bill utilised as a journal slip.

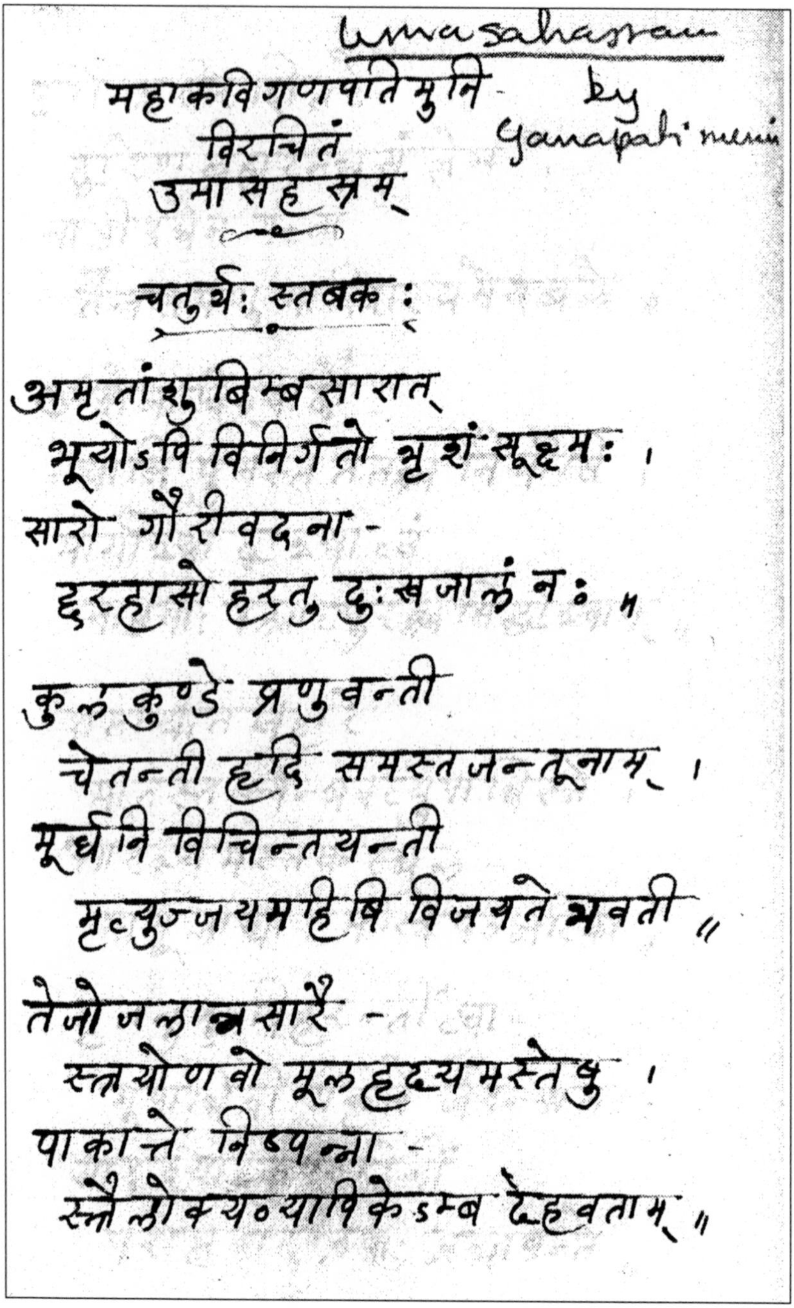

Umasahasram
महाकविगणपतिमुनि- by
विरचितं Ganapati muni
उमासहस्रम्
चतुर्थः स्तबकः
अमृतांशुबिम्बसारात्
भूयोऽपि विनिर्गतो भृशं सूक्ष्मः ।
सारो गौरीवदना-
द्दरहासो हरतु दुःखजालं नः ॥
कुलकुण्डे प्रणुवन्ती
चेतन्ती हृदि समस्तजन्तूनाम् ।
मूर्धनि विचिन्तयन्ती
मृत्युञ्जयमहिषि विजयते भवती ॥
तेजोजलान्नसारैः-
स्त्रयोणवो मूलहृदयमस्तेषु ।
पाकान्ते निष्पन्ना-
स्त्रैलोक्यव्यापिकेऽम्ब देहवताम् ॥

Fig. 35. Sample page of Thompson's beautiful copy of the Umasahasram.

The Journals of Lewis Thompson

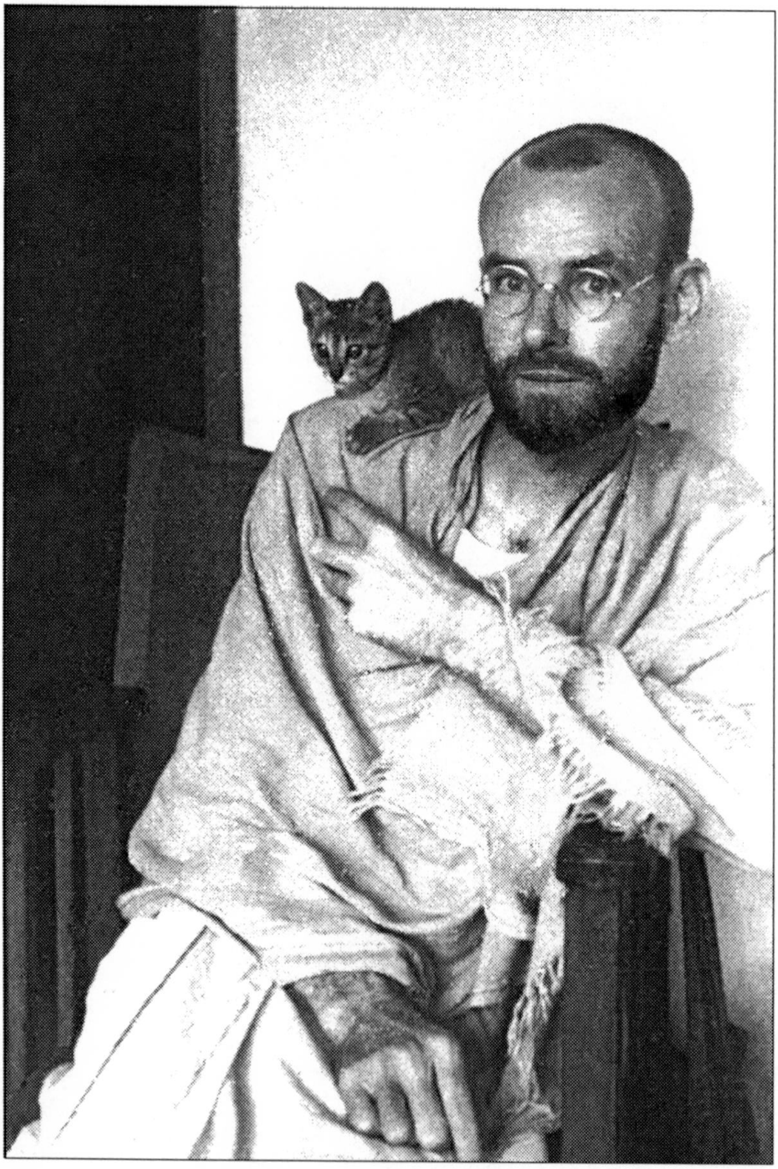

Fig. 36. Lewis Levien Thompson, 1942.

1

Early Years Before The Journal 1909–32

This chapter is a literal transcription of all surviving notes and descriptive fragments relating to Thompson's life until his departure for India. It includes everything that survives by way of record of those years. His family could provide nothing more; his nameless contemporaries have vanished without trace. More dossier than journal, these few pages nevertheless give us valuable information about the young Lewis Thompson. The bare catalogue of significant incidents and key formative influences is published in the same form as it was jotted down, his memorandum for unspecified future use. Like much of the material in this volume, those lists have survived many thousands of miles packed away in Thompson's battered tin trunk—his literary archive—as it was carted to and fro across the Indian sub-continent. The journals were stored after Thompson's death for many years in perfect archival conditions in the loft of Ella Maillart's Swiss chalet in the highest village in Europe. Later, I stored it, and consulted it for a second long period in two of my homes, where I read and transcribed much of it. Very diligent reading of Thompson's often miniscule handwriting was required, as well as knowledge of Sanskrit terminology. Like Robert Walser (an early twentieth century Swiss writer), Thompson's manuscripts are a marvel in themselves, conveying the vivacity and luminosity of his style more intimately than cold print can ever do. I hope that one day a low-cost facsimile process of reproduction will be invented, so that the beauty of the script, and the ingenuity of the 'tabloid' layout in the later volumes of the journals can be appreciated for their own sake. For now the entirety of the archive is preserved under ideal conditions by Washington State Libraries, Pullman, Washington.

Excerpts from letters written to family and friends 'in later years' provide the dimension of retrospective reflection on Thompson's youth.

He notes in his journal the basis on which he mistrusts descriptive recollection: 'What cannot survive as poetry in the fires that purify the whole mind is merely dross.' He finds a passage in Cocteau's 'Opium' which best expresses his reservations regarding the possibility of writing an adequate account of his own life:

> "I wonder how people can write the lives of poets since they themselves could not write their own life. There are too many mysteries, too many falsehoods, too many complications.
>
> What can be said of the passionate friendships which must be confused with love, and yet nevertheless are something else, of the limits of love and friendship, of this region of the heart in which unknown senses participate, which cannot be understood by those who live standard lives?
>
> Dates overlap, years mingle together. The snow melts, the feet fly away; no footprints remain."
>
> —Jean Cocteau, *Opium: The Diary of a Cure*, Trl. Margaret Crosland and Sinclair Road, p.118. London, 1957.

Note: The glyph is used to mark a gap—lapse of time, a change of place, or the break between one theme and another— within a dated entry. Where there is no glyph it means that this dated entry has ended altogether and the empty space designates that tbe next passage following it is a different dated entry. Occasionally, when continuity of theme, or affinity of events calls for it, certain entries have been brought together in one uninterrupted sequence in order to help the reader follow the narrative without the distraction of intervening entries on other themes. Brief editorial interventions are inserted in italics. Very few entries written between 1937 and 1944 (covered by this volume) are undated, even though each journal entry, at that time, was written on a separate sheet, or pinned set of sheets; undated entries have been placed in as close chronological order as possible. Thompson was in the habit of indicating a change of location by writing the new place-name at the head of the first dated entry after arrival. As far as possible this practice has been retained here. Chapter headings have been added for greater facility in reading. Where four dots appear, or three, that does not mean an editorial cut but Thompson's own way to conclude a passage.

Father born at Gosport, 21st March 1866; Mother born at Hildenborough, Kent, 30th April 1872. At marriage in 1908 (my conception, April) aged 42 and 36 respectively.

30.V.43.

Dear Mother,

I've had no reply to mine of June 5th last in which I pointed out that in one letter you wrote that father's father, and in another that his grandfather, was a Jew: which is it? I also asked you please to write a long letter with full details of all you know about his side of the family, and yours. I should particularly like to hear about your mother and father, their antecedents, history, character, sayings, etc.

With love,
Lewis

26.VI.43.

No, Mother dear, the two sentences about ancestors in your letter of 5th April are not at all satisfying: they tell me far less than I know already. I thought that when people get to 71 they love to reminisce. Do please write me a long gossipy letter, with everything you can remember. Leave it on your desk for a week or two and take it up when you feel inclined.

Now I can tell you a great deal more than you tell me. The Jew (or the half-Jew, for now you put him back a generation, and the Irishwoman too) used to keep an Olde Curiosity Shoppe at Gosport, so I've heard. Father's mother (non-Jew) was his second wife. I imagine him a difficult, moody, solitary old man, probably rather dirty, stooping, in sloppy old clothes hanging at the pockets (probably from the bottles of beer he used to bring home from the cobbled streets to drink in bed). Morose and rather enigmatic. And a family of tall, lean, slightly sallow women, long noses with a hook at the end, but rather handsome in their way. Nobody seems to know what they thought or did, whom they married or what happened to them. Father no doubt felt he did not quite belong to this tribe. He was apprenticed to a yacht-maker but ran away at 18, with George Harris, to join the army, and went to Africa and India. He was in the siege of Ladysmith, eating stewed leather. And in India, wounded in the leg (how?), he astonished everyone by leaping a hurdle.

Then *your* father. Quite a different story. He built the village church (it was quite a big one at Hildenborough) and played the organ on Sundays. With great dignity, you told me, portly, with black gloves, he used to walk before funerals, for he was the undertaker too. And I quite believe he had a superior sense of style: his funerals, I'm sure, were models of suave propriety. I even think he must have somehow added a touch of grace or elegance, for by all accounts he had the artistic temperament. I vaguely remember a photo of a handsome man with a wavy golden beard, broad forehead and something of an air about him. Of course he drank and frittered away whatever he had or earned and was a great trial to your mother, but everyone liked and respected him and he had a position in the village. People even said there was "an Honourable" in the family; but there were also, probably wild stories somewhere.—A gifted, charming, rather capricious man, too generous (perhaps, also, too proud) to think of mere welfare. In his inward life alone, having no real friend, for all he was so sociable.

Your mother, subtle, delicate (in health too, probably)—really a finer nature than his and certainly steadier. I imagine her slender, rather pale, with a quiet voice and quiet gestures, choosing dresses of fine muslin, not out of vanity but from natural distinction. Both were highly strung and the atmosphere in that house must have been full of ozone. When you were naughty you were shut out in the garden (I imagine it an orchard) to be stung by the dragonflies—but what did you call them?

What was your mother's maiden name, and what of her family? The big photo of an intelligent woman (?with blue eyes and black hair) that is perhaps still hanging on your walls, I always took to be the 'Irish grandmother'. You told me she was a beauty. I should very much like to hear more about her. Even her name I've never heard.

The uncle Ephraim. Was he your mother's brother? I remember him as the most charming old man, small, delicately made, almost elfin, with exquisite manners and a sweet lightness and gaiety.

Then at Hildenborough (?), when we were still quite small, we visited an aunt of yours. I remember a strange, rather sinister sexless creature in bed, with a gathered nightcap, and on a little table I felt sure it was tobacco for chewing—or was it simply a clay pipe? It was on that visit, no doubt, that we stayed with some other relations, founders of a firm of porcelain filter-makers with an office in London near the Tower. I remember the old-world manners of one of them who, after lunch, took the little boy aside (can I have been ten?) and, stooping, asked considerately, confidentially: "Are you quite comfortable in every way?" (I can still almost hear his voice). I could never have brought this Victorian euphemism on to the same level in my mind with my desire to make water (anyway, I had noticed the glass door at the top of the stairs): it belonged to quite a different world. I admired it as I would a line of poetry. But I felt a moment of superiority when talking of chemistry (he must have heard I was beginning it at school), politely trying to keep abreast of the new knowledge, he said deferentially: "Yes, one liquid clarifies another".

Then the brother Fred you were so fond of. What is the story that by some tragic mistake he died (so young) making experiments in inoculating monkeys? That he experimented upon himself?

The cemetery full of summer grasses, and the summer trees. The quiet village, the quiet house, the half-forgotten life, the old world turning over in the scent of hay and lavender to go to sleep. The quiet voices, decorous habits, gentle eyelids preserving the mellow gold of a world still suave and comfortable, but grown so fragile the least shock would wake it into the modern bustle and crudity.

Do write it all for me: you are the only one, now, who can pass it on. One day perhaps I shall visit, and perhaps with you, the old village, and Gosport, and see what can still be gathered about the old people whose foibles and lovableness still, perhaps, secretly influence our lives.

Love always from Lewis

I suppose by now I have another nephew or niece. *[He did.]*

13 January 1909, born.

c. 3 April 1910: first visit to 'the Priory', West Molesey, Surrey (aet. 1 year 3 months), just before birth of sister Margot (17 April 1910). Stayed at the Priory every year, and also at Westbury till death of Aunt A. (20 November 1927). About six weeks longest stay. Usually two or three weeks in the summer. Influenced sense of time.

No apparatus of even the most subtle and elegant leisure could replace for me now the warm, perfumed air of my childhood at 'The Priory'. The lawns; the earthy richness of the potting-shed; the sound of the loaded wheelbarrow; the delicious, wholesome smell of the gardener; the gravel drives; the cool and stately porch; the loaded fruit-trees; the trailing roses and formal stone steps and urns; the sombre dahlias, dark suns; the white slatted garden seats with the whiter droppings of birds; the acid smell of geranium; the heavy rich warmth of the conservatory. And then the subtle, majestic, aromatic smell of the drawing-room; cabinet drawers with cigars, ivory chessmen, glossy cards; the great Chinese dragon-vase in the corner of the stairs; the wide marriage bed with its folding wings of pink silk; cross-hilted swords (I imagined them Crusaders') under the high window of the hall; the fascinating curved dagger on the wall in the morning-room; the tea-table on the lawn with its sun-flecked cloth and the fragrant hot

silver vessels breathing with delicate waves of steam—all the wide summer leisure that then seemed timeless, universal, eternal. And penetrating all, that indescribable *pathos*, luminosity, of the life of childhood.
1913 (aet. 4): kindergarten. Winter cold.

Fig. 37. The Priory, West Molesey, Surrey, England.

Childhood.

To Woolwich with father, it must have been as a very small boy. Horse-bus entered by steps at the rear. Huge funnels of the boats glimpsed behind dock-walls, high up against the sky. Wide new virgin atmosphere, vast overwhelming ozone, traffic of light and air, penetrating new emotional music, immense poignancy of distance and departure created by those lazy and dramatic vast machines.

Manor Park or Ilford, East London. Wide quays with thousands of barrels appear small as toys. The peculiar still, dull but dramatic light—vast environment of rails, factories, bridges, powerful and forlorn...All made poignantly intimate and lyrical by a smell of vinegar, horse-dung, sawdust, smoke and iron.

Such experience was perhaps an element in my deep recognition, much later, of the vast Rimbaldian towns.

1921 (aet. 12): Aunt N. dies.
To sister Margot:

In a way, I see that I'm not a bit different now from that boy of 12. Perhaps one contains everything at birth and it only has to be worked out, realised, fulfilled, understood. One has to transform oneself into what one is. The child lacks the organs for recognizing himself. Becoming conscious of one's experience one becomes the victim of that consciousness—in over-passing every given, relative self.

1922. (aet.13): 'Westbury", Ealing.
First remembered emission, and Avalokitesvara figure must have been before this date. Lecture on Pythagoras. Harding, 'Buddhist'. Indian and Chinese scriptures. Rituals.

1924. (aet.15): Wembley Exhibition. 'Merleswood'. Terrible 'absent-mindedness'.

1927. (aet. 17): Left school.

1927. B.K. B.G. W.E. *[friends]* Whitechapel. Rambles. Promenade concerts. Beethoven. Op.131.

1927-9 Miscellaneous reading, Central Library for Students: Laotse, Waley, *Chinese Poems*. Renaissance. Humanism. Goethe. Havelock Ellis. English 19th century. Plato: *Symposium*. Blake. Leopardi. Keyserling. Katherine Mansfield. J.M. Murray. Wasserman. Rolland. Dostoievski. Pythagoras. Heraklitus.

Shaftesbury Avenue films—Cabinet of Dr. Caligari, Student of Prague, Nibelungen, Therese Raquin, Jean Epstein's Fall of the House of Usher, Conrad Veidt, Emil Jannings; Lotte Reiniger's rococo silhouettes.

Russian Ballet at Covent Garden.
Moscow Arts Theatre.
Schnabel, Dolmetsch, Elizabeth Schumann, Pachmann, Harriet Cohen, Furtwangler, Mengelberg.

1928. Workshop of Nature á la nineteenth century.
Mecklenbergh Square.

21.12.1928, c. 10:45 am. Father dies of pleurisy, aet. 62

Anne episode, 1930, aet. 21:

A terrible ruinous dumb intensity, the blindness of sensibility without experience, terrible self-destroying, self-martyring gauchness. No worship of grace, nobility and beauty can be more intense and helpless than this youthfulness—self-denigration, self-immolation in the agony of acute but undifferentiated consciousness, and utter lack of self-recognition and precedent; only the callow, obstinate disinterested mind, and femininely sensitive and pliable ego, the complete self-criticism, the undifferentiated purity from which every kind of assurance could only seem a blasphemy.

An important element certainly was the intense repudiation of B.G's clumsiness and sensual egotism.

Impossible arbitrary willed adieu to Anne *[with whom he had a love affair]* who listened with wide-open, luminous, very serious, helplessly-reflecting eyes, while with self-poisonous violence I outraged every grace that was natural to me. All that I said was of course invented, improvised—a poem, forced, perverse, of the state of inexplicable Anguish I was in.

Ln. had said: you are destroying yourself. And perhaps Anne could also at moments have feared that I should in the end commit suicide.

Truant in Kensington Gardens, reading Rimbaud.
The blind arbitrariness of all human work.
Beethoven Op. 130,2,5. Russian Ballet.
Meetings with Bill, talk of 'Magic'. Intense need for and desperate attempt at absolute integral sincerity. Still unachieved, though now (1937) more conscious that the ego is the enemy of 'psychic centrality'; no doubt the solution in the beginning of the true life and 'Magic'.
Last visit to B.G.
1-15 June: Tarascon—travelling players, the Rhone. Avignon—interior corners and crossways, Palais des Papes. Arles—edge of town café, shepherd. Saint Remy—Van Gogh's room in the asylum, part of Cocteau's *Opium* in *Nouvelle Revue Francaise*: he *[Cocteau]* cannot penetrate Rimbaud. Les Baux on foot.
Mrs. Brandt, Russell Square. One day she told me I was easier to talk to now: before, my aura was 'very dark'.
21 Brunswick Square.
December 24-28: Paris. Usual grim, melancholy, transhumanistic will. Solitary meals in empty little restaurants. Louvre: Leonardo's St.John the Baptist, Bacchus, Mona Lisa. Fantin-Latour's Rimbaud in *Coin de Table.* Impressionists. Post-Impressionists.
Covent Garden flower market. Exciting nascence. 'Resignation' from book announced after four years (since 1927, aet.18).
January 1931: deputy at 'reading class' of boys—rough lads. G.E. gives me £25 to reach work at diamond mine, South Africa.
S.E.1. The Abyss. The sun's light a darkness. Objects terribly and mutely dense and symbolic, or transparent under an unnameable pressure. With Mrs. Brandt at Russell Square, terrible involuntary and irrelevant sobbing from days piling up at solar plexus. Sleeping naked, late rising, workmen

in sunshine opposite. Experience of Ignorance. Overpass notebooks! And books. Kept Rimbaud and *Verba Christi.*

The will to surpass everything that sent me forward always into a desert. The one or two books to which I intimately responded I could for that very reason least accept and after a hasty reading left them behind in hotels. I did not understand that this was the reverse of having forgotten them. I finally stopped all reading and writing and destroyed a complicated long manuscript so as no longer to have to struggle with it.

I was alone; always alone, in polar tension with all I most desired (directly expressed in standing opposite the young gypsy in the centre of a little crowd at Les Saintes Maries de la Mer)—out of ignorance, inexperience, absurd innocence, disinterestedness, a devastating humility that was unconscious fastidiousness and pride.

Yet not pride, but will to the Absolute, and which first nullified myself. I was tormented in every direction by the Absolute—the absolute of physical beauty that made me worse than unconscious of whatever natural grace I had, that turned its back on given ease and elegance without having seen it and looked out into a black night where there were only silent stars. Absolute of the Eros that held every desire too mean: an unrecognized ultimate of consummation imposed a white-hot virginity, the x-ray cold of a salamander. Absolute of the Mind reducing all knowledge beforehand to dust, making thought itself pure Labour. Absolute of Intuition too pure to be conscious of itself, ringing always in a void of sound denser than silence. Absolute of Ethos for which God was an idol and the devil merely a clown, a poor mountebank—that could believe in neither good nor evil, heaven nor hell. Absolute of spiritual will for which life and death were merely abstract opposites leaving an irresoluble solitary ghost neither born into the world nor capable of suicide, for whom both were equally unactual, but whom pure clairvoyance at every moment timelessly destroyed and recreated, for whom the Object was always supernatural, overwhelming nostalgia, suffocating pungency of absolute and therefore self-negating Poetry.

Every sound, every sight, rang, shone arbitrary in the Void, with the extreme fragility, irridescence, surface tension of a bubble that has no place in water or in air.

No words can exhaust this for it first exhausted all words.

That whole level of vital experience and imagination whose supernatural intensities, whose terrible ozone, made me feel so direct an intimacy with Rimbaud is gone now, has burned itself in my nerves to a white ash. One goes on to the longer, subtler task of reducing the Mind too, past all sanity and insanity.

When all romantic, dualistic strength and fatality is exhausted, when the ego no longer exploits or is exploited by natural resources, strength is possible and only as a function of inner unity. For every given *personality* the Truth is *based* in the Arbitrary.

The blood is burned dry. Now nectar must flow in the pure and empty veins, in the body of resurrection.

Victoria Station. Usual solitary departure. No objective. The boat, Newhaven. At night. Irrevocable, hopeless, unlimited 'metaphysical' journey—no return possible.

[Lewis' commentary on incidents in early life frequently post-date the event itself. Since these passages fill gaps in the biographical narrative they are included here at the appropriate date at which they were originally experienced.]

5.1V.38.

Sensibility is given, but promptitude, flexibility, presence of mind, are attained only by the organisation of consciousness.

It more and more seems, now, that only the aims of yoga can canlise and satisfy my seriousness.

I have never yet found in my life the basis for complete seriousness. From my childhood I have never felt that things as they are demand it. What I rather discovered, in fact, and could not use, was the immeasurable advantage as well as the solitude, exasperation and suffering it gave not yet to have been compelled to be serious at the level where others already were.

*[*For a time Thompson worked at a bank in Gracechurch Street, locus of many subsequent dreams of the City. The major relationship of this period was with Anne, whose surname Thompson does not record.]*

15.1.43.

I gave up consciously at about 18 when several intelligent friends expected 'great things' from me the idea of any achievement whatever, including 'spiritual achievement'. This was only the rationalisation of the fact that I had never had in any sphere the least ambition. Even as a boy, asked What is your ambition? I would answer (though I could not explain what I mean) 'I am not ambitious'. Yet as my mother testifies, I was unusally energetic and conscientious. In a similar way I have always answered the question What is your aim? by pointing out that an objective is limitation and a function of limitation. —This not because I wished to be 'unlimited', understand, but because in some way, no doubt, I felt the Unlimited. From my boyhood, also, I was called a mystic because of this note in my remarks.

30.V.45

[Letter to elder sister, first paragraph only sent.]

In yours of 25th October last you wrote: 'I feel it a little difficult to write to you after such a lapse of time since I feel you may be bored by many things I could write.' Your letter of 19th March, also, makes me reflect on the tragic self-sufficiency of the English, their extraordinary emotional *pudor*.* One doesn't know if it is pride or humility: is it the depth where they oscillate so intimately that they are one? It was R. *[his younger sister]* if I remember, who had the courage to say she wanted to talk with me, and what joy and tenderness I felt once it was possible. It never occurred to me that your reaction might have been what you so generously tell me it was, or that you might have any reaction at all! Everything was obscured by the fact that I knew I was not, and could not in the circumstances be, understood: I suppose I felt I was chiefly considered a disturbing element. No, I could not even begin to be aware of my feelings: all was one inextricable interlocking of blind act and suffering. It was by this inarticulate concentration, and by the same *pudor*, that I announced my journey to Ceylon, without explanation, I think only the day before I left—and that, correspondingly, no-one asked Why? For how long? Of course it was also true that for a long time, but for the same sort of reason, we had all been—always been—out of touch with one another's thoughts and feelings, and it was impossible to make a bridge at the last moment.

This dumbness is really extraordinary, outside its context almost unbelievable. Yet I see that this impossibility, this *impurity*!, of supposing even for a moment that one can be of any interest to anyone (perfectly married, often, with refusal to admit one's awareness of the blindness or helplessness of others!) still deeply operates in me. But in spite of the essential solitude of my life all these years, I begin to see that this fastidiousness leads to great unconscious cruelty to others, who for their part could never imagine such a motive. Completing its circle upon itself, it becomes self-aware in very dangerous perversity and anguish. I have still very little real experience of others, particularly since my rather intense mind and imagination tend automatically either to subject or else reject them, and in neither, of course, do I find any reality or satisfaction. For many years an imaginative plasticity which identified itself with everyone and responded to each in his own mode made 'objectivity' impossible, and even now this makes it impossible for anyone to see me 'objectively': friends are astonished at the difference of my very appearance in relation with different people. The fact is that no relative individual *can* see another objectively—there is no such 'object': all is defined by the inter-relativity of motive—so often unconscious—and perception. Only those interest me, in practice, whom my imagination can find some excuse to use or delight in as symbols. Perhaps only children perfectly 'understand' this, for they live in the imagination and are pure, 'heartless', still see all as play: they have not yet discovered that idol, the 'object', and so directly mirror the poet, who overcomes it. Mental intelligence, quickness, subtlety I take too much for granted for it to interest me—or, really, therefore, for me to be more than a little wearied in the long run by its absence. One friend found in me for a time 'an untiring kindness', yet this is really only one of several possible veilings of incapacity to accept anything but the intensity my intellect and imagination demand. And this intensity leaves me no time for satire, irony.

But I did not mean to write about myself, only about this strange 'English' silence. What is thus borne in silence is the tragedy of existence itself. Hence the English distrust of philosophy which behaves as if this tragedy, purely a matter of experience, could be mentally explained, even truly stated mentally at all—even called tragedy. And distrust of the artist who makes articulate emotionally or imaginatively—the feeling, rather, that he must be incontinent out of weakness, shallowness, lack of heart and so betrays—that none can have authority to express the silent roots of experience, that in fact there can never be any real occasion for doing so. Whereas religion, even the most eccentric private superstition or caprice, because it respects this inexpressibility and remains inexplicable, is respected.

Perhaps all this is linked with the fact the Englishmen who go in for Oriental 'religions' generally become either Hinayana Buddhists or Muslims: in one case the fact of Suffering is the first 'Truth', there is no metaphysical affirmation, only a pure 'Existenzphilosophie'; in the other the non-rational remains as the unquestionable, inexplicable tension between man and God—which has always tended to consider monistic resolutions of it, in Ibn 'Arabi or Mansur, heretical—as Eckhart, too, in Christianity, was considered heretical.

In poetry, the characteristic English expression, this purism of experi-

---

**Archaicism meaning 'sense of decency'.*

ence the radical 'Anglo-Saxon' realism, resolves its opposite, the wayward, passionate Celtic sensiblility, imagination and quickness of mind, and thus attaining perfect articulateness, overcomes articulation, redefines perfect self-sufficient silence, the White Muteness, the suave, dignified, uncapturable beauty of the Swan. How 'English', then, is my exaltation (like Blake's) of the characteristic English expression, Poetry, as Self-sufficiency or Expression and Experience, as well as the fact that my most economical dialectic is buddhistic. Hence the extraordinary capacity of some of the most gifted English poets to remain 'ordinary men' and the English discomfort (at first) with Keats who tried to isolate the senses and emotion, Shelley who flirted with ideas, and Byron who cut a figure. But the Elizabethans *were* their poetic world, Milton and Wordsworth remained solid citizens (Wordsworth too much so), Blake is a thoroughly wholesome eccentric.

Hence also, in England, the mellow, perfectly self-protected drama, poetry, heroism of what are supposed to be ordinary lives, and the subtle, uncodified humour and humanism that respects this, and which is so enigmatic for the mental humanism of France, the self-dramatisation of Italy, self-sentimentalisation of Germany, tragic irony of Spain.

France 1931. March 9: Paris. Rimbaud's Hotel de Cluny, rue Victor-Cosin. Keyserling lectures at Trocadero.
March: Bergerac. Fountains in little squares at night. The river. The market rosé wine of local hill.
March 24: Sainte Foy la Grande. To Mme. Vigouroux, with P. Preston's introduction. No work in vineyards. Little roundabout at night outside Hotel du Cheval Blanc. Cemetery, moonlight, cypresses. Place with low white arcades. Church and flower market.
April 6: To Marseilles. Low hotels, Arabic scrawled on walls. Endless bare corridors. Russian settlement and church. The docks. Room in Vieux Port. Quay-sides, barrels, bouillabaisse. Sea: the wine lights my forehead. The strong light swarms upon the sea: in all her movements she would not and could not evade.
April 11: Cassis. Little streets, fountains, plane-trees. Incredible lighted, coloured, flowered and scented landscape with red-roofed campanile of the Domaine. Room chez retired sailor-poet. Work for Colonel C. Uday Shankar at Marseilles Opera House. Night-walk back to Cassis. Dawn at a little creek. Petit-dejeuner at cafe´on port. Light, space, Emptiness, wideness, hopeless plasticity of the heart. Little circus.

May 3: Arles. Italian cafe by Rhone. No writing, no reading. Despair. The fields. Montmajor. Cloisters of St. Trophime. The sweet corners where we piss ardently. Van Gogh's bridge. The square. Arles carriages. MS destroyed.
May 14: Martigues. Our blood is poisoned with anger and wretchedness, but things in themselves are naive and perfect. Istres. Night. Wooden castanets of frogs. Complete agony and disinterestedness. Every affirmation awakens agony because affirmation is the clearest voice of partiality.
May 16: St. Michel de Frigoulet. Thyme, rosemary, asphodel. Talk of Mistral.
May 21: Les Saintes Maries de la Mer. 11th. Century church. Lowering of relics. '*Vive les Saintes Mar-ies*'!

La Camargue. Sleeping in cars, railway carriages.
The fields: desolation of light, colour, flowers.

Lyons. Fountain, flowers, café-corner. Staying with flower-sellers. Edgar Alan Poe's house. Bibliothèque (Valéry poems). Gide, *Morceaux Choisis* in windowless hotel-room.

Germany. Frankfurt. Princess S. Kassel, Goethe's house. Firefly woods, rich flowered fields, villages. Harvest, village fair and dance. Autumn crocus. Child Erika, fairytale princess.

The light of my eyes and their knowledge incessantly stumble into sleep. I receive from an invincible distance the dangerous question of trees against the white sky; the frail and insolent flowers awaken and withold the possibility of arrival in delight. I determine and lose at the same moment the approach of certitude in unchangeable songs of iron.
Paul Dahlke's *Buddhism* 1927. Attempt to account once and for all with annihilation-idea on horizon or subconscious since 1923.
Advertisement. Letter from Sir S.D.
Cologne. Brussels.

London. October 3: 16 Glebe Place, S.W.3. Sir S.D. Wood's Harvard translation of Patanjali. Bill again. Lecture at Geographical Society: The Surviving Tradition of Indian classical dancing. At Glebe Place I ask about the cheapest way to, and in, India.
Riding, car, Arabic.

The Narrow Way.
The metaphysical voyage.

present! And he wrote me a cheque for twenty five pounds. Absolutely no obligation, of course, he added: 'I don't expect you to write to me or anything.' In fact (out of exaggerated modesty) I never wrote to either of them...

July 20:

I took it for granted that only I suffered in every relationship and always feared to be *de trop* in my simplest and most natural gestures. Thus I falsified myself, dramatised the merely mental part of me.

Because I did not realise but entirely suffered my own sensibility and the bottomless wounds it could receive I could never suppose others capable of such wounds. I had toward others all the absurd, infinite, virgin modesty of my own unconsciousness of myself, my lack of standards. The solitude I took as a matter of course, the proud and sensitive obstinacy of my mind (how could it have been otherwise?).

My whole life since, from one point of view, has been an insane, ingenious, obstinate, sterilising attempt to impose other values than my natural sensibility and the immediate faculties, the immediate destiny, it could give me.

The terrible supernatural solitude, white ringing hollowness in every subjective direction, grew more perfect, enlarged its vastness, confirmed its intimacy, permeating everything, reducing every object to a thin, luminous shell, sustaining the decor of a calm nightmare, too immediate and inescapable to need to be real, deepening a void full of a light without resonances, devastating, devoid of all purpose and all cruelty.

From the first it was impossible to know what to do. Everything I might have been doing was meaningless, subterfuge, half-consciousness. Everyone had to work, all this work built the world they live in, they could not suspect my lack of connection with it, I must label myself student, que sais-je, I must satisfy their certainty that no-one can live outside some purpose or ambition.

When I must escape unbearable noise or bugs I looked in despair for some place one would have some reason for going to. I had exhausted all my reasons (without having exhausted the Mind).

Utter lack of desire or direction and complete lack of any presupposition for relaxation. Constantly under an impending supernatural atmosphere that looked out of every stone, and reached crisis in certain groupings of objects, light and movement, in the false stillness of every landscape of presumptions; nothing but insecurity, that left me sitting on a kurb-stone or walking always past cafés or entering the church with abstract or sentimental interest because it offered no possible satisfaction. Pressure of darkness. As if the end of the world were imminent—immanent—behind a thin shell and stamped every object with terror and pathos.

And certain poignant moments and scenes in places whose name I have forgotten or how I got there. My impatience appeared as absurd ennui in completely uninteresting little towns out of season and where no tourist ever went. Alone in the cafés where it would have occurred to no-one to approach into my atmosphere I could not want to get drunk, or even get drunk. I searched pitiably for resistance, I prostituted myself in naiveties. Only unconsciousness (if it had been possible) or solemn preconception, rationality and tasks could fill every day. I was eating my own heart. But every day was a delay to make one frightened and sick with failure.

I pursued myself at every awakening with bitter and endless tasks which I could evade in my search but never forget. They were not at the centre but they were tasks perhaps related, they satisfied nothing in me, they were nauseating, bitter, dusty, but I had nowhere to pass gladly and certainly out of them.

It is my frankness, simplicity and joy that are natural...

I read nothing. I stopped for a time deliberately and completely the inconclusive notebook or scrap of paper that relieved my mind and memory of ideas; perhaps it had grown up as a laziness and dispersion of tension.

In Rimbaud I had met with profound excitement for the first time. He made the more necessary and undeniable my most extreme intransigence. I found that none of the books about him were at the level of his problem and his refusal to compromise. It was the first real and acceptable spiritual event that had happened in my life. I could have expected him to appear to me.

None of the duties we impose upon ourselves has anything to do with our real clairvoyance.

I begin to recognise and fulfil my geniality.

My dreams become poems.

All the real, *absolutely unclassifiable*, moments and visions group themselves behind me.

Perfection and exploration of the same exactly penetrating and transnatural beauty...

I sometimes feel the most intense unreasonable joy. I do not understand why everyone is not laughing. Especially—most intimately—the cripple, the leper, the fool.

The tiger is for me so much more simple and natural—and more homely—than a cat.

How much fastidiousness, despair and pride there was in this, how completely it expressed my absolute solitude! And how much always of that youthful blindness, gaucherie, lack of self-knowledge and savoir-faire—that combination of sensitiveness and inexperience, athleticism and timidity, which is the dark night of youth, by which precisely the most subtle emotion and intelligence can only turn back upon themselves in destructive suffering and irony—in which one does not know who one is or who anyone else is.

How slowly, with what complex suffering, what oscillations and reactions, what intransigence and what nostalgia, I woke to realisation of the fact that my standards were transhumanistic! A realisation which in all its consequences is far even yet from being completely mastered, assured and absolute for me.

July 24: To Mrs. Brandt at Jordans near Beaconsfield. Last visit.

How I remember her grave, absorbed, illuminated face, gaze-lost, all her deep and sweet and discreet kindliness (and could my tormented eyes have seen it—her vision and wisdom) embodied in that humble, dignified and silent form. Beautiful friend, give me now indeed the blessing I asked too lightly and conventionally that day.

Returned with Egyptologist, to St. Pancras by mistake. Excruciating. About twelve p.m., returned to Ealing, still unpacked, too late to get to Leigh-on-Sea if to reach Barry Docks in Cardiff next day.

July 25: To Cardiff.

July 26: Barry Dock. Departure for Columbo.

1932.

26 July:	Departure Barry Dock, Cardiff.
Mediterranean:	Last note to W.E. about Peyotl experience.
	Javanese cook and quartermaster. Stories of witchcraft.
	Learning Malay: 'ter lay ang' = pre-sleep state (layang-toy kite)
2 August:	Algiers.
6 "	Suez.
15 "	Aden. Smell of burnt rock.
Ceylon	
24/5 August:	Colombo. The kandyan Bhikku Anandamaitreya.
	Bulatgama, Khawatta.
2 Sept–Nov:	Ellapola. Unposted letters to W.E.
	Rassagalla. Maunam (vow of silence). Notebooks.

1933.

Aet. XXIV.	Last letter to M. Hawks.
March:	Adam's Peak: Flags moving fiercely in the moonlight—Wind and Fire, symbols of the Spirit. It is because everything visible is entirely employed. Forms of sail-cloth over funnel in wind.
	Bo-tree deva: the handkerchief.
27 July:	Balángoda.
	Katharagama festival. Cocteau: *Essaí de Critique Indirecte*, Kafka: *Great Wall of China*.
	Hook-swinging, fire-walking.
23 August:	With Shivalinga at Madulkelly. Hut on hill. Work at quotations on terrace.
	Sinhalese Theatre. Decorating the elephants, Kandy Temple of Tooth. Ganja (marihuana).
14 September:	Tambulla cave-temple. Polonnaruwa. Anuradhapura.

India

18 September:	Dhanushkodi.
	Ramesvaram. Ramnad. Ganga, sadhu guest, temple, seashore—powerful enchanted dream.
	Madura temple.
22 September:	Madras
23 "	Meet P.K.R. for first time. Notebooks. Prose-poems.

1934.

Aet. XXV.

February: Meeting with Krishnamurti at Adyar—the dhoti-angavastra hole, an example of his perfect subtle awareness.

March: Bangalore. Judge. The Jacaranda Tree.

May-June: On foot towards Conjeeveram. Exquisite non-human grace and prestige of pale-gold utsava-vigraha (*temple image*). Vellore. Intense heat of stone hills where at night the cheetahs prowl. Village hospitality at Tiruvannamalai.

Sri Ramana Maharshi at Tiruvannamalai.

Work, anti-humanistic tension, silence. Recognition of static nature of Vedantic realisation, its dependence on metaphysical statement of the problem, and that I am not, or not finally, a *jnani*. All final or central realisation, however, as with Krishnamurti, completely baffling, beyond measurement and definition.

Maunam (vow of silence) in Salem and Cuddalore.

Pondicherry. Visit to ashram. Meeting with Jashvant.

July: Long letter to Sri Aurobindo.

Oct–Dec: Work at University Library, Madras—living on a beach again. Notebooks. Weight 94 lbs (6 stone.10)—average weight in Europe, say 91/2 stone = 133 lbs.

1935.

Aet. XXVI.

21-8. Feb: Dilip Kumar Roy's music. Darshan of Sri Aurobindo at his Pondicherry ashram: impressive, powerful and weighty condensation of spiritual substance, force and light. Look apparently of approval and encouragement.

Madras.

Ambattur: Helping nurse advanced consumptive till I smell blood everywhere. P. and child ill. Squalid vortex of sickness and horror. I rebut the foreign karma and escape!

17 April: Bangalore. Experience ascent of Kundalini. Samadhi. Lucifer, Christ, Zen, Tantrik methods etc.

Brother Suerxis and arrangement of Buddhatissa's very intuitive aphorisms.

22 May: Madras. Brahmin wedding.

June: Ramnad. Nayuurkovil festival. Musiri music. At private country temple, charming Subramanyam *vigraha* (temple image). Ramesvaram: 'caravanserai'. Continuous effort at ordering *Art and Expression* notes. Living on coconut and milk *prašad* daily as guest of Ramesvaram Temple authority. Begin to swim in the sea.

7 July: Ramnad, chez Raja Dinakar, gentleman of the old school. Sense of task definitely weakened. In future less and less room for sustained intellectual criticism and coordination—intellect more and more a spontaneous and sufficiently justified organ.

18 Aug.–on: Another of the recurrent willed orderings and reduction of 1929-1935 notes, whose subjects are still too fruitful and unresolved.

2

Indian Notebook
1933–37

In a boat on the sea glaring with sun I stand up into the dark behind the sky enclosing the whole earth and my helpless phantom—without direction or reprieve.

Letter to a friend.

I stay in India for the same reason I came here—the attraction of an ancient power and wisdom of life that I have still personally to examine and prove.

... It's impossible for me to convey to you the rich, massive subtle, supra-human element that so deeply attracts me in the Indian tradition. —Even behind the sordid modern degeneration.

In the streets where everyone is hungry flowers are on sale by the hungry arranged in the most perverse bouquets. Their perfume fills the street and suspends its sounds. The doors of the houses, even the pillars, are inlaid with coloured glass, hung with garlands, sombre printed stuffs, pictures of child-gods dancing. With my companion I am seated on a balcony of the street hung with flags. In simple dress we enter the wide inner courtyard where the crowd is slowly assembling under trees not visible every day.

An invisible ray builds a vast tetrahedron upon the perpendicular corner of the square.

Sweet, monotonous and crooked music: an unhuman festival. It hangs in the air scalloped awnings and flags—transfigured by an amethyst dew of a rare heaven now present.

I still pursue in the cool nights, the sweet perils and cul-de-sac of a journey begun long ago in dream—an escape or ruin. There it still fearfully speculates and retreats like the cut end of a worm, living forgotten in poignant variations of crisis.

Stars and still cloud. The impersonal cry of a train makes the night seem almost over: for a long moment it flinches and contracts in bitter wonder and nostalgia. The train drags and hurries through the silence like a record of waves played too fast or too slowly. Other sounds are disturbed, spring like flowers, grow into pharaoh's serpents, miniature dragons, freshly decapitated heads modestly prophesying.

All the forms of the world now, crisp, bright, precious, evanescent, burning cold like snow. The fresh, coarse, uninventable sound of young men singing at night. It is like the echo of light on the dockside building outside the 'never seen' and 'never shall see again'.

In what time, what place, what world do the market-women uncover their baskets? By the roadside the little tea-urns are set up; milk silently clothes the black idol; the sky enlarges the inescapable spell.

A child, not yet counting the difference between waking and dream, sings, wanders, plucks a leaf, pisses subtly and comfortably by the wall.

The eyes I meet are quiet and mysterious as flowers or stars.

The sea is an expanse of silver, impersonally beneficent, containing like a picture the far-scattered catamarans, many little sails.

Behind the low grey clouds there is lighted a glow of fulvous roses. Out of the infinity of liquid silver, now very pure and ethereal, a delicate beauty trembles, like a perfume is released—pervades.

The invisible gods have their shrines. In the deep city bees surround the basket of pink roses where the fingers of the hawker move with boredom.

Heavy warm sweet smell of lamps and flowers. The ikon of black stone has a dense and bitter life, as if a muffled perfume. Its immobility is a part of this life, a kind of concentration, so that the rich golden throne is perfect in a mirror. The face is not human, shows a subtly new arrangement of the projections and surfaces that have become the human mask.

Here the darkness in which the mellow flames are still is of a special kind, refers to a special kind of light, a light that would be the full nature and appearance of the god. At night a very delicate paradoxical force can be felt living in the darkness, but withheld and close to itself—too light, too heavy for our senses.

1933 or 1934

The seller of brightly-coloured paper lanterns sits so long in meditation as a lantern-seller (he is Chinese and they have a relation with his soul) that when someone stops to buy it is a great event. With soft contentment, with gravity and dignity as priest of his trade, he shows them all and helps the customer to choose. He knows that the lantern a man selects cannot be without influence in his life. But at the slightly too rare and secretly more and more ardently awaited interruption as he sits on his little stool near the brilliant roadside, he may feel anxiety at the sudden happening and may even seem to have a grudge against the buyer. Then if an unusual customer, feeling this, to increase his own pleasure and that of the old man, is very charming and wants to buy a lot, when he is gone the seller will nevertheless feel that, by this event greater than his mood, his being a lantern-seller is upset, his long role and meditation for a moment threadbare and accidental in the light of all other possibilities in the now hostile, no longer calmly ambient scene. Many such customers would ruin him. And indeed the reigning indifference, pre-occupation and abstract politeness in Western cities has almost entirely destroyed such sellers and priests. The seller even of diamonds or drugs is no longer different from anyone else who practises a trade, he has no special life, environment, tradition. Money has spread everywhere a terrible monotony. But this lantern-seller goes at night to an unfamiliar part of the city, to an unexpected, detailed and special milieu; he has a long and unforeseen history of which he would tell, however, very modestly. Only he can get these lanterns: as if in this foreign land he were a missionary, there are merchants and agents who serve him alone. No-one relieves him at his basket with the stooping bamboo except a seller of little toy drums, windmills and whistles.

In the Indian sun his face has grown darker than those of his countrymen at home. To them he would seem as if become foreign, having evaded the peculiar influence of rays striking at the far East and the cosmos they determine.

6 June, 1934.

There are people who think that the parables of Christ are the direct void of the Spirit, but they have so little understanding of the influence of the spirit upon language and ideas (and therefore one would think of its intention for they too use language and ideas), that they accept at the same level the hymns of Sankey and Moody and Bishop Heber and besides the bible read only Kipling and Ella Wheeler Wilcox. But always this could be an extreme of spiritual superiority, a singular unconscious hypocrisy against culture and the obliging of human effort. And in other respects these people do not appear as humanists. It is possible that they are the angels living among us. And it has always been clear that the angels make no difference: we are not surprised that these people are superior to passion and perversity and to every uneasy human situation, that by love they mean comfort and agreement at their level, mutual concession, or that they accuse everyone of sin. But our necessary humility may prostitute us to them. Oedipus emerges from tragedy, from the perversity of agony and from himself and triumphs only when he can love the Sphinx.

Satisfaction of the *religious* attitude leads to repose for its own sake. Thus the love of God or one Self becomes an absolute limit: now nothing further is possible. Think of Ramana Maharshi.

Madras, 1933.

Infinite dome of the sky, deep turquoise above the brilliance of colour, form and movement. It is the world of the five elements, the darkness of the universe lighted within the limits of the sun.

Here the long street is eternal, expressing nothingness with infinite justice and delicacy, in detail so perfect and charming that all is empty and arbitrary like a stage setting—thus pure delight, calm, depth and freedom.

Everything is continuously pure Novelty and having always presumed All without remainder, in itself exquisitely looks out on Nothing. This form is perfect as the relation between the All and Nothing—Form is pure.

In passing down the recognised street many times before and knowing where it 'leads' I have not yet seen it, but only an image, a metaphor, according with my own preconception—the scene has existed ad hoc for the sake of a limited and partly conscious nexus of purpose and causality, thus only as prejudice. The world in time and space continues and evolves for me only by this causality, a system of substitutes and delays. I have not been free to see the complete and impossible Object, to receive revelation that there is no revelation, to experience the impossibility of background—to transcend every given form of consciousness, all possible contexts. What I now see and enjoy is the form of pure Possibility, its infinite reverberation.

Far sought and soon returned who found a song; far travelled, soon arrived who saw the sun.

March 1934.

A flowering Jacaranda tree in the Lal Bagh, Bangalore.

Its beauty is complete freedom and generosity, is complete repose. It is beyond contentment, all contentment has been justified by it. It has perfect silence because it is perfect expression: its movement is entirely grace. It yields entirely to the wind, entirely interprets it: every occasion rediscovers its grace, its perfection. It makes all occasions—it would make even its cutting down and burning—a delight. Its flowers lie also on the ground.

Their delicacy against the spaces of the sky seems infinite; they are so much bluer that the relation has the effect of a perfume or a bell too sweet to be heard. The sunlight everywhere on its pale branches, exquisitely articulated, is cool and still.

It does not need to move to another place. It has adapted itself to all times and events of the year, it continues as command of them, it *exists* beyond them and its existence is perfectly manifested, it is a pure freedom, it defines nature as pure freedom.

And this is its magic: it exists again in another part of the garden, this exquisite individuality appears and is present in other parts of the world, it has conquered time and space, it is fully present. It greets all conditions, it manifests itself in differing forms, in perfect freedom: by sudden or subtle evasions it can also take leave of itself, it wanders into a new kind of being. It is not limited by itself, it possesses always justice.

An old Zen saying: For Ignorance mountains are mountains, waters are waters and trees are trees. When a man has studied the great tradition and knows a little of doctrine, mountains are to him no longer mountains, waters are no longer waters, and trees no longer trees—that is, they become mere symbols, mere appearances, of the One Reality. But when he is thoroughly enlightened, mountains are again mountains, waters once again waters and trees once again trees.

At night among shadows timelessly forgotten and still, a paper flaps or scurries in a sudden little wind. In the immense self-absorbing night its meaninglessness is strange. It reveals our ennui as a ceaseless question, vast as the night and which we cannot bear: it uncovers an insomnia filling with thin invented acts, with memories and fantasies rejected and recast, the vacuum before dawn.

Dull rainy day in the Indian city. You feel again a forgotten world and the character and thought it makes. Wide parks with intersecting paths and splendid monuments deserted with their trees under drifting grey sky. Everywhere patient reserve and immobility. At the gates the guardian is shut inside his lodge, like a greenhouse locked for the winter. You are forsaken by everything—the shining taxis swish and spray through the wet streets.

I am awakened by the plangent chords and arpeggios, the accentless uncoiling of sound, of the musical box of my childhood.

At a certain moment of eating a mango at Tiruvannamalai (eating a mango it is easy to lose presence of mind!) I have a complex sensation associated with Charing Cross Road. I do not command or understand the connection. The automatism of memory is that there is no connection to command.

I can only consider this a phenomenon of inattention, incoordination. This purely a technical matter: my eating a mango and the attitudes of my absence from the connection and its world of significance could themselves as well be considered inattention. But the question is: Which kind of attention can I most easily and completely command? Complete command must be command of both *and* of their connection.

It is clear that the first task of everyone, saint or soldier, who has arrived at free action has been a technical definition of himself and—so far—a freedom from egoism.

The question is not: Is my sensation the effect of 'myself' in relation with Charing Cross Road, or of Charing Cross Road on a complex state of 'myself' but always something different.

A drug only furthers him who *resists* it. Then it is a detour.

A drug can be enjoyed only by one capable of pure perversity and he will not need it, for it will be neutral. It defines luxury only for those who are incapable of it.

But employing those detours and justifying perversity a man may disentangle himself. There is no luxury in knowledge.

The Buddha, supreme classicist, stringently defining geniality, forbade all intoxicants and stimulants.

Drugs—opium, praise, hope, religion, authority, metaphysics—are the inevitable resource of the romantic. Rimbaud still exploiting ambiguities sustained his evasion with drink and drugs. In Harar, living his innocence and despair, he drank only water.

But so far as he had really been romantic he could react only into silence. His classicism could have continued only as yoga—integral technique.

Alcohol stimulates one's life because it is a product of corruption. It is characteristically the refuge of those who wish to evade life, to flirt with death. They can finally do or endure nothing but this commerce: in their sober state they are like bound lunatics.

Wine is entirely employed by the will for 'Life more abundantly', the will to Resurrection by the man who cannot be made drunk. The miracle of Cana is a symbol of life as Immortality—for which water and wine are the same, for Christ says the same of water to the Samaritan woman at the well.

Consider the awareness favoured by resisting ganja—*cannabis indica* as commonly smoked in India—in which the relations between ordinary 'linear' thoughts themselves become thoughts and so by a squaring, cubing to infinity all possible thought is entirely, immediately and inescapably complemented by Consciousness as a whole.

I took a preparation with almonds, ginger, pepper and milk (solids strained off)—of 2 level teaspoons of dried leaves of local cannabis. About three hours afterwards I made the following notes.

There are timeless gaps which of course you know only on returning from them: you cannot say they are long or short but only that they are subtle.

The mind is from moment to moment absorbed into itself and so between these acts of pure concentration memory ceases to exist.

Concentration in the sense of one of these moments would no doubt lead to a *samadhi.*

The change seems to be due to an increase in the rate of vibration of the prana. Alcohol, rather gross, *simplifies* perception: *bhâng,* [*cannabis in liquid form*] subtilises. Both evidently work by changing the rate of vibration of the vital force. In the West it has been forgotten that this is something in itself supra-physical.

The writing hand allowed to go ahead by habit begins to slide without moving as if over a surface of ice—or rather as if ice covered and made transparent ice all movement.

A vibrating glass, an invisible sea, pulses between myself and any object of sight.

What I see I create and hold in my consciousness. This is dictated to a medium from an incommensurable mental height between Head and hand.

...Or ordinary actions go on, but in another space and time remotely involved within my consciousness.

There now seems to be whole giddy worlds between each successive thought. Yet one is really, though in a specially interesting way, simply falling ill.

...It is in this way that people, all psychic grooves and little mind, are magically locked into a world of their own.

I think this experience not really valuable except, perhaps, to deepen analysis of the nature of the mind. Throughout, a sense of pleasure so far as experience is not questioned.

It is subjection to the surface ego that makes drugs necessary and in terms of this subjection they are effective. Otherwise, when there is no such need for them and their mechanical effect is resisted, they lead beyond the ego or break it down.

Or men use a drug to make weight of the Unknown conscious, conscious our actual experience that in all directions we are lost. The drug is a symbol of the dynamic power of the unknown.

One evening, when we had regained our seaside verandah after timeless wanderings—for cannabis one byelane is the same as another, all are equal in endless newness or ancient familiarity—while someone offered sweetmeats, milk and fruit it was as if my life looped the loop. I did not know if the night had already passed, if I had eaten or not eaten; the whole world-cycle had passed, as if it was now in a new one, new in the infinite ancient perspective of newness, that they asked if I were going to eat. Since that long-forgotten scene in another world I had lived through aeons of thought and experience. Day, yesterday, tomorrow were the same, I was collected in oblivion, the world was an infinitely realised delicious dream, a pure invention, yet all its resources could not fill that timeless presence, were perpetually lost in it.

The states attained by drugs are real ones, belong to the nature of consciousness. When they are not merely transitory, then, it is as if the drug has effectively complemented the usual absence of our consciousness from such states; it overleaps, disentangles, reverses the circle of a certain confusion and helplessness, an unconscious evasion, a certain set of habits;

it enables us to withdraw behind the actor's mask to knowledge of another wider world whose laws contain the play we follow: we recognize but cannot entirely release ourselves to act in that direct, free, unarbitrary world of relationships. Everyone turns to us in the knowledge that we will not spoil the play; this knowledge has become unconscious, a false seriousness whose laws everywhere circle back up on us. Of everyone about us we can say like Rimbaud: 'Ce monsieur ne sait ce qu'il fait'.

But we perceive this in terms of our absence, by virtue of it: from the point of view of achievement of wakefulness, of that direct, free love and practicality, this negation of our absence is a double absence: we have escaped by a side door and either wander or return. If we could not return we were lost: we have only negated the necessary seriousness by which we have the power to consecrate ourselves to what is beyond us.

Subliminal: Bind yourself to the space between two thoughts.

Light is definitive only by the dispelling of darkness. It is not enough to experience or even to arrange indescribable influx or efflux, to be drunk, luminous or cataleptic with an intense ichor—it is necessary to justify and organise these things, to discover and deploy the conditions and nature of this life. One's discovery and organisation is apparently what has been called magic or yoga.

August 1936.

People who don't know me say 'You are doing a very brave thing'. But I had long ago seen that I must either be very rich or override the money question altogether: there was no prospect of the first and I cannot turn my real energies towards doing other people's work. I have more than enough of my own.

I took the only direct course if I were not to cripple or waste my life in inessentials. If it had not been quite simple, natural and inevitable it could only have failed as something false. But then I have always instinctively taken the Christ seriously. In fact, is it necessary to be so 'serious' if you have ever really seen 'the lilies of the field'?

Also I need less and less refuse to admit the view that there is behind it all a kind of inner destiny that must and will work itself out, and beside which all such statements as this are in the last analysis sophistries because unnecessary—except to those who demand because they cannot understand them. The movement to India was no doubt something fundamental. At the surface I had to find excuses and explanations for myself—Uday

Shankar had revealed to me Indian dance and music, or I related it with my early glances at the Gita and the Upanishads and what I read of yoga (this was perhaps nearer the fundamental pattern). But if I had known 'why' I came it would not have been a real or necessary movement. Only the final fruition can 'explain' what does not need *explaining*. But in ways too subtle to describe I feel I am more and more justified, the simple inner justices or inevitability of this course seems more and more unquestionable. Only when the pattern is complete and commanded (and only *patterns* are ever *complete*) can one see the real connections and necessities of one's life; meanwhile—though all comparison with what might 'otherwise' have been is entirely abstract and unreal—it seems to me that I have developed and must develop here in ways that would surely have been impossible or at least very unlikely in Europe. Among other factors, there is such a thing as a subtle but powerful and inescapable atmosphere which favours certain possibilities. And the spiritual atmosphere of India, matured through thousands of years, is something palpable and indescribable as soon as one lands, as soon as one enters this rich life vibrating at all levels between the widest extremes beyond and beneath sense—harsh and subtle, brilliant in dust and sun—flowers and corpses, gods and gonorrhoea. I shall never forget the first days in which we (the other was a wandering pilgrim-philosopher, with whom I came from Ceylon) wandered and lingered like beggars or birds through this subtle, ancient, novel, blatant life, rich, strange, hypnotising and rapturous like a dream. I feel I know now what people probably mean when they say that once you have lived in the East, and especially in India, in spite of all the squalor and dirt, indifference and cruelty, if you ever go away you will always return.

You are probably not interested in the questions I have to answer in the contemporary world. Like 'Why are you not a Communist?' For at the same time, at a certain level of human seriousness, because of the actual general misery and degradation, and since it is not my nature or job to turn first to that (this could only seem to me a *reaction* in terms of history, as Communism entirely is), I feel in a way bound in the historical situation to live as simply as possible. There is work to be done to correct all this misery and exploitation (Communism is another historical formula still in tension with politics): this is indispensable—at that level certainly the only real work, though merely resisting or attacking the evil perpetuates it by taking its cause for granted. Because I know this but have another 'work' and nature I must incidentally entirely respect it—there must certainly be no waste, laziness, carelessness, irresponsibility. Otherwise one is guilty of evasion and self-protection. My position is that although I cannot situate myself at the level of this problem (I am not *a revolutionary* though I may be revolutionary), by my very position I am bound to respect it and the seriousness and athleticism it demands—though they are helpless so far as they can be absolutely disinterested. The failures of this disinterestedness is their occasion: revolution only complements history as the failure of life. Whether you like it or not there are spiritually only individuals and the world will not be spiritually governed until this is recognised again. If, particularly since the Renaissance, this has been refused by greed and by rational*ism* (the modern superstition), denial of the (false) 'individual' because he appears as Capitalist is only a *transition* or reaction—inconclusive movement on the same plane with its cause (and hence its fictitious 'ideology'). Democracy is the greatest and most wholesale superficialisation so far known to history.

But a far more urgent and fundamental reason for living as simply as possible is to sustain Normality as an essential scepticism and economy, which defines Nature in terms of the primary technical problems of rhythm, energy, sensuality—all the transitions, interchanges, balances, modulations otherwise entirely uncommanded.

Also this economic noncompromise has meant and always needs to mean refusal to live in the atmosphere of people who—often by the most subtle and unattackable evasions—deny all values in equating wisdom and comfort. Their whole energy is perverted in defending themselves against the fact that spiritual athleticism and enjoyment exist only in terms of spontaneity and resource, are volcanic for any given state. In fact the whole thing is entirely spontaneous and actual, no explanation can seize or exhaust it, though it can exhaust every need of explanation.

[On several occasions Thompson visited the masterpieces of south Indian monumental sculpture, a group of rock temples and boulder reliefs (7th Century A.D.) at Mammalipuram, on the seashore 35 miles south of Madras. He considered it to be a perfect example of 'transhumanistic' art, equalled only by the great Chola bronzes of the 9th-11th Centuries A.D.]

Temples by the Sea: sculpture steeped in golden plasticity.

It is only by European humanism that beauty has been essentially defined by an intellectual esthetic in dependence upon the relation of the external man with given objects. Elsewhere, and for other traditions even in Europe, it is seen that there are many kinds and modes of symbolism. In humanism mind and intellect define simply because they are the highest and freest factors of consciousness.

The Hindus attribute personal beauty to the subtle element of 'light fire'—*tejas*, brilliance. As soon as the external man of humanism ceases to be the measure of all things the sense of beauty, in its unprejudiced wholeness, has necessarily an occult reference. Images of occult and spiritual beings in India and the Far East make contact with human canons only so far as man also is really an occult and spiritual being, who perceives and uses these forms as a master of cosmic symbolism, of the creative cosmic Imagination. The perfect beauty of the Christ in Celtic legend has a spiritual reference that is not effective in a statue of Apollo.

When the immediacy of beauty is seen to be always transrational the most intense and valued symbols—indeed the only complete ones—are those that make conscious a Transcendental reference.

'*Descent of the Ganges*' is a colossal boulder relief with a central cleft; scores of figures riding lightly to the surface of the rock tend towards the central cleft. With that fusion of richness, power and subtlety which is the general characteristic of Indian art, there dominates a noble elegance. Heavenly beings glide effortlessly forward with the imaginatively sustained flight of certain dreams. Only the animals and men are subject to the force of gravity; the hero lifts himself strenuously against it while the God beside him stands quite weightlessly. The various composition with its reptiles and birds, its *devas* and *gandharvas*, *nagas* and *naginis*, *kinnaras* and *ganas*, is entirely free of restlessness: all, in exalted calm, serve a single aim. Here at once is established the majestic harmony, the sense of cosmic unity, that reigns throughout Mahabalipuram.

'*Rock-cut shrine of Krishna*': The figures in this pastoral have the bland simplicity of vegetation, fat, tender, translucent with sap, that has grown rapidly in richly watered soil: they swell out of the rock with the same unconscious dignity. This limpid complacency is reiterated in the heads of cows that fill the upper spaces: the keynote of the whole composition is as it were the soft richness of milk in a lush Vrindavana. Here there are no gods or serpent-kings: Shri Krishna, the Avatar, is in profound harmonious sympathy with an humanity which he fulfills into its sweetest and most simple consummation. The women are tender, deeply composed, undemonstrative because so utterly self-given and so completely satisfied. Children, the calves whose charming awkwardness is so simply and directly realised, a peaceful old man—all live in Edenic happiness in which there is even no need for tenderness.

'The Shore Temple': In the moonlight, the eroded forms of the purplish, livid stone suggest an architecture of volcanic rock. In the narrow ambulatory the tormented images, capriciously hollowed, rounded, fused and eaten like metal by the scorching salt, seem disconnected from the human world. Immediately below the porch hisses and snarls a frantic sea, filling the whole arc of the horizon. In spite of the ceaseless roaring, surging, spuming, plashing, swirling, and a high, hollow, shapeless ringing and moaning as this body of sound sings over the walls and echoes in the musical stone, this central chamber has its own deep silence and a secret warmth. Upright in the floor, black, facetted, a massive broken shaft—the Linga. Mute grandeur, like the core of a dead planet.

The whole, in this atmosphere, suggests a superhuman discipline and dignity, a passion, a sensuality, for what is prior to Being and Non-being—astringent like the taste of iron.

[The following magnificent piece which treats the demonic and the perverse was first published in "Mirror to the Light". It was originally part of the foregoing reflections on the great seventh century masterpiece, the rock carvings of Mammalipuram. In luxuriant prose, Thompson celebrates the dramatic myth of the Mahishasuramardani panel in which is depicted the fierce confrontation between the Great Goddess, Durga, and the buffalo demon, Mahishasura. The pinnacle of Pallava narrative sculpture, this is one of the few great Indian works of art in which Thompson found the perfect visual analogue of an elusive theme on the very borderline of verbal expression. The mighty forces of the Goddess are arraigned against the horned Titan in a conflict which Thompson reduces to two essential contrary forces of radiant energy and overweening mental pride. prime components in his persistent examination of psycho dynamics.]

The Goddess is surging with endless reserves of effortless, autonomous force; the abstract will of the Titan continues in a void. On the side of the Goddess the forms are rich—inner resource recoiling from its temporary limits in a condensation of ornament, like curls or foam; on the side of the Titan all is tense with mental pride and effort. Round the Goddess the forms are swollen outward by a calm and magistral inner fullness, a force that need not hasten, that remains forever invincibly its own centre; the attendants of the Titan half turn away in flinching doubt and the complications of evasive thought.

Fig. 38. Mammalipuram Rock Carving—Mahishasuramardani panel.

The Goddess, eternally calm and prior to all Necessity, in purely poetical recognition of his effort, launches her shaft against the Titan. Her face has the calm inward smile of love and wisdom. Her far-focused, upward-looking eyes remember only God, her Essence.

In the Titan the ruthlessness of unacknowledged despair has a unified animal head and a sinister, simplified mockery of the human form, a hollow eidolon. The timidly insolent head is really weighted down by its dark weariness and despair. Helpless in an ill-will now fatefully closed upon itself, his entirely repressed longing and need for liberation brings him face to face with the radiant grace of the Goddess: she meets his desperate dream in its own terms in order to free him from it.

For mere man the true Self is a jealous God.—Why does one so object to Jehovah? How naive, how graceless, how lacking in subtlety are all the prophets and devotees. The Babylonish Whore of Whores speaks so softly and charmingly, with such taste and elegance, while John, screaming and ranting, foaming, tearing his hair, heaps up his incongruous metaphors.

The Sphinx—body of a lion, majestic, strong for prey; head of a woman, subtle, questioning—is the rightness of the ego. We face it because we cannot avoid relation with spiritual things, because we become ourselves only by conquering our fate, the external personality that persists relentlessly through Oedipus' greatest ingenuity, wilfulness, intelligence, sensibility, simplicity, perversity, anguish, irony—and even in his abandon, so that these things also are itself.

All who have to presume the spiritual are parvenus. Whoever has fundamental generosity and imagination—who lives them, and this does not imply 'renunciation'—is spiritual and does not need the Word. He is directly 'guided'—that is to say he does not need 'guidance', which is only possible as the appeal to superstition in those who are effectively unready, ungenerous, unable to discover, exploit and exhaust their unreadiness.

He acts from the point of view of what in him is unquestionable—he is capable of the arbitrary and nothing else can satisfy him: he does not need and can never accept 'satisfaction'. Thus he never believes. As he discovers himself belief is more and more meaningless—there is always either superstition or positive Hypocrisy. There can never be any real occasion for belief. The Real is what creates itself.

At any, therefore at all, levels, any hierarchical system expresses incapacity and as long as it continues can never express anything else.

A sure sign of these 'spiritual' parvenus is that they put themselves over against those they call 'worldly men' and presume that there are certain things they can never understand. And they themselves, significantly, become 'teachers'. And they are the ones who will persist in calling the Buddha and the Christ *teachers*.

Real understanding is always entirely personal, because it is not otherwise necessary. It is not transmissible in any given form. Understanding is complete as the sufficient definition of Technique—Spontaneity.

But for any real humility and generosity there are only *men*. I admit it is very hard to find the man behind the sectarian, the pharisee or Brahmin, the intellectual, the artist, the mystic, the brief authority—the ego. But if these are not discriminated 'the spiritual' is defined only as a play on the word 'human' or 'nature', by their continuing absolute necessity. The Christ, supreme Realist, refuses this figure of speech though in terms of language still unexploded (that is, so far as anything can or need be *said*) he must invent others—'Son of Man, Son of God'.

The parvenus, again, are revealed by the vast superstructure of illusion they need to balance their actual evasiveness: they deal in nothing less that aeonic cycles, gods, worlds....

They are as a type insolently ignorant, insensitive and careless in all matters in which less than archangels are involved—in fact everywhere where knowledge can be tested. One might expect them to appreciate and put in its place the discipline of pure science, but with a strange irritability they affect to despise it. However, they accept its humanistic applications and vulgarisations as uncritically as everyone else.

As human beings they are completely inadequate. They have not had the grace or, as a rule, the capacity first to be human. Thus they have never known the specific agony of the human situation—the first effective definition of the spiritual.

They make the Spirit the *romantic* value *par excellence*, an excuse for all sorts of slackness and negative disorder. These unworldly people are afraid to be what the world calls immoral. They have no stability but the religious attitude: are either fanatics or on any real issue moral cowards.

Humility sustains the Sphinx immemorially as a symbol of the inconceivable, bottomless Wisdom before which precisely the most active imagination, the widest and most courageous generosity fight most desperately and in vain.

But is Oedipus himself to become a Sphinx? No: at whatever cost the riddle of the Sphinx must be answered, this bluff must be called. There is only one way: the acceptance of nameless Tragedy, and opening of a dumb secret for the few who can see.

For the spirit there is no such thing as vulgarity, stupidity, weakness, deceit.

This last superiority is the invention and the plague of the fine, the intelligent, the strong, the truthful.

The criminal is in easiest relation with it. Many great saints appear superior criminals. Having the genius of naivety, the *outrance* of the child they emerge from the endless, official, heroic, blind, dignified, pitiable human.

The world is sustained by this action of paradox and all explosions of force and violent transitions continually and secretly happening express its veerings and readjustments.

The man who really knows can at this level adopt no attitude towards others except that of the learner.

Religion usually satisfies—vagueness, and a *need*. Such people can accept, and they can transform, what is given; but something must be given. At their best they can accept without turning a hair whoever with the right admixture of capital letters will proclaim himself God.

This acceptance can develop into a colossal superiority. Their vagueness asks everything, they need to possess the Infinite—in order to practise charitableness, perseverance and other virtues in order to obtain right of presence and authority before all in it can be similarly fruitful. They obey with directness a psychological law, no doubt what Wordsworth called the 'grand elementary principle of Pleasure', which can otherwise only be commanded by complete hypocrisy, as and at the end of all indecision and unhappiness. This conduct can lead to the supreme psychological masterliness, hypocrisy, direct knowledge and inner secrecy of great religious leaders. They demand the same primary satisfaction, consecration, the same immediate happiness as the idol-worshippers, others and others' independence that they do not understand. Thus they make all independence evil or they protect themselves and solve all their problems by the exercise of 'love'. It was against this position that Blake partly spent himself in reacting: these people are not conscious enough to 'love the greatest men best'. Thus they remain vague, lonely and avoided, proclaiming that the world of the Infinite is a suburban church and God supremely present at Sunday School outings.

This is where they catch the psychological athletes, the men of profound tensions and appetite who at last find the first act that expresses them and from which they can proceed, in the non-rational overturning of all values. That is why the men of greatest potentiality and consequence appear out of the religious vortices: culture demands restraint and balance, which can never be final. Thus periodically by religion culture is ruined, and allowed. But any movement in any direction out of vagueness is extremely painful to them. Their God indeed could not exist without this omnipresent Evil One. They have always been conservative and vague in politics.

[Letter to P.K. Rajagopal (P.K.R), businessman and Tantrik 'sadhaka' of thirty years' standing and Thompson's oldest Indian friend.]

9.XI.36

The daughter of one of my friends here, a noble soul and a *sâdhaka,* is a beautiful young girl called Lakshmi whom I have always looked upon as the Mother in a very gracious form. A few days ago, after I had been telling fairy-tales to her and her brother (who is called Krishna), we began to play *swarga*—'Snakes and Ladders'. Sometimes I got quite near to 'Swarga', but again and again the die landed me on a snake and down I went. The snake has of course been an immemorial transrational symbol. Then at a certain point when she herself reached Swarga (from the start she had been easily leading), she spontaneously began to move my piece. It was quite natural for the poet in me to lift the whole thing to a level of direct and subtle symbolism. Of course, one never does such things deliberately, with the *mind.* In this state I understood, as one does in certain dreams in which subtle events and actions are being developed, that I must use the die with a certain kind of consistency in direct relation with her. From this moment she lead my piece steadily past every snake on the board and up many of the ladders until the last throw—4—landed me exactly at 100—'Swarga.'

Only and precisely *superstition* thinks such things childish or insignificant. Anyone who has tried to become conscious of dream—and other subtle experience knows that the most important things can be worked out or revealed in this way.

The fact that, from the point of view of Consciousness as whole, any given level or mode of consciousness is symbolic is used by such systems of divination as the I Ching, the Qabbalah, the Tarot, astrological arudam. And the fact that Consciousness is cogent only as *Chit*, Shakti is represented for ordinary consciousness by the conception that certain *beings* operate the sticks, numbers, cards or cowries. It is in this sense, no doubt, that it is said that Shakti is said to be prior to Krishna, Shiva and all other gods whatever, and alone represents the sole Being in any world of relativities for which Consciousness can only be an absolute. Thus completion of Consciousness intuitively perceived; but it appears also psychically. Here are two dreams:

Subrahmanyam festival. The god at about eighteen, then as a child of twelve, powerful, charming, who speaks. I wish to meet his glance and he does several times look towards me in a big congregation. Emotion of bhakti so intense that I fall to the ground. The divine child comes and tramples my body, awakening the chakras.

Ayyappan, the child of Vishnu by Shiva, the male deity here taking the form of the alluring woman Mohini, appears to me in a dream as a black image whose erect phallus is called Vastu—the Reality. In a byeway like that of a Tamil town or village, surrounded by boys and young men I caress the face of the young god, then closely embrace him.

In connection with both dreams there was also a symbolism of seed and fertilisation.

I realize that in the physical world the most virile boys and youths in a certain sense appear to me feminine and respond so. It is said that subtle and physical are complementary opposites. Thus the subtle body of a man is said to be feminine—like the soul in relation with the Supreme, the Sole Male.

3

Journal About Journal

Thompson began to make regular entries in a journal on February 13th., 1937, as a direct consequence of having recently met the Jnani, Sri Krishna Menon (Atmananda), an event which gave him a feeling of greater stability and continuity.

He had been toying with the idea of keeping a journal since 1935, writing down a series of occasional notes on the problems involved. He called these notes his 'Journal about journal'. He then added to them another series of notes which deal with what he considered to be the crucial technical issue: how to transform the prime component in keeping a record of significant experience—'description'—from a purely factual method into a dynamic means for seizing on 'magical opportunity'. Everything depends on lifting description from the level of the factually prosaic to that of Imagination: 'Description is 'effective' only as symbol'. He jettisons most of the usual conventions of autobiographical writing and restores to the journal its original character of a 'diarium spirituale'.

A journal may entirely exhaust egoism as a scepticism. In proportion to its intelligence it shows the ego as what a man is not and shows its complete accidentality.

A journal can be sustained only for the sake of, or in tension with, the ego.

Otherwise, there is transformation.

Except as Hypocrisy which must finally make it irrelevant, a journal is description, delay and self-circling of the mind. Real action, promptitude, results and continuity are in another dimension.

A journal can only be complete and well-written if you live for it.

Otherwise, so far as it is necessary, it represents precisely what is not well-organised, what is not yet axiomatic enough to have completely commanded all possible modes and occasions of its expression.

If a journal is not a means of absolute sincerity produced by the need of it, it is inevitably complacent, egotistic, and therefore incompletely intelligent.

This journal can perhaps record nothing, essentially, but lapses and vacillations from Normality—the perfect economy sensual, mental, active which is its own satisfaction—or rather, the satisfaction of the most organically direct and continuous will to growth towards the fullness of Reality.

Thus rereading of this journal in the sense of this will to Reality can more and more discourage relapsings and build up a habit of fortification against them. The sole justifiable object of the journal is such a full acknowledgement of mistakes and failures and conscious progressive integration of their lesson.

The ever-inconclusive dynamic force of a journal is tension with the ever-changing ego, which is constant only in surviving at the cost of every slender magical opportunity, every glimpse of an effectivity always insulated by the continuous indecision of the mind. The ego is latent in every sophistry against it and profits by them all.

Intelligence is complete only in freedom from the ego. Otherwise the ego is always observing, judging and critically arranging all one's thought, experience and expression from the point of view of self-defensive standards of poise, sanity, scepticism, grace.

The first quality of intelligence is complete disinterested daring.

But while any inner discord exists there will always be some romantic tension with the possibility of irony, arrogance, sentimentality or self-deceptive humility.

Only what is achieved by the whole consciousness is definitive—does not need to be permanent.

A journal is either the masturbation of an ego or the fact that sincerity can achieve itself only in continual crisis. But in certain transition- stages, blind, desperate—solitude in the womb nourished by darkness, both masturbation and continual crisis may be necessary. At a certain level of consciousness there is always a journal, till we are born for the first and last time, till we are whole before birth and death.

This language will seem to some extravagant and therefore empty. But can narrower terms define a Reality on Earth?

The continuity of a journal depends upon a feminine attitude towards oneself.

A journal is inconclusive because it is necessary only in relation with unachieved rightness, wholeness, living truthfulness and yet this Dharma (ethic) can *only* be Action.

A journal remains possible as self-examination, self-collection, prayer, as the completion and exhaustion of every possible and therefore still necessary humility into perfect Realism.

A journal can at best only define and prepare the possibility of that integrity and technical perfection in which action is action, speech speech, event event. Relation with others also pure and absolute in its own sense—the many-sided yet ever integral Poetry of the Whole Man.

For whom is this journal written?

All need and occasion of expression of oneself depends upon division in consciousness. Economy lies in at least sustaining the level where division is that between one's fully organised self and a greater potential Whole. Then all self-expression becomes yoga.

The relation of an unorganised present self to a greater possibility produces romantic expression, revelatory perhaps but inconclusive and technically inconsistent, ineffective.

Quality of thought, quality of feeling, quality of action—each must be perfect in itself without romantic inter-reference.

A journal can be free of egoism or sentimentality only if it tests and extricates the Potential, the new, the unknown.

Nor can a journal contain the silent thoughts that are acts, that are both the past and the future.

Description proceeds from the surface, with maximum obstruction and the widest choice of falsity.

If my experience is real—intrinsically necessary—description of it is dishonest, surrenders it to the age, to time and memory. While experience is necessary but still incomplete description is a compromise with the ego's uncommanded relation with objects that completion of Experience is to surpass.

Description like judgement, is possible only from an accidental viewpoint representing some uncommanded relation with the true nature of the object described.

It is the indescribability of experience through the delicacy and specificity of every effective adjustment—through the intransmissable integrity on which it depends, that condemns all history of human culture to a common, abstract, superficial vocabulary that keeps alive only a *tradition of thought about* experience, even strictly a scholasticism, while the reality exists always behind it in perpetual novelty and secrecy, influencing history only through symbols.

If an author accumulates details while we still cannot divine his purpose we feel congestion and discomfort.

It is impossible for description to re-arrange things in a vital pattern—that could show a way out of the endlessness of choice. Our choice is movement, but movement itself is irresolution. The problem is to stand still, then for the first time choice is unnecessary and we are not committed—we have really forsaken the idea of description, have overcome our inner bondage to the Object.

Description does not even beg the question, it is merely incapable of question. It is a comfort, a self-indulgence, an architecture employing no dynamism but the lines of least resistance between preconceptions.

Description can never have any *standard* but the picturesque.

All description, including that of dream, is external, partial, perpetuates some division of consciousness, represents something incompletely possessed and understood that cannot be symbolised or commanded by consciousness as a whole. What describes is, in fact, always some kind of ego. Description confuses the symbol. Otherwise all sense experience, by the exactitude of Sensuality, is an intense and irreplaceable symbol.

Why do the simplest experiences of childhood so grasp our imagination?

Because we experienced them utterly, without qualification or reserve, without mental knowledge. Thus in their relation they were entirely symbolic, continuous as Luxury, purely enjoyed in Wonder.

That a thing is red or green is for sight, not for words. Let us not pervert words to the duties of sensuality. And if sensuality is not intact in its own sphere, words will be sick, flabby, corrupted. Integrity of sensuality is essential to classicism—and to Realism.

Perfectly effective description, by its directness and economy, uses every metaphor, and the very relation between nerves, senses, mind and imagination represented in the structure and qualities of language, as something purely formal. Description is *effective* only as symbol—by restoring from imagination the purity of the object as symbol.

4

Early Journal Entries

13.II.37

The relations that the intellect perceives are never organic, belonging to that nascence, that 'intermediary' in which perpetual Newness unfolds.

Recognition that the non-mental—such as that deepening, heightening, enlarging of horizon and capacity into a more vivid, exciting and subtle world of facts and possibilities—is perhaps essentially 'vital'. In fact, I feel now a connection with certain dreams flooded with an indescribably felicitous intensity of odour and atmosphere, heavy, crepitating, intoxicating as if with supernatural possibilities. Here belongs last night's unmentalisable, entirely unliterary sense, in a dream, of the wantonly patterned diamond incrustation of the sky; empathic realisation of rich bye-lanes—vivid mud houses, flowers, palms—an imagination essentially of the same kind as the Persian or Arabian atmosphere, sensuality and philosophy. I stepped from a snake-bite exorcist's cottage and entered as one enters in a dream, into another world. Not knowing where it was—its existing for me entirely *sui generis*, in no space or time—I was shown at the corner of the road its connection with an habitual route and its extraordinary nearness to our cottage. But that same road that I have passed along many times in the car is not the same road. In revisiting that hut I should revisit only a memory, in which everything would have grouped itself in a new light, falsely consenting to be unchangeable.

This occult intensity is related with all the most ineradicable moments of my life, with its transmental poetic continuity, for they have been densely coloured and charged in the same way as such dreams. It is this quality that I so powerfully sensed in Rimbaud and which has operated when I have vividly felt that everything is unreal—by the same token, indeed, by which all mental work more and more defines its arbitrariness. It seems often now that the veil here is indeed thin. A sense, also, of terrible, irrevocable, exciting magical abandonment to a world of unknown richness, resource and immediacies and of inconceivable logic. It recalls certain sensations and perceptions of my childhood, when such experience seems to have been continous and normal.

I suspect something of this behind the rich imagery of Shakespeare, vertiginous if not controlled by the mind. This otherworld atmosphere, heavily charged, spangled with invisible threats, honours and lightnings, seems to swirl about Hamlet in passages such as:

> Examples, gross as earth, exhort me;
> Witness this army, of such mass and charge,
> Led by a delicate and tender prince,
> Whose spirit with divine ambition puff'd
> Makes mouths at the invisible event;
> Exposing what's mortal and unsure
> To all that fortune, death and danger dare,
> Even for an egg-shell.

I take this at hazard: there are no doubt better examples in *Antony and Cleopatra.*

During the day thought—not reaching definitive mentalisation—of strange and tenuous dependence of Western humanistic thinking on the conditions and perspective of rationality: I watch the beginnings in myself of a working shift to 'magical' conceptions based in Being and Action instead of consciousness and knowledge, a world of thought in which its objects and actions are immediately and entirely present.

If I were to become entirely *present* with this actual sunshine the whole illumination could not longer remain the same: dissolution must begin, the rolling up of the heavens like a scroll, the unfolding of pure Luxury. This present awaits our presence.

Over against objects we experience the quality of our absence, the limit of our effective kingdom.

The ego's 'I will meditate' exists entirely outside the controlled, subtle, intense condensation and deployment of forces that can only be immediate—descent and presence of new worlds, simpler, more terrible and beautiful resources and transitions.

For the rich and beautiful landscape there must be water as well as sun, rich Vital as well as Mind, or the Light kills as Heat.

It was tension with the mind that in 1927-1930 etc. put forward desire for austere, even desert, landscape.

I no longer know—have never known—where I am in the incessant play of waves and light, both fathomless: the only thing I have left, in the surrounding delirium of joy, is to destroy piece by piece the raft which is so strangely and interestingly meaningless...

There is a Ship that is born of the Ocean...

3.IV.37.

Silence about all effective gods. They are those whom you *do not remember.*

In this world you are not even a beggar, you are neither beggar nor king.

15.IV.37

Impression after a vivid dream that plant-forms exist perfectly in dreams, are essentially dream-expressions. Works of art in man's waking world, by their relation with nature represent incapacity to live out the dream of natural objects at its level—to complete one's consciousness integrally through and beyond it (Magic).

Essential dream-perception must be integrated into waking life as well as vice versa: their complementariness has to be absorbed by a prior immediacy.

1.V.37.

Bimda, near Rajapalaiyam. Letter to Mother.

Evening in the house of an atmajnani *[first surviving reference to the Jnani, Sri Krishna Menon, in the journal]* where I have been invited to stay till his return. *Atmajnani* is a technical term which it would take a whole book—and more than books—to explain. Roughly, it means one who has recovered and is established in the true Centre of things and whose whole consciousness is organised from there. The *Atman* is the true Self of each and All which is obscured and falsely limited by the transitory superficial 'I', its habits passions and preconceptions. It is impossible to describe the state of such a man, it is too subtle and too profound. The Hindus are satisfied that it is essentially this attainment which Christ was referring to when he said: 'I and the Father are one'. One of the great sayings of the Upanishads is: 'Thou art That', 'Thou art the Brahman' (Essence Reality).

The women of the house are singing in Malayalam the subtle poetry of a kind of devotional romance based by the Jnani on his spiritual experiences and which during the day his son and disciple has been translating for me.

When the Jnani returns, for 2 or 3 days I spend many hours in conversation with him. To illustrate some of his explanations he tells me of experiences of his own which could hardly be believed in Europe where all psychology is based on sense-perception. He greatly helps my understanding of some of my own experience and in fact decisively confirms my growing perception that 'outer' things exists only for body and mind, that otherwise all—including them—is within, in the absolute timeless Consciousness which can only be described as a function of pure Existence and pure Joy. —'The kingdom of heaven is within, it cometh not by observation.'

After I have put to him questions involving the very ground of *atmajnana* and he has recognised my position, with his blessing I take leave of him.

All deep knowledge of such things, and as far as is known all spiritual masters, disappeared from Europe centuries ago, if they were ever really complete there. There is however one master at present in Europe, whether of a high order I cannot say, but he is a Musulman *[Réné Guénon]*. There may also perhaps still be one or two masters of some competence at Mount Athos. Certain Russian masters *[Gurdjieff and Ouspensky]* who have an appreciable following in Europe do not seem to possess or even envisage real Gnosis.

The spiritual master, in Sanskrit, *guru*, as generally understood is in form a man, yet he is the Truth Itself. In theistic terms, he is one who having *really* become one with God so that he has no other consciousness than God's, by his oneness with that infinite love, power and wisdom can help others to reach this union. In Europe hardly anyone nowadays has even a glimmering of what this union with God means—or indeed what 'God' really means—and most will therefore simply not believe it possible, or because they have themselves nothing left but empty words, consider it only a manner of speech. The Christ, who lived in that union—'I and the Father are one'—said 'I am the Way, the Truth and the Life'. Here again, the difficulty is that no-one in Europe really believes this or that there is a Way at all. Failure truly to listen to his words—'he that hath ears to hear'—and compromise with 'this world' have made him an inexplicable exception. His reality, his naturalness and normality, have been covered up in dogma and superstition which cannot satisfy anyone who really wishes to know God, who asks himself 'Who am I?' and what is the meaning of this existence. Yet to reach conscious and effective union with God is the only real end and purpose of human existence, the whole meaning of man. Nothing else—no heaven or paradise, for they exist and are conceived only in relation with earth or hell, and no relative state can be the full eternal truth—will really satisfy his inmost being which as Eckhart said is a 'spark' of God himself, the Sole Substance. 'Thy kingdom come, Thy will be done, on *earth*', the Christ taught his devotees to pray. This final achievement, which leaves nothing outside it and nothing unfulfilled or unexplained, is referred to in the books about Ramana Maharshi as *sahaja*.

The master is the incarnate living Truth before us now 'in Time', who can perfectly satisfy and convince the human heart and mind that there is nothing else but that One Infinite Reality and who can show the individual his own most direct practical way of realising It, of himself becoming in all plenitude of consciousness that One Supreme which is his very Being, his Source and sole true End.

There can be nothing 'new' in this: it has been expressed in fundamentally the same terms from time immemorial by all who have achieved it—by the Upanishadic seers, Lao-tse, the Buddha, Krishna, the Christ, Ramakrishna Paramahamsa (last century), Ramana Maharshi (nowadays) and many more.

Ultimately, of course, the master represents our own True Being, the 'kingdom of heaven within'.

A common European mistake is to call the Hindu teaching pantheism, but it is nothing of the kind. Pantheism supposes that there is no God but the universe, that God and the universe are inter-commensurable; but in the Hindu scriptures the Supreme is made to say: 'Having put forth all the worlds, I remain'. Infinity can never be diminished, or measured: it always remains Infinity, is at once the Absolute and the Transcendent.

Ahimsa (non-violence) first applies in the external world. Deeper than this there is not ahimsa but the inner psychic love by which the animals lay down before the Buddha, by which the peacock and the snake are at peace before Ramana Maharshi with his definitive realisation of the Atman in the heart—the realisation of the inner kingdom in which 'the lion and the lamb...and a little child shall lead them'.

9.V.37. Rajapalaiyam, near Srivilliputtur.

The genial agent of the estate in the hills whose owner has invited me to stay there during the heat welcomes me with a rose-garland and sets about completing arrangements for my ascent tomorrow.

10 May.

Soon after noon I make myself comfortable on the multicoloured carpet of a bullock-cart that is to take me to the foot of the Western Ghats with the two rather wild-looking men who are to escort me and carry the first stock of provisions. Eight miles through the typical South Indian landscape—dusty road, hillocks of baked rock, wayside shrines of stone, a few palmyra trees, a little scrub, women in the gaudiest primary colours carrying waterpots on their heads.

Once, among the foot-hills, we have to turn aside into the bush while in the chequered sunlight there passes by—*ting, tleng, tong*—a train of bullock-wagons with carved axles carrying timber and sacks of grass.

At about three we enter on foot the strange silence of the jungle. We have to mount to 5,000 feet and cover some 16 miles.

Sometimes, on stepping-stones, in the din, cool under-jungle light, we cross torrents whose bed is a chaos of boulders. Unfamiliar wayside flowers appear; some—red with fleshy petals, or high up small white ones with a sweet clove-like scent—have fallen from spreading trees far above. But in the luxuriant tangle, almost every tree festooned with creeper, it is hard to see from which. Sometimes the rocky path is hidden by lush grasses through which we force our way.

Towards sunset we reach a rough hut, roofed with woven coconut leaves, the wall-frames hung with the same dried grass that covers the earthen floor. Here we are to stay for the night.

I descend to the stream nearby and bathe in the pure cold of a rocky pool where it overflows down a great slab to complex eddies below. Above and around, rich, vivid, endlessly varied forms, a careless and majestic luxuriance of life. And overhanging in the sky the nearest peak, clothed with dense trees as if with wool.

While the jungle-logs flame—how beautiful are the colours and forms of Fire!—I eat my usual evening meal of fruit, my companions theirs of curry and rice. The complete jungle silence is spread for miles around us.

11 May.

We set off after dawn through the cold, heavy dew, Everything is wonderfully rich, fresh and beautiful. Up and up, the path turning and zigzagging like a ruined staircase. When we emerge at moments from the dense growth, the folding hillsides all around are patterned by the steady early-morning shadows.

Shrill hallucinating chorus of grasshoppers, the magic music of the place, direct expression of the non-human life in which black panthers and the bison reign. In this silence the most strident note of a bird sounds like a soliloquy. A rich, moist, warm perfume, like that of a conservatory, pervades our path.

The man ahead of me suddenly stops. *'Pambu!'* A snake! A young cobra, dusky satiny green, probes and glides into the cool hollow under a rock.

Overhanging rocks ooze with water. In the rich gloom a tender tree-sprout rises from the dark mould, still in the pale light of its almost transparent leaves, like an apparition.

When the sun is quite high we emerge level with the neighbouring scarps at about 5,000 feet, the whole countryside in a brilliant haze far below. We begin to descend on the other side.

While we rest by a stream with leaning heliotrope flowers under trees of branching cactus, bronze-gold butterflies suck from our skin the minute effusion of sweat.

At about noon we stop to eat on the broad rocks of another musical torrent pressed upon by the towering massed richness of trees and where slow spreading trickles are overgrown on the rock itself with a mass of coral-pink flowers. I recognise in the shelving rock and the path emerging beneath it a scene I suddenly imagined weeks ago on a walk across country in South Travancore. In clumps with a tiny setting of mould begonias grow lustily. And everywhere flicker and float the butterflies, blue-green and black, powder-soft heliotrope, rich cream, deep yellow, white and marigold, diaphanous silver and shell-pink. The *anni*, like a giant squirrel, tawny and black, leaps in the trees.

When the sun is directly overhead the trees open out and we enter a charming grassy, almost parklike scene surrounded by hills, all utterly still as if enchanted in the vivid light.

Before long, when we have plunged into the jungle again, we are met by a man with a big thermos flask of tea, a box of biscuits and a sleek black dog. Still a mile or so more till a wilderness of felled trees, frames of huts and log bridges heralds the final smooth, mudbuilt grass-roofed building where I am to live. Here I am greeted by the three or four very pleasant people who are in charge of the place, and the rest of the family of dogs. A's room, which I am to use, contains camp-bed, mosquito net, table, cane chair, and a cupboard full of beer, whisky, cigarettes, sardines, sauces, asparagus soup, quinine, Tinct. Zingiberis, Kruschen salts, etc., etc., the whole crowned with a range of Zane Grey, Rider Haggard, Scott, Dickens and E. Phillips Oppenheim.

The group of buildings, on what was a year ago an elephant-track, is surrounded by a deep trench. Not long ago a black bear was seen prowling around it.

From a nearby slope there is a wonderful view. To the north for 60 or 70 miles as the crow flies fold upon fold of the hills; to the West a cleft of dense jungle a thousand feet deep. Towards the East Silver Mountain—over 6,000 feet—and half a mile away, the Travancore boundary. To the South, sloping on to home jungle, orange-trees have been planted.

25.V.37.

Imagination.

In the world of a cock, a dragonfly, a snake there are possibilities which do no exist in any other and one has only to observe them, their eyes, their colour, their movement to see this and at last to begin to sense the world in their terms with its strangely concrete prerational intensities and splendours.

Animals as vital beings are unconscious symbols of the purely mental, or (in the case of the higher animals, probably) of the rational. Fear, appetite and curiosity are primary modes for them.

Plants could be symbols of the subtle-physical, or unconscious symbols of the vital.

Both are time-space objects only for the external mind.

If an insect is conscious of only one dimension, as the behaviour, for example, of ants seems to show, then flight perhaps represents in it the force and movement of vital thought or Imagination. Consider the formation, articulation, colour of wings. And at this level human metaphors of 'soaring' have perhaps a basis in nature.

Certainly in animals with their probable two-dimensional consciousness all movements through the third dimension—walking, running, leaping, building—are governed vitally, and at their highest (except perhaps in the apes) only represent the pragmatic—reason for which three-dimensional objects are primary. One would thus expect to find in animals a different coordination of the senses—one of the five below mind predominant or mind organising the five only liminally. The hand of man and certainly, though less obviously, his eyes are organised by a primary three-dimensional sense of objects. Only a few apes, I believe, can bring together finger and thumb: otherwise the whole claw still works, without discrimination of a third dimension. The mandibles of insects, and even of the crustaceans who seem to be very near them, work in one plane. Probably all creatures that can walk upside down on a ceiling—insects, lizards, etc., have a two-dimensional consciousness.

It would seem to follow that insects and animals have not our sense of time—the dimension in which we work pragmatically. The one-dimensional consciousness for its dynamic purposes must have a tool involving at least a second dimension.

Animals, also, can have no sense of their body as a whole and it is evident that insects with their ganglionic structure have from their own point of view no body but only actions. Which is perhaps why they are apparently never still except in chrysalis or as action—watching prey, responding to other unknown action.

A plant for its own consciousness is moved in the first dimension, representing the subtle-physical, an insect in the second, a man in time, representing intuition. Thus in some dreams we descend to a three-dimensional state in which—with reference to our waking state—we get into or out of rooms in no time. Perhaps an elephant in its dreams can fly and an insect is everywhere...!

The only full and commanded Consciousness, indeed, is to *be* Here Now...

The whole of physical space in which one's body moves is contained in one's consciousness so that all displacement in it is only formal. The whole sky of stars may be experienced in this way.

It is this sense, which, perhaps among other things, has for several years completely removed from me something spontaneous and personal any description of new places (I can do it Hypocritically).

One could no doubt very soon come to feel one's consciousness penetrating space. The sense of such a possibility suggests an explanation for the oft-reported voluntary contact between a guru and his distant disciples. 'Penetrating space' hardly expresses the quality of the movement one conceives, for it is not at all correlative with space: it is simply the directed extension of the consciousness that feels space entirely formal, so that it is by its nature trans-spatial, a state in which everything is present or at least immediately accessible to the natural act of thought. For no doubt this dynamic trans-spatiality is indeed the nature of thought. Only submission to the conceptual mode in which we experience objects and even persons in terms of their spatial limits—our identification of Reality with the physical universe—has so far hidden this from us. While all our metaphors are derived from the physical world it has been only metaphorically true.

5

Collected Entries On Rimbaud –Dated And Undated

The influence of Arthur Rimbaud on Thompson is a unified weave of poetry, spirituality and life quest. It was particularly important during the period covered by this volume. All the following journal entries date from 1931-43 with one exception, which is dated 28.XII. 45.

Since these entries are all related to Rimbaud, but are all part of Thompson's integral objective—his spiritual quest—the two men are almost in confluence in this respect, they have all been put together for ease of comprehension. Thompson's approach to the controversy over whether Rimbaud was ever, even at the peak of his visionary exaltation, a "truly sincere mystical 'seer'", is probably the most devastatingly radical counter-blast ever penned on the subject—for he is saying that Rimbaud was neither mystic nor scatological delinquent. His evaluation of Rimbaud is the most total root and branch summary, because he himself came closer than, in all probability, anyone else to living in Rimbaud's Harar—and 'writing about it': embodying the non-literary Rimbaldien attempt to attain Poetry.

Rimbaud's abandonment of literature at the age of nineteen in 1874 was a simple movement in the direction of completion.

The struggle between artist and *sadhaka*—one who is devoted to spiritual exercises—was Rimbaud's great battle. A conflict practically unheard of in the West, it cannot be fully stated in *religious* terms. Hence the great significance of Rimbaud who experienced and worked it out so intensely.

The last words of *A Season in Hell* in which at eighteen or nineteen this genius, who had written incomparable poems, turned his back on literature, or rather, on the attempt to make literature absolute Poetry, are:

'Il me sera loisible de *posseder la verité dans une ame et un corps*'. 'I shall be free to *possess truth in one soul and body*'. The artist has no such aim and means to it. At first the conflict between artist and *sadhaka*, when both are strong, may lead to crisis and a choice; but in the end, unless a purely yogic path is taken, all is resolved. Otherwise we should not have the poems of Vidyaranya, Ibnu'l-Farid and many another 'realised man'. Rimbaud seems to have lived out his hell.

Justifying and exhausting all necessary human myths the Christ recovers the primacy of Imagination, the activity of the Spirit. He is 'the word made flesh'.

For Rimbaud the 'sifflements de mort'—the 'whistlings of death'—of Being Beauteous foreshadow the season in hell, that descent which according to the heretic Marcion delivered the enemies of the God of nature, demiurge author of evil. And so *A Season in Hell* foresees, foreknew the Resurrection:

> Where shall we go beyond the shores and the mountains, to
> salute the birth of the new work, and the new wisdom, the
> flight of tyrants and demons, the end of superstition, and
> be the first to worship Christmas on earth?

It released Rimbaud into the solitary, simple, mysterious, scandalous way of the cross, journey and labour in the Dark Night.

Rimbaud sought to regain the integral magic that is truly natural to us. 'Once did I not have a delightful youth, heroic and fabulous, to be written on sheets of gold...' He experiences the anguish of expulsion from Eden, condemnation to the sweat of one's brow. 'I who called myself magus or angel, exempt from all morality, I am thrown back to the earth, with a duty to find, and rough reality to embrace! Peasant!' In *A Season in Hell* two orders of reality grapple in a void of disinterestedness, by the force of an Imagination, a humility, a generosity capable of the most violent or tenderest *volte-faces*, *voltiges*, self-exaltation, self-betrayal—and none can measure or influence the Reality, the nameless, supernatural intensity and calm about which this all-destroying tornado revolves.

It can at last be embodied only by the Whole Man, beyond the child, beyond the grown-up, the spiritual Adult *transformed* by the Transcendent. '...il me sera loisible de *posseder la verité* dans une ame et un corps'.

There are some who think Rimbaud a great poetic genius instead of a spiritual actuality quite beyond the grasp of comfortable metaphysics.

What Rimbaud showed is the irrelevance of great poetic genius—the true meaning of Poetry.

His whole life in literature and in the terrible search for a duty was an appalling wilfulness. 'My innocence made me weep...' It was this innocence which made every movement an effort of will—irony, insolence, despair—and which collects about every gesture a keen, fierce and as if supernatural beauty. It is the beginning of the Dance.

'Do I know nature yet? Do I know myself? No more words.
I will bury the dead in my belly. Yells, drums, dance, dance, dance, dance!'

He is the 'Etre de Beauté'—the Being of Beauty—in a poem of *Illuminations*. This is the unique human tragedy in its purity, the incarnation of the 'son of Adam who was the Son of God', his consort with the publicans, his war with the reason of the scribes, his sensuality, his compassion, his exasperation, his ambivalence with Nature, his movement towards the possible human geniality, his acceptance of crucifixion—the latest figure of that Christ.

In Kierkegaard's definition 'every individuality which, without mediation, alone, by itself, in particular relation with the "divine" is demoniac.'

And thus it is that Christianity does not abandon the conception of the ego, but enhances and transcends it agonistically in its own direction. This certainly gives as little place for heaven and immortality as did the Christ with the *Now*—crisis becomes pure action.

This necessity is perhaps always undercurrent for the Western Spirit, fundamentally divided as its myth of Eden avows. Not only in Dostoievski, Kierkegaard and Kafka, and others who have affinities with them, in Goethe and Blake you also find it.

The demoniac is perfect in Action, his clairvoyance is action beyond all correpondences. He is outside art from the beginning. Rimbaud as demoniac ruined art. And as European, in tension between the 'neant' and the demoniac (his Season in Hell, which really left a terrible fatigue), he remained, nobly, agonistically, with complete and dreadful humility and reserve, in tragedy from his arrival in Egypt to his death. And his integrity is another of those invisible legacies by which the essential drama of the Western Spirit is dangerously renewed.

Renouncing the continuance of a demoniac activity whose bases prove unreal, renouncing at the same time happiness by surrender, Rimbaud invented this appalling new solution, to live by a heroism completely devoid of pride, by the exercise of his present powers, in complete metaphysical solitude. Rimbaud in Harar is the most profoundly exciting, the most beautiful and the most terrible spectacle of which I have knowledge.

Imperfection can only be changed if you will first sacrifice yourself to it. It is what the Christian Dostoievski so well understood. But the demoniac—and still—Christian Dostoievski also knew that 'whoever will show men that they are good will bring an end of the world!'

And the critics who find that Rimbaud is uncouth, morose, foul, criminal, insane, insensitive, 'coeur de glace, âme de boue', forget that Rimbaud's attempt upon life begins past the Rimbaud who could so easily have seduced them, whose 'facons d'être' can only be completely and complacently insensitive to his agony and his irony.

It seems possible that necessity is their real god and comfort. They embrace art and other possibly genial and dangerous activities in order to hold their arms down and it is this which partly defines Rimbaud's violent ambivalence with art. They are preoccupied with art: the Poet is continually passing outside it. The necessity of the gratuitous is for the Last Judgement. They can believe in any number of heavens but the Kingdom of heaven. They make the parables about it in literature.

Rimbaud is menacing and unnameable for literature by the simple fact that he said none of the things which *can be said*.

He perceived the paroxysmal bitterness and disgust that it is no good delivering parables, or *Illuminations*. He is in tension with the Christian Christ who crucifies him, because he is unconsciously side by side with Christ the Poet and at one with his scandalous, mysterious and violent geniality.

Rimbaud, who found real economy in Baudelaire as he did in Villon, so much the more quickly exhausted what is still romantic in them and that leaves the poet defined as 'maudit' and clairvoyant. His classicism completely facing the human finally accepts silence and despair as the definition of transformation. His integrity, his complete endurance of the human agony, gave him the right to say: 'Now I can say that art is a stupidity'.

For both Baudelaire and Rimbaud the conception of a human perfection is one possible pole of their nostalgia. It is because both by their intelligence, sensibility, refuse humanism as sentimentality and are too genial to accept it as religion or irony that they appear for it pariahs, classifiable only as 'neurotic', 'egoist', 'debauchee', détraqué', 'voyou', 'coeur de glace', 'âme de boue'.

His critics see him at their level. If they could fully see him or even the adolescent photographs, and if they could imagine the innocence and geniality on which it depends, they would understand what is perfectly incidental to Poetry, that 'What are called the vices in the natural world are the highest sublimities in the spiritual world' (Blake)

Vice is simply the failure of Poetry: in accusing himself in terms of the European misunderstanding of the Poet Jesus, Rimbaud condemned himself to hell. Jesus not yet accepted as Poet is present throughout *A Season in Hell.*

Jesus chose Judas, 'a devil': Rimbaud betrayed himself in order to overcome the supreme agony.

28.12.45.

'Il faut étre absolument moderne'—one must be absolutely modern—to forge the irreplaceable, inimitable, instrument for one's present sensibility—and so, first, really to be present, in despite of all past and possible future, and all possible other states—to centre oneself here, to bring all inexplicability, the Reality of Truth and Joy, to crisis here.

All that is literary, derivative, dependent, or in any way fashionable, temporary, must be completely commanded.

1935.

A work has density so far as it represents mystery—appeals to the consciousness for which myth is unavoidable—so far as it looks directly at the human as the subject of the riddle of the Sphinx. In flying away from Oedipus the Sphinx achieved its most sinister and Sphinx-like triumph, its most appalling and prophetic laughter. The riddle of the Sphinx, which for Oedipus seems easy to solve, is its most subtle, complete and cruel deception. The solution, taking the human for granted, is the refusal of the more benevolent presence of the Sphinx as Agony.

This density is for modern times perhaps most troubling and unavoidable in Rimbaud, in whom there is a new meeting and acuter, more desperate, duel with the Sphinx—whose life and work reopen now more subtly and dangerously the abyss that the centuries since the exile of Oedipus have been engaged in forgetting.

1943.

Rimbaud—the universal 'True Man, the Poetic Genius/ (Blake) once more recovered and released. He marks the explosion of modern Western culture and the irrelevance at the same time of a 'new mediaevalism' (in the Middle Ages his relation is with Villon).

As Baring has said, he was 'a super-classic'. This is the relation with the Christ so intense in the Season in Hell. In the Christ the West achieved itself. But he will not be understood till all Eastern 'metaphysic' has been in all senses mastered in their sense—till the Oriental mediaevalism, also, has been rolled back upon living sources.

17.7.31.

Rimbaud. His whole life in literature and in the terrible search of 'un devoir' was an appalling wilfulness. 'My innocence made me weep...'. It was this innocence which made every movement an effort of will—irony, insolence, despair, and which collects about every gesture a keen, fierce and as if supernatural beauty. It is the beginning of the Dance.

He is the 'être de beauté' of the poem *Being Beauteous*: it contains the 'sifflement de mort' of 'Une Saison en Enfer' and the denouement: 'We are clothed again in a newly loving body'.

It is the unique human tragedy in its purity, the incarnation of the 'son of Adam who was the Son of God', his consort with the publicans, his war with the reason of the scribes, his sensuality, his compassion, his exasperation, his ambivalence with Nature, his movement towards the possible human geniality, his acceptance of crucifixion—the latest figure of that Christ.

Rimbaud leaves no preliminary task in which we could forget ourselves. Chaos in the existing order necessary for the coming of the Kingdom.

The only people who, aware of him, disown Rimbaud are those who imitate him *in literature* (i.e. betray him, or rather themselves) or behave as if he belongs to literature and merely enlarged literature. To these two tribes belong modern professional verse-makers or pseudo-poets—pseudo because they all accept some other authority but poetry. Even if they go so far in their cul-de-sac to see that poetry can continue to be possible for them (i.e. can continue to have anything to do with literature) only if it were possible to behave as if Rimbaud's exhaustion of literature had never existed—then there is only one thing left: they must consent to have accepted life only as pre-Rimbaldians. If they stop taking him falsely as a *literary* authority, and if in the face of *Une Saison* and what followed they can no longer continue as imitators of Rimbaud, then they must continue their literary indulgence at peace by accepting personally *religious* authority.

Rimbaud exhausted all the methods of saying on which one might lay one's hands, in wishing to say nothing below a certain level—in discovering (for a moment poised there, angry, in despair, terrible, accusing himself of self-deception) that you can *say* nothing, that no language or substance exists. And real activity can be understood, is *visible*, only to Leisure. Rimbaud remains forever impenetrable to some people and stirs up their foulest exasperation and impotence. Their necessities cannot mirror his freedom, the background of his invention and framework of his agony, which thus is completely an offence to their intelligence, morality, self-satisfaction.

Both those who do not give literature the place in his life that he did and those who interpret him for the sake of an Oriental 'sagesse première et éternel' which he saw as a 'rève paresse grossière'—a grossly idle fancy—evade the solidity of Rimbaud.

22.6.35.

It is perhaps because Rimbaud saw with terror, delight and despair the reality of certain worlds he entered that the 'sophisme magique' of words necessary to suggest his experiences as if for the sake of the rational consciousness seemed to him a lie—hopeless because unnecessary.

Rimbaud—Critics:

They see him at their level. If they could fully see him or even the adolescent photographs, and if they could imagine the innocence and geniality on which it depends, they would understand what is perfectly incidental to Poetry, that 'What are called the vices in the natural world are the highest sublimities in the spiritual world' (Blake).

Vice is simply the failure of Poetry: in accusing himself in terms of the European misunderstanding of the Poet Jesus, Rimbaud condemned himself to hell. Jesus not yet accepted as Poet is present throughout *Une Saison.*

Jesus chose Judas, a 'devil': Rimbaud (also) betrayed himself in order to overcome supreme agony.

Already Rimbaud, desiring objectification actual and not symbolic, turned towards applied science. But this objectification is not more continuous nor therefore less symbolic than that of art. 'La science et en avant'. What we need is entirely *en avant.*

He represented very directly the fact that since the mediaeval belief in 'sainthood', embodiment of Poetry in Itself is hardly possible in Europe. The symbol remains without the reality; hence the partial and thus paradoxical nature of all Western art and its increasing self-consciousness and self-excusing. In Rimbaud the problem became completely conscious, but who else has his passion and his integrity? To anything less he will always appear negative, a 'failure': nothing less really conceives and intends 'the truth in a soul and a body'. The rest have failed because they do not believe in or wish for this kind of success, they do not feel this perfection is the paramount necessity. Rimbaud has aroused in his own way as significantly frantic misunderstanding as the Christ.

Rimbaud, who found real economy in Baudelaire as he did in Villon, so much the more quickly exhausted what is still romantic in them and that leaves the poet defined as 'maudit' and clairvoyant. His classicism completely facing the human finally accepts silence and despair as the definition of transformation. This incidentally puts him in violent tension with the Christianity defined in his life by Baudelaire's failure to dispense with art as an idealism. Christianity here means acceptance of human imperfection in ambivalence with God and the Devil. Rimbaud's integrity, his complete endurance of the human agony, gave him the right to say: 'Now I can say that art is a stupidity'.

Somewhere between 18 and 20 I believe I experienced all that is implied in Rimbaud's rejection of literature—and it seems to me that Rimbaud lived very purely and intensely the modern 'metaphysical crisis'. How is it that after this, and when I had myself abandoned all attempt to write (with music potentially my 'natural art'), I read Rilke, Kafka and Proust in such a way that you may almost have been led to think that I find in them certain essential values that thus make me exclusive? Well, I can't go into this fully, but the essential belong with the idea of Poetry—in principle the immediate, autonomous revelation, the speech of love, universal by its perfect particularity. For the Spirit there is only *nowness*: its immediacy entirely cuts across all that is relatively, egoistically, special or exclusive. So it uses the most transient means. The type of this, and the kind of immediate perception it represents is Zen Buddhism and the arts it has influenced—*hokku*, *sumiye*. The 'natural' type is of course the folk-song. The possibility of Poetry as the only pure, direct and integral human speech is still represented by the Christ. Love is the key to it all: with tact, tenderness, delight, love speaks the language of the beloved: language is perfectly organised—

subordinating all that is merely formal and secondary—only by the sensibility and the extravagance of Love.

6

Extracts From Letters To Ethel Merston

What does Aristotle say about knowledge beginning in wonder—admiratio—delight?

The courage of ignorance is delight.

'...if one were true to the knowledge of one's ignorance, one would be silent.' Well, I'm not so correct and modest, so awfully English: the courage of my ignorance is very voluble. Cocky!

General warning. I have grown up in complete intellectual isolation and probably don't realize to what an extent I use words in special, often highly saturated, senses. It's all perfectly logical to me, part the result of a single organisation of thought—which is really, then, a poem and I suppose can only be so understood!

It's quite unnecessary to harp on your ignorance to a man who believes it's the only true place to start and who is a complete barbarian! (For example: I've written quite a small volume demonstrating the uselessness of philosophy in the modern Western sense, yet I've never read Kant, Hegel, Fichte, MacTaggart and Co. I'll probably look at them when my work is formally complete. I'm absolutely certain of confirmation. Cocky!). It is our real Ignorance alone, which, if we are true to it, (the only real humility) can become real Knowledge. All other knowledge is merely literature!—Seriously, speculative philosophy, like all other merely human activity, can only be valued and judged as an art.

My 'theory of Poetry' is simply one aspect of my sense of and approach to the Autonomy of Reality, the fact that Reality is entirely Self-defining. I say: Reality is that which alone has no need to be real.—Pure Marvel, 'the Concrete of Concretes' as Sri Krishna Prem finely says of Sri Krishna.

In other words: What I say does not exist as fact or theory: it is a practical, unnecessary arrangement of a sadhaka's mind, his re-action to the fact that there is supposed to be such a thing as 'poetry'.

I am not an esthetician or a philosopher, nor in the literary sense a poet. But—because?—perhaps essentially poet in all other spheres. That is why, for example, there is for me no such thing as philosophy.

What is all this about real and unreal?! Can you truly think me such a damned abstract philosopher? On the contrary (though you cannot know how far I carry it, or even believe this), I am an enemy of all abstractions. Is not 'Reality' (blindest of all words) the *Sole Concreteness*? Must it surprise you that I was delicately touched to read of a lovesick swain? Beauty in this world is almost always cruel, for the more perfect it is the less it can be conscious *in itself*. In this world it can only be symbolic and none but lovesick swains will truly learn this. As for me, I live in a state of lovesickness.

To fall into abstraction as soon as one is asked to conceive a more complete reality is impotence and vulgarity—vulgar because it puts a false value on the mind.

Re-reading one or two of our letters, I fear I may be partly responsible for a certain nervousness in the use of words. But what the bluddy fucking hell does it matter what words we use, so long as we express ourselves? And in any case, if creativity does not lie on the side of the speaker, his speech is restored as creation by the intelligence and sympathy of the listener who understands it. In barracks, when I was conscripted not long ago, about the most inarticulate man I've ever met, and utterly uneducated, after a talk with me at once became a fast friend. For me his dense inarticulatedness was an ore of poetry.

As far as I can see I take *no* mental form seriously. When I criticise use of words it may look donnish (as if for mental reasons), but I'm generally aiming at something on another level.—Very often *order* of thought. i.e. the extensibility of a word from Hell to Heaven, or its proper resonant placing between them. Nowadays in almost all one reads words have only an inane accidental surface, as shifting, fortuitous and unreliable as a momentary pattern in a kaleidoscope. It is because, with universal 'education', there is practically no-one left (or audible) who thinks personally, with his whole existence, and so organises his language *in depth*.—Such organisation is always highly personal, and personality (*not* individuality!!!) is as near as possible invisible, unrecognised, for the mechanical and astonishingly feeble (or anyhow fragmented) contemporary mind.

Please don't think that the meaning I choose, in my wilful, eccentric way (yet, I really believe, not entirely so) to give to Poetry—or any other perspective I build—is to be taken as fact or truth. It is poetic—represents vision, spiritual tendency or intention in myself. For others, accepted as dogma, it may be a pernicious lie: anyway, only ignorance could accept it. And it's entirely unorthodox: as far as I know, nobody else has expressed it within this horizon or made the distinctions I make, though I can, as you see, draw upon many who may seem to represent more or less completely what I mentalise in my own way. But this making plausible is done by art, imagination, not by belief in or dependence upon 'facts'. One controls and effectively understands only the ideas one has developed organically, that serve one's integral purposes.—Don't, for heaven's sake, believe what I say (any more than you believe a poem): only see the intention, what it means spiritually. There are enough theories and dogmas as it is.

7

The Gift Of Dreams

From 1933 until his death, Thompson recorded his dreams. He trained himself to write them down as soon as he woke up, regardless of whether or not it was still dark. Since he seldom slept in rooms with electric light, he became accustomed to write in the dark, a few words to each page. These hastily pencilled notes are almost indecipherable (occasionally even to him) but show extraordinary accuracy of recall. In the morning he would transcribe them into his journal and, when a dream warranted it, discuss its content with the Jnani, or send him a copy. He often typed copies for other members of the ashram, as careful scrutiny of dreams is commonly enjoined on sadhakas.

The influence of the French Surrealists is evident in some early accounts of dreams included here. However, his take on dreams is unique to himself and 'within this horizon' he aimed at maximum exploration of his intro-continental dream terrain. Later, he abandoned this technique, fashioning for himself a method which ensured maximum veracity to the peculiarities of dream experience. Until one has read many of these dream-poems it is sometimes difficult to resist the suspicion that the original narrative has been tampered with for literary effect. But careful scrutiny of the original notes with the fair copy, and comparison between dreams and their re-curring motifs has convinced me that, apart from his felicity with words (which makes of many an accomplished literary artifact), he was truthful to his memory. The remarkable coherence of Thompson's dreams amply justifies their inclusion in a selection from his journal, not only because they provide an extra dimension to autobiography and illuminate crucial stages in the dreamer's spiritual development, but because they are often of exquisite literary grace in themselves. They also provide insight into the dream-process, the spiritual significance of dreams and, backed by a series of notes on dream which Thompson wrote from time to time in his journal, present an alternative approach to understanding dream experience from that to which we have become habituated through the literature of psychoanalysis.

An aptitude for inner vision is a charisma of Eastern spirituality, and this should be kept in mind when we read Thompson's dreams, for he wrote in an environment exceedingly rich in dream culture. He was acquainted with some of the principal Hindu and Sufi traditions which closely relate dream experience with 'sadhana' and the highest attainable spiritual and visionary states. Late in life, he decided to collect his dreams under the title "Such Stuff: A Book of Dreams", prefaced by notes (included here) and planned to refer the reader to the ideas of the great mystical philosopher, Shankara, the 'Yogavashishtha', Buddhism and Sufism (notably, the role of Ibn 'Arabi in the development of dream culture).

In spite of the widespread influence of psychoanalysis, the world of dreams is still considered by the modern Western mind to be a realm of unreality, bizarre imagery and fantasy—no doubt 'clinically' interesting—as compared with the 'real' world of conscious waking perception. Elsewhere, in other cultures and other periods of history, dream experiences may be interpreted as the literal equivalent of the experiences of individuals in the waking state. In such dream-supported cultures (including India's), a number of basic assumptions sharply diverge from those of the modern West, which can be reduced to several simple propositions: Ultimate reality is transcendental, and worldly reality, including dreams, is its sign or symbol. No clear and trenchant distinction is drawn between what is and what is not; what is real and what is unreal, what is 'conscious' and what is 'unconscious'. No clearly perceived dividing line is drawn between the natural and the supernatural, possible and impossible. Man's purpose is outside himself and so are the source and the rationale of the incidents that make up his life, both awake and asleep. Revelations and dreams are expected to remedy from the outside what man is unable to achieve from within. Accordingly, psychological phenomena tend to be interpreted as representing objective, non-psychological, supra-personal 'outside' reality. The dream is seen as possessed of cognitive force in regard to otherwise inaccessible sectors of objective reality, especially truths bearing on man's relation to the divine. The intrusion of dreams upon man's consciousness need not necessarily overwhelm him or submerge him in a totally subjective world. On the contrary, dreams and visions can be used as phases and tools for spiritual progress; they are then seen as a waiting, a preparation, an intention, and an activity for commanding the future, a search for a forgotten past, or for establishing connection with divine creation. Such are the findings of modern anthropology.

A Sufi tradition which caught Thompson's eye endorses these observations and someone who dreams clearly is said to have 'the gift of dreams', such as Ibn 'Arabi and Suhrawardi. Abdalghani an-Nabulsi, a seventeenth century Sufi, has written: 'Blessed the one who sees a dream clearly, for clear dreams without mediation of the angel of the dreams are sent by none but the Creator.... Man sees dreams with the spirit and understands them with the intelligence.... When a man sleeps, his spirit spreads like the light of a lamp or the sun.' In its recognition of the objective existence of immaterial bodies, Images, or Archetypes, Iranian Islam named this other-than-human world the Intermediate Orient. The interpenetration of dream-reality and waking-reality, so important to Ibn 'Arabi in his vision of the mysterious 'evanescent young man, the Silent-Speaker', was a frequent occurrence in Thompson's life. The care with which Henry Corbin tries to develop a phenomenology of dream congruent with this venerable mystical tradition is apt: 'The phenomenology of religious experience ought neither to deduce it from something else, nor to reduce it to something else by illusory causal explanations. It ought to discover what form of consciousness is presupposed by the perception of events and worlds inaccessible to the common consciousness.' (Visionary Dream in Islamic Spirituality, in "The Dream and Human Societies", edited by Von Grunebaum and Caillois, Berkeley, 1966, p.403.) Corbin quotes Suhrawardi: 'When you learn in the treatises of the ancient sages that there exists a world with dimensions and extension other than this world of the senses...a world of innumerable cities...do not hastily cry 'lie', because this world the pilgrims of the spirit succeed in contemplating and they find there every object of their desire.'

Thompson read extensively about the cultures, both past and present, which treat this kind of theme. More important, he frequented circles steeped in the atmosphere of 'dream spirituality', the Jnani being especially keen to encourage him in this respect. In fact, dream experience became of such central importance to Thompson's spiritual development that some especially significant dreams occupy an axial position at its climax, the attainment of 'nirvikalpa samadhi' during sleep. His experiences registered on the edge of consciousness were not merely a source of imagery to exploit for mere literary effect, but were the core and even the focus of Thompson's spiritual endeavour at various times. It is often hard, unless the indication is clearly made, to distinguish in the journal between experiences that can be strictly defined as dream, and others which are visionary, or in some enigmatic way supernormal, such as the extraordinary tale of the Midnight Visitor he recalls while staying at Gallela in 1939.

Thompson's orientation, then, towards dream is non-psychological and influenced by Hindu, Buddhist and Sufi ideas, particularly with regard to the way he viewed it as a function of consciousness. According to classical Indian thought both waking and sleeping are subsumed by an all-embracing Consciousness—'Chit'. The Atman is called the Witnessing Consciousness: yoga penetrates and commands 'all' states of consciousness. Indian myth also emphasises the cardinal importance of dream: for instance, the whole phenomenal world is the dream of Brahma the Creator. Shankara, the eighth century Vedantin, held that initiation in dream is the highest of its forms. Thus the significance of visionary dream in Hindu and Islamic spirituality can be understood only as a function of the spiritual ethos, initiatory in the former, prophetic in the latter. A distinction is drawn in both traditions between a 'clear dream' and the 'ordinary dream' of the individual bearing the imprint of 'samskaras' carried over from waking life, past experience and 'karma'. The content of a clear dream cannot be accounted for within the background of the individual's experience; it is seen either as received through divine inspiration or as converse between the individual and his own soul.

The fundamental difference between our modern attitude towards the significance of dreams and these ancient ideas is that we utilise our dream recall as a means of introspection rather than as an instrument for cognition of outside reality. Thompson spends little time 'interpreting' his own dreams, but enters them and inhabits their space in exactly the same way as he inhabits a particular landscape, and sees in both a symbolism which mirrors his own state of being. He often knows that he is dreaming while dreaming, and dreams that he is recording the dream. Waking consciousness and dreaming consciousness actually reinforce each other. The transformation of a dream into significant truth is accomplished by its realisation in words. Instead of scrutinising dream symbolism for information about himself he makes of it a poem which is self-luminous.

While Thompson never refers explicitly to the Dream Quest of the Plains Amerindian, nevertheless it does cast an interesting light on the use to which he put his own dreaming. The Amerindian youth endures a lonely vigil under conditions of great privation and fasting in order to obtain a vision of his tutelary deity. Like the Sufi mystics, he prays for a messenger, a teacher of truth, a companion or spiritual guide who points the way forward in life. The distinctive character of the inner resources thus gained is analogous with Thompson's quest for self-sufficiency and 'inner control' rather than 'outward coercion', or outward submission to a living master. Once again, here is a source of tension between himself and the Jnani, who eventually held the view that Thompson had misapplied dream material in his 'sadhana'.

As to the content of his dreams, they may be said to echo the primordial scenario of all vision quests of a shamanistic pattern: initiatory in character, they involve suffering, journeys, death, dismemberment, resurrection, explicit election to a higher order of being and a psychic isolation which is the counterpart of the isolation and ritual solitude of initiation ceremonies. The dreamer encounters divine or numinous or charismatic teachers, or is inducted by animal guides into some sacred 'otherness', descends or ascends to altitudes or depths of heightened awareness, is granted a brief glimpse into a domain of the marvellous or the superreal. Several times he experiences the ascent of the 'kundalini' subtle energy along the spinal column, opening the 'chakras', inner subtle centres. The latter scenario underlies the whole spectrum of his dream experience, sensitising him to brief repeated receipt of 'nirvikalpa samadhi' and radical modification of the nervous system.

This short chapter is in two sections: a sequence of notes on dream followed by a short selection of dreams spanning the years 1936–41, which have been put together so that the reader may more easily enter the atmosphere of Thompson's dreamscape (the word 'atmosphere' has its root in the Sanskrit 'atman'). As Thompson intended, all later dreams appear in their proper chronological sequence, forming an integral feature of his journal. One is struck by the way they coil or loop forward, and back upon, nodal events in the dreamer's life. One can also see how the dream has a connective function here, knitting together disparate and discontinuous segments, phases or levels in the total pattern of one lifespan. The beauty of these dream-poems lies in Thompson's skill to transcend the purely interpretive level; what we are given is not so much a psychological portrait of the personality as an exploration and illumination of states of being. The Dreamer is the yogin for whom dream is a means to achieve integral Consciousness: the wakened resolves dream in perfect Poetry.

[Notes on dreams:1936–42—Selected by the editor.]

People think the world is real. But all thinking is conventional, there are only conventions.

This world is real to you in sleep, yet you have to admit that your sleep is real. This world, then, is not the whole of reality. So reality cannot be completely explained in terms of it.

That the present waking state and what is seen and done there is the whole of reality or even, except by habit its own begging of the question, the focus of reality at all, no man can say who still dreams and sleeps.

Dream—complex and subtle puns and oracles between diverse modes and aspects of consciousness. We are always dreaming. Complete freedom from dream would be boundless Terror or Illumination.

The dream as accident and incoherence, whose *helplessness* is its only organisation, reflects the failure of waking consciousness to command the subtle and immediate that transcend it—reflects the helpless romanticism of waking consciousness.

One's psycho-physical state may be symbolised in sleep with extraordinary resource and subtlety as a person, companion of the invisible and purely dramatic self of dreams who indeed lives only among his potentialities.

The self that remembers dreams is prior to these two and to the waking consciousness in which this memory is a phenomenon. Conscious in the dream itself, it can change and exploit it as dramaturge. This defines for it the nature of phenomena and their relation with a self.

The mind may become more and more conscious and act more and more freely in dreams, but awareness of them as a whole must be the property of the perceiving Self, command of them a subordination of the Immutable behind the cosmic flux, Who is above all dualities, including subject and object, waking and sleep.

The effort of the external mental will to become conscious of and in one's dreams only mentalises them and probably inhibits the source of transmental dreams or throws them into a new 'unconsciousness'.

One of the chief reasons for the strangeness, vividness, and peculiar interest of dream is no doubt that mental preconceptions are not operative in them as such; so far as they are being exhausted in dream they have no weight there, and the dream is vital rather than mental. A very similar experience can in fact be had in the waking state by putting aside memory and preconception, or when there is vital enhancement or excitement.

Waking life free of preconception recovers the immediacy and Luxury of dream. And dream as a phenomenon of memory disappears: dream becomes clairvoyance unknown and unheard of to waking, a world of another range of possibilities. If all worlds are related by Consciousness, all life is a dream. That life at any given level in any given world is purely formal.

The concentration of this Consciousness must be all-powerful.

Energy can be drawn directly from any form or occasion of the dream. All forms are yantras (geometrical diagrams of divinity), all occasions mantras.

The ego is opposition to the laws of the dream.

Integral consciousness in dream demands enlargement of the active personality and primarily sacrifice of the external ego, realisation of the ego as entirely a construction of external mental, vital and physical nature. This would disperse the trivial dreams that continue only in complement with it and favour those belonging to a richer and more primary inner consciousness.

Whoever has achieved Luxury no longer dreams.

The pure enjoyment of dream and its immediate pressureless detail depend on absence of transitions and backgrounds and necessities. This quality is immediate in spontaneous and disinterested experience.

Your chief power, or at least the best known, is still the waking mind. The first thing, therefore, is to do in the waking state 'the work to be done', and only when this realism is established will other movements take their place in rhythms serving and expressing reality. Only then, indeed, will they be effectively accessible and acceptable.

To say, when awake: 'This is all a dream' when dream in relation to waking is still uncommanded is pure romanticism. Waking is commanded only in the same sense as is dream: Then it has the *sui-generis* freedom and poetry of dream—perfect Sensuality, having no necessity but its coherence, so that its concreteness is pure hallucinating Luxury, commanding all the correspondences it can command.

Only the whole man can master his dream-consciousness: it is not a question of understanding, which always depends upon certain limits of consciousness, but of integration into consciousness as a whole, with all the process of purification and transformation that integration must involve.

As I wrote to a friend, 'my dreams have become poems'. This *can* no doubt mean that they represent, according to the modes of the dream-state, an integral harmony of one's psychic forces in which there is no opposition but mutual support and clarification between dreaming and waking consciousness. Thus such dreams are perfectly felicitous, unquestionable experiences, before and beyond the need and possibility of interpretation. No doubt *vision*, a revelation of the potential Whole Man to his temporal instrument, can be pure, direct and unconfused only when distortion and the need of interpretation are at least neutralised.

Blake spoke absolutely casually of his visions.

Every scene which you view as a whole without preconception has neither beginning nor end; its history exists only in its own terms; walking in this scene you appear as a puppet limited by a certain set of relations. Only so far as your consciousness is limited by the scene are interpretations of it possible and they continue its history.

Mere mental recording of dreams and analysis of them by the ordinary waking consciousness is inconclusive—they must be transformed by the whole man. Here the integrative activity of the poet is more to the point.

The dream, as common experience, is the type of all attempts to express one quality of experience in terms of another—of all poetic and mystical expression. The dream, like the poem, takes form and is remembered only in terms of the waking mind. In the process of poetic expression also the relation set up between two modes of consciousness, waking and dreaming, builds as it were a magnetic field. The *action* of poetry is the deepening and purifying, by this command, of the resources both of the inner and of the external mind in all their possible modes—in fact, the command of Reality. This process of mutual self-enlargement, penetration and fulfillment of inner and outer in the sense of expanded Consciousness, when it involves the Whole Man is called yoga. Ultimately it means union and participation with the One Poet.

The work of art, so far as it is also transrational, is as it were a dream in the waking state which has plausibly to satisfy or circumvent as its 'censor' the demands of rationality. No doubt the waking mind spontaneously values only 'realised' dreams. Only those dreams seem to us beautiful or poetic in which condensation in all its references is perfect and lucid as a completely focussed symbol. It is this strange, subtle and concrete perfection, no doubt, which gives us the sense of the 'clairvoyant' or hallucinating quality of dreams: only these perfect dreams seem to have the pure quality of dream.

Half the task of a work of art is to satisfy and suspend cold daylight mental horizons and criticism for the sake of overflooding immediacy which is so easily achieved in dreams, and in fact the perfect work of art in a very mental culture like that of Europe stands only by a strong, hard, scintillating or astringent critical element and only a very great vital or psychic impulse can reduce this. Take Shakespeare—so often stiff and crepitating with intellect. Modern works, or small but intense things generally, have to be more than half firework—Pascal, Cocteau, Stravinsky....

In dreams we recognise that waking life disguises, that there are only details. The artist understands this. If we realise this only in dreams and in certain heightened states of consciousness it is because our attention then is complete, non-intellectual, elementary. Such attention is clairvoyance.

One of the reasons why the light on objects in dream seems so subtle or dramatic, so strange, is that there is, in dreams, only an abstract, a sense of the passage of time *deduced* (if any at all); and even in the waking state, if all interpretation in terms of memory, reason and expectation is done away, the light on any object at any hour is equally inexplicable and strange. But we seldom see it directly, without preconception: before we have seen it purely, timelessly, we explain it as a stage in familiar gradation from, say, sunset through twilight to night: we see it only formally, already devitalised by sickly rationalism. But in a dream we see it directly, face to face, with no before and no after.

Any attempt to systematise observations about dreams is suspect, for how can it avoid subjecting them to some logic or perception of the waking state? So these notes remain discrete—with no greater interference from the waking state than that which binds each of them together within itself. For even in dreams, or in some kinds of dream, we do use the terms and logic of waking speech, though often with greater rapidity and subtlety. If this were not so, poetry, whose substance is as trans-mental as that of dreams, would not be possible in the same language we use for merely rational prose.

[A Collection of dreams, 1936-41.]

Very beautiful episode of richly scented lily-like white flowers.

Then, by a stream, a very affectionate little soft brown bird passionately pecks and drags at my *dhoti*, drawing me to the Queen of these birds, down by the stream. She laughs because I have already seen her or heard her voice somewhere in the physical world without knowing who she was—not knowing her bird-nature in her human metamorphosis.

Kinnaris of Himavant, the Himalayan fairy-land—bird-women who take off their plumage and bathe as beautiful girls.

From the wide-open windows of an isolated house I have entered a circle of dancing animals. Fiercely dancing tiger. I put aside memory of the idea of fear and face him entirely with my admiration of his force and beauty. I stand aside behind and at the end of a row of mounted teeth or elephant-tusks taller than myself. I greet all warmly, offering *namaskaram* to the tiger. Standing like a man, he responds (it was a question if he would). I tell him he is my guest. He asks me to demand whatever I want and he will produce it. I tell him I want nothing, but to prove his powers ask for an emerald. He stretches himself; then, with concentration, like a conjuror he closes, waves and hides his (human) hand. He explains that the One Power exists only by this will, this concentration. After a little delay he shows on his hand (it was already slightly sparkling as if with minute stray fragments of emerald-dust) a small blister like a hard phosphorescence, pale green like the light of glow-worm or fire-fly. I notice two more hard and gemlike cut emeralds, also pale, in the headdress of one of the tiger's companions, a woman standing near him while I talked with him.

The animals convey to me, especially through the tiger, and I strongly feel, that I have ever the help and protection of their powers, the powers of their realm. Strange sense, almost smell, of the animals, their power and individuality.

They take leave, all with great affection. The water-buffalo rolls in joy and insists on slavering all over me. The tiger goes first by a square black door that opens on a rocky conduit. I promise to leave this door open for their future visits—unless my host's servant shut it.

I keep the intention of using the Moon-forces—the white foam from a cascade in which I wash a series of little dishes belonging to the physical world. Thus I remain conscious at the same time of a physical reference and of a dream in which alone these magical influences are available. But if I allow the dream to get the upper hand I begin to be lost in the deep, clear cold waters of complex volcanic rocky pools or in the influence of a tall, dark, slender girl in a loose white robe, with black hair falling over her shoulders. To avoid being absorbed into the Moon-sphere, after a certain amount of oscillation towards it and back I wake up.

Recurrence after a long series of similar dreams years ago.

I am wandering alone in a vast mansion or palace with endlessly new richly furnished and apparently inhabited rooms. But I never meet anyone.

Looking back at it from a wide corridor with beautifully proportioned and elegantly moulded white doors, I recognise in a room with luxurious sofas upholstered in pale green silk and with high, widely-curving backs a scene from an earlier dream a week ago reminiscent of *The Priory* where I spent the summer at West Molesey as a child.

I think with interest of recording when I wake this remembering of one dream in another.

A very good example of a vivid self-evolving narrative or argument, extremely concrete and felicitous, but as it were arbitrary, inventing itself. Such compositions are so clear and conscious that if only this state could continue in relation with the waking mind they would record themselves word for word. They usually progress as if at the same time being produced and read, and with music of this kind too, as I play the score progressively composes itself on the pages before me, and so vividly that only its complexity prevents my carrying memory of it into the waking state.

Fat book about Zaharoff.

(It is only in 1940, four years after the dream, that a Sufi tells me that Zaharoff, an armaments 'King' and a leader of the 'counted', was one of the Masters of the Theosophists).

It is about his losing or throwing off successively physical, etheric or astral bodies. Experiences and phenomena in the new states. Massive pleasurable interest at the prospect of reading. A sense of the luminousness, as it were, of the rich, clear and unusual contents.

Looking at negative plates of Isadora Duncan. Some relation with or likeness to early photos of Mother. Stage scenes: two or three figures with primitive masks grouped on steps like the Russian ballet.

Isadora, as if in one of the photos, with her little boy, whose face is strangely mature and like Beerbohm Tree. Seated in her lap, in his capricious dramatisation of his affection for her he often looks obliquely behind her where I stand and watch in the room full of night-shadows, mirror-shadows, photographic shadows. He does not see and is not aware of me but Isadora follows his stare every time over her shoulder and looks at me.

I talk with her regarding my half-serious desire to steal one of the negatives. She asks if I have still the bed she gave me and which she had asked me to keep so as one day to help her remember the future.

Most of the photos, close-up of Isadora's head, are still clear to me as I write at about 4 am. Especially one of the young head tilted back—the line of the open lips, smooth cream-coloured skin rich and soft but the forms pure and athletic, vigorously curling golden hair loose at the nape. These photos are really rather like those published of her in her youth. In one or two an elegant companion like Nielson Terry—no doubt Lohengrin or another.

Isadora is so charming in her friendship that at one moment I caress and kiss her face. Perhaps my relation with her has been like that of her pianist... About some of the photos she recalls memories.

Sitting by the fire, about a brass and ebony pot standing in the hearth I say that apart from its ugliness I disapprove of merely decorative objects and think everything should be organic, functional. She asserts a love for decorative things and asks if the silver disc hanging from my watch-chain (of which I was certainly unconscious before!) is functional. I look at it and find OM engraved in Tamil characters. 'How clever you are' I say in the affectionate charm and delight of this whole intercourse. Then, jokingly, I explain that 'OM' is in very special ways useful. Throughout the dream there is perfect clarity of vision, feeling and expression—a very delightful sense of the personality of Isadora Duncan and a deep, tender and sensitive friendship.

I say that the base of all economic value is the fertility of the earth.

Collapsing and burning out underground strongrooms—danger of being involved and trapped. I have a sense of great volcanic force.

Vast and deep shaft where a kind of lift plies up and down, a complex mechanism that from time to time projects and withdraws massive rectilinear slabs that make it very difficult and risky to get past it on a narrow winding wharf. At the top of the shaft I hang by one hand from a slight and not very firm bracket in the incalculable void, glazed with white tiles and crossed here and there by slender rods of iron. But fear is a possibility which I keep in the background even when lurching and diving movements far down in the gulf would attract my sight and dizzy me. On awakening, a state of austerity and concentration.

A small limbed object flies by jerks, falling oddly like a grasshopper. From a distance it appears as a kind of mannikin at most 3 or 4 inches long. Two peripheral women also come up to look.

It is a structure of rough unpainted wood, newspaper, wires, elastic, tin, of the size and more or less diagrammatic of a man stretched on his back. The face is like that of an African fetish. It is a magical creation which flies by virtue of the spells that have been chanted over it. It is covered with talismanic symbols and writings. Strangely lifted by some force that inhabits it like a conscious presence, it flies a little, rests, then suddenly escapes again. *[Resemblance to certain Early Thirties Giacometti sculptures.]* The magical mannikin is lying on its bed in a sort of booth decorated with amateur advertisements of the magician who created it—prosaic price-lists of various magical services and of certain medicines. A fire of logs covering the feet of the bed begins to flame. At first I take this for another automatic manifestation of the magical force, but the two women standing in the booth to the left announce that it is part of their effort to exorcise the being that vivifies the fetish. But the fire does not progress, they cannot burn it.

These gauche spinsters, young and graceless, their dress and bearing suggesting that they are bony and wrinkled, propose to use their knowledge of certain formulae. With serious ritual gestures, outlining a pentagram in the air with a lighted incense-stick, all as an earnest self-imposed public duty, one of them declaims in a loud voice some complicated gibberish, on a classical model no doubt but in which I feel the elaboration is of her own tried invention, held secret and intransmissible. With linked arms and straining bodies and faces the two women fight against the escaping demon, apparently not so much barring its flight as mitigating its violence. The fetish lies there, finally, looking just the same but empty of its strange informing force.

Deeply devotional dream of Tibetan bronze images of deities and yogic beings who come to life for me in a monastery which I have entered playing the part of a demon. This impersonation is a kind of play in which I enjoy the privileges of a child.

With great grace they prepare a special gift for me—a rich, heavy, elaborately worked golden amulet. I remark to them that of course these are local *vigrahas* (images of deities) with only local power, but that they who have become living for me are superhuman. An elaborate tiered bronze altar with many little brass and bronze figures close to me as I squat half curled up on the floor (there is no furniture in the white cubical room) is much less real for me: it remains dead metal. In this great initiation I haven't even room to make *pranam* (prostration). Though the others are not seen, from the beginning the room is taken to be full of *vigrahas*.

The figure nearer to me, to the right, in as easy, rather curled-up, sitting posture on a simple slab (it is he who prepares the rich and heavy gold amulet) is solidly built, massive and simple: he has some quality of robust directness and as if richly acerb or astringent simplicity and undisguise of mood. (I realise, waking, that this identifies this '*guru-vigraha*' with a certain fruitful potentiality of myself).

The second figure, seated cross-legged or at any rate more quietly and formally, is more refined and intellectual, with a reddish robe of delicately patterned silk and a peaked or tiered hat. In a sweet, grave, dignified yet kindly way he detaches charms for me from strings or tassels of his robe.

My relation with this second subtle and elegant figure is delicately intimate, but it is the massive, powerful figure in the foreground that sets the tone of the dream and seems to promise the re-adjustment in my waking consciousness with the kind of force he represents.

Magical dramas. The costumes recall *Kathakali* and Tibet. Many players, as in a ballet—perhaps thirty to fifty in the opposite party seen by me. I have the viewpoint of, and am even partially identified with, the protagonist overcoming them, who is either alone or has advanced from a supporting party in the background. The action is between two opposing parties, as in a *mantra* combat, and victory is not predetermined but worked out in the imaginative fervour of the whole.

In the last dance the enemies of Shiva are reduced to dust. The reiterated 'spell' applied by the protagonist is enforced by cymbals and drums. With arm held powerfully and dramatically outstretched towards and over the opponents, 'Shiv! Shiv! is intensively repeated. They dwindle and suffer as if in tormenting flame. Close-up of their expressions: individual resource and imagination as in Kathakali. For example, one acts 'A garland of fire consumes me'. Till finally they are reduced to a shower of torn-up white paper.

At the end of this last terrific drama (stylised, concentrated, prolonged like every Oriental art) I am intoxicated with an intense appreciation and enjoyment.

In stately gardens two wonderful and very rare birds—'sunbirds'. I especially notice the male, bigger than the peacock—proud gait, very striking bold yet complex design of black and gold bars. He drops it like a cloak, showing another rather different, simpler but equally effective design underneath. He takes his seat (for he is also a man and a king) in a kind of pavilion. He is now wearing a *dress*— shimmering silk or satin pantaloons.

His 'mate' is to sing before joining him and he sits regally at ease to await the performance.

Extensive burned-out factories, seen at another time as a deliberate noble architecture of carbonised and sometimes flaming beams, floorings over gulfs, lean-to's of galvanised iron, roofs, platforms, galleries, stairs, half-razed walls, desolate horizons, cindery slopes and corners—three-dimensional musical scores, as it were, of the works of Beethoven. They are in India and I have long known them in the background of my mind, in my own world, as classical symbols of Beethoven's work.

8

The Subtle Thread

1937. Tenkasi temple.

Certain Indian idols have a controlled and concentrated richness which with dogmatic intuition as it were condenses a new dimension—which suggests beyond the human at the same time a superb intransigence and a triumphant subtlety.

The Hindu vigrahas, in their combination of richness, majesty and elegance, are also surely among the most dense and authoritative symbols of non-human powers.

Alargarkovil, 21.VI. 37.

Sculptures at Alargarkovil. Masturbation. A *Yali* (door guardian) seizing a man's hair in its teeth, lion-paws on his shoulders, straining him backwards, points between his buttocks its long phallus.

The Divine Power and splendour of its Presence has fulfilled every possible perversity and obscenity, it has made them merely decorative, utterly devoid of reference or content. Only egoism and spiritual ignorance remain in moralistic tension with them. Only the confused and romantic religious consciousness, by its sentimental vulgarities, could delay or evade or torment itself in them—obstacles to love for the Divine.

Everything is perfect and justified at its level, in its mode—this is the coherence of the Universe. It can be seized only by perfect imaginative sympathy. Only perfect inner freedom everywhere justifies and shares the Absolute Joy of the Creator.

Adyar, 19. VIII. 37

I write at night amid the smoke of benzoin and sandalwood burning on charcoal against the mosquitoes. Rain hums, sings and tinkles in the garden.

I have spent a good deal of time lately with a troupe of dancers from Java and Bali. In the house hung with rich batik sarongs and littered with trunks and drums, after the performance they sit till two and three in the morning playing mah-jong and gong-gong, while the Russian compère tells me stories of Javanese magic. —A tree embodying a nature-sprite that bleeds when cut. Rain called down from a cloudless sky to wet a square yard of ground. The women with channel between nose and lip who prowl at night as tigers. The old man who stares at him at night in an empty house—a saint dead long ago. He says he has himself learned to hold off rain by scattering rice and salt with certain spells.

The very slow ascending and descending of the dancer in the Balinese *legong*—knees tilted under the rich silk dress, impassive face, eyes closed—gives the effect of a deep dream. The rich gongs, the ecstatic water-sounds of the *gambang* (wooden slats played with a hammer), the controlled abandon of shoulder-movements, the exquisite hands, the vivid fan, add to the deep enchantment a ravishing poignancy and splendour.

A certain walk peculiar to Balinese dance had a fascinating vigour and grace—intense lucid intoxication of resource and *allegresse*.

17.IX.37.

I have suddenly found the complete description of Southern India—its picturesque squalor, its atmosphere, the whole continuum of consciousness of its people, and what is condensed and conscious in the temples: the whole thing is an 'astral slum'.

24.X.37. Dream.

Lecture by a rather ugly man, supposed to be the English occultist Alistair Crowley. I watch his face in which nose and mouth have given place to an abstract black space. He addresses himself to me by name, following a point at which he seems to have neglected the rest of the audience, and I realise that I am probably the only one who experiences this hallucination. It progresses in connection with his arguments, somehow proving them. His eyes shift, now black, now white, as if holes in the flat black mask were moved across a white card behind. I am fascinated. Finally all becomes utterly black while he says: There is only One. In this 'dark night of the soul', hands raised in *namaskaram*, I am seized with a vertigo of reverence and dedication and awake.

14.XI.37. Experience during meditation.

Peripherally organised consciousness seeking and joining with its deepest root—intensification of the attempt at complete truthfulness and awareness, exhaustion and fulfilment of every inner and outer occasion. It seems that by such concentration this 'sector' of awareness must spread, first differentiating completely on the surface, then enlarging throughout the curves of the sphere—widening as it were about the centre into what for every plane geometry must be 'other dimensions', becoming globally aware of them, fulfilling them. Till at last all is fulfilled and progressively united with and as the Centre, all-commanding, all-enjoying.

Withdrawal into another—sub—or super-liminal state during meditation can be guided and controlled only by a formal method. In any other sense it is inconclusive and one grasps the conditions of that state even less, perhaps, than the ordinary frame of consciousness. If its relation with the 'ordinary' consciousness were integrally commanded it would not be *another* state.

Otherwise one can only complete the integration of the present consciousness—the only one we know. All proposal to meditate is a formal and partial *samskara* within that consciousness and can thus, first and perhaps last, only divide it. Hence visions, 'experiences' in meditation. Persevering towards the centre you see that the body can be raised as it were from level to level in terms of that centre, and that the physical consciousness and its level of organisation exists only relatively to the rest of consciousness. Hence perhaps certain physical *siddhis* (supernormal effects).

Involuntary subtle and keenly pleasant upward contraction of perineum (between scrotum and anus). Sensation there, like the intense, silent, frictionless writhing intervolutions of a flame, reminds me of the image 'there is a fire burning at the Muladhara' (lowest chakra, at the perineum). A sense of the whole body in upward current. A feeling that if it increased enough for the body as a whole one might even 'levitate'. Or otherwise that Kundalini must rise within the body. A strong upward suction, tension, flame-current. One automatically stops breathing, with full raised chest, the whole body involuntarily braced. Impression of force and light. Recognition of possible reference to peculiarly Tantrik images: the supernatural concrete in a substance infinitely sweet and precious, hard as diamond but soft and sheened like preternaturally fine gold (as in the Tibetan and Nepali art whose crisp saturated richness, with the subtle Chinese element of intensification of grace, has so peculiarly appealed to me). Rich colour and radiance, intervolving summation of force. The whole face feels tightened as if shining.

There is a tendency for the critical intellect to suppose that states described in yoga books and so forth are always on another plane altogether from anything recalling them that one happens to experience, and to reject such automatic analysis as effete and superstitious. But I notice that most ordinary sadhus and yogis seem to have the opposite mentality—seem ready to take even elementary visual reflexes for something supernatural, their experience owing their cogency and validity to their absolute noncriticality. One wonders if many of the old describers of yoga-process had not such a naivety and that in intellectualising their conceptions to the infinite one is not obviously overlooking the very sort of thing which so many humble practitioners have described to me as 'experiences' and 'results' and which could often so easily tally with and explain 'mystical' attempts to image the nonrational. Though certainly the reported comments of their gurus on these 'experiences' have often an ambiguity which they—or even both parties—seem blissfully unconscious of.

Goodness knows such a naviety is expressed in their chromos of Alpine lakes and lush Arcadias, the Ravi Varma gods and nymphs, German porcelain dolls in 'Buddha'-posture ('I paid ten rupees for it'), clay Krishnas daubed in primary colours, endless group-photos and commercial calendars, puerile plasterwork, crude stained glass.

[After five impecunious years in India on a very meagre diet Thompson was beginning to suffer, as he did thereafter almost continually, poor health. The doctors in the Jnani's entourage treated him for mental exhaustion and the novelist Raja Rao told me personally that Thompson suffered from trembling. He himself noticed his seemingly consumptive symptoms and blood discharges. That he frequently mentions the risks involved in drinking tea and coffee is no great surprise, for Indians know well the attendant dangers: large painted slogans on road tarmac warn 'NO TEA!]

4.XII.37.

Tea produces an excitation of the surface being which, like the effect of other drugs, for a long time afterwards modifies the nervous state so that no simple inner concentration and repose are possible. It multiplies the speed of the *surface*, but for the central being this evasion, confusion, expenditure of energy is a detour.

27.1.38.

It is at the level of the ego that one resorts to stimulants like tea and coffee, it is an attempt to release further energy from the ego-system. Because at the best they work by a romantic relation with extra-personal sources of energy. They work always in a narrowing vicious circle, for they are necessary only to escape from an impasse reached by the ego's refusal or incapacity to surrender to universal forces and rhythms—the incapacity it represents for a truly disinterested flexibility of the whole life. It is the egoic will which cannot accept ups and downs, passages which for its mental consciousness are helpless and obscure. But it will never command them while it still evades them. And this evasion—even if it is supported by disinterestedness in the rest of the being, and by an urgent need to enter into the definitive relation with the Transcendent which alone can consistently organise and employ all changes—can only take place within more and more narrow limits, with more and more penetrating consequences. The completer the organisation the more delicate the balance of the whole being at any given level; the nearer potentiality is to canalisation the more crucial one's vulnerability.

10.II.38.

Need of tea or coffee seems to arise when one must focus attention critically and analytically on the mental plane while there is no direct inner interest or profit, for then attention is disoriented by a wider undirected consciousness which is useless for the occasion.

But today I sense that in the end the solution must be in using the mind consciously within the wider and deeper consciousness. This is connected with increasing direct experience of the limits of the whole waking physical world. One will live, in the physical world also, in a state prior to waking and dream, the timeless inner consciousness of the heart.

The whole present difficulty of vital balance no doubt depends upon a new order. A new phase of the proposed perfect Sensuality—can only be obtained by consenting to shift to another plane and to use the mind undisturbedly and formally from there.

21.II.38.

It is no doubt only because it has been for me my habit since puberty to keep my consciousness sharply focussed mentally in a state where sensibility and criticality are balanced in a state of keen and flexible lucidity that a wider, more general consciousness which destroys that focus seems to me a weakness. It sends me to coffee to help restore it. I tend to associate it with the long inadequacy of my diet, my loss of weight and the debilitating effect of this climate. But it is not necessarily so. It may be something entirely positive—which only an old habit refuses.

31.I.43

Tea and coffee, characteristically modern drinks, flagellate nerves and mind to endless activity—they disintegrate simple enjoyment of life as the self-sufficing, break up perception of the Infinite through immediate sensibility into a whirligig of illusory, unattainable perspectives.

Tea favours a noisy automatism in nerves and mind which will not easily die down and veils natural recollection and spontaneity.

Or, for the most part they are no doubt required simply to overcome torpor in order to meet frantic modern demands almost exclusively at the rational level; for global enjoyment of life is no longer conscious, lucid.

4.XII.37.

Only the intense psychological realism of the whole man—the perfection of innocence, disinterestedness—intelligence absolutely purged of the forms, the literary, the historically or sentimentally continuous—that has made the ego an utterly objective instrument, mask, wardrobe, machine—fulfils the detail, is present in the Moment, makes the marvellous, and finally the Transcendent, more concrete than 'reality', hard, shining, irreducible like Cocteau's living statues.

Early January, 1938.

I have for some time noticed that my handwriting consistently responds to increased inner concentration by increased smallness. And there is a tendency also, then, to increased exactitude.

10.I.38.

It is my imagination that I expend on subordinating my sensibility to the terrible modern Indian barbarism: the simplicity of my life is the reverse of naivety, to sustain it is a severe and complex art—a difficult classicism.

11–2.I.38.

Now, at the end of my twenty-eighth year, my face is beginning to be condensed, refined and sealed by the gravity of the actual as destiny.

Silence instead of *voltiges*. Recognition that one has experience of human beings: the objective view. Before, everyone was treated as if by a child and one did not know that gave one the charm and privilege of one's unconscious youth—a suspension of the laws of gravity, a poetry which everyone was ready to seize and fulfil.

Youth: Experimentality, Geniality, Innocence, Ingenuousness. The need of self-consciousness the sign of Agony. All expression premature, before the fact. 'Living beyond oneself'—avoidance of condensation. Life in terms of the hypothetical, the potential. Life in the interstices of events, in the momentary, in the connection available only to weightlessness—the privilege, perversity, sensibility and obstinacy of the child. 'The private parts of Fortune', a special somnabulant, clairvoyant, daring and idle world, presuming always the unnamed primordial privilege. Magic, intuition, perversity.

Endless disinterested curiosity and self-expenditure—self-enjoyment, self-evasion, self-betrayal.

The tendency to philosophise is a vulgarity of the mind.

The incredible unconscious naivety of people who, though they show no single sign of understanding your simplest reference, say "You are in the stage I was in ten years ago'. They are too unconscious to be humble. They can only be simple. The simple are perhaps the most unabsorbable, the most unreachable, the most impervious of all. Only pure patience and love can understand their place in the world. And may indeed even find them then a symbol, though only a *symbol* of the truth. Just as a child, because he is still unconscious of his destiny, may seem to be a symbol of the intrinsic freedom of the spirit. But in order to achieve it he has to do far more even than to grow up—if he can grow up without losing hold of the possibility of that achievement, without lapsing into the selfish, prudent, opinionated, cowardly, hypocritical sleep of adulthood, the confirmation of all the *vices* of childhood.

Distinguishing between what belongs to myself and what to nature, to the world, I find myself the eternal Child, free of memory and knowledge, whose experience is always pure and complete in spontaneity, who has always conquered Time and Occasion. (This is a gross mentalisation of a fact that I cannot express in its own subtlety.)

This childhood is presence in the world of Symbols to which Time and Occasion, past and future are equally irrelevant, where Man is eternally the Hero, the Lover, the Magician, the King, the Poet, the Demon, the Sage.

(Only when I write this out at about 1 p.m. do I realise that in the meantime I have read almost the same thought in Yeats's *Essays*.)

13.II.38.

'Inner sight' with eyes closed of something like the actual environing physical world is more frequent and steadier now. It tends to happen when the body is entirely resting and one enters but does not surrender to subconsciousness. It is exactly as if one opened one's eyes in another state. But

I don't get any further than seeing with strange, still clearness one limited space.

15.II.38.

One is carried from level to level, from mode to mode, permutation to permutation, of one's consciousness by the currents and adjustments of a life that will not be controlled except as a whole. While this continues—while there is not yet so nearly complete an organisation that one can sustain direct aspiration towards the Transcendent—every one of these phases must be exploited to the utmost. Everything must proceed towards understanding, mastery, purification, till the whole being in all its ranges has been refined, subtilised, reduced to its essential, freed from egoism, made simple, prompt, tireless, clairvoyant.

This applies of course to the whole twenty-four hours, except for the oblivion of dreamless sleep. Dreams themselves, and all the movements of the subconscient, provide crucial opportunity for such work, though it comes to full focus—to its greatest difficulty and greatest effectiveness—in the varying conditions of the waking state, in which the subconscient is active but veiled and the phenomenal consciousness tends to ride upon it self-indulgently like a ship on the waves.

This must also mean living out one's dry periods fully and as such. Otherwise the tendency is to fight against them, to try to get out of them prematurely, by distraction of by use of stimulants which prejudice the 'good' period, for their effects are exhausting and not stimulating in the dry state.

9.II.38

To give up all humanistic values, personal, aesthetic, intellectual with reference to this Indian scene would be a great simplification and saving of energy and in the present state would, I feel, directly aid the turning of consciousness towards its inner primacy.

It is indeed the most obvious thing to do, the only way to understand modern Indian life and use positively all that is otherwise so personally negative in it. Perhaps it is, therefore, because I can never have presumed any result of my criticism of the limits of humanism, that this could have occurred to me before, so that during these five years I have hourly tormented myself in applying standards which are in every sense—but also in my own most positive sense—irrelevant here. It is after all absurd to be fascinated by the transhumanism of the tradition and at the same time to apply humanistic standards to the squalor, irrationality and fecklessness involved in its degeneration. After all, almost any oriental civilisation in its prime vigour would have seemed to a modern European in some respects crucially or defectively non-humanistic. And it is not if one personally sacrifices what is positive in the humanistic tradition, its discipline or its grace. It is only a question of objectivity and practical adaptation to a civilisation whose defects are only different from those of Europe.

The Indian scene must be accepted and used as a continual pointer towards transhumanistic reality.

2–3.III.38.

Seize the immediate source—the subtle thread, stronger than steel, more delicate than perfume, on which all the irreducible jewels of your life are strung. All the rest is dust, greyness, old age, the nightmare of perverse and self-destroying doubt.

20–21.IV.38.

Vital force and passion is essential for the intensities and intuitive resourcefulness of yoga, the burning out of all dullness, and repetition obscuring and delaying the light, directness, subtlety, intensity of all vital perceptions.

It is perhaps no accident that I desire now the brightness and purity of fire and seem to understand those yogis who live with it constantly—flame and clean ash and its purifying atmosphere.

In the still and cloudy night I absorb the subtle force and brilliance of this great Element.

28.IV.38.

It is only the failure in every realm of that entire intelligence and truthfulness, of sensibility and scepticism, of our profoundest Sensuality, from which all doubt, perversity, delay and agony arises. This is the paradox of our position, our incessant inconclusive becoming, the torment of endless process. This failure, no doubt, is the profoundest secret of Baudelaire and Dostoievski and perhaps also, if more subtly, of Pascal and Kierkegaard. In the case of Beethoven it is his uncompromising health and sanity that underlie the heroism and nobility of his spiritual struggle. The purity, penetration and the glimpses of Light which is attained, the strange authenticity, the exalted compassion and joy, of the World that opens in the last sonatas and quartets, threatens, by its extreme tension with them, to exceed and dissolve the intellectual and emotional limits of its musical expression.

There is also the intellectual pride which cannot accept the annihilating transcendental fact that Reality is already entirely present and complete, as traditionally are the truth and the way.

This intellectual resistance is also the refusal of mysticism which makes early Buddhism seem to me the only pure dialectic. I sympathise completely with Krishnamurti's restatement in modern times of the basic Buddhist dialectic. And yet his attitude is so axiomatic to me that I must achieve this centrality in all its consequences.

The Western spiritual agonism must give way to the Eastern spiritual classicism. In this realm alone, indeed, can lie proof that the Christ had realised 'I and the Father are one'. The life of the Christ from top to bottom hinged upon paradox; this is its incomparable intensity. For the West the agonistic Christ is likely to remain the effective truth—until seen from within the realised Eastern tradition to belong to it. If the peace and joy of one's intuition are to be fulfilled and not remain a transcendence of Tragedy, a Nietzchean athleticism, the faith of a poet, it is precisely this which has to be achieved. And in this sense again: 'He who would save his life must lose it'.

12.V.38.

The contingent mental ego depends on the true inner being prior to the mind—the wisdom and direction of the soul. Otherwise there could be no tension but only a complacent dogmatic philosophy, It is, in fact, this tension which has determined the analytical character of my thought, its dialectical accent and rhythm.

I can write this now only because I have begun to glimpse what the 'command of the mind as a whole' which I have so far only dialectically defined must mean in practice. What from below can be foreseen only as command in some absolute and abstract sense can be actual only as the submission of the mind to what is already and always prior to it in our nature—the soul. This central being has otherwise no special interest in or relation with the mind. All that can be called nature, all that is phenomenal, relative, contingent, must become entirely the method and instrument of the soul's search for the progressive union with that Reality which in its indestructible essence it represents.

Yet the mind is right in not being able to accept this soul as given—for it can have only a *conception* of the soul. The soul justifies the mind according to its own purest nature as its instrument. And even thus can the ultimate exigence of the mind be satisfied; for it exists meanwhile and must continue as the living postulation, the urgent representative sense of Reality—a flame which, meeting nowhere resistance, the inconsumable, must even destroy and sacrifice all, reducing all to ash, seeking at last nothing but its own annihilation—martyr for a cause still unrevealed to it, defending sealed despatches to the death.

10.VIII.38.

Every premature simplification of oneself is also, of course, an act of Imagination. One's actual complexity belongs to the realm of Technique, the absolute Technique of Poetry.

It is only by this same Imagination that one does not stringently avoid very simple people, or fools: rather, by its delicacy, one is concerned not to prejudice exchanges with them.

This is one of the victories over fatigue, but like every victory it is merely equivalent with consciousness of the enemy, which it exactly balances. And so, too, every premature simplification of oneself is such a provisional detour, static complement to something in oneself which, if one is to move forward, must be rejected and forgotten.

30.VIII.38.

Image of a God.

You have collected every richness till you burn more steadily than oil. The keenness of every gem is mellowed in that flame. —Splendour, vast chiming sea, annihilates even Wisdom. Your unbreathable perfume, unbearable delight, has stopped the heart.

20.VIII.38.

My application of humanistic standards, even rationality, in criticism of modern India makes my 'trans-humanism' romantic on the same plane with the modern *failure* from humanism.

7.X.38.

When I first entered India at Dhanushkodi, and throughout those wonderful days in Ramesvaram, Ramnad and Madura, I completely accepted and delighted in the novel and powerful atmosphere that I now recognise as a sense of the occult and transcendent expressed everywhere. I felt it directly, it put me at the centre of its logic. Only resurgence of proud and exigent vital and mental humanistic values and the long fight to coordinate them with what lies beyond and must command them can have made me suffer, since, chiefly the negative side of the Indian scene, the modern failure of vital and physical expression, debility, degeneracy, fecklessness, insensitiveness, even cynicism.

12.I.38.

Conversation with the mantra-Kundalini sadhaka Mudaliar on yogic top-centre head focus. Trying to describe the sensation of effort there, and perhaps the *form* of the centre. Mental effort cannot find an adequate symbol, which remains as it were in another dimension. But all the time there was in consciousness an immediate image—association with a section of a bluebell-like flower and the Leo-sign.

When I draw it on the sand the Mudaliar says: Yes, it is like that, an inverted *lingam*. I compare it to the pineal and its stalk.

He agrees to my correlation of our terms: I am, first, Consciousness in the head, work essentially there and draw up in support the 'psychic *prana*' whose other stations are therefore sub- or para-conscious for me, and thus expressible entirely psychologically in mental terms, as thought and poesy.

'Psychic *prana*' is closely related with the sex-force. The bindu (*yogic name for semen*) really comes to the brain.

Madras, 23–24.XI.38. Dream.

London. Some festival or play. I dance my anticipation on the way to it. Feeling of power and elation. In a great underground railway-station, the escalators descend, I find a group of foreign artistes, one of whom, a young man, agrees with my dancing impulse and is not afraid of manifesting it in public.

We two seem to have descended into an underground labyrinth. It takes complete form as an endlessly branching alveolar multiplication and interdivision in endlessly varied shapes, spotlessly white hard glass. I think of public baths in France and see at once, lying on a long shoulder or ledge in this strange, rather oppressive architecture, a kind of bath-brush, bleached and worn with hot water and soap—the only object in the endless aseptic abstraction.

My friend, ahead, is out of sight when water begins to mount from below—some block somewhere, I think. In danger of being drowned, it is almost impossible to find one's way out of such a dense and endlessly renewed labyrinth whose construction is unknown to us and in which all sense of direction is lost, so that only chance and despair direct one's movements. I feel very anxious for him. (At first we had descended and moved forward in confidence, but then the great complication had not begun to multiply and close us in—the chambers were wider, simpler, more progressively tunnel-like.)

The water begins to fall also from chambers above. I feel no fear but only anxiety and the pragmatic impulse to find a way out, though I hardly think it possibly.

The dream possibly symbolises, on the physical level, the alveoli of the lungs *[Thompson was afraid at this time that he might have T.B.]* and perhaps some action of the heart. Before sleeping I had noticed, as I sometimes have before, two red places on my wrists near the pulse and vaguely remembered having read of such 'nerve-points' as symptoms. The dancing with which the dream began—not at all unusually—may also refer to the heart.

Madras, 13–14.XII.38.

After her performance a handsome brahmin girl I know, a singer, towards whom I have never in the waking state, nor before or since in dream, entertained the slightest sexual desire, though indeed, if anything, because—my relationship with her is a privileged one; and in any case she does not attract me physically, has visited me one evening when I was out. Hearing of this I go to her. We are seated on a kind of couch. My usually completely non-sexual attitude is modified by a strange, massive yet subtle eroticism.

She speaks English quite fluently though this is not actually the case. All is very conscious and clear, reverie rather than dream, though I am certainly asleep.

She gives me a fruit, then afterwards one of another kind, more or less pear-shaped. She peels one to show me how. At the bottom a little astringent cellulose that has to be removed. She marks the fruit intended for me with her teeth, as in the *Kama Sutra*. It is very juicy and, laughing, trying to avoid falling drops, I suck it rapidly. This deep and prolonged contact with the part she has bitten comes to seem the symbol of a passionate kiss.

She tells me that if after fatigue you want long rest without sleeping you should drink two cups of good tea. Behind our divan there is a rather Chinese street with a teashop.

We had been discussing her performance. She complains of general lack of public appreciation and that the programme is too short. Sympathising, I show my understanding that it leaves me for a long time excited, for one has hardly begun to give one's best.

The Jnani's explanation: the actual non-sexuality towards the girl might just as well represent a complete lilaic Tantrik heterosexuality, and this joins with my attitude towards the young woman as the Goddess.

Tiruvottiyur beach, 24.I.39.

The senses freed from their objects may perceive nature as an ocean of consciousness in which their subtle modifications become the endless, multitudinous waves, swirlings, clashings, interpenetrations, swoonings, intensities of joy, and a perpetual ever-novel interplay with Light.

9

Return To Ceylon

While hardly any written record survives of Thompson's first visit to Ceylon in 1932, there is an interesting sequence of journal entries which covers the holiday he took there for six months in 1939. This interlude gave him an opportunity to recuperate from the physical depletion he had undoubtedly suffered for several years, the lowest point being the period of semi-starvation in 1934 when his weight dropped to ninety four pounds from around one hundred and thirty five pounds.

This return to Ceylon appears to have been a period of quiet study and reflection, in spite of numerous visitors, living alone in a large bungalow on the estate of Thompson's friend Ellawalla in beautiful countryside. Nothing eventful happens: the journal concentrates on inner movements, while the long opening letter to his mother sets the scene and the prevailing mood of calm dedication to a contemplative life is maintained throughout. This period represents establishment of what Thompson called 'Normality' and it will be noticed that there are a number of such phases when, briefly, he recovers psychic and physical health, experiencing a rare feeling of having sufficient energy to concentrate on his various tasks. During his stay at Mahawalatenna the Second World War broke out; characteristically, the first reference—an oblique and passing allusion to it—occurs in 1940. However, it is always a risk to assume that nothing much happens in Thompson's life merely because there are no overt signs in the journal.

2.II.39.
c/o Rao Sahib Sri S.R. Ranganathan, M.A.,
15 Sami Pillai Street, Triplicane, Madras.

Dear Mother:

I've been staying since August with the librarian of the University Library, an old friend of mine. His mother and his wife accept me as one of the family and his little boy calls me uncle. S.R.R. says I am to stay there as long as he does.

I often see P.K.R. and his wife. He still provides all expense outside the house, buys my clothes, is always on hand to help. He appreciated your enquiry.

Both these men, each in his own way, understand and approve my attitude to life and the interests that make me stay in India.

But everywhere I find the same beautiful hospitality. Last week I went to Tiruvottiyur, about 8 miles North of Madras where a great saint is said to have got some urchins on the beach to bury him and who never appeared again. In some such way many great saints in India have entered into a final union with God. One disappeared without a trace from a locked and watched room and even a sceptical European officer could find no explanation. I went to this place for a change and for solitude but finally had to come away because everyone began to invite me to his house and wherever I was people would come to visit me and ask if I needed anything.

While I was sitting on the beach one evening a young man of 31 with a keen and intelligent face, came and offered me a copper vessel full of milk while his wife timidly untied oranges from a little cloth. *[Although Thompson would never dream of telling his mother so, he was respected wherever he went in India as a sadhu and treated with graceful piety and the good will which Indians always accorded such genuine seekers.]* The day before I had had to talk to so many people that in self-defence I was observing silence. Someone must have told him this. He made no attempt to talk but we looked laughing into each other's eyes. I was in a mood almost of ecstasy; in the movement of the sea as I watched it I felt the endless multitudinous waves, swirlings, clashings, interpenetrations, swoonings, intensities of an inexhaustible joy.

The next day he told me how he had learned alchemy through visions in which he went to unknown places and looked over their shoulder at men in all kinds of costumes while they pursued their secret alchemical experiments. These visions, which he had at the age of twenty-four, developed from concentration on the *Ajna-light* in which sacred letters would appear in Tamil or English.

He has also experienced a great fire in the heart and various subtle sounds. He seeks guidance in *yoga.*

As a boy of eleven he had woken up one night, and had a vision of the Tiruvottiyur saint—the great Ramalingaswami—long after his disappearance from the locked and guarded room, but of whom he had not previously heard. Ramalingaswami was so beautiful, about five feet or less in height, that at first he thought him a woman, his skin shining like gold. My friend approached where he stood by a wall and disappeared. This made a great impression on him and ever since he has been seeking the guidance of this illumined soul. At last, in Burma, he entered the jungle resolved to die if the Swami did not again appear. After fourteen days without food he had a vision of himself being buried in a tomb. But he broke it open and emerged. Then he began to overhear, in the remote and dangerous jungle where nobody goes, voices in the distance discussing in Hindustani the method of 'tying' mercury, one of the crucial processes of Indian alchemy. He then had a further vision of a speaking statue of Subrahmanyam who told him to solidify mercury, involving the use of the fat of horse, crab and tiger.

At twenty-two he had been challenged to cure a case of leucoderma and undertook it. He was then doing *pranayama*. In a vision he was told to study *Siddha Shastras*. Visions of various kinds still continue—for instance, while crossing a bridge in the ordinary waking state, of a four-armed goddess.

Perhaps because I had promised to put him in touch with a source of help in the occult yoga practice he had also stumbled on, and perhaps because he had been suddenly told in a vision to go to the place where he met me, he began to his own surprise (for such men are naturally secretive) to tell me much about alchemy and his ambition to immortalise his body by means of alchemical medicines.

'Tied' mercury, for instance, held in the mouth stops emission of semen and gives power of walking indefinitely without fatigue. Laid on the back of a cow it stops her milk.

He has made and successfully used some of the Siddha medicines, including one for rejuvenation that turned a patient's grey hair black; another for immortalising the body (which is then shadowless) that peels off seven skins. Frightened at the first peeling in which his skin came off 'like brown paper', he abandoned it, but intends to try again.

Iron filings washed, treated with lime-juice and dried produce reddish powder, This mixed with copper sulphate and other salts and juice of lime again, left for three days and then washed; the melted residue is 'very pure' and 'heavy' copper with some of the physical characteristics of silver.

He can make gold from various other metals, and silver by a process employing white arsenic. He told me that he was at present living by selling in the market his alchemical gold, for it stands all the standard tests. Yet he sees that all this is meaningless spiritually and seeks the true light.

He can turn metals and bone into lead. And lead from the teeth in a human skull is good for insanity.

He was told in two visions by a young woman some months ago to leave his home in Salem for Tiruvottiyur. Though present, his wife saw nothing.

One evening he began to demonstrate to me one of his processes of transmutation and even appeared willing, now that he thought of giving up his trade, to allow them to be studied by a friend of mine who is a research scholar in chemistry. He left his vessels in the temple where I was then staying, for the mixture must stand for three days.

Perhaps he repented of his confidences, for he never came again and because he was a stranger to the place no-one could tell me where he lived. He looked so honest, spoke so sincerely and gave such details of his success that I can hardly believe it was all untrue. Certainly in India everyone believes alchemy possible and there is quite extensive, though very cryptic, literature about it.

There, very shortly, is one of the tales I might tell you if I were seated with you by your fire with the snow or rain outside.

I forget what I sent in the last letter—probably a kind of fragrant root that is used here in garlands for the gods.

Love always from
Lewis

Added to the journal in 1942: It is only now that I realise that in leaving the little bowl of liquid with me and then disappearing (no doubt to avoid further questions) he had perhaps meant to pass on to me one at least of the secrets of alchemy. Was it for this purpose that he was directed to me in vision?

Of course, I considered the bowl his and that I was not free to dispose of it. And certainly this idea never occurred to me.

Mahawalatenna,
Near Balângoda,
Ceylon.

15.V.39. Letter to his mother.

For some days I have been staying here in a big house that is nowadays very seldom used. It is the ancestral home of a friend who now lives in Balângoda. On the walls you see photographs of his people—'Durbar of Kandyan Chiefs, 1908', processions of elephants, etc. I have a stock of foods, milk is brought every day and I do my simple cooking—sometimes—on a little Primus stove.

From my writing-table near the big French windows I see, through an arch on the verandah, a delicate pomegranate-tree with its brilliant flowers. Except for their waxen calyx they are frail like the poppy and the colour has a similar luminosity, though it is a little nearer orange. Mingling with its slender, almost briar-like branches is a compact and glossy orange-tree hung with heavy dark-green globes.

I think one could enter into a conscious relation with all this teeming life. I don't wonder, anyway, that the peasants find fairies or nature-spirits living in certain trees.

Plenty of animal-life, too—troops of monkeys swinging from tree to tree or light-fingeredly foraging on the ground; birds, butterflies, beetles like jewels. A fine cobra emerged the other day from under the verandah steps and this morning I startled a lizard like a young alligator, longer, tail and all, than my arm. He ran up a tree and sat, comically humourless, moving his ante-diluvian jaws. I am told afterwards that it was an iguana.

The village headman, charmingly, has brought me every day with his own hands a bundle of bananas.

A quarter of a mile from the house there's an extraordinary landscape—almost too rich: at the far horizon blue mountains lightly ribboned with cloud, in the middle distance hills fleecy with jungle, in the foreground a riot of trees, shrubs and grasses—all under the high, empty turquoise sky.

18th. Last night I had a dream of father in which there was a very tender and friendly relation between us. As we walked up the Strand he put his arm for a moment affectionately about my shoulders. He told me he had paid ten pounds for my hunter watch. Then we went into a whole series of shops trying to get the right kind of strap for it.

19th. Your letter of the 9th. was sent on to me today from Balângoda. The lilac and bluebell still smell faintly sweet.

I first arrived in Ceylon on the 24th. August 1932—nearly seven years ago.

I came to Ceylon this time with an Indian friend. I thought I had told you exactly how the meeting with him happened just when I had begun to think of coming. I was his guest from the start in India and for a time in Colombo too.

One feels perhaps a little less caught up in the inhuman economic system here than in Europe. Anyway, I think one should be as little preoccupied with things as possible. After all, life *is* more than the meat.

I cannot be *entirely* happy until I have in some way 'realised Truth'...But several people, for what it may be worth, when my way of life has appeared, have said, looking at me, 'Well, you are happier than any of us'. Several have said, 'If I were young again I would do what you are doing'. Even on the boat, in fact, a Corsican and an Englishman spoke once more in this way to me. I think that if people could only get together and think things out, instead of being caught and hypnotised in their various groups by a colossal machine, they would 'liquidate' the whole thing and try to build nearer to first principles. I think that almost everyone feels deeply, if vaguely, dissatisfied. Even those who get the greatest material advantage out of it are hardly, God knows, happy.

I have met three Germans hereabouts who have become Buddhist monks. They are all elderly and apparently cultivated men. They seem to feel that there's little else to do nowadays. ...Well, I have not their certainty in a clear path. I have to reach my own in my own way.

As for my eyes, I get them tested free at a Government hospital. Last time, when I needed them, P.K.R. bought lenses and frames.

My memory is that an oculist suggested that in old age, when the natural shrinking tendency had corrected it, I might be free of myopia.

An astrologer, reading from my horoscope, told me the other day that you would live for many years yet!

23rd. The village people are really charming in their little acts of kindness and attention. Just now another instance. During the afternoon I went to a little shop that is also a tiny café and asked for coffee, which I do not usually drink. (My host has left me a stock of money.) They proposed to prepare it with a really rather ancient and almost colourless powder. I excused myself and went and asked at the only other shop in the village and they had none at all.

An hour or two afterwards an old man whom I have seen several times, though I have no idea who he is, comes with two little parcels and, bowing and smiling, presents them to me—fresh, rich-smelling coffee powder—perhaps he had even specially to roast and grind it—and some of the home-made sweet-meats that you find, I believe, throughout the Orient.

This afternoon someone went four miles to and fro to get me a new waterpot and was then too modest to bring it himself. His messenger absolutely refused to take him any reward.

Even the children gather fruit for me from the trees in the garden—chiefly the *jambu*, surely the kind of thing Alladin must have found in his cave! It is such an extraordinary bright and glossy pink that when I was first shown a bunch without leaves I thought them artificial: as you wash them in a white bowl, the reflection of this delicate and yet vivid colour seems to tint all the water. Their white flesh, at the same time tender and crisp, is acid-sweet and has a subtle flavour of cloves.

The post office is also the village school and the postmaster is one of the teachers. Sometimes when I go there at about 7 a.m. I meet some of the children coming to the big well in the garden where I bathe, to get water for their teacher's flowers. They wait till I have bought my stamps and then, crossing the erratic path of many butterflies, we return along the sunny road in great glee, delighted with each other.

5th. June. Returning to Balângoda for a few days I find that I have slightly gained in weight and I feel generally better than I did in India.

12th. I have now returned to Mahawalatenna and expect to stay here for perhaps two or three months.

The papers say you are having a heat-wave—temperatures in the 80's. It seems to me delightfully cool.

I expect you feel better, anyhow, when the sun is shining and can be felt.

During the last week I have gained another pound in weight. Since in India I am generally losing, this is a very good sign.

There are so many trees loaded with various kinds of mangoes, and now that the rainy season is beginning the nights are so windy, that the village children can hardly keep pace with those that fall. As for me, my kitchen is perfumed with them. I eat them for breakfast, with milk—otherwise they are very heating. Nowadays I drink about a quart of milk every day.

14th. I had delayed this letter expecting yours (of the 4th., which reached me today) and the enclosed snap (with my host in his garden at Balângoda, taken a few days ago just after sunrise).

I can sympathise with what you feel. But it is indeed true, as the Buddha and other great teachers have said, that only suffering can come out of emotional attachment. Love, which is not attached to one rather than another and which is its own completion, is the expression of Freedom and Joy. It needs nothing, it can only give.

It is not that I am looking for a life I 'like', or that I '*choose* to be cut off', or that I '*despise*' money.

I prefer not to label or too much explain myself, but there is no doubt some justification to friends here and in India who at once take it for granted that my life is, at bottom, simply a search for and attempt to realise Truth, to find and live an absolute Reality.

This urge long ago broke for me all attachments. If you think of it you will see that I am a good deal more alone than you are, but you feel it more because you do not perhaps fully understand that whatever we cling to is transient and denies and veils from us our true immortal soul which by its nature always lives in Heaven, in Eternity, and knows it *needs* nothing temporal. One cannot possess—or think one possesses—children or money or anything else for ever. It is better to turn to the Eternal, where we belong and must, however long we delay in delusion and ignorance, in the end return. Thus until we can give up all blind and sorrowful attachment and recognise and live in our true nature of joy and freedom there cannot be the kingdom of heaven on earth.

As for returning to Europe, whatever we may do with our merely external will is superficial. Let the event shape itself. My departure from Europe took place on many levels and so, or by their unity, must any real return.

One may love others but one can only *live* one's own life and to make others a condition of that true personal living and self-fulfilment only invites incompletion, fear, dismay. Love is the radiation of strength, attachment a sign of weakness, incapacity to live one's own joy and truth.

I know it is not easy to overcome emotional longing, to centre ourselves in our own truth and peace and live there as a centre of light and energy, but until we can we are only tossed hither and thither, confused, bewildered, catching at straws, indulging in extravagant dreams and fantasies, restless, having no real happiness and therefore unable anywhere to see it, in fact refusing it in the blindness, impatience, perversity of our struggles. That peace, joy and certainty is in us, deep in the heart, where no storm can reach, where an eternal hymn of joy and love rises to the Supreme. In the deep heart there is such strength and sweetness that, so far from longing for anything, it could rather embrace the whole suffering world. This is the true nature of the soul, and especially of the Mother's soul.

So I bow down my head in your lap and rest in the great and calm and protecting love you have to give.

Your child Lewis who is one with you in Eternity, where there are neither mothers nor sons but only the Father-Mother of all.

19.V.39.

The apparent asceticism of the saints is no doubt explained by the ease with which the ego and external personality, especially when the vital is powerful, tend to live for themselves, and the difficulty in these conditions of finding and establishing a deeper centre.

This centre may be felt as its opposite pole when vital urgency has been exhausted (as in Baudelaire) in the fatigue following debauch. Thus 'sin' is not only inevitable in the violent conflict with dualities but even inwardly necessary and inwardly produced in order to awaken the soul sleeping in Nature. Christianity, which, in Europe, historically first discovered the soul as a principle of consciousness, could hardly have emerged from paganism in any other way than by this fulcrum of 'sin'. The pagan geniality was incomplete and incompletely conscious: paganism could not therefore have grown by Geniality. The mystery-cults were its last word: it could provide no further dynamic integration of an immortal principle. A great new romantic furrowing of the soil was necessary. But we have to recognise that that period is now over. Otherwise, instead of a greater classical integrality, there can only be a false and impossible attempt to return to paganism, a new rational, Alexandrian paganism. Between the old, genuine, unrepeatable paganism and this new barbarism was D.H. Lawrence born. And the truth of his position was possible only by the decay of Christianity, its incapacity to renew and re-interpret itself.

20–21.V.39

Very illuminating and psychologically 'real' dream of struggle with an advanced type of egotistic hysteria, the subject deriving from Aunt A. and Lady B. Thinking it over I finally see that only the psychic has great power in this realm, is the light and force which the greatest devil cannot pervert or evade.

In a car which had not been completely covered against rain, on the way to the station at night, with absolutely egotistic and unresilient self-pity this woman complains of inattention, though I say we can fix the cover ourselves and succeed in doing so. Then I begin brutally to explain how like a spoilt child she is. But with all the resource and cunning of entrenched egotism, and a life-time's practice in this role, she rebounds under every blow, using its force on her side, transforming its meaning as a masochist transforms the sadist's cruelty.

Continuing the kind of clairvoyance this dream produced I saw that the ego makes us all more or less neurotic. That with Miss V., taut like a wire and continually overpassing all her own personal life-saving flexibility of emotion in the effort of response to Lady B., one might even have plunged to the heart of the matter, warning that the dissatisfaction of her employee's life could only in the end lead to neurosis, if no help from the 'spiritual' things she was interested in could be accepted. That she used her money to put everyone beyond moral authority over her; but that the efforts of a psychiatrist, for example, who should refuse her fees because of the ambiguous relation with her money-power would not be accepted as a 'good work'. Great tact, experience and inner force is required in dealing with devils who do not wish to be converted, for whom conversion is death, who are very resourceful, slippery as eels. Themselves, in their own realm of the ego are like great actors, learned psychologists. The Christ's methods should be studied...

Lady B.'s 'confidences', 'self-analyses' to me questions one to some extent outside the humanistic series. One's incomplete clairvoyance and presence of mind in such cases always derives from one's own ego, its seductibility, its darkness, absence of mind, delays—on which these people, with deep, life-preserving cunning know how to work. In fact they turn all social and emotional forms, and intellect itself, to their ends.

Thus the impurity and insatisfaction in my relation with Ellawalla has always been from the weakness of egoity in me. The subtlety of such relationships by which elements from both sides are equally necessary and are delicately poised. One could almost believe, with the astrologer J., that their developed perfection could only have been produced by elaborate karma in a former life. The difficulty is in proportion with solidity, the real tensions, of relationship in which inward progress for both parties is made: it is like a subtle duel between exactly complementary opponents in which the smallest advantage must grow out of and transcend the best force and skill of both.

All this deepens as it were from the occult side one's sense of the need of integrity, centrality, 'guiltlessness'. For example, the oneness with themselves of Kahuna psychiatrists driving out obsessing spirits; and it is no accident that the 'Pirit' stanzas for a similar purpose here in Ceylon are from words of the Buddha as one powerful to help men and demons. The power of the saints...

Mrs. Brandt's quiet and sweet wisdom during my own 'fight between Good and Evil'...

The importance of a personal centre deeper than the ego—the only authority—in dealing, also, with the egotism of a mother's love.

22–22.V.39.

Meditation: Relax. Reject, throw off as a crust, get behind and within, every idea, memory, form and mode of consciousness—including sleep. Deep gravity. Here indeed all metaphors concur. Image of descending by a dark narrow way as if deep into the earth. Various levels of consciousness, each with its ego and system of expression, left behind like outer layers. Centralisation of force—apparently towards the heart. Delicate and at the same time massive process of application, easily unbalanced, confused, bifurcated, overlaid, dissipated, lost.

Return everything to Nature—body, mind and all...

Thought, even after this small exercise, seems to have unusual vividness and power. Imaginative memory (of a person, for instance) is almost hallucinatingly solid, specific and clear. As if everything were refreshed, simplified, freed, organised from a deeper source.

25.V.39.

Spiritually, no doubt, this nervous debility questions self-will. Is the vital to be surrendered to the ultimate spiritual purpose?—If only the mind were clear and satisfied. Or the soul sufficiently awake to impose surrender upon both.

But all this, as I write, is still theoretical.

Study can only be a sterilising burden and task if it is conceived by mental will: it must be done by a central aspiration as work and sacrifice towards understanding and command of the mind. Everything—all action, experience, expressions, objects—must be considered and used from the point of view of yoga. This alone can in all spheres straighten out the path and stabilise one's deepest destiny.

Remain in contact with the soul: give it first rights over mind and vital and all the many petty egos with their contradictory worlds of dull or fragile compromise, delay, evasion, confusion that are to be purified away.

Incapacity to organise all as *sadhana* is perhaps only refusal to see that things must be done by stages. The imperious mental vision of the Superego's will, incapable of having all at once, produces sterilising, even disintegrating tension. Perhaps a little kindness to oneself—not complacency, but confidence in the Divine Will in everything, the Will for which none of our standards, scruples, difficulties can be a measure.

Forcing of the pace is no doubt a mistake. One should give oneself all necessary time and scope for study and general experience—a natural, integral rhythm must be found.

26.V.39.

It is most important not to conceive or try to achieve everything from below. Imaginative stimulus (as I find again today in rereading a few sentences of Henry Miller on Anais Nin) may produce a great heightening and change of level, and therefore potentiality of consciousness and energy.

The tamasic (torpid) element of inertia may appear in very subtle form and at higher levels in proportion as one's normal conscious level is raised.

Freedom from plans and preconceptions helps reduce *tamas* and keep the consciousness open to energy.

2.VI.39.

1. Finish rapidly with Europe and first cycle of Aphorisms.
2. Meanwhile learn Sanskrit and Hindi.
3. Study Vedas, Upanishads, in the Himalayas (Almora).
4. Rest of the tradition—Buddhism, Tantra, Vaishnavism—in its own milieu.

Study:

1. Complete European survey from Egypt to modern times first.
   The language of my thought is formed by that tradition, so it must be first commanded.
   Middle ages at some R.C. monastery? Enquire at Trivandrum.
2. Rapid general survey of Oriental tradition.
3. Meanwhile learn Sanskrit and Hindi. At Benares? Enquire of friends in Trivandrum.
4. Empathic *Erleben* of main Indian schools *sur les lieux*—completion of synthesis.

13–16.VII.39.

One may be less oneself than others and yet see their limits, or at least those that are visible to one's particular organisation. And is it not also complacency or pride not to suffer from the defects of others?—In those who evade the conflict between head and heart either heart or head is bad or lazy.

When one cannot accept oneself one cannot find anyone else real or solid either, or it's always a sort of solidity that is irrelevant.

One cannot accept others in one's blindness, as blind men lean against each other. One can use others as the small change of one's egoism. But to *love* one another requires vision and wisdom—one must have touched the reality.

Meanwhile, is not the tension towards perfection that Plato reveals as the inner meaning of the Greek *paiderastia*, the dynamism of every living paideuma, the dynamism of every life-culture, Parisian or Athenian, an indispensable discipline—the true preparation for a Christianity that shall complete and not betray so much powerful elegance and beauty? And does not Christianity otherwise favour false humility, hypocrisy, failure of Sensuality?—With the new light there also entered a flood of Judaic darkness that brought to the surface, as Nietzsche pointed out, resentment and bad conscience of the horde of Roman slaves.

Premature acknowledgement of Christian values has since my twelfth or thirteenth year forced on me a long detour in the wilderness from which only now, at thirty, I begin to glimpse the possibility of emerging. It is not for nothing that I found Rimbaud significant, whom the terrible struggle of human force and elegance with the unknown angel touched him in the thigh and robbed him of power. And this also why the anguish of Pascal, Dostoievski, Kierkegaard, Kafka, Chestov, Gide has been so near to me.

15.VII.39

Connections:

This morning I thought of asking Kalua's wife to dish up my *khitcherry* in the vessel she has generally used to cover the black cooking-pot and that so that I should escape the rather tiresome politeness of cleaning the latter before returning it. But I did not attempt the task of conveying this by pantomime—we have no common language. I incidentally wondered for a moment what she would use to cover the vessel.

Towards noon she brings my food dished up in the vessel and covered with a square of plantain leaf.

Mrs. D. at Trivandrum was convinced that Indian servants habitually read one's thoughts and that this is how state secrets become the talk of the bazaars.

When I consider it I realise that this thought, like those that were so effective in similar circumstances at Opara, was concentrated enough to involve temporary suspension of sense-perception. And the condition Yeats records as favourable for telepathy was fulfilled: intending to ask J. to translate for me next time he should come, I had completely dismissed the idea. But apparently it fulfilled its own direction!

27th. Today, for the first time since leaving India in April, because visitors prevented more serious work I began to re-write some notes of studies and chose European philosophy.

In the afternoon, I received a letter from Pisharody (the first time he has written to me) asking for information about European philosophy.

29.VIII. Last night, rather to my annoyance, for I do not admire Gounod's music, I found myself remembering for the first time for years the 'Salve di mora casta e pura' from his *Faust*, the vocal score of which I once possessed.

Today when at Mr. R.'s house I turn on the radio for the sake of something else, I find Gigli singing it. Though I read through the programmes ten days ago I had certainly not consciously noticed this in the *Radio Times*. I did not know and should not in my cursory glancing have recognised the Italian words: I remembered 'All hail, thou dwelling pure and holy' from the English libretto.

21.VII.39.

One-pointedness, continuity and progress in work, gears gripping, integral transformation towards fulfilment, are possible only to the Leisure of perfect dharma, perfect Normality.

Thought not thus supported continually circles upon itself, multiplies itself in delays. As my highest level of recognition, Aphorisms demand the support of perfect Sensuality, Truthfulness, Centrality, and the Clairvoyance and freedom of Energy they give. They are not otherwise economical, serious, integral but become an obstruction, a burden, a confusion, an egoism of thought and literature.

In all external affairs, and especially as regards the body, there must be the perfect realism, intelligence, respect and employment of subtle conditions, discipline, technical hilarity of a dancer—of the artist I *contain*.

And now I abandon to Nature, to the flame of sacrifice of Shiva's Blissful Dance, all action and thought that has gone beyond my control.

24th. *Tapas*. Economy in all action and talk. Where talk is socially necessary get the other to do it. When you have to talk yourself make it an exercise in presence of mind, psychological realism, examination and expression of exact internal truth, watchfulness against egotism, rejection of it, purification.

The *internal* nature has to be commanded.

Here and now there have been provided perfect conditions. All that delays and confuses is to be eschewed. Purification by conduct and by meditation; work as purification. Purification is singleness, freedom, vision, energy, transformation.

There must be no other and lesser object than this purification, no attachment to means and plans: everything must be yoga.

[A careful reading between the lines reveals that the interlude in Ceylon gave Thompson the time and recouped psychic energy to reflect on his relation to India. All along he had sought, in a number of powerful and remarkable men—Ramana Maharshi, Sri Aurobindo, Krishnamurti, Krishna Menon—for an exemplary 'way'. The physical and esthetic conditions, the poor diet and the almost total lack of sophisticated friendship with people closer to himself in temperament grievously devitalised him. Like others before and after, Thompson craved that seemingly impossible elision of utmost Western and Eastern refinement in a terrain where the Seine flows into the Ganges. For some time he had reconciled himself to the fact that neither the way of the Vedantin through knowledge as exemplified in the magnetically serene Ramana Maharshi, nor the Teilhard-like yogic synthesis of Aurobindo were appropriate for a man of his passionate temperament. He speaks in a telling phrase of 'the terrible dividing apparition of Sri Aurobindo's sovereign calm and power'—and then crosses it out. In fact, he had been rejected by Aurobindo on the somewhat melodramatic grounds that he 'was an "asura"—in other words, that he was a demon. This was a common misunderstanding of Thompson's passionate sincerity and readiness to come to grips with any problem, intellectual, esthetic or emotional—evidence not of cold cerebration but its exact opposite: an inexhaustible reservoir of unrecognised love.

He now realised that the prolonged effort put into his 'Art and Expression' notebook had been a huge and inconclusive mental detour and to persist would end in what he called 'perversity'. It would seem that the cerebral element at Aurobindo and Ramana ashrams brought out the worst in Thompson: a sterile, even redoubled cerebral intensity. This he desperately desired to curb. He now pinned all his hopes on Krishna Menon who, in spite of the name 'Jnani' Thompson had given him early in their relationship, seemed to offer a way out by emphasising his need to develop a balance between the head and the heart—namely that the heart be 'raised' in order to release suffocated emotionality.

8.VIII.39.

[Thompson recalls an incident in London ten years earlier of:]

self-isolation from human influence... I came late to Anne's birthday after hours of cruel overtime at the Bank, in a very different mood from the rest, expecting her to be alone and so tired I could hardly speak. I brought a new current; they could not assimilate me, I was too hollow to attune myself.

The immediate demand in any case is to recover the vital-physical force necessary to live my life at its own speed, at the level of intensity without which it does not exist and will be covered and damped out by time like ash. The trans-realistic will, one's energy consumed in driving continually beyond oneself, one's capacity, one's gifts, one's life; the tremendous tension and suspense between the human, esthetic, vital, cultural void and the phantoms created by an imagination of Reality still prior to all realism, too innocent, too passionate; endless self-negating struggle with a hundred uncommanded insistent values, kinds and ranges of knowledge and experience. And all the time the body weakened by every sort of poverty, ugliness, provisionality.

Must get my footing once and for all, intellectually and personally. Must gain strength for intensive study of Europe, Sanskrit, etc., so as to be able to leave the South. Test all and myself, and emerge into the world of intelligent and living human beings, the vortex of expression, the colour and vibration, the intense music of life. Ended this exile among peasants and superstitious innocents, among vegetable riot uninterrupted by man, a sun whose passion he can no longer resist, as once he rose to its keynote at Ellora and Konarak temples.

9.VIII.39.

For the ego others are mental, erotic and sometimes even physical symbols, *abstractions*.

But it is necessary to be completely aware of the intrinsic specificity of everyone.

Reality cannot be personally embodied and expressed until there is perfect unity between disinterested sensibility and psychological realism—until they are subsumed in the understanding and immediacy of love, direct transegoistic vision and power.

17.VIII.39

Nocturne. Stillness is still—and hums, absent behind its hiding in the sky. Pure winds wide wide in the O of space—sweet lyrical full open blossoming. In this night-world, its own name, what unnameable object and element, Banner, Person, Appurtenance?

In all directions every object is single and magical, an absolute.

17–18.VIII.39

Prose-poems with 'metaphysical' metaphors like ' The moon signs the night' correspond with the abstract fantasies of auto-eroticism—in a similar way build a temporary relation between mind and physical sensation. As in abstract formal art generally—the opposite of recognition of *persons*. It is also in the *jnani* seeking the Impersonal who in detachment may let sexuality work itself out in him. But the *bhakta* must be faithful even physically: he sees the Supreme as the Complete Person, the Prior Concreteness, with whom he has an integral, exhaustive, dynamic personal relation.

10.IX.39

Live in relation only with those whose atmosphere is positive to you, who are interesting to you, who in some direction take you seriously, and who thus allow release of natural geniality. This essentially means yogis and sadhakas. Even solitude is less positive than this; and besides, complete solitude is hardly obtainable and could be entirely positive only by final consistency.

15.IX.39

The old poetical interpretation of the signs of Oriental life, even the peculiar kind of squalor, in the sense of an intense dream made it possible for me to remain at my own vital level. Humanistic interpretation of these signs by surrender of former isolation only suffers from their utterly negative meaning—for they express puerility, fecklessness, insensitiveness, limitation. Or at least all the positive that belongs to the same mode of life is baffling, antagonistic, inaccessible to any humanistic consciousness. It is, apparently, the shadow of the occult capacity and the transcendentalism expressed in the Hindu tradition and by the yogis who move in this intense, garish, uncompromising decor. And which expresses itself in the intense sculpture, the concentrated ritual details, the crisp formalism, of the temples.

It is this same temperament that experiences the sexual richness and intensity as Kundalini, occult power, Mother, root of the world, who is to be incited into wider and intenser spheres of consciousness and experience.

Undoubtedly I have a relation with this intensity. As poet, as potential yogi, I have entirely to acknowledge and employ it.

The whole thing is an aspect of the problem of humanism that was first clearly mirrored for me in Rimbaud.

It is the same impulse that seeks concentrated foods—sweetmeats—typically, of almonds and ghee—and, as long as this impulse remains romantic, drugs like ganja. In a word, the whole Tantrik tradition.

18–19.IX.39. Dream.

London, Rimbaud's 'Biblical city'—vast spaces, lights and glooms—docks, causeways, cathedrals, sombre power and elegance. In crowded Gracechurch Street in the City I roll up my sleeping-mat from the pavement after a bank official has passed. I watched him pause for a moment to light a cigarette on the steps of the entrance to his offices, a solid figure with hard preoccupied face—the ease and satisfaction of a place in the world, a recognised 'work'.

At another phase all the City streets are absolutely empty.

Phantasy of meeting an Irish vagabond on London Bridge and improvising so perfect a continuation of the peculiar lyricism and pathos of his life that I risk finding me a lifelong friend, while for myself the whole thing is a poetical exercise without foundation—that cannot change or lighten the far deeper tone expressed by the heavy and giant forms, the majestic nostalgia, of the vast Metropolis.

25.IX.39.

Establish the Centre. Otherwise there are only temporary functional ganglia in mind, vital, will, which the whole man cannot for a moment believe in and which therefore weary and disgust and poison him.

The conciliatory smile of pleasantness and easy charm must be done away—live deeper, look deeper, the smile a rare and true blooming and light.

It is easy to make fun of D.H. Lawrence's language, of all tenderness and privateness. But the private must be kept private, roads for use clear and hard.

Gallella, Ceylon, 10.X.39. Dream:

While I am walking through a town which is a mixture of English and Indian I pass some gaudily dressed women singing to a drum a ballad in English about the war. When I have gone on some way, in a rather narrow and more rural lane,, like a band of Bacchantes they overtake me—gipsy-like women of Northern India, in garish yellows and reds, wild, strong, excited, so that I wonder what they will do. They surge round like a lot of mad prostitutes and shake over me, Holi-wise, some liquid from above. In defence I call them *Amma* and finally, in reply to this thought of them as Mother, one who has marked *tilakam* on my forehead cries 'Lakshmi Narayana!'

They seem to be friendly though very noisy and disreputable, and we go on together. I am asking them where they come from, taking one by her sleeve to hold attention, when we are overtaken by an apparently English soldier in smart uniform. I am rather ashamed at what he must think of my company and repeat my question a little self-consciously. But he passes slowly, lingering, and finally smiles and joins us.

By the roadside, a little beggar approaches. He is rather like the Irish vagabond of the dream of 18th, September. He holds out his hand—by accident or from leprosy it has no fingers or thumb, to display a tiny cream-yellow disc like a tick or louse. He throws it into the muddy road of a little desolate rural bridge that rises in front of us. I see evolving, multiplying, displaced from below out of the wet dirt, a little slithered pile of copper cents and other coins, and this continues with a sinister, slow seething, swarming insect-like movement as if lice were pullulating. One feels he is demonstrating that 'all money is dirt'. The women are fascinated and awed, but without losing their feminine egoism. I am paralysed by an uncanny fear and for a long time cannot move my foot to retreat.

The little man has all the time said nothing and remains in the background of his effects. I am not sure if he picked up the tiny abstract creature and threw it down again, but the change is now into long yellowish worms. They multiply prodigiously, seething, growing longer—foul, evil: you feel they spread some horrible plague.

We retreat. Muddy metropolitan street—asphalt, iron, silence, all grey, gleaming, overcast as if with rain. At a corner we find a policeman, English, with khaki *topi* and cane. He reprimands the little beggar who grudgingly, with hypocritical humility, calls off the worms, now advanced like a shallow, muddy river halfway towards us, and they cease.

Since he seems to know him, I ask the policeman about this strange 'beggar' and he begins a long yarn about having first met him on board ship in an Indian port where such fellows sometimes appear. Meanwhile I keep an eye on the man. He is only about four feet high but slightly made and does not produce the impression of a dwarf. He is covered head and all in a nondescript cloth that hides the upper part of his face. I can only make out a rather long nose. The straight mouth and strong clenched jaw which were otherwise chiefly visible (bristled with grey but all stained as if with dribbled tobacco-juice) are hard, cruel, bitter, almost evil; but I feel that the man may be some eccentric, even self-denigrating, a kind of saint or perhaps yogi or *tapasvin*. I try to memorise this face. I also notice a rather big brown hand (with fingers now, and a sadhu's long, rather dirty nails).

He is very much shut up in himself, as if hating to be questioned or disturbed, but I see him assiduously brush the dirt and manure off some labourer whose coat is soiled. The navvy takes no notice of the insignificant, humble little body. It is as if dirt had some occult significance for him.

Finally, on the nearer side of a black stone bridge in the rainy evening of an industrial town, he lies down like a dog (and now almost as small) in the puddled asphalt of the street-corner, a kind of backwash, where the road widens as it leaves the bridge. I watch him carefully, covered with his grayish cloth; but insensibly, before my eyes, he melts away till there are no longer even rather unusual bumps and pits in the weatherworn macadam; no, to my great awe and astonishment there is really nothing. The policeman also passively witnesses this. I go to look more closely and lift a corner of the torn macadam. Underneath is a big lighted manhole with a sketchy grating through which so small a man could have passed. Below it looks like an engine-room—railings and galleries.

I go off with the policeman past Covent-Garden-like fruit-warehouses (closed with upright planks) which today are being used as Sunday-schools. I overhear a statement that these are facts that contradict rebirth and think to myself that it would be better if these teachers were to explain what the Christ meant by 'rebirth'—spiritual regeneration, birth out of the ego!

We look for some place where we can sit and drink tea while the policeman tells his story.

According to the Jnani the women in dreams of this kind always have power—the harlots representing Tantrik and yogic *samskaras* from my former lives. Money is equivalent to dirt and dirt means dispassion. In spite of the policeman there is nothing worldly in the whole dream.

19.X.39.

Without supporting dharma, without minute technical ratification, one remains a spinner of words, a dupe of words, one is brought to death by words, to material and spiritual perdition.

19–20.X.39. Gallella, near Ratnapura, Ceylon.

One night while I was living in a wild and lonely place, long after I had gone to bed there came a knock at my door. I got up in the dark to open and while I was preoccupied with wondering who it could be, jarred my hip against the sharp corner of my writing-table: in the morning there was a small round bruise. I had not been able to sleep and was calmly collected and alert.

I opened the door onto a figure of whom I could make out nothing exact as it stood facing me with its back to the uncertain light outside. But immediately with a lance he pierced me through the heart. When the long javelin was withdrawn I still felt no pain, only a kind of warmth remained. I was not surprised or disturbed by this, it seemed just an incidental event, like dropping and retrieving a box of matches.

I stepped forward into the vague light of the night-sky to see who my visitor was but he had already disappeared. All around, the midnight hills were asleep.

I felt no wound, nothing was changed, my life continued. I have sometimes doubted the whole thing, tried to believe it was a dream. But the further it retreats into the past the more clearly and arbitrarily my present life is defined, till at last I wonder if on the contrary it is not the only real event that has ever happened to me.

23.X.39.

The Supreme *Person* is for the mind utterly mystical. This level must be reached. Let us not erect false mental images.

7.XI.39.

Humanistic romantic Montaigne-Rousseau-Goethe kinds of interest in contingent psychological relations and process must be completely surpassed—liquidated in the dimension of the Transcendent for which Body, Action, Expression, Mind etc. are all entirely sui generis—Occult.

Every force and faculty is inconclusive, romantic, dividing while it can still be used by the ego. The ego is the great leak, the great confusion, the great evasion.

Direct Organisation of the modes of consciousness in their own terms—occultly—is possible only by direct relation with the Transcendent.

8.XI.39.

No: in any flexible development, in the rhythm of any integral yoga, one will need from time to time to come to the Vital and work there. The mind must be known from the point of view of the Vital as well as vice versa. And resistance to such an alternating rhythm in which they are to become mutually conscious can only produce disorder, obstruction, illness.

It is no doubt such a rigidity that has so attenuated my nervous energy.

14.XI.39.

Dr. T. Nallainathan reports:

All symptoms, including fevers high and low and exaggerated reflexes, due to hyperadrenalism following mental excitement.

Rest, good food, B vitamins.

There may have been a TB lesion, but postmortem anyway discovers traces of TB in 98% of people. Very good, deep breathing (better than that of many an athlete) counters this tendency.

Pulse rate 100 (normal 72. Insurance companies require reason for pulse rate over 90).

10

Meeting With Yogaswami

Blood pressure 135 systolic, with increased thumping pulse-rate. (Normal, c.120. Range 103–141).

Weight today 113 lbs.

Before he left Ceylon, Thompson went to the northern tip of the island to meet a well-known eccentric sage by the name of Yogaswami. This is the longest such account in his journal, and was written in response to a request from his doctor. It may be noticed that, in spite of his eccentricities, Yogaswami's entourage included the usual sprinkling of retired senior officials who, everywhere on the Indian sub-continent, attach themselves to saints and sages, providing financial support—respectful and sincere in devotion to those whom they regard as realised souls. Both in conduct and in the mode of his description, Thompson invests the proceedings with the appropriate combination of lightness and depth which belongs to the domain of the fairy-tale; this accords well with the atmosphere surrounding such far from unsubtle figures. Even the most sophisticated Hindus never lose the knack of a child for slipping, whenever circumstances call for it, into a 'willing suspension of disbelief' that is both playful and attentively receptive to any manifestation of fairy-tale naivety, though it may strike grown-ups as no better than harmless idiocy. Thompson, with his penchant for the folkloric simplicities, would say that Yogaswami made a deep impression on him as an exemplary figure in the ancient tradition of the holy fool or wise simpleton.

17.XI.39. Jafna, morning.

When I arrived his little house was empty but almost immediately he came from outside the compound singing. I was at once struck by the peace and strength in his bearing, the authority of his eyes, his fine geniality. I was prepared to be driven away but he received me very kindly, invited me to sit opposite him and repeated heartily, 'You're ALL RIGHT! Very good boy.'

Mattuswami Pillai told me afterwards that this is '*his mantram*'!

Besides one or two brass utensils for puja there was nothing to be seen in the neat thatched hut but his simple bed spread over a deer-skin on the polished cement floor. He wears only a *dhoti*, his long white hair drawn back and knotted behind, his active hands sometimes twist back into itself the full and fine white beard. His body, of medium height, though his dignity and grace make him look tall, is plump and well-preserved. He might be sixty. I am told he is Jaffna Tamil.

Afterwards I have leisure to note the high and wide forehead, the fine but strong hands, teeth and mouth, the calm, bright, penetrating gaze, the beautiful rich, deep laugh.

I had come to him a stranger, without warning. But I am told that he easily perceived the nature and purpose of those who visit him and drives away those who come with unworthy motives. While I was with him a woman's voice was heard outside, persistently. As persistently the Swami put her off and finally sent her away. Since I had told him that I do not understand Tamil he explained: 'She wanted to ask me something worldly'.

Mr. Murugesan at Bâlangoda, an orthodox Hindu, told me that once when in his presence he thought to himself, 'Why doesn't Swami wear *vibhuti*?' the latter at once sent for some, remarking 'Mr. Murugesan thinks I should wear *vibhuti*.'

Here are some of his sayings:

The kingdom of heaven is within. Pravritti-nivritti (manifestation-release)—he shows spread and collected finger-tips—is the whole axis and rhythm of the universe.

God has become the earth, the sky, the sea, all this wonderful world. All that is is right.

(From a disciple I heard these sayings in the same spirit from the Swami's guru: 'Nothing has happened, everything is as it was. All this was over long ago. There is nothing wrong in this world. Everything is right. There is nothing wanting in this world. Whatever is is right.')

Fighting also is good; it is also a discipline, a yoga; the young men need to fight.

Man must suffer, suffering is good medicine. When there is suffering, laugh. Only the body feels pain or pleasure.

Tat twam asi; aham Brahmasmi. 'In the beginning was the Word.' That Word is OM. Use it.

We *is*, not we are.

Be quiet, go deep. Day and night there must be self-examination, it is not a short or easy task. Go about, see the beauty of Nature, see God everywhere. Neither love nor hate. If one comes loving, it is good; if beating, it is good. Seek in yourself, concentrate. Don't beg help or information from others. Don't boast, don't speak of these things to those who are not really interested. Be sincere, be brave, love all. Don't worry, hurry, sorry. (He repeats this, laughing at the unconventional English. Control the organs, control the mind. First obey, then command.

(This and what follows met the fact that I had nothing to discuss with him but, in spite of scepticism about its real need or possibility, had thought that the only relevant question would be if, from his status, he could see me objectively enough to give any personal advice.)

You are too lean. You must eat *good* food, little but good. *You can eat* eggs (his emphasis), they will not hurt the Atman.

We are the Mother of God, we support Him in this body.

If God should come, ask Him to be seated and remain calm.

Yours is a good age for finding Truth. The next three years are important for realisation.

At last he says, 'It is time'. As I am about to go he picks up an hibiscus flower offered in *puja* and tuck it into my breast pocket.

Evening.

Until you realise you must be very quiet. Stay in one place. Rest. No hurry. Don't care for birth and death. We watch all things come and go. Study many things *inside*. Go deep, find rest. It is there, I see it: only the outside is unquiet.

The whole world and all the gods are within. (I had at one moment thought of asking a question about the nature of the gods.) The spine is Meru, head Mount Kailash; Shiva and Parvati are within us.

We are not the body, all is from within. Throwing aside the body we can be in England or Germany.

You must have at least four hours good sleep. Sleep is samadhi.

This is a nice world. You can take anything you like—sugar-cane, tea, fighting, yoga, name and fame.

Today we chance to meet, there is *darsanam*: I see myself in another form in you, you see yourself in me.

(It is Skanda Shasti today, when Subrahmanyam overcame the *asura*. Camphor is burned. Cross-legged, erect, hands in *namaskaram* at his breast, the Swami sings a Tamil hymn, the others repeating after him line by line. He interrupts himself to say with his brilliant smile: 'We are worshipping *you*.' Later, he gets up and takes me into a little side-room to show me 'all his possessions'—in a leather wallet half the size of a schoolboy's satchel with a strap for slinging it over the shoulder.)

He repeats: You are a good boy—nallu paiyan, nallu podiyan...You are a clever boy; you understand. Become as a little child, become like him (indicating a boy about twelve who was present with his father).

18th., morning.

I walked the two miles or so. Afterwards Mr. Muttuswami Pillai told me that when he has walked a good distance the Swami used to say he had earned something. As I approach he calls 'Come, come' and I enter and sit down. He introduces the Speaker of the State Council, and a retired judge and retired headmaster who enter a little later. He asks if anyone has come to see me this morning. On my return I find that after I had set out to go to him a devotee had left for me according to his instructions eleven rupees for my journey. When he asked yesterday if I had enough money to get to Malakkarai by the 20th, I said that I was not worrying about it, that no doubt it would come. He gets all present to contribute and hands me over, note by note, nine rupees. He handed back one rupee to the Speaker, who in fishing six rupees out of his pockets apologised that this was all he had.

Before this he had given me a fine *veshti*, one of a pair apparently just presented to him by the Speaker. My clothes are just now all wearing out but I have mended them carefully and only close observation could have noticed it.

There seemed to be no question of refusing all this and indeed I felt deeply privileged, if a little overwhelmed, at his care for me and to receive these gifts from his hands.

Samadhi is artificial. You are the Reality.

When you know the Reality you see that nothing is right or wrong, moral or immoral. We do not know anything and Reality also does not know.

Know the knower.

(He tells me he is to come to India next month and that he will see me.) I see you everywhere. You are my nearest and dearest friend and I am yours. I worship you.

(His eyes seem always to express something much deeper and less qualified than anything he says, something more austere, and changeless.)

(The judge, who has been reading a verse from Tayumanavar offers to translate and explain for me but the Swami prevents him.)

If you understand I understand: the mechanism is the same in all.

Give up everything at the feet of God.

Study, don't be idle; idleness is a sin. (I have struggled a good deal over the idea of surrendering all my mental tasks.) Work is rest.

Go everywhere, roar like a lion. We are all playing like children, it is a dance. (Meeting my thought, he added:) The dance of Shiva.

The plants outside are hearing my voice and listening: it is their *tapas*. They are also servants of God and seek to be one with Him. The whole world is *Yogam*.

Be true to yourself, that is all.

Christ, Buddha, Muhammad are in your body. All religions are one.

He recites the Three Refuges and the first Sila in Pali, the beginning of the Lord's Prayer and the *La ilaha*.

Aham Brahmasmi. Tat twam asi. Think that.

He offers *namaskaram*. I feel 'it is time' and take my leave of him.

11

Tasks And Detours

4.XII.39.

Wherever you are you are alone with God. This direct aloneness is continual prayer and adoration in which the whole creation blossoms like a flower.

7.XII.39.

In spite of Eros-ego-Spirit difficulty, intensity as askesis, auto-punition in tension with super-ego, etc. etc., prolonged formulation of the vital problem has fundamentally been mental evasion of Sensuality. The basic fact is that 1930–32 intensity has been betrayed in India by poor and scanty food undermining the vital-physical and it is this that has to be corrected. All delay and complication, like a pullullation of fungus on a sickly tree, derives from failure of Sensuality. Tea and coffee for instance were first needed for temporary recovery of the energy undermined by physical and esthetic starvation—vicious circle.

13.XII.39

Watchfulness: reject every negative, evasive, impure (especially egoistic) movement.

Examination of motives—their immediate weight, form and quality behind all specious constructions of mind and will.

16–17.I.40. Dream.

Violent interaction, like a ramping motor, and as if sexual, of two apparently mechanical objects produces a third sinister crab-like living thing with rhythmically distributed 'claws'. —Inter-exhaustion of forces with insect-like tenacity, crustacean weight and coldness.

17–18.II.40.

Clinging details—circumstance, hesitation, thought—frail, but persistent like a cotton thread on serge or shavings coiled about a plane. Sweep clean and see the work that must continue.

In every least movement and action remain in sole direct relation with God, with the Completeness of Heaven (His Eternity, His power and glory) and with the immediate potentiality of completion on earth ('Thy Kingdom come, Thy will be done').

Dependence upon oneself, or upon man, is 'atheism', ignorance and can only lead, in relation with one's suppressed spirituality, to romanticism—sentimentality, rage, passive Anguish, negative hypocrisy, involution of energy in self-deception.

18.II.40.

All fear depends upon limitation of consciousness. You cannot fall out of the Universe, nor will Reality separate itself from you. There is only the possibility of ever-deepening, ever more conscious union, of fuller and more resourceful enjoyment.

20.II.40.

The stones, the burning flowers, the spaces in the sky, are fragments of my riven or my squandered heart. I remain the void that neither contains nor is contained by them.

26.II.40

First of all, in the hills, several days of complete rest—pause in the whole chain of time and place from birth. Let all tensions, all provisionality, disentangle; recover one's rhythm, one's breath, one's blood, one's simple eyesight—the wide sky, the direct, detailed eloquence of light, the brilliance and reverberation of everything—presence of the real future in perfect economy and zest.

Sense of task, cramp of mental will, must be completely blown to the winds—recovery of immediate Sensuality.

While there cannot be action by Love and Delight you first need *Rest.*

2.IV.40. Meeting with the Jnani.

Only the ego introduces the possibility of evil and transience into the sphere of beauty and enjoyment. Otherwise they are the Divine itself.

Radical confirmation and agreement. Has not that Divine Being himself shown me that Delight is the heart of his world?

Subtle Eros developed, fearlessly fulfilled, when there is no hankering for gross sensation, leads to *mahabhava* (Trance of Delight), besides which *nirvikalpa-samadhi* is distasteful. In this state one may be absorbed for days, appearing to others insane.

For the realised man sexuality becomes *lila* (Divine Play, as in the play of Krishna-Lila) in the divine sense. There is no longer emission for the sex-centre is transformed. After such intercourse without emission, there is no tension, but enhancement of energy. A touch for one at the level of *mahabhava* transforms at least for the time and often permanently all gross desire.

After recounting of *mahabhava* experience, told before to no-one, not even his wife, the embrace, deep breath, sobbing, crying. He rushed away, stumbling, stamping as if blown off his feet and finally, banging the door, regained his room—too deep and great and loving for me to respond. Or perhaps only cold objectivity remained because everything else was absorbed. I was left simply, deeply confident and happy, released.

3.IV.40. Letter to Alex.

...Perhaps *all* continuous writing or thinking at whatever level soon becomes an exercise in expressing the unimportant, for nothing immediate and essential can be discursively described. —Integrity of personal poetry that seizes, objectifies, commands, enjoys only what is significant to one's purest Sensuality—that allows no state of transition, provisionality, no substitution, indulgence, compromise, anything of lower organisaion can fill the void, but remains in constant tension with the Transcendent. For this integral Sensuality, by what it refuses is also necessarily an askesis: Shiva the Dancer, abandoned in his terrible, all-creating, all-subsuming joy, is also the Supreme Yogin.

...Only such economy gives enduring force—Villon, Rimbaud, Cocteau; it is even the only true measure of quality: before this intensity the question of size, of 'greatness' in the ordinary sense, almost entirely disappears.

Penetration fulfils and subordinates the most powerful intellect and makes it secondary—even, for the unintellectual, apparently non-existent.

And by itself *intelligence*, the great temptation, can only dissipate this singleness, reduce it to crumbs.

8.IV. Chengannur. Today (for this may interest you) really prolonged and heavy rain. Let us hope some fell at Anma.

16.IV. Chengannur to Kottarakara. Baptised through the window of the bus by flying spray of albumen from a basket of eggs on the roof. I don't know what surrealist or psychoanalytical symbolism may hide in this. We all grinned a good deal anyway, wiping our matted hair.

18.IV. At Rajapalaiyam I am sorry to hear of the death of your English cow, apparently through a miscarriage. Long argument last evening between Johnson and a veterinary doctor from Srivillipputur who said he absolutely could not go to the estate without official leave.

C.F. Andrews's book on Sundar Singh, the Christian sadhu, a converted Sikh. Weak, diffuse, possibly sentimental in the peculiar Protestant way. But *The Sadhu* by Streeter and Appaswamy, as I remember it, was rather better and if you don't already know it would interest you as a Christian. The beautiful autobiography of a Hindu sadhu, Sri Purohit Swami (*An Indian Monk*, Macmillan), or Rolland's life of Sri Ramakrishna Parahamsa, would be good for comparison.

[While Thompson lived in South India he received material support from a number of friends including Dr. S.R. Ranganathan in Madras, Alan Chadwick at the ashram of Ramana Maharshi at Tirunvanamallai, S.N. Ure at Trivandrum.

Dr. Ranganathan's reputation as a library scientist was based on his complicated system of library classification (long before the days of computers). He had been a Theosophist and Thompson was instrumental in directing his attention back to India's classical tradition. A high-caste Brahmin, Ranganathan bore an impeccably painted Ramanujan brow-mark to the end of his days, even when travelling abroad (where I met him at UNESCO Headquarters in Paris in 1963). Many years Thompson's senior, it was nevertheless the librarian who persuaded his young friend to edit his difficult masterwork on library science. It was Thompson who persuaded him to publish an account of how his system of classification came to him on a visionary evening walk: 'I asked Thompson to edit my book, because even though he knew nothing of library science he had the most incisive and razor-sharp mind of any man I have met. Yet I must say that he had also uncommonly deep spiritual insight and whenever I wished to ascertain the worth of a particular sage or teacher I invariably consulted Thompson. His judgment in such matters was unerring. I owe my meeting with Sri Purohit Swamy, who collaborated with Yeats on a translation of the 'Upanishads', to Thompson's good offices. He assisted Purohit Swamy with the editing of his work after he went to Benares. Thompson was completely accepted in orthodox circles and gained access to holy men and shrines in remote places where even I, a Brahmin, was excluded. He had a radiance of being that won everybody's heart.'

The circumstances in which I met Dr. Ranganathan are an indication of the deep affection in which he held Thompson. My wife spotted him in the library of UNESCO, a very elderly gentleman exhausted by jet-lag, and asked him if he would kindly talk to me about Thompson. He readily assented, somewhat astonished to find anybody in Paris who had heard of a man who had died fourteen years earlier in India. He immediately cancelled all his appointments and joined me for lunch at the Delegates' Restaurant, where he shyly drew from his pocket an article of great sentimental value which Blanca Schlamm had sent him after Thompson died—the wallet Thompson had made to his own specifications many years before in Madras to contain the paper slips he carried with him, and on which he would write his aphorisms when inspiration struck. Ranganathan carried this wallet with him wherever he went after it had been bequeathed to him. He became completely absorbed in his reminiscences of the remarkable Englishman, and we talked for many hours in his hotel room, oblivious of our surroundings, of Thompson's life in India. Late at night, I returned home by underground train, only to find my street packed with policemen armed with submachine-guns, blood spilled on the pavement. It was the height of the Algerian crisis in France and it is a characteristically Thompsonian touch that Ranganathan and I had occupied a night of massacre in deep discussion on topics far removed from the terrible events raging around us in the outside world.

P.K. Rajagopal was Thompson's oldest friend; they met within days of the latter's arrival in Madras in 1933 and remained friends until Thompson's death. Rajagopal was a brusque businessman to all outward appearances. But he had another side to him: for many years before they met he had been a deeply serious Tantrika, claiming direct visionary guidance from the Goddess. Subsequently, Thompson introduced him to the Jnani. He remained a fervently loyal disciple of the Jnani until he died. A lengthy correspondence, with a stream of advice from Thompson on spiritual matters, might have survived but for Thompson's request that Rajagopal destroy each letter immediately after he assimilated its content. The relationship was stormy, but Rajagopal remained loyal to his friend to the end and provided assistance in the preservation of Thompson's manuscripts after the latter's death.]

24.1V.40. Letter to Rajagopal.

I now see that my long difficulty in 'accepting you' (!) and the whole situation (I was for years in tension with you) arose from a desire for autonomy, extreme unwillingness to admit anything but my own thought, will, initiative—refusal from the start of anything so passive as the the possibility of anything *happening* to me, of one's being conditioned by any environing universe. The problem of one's subjectivity raised everthing to a plane were no outer object or person could be quite real. This state blinded me, in fact, to the autonomy of others as something that might have any effect in my world: I had to treat them as puppets and could never take refuge (such was my disinterestedness—or pride) in any idea that they might have, their own sufficient motives and satisfaction in their action and attitude towards me.

All this only incidentally expressed a general, old and very deeply rooted sense of a need to *command* Nature and events, the attitude (if you can imagine it!) of a *Buddhist Paracelsus*... But as I get a little nearer inner equilibrium (though I have not yet found—or even yet accepted—its ultimate conditions) I can be a little more realistic. But when the nature of one's own existence is entirely in question the Other is a mystery that can only be held at arm's length: one is, precisely, in a state of *tension* with it. I use this metaphor more exactly than you perhaps think—to suggest an unresolved polarity or deadlock of forces.

And now that I begin little by little to reconsider my equally unrealistic economic intransigence, I see how altogether symbolic your relation with me has been.

13.IV.40

These seven years without money have surely sufficiently taught me patience and humility—have sufficiently controlled blind natural impulse and demand.

8.V.40.

If my life is not *sadhana* (spiritual exercise) what is it? —Confusion, evasion, vanity, anguish.

And if it is *sadhana* let it be conscious, expert, sincere. This first Truthfulness must be sustained at every moment as the dividing line between order and chaos, simpleness and duality.

11.V.40. Letter to S.N. Ure about a dream.

Well, no doubt, deep down, there is that nostalgia for an old order, grace, elegance, intelligence, suavity—which, in the dream, like a delicate but suffocating perfume wells up into tears—and nowadays, along with

Kierkegaard and Vallabhacharya, I sometimes read Jane Austen. How difficult it is to synthesise all one's personalities and in the attempt at singleness does one perhaps only mercilessly sterilise oneself? —At least that satisfying singleness seems possible only if one can reach, in oneself, great height or depth...

When every colour is absorbed, held back into a total synthesis—every occasion one of silence—the white light is blinding, burns like ice.

Women prevent that, make us manifest our many colours: they fear the terrible empty echoing of that self-destroying whiteness. Without true women perhaps no man ever gets to know himself *in the world.* Birth in the world is through woman.

I am still apparently in the darkness of the womb where all is potentiality—poignant, exhausting, unproductive, self-involved like dream.

... 'My mother, the Holy Ghost' Christ says in the Gospel of the Hebrews...

The hills nowadays are to me just hills and I so seldom wake up into that condition of delicate awareness (it is the very tissue of one's childhood) in which they are living, subtly magical symbols, reverberating as it were with a sweet soundless music.

12.V.40.

During my abstract vegetable meal today the ghee for a moment combined with some other element to produce a quite rich and satisfying flavour—something absent for the last seven years from my mentally simplified, and because of circumstances anyway extremely poor, food.

I believe it was this momentary sensation in its effect on the system that has suddenly restored to me a certain vital richness, solidity and colour and a subtle kinesthetic-sensuous awareness of my body that changes (subjectively, of course) even its visual value and returns me as it were to a sturdy Mediterranean brilliance, impasto, vibrato. This encourages my general tendency to return to my natural sensuality in food, environment, experience—no longer to deny the gods of life—to come out from a wilful mental shadow.

Spiritual knowledge is to *change* our relation with physical, vital and mental but not overthrow their truthfulness on their own plane. And they cannot be transformed by mere mental imposition.

13.V.40. Vellimalai.

This leisure could be sustained by *karma-yoga*. But otherwise an occasional 'sabbath' of complete relaxation is essential. For how many years—10? 20?—have I been cramped in a ceaseless tension, a ceaseless subconscious preoccupation with work and with certain symbols and *definitions* of spiritual potentiality!

But by this relinquishment all appears as Poetry: the false willed continuity of the uncertain ego defining task is broken.

Pre-occupation is one of the most obscuring forms of confusion.

13.V.40. Malakkarai. Hindu new year: *Guru Puja*—veneration of the master. Washing of feet, garlanding, burning of camphor, throwing flowers; the sweet grace and dignity of his wife performing this, the beauty of absolute devotion; clasping hands, black hair long abandoned in deep emotion at his feet. Then, at last, out of deep immobility (only an occasional very deep breath marking perhaps a change or intensification of state) the Jnani gets up. The strange stirring impression of that walk as if in this high absorption the body has been left to control itself. Slowly, precariously, as if moved by some other will, he passes by the crowding disciples and throwing from his garland leaves and flowers. Risen once more after a return to his chair he stands at the foot of the steps where I cannot see his face, gazing upon those below. At the throwing of flowers there was already deep, but mostly controlled, emotion; now, before that silent gaze, they break into a peculiar deep sobbing; you feel the ego has been broken down. He turns a little and in another group the same strange unwilled reaction follows. As I watched I could not help ascribing it to some extent to the rather passive emotionality of some of his admirers. Finally he turns towards me where I stand separately with his son. And that extraordinary, no longer human gaze, with its subtle, deeply peaceful power sends a peculiar thrill through me. I meet it; it is vast, deep, luminous, absorbing and sweeps away all but a tenuous thread of one's outer consciousness.

When he comes out later to give upadesham I recognise that this gaze is an intensification of the usual expression of his eyes.

It is curious that I still remember his eyes in that state as if ash-blue or silver with intense light, though like almost all Indian eyes they are actually dark brown.

Perhaps pupil and iris were so abnormally 'emissive' or 'absorbent' that only the impression of the whites was retained in physical memory. But I can hardly believe this: the impression that very vividly remains is of the two irises pale and intense with a peculiar almost metallic grey, like the colour perhaps of a thin film of ash on white-hot platinum.

In the previous guru-puja when his eyes were so deeply supra-personal that one somehow could not directly look at them (I made a mental note to try next time), they seemed to have become darker than usual, especially along the line of the lashes.

The net effect of this morning's experience is a feeling of joy—that all is, and always was, well. And this joy tends to express itself as the simplest, most spontaneous, most unqualified love, a love which therefore entirely contains all possible demonstration.

15.V.40.

We live and move in God: the thing is to do so no longer blindly but in deeper and deeper consciousness.

16.V.40. Vellimalai.

In the jungle.

A little stream outside my window in the night whispers and dialogues in the various voices, male and female, ringing or sibilant, calm or breathless, of a radio play, with its pauses and climaxes, suspense, its dramatic accelerandos and rubatos—always with that slight metallic heaviness, the artificial continuity of reproduced sound, like magnet kissing magnet.

17.V.40. Rajapalaiyam.

Self-excitement in speaking corresponds with auto-eroticism—which only negatively mirrors the possibility of *lila*.

20.V.40.

The grim poverty, the harsh and lurid squalor of Southern India, the crudeness of manner of the people, no voice, no gesture modulated, so turn back one's senses and imagination upon themselves that this country could inspire only poetry written in blood.

25.V.40.

The old capacity to detach each environment from past and future, automatically to break all links, to live in a void of intensity, seems to have failed. This is no doubt a sort of fatigue due to having remained too long in association with the same place and people.

26.V.40.

An immediate effect of this increasing recognition of my true destiny is that it now becomes quite easy to tell objectively the external story of my life—the detail of circumstance and Anguish is so clearly incidental in that very objectivity to the second, hidden, essential, secret destiny present from my childhood and that later on, in a void of Anguish too pure even to know itself, produced its own liberating events.

Yet till that Anguish is fully justified, the other shore in that irreversible dark journey firmly reached, its tension of silent storm has still remained in the atmosphere.

27.V.40.

No longer strength to formulate the deepest movement—that whole level fallen silent, fire under ash, storm collapsing upon itself in greater and greater darkness without lightning.

Vital weakness counts the hours of the day, has always failed before we can begin.

29.V.40.

What have you accomplished all these years? Besides a possible slight, merely natural, growth of intellectual and expressive power there is nothing but the increasing complication of inward and outward weakness. Even the force, now, *deeply and precisely* to examine your state you lack. O long detours, involution, substitution, evasion...

Only strict moment-to-moment discipline can save you, break these frightful webs and bring you out again into simplicity and clarity.

Yet how much of that sense of simplicity and intensity was after all no doubt sheer youth (as at the time one cannot know) and this working out perhaps of the confusions and weaknesses there...

Make once more a clean sweep of all that is confused in the past and beyond your control; by not adding to it and all its associations die.

30.V.40.

No, this youth is the real childhood, the immortal simplicity, the unquenchable native sincerity of the *soul.*

Without this root—that surpasses because it is prior to it—all attempt at 'discipline' has only failed. And had it succeeded it could only have made you a monster of mind and will. If it could have been complete it might have damned you.

The soul simply sees that a mistake, as with D.M., has been made and, secure in its own light and power, can let it go—where it goes anyway—in Nature. The ego in trying to rectify can only continue a mistake—elaborates it in even more inextricable refinements of anguish.

31.V.40.

This is the condition that so often prevents work: food *nervously* disturbing; pulse very fast, head quite empty of light and force. Attempt to concentrate is like forcing a man in feverish pain to keep still: one is uneasy, fragmentary, incapable of enjoying any kind of literature (supposing the choice so wide; and music, alas, is not available here), yet rest seems poisonous.

It may be some unconscious spite or resistance that so often produces this condition when there has been a resolution for work—the deliberate willed, formal work of organising aphorisms in themselves spontaneous. A very subtle feeling of vacant repulsion, almost of nausea, can be localised at the solar plexus: the vital wants to gallivant, saunter, divagate, it wants the new, freshness, spontaneity, easy wit and sensuous gallantry or delicate occult perception. This state could easily be cured if one would deviate into a long and various letter (and if there were anyone to write it to) but it rears at the stern, ashen Apollonian task, mere intellectual labour.

Even writing this, so far as it accepts this state in order to describe it, has made me feel rather better. Yet the vital if it is allowed its way will have only an idle, fragmentary day, for here in the barbarous unbeautiful jungle, all art, music, complex human spectacle, intelligent conversation is lacking. Then it begins to long for the old life of cultured cities, London, Paris, where every kind of vital or intellectual distraction is at hand. It complains that nothing is wrong but years of nervous, esthetic, emotional, intellectual starvation: the mill would make bread of its own stones.

1.VI.40.

My puritan upbringing, the Protestant scepticism... For when Nature itself is denied, God necessarily becomes abstract, a monster of mind and will. How much better, though it remain within the limits of religion, the Catholic way of recognising, first with the soul, or by faith, what belongs to the Spirit and judging all other incidentals liberally from this foundation.

The Puritan can seldom be a true mystic because of his first failure from realism. His theoretical moral will tenses the whole nature in an absurd cramp. It allows the smallest 'failure' to question or measure one's whole spiritual destiny. In fact, as I know very well, it can entirely prevent one's recognising it and riddles one with scruple and scepticism. All because nature and not the soul was considered first.

How very slow I still am to recognise this! Lack of spiritual education! —If I could have understood it in practice from my boyhood, what years of difficulty and exhausting self-torment—till now—it would have saved me. How differently (this is a mode of expression) my whole life might have developed! For such inhibition has very wide results: it affects the whole sphere of expression of the personality. —Intellectual and artistic self-criticality and scepticism too. How far I still am from accepting in practice that artistic expression is natural to man, from giving it room in my life. Yet since an artistic nature was really there from my childhood this repression has cost me all my energy to deal with it. This has been the whole problem and delay of my years in India. How much, how ingeniously, this tension with my natural temperament has made me suffer! For it puts me (paradoxically) in the greatest tension of all precisely with the fullness and richness and power of its opposite, the deep recognition of Shakti. And it forces me therefore to put the wrong colour and accent, almost certainly, on the need for complete command of sexuality. Yet intuitively, as my aphorisms on Eros and Sex, on Morality and 'Sensuality' show, I know all this perfectly well.

But this inner tension has no doubt deepened me and it is this experience that values the penetration of Pascal, Dostoievski, Kierkegaard, the anguish of Baudelaire and Rimbaud.

I see that even now I have not fully grasped the implication of what Brother S. told me of the attitude of an Himalayan guru towards the amours of two of his disciples.

Is it not perhaps one of the chief devices of the devil that through our own purism, fastidiousness and, yes, after all, our pride of mind and will, he makes it impossible first to recognise our spiritual destiny, our relation with God—that he makes God a Calvinistic monster of abstract perfection with which we remain forever in tension? And of course this very attitude tremendously deepens the timbre and repercussion of the smallest weakness. Once it is overcome, how easily the molehills thin out!

To confuse Eros and Spirit shows such lack of taste, is such bad style!

It is characteristic that I make this observation only now when I have so analysed and attenuated all spontaneous desire that only perversity, the wilful folly of indecision, unpurified scepticism, false curiosity and every sort of mad, self-despiting sophistry, Donne's heart 'which lov'st to bee/ Subtile to plague thy selfe'—in a word, the devil—could tempt me.

2.VI.40.

Through all uncertainty and inconsistency this journal is as it were a documentation made for higher authorities who, even while they are not recognised (they are still hidden and unknown like those of Kafka's Castle), are more interested in their subject and his behaviour than he can be himself.

[The entry for 13 June 1940 reveals the workings of LT's mind. Firstly, it was written just after 300,000 British and French troops were evacuated from Dunkirk, Britain's darkest hour, when it stood alone against Hitler—one of those rare instances when LT even refers to world events as having some influence on him. Secondly, it has a strong masculine slant connected to his use of the term 'vital', which is, in part, in his usage, connected with the male 'eros'—particularly here with the sexual 'eros' that he wished to subsume in his spiritual quest. But the actual written text, unusually extended over eight sides of four paper slips in his standard size of slip, also provides a reasonably legible example of his practical solution for reaching speed while writing out a thought through his own personal system of abbreviation. The MS and our printed transcript run parallel, so that LT's abbreviations and deletions can be more easily studied.]

13.VI.40.

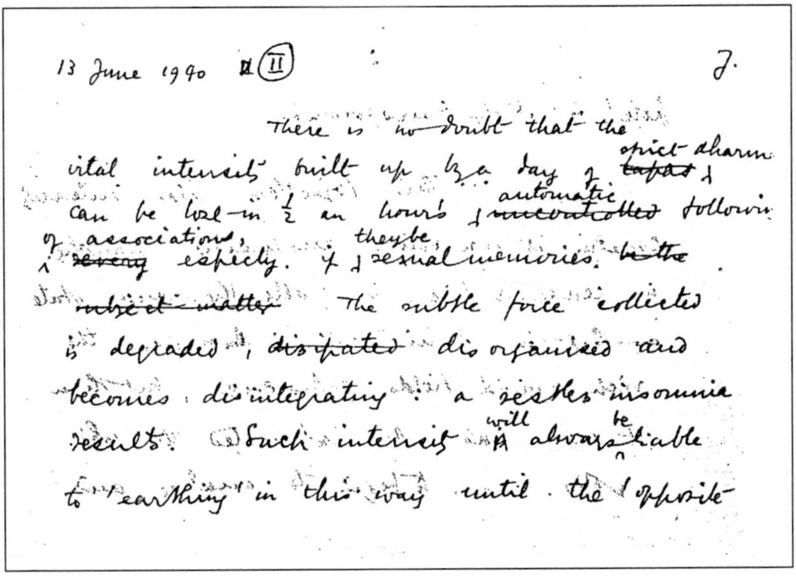
13 June 1940 II J.
There is no doubt that the
vital intensity built up by a day of strict dharma
can be lost in 1/2 an hour's automatic following
of associations, especially if they be sexual memories.
The subtle force collected
is degraded, disorganised and
becomes disintegrating: a restless insomnia
results. Such intensity will always be liable
to "earthing" in this way until the opposite

Fig. 39. Journal slip No. 1/8.

There is no doubt that the
vital intensity built up by a day of strict *dharma*
can be lost in 1/2 an hour's automatic following
of associations, especially if they be sexual memories.
The subtle force collected

is degraded, disorganised and
becomes disintegrating: a restless insomnia
results. Such intensity will always be liable
to 'earthing' in this way until the 'opposite

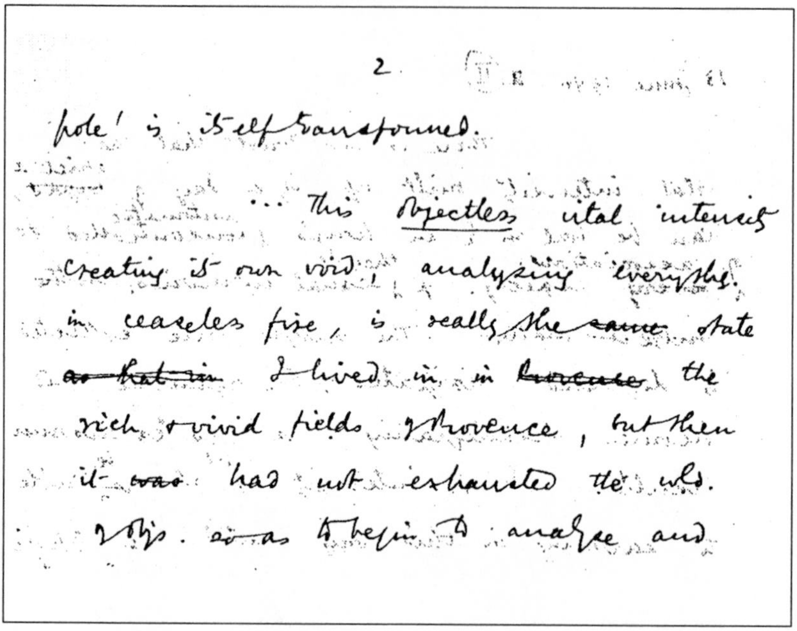

2.

pole' is itself transformed.

... This objectless vital intensity
creating its own void, analysing everything
in ceaseless fire, is really the ~~same~~ state
~~as that in~~ I lived in in ~~Provence~~ the
rich & vivid fields of Provence, but then
it ~~was~~ had not exhausted the wld.
of objs. so as to begin to analyse and

Fig. 40. Journal slip No. 2/8.

pole' is itself transformed.

...This objectless vital intensity
creating its own void, analysing everything
in ceaseless fire, is really the state
I lived in in the
rich and vivid fields of Provence *(in his early twenties),* but then
it had not exhausted the world of objects so as to begin to analyse and

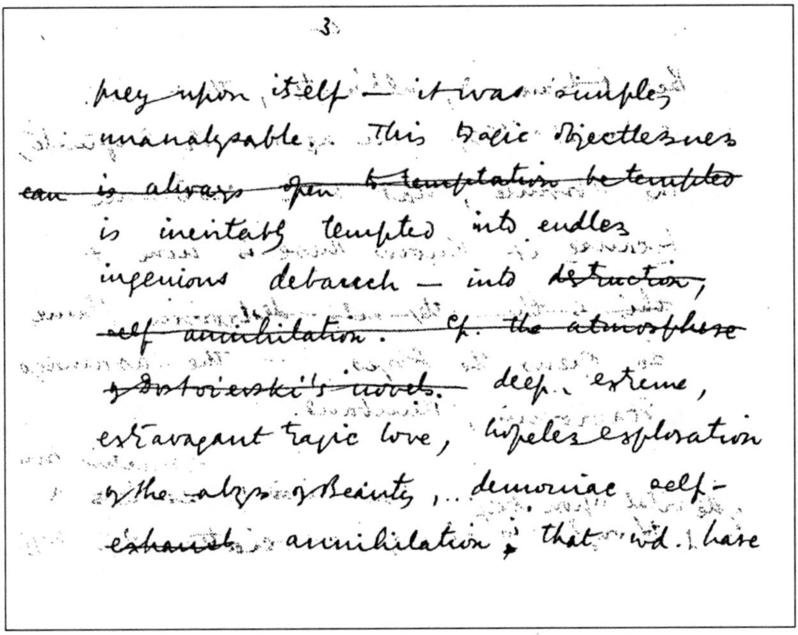
3
prey upon itself — it was simply
unanalysable. This tragic objectlessness
~~can is always open to temptation be tempted~~
is inevitably tempted into endless
ingenious debauch — into ~~destruction,~~
~~self annihilation. cf. the atmosphere~~
~~of Dostoievski's novels.~~ deep, extreme,
extravagant tragic love, hopeless exploration
of the abyss of Beauty, demoniac self-
~~exhaust~~ annihilation; that wd. have

Fig. 41. Journal slip No. 3/8.

prey upon itself—it was simply
unanalysable. This tragic objectlessness
[*LT sometimes used words like 'objectless vital intensity creating its own void' to define masturbation*]
is inevitably tempted into endless
ingenious debauch—into
deep, extreme,
extravagant tragic love, hopeless exploration
of the abyss of Beauty, demoniac self-
annihilation that would have

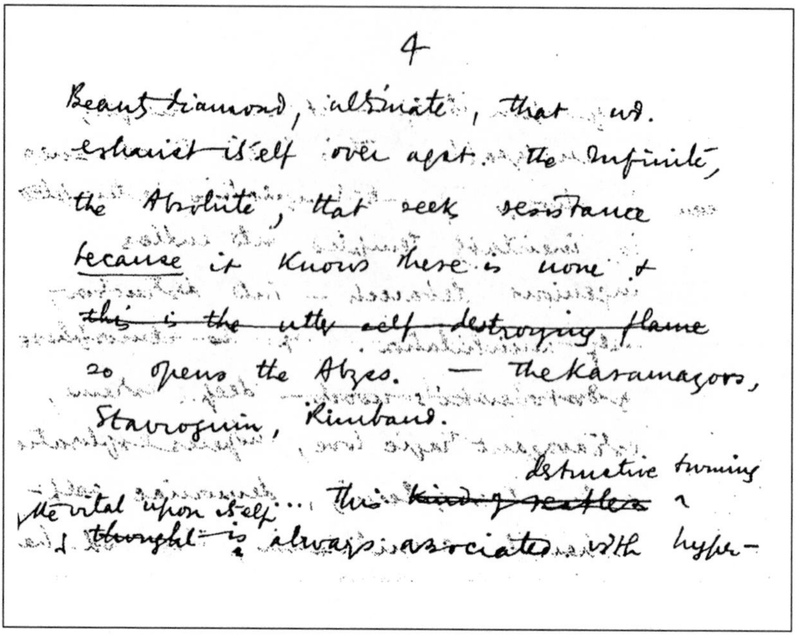
4

Beauty diamond, ultimate, that wd.
exhaust itself over agst. the Infinite,
the Absolute, that seek resistance
because it knows there is none &
~~this is the utter self destroying flame~~
so opens the Abyss. — The Karamazovs,
Stavrogin, Rimbaud.
destructive turning
the vital upon itself ... This ~~kind of restless~~
~~thought~~ is always associated with hyper-

Fig. 42. Journal slip No. 4/8.

Beauty diamond, ultimate, that would
exhaust itself over against the Infinite,
the Absolute, that seeks resistance
because it knows there is none and
so opens the Abyss. —the Karamazovs,
Stavrogin *(Dostoievski's characters)*, Rimbaud.
This destructive turning
of the vital upon itself is always associated with hyper-

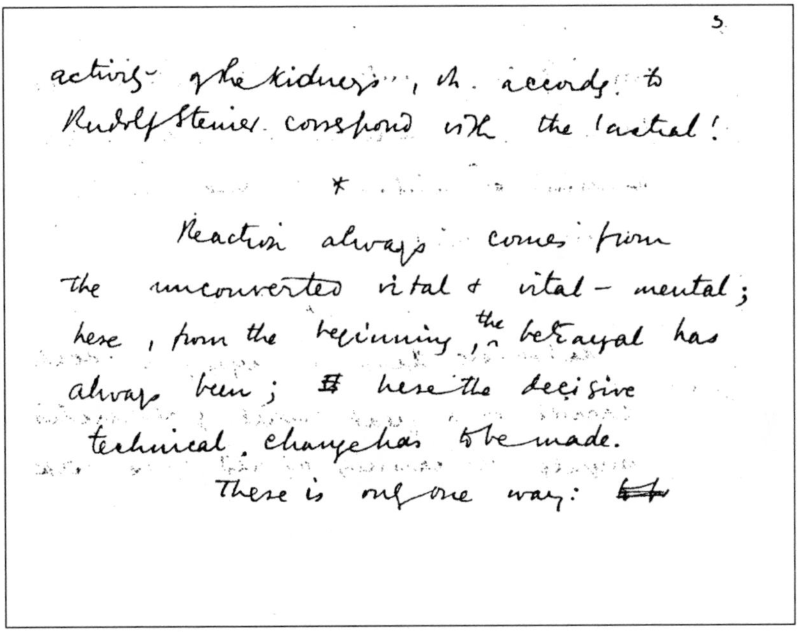

5

activity of the kidneys, wh. according to
Rudolf Steiner correspond with the 'astral'!

*

Reaction always comes from
the unconverted vital & vital-mental;
here, from the beginning, the betrayal has
always been; here the decisive
technical change has to be made.
There is only one way:

Fig. 43. Journal slip No. 5/8

-activity of the kidneys, which according to
Rudolf Steiner correspond with the 'astral'

Reaction always comes from the unconverted vital and vital-mental;
here, from the beginning, the betrayal has
always been; here the decisive
technical change has to be made.
There is only one way:

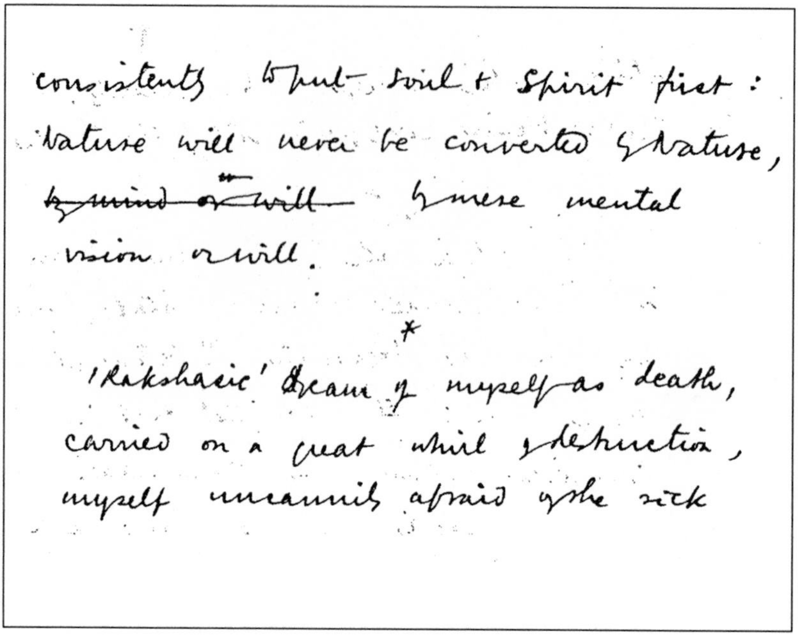

consistently to put Soul + Spirit first:
Nature will never be converted by Nature,
~~by mind or will~~ by mere mental
vision or will.

*

'Rakshasic' dream of myself as death,
carried on a great whirl of destruction,
myself uncannily afraid of the sick

Fig. 44. Journal slip No. 6/8.

consistently to put Soul and Spirit first:
Nature will never be converted by Nature,
by mere mental
vision or will.

'Rakshasic' dream of myself as death,
carried on a great whirl of destruction,
myself uncannily afraid of the sick

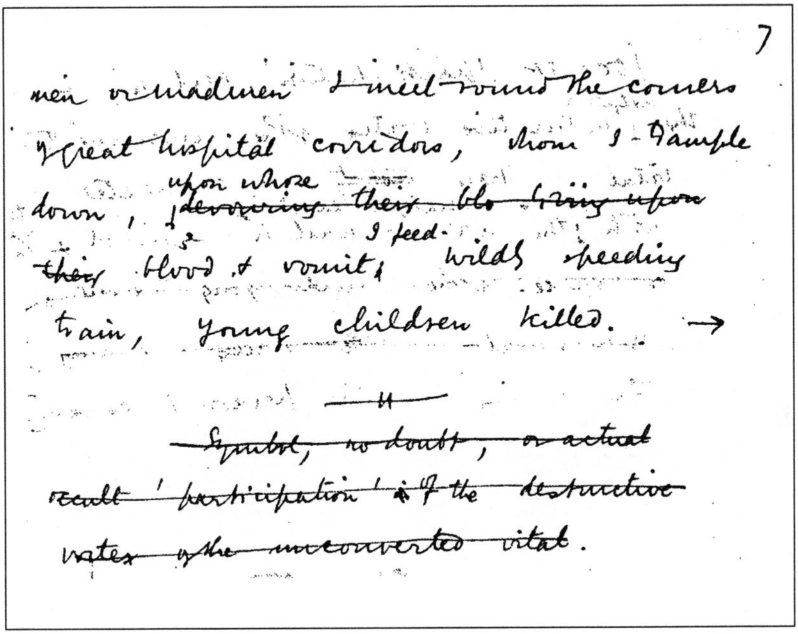
7

men or madmen ~~I~~ meet round the corners
of great hospital corridors, whom I trample
down, upon whose ~~devouring their blo bring upon~~
~~their~~ blood & vomit, I feed. wildly speeding
train, young children killed. →

— II —

~~Symbol, no doubt, or actual~~
~~result 'participation' in the destructive~~
~~water of the unconverted vital.~~

Fig. 45. Journal slip No. 7/8.

men or madmen I meet round the corners
of great hospital corridors, whom I trample
down, upon whose
blood and vomit I feed. Wildly speeding
train, young children killed.

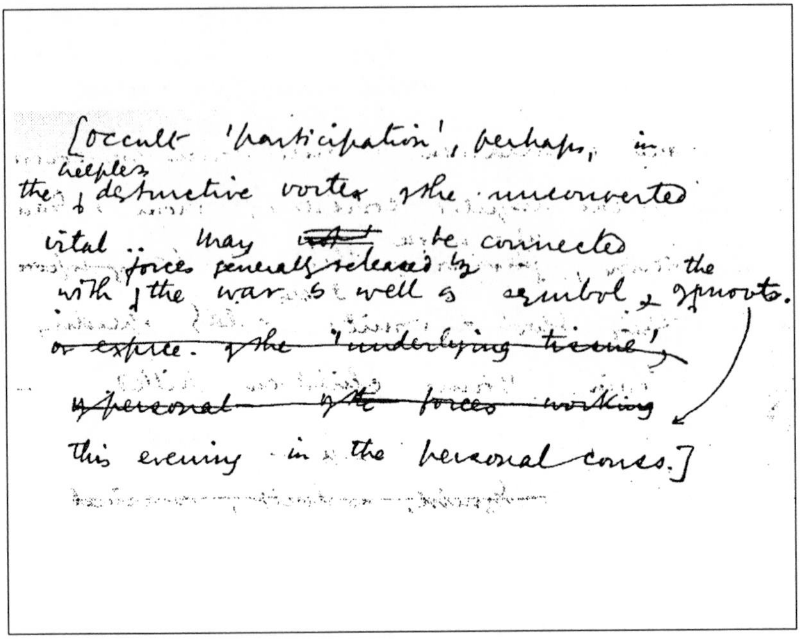

Fig. 46. Journal slip No. 8/8.

(Occult 'participation', perhaps,
in the helpless destructive vortex of the unconverted
vital. May be connected
with forces generally released by the war as well as symbol of the movements
this evening in the personal consciousness.)

16.VI.40.

I suppose the greatest twist, perversity, weakness is even to pretend that you could talk to others seriously. It is because you know you really cannot, out of desperation, perversity, extremity, failure, that you ever even imagine it and certainly it becomes weakness and brands your whole life when you mentally blame them for it.

This is not to affirm pride. I only mean, what is so obvious, that you can't talk to others on the basis of the actual vast and terrible spiritual Ignorance, 'the abyss'. And there is disgust because everything conspires to set value upon mere egoistic, unscrupulous cleverness, display; on stupid, insensitive dogmatism; on false wit and humour; on the conspiracy of evasion which in the English becomes a discipline, an art, a mode of life; on every kind of blindness, dishonesty, hypocrisy, carelessness, incapacity for Presence, for the complete responsibility which alone could free itself of responsibility, that false, helpless arrogance...

22.VI.40.

Subconscious response.

Cold, rainy and dark. I think it is like living in a Northern country. The next moment I find myself whistling a fragment of Grieg (*Peer Gynt*) that I have not remembered perhaps for years.

6.VIII.40. Ramana Maharshi Ashram.

Boys chanting Upanishads.

In their voices is expressed an almost brutal freshness, the saturated fragrance of the seed, yet sweet, tender, almost pathetic because so unconscious of its own qualities, so self-defined, helplessly experiencing the world in its own way.

Believe in the Christ; not believe Christ—give him credit for having meant what he said and did. The first is religion, the second spirituality.

6–10.VIII.40. Tiruvannamalai.

The novelist, Raja Rao, a disciple of the Jnani:

'You are in love with your demon. You are sincere but not quite honest.'

11.VIII.40. Madras.

All that can truly be said at present is that it is the mind that supposes (and thus for inner experience actually prevents) great levels between itself (and its idea of others and the world) and God. But if the immediate presentation is directly a manifestation, 'Maya' only (and precisely) an *infinitely thin* veil...

The difficulty for an Occidental consciousness of judging the psychological presumptions in its audience that oriental texts make—the precise value, weight, context, application of its emphases, the place of Hypocrisy in its affirmations. An Occidental who had realised by an Indian way might perhaps distribute all the emphasis quite differently because the relation of his realisation with his natural mental and emotional values, with his humanism, would be different. The acceptability of Krishnamurti, the attraction of Sri Aurobindo, both of whom were from their early years educated in Europe...

Perception of immediate manifestation can be constant for the embodied being only for the heart.

Perhaps it is no accident that this subtly new sense of things that I experience on my way to the station follows my taking leave of Bhagavan (Ramana Maharshi) and the sweetness of his glance and smile—the more moving because I had felt, all my stay, rather out of tune with him, cut off in my own problems.

Mind—the practical, intellect—the ideal—faculty of division, of partiality. Reality is whole and immediate only for the heart.

This is the necessary surrender, this is the only spiritual ratification of Hypocrisy in entire employment of a mind now entirely irrelevant, for all its references (purely relative) cancel each other out—are still sustained (the whole story of human thought and expression) only by those still caught in them, in the infinitely superficial by which anything is other than God Himself, container of all modes.

And if there is to be fulfilment of the world even in its own separate sense—Transformation, the kingdom of heaven on earth, this first union with the Supreme in the heart is an indispensable base. 'Separate' means 'separately' affirmed now for the sake of God, as his special manifestation.

18.VIII.40. Letter to a friend.

In poetry there must either be intellectual convention to resist and condense what is otherwise too wide, impetuous or tenuous, or else the emotion or experience must be a breath strong enough to 'blast its form upon the trumpet'. —Either an athletic wedding between intention or possibility and the exigencies of form—in which both are organised into a new kind of order (intensity desiring and creating out of its own sensuality an elaborate resistance—like the *tapas* of the Supreme Poet)—or else, in the case of a 'free' form, it must be so organic, so living a nakedness, so purely self-defining that not a comma can be changed without maiming the whole—it must be pure *mantra*. This is in fact the most highly organised form. But because modern language at least is mentally determined this absolute lyricism is not really possible in art—as Rimbaud, who so powerfully attempted it, discovered. He found in fact that Poetry in its root nature belongs to the Spirit, and to Yoga—that his problems never had been literary. If this absolute lyricism is attempted classically (within the limits of a humanistic art—as e.g. in Cocteau's *Ange Heurtebise* or in Picasso's middle and later work and perhaps in Stravinsky, it really invents new and subtle conventions.

Otherwise one has only made a sketch for a poem. And that self-indulgence itself dissipates the real poetic tension in which 'inspiration' and 'intellect' must combat and serve each other so as to produce a form which however subtle, is self-enclosed in perfect economy, irreducible like a jewel or a flower; for hard or delicate, born of water or of fire, by their unitary perfection they either are or are not.

Though I wrote verses from my tenth year I am not of course in the literary sense a poet. My deep recognition of Rimbaud confirmed the refusal to write, that my own Anguish had produced several years before, at about eighteen, and even if there were question now of anything but a kind of intellectual recreation I should therefore have no technique: my energy has gone now in other directions.

25.VIII.40.

To see everyone as the Beloved you must have found the Beloved. Meanwhile, it is only the cruel, demonic mind (Buddhism, Advaita *as philosophies*) that would override the heart's love of charm and beauty. But this abstract equality prematurely forced upon an hierarchical manifestation only blasphemes the whole meaning of creation, and by sterile spiritual pride would seek to deny one's place in it.

Yes, I am demonic so far as I recognise that one can only be a Saint (by the vision of God)—one cannot become one, such a sterilisation is a vanity of the mind, yet another of its exigent cruelties against the heart and all of God's Nature.

Suddenly, I remember Yogaswami's advice to me to enjoy Nature!

19.VIII.40. City Beach, Madras.

Meeting with a holy man—Yogaswamy.

He immediately gives jasmine and explains the essence of all is like a perfume, immediate, beyond form.

Atmasvarupa one in all forms. This is very great truth. All avatars like different manifestations of one electricity. Your internal movement is going on normally.

You are my own son.

Eat good food.

Shave.

Wear European clothes.

Well, watch for the suit when it comes!

All religions one, don't prefer.

Your mother worrying about you. (What can I do?) Write.

You come of a great family. I knew your father, a devotee, great *jiva-Karuna*. Used to dine in some hotel in London. Once he gave me food. That's why I call you my son.

I met you in Ceylon. You were fatter then.

Brahman and Shakti are one.

I will take you back to London.

You have been through great troubles. Necessary as test. I have always been with you. You broke off your studies as a boy. If you had continued you would have achieved distinction.

Don't read too much, it dissipates *shakti* (energy). Concentrate on inner realisation.

Hand—*Sat*.

Ivory snuff-box seen on it—*Chit*.

This relationship enjoyed—*Ananda*.

Gesture: 'Once we slept together'.

See all as *I*, not as mine. Then there is perfect peace and power.

22.VIII.40.

The beach episode was simple like the perfume and the flowers he offered; yet it happened in the context of my stringent mental debate about the Eros. One's life can be pure and ultimately organised only as Yoga—on the basis of complete surrender to the Divine, the will to integral realisation. This surrender is the first *movement*. Otherwise one is indeed mentally 'living beyond' oneself as Sir Denison Ross remarked to me when, at twenty-three, I was about to leave for Ceylon.

27.VIII.40.

Second meeting with Yogaswamy on the beach at Madras.

Spiritual solitude, great love. With what clairvoyant despair, knowing that it is impossible to move otherwise than towards the Mystery—with what excess of passion and tenderness does such a soul and body feel the most accidental sweetness of other souls and bodies! Of what vibrant abandon, extravagance, invention it is capable! Yet still greater is its knowledge of the uselessness of such extravagance.

For such there is rest in no human arms.

The Saint whom I greet with love. Asked to explain what is my inner state that he speaks of he refers chiefly to love and says that there are only six souls in Madras in this state. That unlike the yogi, I who need no special *sadhana*, should shave my beard for it 'draws from the blood' energies needed within.

But over the terrible paradox of words, the mental dualism, exhausting irresoluble combat—he will not meet my resistance, says that 'discussion' is useless or must be continued when we meet again in seven years time. I complain that he uses words, makes statements like 'You must marry, you will not attain *jyoti* otherwise', or 'I have been with you formlessly during these years in India; I met you in Svarupa in Ceylon and now in svarupa of svarupa'.

But he will not resist me in my effort for understanding words on their own plane—in my taking him so intensely seriously. For either I must accept his words (as I might anyone's) without understanding—superstition, abdication of the very intelligence to which words are addressed—or, if he uses words at all, he must help me understand from within.

'Make no difference between I and thou; be always You', he says.

I do not know but want to understand if I am in relation with him who he is. But if there is indeed, as I believe and he seems to agree, nothing else to be done but to go forward oneself towards realisation (by which alone one becomes that Understanding), what can such advice and predictions and ex cathedra statements do? On the one hand they make no difference, on the other they could be accepted only by oneness in understanding with the consciousness for which they are true, or by completion of the realisation he says I am seeking.

At every point in my detailed attack he answers but instead of taking up my narrowing of the equation, replaces its x by y or z!

Why if a form of manifestation—speech—is used at all should not all that can be brought to crisis there? This at least must be the endeavour of one who is serious but still not utterly free of dualities. 'Break my mind at this point' I ask: 'it will be only too ready to accept a true self-exceeding.' (The much greater satisfactoriness of the Jnani in this situation.)

The mind cannot be *surpassed* by superstition. Love is another thing; the methods to kill the mind must resist it in its own sense. If there could be only love there would for that man be only God and how should he use the mind? Well, perhaps, quite mystically and inconsistently or with arbitrary authority as does the Saint!

3.IX.40.

The whole point is that for me the spiritual problem is really the first and most pressing.

Yet in the present situation, in tension with all other problems, I can never collect the energy or even the most elementary material security in which to think and live it out continuously. My thought and experience all these years have literally been snatched, in the street, at night, in contrived and precarious solitude, in impossible material and psychological situations, from the pressing preoccupation of all other problems. For though I had been driven to the extremest simplification of my external life, in fact at last to living absolutely without personal resources, I soon saw that incidental physical, economic, emotional, esthetic, intellectual difficulties are *world*-problems. Yet one cannot take the weight of the whole world upon one's shoulders and even if one does it can only crush one into negativity. Very slowly, out of complete personal abnegation, and though I certainly have no *desire* to exist, I come to recognise that in the world I also exist and must continue, I have a place. I saw the romantic inconclusiveness and non-sequitur of suicide in my adolescence, at the beginning of my Anguish.

It can only be said that this tension, suspense, uncertainty has 'produced' nothing but negation and suffering, physically, emotionally, esthetically, mentally and intellectually.

Does it mean that no-one, in this dreadful world of human ignorance, is free to live—except in terms of greed and fear and mutual exploitation?

4.IX.40.

Only complete surrender, complete self-dedication can bring all under the spiritual, can make all yoga. And here indeed the fears of the intransigent mind are irrelevant. If there is deep sincerity—and that alone is to be completed—yoga must include all integrally necessary experience. And anyway the mental will is spiritually impotent and only sets up a sterilising tension.

12

Glimpses of Ramana Maharshi

At this period Thompson was a frequent visitor to the ashram of Bhagavan Sri Ramana Maharshi in Tirunvannamallai, a town with a large temple in the Tamil style. The ashram was situated at the foot of the most sacred hill in the region, Arunachala, where the Maharshi had lived as a hermit since renouncing the world in adolescence. He was the most respected of Indian sages in the nineteen thirties, famed throughout India. Every serious seeker at that time made a point of visiting him, to experience the ineffable peace that came to be associated with this gentle man. The Maharshi seldom spoke, but when he did his brief and cryptic replies to questions were couched in the austere terms of 'advaita vedanta'.

His fame spread far and wide, drawing the attention of the great and eminent from all corners of the globe, including Carl Jung. He wrote little, mostly in the form of questions and answers, or in aphoristic form.

Thompson was less attracted to the astringencies of 'advaita' (non-dualism) than the serene and rich quality of the Maharshi's silence. Daily he would sit with many others in the hall of the ashram, silent at the master's feet, in meditation, working over inner problems in the prevailing atmosphere of seriousness and tranquility. In a letter to Ella Maillart, Thompson wrote that 'I have never identified myself inwardly with 'advaita-shastra' (the texts of the vedanta school), though it is complete, flawless and inevitable on its own (intuitive) plane, and that a perfectly real one—indeed, no doubt the highest available to man 'as man'.' Thompson hardly wrote anything at all in reference to the Maharshi, save for his account of a remarkable visionary dream in 1943 (included here at the appropriate date). In the following the Maharshi replies to his, and other's, questions.

19.III.39.

L.T.: What does Krishna mean in the Gita when he says 'I am the foundation of the Brahman?

S.R.M.: Find out who is that I.

L.T.: Regarding the Immanent, Cosmic and Transcendent Divine, what is meant by 'seated in the heart of all beings; Brahman, Visvarupam I remain'?

S.R.M.: On the basis of thinking yourself an individual different from the Brahman you think the Brahman different from the Purushottama.

L.T.: What then is meant by 'When one has become one with the Brahman...the one supreme bhakti (devotion) towards Me'?—Is there any difference between the devotion one may have before realisation and that possible afterwards?

S.R.M.: Abhyasa-bhakti is not real bhakti. In the verse of the *Gita* describing four kinds of bhaktas the jnani is said to be the true, the greatest bhakta. (Later S.R.M. adds) He is Myself. Bhakti is the very nature of the realised man.

L.T.: Is any further progress possible?

S.R.M.: No. There is no duality; he is one with the Divine. (After a long absorbed silence) That is effortless bhakti. Nityayukto.

26.I.40.

L.T.: Bhagavan speaking to others must do so from the point of view of *ajñana* (relative knowledge), otherwise there is no occasion for speech. Is it perhaps like a man awake speaking to others who are dreaming but hear him in their dream?

S.R.M.: Is the questioner jñani or ajñani? (After about five minutes' silence) If you dream that you speak with Bhagavan, when you wake up do you ask him if he spoke?

7.X.40.

Harindranath Chattopadhyaya tells me that Ramana Maharshi, asked to explain how the world appeared to him, said that the darker the cinema the more real the pictures seem but that in bright sunlight though they are still there they become transparent.

24.X.40.

Ramana Maharshi, just before sleep, to others:

To find an object in a dark room you need a light but if a man seated in a dark room is asked who is there no light is needed for him to answer 'I'.

2.XI.40.

The whole room is prayer. Every movement, aspect and event entirely prayer as the figures of a dream are entirely within the consciousness of the dreamer, formed and saturated of his mood.

2.XII.40.

The winter days here are very beautiful—like a quiet English summer but much brighter. The sacred mountain is still, luminous, ethereal under the blue sky yet always curiously self-concentrated.

24.II.41. Festival of Shivratri.

People make pradakshina (circumambulation) of the Hill. A friend and I decide to go a little way, silently, the body walking of itself. When we turn back, 'against the current', it is like wading against a river or stroking a magnet with a piece of iron. We both remark on it and stand still for a while. A furlong or two further on the effect diminishes but we still feel the weight of our body as if on a hot day.

24.III.40.

Complete 'verticality':

Chadwick tells me that once when Maharshi was alone he asked 'Is this manifestation an individual or a cosmic dream? Maharshi replied in Chadwick's own words that it is an individual dream and added after a few minutes that the 'Cosmic' is introduced only because people cannot understand this.

Maurice Friedmann once asked Maharshi if he would see the same factory at Bangalore as Friedmann sees. Maharshi asked: 'Do two men dream the same dream?'

25.IX.41.

Ramana Maharshi replying to a questioner (Dr. Mees.):

'Mayavada and Shaktivada the same: Shaktivada only consciousness and Mayavada a projection of consciousness. The term Mayavadin (a descriptive term applied to Maharshi by the questioner) cannot apply to us: Maya* is not posited by us but by you. If the negator of Maya is to be called a Mayavadin, then those who deny God should be called theists!

**'Maya' here means the whole phenomenal universe, and according to advaita vedanta it is illusory—the most vexed question in Indian thought, with different shades of meaning in the various schools.*

Desires born from memory are endless and really represent my own Eternity, that the whole world is within me.

[The following dialogue between Lewis Thompson and Sri Ramana Maharshi appeared in 'My Life and Quest' by Arthur Osborne (Sri Ramanasramam, 2001), a book of some 600 pages recently unearthed.]

L.T.: Srimad Bhagavad Gita says: 'I am the prop of Brahman.' In another place, it says: 'I am in the heart of each one.' Thus the different aspects of the Ultimate Principle are revealed. I take it that there are three aspects, namely (1) the transcendental (2) the immanent and (3) the cosmic. Is Realisation to be in any one of these or in all of them? Coming to the transcendental from the cosmic, the Vedanta discards the names and forms as being *maya*. But I cannot readily appreciate it because a tree means the trunk, branches, leaves, etc. I cannot dismiss the leaves as *maya*. Again the Vedanta also says that the whole is Brahman as illustrated by gold and ornaments of gold. How are we to understand the truth?

Sri. R.M.: The Gita says: *Brahmano hi pratishtaham*. If that 'aham' is known, the whole is known.

L.T.: It is the immanent aspect only.

Sri. R.M.: You now think that you are an individual, there is the universe and that God is beyond the cosmos. So there is the idea of separateness. This idea must go. For God is not separate from you or the cosmos. The Gita also says:

> The Self am I, O Lord of Sleep,
> In every creature's heart enshrined.
> The rise and noon of every form,
> I am its final doom as well. *B.G.X.20.*

Thus God is not only in the heart of all, He is the prop of all, His is the source of all, their abiding place and their end. All proceed from Him, have their stay in Him, and finally resolve into Him. Therefore he is not separate.

L.T.: How are we to understand this passage in the Gita:

'This whole cosmos forms a particle of Me.'

Sri. R.M.: It does not mean that a small particle of God separates from Him and forms the Universe. His *Sakti* is acting; as a result of one phase of such activity the cosmos has become manifest. Similarly, the statement in *Purusha Sukta*, 'All the beings form His one foot (*Padosya viswa bhutani*) does not mean that Brahman is in four parts.

L.T.: I understand it. Brahman is certainly not divisible.

Sri. R.M.: So the fact is that Brahman is all and remains indivisible. He is ever realised. The man does not however know it. He must know it. Knowledge means the overcoming of obstacles which obstruct the revelation of the Eternal Truth that the Self is the same as Brahma. The obstacles form altogether your idea of separateness as an individual. Therefore the present attempt will result in the truth being revealed that the Self is not separate from Brahman.

13

Like Orpheus—A Charmer

At the ashram of Ramana Maharshi in 1941 Thompson met and became close friends with the distinguished travel writer, Ella Maillart. Of strongly contrasting temperament, they formed a bond of enduring mutual interest in Ramana Maharshi and, subsequently, after Thompson introduced her to him, in the Jnani, Sri Krishna Menon. Ella had been given a 'mantra' by a Tantrika, Vishwanatha. When she told Thompson, he was disturbed enough at what he considered an unwise course in this particular instance to seek the Jnani's advice on her behalf. The Jnani at once suggested that she drop it and request Vishwanatha to 'take back the 'mantra'. Thompson, though six years her junior, was more experienced in such matters, so she trusted him and took the Jnani's advice. Eventually she met the latter at Malakkarai and became a devoted pupil until his death twenty years later.

Ella Maillart, of Swiss-Danish stock, an athletic, outgoing and versatile woman, was encouraged when quite young by her writer friend, Alain Gerbault, to take up yachting, represented Switzerland at the Paris Olympics and was for four years a member of the Swiss national ski team. Her first venture abroad in the nineteen thirties as a writer was to live for a time in Moscow. On the proceeds of the book which she wrote on her experiences there she subsequently went to stay with Kirghiz tribesmen in Turkestan. In 1934, after a visit to Manchuria, where she met Peter Fleming, then a correspondent with the 'Times', they both set off from Peking together on an epic journey westwards. They travelled under great hardship through outer Mongolia, Tibet, Sinkiang, and through the Pamirs to Kashmir, and from this celebrated journey came the book that made her name, 'Forbidden Journey' (reprinted, London, 1983). Later, she travelled through Afghanistan with a woman friend and when she met Thompson was writing an account of this anguished journey in 'The Cruel Way'. She consulted him on its writing and he devoted much care to its editing. Characteristically, he profoundly disagreed with her attitude towards her companion, a deeply disturbed woman drug addict whom she felt called upon to offer help; Thompson felt that the exact contrary would have been more appropriate and that Ella had much to learn from 'her'!

Soon after meeting Thompson she concluded an account of her life in her book, 'Cruises and Caravans', with the following paragraph:

> 'Here in India I have started on a new journey which, I know will take me further than before towards the perfect life I was instinctively seeking. I began this journey by exploring the unmapped territory of my own mind; and now, in the light of what living sages teach today, it takes me forward to a Reality so wonderful that to love and obey it is the greatest adventure and the greatest happiness there is.'

[Ella reintroduced into the imaginative current of Lewis's life that vital component for which he had so long craved—even in his beloved India—a certain European luminosity of spirit, a rare flavour of mountain spirituality as cultivated by poets, 'savants' and travellers—one of the West's least recognised veins of lyricism.

After Lewis's death, Deben Bhattacharya and Ella took possession of all his papers and I brought them to Europe in 1954 for Ella's safekeeping. There they remained for some years in her mountain chalet, a haven of tranquility in the Valais high above Rilke's Chateau Muzot at Chandolin.

Ella Maillart included a photograph of Thompson in 'Ti-Puss' (1951), a book about her life in India during the war and which she dedicated to him. 'Without doubt one of the most remarkable men I have ever known', she describes him, 'and like Orpheus—a charmer'.

The following letters were written in the early days of their friendship. Occasionally described with humorous drawings, they reveal a blend of warmth, passionate seriousness and playfulness. Printed here as a group, this start to their correspondence continues later between journal entries at the appropriate date. As with other close friends, Thompson's letters became increasingly critical, but in spite of this he repeatedly affirmed what is at all times very clear—that he remained deeply affectionate and loyal to a woman who is greatly respected.]

29.V.41.

My dear,

It's surely no good going anywhere for seven years: the pilgrimage is in experience. Shakespeare!: 'Ripeness is all' and you ripen on your own tree, on the roots of the deepest and most precise (and in the artist's sense most difficult) Truthfulness. —For which all else is only rain and sun and breeze, not at all to be *believed* in, but through which one spreads and laughs.

If you cheat yourself you will suffer, that is all. And by suffering you recover in compassion the Edenic purity of heart. Adam, the Androgyne, is this purity unconscious, self-bound in its own perfection; then comes Eve, dualism; finally the Bodhisattva, again Androgyne—see T'ang and Sung bronzes for instance—is the same purity conscious and radiating, having subsumed into itself all possible experience. This, a poet may say, is what is meant by the Bodhisattva's not 'entering Nirvana' till all beings are liberated. This experience takes up the whole relative mode of time, the whole 'future'. The Bodhisattva is the sun become entire radiance: once more Presence (Nirvana) is veiled by its own effulgence—a new power and sweetness and delight is born. Ah, Infinity of wonder!

Of course 'I want to be happy' is the denial of happiness, which is a pure presence: it expresses, and in expressing seals, an irremediable poverty, perversity or ill-will. And happiness is anyway indifferent, something neutral, the least one can have. It is out of Joy that all came, in Joy continues and in Joy returns. The radiation of this Joy is Love and Love is Joy self-reduplicated as Delight—the Eternal Play of Krishna and the Gopis. The Gopis' least-possible transparent happiness, their natural aristocracy, is the state of *advaita* (the non-dual).

All talk about *advaita*, my kind of postulation of it, according to any mode of consciousness, is obviously a denial of it. Except as Hypocrisy it is simply a vulgarity, gross lack of taste. Vedanta is not for the menial, the man who cannot even be happy. For him, the consolation of religion. If you question Vedanta the answer is 'It has evidently nothing to do with you'. People who can't enjoy poetry ask why it should be rhymed. The purification of the mind is the self-exhaustion of all postulation: one must become Poetry. But the very possibility of this does not arise if there is not elementary Geniality. The disciples of the Buddha in the *sutras* are called 'noble', 'of good birth', 'well-favoured'—in other words they are not in debt to their life.

And here again, whoever has not Geniality cannot appreciate real Anguish. Many bhaktis say that absence from the Beloved is the most intense, and therefore the most valuable, of all spiritual states. Yes, it is absence from the Beloved, the utmost tension, the keenest, sublimest music.

Europeans so often import their barbarian post-Reformation poverty into interpretation of the simplest Indian text. They forget, because they have never known or cannot see, Ajanta, Kalidasa, Vatsyayana, the rich soil out of which the spiritual lotus springs. Besides, per contra, there is a beauty of austerity and many talk of Bach who like the cinema-organ.

My fatigue evidently represents some maladjustment and to that extent untruthfulness: I must consent at last to be myself. We shall see...

Spiritually—first and last—as I have said before, there are only individuals. The 'mass', the 'world', 'humanity' is the illusory product of every *one's* evasion. Love is of one's neighbour, it is the complete opposite of the unsatisfying abstraction in which the modern world more and more lives (or dies).

'Si chacun...Mais ce n'est pas possible'. There's the fundamental evasion and won't-playism. People don't really mean 'réalité'. 'Seek ye first the kingdom of heaven and all else will be added to you.' As the Veda says, all comes from *the Surplus*. 'Solomon in all his glory...' It's useless to repeat these things. It's like talking to a man who is not in love about the wonderful beauty of a woman. If you are in love you see, if not—well, all your arguments are irrelevant.

This Western illusion of 'action'. Have they no humour? —Where has it lead in all these centuries? They get us into an insane mess and talk (once more!) of 'aide à donner'!

Always someone *else*. But individuality is an immediate fact, the immediate paradox. In all its philosophy and psychology modern 'thought' is false to the first fact of consciousness, of 'subjectivity'.

All compromise is built on and ratifies evasion. If you compromise between eating and not eating, loving and not loving, or in any other simple matter, what are you?

One is born and dies alone and alone must break the circle of birth and death. Nothing has reality except so far as it represents the One. The 'prince of this world' rules the kingdom of evasion from this fact. Besides, no-one who has not completed for himself the primary fact of the tragic solitude of individuality can love, but only needs love.

*Monod's is the 'horizontal', 'worldly', view out of which there is no issue. Everything, and man first of all, is determined 'vertically', spiritually.

* A French philosopher

Since the Middle Ages this has been put aside in Europe, That is the sickness. No-one any more understands Jacob's ladder or even Jack and the Beanstalk. Compare Gothic cathedrals and modern buildings, all *flat* but not honest cubes. Men fight now on their bellies or crawl in a tank and fly only to bomb the earth to keep the others down. Back to the slime!

—And so on: ti tumpty-tumpty-tum.

Your *charming* Lewis.

12.VII.41. Tivandrum.

Dear Ella,

The other evening, speaking to others while I was present, the Jnani gave the following interpretation of one of his verses:

> At first conceding to others and considering what they think and feel though not because one needs or desires to, one loses one's own centre. This centre restored by the Guru, I still live for others but now with joy, for the ego that before was dissatisfied has now vanished.

Much else that he has said recently in my presence—especially to the effect that 'nothing exists but Poetry'—seems to correspond closely with my thought and experience.

Last evening I had an opportunity of mentioning you to him and spoke of you at some length. I added that you had some thought of perhaps visiting him some day, but that at present you are busy on a book which you are trying to do as karma-yoga!

I hope it goes well,

Affectionately,
Lewis.

13.VII.41.

I wish I could remember exactly the Jnani's praise of such tears as yours.

Of course you were always right about me but as I must have said some time or other one cannot give *oneself* sanction: this is the disinterestedness of the Heart. My tension was with an individuality that both head and Heart had reduced to paradox. I was all the time on thorns.

I had remarked before to the Jnani that it is one's very disinterestedness that cannot give oneself sanction, cannot allow one's natural right and abandons one to the endless ingenuity—and apparent perversity—of Imagination in which one absorbs and exhausts all the subtle possibilities of the phenomenal world—all that in its limitedness is irrelevant to one's Actuality. One can always do anything for others (even achieving realisation!) but to do anything for and as oneself is impossibly dry. The law throughout is Love—this is the heart of the *guru-shishya* question. For Love sustains the pure Eternal Play of everything.

A feeble expression would be: I am allowed to acknowledge now that I have never really cared for anything and at the same time have always known that everything is pure Delight.

There have been no 'moments' in one's phenomenal nature: only there is a profound re-adjustment with the Peace that was already there—as Yogaswami also told me. The re-adjustment takes place at a depth far beyond one's mental, psychic and physical nature. Everything remains the same but now the Sun is acknowledged. *As Ramana Maharshi has said, the Heart corresponds with the Sun, the mind—reflected knowledge—with the moon.* It is extremely simple, subtle and concrete. And of course a certain joy and light and calm begin to flow into one's individuality: in other words they are no longer questioned or obstructed.

No, the [*indecipherable*] is perverse. The positive thing that he deflects is a certain quality of power and intensity which are free and harmonious only in direct relation with the Source, the Absolute.

The Jnani especially arranged for a photograph to be taken of me and says that it *[reproduced on cover]* shows something of what he wanted expressed—that something from the far Background looks out through the eyes. The rest of the face, he says, expresses a certain abandon or recklessness.

It also certainly shows how great a work of integration remains to be done but he says I shall achieve it. He says that in my natural 'method' I am jnani, bhakta and yogi. And that neither of us can break the relationship between us.

You must come one day and visit
this sweet and wonderful man.
With my love, dear Ella,
Lewis.

22.VIII.41.

Dear Ella:

You must come to Travancore [*Kerala*] one day. Rich vegetation, altogether very much like central Ceylon—coconut, areca, plantain, brilliant paddy-fields contrasting with red and pale cinnamon roads and earthen walls. Temples and little old houses (not all, alas) like caskets of carved wood. Teashops of many levels and corners divided by cretonne-covered screens. After the arid and graceless Tamil country the people look handsome and blooming, sleek from their twice-weekly bath of coconut oil. Throngs of girls with jasmine in their hair going to school. Travancore is proud of its literacy. The bus-conductors are mostly young graduates and address you in charming English. A few steps from this house a pond full of magnificent red water-lillies.

In a subtle conversation with the Jnani we went rather deep and I had to acknowledge that I do know something of my own myth or legend, as it has sometimes flashed upon me. I have sometimes thought that the secret spiritual life of every being—the mode and trend of it that express his innermost nature and destiny, his unique relation with the Supreme—might be expressed for his or others' phenomenal nature in a myth. Only in terms of this myth could his least true action be properly understood.

The whole secret of the 'Guru', for me at least, is that relation with him is utterly one of profound and joyous *love*. He sets one free to become oneself because he completely satisfies and ratifies one's *disinterestedness*, the sense of *líla* (divine play). He can make it possible, in fact delightful, to do what one would never do for and as oneself because he completely justified one's inability to do anything or to accept or obey anyone for the purpose of 'Realisation' or anything else. There is the inability by which before all self-conscious seekers one was bound to say one is not a seeker, the disinterestedness that must protest at all division of the world into sacred and profane. As if anything could be either sacred or profane for God, for Reality. The 'Guru' confirms what one knows, that realisation—or anything else spiritual—cannot be in however subtle way a *need*. He meets and affirms the Child's Innocence and freedom from preoccupation. If *method* is not *líla* it is merely a delusion of the ego, another of its little self-shut stupid meannesses.

12.IX.41.

Dear Ella,

I have little doubt that what from the point of view of the European will-to-action appears to you indifference but which is experienced as a quiet autonomous joy is simply the sensation of your fundamental disinterestedness, a purely spiritual quality which therefore cannot be measured phenomenally. To one's outer consciousness it can only appear negative. It is this disinterestedness that first and last recognises *líla*. I remember my truancies from the office where I was supposed to work—Kensington Gardens in the pale Spring sunlight, the universal preoccupation like a play of marionettes. Yet one had no conscious knowledge to justify this direct perception. And later workmen building outside my window both in Gower Street and Westminster threw my anguish into soundless, exquisite relief. On his last visit, for afterwards he was in terror at this obstinate, bright devouring vacuum, the only friend who remained asked: 'But what do you do all day?' I could not reply nor turn away.

I think the 'herb' [*marijuana*] has nothing to do with the causeless joy you feel and I can say quite definitely, now that the Jnani has explained them to me, that the experiences it may seem to have supported in me were purely spiritual and as I have always known were not at all *due* to the plant. Of course this is true of all drugs. Even when they are submitted to their effects as functions of one's consciousness and the kind of resistance to the effect that was automatic in me, no doubt simply enhances that consciousness, though perhaps in an unfamiliar direction.

Sri Krishna in the Gita speaks of himself at several different 'levels': the Self is certainly, in the sense of phenomenal action, actionless. Though one might as well say that It alone has pure, absolute, Action. As Krishnamurti has said, the realised man acts but never reacts: all conditioned action—what we ordinarily call action—is really nothing but reaction, and this is why it really changes nothing. Whereas in the Absolute there is nothing to change— 'action' also is Absolute, *Líla*.

I read parts of your letter last evening to the Jnani. He said: 'I have some interest in her'. As I know from certain things he has said about the 'interest' of a realised man, this means a great deal.

The other day a disciple was admiring with tears the marvellous love and generosity of the Jnani. But since his help is chiefly needed precisely where the recipient is least conscious, and because of his delicate reticence, it may never be known.

'I feel so vacant, when shall I be inhabited?' A few days ago a *sàdhaka* wrote to the Jnani complaining of loneliness. In his reply he said that this loneliness, 'the pain of separation', is a Divine Grace.

Your English seems to be improving.

L.

7.IX.41.

I find that I am generally taken too literally. But I am, it really seems, essentially imaginative, and believe that all experience is really.....

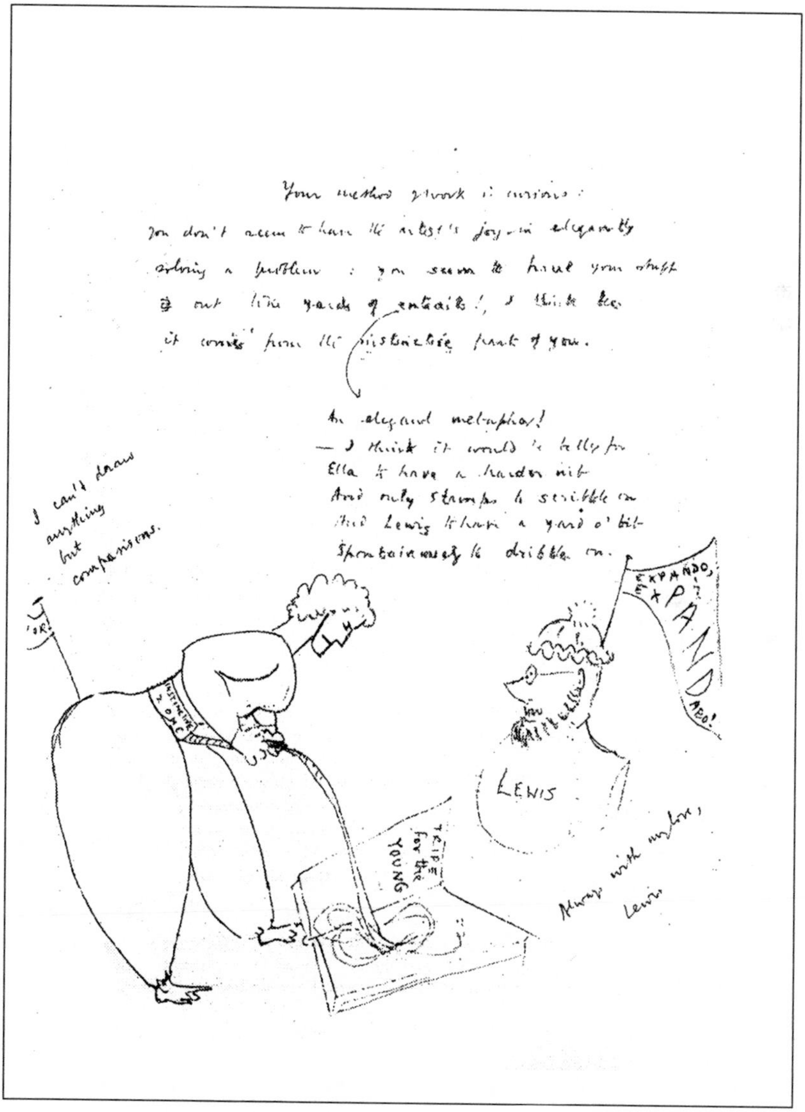

Fig. 46. Cartoon revealing Lewis' playful nature with Ella.

12.X.40.

A young friend of mine told me the other day how while he was resting outside a cave on a hillock near Sri Villiputtur a very old woman appeared and beckoned him. Her cheeks were so hollow you could have hidden your thumb in them. Somehow he felt very afraid and tried to call his companion who had gone away down the hillside to gather lemon-grass, but he could not open his mouth. Once inside the cave she turned and kissed him. He was frozen with a sort of horror.

'Wretch!', she cried, 'do you not remember me? Now I am bent and old you forget my lovely limbs, my scented hair.' He could neither speak nor understand. But by a sudden change of mood she threw herself at his feet— 'Forgive me, forgive me!'

From beside a fire burning at the far end of the inner cave she brought a broken skull. She held it out toward him and the water in it held an image of two lovers in a swing. Then there unrolled the vision of a young Chola nobleman who fell in love with a very beautiful girl with whose family, however, his own had a deadly feud. The young man was betrayed and murdered by the girl's parents. The girl ran away to this cave and became a yogini. By the powers she acquired she was able to hold off her death till her beloved should be reborn. But now, since he could not love her in her aged form, she would sacrifice her 'immortality' and be reborn herself as a beautiful but poverty-stricken girl. Finally she gave him a *tali* and...somehow he found himself outside the cave with it still in his hand. He could never afterwards penetrate to the 'door'.

When he told his father this story he in his turn said that once when he was resting by this cave—he was an official in the district—a hand appeared and gave him a small round object which had since been kept in the family puja-box—where the *tali* now joined it. Members of the family kept it for a few weeks but finally, after my young friend had met the guru who initiated him into the Tantra, it mysteriously disappeared.

My friend was so impressed by his experience that he had refused to marry, but the guru told him to disregard his vow and he did later marry a girl chosen in the ordinary course by the family.

6.XI.40.

The *cerebrality* of Southern India. For instance, entirely abstract, trans-esthetic furnishing of rooms: though they are not *furnished*, but objects abandoned by a consciousness entirely self-centered, they remain purely symbolic. This hardness, this spiritual virility, favours the purest, most dense and conscious classical art.

15.I.40.

Doubt, qualification, is all of the mind and unpoetical. And the mind tends to neglect what is open to possible doubt, however clear and vivid it may have been in its own way.

For example, S.B. last evening sitting opposite the handsome Rajput youth, S. After looking at him for a little, under the pretext of brushing back a loose hair, she quickly, surreptitiously kissed the 'marriage-bangle' at her wrist. This was very precise but so rapid and delicate that one could easily think one had imagined it and the whole connection, though it expressed so well at the same time her generous vital nature and her sweet and simple faithfulness to her husband. One element of the pattern may even precisely have been that she had felt my perception of her sensitiveness to S's rather voluptuous good looks.

26.I.41.

A Sufi friend tells me that Réné Guénon is a Master though he has not the function of taking disciples. He has not himself therefore any present Master and this, S.A.H. takes it, is what is meant by his declaration that 'personne n'est qualifié pour nous adressées un "rappel à l'ordre", notre independance étant absolu.'

S.A.H. shows me photographs of Guénon—very delicate and distinguished, the embodied subtelty of a royal type. Raja Rao who met him said he was like a Bengali aristocrat.

One sees that his astringency, almost acerbity, come precisely from his delicacy, from a very sensitive and upright mind. Deep-set, softly luminous eyes. Suggestion of specially gentle and subtle humour. Quick, resourceful, dialectical mouth, lips slightly pointed like a faun's. Electrically bristling moustache, soft hair. Sensitive, supple hands. Frail, rather narrow shoulders. Sometimes looks very French, sometime quite Oriental, in either case giving the impression of having been formed by centuries of experience.

The face, in its shape and planes and several elements, suggests a highly-organised complexity releasing rare, even exalted, faculties of perception.

The effect is of a very highly organised and delicate instrument—an organisation entirely sensitive to *Possibilities*—of a rare and perfect flower, king-lily with a subtle and exotic perfume. Musa Sahib says that he has reminded several of St. Bernard.

Effect of great purity as if a very exalted light were shining upon the face. Curious youthfulness.

19.IV.41.

Conversation with a Sufi.

The primordiality, Edenic innocence of Hinduism. The childlike simplicity of the Jnani's handwriting. The sense of inferiority of the average Hindu before Occidental sophistication. Hence, often, his desire for 'Western' education and his absurd vanity—and incompetence—when he has it. Even the rich Gupta period, no doubt, was not sophisticated in this peculiarly Western sense. The positive quality of European sophistication is fulfilled in Islam. Christianity of course denies this sophistication and this is one of the reasons for the failure of Christianity to integrate the Western psyche. From the Christian point of view the sophisticated man necessarily remains worldly.

It belongs to the 'polar' nature of Hinduism representing the primordial Tradition that the Hindu finds it practically impossible to take up another's position. This rigidity is in fact expressed in the caste system. For example, the incapacity of an Advaitin to understand a Dvaitin positively; from the individual point of view this is evidently something negative.

—Whereas in Islam good manners, in the sense of meeting everyone on his own ground, is of prime importance.

Islam is really not comprehensible from the outside: the only way to understand it is to become a Mussulman. Like a cube, like the Kaaba, it represents the 'squaring of the circle', full expansion on the earth in the last days, and presents everywhere outwardly an impenetrable face. This corresponds, I suggest, with the 'masculinity' of Islam: other traditions are comparatively feminine in that they are accessible without complete self-identification. I connect this with pederasty as an Isalmic mode. My Sufi friend says that among many Persian Sufis the pederastic mode has in fact been much developed as a means of spiritual experience and expression. Unless there were corresponding—at least 'vital'—external facts this would evidently be no true symbolism but only a vain mental game. Embarrassed Western translators, who can as a rule only see the negative side of pederasty, write 'she' for 'he' in such poems!

24.V.41. Letter to Ella Maillart:

Vedanta undoubtedly represents an important mode of 'the truth'. Is it possible that like so many Europeans F. thinks there is such a thing as Indian philosophy? whereas philosophy, of course, is entirely a modern European invention beginning only, say, with Socrates—the ugliest and most virtuous of the Greeks who had to get his own back somehow. —I mean, of course, that 'advaita' is, or claims to be, nothing without the corresponding means of realisation. If one is concerned with realisation one need not talk against talkers or degrade the 'darshana' to the level of their idleness. It's only too obvious that most contemporary Hindus are in the last stages of deliquescence, but how can that interest one?

Modern India: The struggle is between the direct human truthfulness, real by its truthfulness whatever its unconscious limits, of for example Villon, Pascal, Beethoven, Baudelaire, Kierkegaard, Rilke and the claim here to superhuman knowledge combined with complete lack of civilisation (language, to begin with, is completely degraded), completely coarse and monstrous sub-humanity—abysses of stupidity, fecklessness, laziness, complacency, and the appallingly cynical Brahmin insolence, insensitiveness and pride.

...But is not everyone who is still unpretentiously human torn between will and sensibility, Intuition and thought, Spirit and Daimon, pure Imagination and desire?

I'm not much worse here than anywhere else, though the damp air stimulates my phthisic tendency. The centre of the trouble is in one's vital and emotional nature: one gets into an extraordinarily subtle 'vibratory' state in which one's energy simply exhausts itself like a self-devouring light or foam. This also produces a rarefied amorousness in which one is exquisitely conscious of a kind of quick of sweetness, of darlingness, in everyone of which, however, everyone is stupidly unconscious—whole worlds of indescribable subtle vital specificity deepen and scintillate about every person, even every object. It is astonishing what a weight of 'sukshma' potentiality eyes, lips, hands, gesture, costume, a street corner can bear. But if you act in terms of it—you are at once forced to remember that everyone is asleep in the physical world—like angels chloroformed, following physical and rational connections like somnambulists. And besides, to act in this way would divide one, for one's highest being is far beyond the mind, let alone the vital. The whole modification of energy no doubt represents a transitional failure of unity with the 'highest planes'. Of course, the 'higher' you go the more this unity depends upon true vision of God and worship of Him: otherwise, to move out of the physical is perilous. Most people, it must be said, have only the automatic mechanical 'unity' of their bondage to the physical.

14

A Visit to the Jnani: 1941

Between 1939 and 1941 Thompson goes through a period of subtle change. The turning point seems to be the moment when he takes leave of Sri Ramana Maharshi and sets out on a long visit to the Jnani, Krishna Menon, in Trivandrum. The day-by-day account of their meetings is set out in some detail and with the exception of several technical discussions, is included here in its entirety.

Considering the formal restraints imposed by such a relationship between a seeker and a spiritual master, it is a remarkably intimate picture that is built up in a few pages of the nature and subtlety of exchange between the two men. Everything that happens during this visit is charged with importance for Thompson, and it becomes apparent from the course of events in the following two years, that it is the most important relationship of his life. For a man widely recognised as 'realised', the Jnani is unusually close to Thompson at this time, and the account of their long private talks conveys something of the distinctive flavour of what this particular master had to offer which nobody else at that time—not the Maharishi, not Sri Aurobindo, nor Krishnamurti—to name the more important masters Thompson had already encountered in person—could give him. There are innumerable 'schools' and 'styles' within the Hindu tradition, each with its partial resemblance to other spiritual paths, other traditions in the world at large. The special character of the path provided by the Jnani has something to do with his emphasis on the Heart, and there are clear indications in Thompson's account of an 'advaita' style through which runs a powerful, but paradoxical undercurrent of rapturous mystical devotion (bhakti) and with it, of course, elements of 'advaita'.

Perhaps the most important feature of this dialogue is the emphasis which the Jnani places on 'outward expansion' in the world rather than on the more conventional way of the simple 'jnani', what he calls the Return to the Background and its connotations of total renunciation, contemplation and quietism. This, perhaps, suited the 'divine recklessness' which the Jnani recognised as an important feature in Thompson's make-up. In fact, one senses here a response of the Jnani to the specifically occidental characteristics which are so pronounced in Thompson. Ever since Ramakrishna Parahamsa in late nineteenth century Hinduism, or at least amongst certain of its prominent masters, there has been a tendency to break out of the conventional mould of strict othodoxy (though convention may have prohibited accounts in earlier times to record non-conformity), as if in response to pressure from Western seekers, and the influence of the West on the modern Hindu seeker too. The Jnani seemed to be aware that he was taking a risk in treating Thompson differently from his other disciples, including the Europeans. He accepted Thompson on a basis quite different from everybody else, at least in private, insisting that the particular bond between them could never be broken. He clearly makes a distinction between what he tells Thompson and what he tells others. In any case, Thompson was his most articulate and advanced pupil, as is borne out by the depth of the Jnani's own emotion, to the point of trance or mahabhava in response.

The profundity of the discussions Thompson held with the Jnani as reported by him with characteristic accuracy (based on his daily notes of what had just transpired) during this visit, are the high water mark in their relationship. The subtlety and, if it is not, in Western usage, too worldly a term to use of spiritual dialogue between people of high calibre, the Indian-style sophistication with which they mutually pursue a complex train of thought is quite remarkable. If evidence is needed as to why Thompson had such a high respect for the Jnani it is to be found in this chapter.

Each dialogue or incident is almost prophetic, in one way or another, of subsequent developments in the relationship. One gets the feeling that, just beyond conscious awareness, Thompson is filled with presentiment of the future, that the Jnani may even have been in a position to know the way events would ultimately unfold, and that both men sense that the course of their discussion already possesses symbolic significance, the meaning of which will acquire special importance in retrospect. The dreams recorded at this time usher in a new phase of visionary experience. This commences three weeks before Thompson's arrival in Trivandrum, with a dream that occurred at Tiruvannamalai where he was staying in June 1941 at the ashram of the Maharshi. In this dream, Thompson's head is cut off—the first of a series of similar dreams which continued to the end of his life.

Two days after this dream, Thompson received a letter from a French Sufi friend which is one of the rare instances we have of a critique written about Thompson by one of his contemporaries (the reply to which is included here). As this letter encapsulates the central dilemma Thompson faces at this stage of his life, the chapter opens with it in the original French.

16.VI.41. Letter from a Sufi friend.

'...je pense que vous m'excuserez de vous parler de vous comme si vous étiez une tierce personne. J'ai l'impression, quand je vous vois agir ou vous entends parler, que vous n'êtes pas libres, mais ceci d'une façon subtile. Disons, pour employer des images, qu'il me semble vous voir agir dans an oeuf de cristal, ou bien dans l'intérieur d'un réseau invisible, ténu, parfaitment souple, mais infrangible. Vous faites tout ce que vous voulez mais...à l'intérieur du cercle seulement. Et je pense qu'en vous l'être sent la vérité des grands espaces, et que de cette contradiction entre l'étre et le pouvoir nait ce que j'ai rendu—très imparfaitement—par le mot 'inquiet'.'

I trust you will excuse me for speaking of you as you were a third person. I have the impression, when I observe your behaviour or hear you speak, that you are not as open as you make out, but in a subtle kind of way. Speaking figuratively, it seems to me that you see yourself as enclosed within a crystal egg, or even colored in an invisible net, plausible, suavely subtle, but inviolable. You do whatever you like, but only inside the enclosure. And I believe that in essence you feel yourself open to great wide spaces and that this contradiction between being and energy is born out of what I would call—very hesitantly—'disquiet'.

[Readers may recall that Thompson was fond of quoting Goethe's belief that 'disquiet' is the better part of the man.}

16.VI.41. In response to

What you so subtly perceive and express about me corresponds curiously with my own dawning recognition during the last year or so that I have always refused to take the relative world seriously, have always seen it as only one temporary formal organisation out of an infinite resource of possibilities. Yet it is true for certain souls that they can begin to consider any given world at all only when they are first certain of the Supreme and it has been only very slowly in my case that somewhere within me such a certainty begins to take form. Meanwhile I am not yet born into this world, but as it were directly into a mid-world; I have myself said that I am in this sense 'still in the womb'—in your 'oeuf de cristal, reseau invisible', that I have not yet set my feet upon the earth.

One can be utterly serious in the relative world only in terms of the Absolute—that is when one's life is entirely and only sadhana. In the meantime one remains in suspense, the given is a torture of provisionality and it is very true that this is a state of Anguish, of inquietude. Your perception is quite acute.

My individuality really is a 'z' in an unresolved equation, I really am for myself also 'une tierce personne', a very fluid irrational *persona*—an interim term which must completely disappear.

[The following entry is a fine instance of the poet's presence behind a seemingly quite simple descriptive piece. Ella is setting out to meet the man who would become her guru. Every word, from the peacocks onwards, is a subtle emphasis of the occasion's momentous significance. Her pensive and laconic comment reveals her intuitive recognition of the portent as a perfect syncronicity.]

3.VII.41.

In the morning all the peacocks came to the garden and the most beautiful began to dance.

After 8 o'clock, where the Maharshi sat in the calm moonlight: 'I think of going tonight: may I have your leave? — 'To Madras?' — 'No, to Travancore'. He sat up and gravely, attentively, as if he felt that this was not the ordinary leave-taking, with a slight movement of the head gave sanction. I bowed before him.

On the way to the station with Ella we overtook a small lighted procession: a beautiful young girl adorned with flowers and jewels for her marriage, reserved in a dignity of wise and conquering passivity, upright like a queen in a little carriage. —Ritual dramatisation of an eternal mystery, an inextinguishable symbol. After a time, echoing my thought, Ella said: 'The bride goes to meet the Bridegroom'.

4.VII.41. To Trivandrum.

The part, the individual will, cannot attain wholeness. The individual will can only surrender to the Whole and serve it. This is its completion. By itself it serves death.

6–9.VII.41. Trivandrum.

The Jnani receives me as always with great love (the house is as it were perfumed with richness).

I can only very roughly summarise what he said with far greater subtlety:

—That no traditional affiliation, guru or *sadhana* is necessary in my case. He laughed at the picture I drew of my irresponsibility, lack of seriousness and realism, even spiritual obstinacy and pride as seen from the orthodox point of view and said that it is the reverse of the truth. All that needs to be done is to become conscious of the Heart which has all along guided me and prompted all my thought and enquiry, for they are not at all from the mind. This can be done simply by thinking of it. In my case 'nothing can go wrong'.

He feels sure that if I had put this 'question' of whether I am doing all that is necessary to Sri Maharshi he would have said the same thing.

He said that I am doing all that is necessary 'unconsciously' because I was unconscious of this guidance from the Heart which only needs to be recognised. My natural position corresponds indubitably with the Truth. 'You have the essential abundantly in your heart. But all do not possess this and need method and master. The sole object of any *sadhana* is to raise the Heart. Mental recognition by itself is sterile and can never touch the Subject-matter. For the sake of those who need him a realised man may avoid saying that he has no disciples. But if he is asked point blank he cannot say he is a guru.'

He says that the infinite omniscient Being, the true Self, that I sense 'above the head' (though that corresponds with a certain truth) is really in the Heart.

He stresses the unqualified Love that is one with 'functionless Consciousness'. This Love is 'God'.

He allows me to come to his village though it is quite unnecessary for me to stay near him. 'I (of course not the relative I) am in your Heart.'

To a pupil of Réné Guénon:

The Jnani said that I might convey his essential affirmation that 'Hinduism' fully and properly understood does most certainly intend and provide for the most expansive fulfilment. 'There is absolutely no essential difference between the path that he /Guénon's pupil/ is following and the path I followed.'

He said today that the only surrender necessary in my case is that of the head to the Heart. And that in my natural 'method' I am jnani, bhakti and yogi—as he would also prefer to be considered, instead of simply as jnani.

Referring to my dream of 13–14 June of my head cut off and kept separately (I still see and speak), he tells me of a similar dream by a *sadhaka* recounted somewhere in Sanskrit. It means that one is ready to overpass one's limitations. He said to me joyfully and emphatically: 'You *will* achieve the ultimate realisation. There 'in' the Absolute *and elsewhere*, on every plane *in its own terms also*, as you demand.'

During his *sadhana*, three days before a glimpse of the Absolute, he dreamt his own death.

8.VII.41.

It is one's very disinterestedness that cannot give oneself sanction, cannot allow one's natural right. It abandons one to the endless ingenuity—and apparent perversity—of Imagination in which one absorbs and exhausts all the possibilities of the phenomenal world—all that in its limitedness is irrelevant to one's Actuality, in order to sustain the definition of it as *Lila*. One can always do anything for others—even achieving realisation! But to do anything for and as oneself is impossibly dry. The law throughout is Love—this is the heart of the *guru-sisya* question—for Love sustains the pure *Lila* of everything and that is why the delight and anguish of Love is the Supreme *Lila* of Radha-Krishna. Here the greatest intensity also is fulfilled.

I had remarked thus before the Jnani told us that, at first conceding to others and considering what they think and feel though not because one needs or desires to, one loses one's centre. This centre is restored by the Guru, 'I still live for others but now with joy, for the ego that was dissatisfied has now vanished.'

What follows about Poetry and Imagination has not been said by the Jnani in my hearing before, but it corresponds exactly with a point of view I had been developing by myself, long before I met him and which I believe has always been in me. I have said in effect that 'Reality' is pure, self-defining Poetry:

'If there is something of the Poet in you, you are near the Goal. There is Poetry everywhere, even in misery. Nothing exists but Poetry. Poetry is Harmony. Everything in this world is the manifestation of this Harmony. Even *Jnanins* express themselves in poetry rather than prose. The meaning of the poem is the intellectual element only. But the essential is splendour, glory, beauty that appeals to the esthetic sense. Yes, as someone present suggested, '*bhakti* is Poetry'.

By Beauty you are drawn towards the Infinite. There is no self in Beauty. You are attracted because you do not want the self in you.

What is veiled is Imagination in any form When there is the Poet's Imagination you are taken towards the Goal—the Heart is there.

In this way one can expand from the phenomenal world and reach the Absolute.

There is the general flow in every man from the Source that 'projects' phenomena. Don't obstruct it by putting your *shankara* there: let it take you on and make you All.

A *bhakta* reaches the Absolute in his own way and none can conceive the depth of his realisation. If then *bhakti* and *jnana* are combined, what fullness!

This evening, in his beautiful, resonant voice, he sang many *slokas* from his Radha-Madhava. I have never seen such a concentrated energy of sweetness and light, such simple, profound and exalted loveliness.

9.VII.41.

He told me that the space between the brows (it should be hairless and neither too projecting nor too depressed), the expression of the eyes, and the nose are the chief indices of greatness in a man's face. At the apex of the triangle whose base is at the root of the nose the individual consciousness is absorbed.

When I showed him the Frankfurt photograph of myself (1931) he said that though of course forehead, eyes and nose are there a great change has taken place since then (when I was 22). He asked to keep it. (Available for reproduction).

During the evening when he had to refer to my 'destiny' I noticed that he immediately though unobtrusively checked himself. Later on he told me that there is much about it which for various reasons cannot at present be revealed to me but that in any case I shall come to know it by myself.

As for the book he was being pressed to write he tells me that it is virtually impossible to write of the Absolute: pen in hand before the page he has tried several times but he is at once absorbed and nothing remains. Poetry, which is quite spontaneous, may be possible at any time. Yet of course it is always possible to answer questions posed in terms of the phenomenal consciousness (though even then, he has told me once before, if a question relates directly to the Absolute and is at the same time not merely theoretical he has often great difficulty in remaining in the phenomenal consciousness to 'answer' it. *[The jnani would go into samadhi with Thompson's line of questioning, affirming this point]*. As for the relation of the *jivan-mukta* (realised man) with the phenomenal consciousness, in a later conversation he gives the following examples: 1) When a man approaches a mirage it disappears. When he has returned to his former standpoint (as *sahaja* realisation demands) the mirage reappears but he not longer believes in it. 2) The trompe-l'oeil: though it deceives your senses you know all the time that it is only a picture.

11.VII.41.

He wanted a photograph of me that (unlike the 1940 ones taken in Madras) should show the essential; he arranged that his disciple, the painter who did his portrait at Malakarrai, should superintend the taking of it. He approved the proof print, *[reproduced on cover]*, remarking that something of the far Background looks out though the eyes and that the set of the face expresses a certain recklessness. Though I only just caught the words my memory is that he said 'a divine recklessness'. I told him I was 'thinking' of him (a kind of psychic 'reminiscence') while it was taken and later he remarked: 'I may say I was present there.'

He said to me: 'Even supposing you were to have a guru, neither you nor I can break this relationship'.

I mention the almost constantly conscious identification I feel with him and he say he also feels it.

The method of 'direct perception' that the Jnani advocates evidently corresponds with my natural intuitive attempt from the beginning at 'completion of Experience' in terms of immediate consciousness, the 'completion of subjectivity' that I have worked out in my aphorisms since 1929.

17.VII.41.

The Jnani is struck at finding several times in Sri Ramana Maharshi's works precisely the same idea as his own and also, of course, from experience, not from *sastra*. (If diacriticals are not used—then *shastra*).

He tells me that he looked into *sastra* only when his *sadhana* was over and even then very little. He does not read Sanskrit though he understands it fairly well. Pandits who have talked with him have found that his direct perception does not contradict *sastra* and he is of course perfectly capable of expressing himself in *sastric* terms though he finds it uninteresting to have to do so. He finds that *sastra* often over-complicates matters and agrees with the Maharishi that it is useless to sweep up fragments in order to throw them away.

19–20.VII.41. Dream.

Festival; *Pradakshina* of a shrine; flowers, exalted *bhakta* emotion.

Ramana Maharshi in a dream about a dream of mine. The sign of the end of the *yuga* (aeonic cycle) is that animals no longer respect man but will snatch his food. Great exodus of man with all the animals in haste under rain for shelter—as the Maharshi goes underground into the earth, walking with relief and leisure where all is darkness and obstruction.

The Jnani says that this is exactly symbolical of the Maharshi's method.

25.VII.41.

Intellect (*buddhi*) cannot by itself transcend its limits: if they are transcended, so that intellect becomes a means of realisation, it is the Heart that has achieved it. Every realised man will affirm this.

Intuition, inspiration are always from the Heart, never from the intellect as such.

Ordinary jnanis pooh-pooh the Heart and therefore find it very difficult, later on, to establish themselves in profound thought and meditation on the Truth. It generally takes years to establish oneself at this stage.

The Tamil *siddhas*—the 'realised'—have again and again emphasised the necessity of deep feeling.

26.VII.41.

Lila: in thought, action, omission, speech—the genial economy and precision of art in terms of direct intuition and sensibility, things as they are, not at all a false and abstract economy predetermined by the rational will and imposed on rational or extra-rational. Fulfilment and subordination of mind and will in the clarity of perfect intuition and sensibility—illumination. This cannot, then, be initiated by mind or will but is to be done in a more direct, spontaneous and subtle way, without paradoxical limits, by the rule of the Heart.

I came to describe to the Jnani the Wellawatte experience, which took place one evening in Ceylon with the sadhu Shivalingam just before I entered India. It was preceded by a state in which everything is Thought: every object and even the thought of another, which one seems directly to contain, is the Self. Looking at each other in this state, language becomes useless, we could only laugh. Then: the One Infinite experiencing its Infinite Oneness—unbearable, dreadful 'ecstasy': the only possibility is to attempt by some extreme ingenuity, some incredibly rapid and subtle turn, for a moment to escape, to hide from, this one Self, to become Other, though one knows it is not really possible. One understands that this is the whole *lila* of the endlessly varied manifestation—and its deepest seriousness.

The Jnani affirms, what I had never for a moment suspected, that this is *mahabhava*.

It is the nature of *mahabhava* to reverberate almost indefinitely: it is the 'state' in which the Absoluteness of Love is directly experienced and, so far, expressed: one becomes that Absoluteness.

28.VII.41. Dream.

Connected with my proposed professorship at Benares. I come to the Ganges, a wide luminous blue river which I intend to cross to the bright town on the other shore. It is shallow enough to wade but I realise that I shall get my clothes wet. Two mounts pasted with photographs of friends fall into the water. I decide to sacrifice them. A little old woman with me will offer them. While she is ducking up and down as at a ritual bath I feel that she has only two or three 'breaths', or years, more.

29.VII.41.

Virtue and vice, says the Jnani, are entirely relative, belonging only to the middle consciousness: there is no morality in sub- or super-consciousness. What raises one from ego may be said to be virtue, what strengthens it vice.

30.VII.41.

It is possible to enter *nirvikalpa-samadhi* without suspension of breath and it may therefore not be known to others. The Jnani had *nirvikalpa-samadhi* even while he was Prosecuting Inspector and his *sadhana* was over even before he became Assistant Superintendent of Police.

In the Jnani's *nirvikalpa-samadhi* the yogic Witnessing Consciousness remains. The Witnessing Consciousness cannot say that between two thoughts there was either something, or nothing, or sleep; yet without this interval one idea could not become another. He agrees with me that this shows the whole continuity is *Lila*. Once, at Chengannur, after the *sadhana* period, this interval was expanded for three to four months. (Once before it had continued for three days during the conduct of a case). It was entirely spontaneous and corresponded with no wish of his. In rising, bathing, eating, going to the office, retiring, his former habits were continued with clockwork regularity: if for example food was not ready at precisely the usual time he would go to the office without it. During this period he would talk on spiritual matters, though past a certain level there was silence. No cause, no effect; no time and therefore, he agrees, no aging—if this state continued one would be physically immortal; no space—during this period he moved to and from Nagerkoil. After his emergence there was only circumstantial evidence—evidence for the rest of the world—to 'prove' that he had continued to exist during this period—testimony of family, clerk and friends, the office diary in his handwriting. This state was of course beyond *nirvikalpa-samadhi*—no Witness-principle. In fact it was not a 'state' at all but the Absolute. He agrees that this experience represents the fact that there *never 'was'* any manifestation!

31.VII.41.

The Jnani is Tantrik in that instead of retreating to the Background as the passive Purusha, as do some *Jnanis*, he 'absorbs' the object. He was very interested when I mentioned S.V's deduction from my horoscope that I did Tantrik *sadhana* in the life previous to this. He tells me that he spontaneously saw the same thing on the day after my first visit in 1936. He makes me understand without actually saying so, that he saw more than this which is not at present to be revealed. 'You will have to complete your former practice.'

Three-eyed women in my 'dreams' are generally the expression of past-life yogic practices. Hence my present indifference to them. If one succumbs to their influence one may get magical powers and one's influence in the physical world will be evil. But such women are not necessarily sinister: they are emanations of the Shakti Herself. A sure sign of their nature is a feeling of happiness at the sight of them. My recurrent dream since boyhood of exploring richly appointed rooms probably represents power gained by this former Tantrik *sadhana*. Correspondence of this with childhood at 'The Priory'.

My so-called 'asuric' intransigence and plastic imaginative sympathy are not at all opposed but aspects of this one Reality. If 'asuric' will is to grow it grows from this element beyond it: remaining what it is on its own plane it must serve that priority.

3.VIII.41.

Against the forgetfulness, carelessness, folly, superficiality, of the ego:

You are given food, shelter, clothing; no one compels you. Your sole work is to reach union with the Reality, the infinite freedom, joy and knowledge of that union. To this must be devoted the most sincere art and intelligence, unfalteringly, at every moment, with Leisure, joy, illumination. This is your *dharma* and your pride, by this you are judged.

4.VIII.41. Dream.

Ramana Maharshi crossing the sloping roofs of a rather sombre hill-city. Changing direction, he makes towards the tower-like corner where I stand.

He is with his attendant and some young cattle. They meet a second train of cattle who, head down, charge the first. The Maharshi and attendant are thrown down and trampled. Blood and brains. Having watched this with helpless horror and grief, I rush for a doctor. Already people think he is dead. I find him seated calmly, his head uninjured or injured only superficially. He says it shook his heart but touches his left side near the stomach. I am sobbing dreadfully, quite suffocated with grief, yet in a sense I have been throughout a detached spectator. Seeing my state, and no doubt to console me, when I ask if he would not like something to drink he allows me to go and get him some lime-juice.

This followed a dream of a miracle in a shrine connected with Saint Catherine. The Jnani remarks to me that it would be good if on one's way into a temple a certain girl could be stationed so that as one looked into her eyes in passing one's consciousness would be raised.

5.VIII.41.

I recount the dream about the Maharshi and the Jnani tells me that cattle in dreams generally symbolise tenderness. When I suggest that the conflict of two streams of tenderness in which the Maharshi is overthrown may represent a withdrawal of his influence. The Jnani tells me that between eleven and twelve thirty this morning he had a vision of Ramana Maharshi in which something passed between them. Dazzling light from the Maharishi's eyes met and fused with light from himself. Then the Maharshi became 'a ball of light' that rolled away down a slope. Returning, he appeared without light in his eyes. The Jnani thinks that the Maharshi has been interested in me.

The Jnani does not tell me now and will not hereafter the ground of his knowledge that out relationship, even if I had accepted another guru, cannot be broken by either of us: I shall some day 'indubitably experience' the truth about it myself, and by indubitable experience he means something more than vision.

His disciples' position [*concerning conventional attitude toward the Jnani as guru is correct*]; so also is mine. His great fear, before, that I might discuss the *guru-shishya* question with them was that it might result in their confusion while he could not warn either party against it without raising that very question.

When he tells me that his meeting with his guru took place by a culvert, I remark that I had imagined it so from his son's brief account, in which, however, this detail was not mentioned. I describe the low parapet, to their left, and also my impression of the Swami as tall, lean and very 'fair'. All this, the Jnani confirmed, is correct: he was of my height, thin like myself and as fair.

Leaning back in his chair (it was at the house in Tanchiyur), he appeared to enter a *samadhi* and remained so for perhaps a quarter of an hour; then opened his eyes and looked round for a moment but slowly relapsed, the eyes turning upwards and closing again. During this time I passed through various phases of a more or less concentrated state. Perhaps fifteen or twenty minutes more passed when he re-emerged, or at least opened his eyes, and after a minute or two suddenly came to me where I sat and with both hands, front and back, stroked several times downwards from my shoulders towards the heart. When I bowed, clasping his feet, he placed both hands upon my head. Returning to his chair he fell back stretched out fully as if exhausted or as he might upon his bed. A few minutes later, walking as he does after *guru-puja*, or as I once saw him in *mahabhava*, he went inside.

6.VIII.41.

Maithuna: The Jnani says that, in a man with any 'esthetic feeling', sexual intercourse demands primary attention to the pleasure of the beloved and therefore lifts him beyond the lower self. It is by such self-sacrifice that the Supreme is the Bridegroom.

Such intercourse at its highest can become a way to the Absolute. He agrees with me that erotic experience may reveal aspects and consequences of the Truth hardly attainable by other means.

What he has said about my Tantrik *sadhana* is not opinion but the Truth. I was born this time in Europe because the tendency to action which had prevented my devoting myself entirely to *sadhana* before was still predominant. It was very soon exhausted, however, and I had to return to India.

He says that I shall receive help in *Tantra-marga* though not necessarily from a guru. I do not need *mantra* or *puja*: in its essential Tantra is at one with all *jnana* that is not content with mere Return to the Background and I shall complete this possibility.

[Thompson then added a footnote during a visit to a Sufi festival at Ajmer in the following October, where he compares the Return to the Background with the Sufi 'journey to God', 'journey in God' and 'journey from God back to the world of manifestation invested with the attributes of God'. 'Travelling from knowledge to certainty to the intuition thereof—'essence of certainty'—then journeying to the fact thereof—the 'reality of Certainty where the Truth is.']

6–7.VIII.41. Dream.

With great difficulty I shape the face of a *vigraha* (image of a deity) out of wet sand in order to show how eyes and mouth in the bronze are incised afterwards.

July-August. 41.

[The use of the word 'avadhuta' in the sense of 'holy fool' is, I am told by several scholars, wrong. But I am not so sure. It may be correct to a certain sect, or in certain localities. I doubt if Thompson came to use it in complete ignorance. In any case it appears that this is the meaning which the Jnani gives it in this talk of eccentric avadhutas in consequence of Thompson meeting with one in Trivandrum:]

Avadhutas are generally illiterate and incapable of discriminative thought. They are therefore taught by their guru to overcome body-consciousness by courting blows. They thus often reach the psychic plane and in that state, unconscious of others, with vacant eyes they babble as one may in dream. Such *sadhakas* have themselves told the Jnani that no blessing is to be expected from them. But if they are recalled to the physical plane, perhaps by touch, they may truly bless.

On the way I overtook the Thaugal, 'Kili' as people call him. These *avadhutas* are quite surrealistic: old cotton-reel and razor-blade on a twist of cloth under his beard. In the teashop he repeated Hindu, Christian and Muslim triads: the Muslim one was 'Allah, Muhammed, Mahijiddin'! He picked up Guénon's *Man and his becoming*, pressed it to his eyes and breast again even after I had told him it was not the Quran (he doesn't understand English, opened it upside down and marked a page on which I found nothing very special) and he insisted on carrying the book under his arm when we left.

Perpetual vital blaze—words, gesticulation, shining eyes, half-idiot half-ironical laugh, Tamil verses at top speed to the last resonance of breath and all with a kind of sweetness and charm. He wanted me to come with him. I asked him instead if he would come with me.

'Is it a Christian house? Women or men? Householder or *sannyasin*?'

We caused great delight as we went hand in hand through the streets (he made me hold his hand in a special way, simulating, I think, the marriage ceremony) — Kili singing, dancing, chattering, imitating my walk in the funniest way, then trotting along demurely like a good little girl, making strange woeful noises, burlesqueing European music. I was surprised that he actually entered the Jnani's house. He sat down on the floor and suddenly became silent, writing with his finger in Malayalam in answer to the Jnani's questions. After a few minutes, when he understood that we were to talk, though the Jnani had invited him to stay he asked permission to go.

The Jnani told me that when Kili had once appeared to him in Suksma (etheric) form he had understood his *sadhana* and the stage he had attained, though he forgets it all now; but he is sure from what he saw this time that the Thaugal is a sincere seeker.

Kili stands at the threshold of a wineshop in the High Street. I salute him and he embraces me, sniffing as they do in Ceylon. Prostrating to the moon, *puja* to a statue. Back the way I had come to a den where *arak* is served colourless like vodka and so fiery that even Kili cannot drink it without coughing. I manage to get a mouthful down and hand the rest to Kili. He also makes me eat meat. Then off again for cigarettes. We meet K.K. Nayar*, followed by a crowd; proper and respectable, he is a young M.A. who has not seen me for a year or two. He has the courage to continue with the madman, but Kili finds this irksome and gets rid of him. He proceeds along bye-lanes till he stops at a lighted shed in a coconut grove. Another den where also he seems known. Toddy, a foul-smelling foaming white liquid, is served in porridge-bowls of which he drinks two, and I have no money. Off again, Kili makes signs that his head is whirling—very affectionate—sometimes wanting to walk unsupported. At last I induce him to sit down but after a few minutes, signing that I may go back, he trots and sways off alone into the outskirts of the town. I make my way back devoured by bugs and saturated with Kili's peculiar smell.

15–16.VIII.41. Dream.

Powerful trains forge with a grand music through great lighted tunnels deep in the coloured mountains.

16–17.VIII.41. Dream.

A hill minutely covered with writing, as if on every stone one sees a word (it is difficult to read): directions for some alchemical process—tincture. A sudden sharp flash at another high hill at some distance to my right in country rather like that around Tiruvannamalai but more vivid and ochreous. Heavy dark smoke plumes forth, curls and ascends; an explosion as from

* K.K. Nayar came to a talk I gave in 1983 at Pune. During question-time he introduced himself as having known Thompson and declared that he had obviously worked for British Intelligence!

dynamite and several flying rocks are flung up; a very big piece of something that seems not rock hurtles flaming down to a little river or canal near a bridge. Where it sets on fire a boat. No means of livelihood of its owner. In a few minutes people gather in excitement and put out the fire while the boat is still only slightly burned.

On the boat is a great bird like an eagle, its wings ablaze. I watch with horror from the distant little valley by the first hill while the owner, instead of casting the bird into the canal, pets it and lets the wings burn till the bird (I imagine its agony) is blackened along the sides. A close-up of its brown eyes in the smooth brown-feathered body, still softly living and in gentle wonder rather than anguish. I give an account of this to someone.

Writing on the hill—What in Ramana Maharshi was not
penetrated by me.
Owner of the boat—my ego.
Boat—a. My body, or *samsara*. b. *Jnana*.
Eagle and second hill—the Jnani.
Fire—my lack of faith and
a. devotion which continually does violence to him.
b. Jnani's grace by which he limits himself for me.

17.VIII.41.

A plant breathes by its leaves. The fronds of the coconut spread like gills. Other trees are shaped like lungs.

24.VIII.41.

The coconut palms, the stars, the whole landscape looks minute, like something under the microscope.

8.IX.41.

[Letter to a friend on concluding talk of this visit with the Jnani.]

I must report some of my conversation last evening with the Jnani.

L.T.: Diatribe against the all-levelling abstraction of false advaitins who, in their return to undifferentiated slime would make, for example, beauty and ugliness the same till they lack even—and precisely!—the sensibility of a child. Reality (this is also certainly the Jnani's attitude) is not at all the 'Absolute', a postulation of the relative consciousness but 'in itself' entirely the Transcendent. In spite of the fact that everything relative is contingent, conditioned (relativity its own network of causes), the uniqueness of everything given, no matter for what consciousness—no two leaves on the tree the same—is the direct sign of the Transcendent. The Absolute Self-defining

Concreteness of 'Reality' would perhaps be better safeguarded by saying 'There is only He'.

J.: Certain jnanis bring beauty and ugliness to the same level to guard themselves from the pitfall of the senses which, isolated, submerge more subtle faculties of experience: this is necessary for people who have not been subtilised by experience, who cannot see that Beauty is never *in* the object but always entirely symbolic.

L.T.: Yet sensuality is also a reality and wholeness that demands the integration of all possibilities. Integral experience never denies but rather satisfies what it has surpassed: in surpassing limitations it completes the *symbolic* character of relative experience. In fact it is always integrality that is prior to the relative and thus all experience is essentially imaginative, an *exploitation* of symbols, poetry, only an animal is *held* by his senses.

J.: But practical *shastras* do affirm the path of integral experience. By 'relative' I mean that the existence of any object can be established only by reference to the subject: a change in the subject produces a change in the object.

L.T.: Well this falls within the scope of my definition: subject and object are also complementaries in the network of always partial, inconclusive cause-and-effect that I call relativity: the ego, the relative subject, is an object, an experience, entirely interdependent with all others.

J.: But it is *you* who say that 'uniqueness represents the Transcendent': this uniqueness depends on your perception.

L.T.: But this perception is also relative by the same token. No 'I' perceives the Transcendent: 'There is only He'.

J.: So Uniqueness and Perception go together and cannot be discussed!

L.T.: Everything 'given' for any possible given consciousness is entirely 'mystical'! There are no connections. 'Every day He is in the state of Sublime Creator. There is only He'.

J.: Why not 'I'?

L.T. Before His Sole Concreteness the ego, which is pure insufferable paradox, can only be done away. There is no question of 'union' with Him: He is entirely His affair; I am not even nothing, yet my whole meaning is Himself, for there is nothing but He. —In saying 'He' I am simply concerned, you see, to respect Absolute Concreteness, to avoid abstraction. All such use of words is anyway poetical, one is not at all conditioned by it. This 'only He' is, if you like, the attitude of absolute Passion!

J.: Well, the false 'I' must also be done away. Using 'I' you will find it easier to merge the paradoxical individuality.

L.T.: Yes, of course, it gives the process centrality.

J.: You need certainly not have any 'conception' of the Absolute. But to feel something you must bring it close to you. In *shastra* three stages are spoken of: *tasyevaham*, I am His; *tavevaham*, I am yours; *tvamevah*, you are myself. A man of enlightenment has said: 'When my existence is in the body I am His; when in the mind I am part of Him; when at the root of all thoughts I am Himself.'

L.T.: No doubt mind and thought here must be taken as representative: even in one day one may experience innumerable 'aspects' and 'relationships' and there are also perhaps endless non-mental modes of experience. There may also be an oscillation between the masculine and feminine elements in one's being—between the passive, receptive, adoring and the active, possessive, willed.

J.: Yes, there is always a mixture of *jnani*, *bhakti*, *yogi* in every *sadhaka*. Ramana Maharshi's enquiry, for example, involves one-pointed concentration which is yogic.

L.T.: Whoever can deliberately concentrate his whole life long on one idea must be either very stupid or an asuric monster. The infinite richness of Reality is expressed in beginningless and endless *Lila*.

J.: But if that one idea allows all activities, takes you to their root and deepens all experience....?

L.T.: Then it certainly cannot be an idea.

J.: No indeed!

L.T.: Only the Reality can concentrate upon Itself!, all is indeed Its manifestation.

J.: You have only understood this, in practice, as experience. If you allow your thought to proceed as before and realise that all is the expression of the Reality you only give your activities a deeper meaning. Or else you must get to the root of the standing obstacle, the mind, and so annihilate the ego, that which does not exist yet wants to claim everything for itself. The mental will can be converted. Offer it arguments and it must agree; it will never be able to offer counter-arguments. Will, the progeny of Reason, must agree to Reason. Or the suggestion will come from within and the will must agree. The path you choose cannot be in conflict with anything I have said.

L.T.: I have long known what for me is *the* direct path. It is so simple that it took me years even to see that it demands that everything be done at once, this moment: the path is the goal! and this is how I could never find room for method but could only in anguish blame without admitting impossible weakness, failure, evasion, fatigue. I was depending upon my only immediate means—Anguish, passion, intuition, but it may take time for other elements of the being to see and accept the essential. I find that willed effort along a mentally determined line disturbs this irreversible focussing: other elements react. The will can only *serve* an integrality that is ultimately its own cause.

J.: Yes, one must wait till what refuses comes in of its own accord. There must be no tension or strain. But the so-called quarrel—between us—is also a positive sign: a position which without it you might have reached only in ten days, by this intensification may be attained in five.

L.T.: I have often thought that by *resisting* the Reality by all means, one deepens one's realisation, for this resistance, out of passion, can only be for the sake of Reality.

J.: *If it can be done consciously* one certainly shortens the way. (He quotes the example of the demonic Ravana in the *Ramayana* epic.)

L.T.: Yet perhaps only a simplicity of the 'size' of Ravana's is really capable of this. What I often obscurely felt is perhaps rather that, one allows oneself away, repressing every deliberate, conditioned movement, and is devoured before the Reality with which one remains in absolute tension, till at last, though one has 'done nothing' and has never played the role of *sadhaka*, only the thinnest shell remains and the movement that breaks is still both too subtle and too concentrated to be deliberate. So in one moment, for all has unconsciously been done, there is full day. In this way, will, the most superficial, and usually the first means, is the last to give way so that, not recognising oneself, in the meantime one experiences oneself *directly* as *asura* (demon)—a possibility I faced at Pondicherry [*at the ashram of Sri Aurobindo*] and which, though it was terrible, at the same time greatly enhanced my sense of *Lila*. I did not realise that I was simply experiencing my own disinterestedness for which all extremes are present and which corresponds with infinite Joy.

J.: I can deeply appreciate this though it was not my way.

When we had been discussing Brahman and Purushottama a point was at last reached when the Jnani said:

There is very seldom occasion to say this, but—when a question is put to a *jnani*, the question and the questioning, the words, the meaning, the answer and the manner in which it is given, is all one whole—He Himself: 'the whole is contained in him'. It is only by speaking as if from the phenomenal viewpoint that the *jnani* appears to try to answer questions with a labour that no other can conceive, by every device of logic and example he tries to perform the impossible task of bringing phenomenon and noumenon together in the questioner's mind. 'The whole is part, the part is whole, *there*. Left to himself, the *jnani* simply sees himself—but the ideas of 'seeing' and 'himself' are limits here. This is beyond speech. And there is no change. You may argue that there is something beyond and the *jnani's* intellect may not be able to answer, yet he is not at all shaken from his position—for it is not even direct perception but 'direct oneness'. From the phenomenal point of view one may arrange things as to have always a Beyond. Even when in the phenomenal plane the *jnani* agrees to act a proposition it is only in accordance with the limits of the intellect. Thus when the highest is in question it is speechless communication that communicates the position in which two *jnanis* are. (When the Nagercoil 'Mother' visited him they said no word to one another: for three hours, both thrown into 'That state', they remained in silence. Some will say she is not realised because her guru told her she would have to continue in this phenomenal world till certain things drop away. She has to agree she is perfectly happy and wants nothing beyond. She reached realisation simply by service to her guru, quite without *sadhana*. He was certainly a very great man—*yogin* and *jnani*.)

Every action, object, event, thought and experience, including this writing and this idea is That, is to be entirely preferred to the One Changeless Reality.

All these are external proposals: experience everything as That.

Hitherto the mind, wishing to retain its own egotistic will, has put itself outside every real experience by mentalising it at all costs or actually replacing the experience by a mental expression of it.

Time is the fact that spiritually one in continually starting afresh, continually re-collecting oneself from dispersion.

Two or three days of fierce inner contention had exhausted me but in his presence I was restored. I found that the attitude of experiencing every thought, act, event as That arose once more spontaneously. Yet it is very subtle, a summit of harmony; if a powerful thought or feeling is allowed to run by itself the door is shut and profound harmony must be established again before this spontaneity can be recovered.

23.IX.41.

Dr. Srinivasa Rao, who treated Sri Aurobindo after his recent accident and spent many hours every day with him, tells me that he said to Aurobindo about me: He is devoting his life to study of spiritual things and is earnestly trying to live a spiritual life; why is such a man refused admission to this ashram? Sri Aurobindo replied: 'He is too egoistic and too intellectual.' One of his lieutenants said: 'This ashram is not for people of his sort.'

5.X.41.

Sri Aurobindo would not have made this remark, nor could it be true, if he were my guru. But the remark represents that possibility of my damnation, thus it defines, precisely, the protection actually given by the guru.

27.XI.41. The Jnani's birthday.

Certain even of his family and relations are not allowed to be present at guru-puja /customary worship of the guru on his birthday/. The chief point, apart from the special nature of the manifestation, is that the Jnani is not individually responsible for or aware of his activities on such occasions and they cannot be foreseen. Only those therefore who are sympathetic and understand something of spiritual states can be allowed to be present. He had absolutely no hesitation in the case of myself.

15

First Pilgrimage to Ajmer : 1941

Trivandrum to Ajmer by Rail

October, 1941. To Ajmer. For Ella Maillart. *[Translated from Thompson's French.]*

In the train a little after Gooty (what a name), dear explorer of the unknown, I am getting bored and too tired to continue reading the charming Réné Guénon. So I'll start gossiping with you but not in English (nor in French, you can see, or will see) because I will probably comment on my fellow passengers.

Today is the first day of Saraswati puja and that accounts for the vina wrapped in an apricot sari on the luggage-wrack and the fact that two people have just begun to sing.

Opposite, a young man whose upper lip betrays a remarkably passive sensibility: his gentle eyes do not appear to find anything much to satisfy him in *Filmindia*. What possibilities for deranged or confused poetry exist in this world! Farther on, a charming woman, from the pride and delight of her companion I take to be recently married. She has neat and intelligent features, really beautiful. She buys jasmine to replace in her hair the flowers which are now faded.

At Guntakal a wrinkled Muslim vendor truly supposes that I should want to buy a child's toy. Guénon says all Orientals believe that Occidentals are children.

A little boy with diamond earrings takes a great interest in this typewriter.

—Things are happening like a parody of your books!

The young man is now hunting through *The Murderer Lovekill*. 'Mr. Lovekill stroked his revolver malevolently.'

Outside the window, always the same waste of cactus and scrub; blue hills on the far horizon.

The objects of the physical world, if they could be viewed in another state of consciousness, would appear inexhaustibly mysterious. But already, when one observes them without preconception, they are seen in quite another state, for the logic of which they are purely, densely symbolic—exactly as would 'visions' be for the state of consciousness centered in the physical. But this way of seeing surpasses the logical connections of the physical world which can no longer, in consequence, serve to express it.

In the new train at Dhond, five in the morning, October 28th, no Inter. Class. I'm thus in third class since I'm not sure that I've got enough to pay for second. Everybody filthy. Prodigious mountains of baggage, little packages tied up in cloth, these knots always seem to suggest the touch of graceful fingers. One of the boys in the group to which this baggage belongs has strangely beautiful hands, a deep dusky brown, the nails tinged with henna. A little girl sings to herself: 'La la patti laiya'. The blueish dawn light comes in, the morning breeze stirs. A sweet and delicate tenderness suffuses the heart and vanishes like a perfume. The train sways. Slowly, after a night of tedium, people start talking. One rests on the knee of another a peaceful hand. How beautiful all these human lives!

At sunrise an old man offers *namaskaram* to Him and prays.

When I try to switch off the fan every hand is stretched to help me.

Blind beggars with castanets climb in on the wrong side of the train; people here seem to be less generous or perhaps they are poorer than the Tamils. The houses such as one glimpses are mean hovels: stone with sheet-iron roofs. Almost everyone wears clothes which are dirty and often tattered.

> Great India Peninsula Railway
> NOTICE
>
> Warning is given that it is a common practice for Railway thieves to pretend to go to sleep on the floor of a carriage and when passengers are asleep or inattentive to open and extract articles from bundles and boxes placed under the seat.
>
> In order that they may not be the victims of professional criminals, such as poisoners, swindlers, thieves or pick-pockets, passengers are warned not to accept food or tobacco from strangers...

Frenetic chanting, comic, impassioned, to the rhythmical clink of little cymbals. He too, the third in half an hour, is blind.

There are plenty of Hindus here as they are imagined in Europe—just like gypsies. More cunning, less peaceful than people in the South. Not so deep, either, I would guess. Less self-contained. When I offer him a cigarette my neighbour gives me, in return, some areca-nut. A Tamil would find that indelicate, too commercial, or—too obvious, too artless. All the eyes here seem to me more brilliant, more focussed. The women are half-veiled with their saris. Big pearl rings pass through their nostrils. Colours are more gay than rich.

Ratlam, October 29th.

Spent the night in second class. Everything more sordid than in the South. Flies. Clothes always dirty. Tea but no milk. Fruit very expensive. Even brighter colours: acid crimson with brilliant yellow; lime green; turbans like multicoloured nougat. Ganja is smoked. Waistcoats of patterned quilt or with sequins and embroidery.

When I approached Hindu cafes I was taken for a Muslim. When, at Khandwa, I asked for milk they said there was none and when I pointed to some that was being boiled they said it was no good: 'Achcha nahin'.

A charming and simple police officer—a big baby—came and told me he had coughed all night long, supposing that I might be a doctor. His voice croaked and I could see that his throat was inflamed. I told him he must see a doctor as soon as possible and, meanwhile, take a spoonful of honey every fifteen minutes. They say honey is obtainable here. The interpreter in this exchange gave me the address of a Shastri and yogi with many disciples who lives near Ajmer.

In third again with small compartments hung everywhere with colorful garments.

Since this morning, the landscape as I had always imagined it—completely flat right to the horizon.

At Neemuch I obtained chapattis, quite good although without ghee. A small boy who saw that I did not like the highly salted curry ran to get me some mango pickle. With fruit this was sufficient for me.

A surrealist woman veiled in a yellow sari, its border worked in metallic silver piped in blue; heavy manacles and fetters of elaborate silverwork; her pale hands, cruelly made up with henna, dark brown, appeared soaked in the long-since dried blood of crime. All the small children, eyes heavily outlined with khol, have the air of perverse intelligence. It must be this implacable sun which intensifies everything. It weighs down, it stifles. In resisting it one becomes passionately perverse. Intense love of Apollo who created shade.

A supercilious camel, thoroughly ill-tempered. Houses of undressed stone, half-ruined; tiled roofs. Crops of maize. Small grey-green tree powdered with flowers of dusty yellow. Thorn-trees, grass burnt dry.

The women are sad, patient, fatalistic.

A hill fort; flags which flap languidly in the breeze.

Young man with a silver pommel to his sword. A prisoner escorted by two policemen. They sell roasted maize here. Terribly hot: for the first time on this trip I perspire visibly.

I can see the strength to continue this for months will make me become a famous author. Truly too hot to read, to think, to sleep. From a milky blue sky it suddenly rains.

At Chitorgaon, an officer of the railway company: O. 'Whsidhtk hfyr oiecy?'

L.T. 'Malum nahin'.

O. 'Bhutanpersiapeshawar?'

L.T. 'Nahin.'

O. 'Arab? Turkey? Padre? Are you French?'

L.T. 'No, English.'

O. 'When will this war end?'

L.T. 'Heaven knows. After America comes in, probably.'

O. 'You think America will come in?'

L.T. (sagely), 'Bound to, if it goes on long enough.'

O. 'Is Russia finished?'

L.T. (who has not read the paper for a week), 'Not quite.'

The officer gives me a respectful salute. He has seen the typewriter: I must be a very well informed journalist.

The soda-water vendor, when he wants to light a cigarette, makes fire with a piece of iron curved like the handle of a drawer round the four fingers of the right hand: he strikes it against a flint on which he holds, with the thumb of the left hand, a twist of cottonwool. That doesn't work, so with a stroke of the iron he gives the flint a fresh chip so that it will strike more sparks. At last one drops on the cotton: he holds it out of the window into the wind made by the train; it burns red. Eventually he extinguishes it with a little iron rod.

This amiable Robinson Crusoe makes tea on the train and invites me to have some: it is excellent. He knows all kinds of things which he would be quite unable to explain but are reflected in his face; one day, completely mastered, he will be irradiated with them.

He explains that his cotton, at one pice, lasts as long as four boxes of matches at two pice a box. He smokes a great many beedies. He is often alone in his separate compartment and no doubt bored. At stations he serves 'raspberry' soda of a horrific colour. But everyone is a poet: the colour is symbolic, the taste also. Children, for example, like it much more than the real fruit because it appeals to the imagination. Only the imagination of the Good Lord can *totally* delight in real fruit.

9.X.41.

Harindranath Chattopadhyaya says of Farzand Ali Shah whom he saw in Hyderabad when he was about seven (the old man was 120 then) that you sensed him coming from a distance through the air, progressively condensing into form like a frozen wind, till there he was, seated before you, grasping your arm and repeating with intensity 'Allah! Allah!'

Another *faqir* once, at his father's house, produced from beneath a cloth spread across his knees whatever guests asked to eat, from mangoes (out of season) to hot rice and finally offered beautiful garlands to C's mother and sisters. He said that invisible beings (djinni) brought what he desired, but always paid for what was thus taken from others.

About five years ago at Alleppey C. met a very ordinary-looking Moplah who was said to have similar powers. When C's son asked for oranges the Moplah went to a window a few feet away from C. and raised his hands, open palms together before his face. When he lowered them and turned there were six oranges.

Somehow the whole thing seemed quite natural. This flying was never done in daylight. Once C's father went with him to a little hut at the top of a hill. He went inside and told C.'s father that when he saw a flash of light he was to take his shoes to a friend's garden some way off where he would find him—as he did.

C's father says that he saw him separate his head and all his limbs. He had never done any special practices: the powers were transmitted to him by his father and Ali Shah handed them on in his turn to his own son.

The Tomb of Mu'inud'din Christi at Ajmer in Ramzan

[The great annual pilgrimage to the tomb of Mu'inud'din Christi occurs during Ramazan, when Muslims eat, and drink water, only after sunset. The Monsoon over, the temperature would be very hot in daytime Rajasthan, cold at night—a very different climate from the one to which Thompson was accustomed in the southern tip of India 1300 miles away. The great saint, Aftab-i-Mulk-i-Hind (1145–1235), Sun of the Realm of India, was revered by the Mogul Emperor, Akbar, who went on pilgrimage to Aftab-i-Mulk-i-Hind's tomb every year from 1562–1579 on foot, a journey of 250 miles. Pilgrimage was immensely popular with the faitful of all religions, and a round trip of 500 miles was common practice among countless millions, often twice or three times as long.]

Marble courtyards polished and eroded by the tread of centuries of bare feet; rich door, golden finials. The ribs and drum of a graceful white dome are patterned with nobly stylized golden flowers.

Within, by the soft living gleam of long tapering candles of brown wax, walls sombre with dark green and gold; ballooning velvet baldaquin like a heavy flower under the dome; silver screens about a long high mound heaped with jasmine and rose. People stand silently in prayer or meditation; continually intoning, others circulate who humbly and passionately kiss the silver posts and balustrade. Some bow their heads under the scented cloth of brocade, voluminous beneath the weight of flowers.

The soft fire and gloom of beauty serves a magistral influence of love and graciousness.

Endlessly varied surrealistic perfection of the lanes about the Dargah (royal court) and their life and people—flawless enchainment of stage-settings, full of perfectly posed and lighted detail. It is as if the spiritual force (*baraka*) of the saint's tomb had made everything directly plastic to psychic consciousness. Imagine a pillar-box on a bent tripod, subtly transposed and distorted like an assemblage invented by Picasso; and so with every grouping, every object. Nothing can be reduced to pragmatic terms, everything is inseparable from the aura that forms it. Hence this continual felicity, the infallibility of dream that absorbs all into its own ever-new, ever-marvellous, ever-refreshing harmony.

Space takes on a dimension of innerness, is hollowed and modulated with a 'Magian' resource in porches, niches, alcoves, ambries, embrasures—endless honeycombing self-penetration and latticing.

The street, under awnings, has the vivid intimacy of an interior indefinitely various and prolonged. Flat bread, savouries, *kawabs* on spits are made and eaten under your elbow as you pass; fire tongues the air; people sleep, read, are shaved, massaged, shampooed, sit knees up on iron chairs smoking cigarettes. In corners and gateways, at the foot of steps, on little platforms, they play cards, pass the hookah round, kiss and pull at the funnel of *ganja*. Piles of sweetmeats, vibrating like hot metal with the zigzags of giant wasps. Piles of flowers, overwoven by the weightless, concentrated arabesque of bees.

The lanes twist, slope, redouble, divide, are coigned, stepped, ramped, recessed, flagged, canopied, bemirrored, inscribed to follow every local and momentary need; complicated also by the awnings, verandahs, balconies, belvederes, painted facades and jutting storeys of interpenetrating individual lives.

Rajput women, high-breasted, elaborately bangelled and ankletted, with tight trousers or a rocking sea of skirts, head and shoulders covered with a light gesture of acid yellow or cerise. Muslim women veiled from head to foot in a sort of white burnous with a little white lattice for the eyes; turbans like toffee, ice-cream, barley-sugar, multicoloured nougat. Little boys with gold-embroidered caps, flowered jacket and white jodhpurs; beggars, faqirs, pilgrims, hawkers. Water-carriers with a swollen legless goat-skin stoop and hasten over a little stick like a foot-rule. Camels—melancholy, supercilious, flattened like shadows; clipped white sheep with bells, dyed rose or marked with orange stars and crescents. —The unresolving drama continues, constant, musical, multiple and secretive like a river, or like the court and palace of an invisible king.

> The musician's sweat is for you the honey of song, O Sword that pierces beyond all knowable beauty. You who hold his heart in love and hate and waywardness have made his song a glittering silence.

> And save me from these singing boys with drums,
> Their careless, ringing rapturous, eagle cry,
> Their spiteful freshness, dreadful tenderness—
> Not angles and not devils and not men.

October 1941.

Under the influence of music before the tomb (normally forbidden in Islam, but the Christhis make use of it) with closed eyes a faqir works himself into ecstasy. His heavy dance has at last exactly the vigour and abandon of the sexual act; frenetic acceleration sums a climax at which he falls exhausted.

When after a few minutes he sits up he appears so different that at first, having in the interval looked away, I wonder if it is the same man: though his previous state seemed entirely passive, a certain effect of power and illumination has faded away; the outer individual that is left has the passivity of an accidental.

At midnight the crisp *tak-tak* or hollow burbling of the drum begins and the sweet snarling and bleating and plaintive nasal rippling of a reed pipe, with the occasional shimmering clang of cymbals—the music established in the gallery of the high gateway by the Emperor Shah Jahan. It ends with a deep thunderous rumble from the biggest of the bowl-shaped drums, with at the other end of compass a prolonged, delicate, other-worldly trumpet blare. It is like the sound of the earth gyrating on its axis in the void; a cry, exalted and forlorn, at the battlements of space and time.

At three in the morning groups of young men following a green flag through the lanes sing in chorus, with biting passion and ardour, a strongly rhythmed four-square theme out of which arises at intervals, solo, a rapturous, entranced, richly beautiful aria.

[Although the style of this account resembles Thompson's treatment of his dreams, the reader might protest that he is doing precisely what he said was the wrong way to write a journal: using description. However, as in his dream narratives, he is attempting to achieve his objective: to go beyond the ego, the individual, and what he calls in Journal about Journal: "Description...from an accidental viewpoint". The key word in his account of the entranced, supra-individual state of the faqir in the ecstatic throes of dance, is the state he returns to at its conclusion: the "accidental". Description, he says, is nothing more than a surface view of the individual, has the "passivity of the accidental". In fact, his whole piece is a vivid example of how he sees right through surface accident to a level of perception in which the uncommanded object is "transfigured". "Hence this continual felicity, the infallibility of dream that absorbs all into its own ever-new, ever-marvellous, ever-refreshing harmony".]

16

Samadhi

21.XI.41.

This evening the Jnani, placing his hand on the crown of my head, said: 'Your name is Chillilananda'. (Chit–Lila–Ananda, Chillilananda in Malayalam). 'This is your *mudra*, it represents your relation with the Reality; you have only to think of your name to be taken There.'

Later, mentioning this *prasthanam* in which Love and Knowledge are equally stressed, he said that of course '*Chit* here does not stand for *jnana* only but comprehends everything'.

This name came to him in a special state. He has never given anyone this name before: it is quite 'fresh'. It is not a 'Hindu name', does not mean one is Hindu, but a suprapersonal name in terms of the Truth. He has never heard of it elsewhere and it corresponds with the truth of a personal position. It is not a *diksha-nama* (initiation name). It merely met my old *samskara* that it would be convenient, living in India, to have an Indian name.

[To his mother Thompson wrote in explanation:]

It is my 'spiritual name' and expressed my relation with the ultimate Reality. It is itself a name of that Reality, so has nothing sectarian about it. In India the ultimate Reality as conceived from our point of view is said to be Sat-Chit-Ananda; that is to say, it is Absolute Being (represented by our life), Absolute Consciousness, Self-awareness or Intelligence (represented by our thought) and Absolute Bliss (represented by our feelings)—these three are three in one and one in three—they correspond in fact with the Persons of the Christian Trinity, in which, I suppose, the Father is Pure Being (Eckhart's *Esse est Deus*), the Logos the Son, and Divine Love, manifestation of absolute self-happiness, the Holy Ghost. Since each tradition is an organic whole, exact correspondence cannot always be made at any given level.

Lila—Divine Play—expresses the fact that the whole manifestation is entirely self-defined and non-necessary.

Chit is taken as the dynamic aspect par excellence of the Reality—its manifesting force which, as the Divine Mother, appears under various names in all major traditions.

Of course these words are Sanskrit.

It may amuse you if I describe the room I shall, I suppose, be living in for the next few months:

In a corner by the shuttered window, a plain writing-table where I sit in a pair of very wide and loose cotton trousers with a red girdle—in the Lucknow fashion (though outside I generally conform—with a *dhoti*). Though it's not hot (only 90 degrees Fahrenheit), there's no need to wear anything else. To my right a bench with books—poetry and belles-lettres in French and English, translations in Hindu, Chinese and Tibetan scriptures and some Sanskrit. Beyond, by the door, a green deck-chair and a cane stool. Behind, a folding wooden bed, also seated with cane. It is covered with a length of supple bark, the inner coating of a tree: this is used by yogins and contemplatives in India to insulate them from the earth and preserve the 'magnetism' of the body—I got it when I expected to be sleeping on the ground. Over that a very gay mattress, a cubit wide and of the thickness of a quilt (now, in the daytime, rolled up). On the floor by the bed a small tin travelling trunk in which I keep my books and papers that have accumulated now that I no longer lead the vagrant life I used to. The door at the back leads to the kitchen, one at the side to my friend's room. In front a small verandah and another little room at present used for his trunks. The floor is of earthen tiles, the walls washed with a cream colour. The room is very high, so on the big blank wall I have hung a rich and brilliant cloth from Ajmer—broad zigzags of black and red with a complex design of yellow, blue, green, red and white spots. A cord with a towel and loincloth on it completes this rather gypsy-interior. On the other wall a rich and sombre Indian picture of Shiva Nataraja, the Supreme as a Dancer. Outside, a radiant landscape of hills and trees.

[To complete this description, additional details were described in his next letter home, after Ella Maillart came to stay:]

Since a friend, a sincere and original woman, traveller and writer, has joined me here, I remember how much domestic details interest you:

I have still a contribution of 25 rupees a month from a friend and this is enough for me to live on in this country: I expect soon to try to publish essays and so on fairly regularly and to live by that. We rent a very pleasant little house here and our joint expenses every month amount to about 60 shillings, for we live very simply on vegetables and milk and fruit and a few eggs, so this also includes wages and food for a servant to cook and sweep.

We get up at four every morning and meditate or study sacred texts, then (for my friend's program is slightly different), before sunrise I bathe in the fine river here fringed with rich tropical palms. Breakfast of porridge, fruit and milk at about 7:30, then work of various kinds during the morning—study, writing, etc. —till lunch of rice and vegetables and curd at about noon. Then an hour's relaxation and an hour or two of rest lying down before tea. Then we type our notes of the previous evening's conversation with the Master and perhaps write a few letters. Just before sunset I am at the river again where I wash my simple cotton clothes on a stone and play in the water with the children of this little village (some miles from the post office). Then fruit and milk and perhaps some sweet my friend has concocted, before we go to the Master's house.

Neither of us has read a newspaper for many weeks, but we hear sooner or later the main points of the news.

22.XI.41.

That is not realisation, the Jnani has repeatedly affirmed, which does not embrace, explain and fulfil the richness of all the countless spheres of reality and all the worlds that can ever come to be. In this attitude I have myself stood firm from the beginning: I do not want simply *Liberation*, a mere necessity of bondage!

6.XII.41.

At present you free yourself from space, time and samskaric conditions only unconsciously, in sleep. *Samadhi* is temporary. This freedom is continuous only as *Lila*.

11.XII.41.

The first qualification of a Tantrika is shamelessness. The essential of Tantra is that it sees process as Reality Itself—recognition of *Lila*. This shamelessness really represents complete surrender. Shamelessness is integrity: it does not do what is unnecessary.

17.XII.41.

Talk with the Jnani. He had taken it that the question had been settled once and for all at Trivandrum in July—no guru *or sadhana for you!* At Trivandrum I asked him to be completely frank and open with me and he has since 'taken the liberty': otherwise he would have expressed things very differently.

One must never reveal to others what passes between us in our particular relationship, 'for others are not in your position. *For you* there is no guru.'

'This guru-question need not be discussed: no solution will be reached by discussion with the outer mind.

'It is not possible for violence to be done to me. You have done violence to *yourself*. I do not want disciples, I do not want to exist in this world. I do not exist in this world.'

As for dreams, he had told me before the main principle: all dreams must be taken to work out one's waking *samskaras*. Only what cannot be accounted for by one's waking thought can belong to another range, such as in his interpretation of this Kundalini dream:

Big rich house with potted flowers. At some moment talking to the Jnani I touch his feet and lay my head on his knees, weeping. He tells me not to discuss with him the guru-question. Making notes and finishing a sentence I had lost the thread of what he was saying. He went away quite disinterestedly, not as a protest but as if because it was useless to go on speaking when I was not attending. He sat on a verandah in a sort of Mediterranean richness of light and flowers, wih a vivid and beautiful cheetah-cub. When playing with it he placed its head upon his, or its front paws and breast on the top of his head. I entered the verandah and then, receiving me lovingly, he put his head down on my lap and with one hand very gently stroked upwards from the base of my spine—then with both hands. A subtle vibrating current of vivid fire and enchantment passes upward with his fingers and this movement is repeated several times till at last a great flash, as it were, from Kundalini *chakra* passed upward and I feel that very centre has been opened—release of vital force. Going back into the house he is received by his wife—he seems to be in curiously powerful mood and looks strange. Overcoat and collar turned up, big spectacles. Going away, I think the subtle relation had links with what was being spoken of or with the occasion of my kneeling at his feet, that he had perhaps for some time intended to do this when the opportunity of touching me should occur.

In the dream, still taking it for reality, I say something about questioning him on it in Malakkarai.

The Kundalini sensation was much enhanced when I breathed in.

I went through the whole thing with him—one doesn't ascribe this to oneself—the disinterestedness that is bound to give most weight to what is opposite to one's natural point of view, the necessary preferring of others' (for example, the *bhaktas*') position to one's own; but at present, in outer consciousness, imagination of other possibilities—the transcendental nature of the guru—indistinguishable from any other mental forms. One is only on one's feet in one's most economical truthfulness. All confusion is really from not fulfilling it alone, for this would lead to all fulfilment; anguish, polarity with possibilities which, if real, can only be integrally reached.

The thing is to go forward patiently on one's own true base, without tormenting oneself, then the fullness of the truth will be revealed. 'You *will* be free of confusion henceforward, you *will* come to know all.'

With his own guru, he has only described to me his 'conversion' by his humility and sweetness, but (he told me with emotion) if he had fully understood him from the first his *sadhana* would have taken a different course: it was only years afterwards that he appreciated him for what he really was.

Last night's dream: something must certainly have come from the Jnani. Psychic experience of him would not solve my problems.

18.XII.41.

As I bow at his feet as he stands, he bends his head to touch my back and afterwards touches head and nape. Rising, I say: 'One day I will understand you. He, with emotion: 'No. We are one.' And he went away in tears.

24–25.XII.41. Dream.

The Jnani standing in a kind of park. As he looks at it, a peacock at the end of a willow-branch, slowly overcoming its timidity, approaches him.

21.XII.41. Kathakali dance-drama, village of Tiruvella.

The crowd, rockets zithering like scissors through heavy silk, reaches a silent, astonished consummation.

In the retiring-room supernatural characters, with long, reddened eyes, faces green, or red, black and white, with elegant or terrible white frills about the cheek-bones, unsmilingly appraise themselves in little mirrors.

They are waited upon by mere humans with uniform brown faces, who tie ornaments above the bulky dress and a piling aureoled headdress above the intense mask with its winking eyes. A cruel woman with a delicate arabesque about the jaws dusts spangles upon a dancer's lifted face.

In the portico of the temple a dense crowd. A heavy cloth with bold red and black designs held before a great brass lamp.

The living flames, the warm and changing breath of light and a furious, peremptory, trenchant, clashing staccato music, supported them in their superreal cold.

Behind the curtain (I sit at first on the stage, like an Elizabethan blood) the first character solemnly postures—invocation to God, homage to the guru. One sees the connection between the rich Indian elegance and the slighter, more rococo grace of Javanese dance. Slowly and gravely, but already florid, the song begins.

Apparently Kathakali preserves the tradition of the Upanishads' high-spirited rishis—intensely alert with gay intelligence, all their movements swift, sparkling, economical, energetic: action is so intense and frictionless in them that you feel they have no external rest but in *samadhi* or deep contemplation.

How much more true a culture this stylised village art represents than the insipidly pseudo-realistic talkies, *circenses* of the degraded modern *demos*. But in its long descent Kathakali has no doubt grown rather slack and shapeless and badly needs editing: almost every episode is prolonged and elaborated to pointlessness.

Or Kathakali must be supposed to act like a very slow drug. It lasts all night and has the delays, the long self-hypnosis and self-involutions of dream. Yes indeed, it proceeds by figures and images, its narrative is non-temporal; like Indian music it sustains a timeless intensity.

Drums, cymbals, gongs crisply punctuate minutely gestured exposition or dialogue. But from time to time the pitch is raised to continuous climax, till the singer's voice emerges from the ecstatic clangour to carry the story a little further.

Baka and *Bhima*—the green-faced sattvik hero with his proud gestures and noble high-spiritedness; the *rakshasa* demon with his guttural roar: finicky taloned hand to-fro in precise rage at the curtain. Till at last, dragging it down and plunging forward, under the great nimbus of his *kirita*, he is revealed—prodigious, voluminous, arms feathered like some monstrous bird, face red, black and white, dehumanised by fragile white combs about the cheekbones, with knobs of pith on forehead and nose, with little designs of a nightmare arbitrariness and precision. The fanged, wickedly flexible mouth is more clearly the face of many a financier, drug-king, art-merchant, politician.

Heads a little drawn back at this furious display, the audience, like a child wise but not too wise, is only half skeptical.

The daivik hero enters: how delicate appear the forces of good! Elaborate boasting, threats, contempt; the combat formal as a waltz or else complex and turbulent; the *rakshasa's* finally voiceless cries and vivid grimaces of pain; triumphant circling and prancing of Bhima, till the figured red curtain is held arm-high once more before the flaming lamp of brass.

As we return to the bungalow to sleep (it is long past midnight) the clanging cymbal, the passionate voice of the singer, the attention of the crowd, sustain an exotic oasis, a ringing centre of light and energy, in that silent and unconscious night.

7–8.I.42. Dream.

I help D.M. to haul a big cubical grey-white block of stone out of a well. As I pull with him the rope unravels near us and divides. The block is seen lifted high above the well-head. He has to send it to someone and I point out that the heavy stone will break any crate that may be built round it.

The Jnani agreed that the cube is the Hermetic 'squared circle'—like the Kaaba the symbol of realisation complete in terms of the earth. And 'Truth is at the bottom of a well.'

8–9.I.42. Dream.

Throughout sleep, it seemed, I was conscious of my state of intention during the day—waking a state like others, like dream.

18–19.I.42. A copy of this account of the night asked for by the Jnani.

Rigorous attempt in meditation to attain the Ultimate. I am seated, simple *asana*, in a slightly hollowed circle on the ground, the Jnani to my right, apparently standing outside the circle, and looking on with interest.

It is at the second stage of an accompanying chanted verse that I begin to make a great effort—really rather doubting if I can reach, or holding concentration into the head I lost myself, passed beyond myself upward through the crown of my head.

As I emerge, the Jnani, raising me from the ground as one might a man who has fainted, embraces me and kisses my lips. But I realise that I do not respond on his own exalted plane to the kiss. At some stage with laughter, I 'come down'.

20.I.42.

The Jnani asks if I remained conscious or was really lost and I reply that there was really no lapse from consciousness in the highest sense, though there was a gap from the point of view of the mind after the culmination of my effort.

The Jnani affirms that this was undoubtedly *nirvikalpa-samadhi* and tells me that in an experience the night before it happened, one of the family foresaw that I should soon attain it and when he was told he agreed that I was near it. 'The experience we had here' was exactly the same as that I have noted above except that, as for my response afterwards, 'your tone admitted what your words refused'.

He says that the 'shock' of the heart, in relation with this experience, means that the *nridaya-granthi* ('knots' of samskaras) are being destroyed, and this is confirmed by my having fairly often before sensed the ego quite objectively as a whole on waking—an experience which he assures me is more valuable than *nirvilakpa-samadhi* and points away from realisation entirely in *samadhi* to an integration of the Reality in terms of body and mind.

21–22.I.42. A copy of this account of the night asked for by the Jnani.

> ' In Christ all the Creatures are one man, and that man is God.'
>
> Meister Eckhart

A golden mask of the Christ, connected with the Word. Afterwards a brilliant golden statuette, slightly bent and leaning in the posture of a Pieta. The smooth head, high at the back, slopes towards the forehead. In the waking state it reminds me of the Jnani. I realise later that something in the outline of the jaws reminds me of the Mother at Pondicherry, and the whole very directly of Sri Ramana Maharshi in certain of his aspects. Wide straight mouth, simple, strong and grave; rather wide cheek-bones; the whole very specific and real, profoundly and subtly modelled by deep feeling. I still remember it quite clearly a week later and feel that I shall never entirely forget it.

The living face was seen separately from its image in the statuette, against a background corresponding with Woodford Green, which refers to a period, from, say, twelve to fourteen, when I thought much about the Christ.

Strength and sensibility of one established upon the Earth—a king of wisdom and greatness all of feeling, soul and will, and with great depth and peace.

It is the Christ as *Man*, the consummated Adam—the Face of all humanity and ultimately the Sole Person, the Purushottama.

It is strong, subtle, silent, nude, like that of an old peasant, sailor or mountaineer—with the sweet gravity and simplicity of the earth—deepened, strengthened, sweetened and subtilised by the wisdom of experience, something deeper and older than himself that in the sailor or mountain guide would have come to inhabit him, of which he has become the vehicle and which he possesses by his personal integrity, humility and purified truthfulness.

It might be the face of a man of fifty, but its main character is so strong that one does not notice the quality of the skin or if it is wrinkled, though it seems ripe, healthy and a uniform, in fact quite Indian, brown such as only a life-time of sun could give a European face. Beardless, it is beyond sexuality: its mature strength contains and surpasses the qualities of man, woman, child.

Great understanding and sympathy without the slightest sentimentality; great patience without slowness, and unconditioned by any aim; great wisdom without intellectuality; a peace that seems the *source* of all joy, itself too rooted collected, uniform, ageless to manifest anything but itself. Sun and wind play over this face, whether gently or ruthlessly, without changing it.

Leonardo da Vinci's study for the Christ of the *Last Supper* is like a very refined, attenuated and sweetened version of some qualities of this face, but without the weight and directness and nakedness of primordiality—of the direct, familiar yet profound humanity, all realism: da Vinci's work is frail, precious and ideal.

When the face begins to live and move—another connection with the Jnani was the action of chewing—to hide it from others I veil it and carry it in my hand to a church where such are used as 'ikons'.

Later, it is the idea of going on Sunday to a church I used to attend as a boy, on the way along the road skirting the Green at a place I have not remembered, perhaps, since I left Europe more than nine years ago and even many years before that. I hear the strong cultured voice preaching in the open air. I realise that there is nothing for me here, that I shall return home.

This was followed, I cannot remember whether waking or 'asleep', by the following memory of my schooldays:

Going to the 'Warren' at Loughton for games. The child is frail, it was a long walk uphill. He acts in terms of a very subtle and mobile vital energy, directly linked with feeling and imagination. In terms of this mobile current, a kind of delicate light or aura, it is therefore much easier to do such things as necessary walking to and from school with other children, supported by talk and play, the whole common subtle interchange.

The child accepts without discussion the rulings and arrangements of elders, because they lie outside the range of what interests him or he can clearly think—he is passive to an unknown psychological world which is not yet objective to him, for he has not yet organs (a developed mind) to objectify its growing life in himself. Meanwhile he is essentially a creature of the vital and the soul, moving in terms of a delicate, luminous psychic universe which for grown-ups has been limited and taken up into rigid formalisation by the mind. But the possibility of this mind hangs over the child so that he is passive to his own world also—expands it and explores it not consciously but spontaneously, as the wind spreads and travels without losing itself, not enlarged by its travelling, but only changing form.

22–23.I.42. Concluding account of nocturnal experience recounted to the Jnani.

A little old woman who is not in this life—perhaps my former guru—and only rarely appears, undertakes to show me something. On the way to a little-used room she tells a young man that she is more than a century, hundreds of years old. In the room, silently and complexly, she concentrates, one after another, upon photographs till all the people in them appear as they were many years before—younger, with different expressions, and in the case of a rather undeveloped person, as a kind of monkey in human dress.

The scene where, before this, I embrace her with emotion and some reference to my fidelity, is, I realise on waking, something like my mother's bedroom in a house I lived in as a boy. But this strange woman beyond or outside the human state is not at all like my mother and evidently contains other, perhaps Tantrik, elements.

24.I.42.

I continue to note these tendencies in order to aid with my imagination the effect of the *samadhi* and as a way of keeping in touch with it:

The mind is like air or water: every movement has an immediate fullness of effect but subsides immediately and completely, leaving no trace.

The air or water itself is as it were an inexhaustible unmanifest laughter. It cannot weigh upon any act or occasion in order to achieve intensity, for all are equal and equally evanescent: all that can happen is that each occasion is a greater *volume* of water, a deeper wave, or a lighter, more iridescent, joyous and delicate scatter of spray.

It is this no doubt that expresses itself in greater and greater concentration, so that every thought tends to fulfil itself immediately or exhausts its consequences in a *savikalpa* experience.

29.I.42.

Everything is the perpetual Wonder of the Reality, pure Marvel constructed of Marvel, but Void and fullness and neither—outrageous without being shocking, sweetly interesting without exciting interest, keenly and massively delightful only as a reflection of Peace.

In every moment, *as* every moment, innumerable worlds of consciousness, experience, expression, arise, condense and work themselves out.

The physical world is like an untrembling reflection, a boundless sea or mirage—as clear, as constant and as evanescent: at the slightest 'vertical' penetration it proves pure, undifferentiated Air, inexhaustibly cool and sapid Water.

(The defect of this figure is the suggestion of something outside the water to be reflected!)

Retrospect.

The fact that this experience took place incidentally, as it were, in the psychic consciousness, I take to show that in the waking state the intention has always been *sahaja* and nothing else.

The Jnani's comments on the vision of the Christ as Man:

'The whole Truth is portrayed in that experience, every aspect of it is there.' He read it two or three times and said he will get much from reading it again.

'It gives an outline of the whole inner movement of your life which brings with it your past lives as well.

'It has meaning individually and cosmically, and the Truth Itself is also very clearly expressed in it. You had a vision of the real Christ—that Christ who comprehends within Himself the whole Truth.

'Such an experience, if not at once fully understood, will be made clear later and mental constructions upon it will be corrected. It is different from all your other experiences and the record of it should be preserved.

'I see nothing in your aphorisms that necessarily conflicts with the point of view of pure *jnana*. Your *intention*, then, in wishing to 'give up' sleep, must appear yogic.'

'From the standpoint of pure *jnana*:

'There is no need to change any of the three states (waking, dream, sleep): all are effortlessly enlightened from the Source.

'Leave everything as it is, without doing anything. The rest is not for us to discuss, decide, attain. There is absolutely nothing to be done hereafter. But this does not mean that you will not be doing!

'Whatever one may do can have no reference to the 'Ultimate beyond', for from that standpoint doing and not doing are the same.

'What you learned waking you forget in the dream and sleep. So the *jnana* you had in *nirvikalpa-samadhi* is forgotten, but the Centre is not lost: only the mind is not taking hold of it.

'If mind sleeps, no matter.

'You want to correct your states like a man bitten by a mad dog who in order to become a man again tries to cut off his tail.'

He agrees that 'I was always as I am—no *sadhana*, no *nirvikalpa-samadhi*, no realisation.'

'Those who have experienced a 'subtle illumination', who have an unshaken conviction that they are other than they thought themselves before, may also sometimes be said to be realised. Those who on the *samadhi* path have had this illumination may want to purify the mind and reject certain thoughts as a yogin would do, till the mind becomes purely light-discriminative and, purged of *vasanas* ('imprints'), is absorbed. But the body has been left out of account: why should it not also be transformed? And anyway, why this process? Because the mind sometimes thinks of things other than the Reality and it is not seen that thoughts are also the Reality. What is there to show you that your thought is *not* That?'

'From the point of view of *yoga*:

'Yoga intrudes into *jnana* only if you are to be left as a corpse in this world: if as a 'result' of realisation is another matter. A yogic tendency may make one wish to be conscious in sleep. Overcoming sleep is a yogin's way and without yogic practices would injure health.'

Of course it is not really a question of 'giving up' but of 'transforming' sleep.

Letter to a fellow disciple of the Jnani:

... A certain penetration of the waking state from beyond had been taking place for a long time. I see that all my thought, and particularly all that I have written (journal, aphorisms) since eighteen or nineteen, has really been organised from the point of view of *nirvikalpa-samadhi* and the Jnani remarked this about my thought soon after I first met him. It was for this reason that *nirvikalpa-samadhi* could not for me, either, be an aim, and no deliberate steps could be taken to reach it—everything was done 'from below': the requirement is *sahaja-samadhi*; everything else is from the start, potentially over-passed.

That is why left to myself I should have made nothing of this experience, why it literally never occurred to me to tell you of it, and why when P.N. (a disciple), informed by the Jnani, recognised its importance, I could only say, perfectly sincerely and as a matter of course, 'It is really nothing: everything remains to be done.'

As the Jnani says, it establishes a centre from which one will work hereafter. In other words, real concentration now becomes possible, the natural concentration that will establish *sahaja* and fulfil all predetermined perfection—the Jnani says inevitably and without effort.

He tells me also that I have experienced *nirvikalpa-samadhi* before, only was 'not aware of it *as such*', and in Ceylon in 1933 I entered *mahabhava*, which I had never heard of then. He says it is usually necessary to enter *nirvikalpa-samadhi* several times in order to reach an effect for the outer consciousness which in this case was obtained at once.

'The notion of realisation, I told the Jnani, 'seems to become a dream, and one begins to wonder who it was exactly who had that idea.' To this he responded: 'Yes, quite so!' As I have always said: Realisation is the fact that realisation is not necessary—its reality is the fact that the point of view from which it can seem necessary is irrelevant to it and the only 'obstacle' to it.

I have no clear memory of having ever lived for five minutes together with the perfect truthfulness, awareness, resource that can alone satisfy me. My whole life, from my own, inward, point of view, has been an endless, subtle, complicated, effortful failure. One is entirely perfect now and ever or not at all. From the point of view of *jnana* it can only be a question of becoming aware of perfection, of removing the irrelevant limitations of mind and will—sleep as a condition, for only the Whole, only Unity is perfect. The 'I' will never be satisfied; it is itself imperfection, the impossible, paradox.

17

The Black Lion

30–31.I.42. Dream.

Exploring what in the dream I call Egyptian and Babylonian worlds, though they might also have belonged to any powerful forgotten civilisation. I am led by a yogin who tells me he has discovered a way of reaching them. We climb difficult, roughly split or hewn rocks, and somehow penetrate reserves of vivid powerful images unknown to those who see only surface remains.

January 1942.
Temple festival at Chengannur: Shiva's hunt.

Shiva, Parvati, Ganesha, Subrahmanyam, Bhagavati—concentrated ikons on five elephants, with red and gold parasols against the cold night sky. The yellow gold of lighted bodies waving *chamaras* (fans) upon a granite rock spined and blooming with life. Or under the great trees, lighted with dream—clarity by rapid spiring flames, five-or eight-fold upon rays of iron at the corner of heavy poles. Dense, sweet-smelling, silent crowd.

The *nagaswaram* player, a man of twenty, plays his long double-reed pipe with a peculiar richness and brilliance and corresponding in compass more or less to the old *oboe de caccia*. Shining hair loosely gathered at the nape. Svelte, graceful, wide body, red and gold embroidered cloth about the hips, below the knees. Fine wrists, the strong delicate fingers with pink nails upon the long simple black trumpet, pointed towards the sky with a pure and ancient posture of the arms, the strong, supple shoulders, the sufficiently muscled torso swung across and down and up again, the acerb, zestful, vibrant, youthful sound given a new edge of colour, smeared through the air like fresh blood. Brilliant, concentrated style like the feline sleekness and compactness of the whole body, the concentrated face, the curved nose with keen nostrils, the long narrow eyes, finely modelled cheekbones and jaws, sardonic lips. The small ears set off with diamonds, a thin gold chain falling a little below the collar-bones, a little golden talisman on a thin red cord about the slender, tapering arms.

The face hard, proud, cruel, passionate, absorbed; the light, delicate taut body lifted upon the toes, turning from the hips. The waist, the shoulder in the cascading, passionate, impervious, violent caresses, juggling and sword -play of biting, exalted, ringing or searing sound, sustained ever-fresh at the extreme ictus of passion. And counterpoints by the metallic double-tipped *mridangam* drums, cold, brilliant with learned and dramatic fury.

Back through nocturnes by Watteau. Forests and villages dumb with moonlight and space suspended by that secret, absent, indirect silence.

Tea and coffee, characteristically modern drinks, flagellate nerves and mind to endless activity—they disintegrate simple enjoyment of life as the self-sufficing, break up perception of the Infinite through immediate sensibility into a whirligig of illusory, unattainable pespectives...Or, for most, they are no doubt required simply to overcome lethargy in order to meet frenetic modern demands almost exclusively at the rational level; for global enjoyment of life is no longer conscious, lucid.

2–3.II. 42. Dream.

I revisit Ramana Ashram. They say I am in debt for twelve days' food there.

Ramana Maharshi in a new high chair:

'If I ever go to the Jnani it will be as a friend.' (The implication was): 'In spite of what I hear about him.'

Then to me as he walks away, with the slowness and precaution of an old man: 'You will have extraordinary experiences there with the Jnani, extraordinary experiences.'

This makes me feel that I must deeply examine everything—and particularly myself—at Malakkarai and not necessarily believe what the Jnani says about the *nirvikalpa-samadhi.*

When realisation is spoken of, the ego is still there—it can only be spoken of in relation with the ego: there is not yet only the Truth, Self-luminous, having absorbed all.

3.II.42.

The onesidedness of literature: The rich, massive world of flowers, perfume and strong Sanskrit letters, of elephant-grey, cardinal and gold, of fuschia, laurel and musk, that opens to the inner sense at this moment would demand for outward expression a fusion of the painting of Bagh and the music of Tibet.

5.II.42.

The trees are asleep but intensely dreaming. The moon, sun of that concentrated dream, is rising behind them towards the zenith of her reign.

Unemphatic music of insects, sistrums, pipes, silver cymbals and xylophones.

But binding all into a conscious beating hallucination (endless, inescapable), the vivid, lively but unhurried pulsing of a drum.

It suggests some rite on the border of the human, with accessories at the same time fearful and grotesque—blood, feathers, a severed goat's head, symbols like toys but with non-rational clarity and directness.

12–13.II.42. Dream.

Til Beauc, sailor-poet, Provence. In a little restaurant he prepares omelette and some local dishes. Coffee, vin rosée.

Atmosphere of youth, colour, elegance, joy, zest, clarity, poetic possibilities. As it was in reality, but youth then not knowing its own prestige and beauty, its rare sunlight and ozone, but reduced to zero, to anguish, by an ideal perfection. I remember Cassis. Radiant air, sparkling sea like a sapphire wine, pale tortuous olive-trees, keen flowers, red earth, thyme, marjoram; the bright bars, the little harbour, the little circus, cuttle-fish bones, roped-soled espadrilles. Had the sailor-poet I lodged with a name like Til Beauc?

One had no experience or rational perspective or self-consciousness, but one's life was an ambience of delicate and immediate vital sensations and perceptions not now obtainable, a sensibility sterilised, placed in a void, by its absolute, suffocating disinterestedness—as if a very subtle elixir inhabited one's breath, blood and nerves.

21.II.42.

At Nagerkoil we brought a great saint, one '*in sahaja*', an old lady inexpressibly sweet, simple, dignified—queen and peasant one—to visit the Jnani. He had hardly looked at her when speaking like a child, the words bubbling, as it were, with surging rich emotion, he asked: 'Mother, may I go in? —but already was overcome and fell down on the floor. With infinite simple love, joy and wisdom she fondled him, his head upon her breast; then, as the state deepened and there lay there a figure denuded, beautiful, august, she came and sat beside us, remarking (as a mother might to a neighbour, simply sweetly, 'He is sleeping. The *jiva* is gone to the Absolute.'

Last time it was she who lay down, overwhelmed.

Before she left she went back and embraced his wife.

We took her back to her house and when we returned the Jnani was seated beside his wife on the mat that had been brought for him to lie upon. He was still, as it were, immersed in nectar—rich, radiant.

15–16.II.42. Dream.

With the Jnani in sunny streets freshly bright as if washed by rain. Very bright clothes hung out are associated in the dream with the Tamil country. A certain bright shabbiness everywhere, and the peculiar atmosphere of the dream remind me of glamorous 'astral slums' I have 'visited' before, though here the tone is lighter and a rather heavy sinister intensity is absent.

Walking back to his usual house he stops and I am very close to him while he speaks in an access of confidence. He is shrunken, wizened, very yellow. When he draws me to him I feel him stiff, immovably clenched, as if with a deforming calcification of the bones. It gives him pain. He tells me it is due to the cocaine which he has been taking for years. Cocaine, in a special experience, was the immediate cause of his realisation.

He is impregnated with cocaine, yellowed within as well, it seems. He holds me closer and closer—I get the bitterness of his skin—till finally we kiss. I felt thoroughly no physical or emotional excitement. His kiss is deep, prolonged, intense, with a peculiar movement of the lips and tongue. I wish to withdraw and say 'I can't bear this kiss', but he insists and continues.

He tells me that his wife of course knows this secret of the cocaine and asks if I know why on Fridays he always gets others to talk with him on spiritual matters so as to raise his mind to very subtle levels. I understand that it is because on this day he takes the cocaine and would like to profit from it as much as possible.

Throughout the experience I seemed to have my full normal consciousness, behaved quite consistently and had no doubt that all, though so strange was completely real. Sense of the complete transfusion of the physical world by *sukshma* (etheric) realities, the impossibility of seeing 'the physical in itself'. The fact that it was more than an ordinary dream is also supported by the fact that most of the external materials were from trivial *samkaras* of yesterday only, having no weight in themselves, while the other elements—kiss, cocaine, and the whole peculiar atmosphere of the dream —were not analysably due to ordinary *samskaras* at all. I awoke, at about three-thirty with a very strong, persistent and intimate sense of the Jnani.

Like another recent one, the dream very subtly suggested, in its net effect —and directly to my sensibility, not by inference—that I am being in some way as it were 'handled', diverted, even exploited by the Jnani.

17.II.42.

Conversation with P.N.

I reminded him that (as I have so often affirmed) realisation has never been my object and is for me strictly and precisely an inevitable Nothing: there is only Reality: the only truth, then, is for me to pursue and complete my own truths: if there is any question of realisation I can only say I would rather take ten births my own way than realise at once for the sake of realisation. What, anyway, can desire or value it but the very ego it makes irrelevant.

19–20.II.42. Dream.

A school of dancers. The guru, who reminds me of the Jnani, is seated with legs up on a chair. On the floor I am seated beside a very beautiful girl. I do not myself seem to be a pupil, but friend or visitor. Without the slightest provocation or even interest on my part she kisses me passionately.

We are to get married and the greatest happiness is promised. Though I appreciate the girl's charm and beauty, I feel entirely detached.

A kind of temple or church, in early Renaissance style, walls and floor of white marble with panels and mouldings, lucid, elegant forms, cool colour including light blue, but with a note of rather rigid Byzantine richness and formality.

In an apse to the left as one enters, the Jnani, richly clothed, sits high up, as if enthroned, with others, behind an open-work screen of worked metal with brass or golden finials and ornaments.

The altar is felt to be at the end of a similar wing opposite the right; it is only dimly, though coolly, lighted and one can see only a little way into it.

I realise, then, that for the marriage I shall have to turn my back upon the Jnani and face in the opposite direction: I cannot bring myself to do so. The presumption was that he approved of this marriage.

I turn towards him in doubt and when I look back it is at a tall, upright, very concentrated and powerful figure, the priest who is to perform the ceremony. He gives the impression of a being with very high occult powers and even an appearance of great spiritual prestige. Short tightly curling rather square black beard; very thick dark eyebrows, or the eyes are so big, wide and dark, seeming to cover the whole breadth of the face, that they give this impression. When my gaze plunges into these eyes, as if compelled by their extraordinary power, I think one might lose oneself so, for they dizzy and disorient like an abyss; yet I know I cannot really lose myself but even deliberately allow the rather pleasurable sensation, as if I wished to measure this being. He wears a kind of cassock, severe, of a strong deep brown. The impression of his dense occult power and authority completes itself in the waking state in the idea of the Antichrist: the hieratic face, dark with the formal, concentrated blackness of hair on the ivory skin and with its great hallucinating eyes, is very like certain Byzantine Christs.

I realise that this being is strongly hostile to the Jnani and this marriage is a trap. As a kind of test of the 'priest' I begin systematically to torture him.

I have pierced his left foot with a kind of javelin, all very deliberate and with a kind of exalted strength. It seems that he will be undone if I pierce the right foot also and there is a special occult resistance to this. He has accepted and borne all hitherto as if with the certainty that he will not be defeated. It is like the crucifixion of the Christ.

I wake with images of ever-renewed flowing of blood from the wounds I have inflicted or rather of pink corpuscles in lymph as from an exhausted wound and like the 'blood and water' that flowed from the Christ wounded with a spear—discrete and granular like the flesh of orange or pomegranate.

Immediately on waking I thought: here is an experience in some ways opposite from the 'cocaine dream' and with the common detail of a kiss.

There was no special *sukshma* (etheric) atmosphere.

Waking, I chiefly remember the very powerful impression produced by the 'priest'. This impression could be related with Ella's explanation yesterday that in the Trivandrum 1941 portrait photograph I seemed to her like a stone block of ruthless hardness and this is the side of me that she thinks would be developed by yoga. I do not myself see this hard will in the photograph but when she points it out I could perceive, at a certain level, the truth of it.

I stand up and at once in my erectness and my whole 'atmosphere' I feel something that might have been transposed and isolated as the 'priest' and I now realise that he was of my height and build.

1–2.III.42

During the night I was pierced by a moment of extraordinarily keen yet simple joy and illumination. Can it be the beginning of transformation of sleep into *nirvikalpa samadhi* or *nirvikalpa samadhi* appearing in the Heart?

2–3.III.42. Dream.

Subrahmanyam shrine high up on the steep face of jungle-covered mountain. I think of going there to spend some days in meditation or yoga. I meet an entirely black lion coming *apradakshina* round a little temple at that point on the mountain-side. I decide to go on in spite of it; I am unharmed. *[Apradakshina means 'counter-clockwise circumambulation' and is therefore conventionally against the spiritual grain, but for that reason regarded as of great potency by certain 'left-handed' sects.]*

14–15.III.42. Dream.

Envelope finely outlined in black from Margot: Mother dead.

18.III.42.

Continuing weakness for the last fortnight is an opportunity to organise oneself entirely in terms of spiritual strength—'sensuality' in Dame Julian of Norwich's sense to be commanded by 'substance'—transformation of the temporal nature in terms of the timeless Spirit—establishment of *sahaja*.

What is wanted is all that encourages delicate sui-generis impressions and resources of vital sensibility and imagination (like those released by poems of Cocteau, by thought of the life of kathekali-dancers)—all that in the Jnani's sense is related with Moon rather than Sun, Sensibility and Imagination rather than Thought and Will, with Heart rather than Head—all that is immediate and trans-mental, that casts upon mental language its own rhythms and richness and precise and subtle imagery. —Everything cooling, timeless, untensed, spontaneous—the colored substance of things, the vital sap, dew, *amrita* (nectar) from the thousand-petalled lotus upon the Heart.

23–24.VIII.42.

The whole strain of sex is from tension within the mind—tension between the cerebro-spinal and sympathetic systems—lack of geniality. If there is complete consent, the high-pitched, self-exalting tension can be avoided. Whether sexuality is to be indulged or not, sex is the power of the

Eros as it manifests at the physical level. But the Eros *as a whole* must not be questioned on this basis. Let each level remain whole. Only D's sound and sensible realism; my unrealistic, paradoxical and hopelessly complicating self-tension. My inconclusive tenuity, 'fragility', sterile subtlety is no doubt from denial of the physical in its own sense. The physical in itself must also not be disturbed by mental curiosity and experimentation.

...The relation between mental ingenuity in sex and experiment with drugs...

The forthright realism of *vajroli-mudra*—yogic flushing of the bowels—should always be taken as typically the yogic attitude in relation with the physical. No *technical* perfection is possible without perfect realism.

The physical is to be related with Centrality. But it must first be acknowledged as physical.

Meanwhile it remains true that my nerves have been weakened, partly by this tension and that higher and wider mental and spiritual realisations, if they are also perfectly genial and not romantically defined by will and tension, spontaneously and joyously integrate to their purpose the basic sexual energy. This spontaneity and geniality will appear in perfect human love, compassion, humour, understanding: it must contain the human as it is with all its possibilities, not only beyond all prejudices, criticism or judgment, but in the most prompt and tender consideration.

25.III.42. Letter to the Jnani.

The sensation of seeing the ego as object reaches a stage so subtle that I cannot afterwards remember or describe it. It almost seems to be Man himself in the highest sense, as Purusha, who is an unreality, quite arbitrary. I do not succeed in seizing it.

15–16.VI.42. Courtellam. Dream.

A dream really too special to describe—style and sequence unlike anything else:

The great proud King, twenty feet tall, simple, bright, effective like a giant village Ravana of wood and painted paper, advances in procession into the house. I, who witness and have dramatised all from the beginning in earlier episodes—a tiny human creature—look up at him and flatter him. He is proud, genial and stupid like a kathakali demon. He quotes some remark of mine about the effect of music on processions.

Four friends in a strange empty house, by the entry of a power which has now become this king, have been bound down on couches, tied like toys in frames of wood and string, in unnatural attitudes—rebellious, perhaps blaming me. For all this follows their fear of and enmity towards powers which I welcomed because I knew they could be overcome by understanding and love. All began with a companion's fear in the strange grey and glossy, sombre, blue house at night. Refusing to accept the wave of his terror, I led him back to the other. But the occult influences immediately followed and I absorbed them.

One of my four bound friends make *namaskaram* to the great King. Desire to ingratiate himself for safety's sake has produced in him a kind of sweet, graceful and vital sincerity.

As the procession advances it begins to exceed itself in over-topping grotesqueness. I am at the same time the consciousness of the King and of the rebel who began this movement. I lead the King at a quickened pace uphill till his whole world begins to disintegrate, forced to a speed too great for its conditions. All, stage by stage, in a humorous rapid rhythm, topples, falls to pieces...

One of the King's retainers, however, an old woman, remains faithful to him. She appears as a brass *chembu* of water which, with deep emotion—still strongly felt on waking—the King pours through a little hole into a kind of closed well or cistern for the future of departing souls.

'Be blessed—God bless you—may you reach eternal happiness.'

Then, still with great emotion at this survival of a being made real by devotion from an unreal world and an unreal object, he, now abdicated, seeing the pity and surprise of a nearby artisan in his wayside shop, reverses the vessel over his head to receive the last sacred drop.

23.VI.42. Letter to Ella Maillart.

One tends to fall into a special style with everyone one knows—a sort of working compromise with many factors; yet this style may become a veil and in one's own heart one never really accepts a compromise—always largely with one's own weakness. And such a habit may also irk the fact that like a Hindu god one has innumerable aspects. It may become tiresome to appear always in the same way: after all, one betrays others' sincerity also if one makes their comfort the chief consideration. Yet it is true that one can (*if* one can!) only be continually quite direct—and consistently inconsistent—'before God'. From this relative point of view one's essence is always a secret, a solitude.

You write: "in the egoless state return over a past action would surely be impossible, as we would have acted without ego and therefore there would be no concern about it?"

The wave is only ocean, yet on the surface it seems to have continuity as wave. Once you introduce the idea of the ego you see this continuity, the optical illusion works. Otherwise, the ocean heaves entirely vertically: every act is direct and spontaneous, there is no looking back—the whole universe with all its inner relationships is created anew at every moment and time is one of those inner relationships! In the egoless state there is no past to return over. Your question contains a confusion. Because for an ego there appears to be a returning, it does not follow that there was ever concern—that also is imported by the ego. If you had acted without ego, the ego that questions must have arisen *since*—it alone imports the idea of time. Otherwise the question does not arise; if it arises, like all questions that deal with something more than names, it is unanswerable on its own plane.

27.VI.42.

P.N. tells me that the Jnani once said to him: "I know your nature, but not at all what Chillilananda's true nature is."

Perhaps because I have no individual nature but that of the artist, and so for me nature is entirely formal. All that I appear is imaginative improvisation.

End of June, 1942. Letter to Ella Maillart.

I am perhaps more conscious, and blame myself, more than you think for my imperfections and the imperfection of my speech and behaviour with you. It is clear for all to see that I am *very* far from being an harmonious whole.

My dear, you have never bored me and I do not see how you ever will. As for the question of 'mind', the beauty of yours is that it is one with your central sincerity and aspiration and so a lesson to me who am too often tempted to be complicated, perverse, pedantic or downright specious.

The speed of my mind really corresponds with an intensity far greater than my nervous system can generally sustain, and so it sometimes tends to race, extravagate (yes, there is a verb!), throw out sparks: it is only at a rather high level that I can be fully myself and so it is rarely that I find an acceptable occasion to be really spontaneous. In fact, I am never even for a moment fully myself—who is, after all, short of *sahaja ('spiritual spontaneity')* ? What is required, of course, is to tune the lower or surface strata of oneself to the pitch and amplitude of the greatest depth or highest intensity. It is such a singleness, no doubt, that explains the tendency in the Jnani for the whole ocean to respond—in *mahabhava*—to an occasion that need only, it would seem, arouse a wave: 'the ocean is in the drop'.

Do you know that when with your organic sincerity you ask me any question I often feel somewhere a little embarrased and ashamed, and that I feel I have never been able to give you the simple and genuine answer you deserve—or how impossible it is for me inwardly to accept your generous consideration of my ingenious or complicated or spur-of-the-moment responses? I admit that I do more and more try to do you justice as far as I can, but I am not simple and global enough to succeed as one should—on the one hand too sceptical and analytical, on the other hand such an incurable poet or *lilan*! You perhaps don't realise how positive I am in my half-joking remarks about your weight and solidity: for myself, because of my volatile psychic nature rather butterfly than bee, at least solidity can be symbolically appreciated!

As for offhandedness, I'm not the one to fail to appreciate it: I'm all for getting rid of unnecessary ceremony. I think I remarked to you once that it is only those who are in some way one with us that we can—thank God—forget, for we have to make no effort to remember them!

28–29.VI.42. Dream.

I say to myself, and wake with the words, which I almost exactly remember: 'Whether I find myself in some other world, or continue my presence here, it is easy to bear, for I have laid the responsibility for it upon myself and it can make no real difference'.

5.VII.42. Dream.

Before waking I was continually repeating, backwards and forwards, REWA, a name I have never heard. Murray's Guide gives it a small state South West of Benares.

[This is a very curious dream; it followed a dream about finding a job. Within a few years Thompson would be helping Raymond Burnier and Alain Daniélou with their work in their rented Benares quarters at the palace of the Maharaja of Rewa. In 1999, the last time I saw the palace, it had long been empty and bushes grew out of the windows. In the 1940s and 50s the two men acted as hosts to the eminent, and it was, de facto, a kind of cultural embassy.]

10.VII.42. Letter to Ella Maillart.

As for my 'few experiences', if I were to tell you them precisely you would see that not one was a love-affair or a search for pleasure. The Jnani knows—and appreciated—one of these stories that I told him in detail, and in general of such experiences he said they have been pure *sadhana*. No *simpliste* word or phrase will explain them. I myself, at any rate, cannot completely fathom their symbolism.

I feel I could do very well with a period by myself—I have so much to bring up to date. My deepest attitude to all this guru and Truth question belongs to my solitude (even perhaps to what the Sufis call a man's Secret, which only 'God' can know): I cannot, really, express it to others. Let it be worked out...

11.VII.42.

In a dream the Jnani tells me I shall begin to have a power of knowledge beyond *shastra* (reaching a level not covered by Hindu doctrine)—in a very subtle mode. I understood in the dream what this faculty would be but can hardly express it now—an understanding of relativities too subtle, profound and intimate to be expressed to others. I asked if it is related with the fact that I now notice, often several times a day, that people reply to my unspoken thought, but this suggestion was passed over.

He also told me I shall soon have some gastric disturbance. This morning I read in Raymond Roussel a description similar to an access of nervous vomiting two days before this.

Dream of Norton, a London friend. Two days later Yogananda meets me apparently by chance and, having for the time forgotten this dream, I noticed that he looked quite like Norton.

July–August, 1942.

'It seemed to Proust that by forcing us to relinquish a life at the centre of our being for a vague existence upon its periphery, friendship causes us to dissipate our ideas, our personality and our energy in a series of excursions which are not only profitless, but wasteful.' (Derrick Leon)

It is certainly true that with many people who have no very developed mind or even imagination, immediate relation is possible only 'vitally' and so complete only erotically. One responds to what they consciously are at present vitally or not at all. And I can never act on any assumption that I am essentially different from others.

Any division of people into sacred and profane, enlightened and ignorant, worldly and unworldly, 'evolved and unevolved', intelligent and stupid, seems to me not only ungenerous and in principle unjustified (Man is always Man) but a sign of smallness and lack of Geniality. I have never seen it correspond with anything but a defect in the person who considers himself one of such an elect—it corresponds in fact, quite simply, as a rule, with a *need*: it is a compensation. To see differences objectively where objectivity is relevant is quite another and more superficial matter.

Treat the external character of others absolutely objectively, as an incident of nature: sympathy and understanding, if they are to be real, must also be entirely objective.

[Letter to Ella Maillart concerning defence of Aldous Huxley's vedantin position against critical articles by journalists written from a Christian viewpoint.]

Little Protestant shopkeepers and players of golf take the meaning out of everything. Find out where you belong!

To deal with spiritual questions one must have great faith, real intuition or at least full and exact knowledge. *No* kind of serious *sadhaka* wastes his time in vague and woolly discussions. You surely need, to begin with, a knowledge of Christianity and grasp of its peculiar qualities and limitations in relation with the great Oriental traditions far greater than any possessed by (these journalists). The trouble with them seems to be that they have none of these things but only a sentimental belief in their own and each other's parochial importance. It's all mere religiosity. In a spiritually organised society they'd be taught what is good for them and have nothing to discuss. Otherwise, to get out of the modern Western confusion requires a great deal more than endless unfounded amateur discussions of happy phrases and books by superior journalists like Huxley and Gerald Heard. The whole thing has the most depressing suburban feebleness and *fadeur* (insipidity). Like a school of mice.

The time to *discuss* prayer may come, perhaps, when one has followed the advice of St. Theresa and all the rest. Otherwise, clear intuition can place it well enough for one's purposes. If you don't know how to place it, better either pray or leave it alone. If you must merely think of it, at least inform yourself on the subject.

Does Chaning-Pearce really think that, barring the Christian path, there is no salvation possible to the millions of beings to whom the Christian teachings are completely alien? Who cares what he thinks?

20–21.VII.42.

It is the ego that betrays dreams and all supra-or extra-individual experience by thinking or talking of them with insufficient consideration—by frivolous *gâcherie* ('balderdash', 'bilge').

Dream: As an invisible ghost sixteen thousand years old, imprisoned at the bottom of a lift-shaft, I ask to be allowed to visit a certain office, where my voice causes surprise.

10.VIII.42.

The idea of being absolutely frank and spontaneous on all levels and in modes with any human being is an illusion, an evasion: it is only possible through the greatest of all human tasks—simply to be in all ways true to one's purest and deepest self.

14.VIII.42. Malakkarai.

Old sadhu sleeping after the meal. How strange on the frail, shrivelled body no bigger than that of a boy, the elaborate head, fine, taut, precise, with white beard, and curly hair in matted cords two or three feet long. The effect is almost like that of a gnome or of a human form with animal head or of an elaborate silver plaque and headdress upon the face of an idol of black stone.

26.VIII. 42. Letter to mother.

'You are free to live for yourself which so many are not able to.'

Outwardly, I am subject to the same conditions as anyone else. Freedom is an *inward* fact and anyone who was prepared to risk starvation could have done what I did. It is a question of faith.

'It is a great comfort to me to know and feel that you are living a good life and happier than you would have been in England....I don't think anyone living for themselves realises the joy of doing and living to help others.'

I think you are beginning to admit that I have not been living a selfish and irresponsible life seeking external happiness (an idea anyone who has known me in India could only laugh at) and that there is no question of your 'nobly' reconciling yourself to the fact that I find happiness away from you. I have explained to you several times that I have not been seeking happiness and do not consider it in itself anything ultimate. Though the purpose and direction of my life were already clear in boyhood, it is only in the East that the attempt to find out what *is* the 'self' and the meaning of one's existence is still at all generally understood as the essential human activity. It is also recognised that only such a quest can justify the breaking free from all human ties. I perfectly well understand and at its level sympathise with your natural grief at being separated from a son—a passive grief not resolved by any greater purpose; but if you can understand the 'impersonality' of my motives, I think you will see that for you too there is no need for it. Our life cannot be explained only in terms of this world. Nothing is properly understood until it is directly related with God. Only then is there lasting peace and harmony.

You cannot in the natural course of things remain indefinitely in your present body and it is only that body after all that determines your relation with me as a 'son'. When your body that gave mine birth is cast aside, am I your son? Are you only the body? Is it not time to ask what is the real meaning of this existence, your true immortal self independent of birth and death and all transient relationships?

People don't like their life, with no absolute joy or knowledge, yet how sentimental they are about it and how steadfastly they refuse to change it—as if death were their sole end and meaning!

I need not go into long arguments about the illusion of helping others before one is free and at peace with oneself. "The blind leading the blind." "The kingdom of heaven is within, it commeth not by observation." You yourself write in another place of helping others: "I ask myself why we do it?" It is evidently, as a rule, simply an evasion, a substitute, a burying of one's head in the sand, self-deception with a 'virtue' one knows very well is not a pure virtue at all; one is not really free or prepared to undertake the far more difficult work of changing oneself, yet one will not serve others with joy and love, out of a free heart. Why otherwise, do people continually *complain* of their occasions for virtue? The fact is that man as such is not sufficient to himself and no human life can be perfect, can be fully itself, unless it is based on something supra-individual. If what is done is not a prayer to God or governed by inner awareness of His Presence attained by solitary meditation, of course it is bitter, vain, exhausting—continually raises and continually suppresses the question "What is the meaning of our existence?" Man as man is not sufficient reason for doing anything: to serve him is slavery; but the 'neighbour' is man in God's image, the eternal soul.

The friend who stayed with me (Ella Maillart) for two or three months earlier in the year is purely and simply a friend, a companion met with on the way, seeking the Truth, because she felt years ago the hollowness and folly of the life in Europe and the meaning of man's existence must be something more than to be born, to eat, to work, pray to an unknown God, sleep and die, understanding nothing at first hand of his own immortal being.

In trying to be brief, I have sometimes expressed myself rather crabbedly or crudely, not at all as I might if we were face to face. But if anything in this letter even for a moment however dimly strikes a chord in your heart, please ask me about it so that I may try to make it clearer and more concrete.

1.IX.42. Dream.

(Ate mushrooms yesterday for the first time in years. I learn afterward that they tend to grow on ground fertilised by horse-dung.)

Chariots with mushroom-white horses, like their drivers about one and a half times the usual size. Wide box-shaped carriages entirely enclosed with glass. Seated within, nobles or officials in rich robes of white fur or wool with touches of blue, and silver circlets about their headdress. The rearing and plunging great quarters of the horses collide. A completely nude warrior, simple and magnificent, such as these princes like to see. Thinking of photographing or painting these superb animals and the whole suavely cool and massive equipage, I fear I should be thrown down and trampled beneath the swift wheeling and intershocking of teams of six or seven horses abreast. And at once, only just escaping, I seize a kind of pommel or some other projection there while the rest of the vast manoeuvres continue towards the wide luminous street of a port—which as we advance gives place to a kind of coloured amphitheater by the sea, a bright post-impressionist fair, with little artificial aeroplanes (some that fly free are like birds) like painted wooden insects, less svelte than dragonflies, that whirl in circles about glossy red poles. At evening the streets of this strange Nice will be flushed with rose-water: some still remains tomorrow morning.

20.IX.42.

The Jnani affirms my whole trans-advaitic position. I shall not be at all heretical in elaborating it. We mean the same, but I speak from a different angle. The dialogue between *bhakti*-imagination and 'direct knowledge only' carries me deeper. *Nirvikalpa-samadhi* has not been repeated because my aim is beyond it.

The waking state is dream for the dreamer; it can certainly be remembered in dream as dream is in waking. Lucid conversations with all, and more than, waking consistency and resource take place in a state between ordinary dream and *savikalpa-samadhi*. Dream is certainly more profound, more 'real', than waking but neither depends upon the other: they may be said to converge independently towards a third superior state.

He agrees that focussing all into the waking state instead of enlarging in the *sukshma* experience must gradually widen and subtilise waking, a type of *sahaja*. Sahaja is defined as changelessness, possession of a Reality, in all possible states. I say it is "the presence of the Transcendent". Nothing else can be said of it, for in its whole nature it is precisely beyond explanation of the need of it.

23.IX.42.

During the meal with the Jnani at about 2 p.m. today, I discussed with him the question of energy. He agrees that it is the heart-centre that co-ordinates the energies of the levels above and below it. He says I may meditate (seated erect, best time between 4 and 7 a.m. and at sunset) on the right side of the heart (about two fingers'-width from the centre of the chest. After some time, the *anahata chakra* will open. But there must be no strain and if there is no inclination, no free flow, meditation must not be pursued.

The centre on which one is asked to meditate at the Aurobindo Ashram in Pondicherry is not this to the right, the deepest. (The Pondicherry yoga seems to start from the lowest, dualist level—in correspondence with its aim at divinisation of the physical).

27.IX.42.

Co-ordination of energy.

The Jnani says that it is at the Heart-Centre that *prana* and *aprana* in my case tend to get mixed. Opening of the *anahata* will certainly give perfect co-ordination of energy—a constant flow that can be focussed at any desired level.

This may also be attained by watching the breathing till spontaneous *kumbhakam* occurs (retention or stored breath)—then it should be allowed to continue. This should be done *only* morning and evening and in both practices there must be no strain.

[The Jnani's instructions were timed in response to Thompson's receipt of his calling-up papers. Following widespread civil disturbances and the arrest of the Indian leadership of the nationalist movement, the British authorities were tightening up their recruitment policy, revoking Thompson's previous exemption. Bizarre as it may seem in the context, the very next day following this journal entry he was on his way northwards for military service. Nevertheless, he continued with meditation and yoga during the ensuing weeks according to the Jnani's instructions but does not describe the result for two weeks, due to his conscription.]

18

Diary Of A Conscript

Thompson was called up for military service on October 1, 1942. Wearing his customary white Indian pyjama and kurta, he set off by rail to report at Royal Army Medical Corps barracks at Devali, near Nasik, north west of Bombay (now Mumbai). He wrote a diary which he sent to the Jnani, who had, of course, experienced British-style training in the Tranvancore Police Service.

28.IX.42. Cochin.

The only good thing about this 'hotel' where you bathe on a broken door in the middle of a surrealist ruin is the fact that it overlooks the street of the White Jews. Graceful lads in brightly striped pyjama-trousers saunter hand in hand, a soft shallow round silk cap of yellow, rose or blue charmingly tilted among curls. They are all related by first-cousin marriages, perhaps for centuries. Many of their number are insane but some of the children of these Spanish and Mesopotamian Jews are remarkable beautiful.

In the evening I went down and made friends with them. When I asked one of them where I could buy the delightful caps he took me to his house with big Dutch rooms and sorted out four or five from under pillows and mattresses of a pale electric blue. I bought one of the dark blue velvet.

They took me to the synagogue which has all the marrowy Jewish richness. Afterwards at the house of the Warden of the synagogue we talk of Qabbalah and Hindu doctrine and dreams and Indian saints. The service has the unhurried, accentless intimacy of a family gathering. On a carved wooden bench in the alcove of a window a man, half-seated, half-lying, takes up the tassels of his ritual silk shawl Qabbalistically knotted with the Name of God, his pale blue cap and almond skin tuned against the yellow walls.

I breakfast and lunch with a hospitable young Jewess who sends for her private boat to take me across the Harbour to the Station. On the white awning reflections from the sparkling water keep up a continual lightning.

[This is the only occasion when Thompson records a connection with his Jewish ancestry beside brief references to it in letters to his mother. The quarters of the Cochin Jews were a well-known feature of the town, with the strong evidence of Dutch architectural style, particularly the charming little narrow street of the so-called 'White Jews' (to distinguish them from the 'Black Jews' who had Indian blood, or were Indian converts to Judaism). Most of the Jewish community eventually emigrated to Israel where, as 'Oriental Jews', they were discriminated against. Thompson often wore the little velvet cap. Ella said he looked like Rimbaud wearing a similar cap in scratched old photos taken in Harar, Ethiopia. Thompson had extremely few possessions: besides a couple of dozen books and a change of clothes, no more than around eight small objects, each of which was important to him in a special way. How they were arranged, he said, had occult significance. After he died Blanca distributed these objects to his friends with great care, but the cap Blanca sent to an elderly Austrian Jewish friend of hers who cherished it.]

3.I.42. R.A.M.C. Depot, Devlali, Nasik.

15 recruits–all Anglo-Indian, most in their twenties–in the big barracks-room. Others, training done, at the other end.

'Join the Navy and see the world; join the R.A.M.C. (Royal Army Medical Corps) and scrub it.' I've already swept the barrack-room—forty yards long and five wide—and scrubbed the dining-tables.

Corporal Hill, from Bridport, Dorset, a long, stooping, bird-like, blue-eyed man, is a good sort. A bird carrying the word 'Mother' tattoo'd on right arm. 'I always respect a Britisher...I can see you're a respectable type of man.'

Lecture by him, foot up on bed, hand in pocket of shorts, eyes following swing of cane. When they glance up they are absent, indirect—very slow delivery, the British self-consciousness:

'Believe me, it's the grandest life there is going. You can neverav too much training. You've got to be tough...It hasn't done anyone any arm yet. Squad-drill—this probably sounds very formidable to you. Why do we av ter do that? Squad-drill is a combination of the mind and the actions of the body. You receive an order, you've godter *think* what the order is...The British Army is the smartest in the world. Squad-drill is not to exercise the instructor's lungs...you've godter be shouted at. On parade, *on* parade; off parade, *off* parade. I'm pre'y strict. Giving orders to one's mates learns you to develop your voice. Nice little bit of fun.

'The R.A.M.C. Training Manual is a wealth of information. Everything from A to Z.

'The barrack-room is your home and it's mine. No harboring up germs and disease. You might be sleeping next to the biggest rogue God ever put breath into. But it's a community.'

Charpoys (rope cots)—with bugs. About 40 in this barrack-room. Tiled roof, quarter-walls of brick, the rest 'tatty'—the sun beats in strongly (hot here), cement floor. 'Uniform in the Army is the great thing.'

'This book of regulations is like a lumpa gold in me ands. I'm not immakilit because I've got two stripes on me arm...Don't for gawds sake get caught.'

All are trained as nursing orderlies third class.

'*Tuck it in*!: wodyer think a mosquito-net is—a bluddy ornament?'

'Tea' is a muddy dark brown liquid: can't find an adjective that quite describes its taste.

Dinner: Minced-meat-mashed-potato, carrots, onion, thick shiny dark brown fluid; oblongs of a dodgy composition containing a few raisins and an unnaturally yellow liquid tasting of raw 'custard-powder'. What you can't eat ('My dog has better than this at home') is received outside pell-mell on sheet of cardboard by various poor souls.

Corporal told me I must change my 'Lucknow' pyjamas.

McM. lent me a pair of white drill trousers. He is on the whole the most interesting of this squad. Strong, handsome, brown eyes, delicate jaw and cheekbones. Slanting smile, upper lip too tight; rather vixenish teeth. 2 years out of school in Darjeeling. Father Russian, mother Irish, great grandfather General McM. of Indian Mutiny. Counts as an Anglo-Indian and has Anglo-Indian touchiness. Joined the Army because he wants excitement. Believes in Nirvana, but has very vague ideas about it.

On either side of my bed, N. and G., Portuguese-Chinese from Hong-kong, friends from childhood, affectionately throw shoes at one another. By air from Chungking.

Bluddy—fuckin—bugger—cunt is simply an impotent emphasis, purely musical like the endless pom-pom-pom of the Salvation Army drum.

The bathing-sheds are doorless cubicles of corrugated iron. Looking for an empty one, along a dulcimer of buttocks, white, cream, brown, of various heights and sizes, bodies stooping under the shower.

5.X.42.

Educational test. Three subjects for essay. I chose 'My Journey to Devlali' and wrote an I hope entertaining mixture of facts, observation, history, *belles-lettres*, with mention of Vidyaranya, Cézanne, the war, a sentence from Cocteau, a German word, a Latin one and several Sanskrit thrown in! I called the Cochin boys "rather languid"!

Farewell party to Major P., former C.O. Recreation-room packed. Ping-pong, draughts. Two pianos vamping with cymbals and drum. Interesting to be there and not there, to savour this wave and at the same time to feel it Water—the inexhaustibly marvellous Reality. 'Nectar' is indeed the only word. This Actuality is prior to all imagination. N.C.O.'s carry tea and sandwiches to the men. I have several times been asked what I was doing 'in civvy street'.

Solos, songs at the piano, accordion. 'I love the moon, I love the sun. I love *y-o-u*'. 'My little blue-eyed boy'. Soldier 'toughness', 'manliness' is no doubt really complementary with often largely subconscious Western 'sentimentalism'.

Finally, in chorus, 'The Man who broke the bank at Monte-Carlo', 'John Brown's Body', 'He's a jolly good fellow', 'Auld lang syne'.

Overheard:

'Seven years for sodomy.'

'What's sodomy?'

'Fuckin one another. It's the biggest sin you can commit.'

7.X.42.

Medical Inspection. Heart and lungs. On and off a chair 15 times. 'Put down your trousers.' F.F.I. (free from venereal infection). Over chest again doubtful.

8.X.42. Dream:

Living mask, of a toad-like non-human being identified with an unpleasant person here everyone calls "a dope", spontaneously catches fire and burns like sealing-wax. I shall have from it a yellow-red powder to cast against him if he appears in another form, or to eat homoeopathically. A visiting sadhu understands that this is alchemy.

Life-stories, ambitions. It's clear that people need tiresome and laborious experience because they've no imagination.

Attestation Form. Asked to choose between R.C., C. of E., Nil, Hindu and 'mother's religion', the officer chose C. of E. Willing to be vaccinated? 'Should prefer not.' Did not enter name in Oath to serve King.

I've so far seen no newspaper in this barrack-room nor heard any talk of the war.

Around camp: Peggy O'Neil, Inky-pinky parley-vous, Bicycle made for two.

Canteen. P., 25, born in Wolverhampton. Fresh and round as an apple. Periwinkle eyes. Tells me his name is Bill. Has a great friend called Lewis whom he's lost touch with. I was so intent on giving the proper sympathetic hearing to this that I quite forgot I can say the same.

I've been exercising my talents as a listener. 'Come an av a talk', says Daniel Gillifer, the Orderly Sergeant's orderly. From Derby; in the army since eighteen; really rather primitive, like a half-cooked potato. 'I may fock an blind but I knows good from bad.' Says the war will end this year or within the first three months of next. 'And when I get back to the missus and the two kiddies (God bless em), I'm goin to write a book. An d'you know what the endl going to be? —DESTRUCTION.... In Lunnon I know a lovely dame—Irish she was—fock'n glorious. Used to take er to the pictures; I got me fock'n arm round her. They say the married men's worse-an the single ones! 'I ave'ad a poke at my wife for thirteen months. When I see er again I'll open it up an spit in it.'

9.X.42.

Pay-parade. C.O. hands me ten rupees, rest of sixty rupees per month here to one's credit for leave. Asks me if I am not rejected 'for medical reasons'. I said I've heard nothing of it. The office tells me the matter is still under consideration.

Simple, slow-speaking Lancashire man stares and stares as if I were some unknown animal. 'How can a man voluntarily live nine years in India and wear Indian dress?'

10.X.42.

Drill-instructor on the square: 'Yer might av broke yer mother's art, but yer won't break mine—I aint got no art.'

Gillifer: 'If when yer go ter sleep yer concentrate that yer in the air, yerl wake up near the bluddy roof.'

11.X.42.

This morning I got confidential information from a clerk in the office that, no doubt for medical reasons, I am not being approved and shall therefore certainly be discharged.

If this is true, I shall make a little tour in the North before returning.

14.X.42.

'Watching the breath.' It piles to a deep fullness, till you are plump with its energy. *Kumbhakam* was not automatic: near that point I kept on shallowly breathing. Then in a way almost impossible to describe, you come close to yourself: the inner feeling of space is changed—space is more subtle, wide, intense. In this fine, rare, powerful darkness a focus nears and swims. (There was a slight tendency, before, to concentrate at *ajna chakra* between eyes)—I avoided it—and this dark centre edged with cool unradiating light seemed to drift from there.) The sensation is almost exactly that I had quite often as a child on waking from a nightmare, or in certain "dreams" in which space condenses or expands into an abyss.

I felt rather sleepy after this (around 4 a.m.; part of the nature not ready, I suppose), so did no concentration at *anahata*.

[Discharged as medically unfit, Thompson went on a short visit to Bangalore where he stayed with the great classical dancer, Ram Gopal, where he completed his Devlali diary with this brief note, followed by a letter to Ella Maillart.]

20.X.42.

On the way to the recruiting office, fearing that my discharge may have been withdrawn (as I was told on the way by a private from Devlali) and finding a 'transformation' flower just fallen, addressing the Devi I prayed that I be discharged—and helped to do her yoga.

Letter to Ella Maillart

I am so glad I went to Devlali; it was far from meaningless. I think of a Lancashire man there, fresh, sound, serious with that salted glee you feel in Cretan or Etruscan sculpture—something ancient, indestructible. I think of a song of Gracie Fields, and the music of *Sous les Toits de Paris*: out of the swarming megalopolis, out of the mud of the streets, springs up ever anew the deepest seed. —O, Man is indestructible, Ancient, Marvellous.

I am grateful that I know the background of the simplest man, the tar and the horse-dung streets, the docks, the pubs, the grim desert of the elementary schools. Writing in such a mood one is sure to write nonsense, but let the classic mind rest: Gracie's songs are nonsense, but through them ring the simplest emotions, the folk-Spring, verdant, out of which all wars and culture surge and into which they pass—the heart of Man, untellably tender, untellably cruel, untellably courageous.

—Your sailors, peasants, mountaineers.

Even our specialisation is necessary. Think of the apparently contradictory parts of a violin. All serve its beauty and the singing melody.

19

Parting Of The Ways

20.X.42. Bangalore.

Guest of the celebrated classical dancer, Ram Gopal. Ram (XXV), born November 1917, mother Tibeto-Burmese, father Rajput. Told me I should learn to dance, that much would come to life for me in this way.

Dream.

With a woman whom afterwards, tenderly and passionately I would kiss, in a rich room, playing a strange instrument whose mechanism I do not understand, with three rows of pedals and a thin, subtly shaped metal tablet instead of keys. It transmits the most subtle nuances of touch and tone, even the timbre of the sound changing in response to the nature of one's pressure.

22.X.42. With Dr. Ranganathan in Madras

A Brahmin interior has all the spontaneity and saturated non-rational directness of a child's drawing. In form, admirably abstract—death to sentimentality.

23.X.42. Letter to Ram Gopal.

At the Raja of Chettiar's palace at Adyar, Balasarasvati recited Sanskrit *slokas* (Abhinayam). (The greatest exponent then living of the Indian Classical dance, *Bharata Natyam*.) Simply, without ornaments, on the marble floor, facing the ascending moon and the calm blue night of the river, she sang for herself in a small sweet voice generations of dispassionate sympathy and service. Her art is really exquisite, noble, fluent, mellow with the last simplicity of art concealing art—art become itself, all Nature's depth behind it made translucent to the grave flowering sweetness and complexity of a great spiritual tradition.

2.XI.42

> The avadhuta is he who is without any rules, gets his food following the way of the boa constrictor—said to remain in one place only on account of its huge body—from all persons save those of ill-repute and outcastes, and is ever engaged in the realisation of the Real.
>
> Naradaparibrajaka Upanishad

Dr. Ranganathan heard from Turiyananda, disciple of Sendamangalam Avadhuta Swami, that his guru asked him to use the *malai-pambu*—'inert python' method—of complete surrender even in the most material matters. To be above the temptation of asking for food, he chose a rock in the Arabian Sea off Gokarna on the South Kannara Coast where even the fishermen had no reason to come. He resolved to test the *Gita* sloka 1X,22: Ananyas chin tayantoma... —Whoever single-mindedly thinks of me, ...his daily life is my care.

A month went by; he grew very weak, but refrained from beckoning to the fishermen.

One day when he was in a semi-conscious state, a dancing-girl from a nearby temple came in a boat and put food in his mouth. When she had done this for three days and he was a little restored, he asked her why she had come and she told him she had dreamed that a sadhu was dying and came to verify the truth of it.

10.XI.42. Dream. Margot.

Ascending with Renée and Margot [*sisters*] in a kind of balloon higher and higher into the sky till we pass beyond a point where we can ever return. I begin to keep a diary.

14.XI.42. Adyar.

It takes a minute for a scatter of water to fall a few inches: I watch the deploying silver shapes. As I pass a wood-cart, some part of it, or of the wood under its wheels, withdraw sharply-folded legs like an insect's. I realise I must be in a special state of consciousness in which this secret life is visible.

8.XII.42. Tiruvannamalai.

Talking with Kitty Osbourne, aged six.

She says: "God can't be everything without being Himself." A perfect argument against pantheism and those who see it where it is not; and it very clearly shows that pantheism is simply a form of atheism.

16.XII.42. Thukalay, South Travancore. Letter to Ella Maillart.

There was a small *guru-puja*—some thirty present, including about twelve women. Since you do not know the 'normal' course, you might not understand the garland thrown off with a marvellously deep and simple gesture of divine impatience—rather as if 'This can no longer be borne'—by that dense, non-human being—to lie contorted among the lamps and incense-stands, while he passed rapidly out, still wearing most of the heavy ropes of rose and marigold that he usually plucks more fully upon the assembled devotees.

17.XII.42. Takkale.

The Jnani says that experience of 'gods in the valley' (*Golden Flower* Chinese Yoga) voices which I heard last evening at the *samadhi* (tomb) of the yogini here, was due to my attempt to concentrate at *ajna*—following the *purnima-drishti* (upward and inward-turned gaze in the picture of her there. This may lead to apoplexy unless there is right guidance or certain very special conditions. *Pratima-drishti* (eyes half-closed and not observing objects or receiving light from them) is quite safe, or *trataka* at a point a foot or two ahead as one is seated. Actually the point just above *ajna* that I felt was the Shiva-raja-yoga *nadatmaka* centre—according to Tantra the *Nada* centre, below which is *bindu* (raja-yoga *ajna*) and above, *Kala*. The peculiar dense coolness was of "the moons" there. (Sammohana Tantra: '*Ajna* is the seat of the mind—*Manas*'.) Perhaps the cool light as of a thousand suns. *Ajna* itself is entirely beyond the world of form and such experiences really belong to other centres, though they are ascribed to *ajna* when one is consciously there. The Yogini was not established higher than *anahata* and passed into *mahasamadhi*. She will no doubt be reborn to cross the transitional *visuddha* to *ajna*. Perfect establishment at *ajna* leads at once to *brahmarandhra*.

17.XII.42. Padmanabhapuram.

The Jnani, some time ago, told P.N.: 'Europeans always come out with everything; Hindus, contemplative, though they may think much the same things feel no need to "express" everything.'

—Hindus, the people of the direct way—primordial—whose mode is singleness, spontaneity, know nothing of the *maladif* (morbid) Western 'expression' as an activity of the ego.

20.XII.42. Takkale.

My putting my head in the Jnani's lap like a child threw him into a state in which he lost all outward consciousness: all was Ananda. If my *bhakti* could do that, there can be no doubt of its reality. When disciples only formally prostrate, though he cannot be said to love them less than me, he remains in the phenomenal consciousness without moving; like a rock. It is not consciously that he blesses in the superconscious state into which such an action "throws" him (he seems to say he would never bless consciously, for he does not acknowledge disciples different from himself). Thus it is I, he says, who bless myself.

I would say, of course, that it is the Infinite responding to the finite.

26.XII.42. Dream.

I am astride one of five or six magnificent rich-brown horses (sleek, glossy, compact with strength— Indriyas?) yoked closely together to a sort of chariot. Their owner points to a sphere like a moon in the sky where the slight elegant forms of three younger horses, still in the stage in which they have wings, make a graceful, flying rather Blake-like pattern. The one horse to my left bears high on the middle of its forehead a single delicate forward-curving horn—misty, transparent, so faery-like, in fact, that it might be 'the horn of a hare'. They are very noble animals and I feel the greatest love and admiration for them.

Earlier: My cheeks have been smeared with *sare*—I am not sure of the spelling and wonder what is the difference between this and *rasa*.

Of the horse dream the Jnani remarks that he who directs the five senses and the mind, and he who stands aloof—the charioteer—are now one and the same. He agrees that winged horses in the sphere of the moon (Imagination, Poetry) may represent Pegasus (Inspiration). P.N. suggested that the curved horn may represent the crescent moon. Then perhaps that horse represents Mind and the next which I ride and from which all is seen, Sight.

29.XII.42. Padmanabhapuram. Dream.

Vigrahas, now after a long interval, in an Oriental shop. A very small one, Shiva Nataraja, in an unusual posture, is rather rough. Looking for a better image of a dancing god to give Ram Gopal for his birthday, I enter a big carpeted showroom with glass-fronted cases full of images, of the usual copper metal, some no bigger than a postage stamp and none too big to hold in the hand. Some are Tibetan, a whole set Balinese, all embody a rather Tantrik atmosphere. One of a Tibetan yogin in very elaborate dress, supported in his meditation by a slightly sloping cushioned back in shape rather like those behind privy-footings in late medieval Padmanabhapuram Palace.

A massive, very complex Ganesha or some other dense and powerful god, wearing a Tibetan headdress, leans forward, impending like a hood with weighty richness, over a Devi rooted and huddled in bashfulness and surrender—all her complexity (elaborate dress and ornaments, delicate fan-shaped headdress) folded upon itself like a crammed bud, chrysalis, Japanese water-flower. Yet this image was understood to be of the *maithuna* kind in which Shakti embraces Shaktiman in the furious *harsha* of immeasurable bliss.

I think while I look at them (never finding exactly what I want), though each is interesting, that all these images express latent psychic possibilities.

All the time I have to get back to my office at the Bank—distraction from psychic leisure and consistency. It is nearly three o'clock: I have long extended my lunch-hour. It will need considerable face to appear so late with work unfinished, especially since I shall have to go out again at once to prepare tea for Mother in her house.

Waking, I feel these endlessly varied images with their curious power are a direct expression of my mood. They represent a certain inward psychic richness or complexity which has yet to unfold and become active in its own peculiar sense—the heart's rich joy of beauty incompletely fulfilled.

The Ganesha had something of the Jnani's richness and bull-like non-human massiveness. From this point of view the effaced Devi represents my incapacity in the waking state at least, to respond fully to him.

The dream seems to take up the Jnani's agreement with me that friendship with Ram Gopal would greatly help psychic blossoming: applying to both of them, it expresses the single theme of complete spiritual expansion—*sahaja*.

[Scrutiny of the actual manuscript of the journal indicates that in 1943 there is, again, a perceptible, if subtle and elusive, change in Thompson. This obviously had something to do with the emotional intensity of his post-samadhi 'no-sadhana 'sadhana' '. The handwriting becomes more fluid—'molten'—the slips of paper of irregular size, the content often almost indecipherable. Clearly, this very pronounced illegibility, such a contrast with the preceding years, has visible connection with the events described. Suddenly, everything seems to be in a fluid state—great oscillations in mood occur, either radiant or full of gloom and shadow. The Jnani, too, seems even more 'various' than in Thompson's earlier accounts, generating a mounting unease in the volatile and gifted pupil. Yet, any interpretation

such as one may be prompted to put upon events of this year, so momentous in its way for Thompson, inevitably eludes the 'truth' of the situation. The hauntingly strange and disturbing 'cocaine-yellow' dream appears, as events unfold, to have been a harbinger of disturbing events to come. But, however much one is tempted to interpret the document, Thompson's own words are all we have with which to understand the extraordinary opacity and complexity which unfolds in the consistently precise record of events as they occur. Perhaps the importance of the journal here is that every detail of the strange story has the unsettling immediacy of direct experience, with all its ambiguity, rapid shifts and dissolves, its unfocused, almost directionless and momentary chaos, just as all spiritual crisis in the lives of individuals is experienced: too fluid for hindsight to do anything but distort the actuality.

For once, too, Thompson's consistently orderly manuscript falters. Quite apart from its sheer illegibility, 1943 is full of visionary experience of so strange a kind that, as if deliberately, the author has abandoned the system of marking entries to signify descriptions of dreams; introducing descriptions of actual events in the waking state without precise indication that this is so. In consequence, it is occasionally almost impossible to tell in what state of consciousness a given event was experienced. Perhaps he was not concerned to make, or record, any such distinctions. Either the Jnani has also changed in response to his pupil, or is perceived by Thompson in a different light, but the difference is subtle, even so.

A reflection of this heightened mood is palpable in Thompson's account of the dream which follows, perhaps one of the most remarkable he ever had, comparable with the 'icon-like' vision of the Christ in the dream he had at the time of his 'nirvikalpa-samadhi'. This is a 'clear dream', and I think it likely that it was of profound significance to the dreamer. But as so often happens he makes no comment. However, that does not indicate that he discounted its exceptional visionary clarity.]

January 1, 1943

Ramana Maharshi, appearing young, radiant, in complexion European, comes forward among the congregation in a sort of church, as if with his back to the altar. He is kneeling among the worshippers. In an ordinary voice (for 'praying to God' is his ordinary consciousness) he begins to pray, as far as I can remember, for peace and happiness for all.

I seem to go with him to a kind of cell as if in the heart of rock—granite walls like those of a monolithic temple. There is a right-angled corridor around the solid cubic core of rock leading to a shrine of Shiva where

Ramana Maharshi lives. I glimpse a larger room or even whole temple beyond, full of light—a beautiful pinkish-yellow light with also a suggestion of electric blue in it. High up on the walls of this passage, as one sees inscriptions in the *prakarams* of Tamil temples, Ramana Maharshi has written in pencil an account of thoughts and experiences of his on certain special occasions, of which today is one. I think of transcribing these inscriptions, and it was partly for this purpose that I have come here to Ramana Maharshi's own hidden domain which is not generally known of.

He has gone a yard or two ahead in the second side of the corridor towards the shrine (each side is only about four paces long) and I am standing a little more than halfway along the passage towards him (there is hardly room for two to pass). Evidently from the shrine, suddenly, with a supernatural force, there comes a form like an elephant but with only one axis and leg, and it is also somehow truncated at the top. I take it for the Goddess and following its sweeping course along the corridor, offer *namaskaram*. At this act it is dissolved in its onward course in the third corridor and disappears. At the same time I feel that Ramana Maharshi takes it as Shiva.

Again, another powerful form which I cannot now remember comes from the shrine with great force and sweeps through the corridor; or perhaps it was only secondly that a great pink and grey elephant-head which I take is part of a complete animal not seen face-on comes straight upon me with upraised trunk and open mouth. I welcome it, in spite of its overwhelming force and recognizing it as Shiva allow myself to be swallowed up and merged in it. Throughout, Ramana Maharshi seems to remain standing passively in his corner.

24.I.43. Trivandrum. Dream.

Leaving a Tibetan monastery on pilgrimage. Ceremony; kindness of pilgrims to one another; devotion to the two principles—Wisdom and Method. I am dressed in a pale blue silk gown, over it a red-brown robe.

We descend the stepped slope outside the monastery; emphatic colours in the clear air.

First stage of the journey: wide, mountainous country with cypress-dark trees. Our approach to Penel is announced by music from a small wagon in front of us—black lacquered wheels, curved roof supported by dark wooden pilasters, between them rich red hangings like satin carpet. Within, a great shining brass bell. The music has strong but sophisticated rhythms, simple but fundamental themes economically combined. I am so pleased with it that I take out a little notebook and begin to try to describe it.

Waking, I find my pencil moved from a side-table into the bed, as if I had physically tried to do so.

8.II.4 . Letter to Ella Maillart.

As you know, I see with Blake that all 'religions' are creations—poems of 'the True Man, the Poetic Genius'.

What is really negative in the ostrich attitude of Europeans in ashrams here is simply its puerility, pettiness, lack of imagination, lack of free and genial energy—in fact its 'bourgeoisisme'. I have always the feeling about such people that there's some well-disguised point where they are cowards and traitors, would let anything or anyone down for their own safety and comfort. Their whole life is really a maintenance of safety—an 'eat and drink for tomorrow....' business. The more intelligent they are (or might be) the more deliberate and contemptible is their short-sightedness. They make a sickening virtue of laziness, timidity, inhibition, lack of geniality—the incurable Mediocre who are the 'great' this world can recognise! Men who risk nothing because, at bottom, they've nothing worth risking. Pictures held together by their varnish, by surface excuses and activities (which change like fashion), who naturally try to make out that the varnish is all.

Anyway, people who are afraid even of freaks or of appearing freaks have no guts or generosity. Even their 'love' has a safety-catch, if it's not a safety device.

I think, by the way, one more and more sees the point of injunctions about keeping it to oneself that one is doing anything in the way of *sadhana*—or else, same thing, doing it in a place where no-one knows you. The truer it is, the more displayed and the more invisible—the more transparent.

21.II.43. Nagerkoil.

After the experience one evening at ?, before I went to Ajmer, the Jnani had for three days to deal with the gurus of my former lives: Chinese yogic *sadhana* with a woman guru; Buddhist sadhana; Medieval Christian—'Here you reached a certain level; a Tantrik Master instructing others in ritual with a knowledge of Sanskrit and yoga. Otherwise, Devi worshipped informally in many forms just as now. (Referring to erotic component of dreams of him last year, you may have been my wife in a former birth). Sexual *vasanas* (traces, residues) do not explain the cogency of these dreams'.

24.II.43.

Dear Chandran,

I went to Nagerkoil the other day, found *Araichimani* (a Tamil movie) and went twice to see it. What a surprise it was when in the scene of worship at the *patasala* you begin to sing in a man's voice! It makes me realise how long it is since I last saw you. How old are you now, exactly—XVII? The grace you had as a boy is still there, but now, of course, there is a new note to it. You may be sure I closely followed every movement. I particularly liked the scene in the court before the King—though unfortunately, not knowing Tamil, I could not understand what you were saying.

I got the cinema people to cut out for me from the film a 'still' close-up from the end of the sequence where you are looking at the 'living pictures' so that I have an enlargement made from it.

I am told you had something to do with the music in the film. One passage particularly—a series of strummed chords where you stealthily enter Kala's garden at night—exactly corresponds with the psychic atmosphere you suggest throughout the film. According to conventional ideas of nocturnal music it is too insistent and loud. Yet it very well suggests the freshly youthful erotic excitement of the situation. It corresponds with the "magic glare" of moonlight. The tight sleeves of some of your costumes stylise you in a curious almost Persian way and emphasise your strong musician's hands.

27.II.43. Letter to the Jnani.

I have no satisfaction in my relation with you. You do not seem to me *overwhelmingly* real.

The sense of those hostile dreams is always present with me as soon as I look below the surface.

5.III.43.

As I was sitting in the restaurant drinking lime-juice which I had prepared myself, an *avadhuta* whom I have not seen before, alert, with bright eyes, apparently under forty, dressed in old rags with a soiled towel about his loins, suddenly entered from the street and stretched out his hand for the glass. I at once passed it to him: he drank all that was left. He felt my pulse and said several things in Malayalam, beginning with "Onan illai" which I took to refer to the fact that I am not feeling very well. I gently took his arm and replied in Malayalam. Then he tried to say something in broken English about going to and fro in the streets and about God. He touched my book on the seat beside me, then bowed his head to the table before me. I felt a gentle sympathy towards him. When I turned to get the restaurant people (who said he was mad and wanted to turn him out) to translate he said 'Fools'! and went, after we had exchanged *namaskarams*.

19.III.43.

Jnani: '*Bhakti* removes mineness, *jnana* does away with I-ness; thus both attain the same end.'

26.III.43.

Think your own immediate trans-rational thoughts, not thoughts of reason as if for others.

The *avadhutas*, in this, manage better than I!

1.IV.43.

Jnani: 'It is better not to tell one's experiences even to other disciples of the same guru. Except in regard to higher matters and when you feel you can tell another without causing anxiety or doubt—then you do no wrong. For instance, you can say you had *mahabhava* or *nirvikalpa-samadhi* or *savikalpa-samadhi* in general terms. But friends may repeat and so spoil its sanctity, making it commonplace.

'One is never to give the name of one's guru—traditionally. The only permissible question on this subject is: To what *parampara* do you belong?—emphasising what is well recognised, that there is no obligation to answer it.'

Ella tells me that the Jnani said to her the other evening that he cannot speak to me as he ought, for the sake of the others whose position is more conventional.

Referring to my new tendency, he said: 'It is very good.'

When I suggested very tentatively that it may be the first beginnings of *sahaja* he said emphatically: Yes, it is just that.

Babu-Jan, the healer, personal physician to the Jnani, told P.K.R. about my health that 'it is his fervour that exhausts him. It will be the very cause to strengthen him hereafter.'

12.IV.43. Dream.

Sleeping between 3 and 7 p.m. Ramana Maharshi opens the closed doors of his little room in which he has been sitting with Chadwick in meditation.

At the other side of the room, where he is to come forth to a great concourse soon to be assembled, I stand gazing at him in tears, having left him and Tirunvannamalai raggedly, imperfectly (so I feel). I find myself on the temple-roof of his room with a young Brahmin *pujari*. I ought not to be there really, but he accepts me and goes to get a red stuff with which he ritually paints my face, applying it with his fingers.

20.IV.43.

Chengannur festival. Circling narrow corridors within the rotunda roofed with plates of copper, concisely rich, carved wood and black stone, the Queen of the Worlds, intensely focussed, stands golden in a glory of jewels, lights and flowers, pink and almond blossoms continually cast like bursts of spray at her feet. The hieratic gestures of the seated worshipper are a complex, zestful dance enhanced by drums, cymbals, the passionate lauding of the *nagaswaram*. You stand among hanging ropes of flowers and lamps of brass, before the double mount of steps against the plinth, the balustrade formed by the curving tongue of *makara*-heads convoluted with crisp power.

Black stone, black night, dazzle of gold and red, shivering gongs of lightning, pale amethyst, open a cold sky.

The cast spray of flowers continually scatters against her feet.

Golden lights, warm perfume, *stotra*, *mantra*, *mudra*, clothe an unflickering height of presence. Soon all is a subterranean blaze of orange flame; supple shoulders, torsos, hands bow in praise and adoration.

26.IV.43.

The Jnani on the *Child*.

'For the Child all is the immediate Present. The lowest rung of the ladder is the child, the topmost is the Child: you begin as a child and you end as a Child.'

3.V.43.

A young girl singing to the vina, the supple body made sweeter with rings, necklace, bangles, flowers. The Supreme Reality a lovely girl, more delicately capricious than water or wind, with a direct, monumental wisdom, frail and triumphant as a flower.

At once the *prana* is harmonised into a serenely mounting yogic movement. Indian music is the direct embodiment of the very movement and quality of emotion—the *gamakas* its direct shape in the nerves.

4.V.43.

During his *sadhana* at Trivandrum, the Jnani would walk from his house to the court. In those days he would not, as now, speak on worldly matters: only in the court-house would he be a worldly man. He would go and come with closed eyes and without the blind man's guide or stick. Yet there never was any accident—as Tampan observed, following him for a few days. The Jnani would go quite straight, carts and vehicles changing *their* route. Once a driver could not turn his cart but the horse stopped dead till the Jnani had passed. 'All these things, you may take it, were guided by an unseen force—someone else took care of me.' His business at the court-house never suffered, though everything else did—no desire to eat, bathe or sleep.

7.V.43.

Arrival of the Muslim healer, Babu-Jan, to attend the Jnani's ailing wife.

Fullness between eyebrows and eyelids as in the life-mask of Blake. Also partly responsible for his Chinese appearance.

Ella says he is like the Afghan-Nazara type—Mongolian soldiers left in the North West by Ghengis Khan. P.N. says he is like Bukharis he has seen.

Grizzled head, almost entirely bald. Straight back, bow-legs, below my shoulder in height. Little paunch, small feet, plump, short-fingered hands. The flexible mouth, teeth mostly gone, moustache clipped above thin beard on the chin and by the ears, broad cheek-bones. Dense, compact, powerful and serious, with deep eyes, he might be the African magician in the story of Alladin. There is something in this self-concentrated figure that attracts everyone's attention in the street.

Long white jibba and pyjamas, embroidered green shawl about neck (lump to the left), hard gold turban compactly folded and stitched upon a woven straw foundation, slippers which the bow-legs tread down on the outside of each heel.

Very quiet, measured, gentle, persuasive speech; humorous, loving smile.

7.V.43.

Conversation with the Jnani that would need 'volumes' to describe on all planes.

This exhaustion of Perversity, the Opposite, this 'carrying out the unbearable, the Impossible', is *right*, inevitable, though not all do it. He affirms and understands: 'Is there not something in me that responds?' It has been germinal in me from long ago. It involves the subtlest, extreme paradox everywhere. It lies beyond the sphere of words, he can say nothing about it. The *shastras* give only vague hints, for clarity on such a matter would be dangerous for those who have not reached this level.

His own 'hostile' experiences of his guru were on all planes. I am the only one who has had such of him.

He agrees that strength is now needed to complete my aphorisms. Then for yoga, with necessary changes in mode of life, conservation of energy by not talking.

9.V.43.

P.K.R. (who accompanied the healer from Madras) tells me that B.J. has said 'Thompson is beyond his guru—at a certain level his guru does not understand him.' I cannot believe this, though it may in a way appear so. I can myself hardly grasp the full depth of the drama being played out with the Jnani.

In my absence B.J. requested my presence for three evenings at his prayer.

Jnani: 'Yes, his energy must be organised.'

B.J.: 'Thompson is the foremost here and should be helped. If only he gets wings, Thompson will fly like an aeroplane and leave everyone else behind. There is no comparison between him and the others.'

B.J. also said that I should spend about a year in silence. This is my idea too! He says 'God hears the sound of the black ant's foot on the black stone in the black night. Only with this thought in mind do I then venture to speak.'

In the afternoon P.K.R. translated B.J.s talk with me:

'Whenever you feel dejection, mental or physical, think of these two things: 1. Only when those who pour love on you are in all ways well can you also fare well. 2. You will have quick proof that you will lay your hands on those things that you wish to know and do.

'Whenever you wish to question anyone, observe silence for a few moments and accept or reject what they say as you decide for yourself after a few moments of silence. Some will speak truly, some otherwise: let the corresponding impression be objective for you. When you wish to utter a word to anyone, bend your head, look at your toes and then speak into their face. But if there is no time for this, at least look at the tip of your nose before you speak, so all that is outward will then disappear. This will establish perception of oneness.

'Acting, speaking, remember that God or guru are your shadow.

'Sometimes the guru may not answer your question and one of the reasons may be that the disciple has outgrown the guru. In that case, don't think of it that way.'

10.V.43.

I was seated behind B.J. in the room of the Jnani's wife (she lying on his bed) while he recited his beads (*japam*). After a minute or two, some sense of a kind of dense warmth, almost physical in quality, as if proceeding from B.J. entered me from below. For a phase during which, though only superficially, I 'became' a rather powerful form of the goddess, I remained very much myself, though I became more concentrated and inwardly alert than I was when I entered.

11.V.43.

B.J., last night during his *japam* saw me in vision as a child held in the crook of the mother's (Jnani's wife) arm near her shoulder. The Jnani says the Devi has a special affection for me.

This evening, when I entered with B.J. she gave me a rich and deeply loving look, the more impressive because of her habitual reserve and poise, which gave it great subtlety.

12.V.43.

Ella says that when I came out of the mother's room with B.J. on the first evening I looked quite changed—instead of rather haggard and tense, peaceful and self-contained, with a slight healthy flush.

She says, as Earl and Achsah Brewster did at Pindi, that I sometimes remind her of D.H. Lawrence, though I never look so tormented as his photographs show him. *[The Brewsters were the hosts of Lawrence in Ceylon.]*

13.V.43

B.J. told the Jnani that from the first day, during his *japam* in the mother's room, he has had visions of Bhavani Devi and the Jnani says this is the equivalent of *savikalpa-samadhi*. The Jnani also told B.J. that I am the Devi's child. Bhavani represents the mode of rich, kindly sovereignty I have felt on these occasions.

B.J.: There is a current from the guru to the disciples which works in them but which others do not share.

Festival of the goddess Kanya Kumari at Cape Comorin.

The Goddess at ease in her arching palanquin—golden limbs, a little long, a little thin (she is a tender, gawky girl); arm and subtle hand loosely behind the head, right foot spaciously upon the other bended knee. The fanned-out skirt distributes heavy arcs of jewels; silver palanquin and cloth of gold (both closely wrought) are salted with vivid yellow and cerise.

These limbs so regally disposed of the intense puppet built with art among her silks, are loosely connected underneath with string; the hollow ungilded ends, tubes of polished iron, are hidden among the cushions. The golden-apple breasts, the mitred head—smiling, weighty, concentrated with unchanging power and peace—are masks upon the standing ancient *pancha-lohya* form at last revealed unbinding from its cords. Soft silvery copper, tenderly polished, eroded to sightlessness (fingers sharpened, melting like frail ridge of frozen snow) with the delicate friction, during centuries, of water, honey, oil, silk, perfume, flowers, adorning of adoring hands.

Dream at Cape Comorin.

I walk southward along the sands. There is an infernal light, golden like the flame of a lamp, about the height of a man from the ground, an influence at the same time radiating and attracting. Entering its mood, I begin to chant in a loud voice some formal word.

16.V.43. Dream. Cape Comorin.

In a Buddhist monastery, seated with five others in a low, carpeted, unfurnished room, one of many opening out of each other in a rose. Silent, spending hours in the absorbed interest and satisfaction of yogic meditation.

17.V.43.

Friendship is an art and I am concerned not with art but with personal truthfulness—I see art not as a humanistic Westerner but as an Oriental, in terms of *yoga*. The westerner would call this a supra-personal truthfulness that cuts through all else, for it presupposes a spiritual, not a human, perfection. But for the limited individual taking himself and others for granted as they are, there can only be the perfection of a given art, a small tragic (really pathetic) perfection—even then almost impossible to sustain in the shifting, fragmenting world of relativities.

21.V.43. Dream.

Dissatisfied at my relation with Ramana Maharshi, or rather with my clumsy, helpless failure to make my feeling in the changed circumstances clear to him, I approach the Ashram. There is a sort of fair, the ground packed with people in European dress, mostly women in blue. Since there is no room to walk, the Maharshi is being carried through the crowd in a palanquin, jostled to and fro inside so that he cannot as usual sit serenely. He is brought to the point of the wooden paling where I have managed to get, his face about a foot from mine. I make *namaskaram* with emotion at this special opportunity to express my real feeling, I am in tears, but do not think of saying anything. He is sympathetic, recognising me with all the old deep familiarity, but drolly, in his dry Tamil way, says to attendants and others that this is not the auspicious way to pose for a photograph, and that I want to see the star Rohini, associated with a little red cow rather than with Krishna. And he repeats this again and again as if cajoling a child and to change the trend of my mood, I smile through my tears, but with a purely mental response. I do not feel consoled or at all interested in Rohini: the same tragic situation remains—ultimately the living spiritual isolation for which the 'professionally spiritual' with all its safeguards and its presupposition of others' limitations—the hypocrisy of its 'Love'—is exasperating and even seems cruel and evil.

The Maharshi has as escort a double file of tall young men whose black costume and way of dressing their hair has been designed by some foreign organiser.

When the deepest tendency is towards self-perfection, relation with others can only be symbolic, or fulfil the formal necessities. Subjectivity cannot be carried into this sphere without becoming egoism. Such relations can, indeed, only be art, but art as a mode of the skill, presence of mind, objective of *yoga*.

28.V.43.

At a time when I have only 25 rupees left in hand I looked in at a shop in Chalai Bazaar the other day to see if there were by chance old *vigrahas* of some artistic merit, though I do not really want to possess such things in any case. There was one of Kali which I noticed because it was a good deal above the standard of what one usually finds, not because I spontaneously like it. The man swore he had given 12 rupees for it and asked 15. Out of indecision (though to spend 15 rupees in the present circumstances is mad) I left a retainer-fee of 2 rupees and afterwards—going from one sleepiness to another—vaguely thought that the Goddess must give some sign or help if the image is to be bought. Yesterday morning I had a card from U.D. mentioning that in sending back the balance of money she had sent me for purchases for her, I had forgotten to keep 20 rupees she owed me. I finally took the *vigraha* for 10 rupees; and in fact the man who had paid 12 rupees for it could not hide his pleasure at receiving this amount!

The following dream (after purchasing the Kali image) corresponds with the cerebral torture of the action of coffee drunk in defiance of all prudence after supper: Dream: Ella and I come back with horror to find the pet dog lying on its back in blood, half-killed by some marauding brute, its loins eaten away, the kidneys extracted. Something similar has happened to a tiny kitten or puppy. It rested with me to put them out of their agony...

But they can run madly, blindly in their torment and I keep losing them while I search for something to end them with. I look in a cupboard behind the dining-room fire for a coal shovel heavy enough to smash the dog's skull. My mother supposes I know where it is but I am not really familiar with the house. The dog has got trapped at last in the dining-room and with much anguished manoeuvring, though he desperately wants his death, I get his head half projecting from under the table and try to get in a good finishing blow. He half withdraws, half gives it again, standing there, nervous system deranged, perhaps not feeling the pain of my repeated blows, but they are like sheets of paper falling for all their effect. All the time the kitten awaiting the knife, may escape in mad torment again to some inaccessible place. I call "Mother, Mother'" for her to come and help me.

A parable at a very low level, to the effect that what is to be destroyed is *samskara* and childish unexamined motive! And of course the possible 'symbolism' of the Kali figure at this juncture radiates in other directions also—the 'possessed' outbursts to the Jnani and all that lies behind it—the necessity of yogic completion.

Only the 'living' Krishna *vigraha* (an earlier purchase, unique) the Jnani says I should keep. *[He returned the Kali image to the vendor. After his death, Blanca kept the Krishna in daily worship for 35 years.]*

2.VI.43. Letter to Ella Maillart.

I say that in a conscious *man* nothing can be fully explained 'from below'. The modern mind, all surface, knows nothing directly about the Eros: I take the term from the last civilisation in Europe that recognised it as a matter of course.

For the rest, my myth about it—and only myth can codify what stands above and outside reason—is the Vaishnavite one that the One Person, the only real Beloved, the Transcendent, is the Sole Male and all 'souls' feminine. On the plane of relativities, therefore, the true man, or one who at least wills classic wholeness, finds other souls feminine, yet symbols of the One Man. He sees his own nature, truly, as feminine because therefore he expects nothing from nature as such—he is interested in Man alone, Man alone can be interested in Man, he sees Man everywhere. He has already taken the point of view of Heaven, in which there is neither marriage nor giving in marriage. From the point of view of sexuality the One Man is 'androgynous'.

This view cannot be explained by what did or did not happen to him who holds it as a child, but itself, rather, must explain what 'happened'. Man is not a jelly-fish. At what level does such a child start?

And what, then is Woman? Remember the myth that I am a Tantrika! It is a Tantrik text that asks: 'What need have I of any outer woman who have a woman within myself?'

7.VI.43. B.J. the healer.

B.J. comes to my room at the hostel and we talk of the rich Love and Beauty I felt at the tomb of Mu'inud'din Chisti at Ajmer. *[There is a long account of a second visit to Ajmer in 1945 which will appear in Volume Two.]* Then I had no eyes to see the saint and the saint had no tongue to speak to me. 'But the life-force is one in all: consider me the saint. They are ripe whose voice is like honey, their gaze full of sweet milk. You are P.K.R.'s greatest friend; though I am a poor man I will do something for you. I will see that there is transmitted to you the richness and love you felt at the tomb.'

He looks at me steadily for a minute with a deep power in his eyes.

'You will meet your mother. You will be of use to others in a way you cannot now imagine.'

17.VI.43.

Gurugita: '*Gu* means darkness, *ru* means that which dispels it. Because of this destruction of darkness he is called *guru*. *Gu* means what is beyond all *gunas* (qualities), *ru* means that which transcends all *rupa* (forms), therefore he who is without *rupa* is called *guru*.'

19.VI.43.

About four hours of 'vehement hyper-dialectic' again with the Jnani.

He affirms that it is impossible for him to lower the tension of the paradox by withdrawing what he said about my experience at Malakkarai. He says this *nirvikalpa-samadhi* (or *turiya*, expanse of the mind)—compare what he said then—corresponds with the Absolute: according to *jnana-shastra* one who has experienced it is a *mukta* (liberated man). But there are stages between this and 'the Ultimate'.

He replies so little to my 'dialectic' because he knows I was following this path before I met him and because that experience gives me a centre from which it can be resolved. Quite apart from the fact that, if I can resolve it, whatever may be said is limited to the spheres of understanding and imagination.

Simply, I say: One wants to be whatever one is *wholly*: only wholeness is 'real', is satisfaction. I am not interested in understanding or imagination, but only in experience.

I protest against his usual statements about wave lapsing into water, surface into depth: the paradox is that the only occasion for saying this is the wave. I say that water must become wave: Wholeness is the state in which surface and depth are one. Where the 'supreme Mystery' is true, there is only appearance—only *Lila [Divine Play—the whole Cosmic Dance of Life, especially of the world of appearances.]*

19.VI.43.

After hyper-criticism with the Jnani, from which I got back at about midnight to my room till past three o'clock I could not sleep, my brain conscious of its strained substance in a sort of cold fever, the whole thought-world, wherever one turned, of one mode with the inextricable-subtle-paradox-on-all-planes of the conversation.

At last I evidently fell asleep, and had this dream:

Continuing the conversation with the Jnani, P.K.R. (P.K. Rajagopal) has told him something like my way of intense dialogue with the 'guru' prevails in an Arab *parampara*, some of whose members are at Ajmer. They are all tense and overdriven and look it. At this point, the Jnani, who has come and seated himself beside me in a chair to my left, with a kind of exasperated benevolent violence, that I may lose my tensity, suddenly puts his forefingers into my mouth and rubs along the teeth. Then he gets me, by an effort and with strong clear breathing, to put back the uvula (by itself, not with retroverted tongue as in yoga) to close the hole (as recognised in yoga) just above and behind it. With his forefinger he checks that it is closed. He also with his fingers, for a moment, lightly looses me about the stones.

In a way such methods recall B.J. rather than the Jnani.

20.VI.43.

The Jnani on this dream: 'You have caught, in essence, my thought last night. I have been taking a deep point of view that your tenseness must become loose—either by your going into *samadhi* or by a deliberate effort of your will-power. This thought I took when I was neither dreaming nor waking. After midnight and before 3.30. At 3.30 my wife got up and I was disturbed, but afterwards the current of thought continued the whole of last night—I got up from that atmosphere this morning.'

He was saying this evening to Ella that faith is alright for *bhakti-marga*, but for jnana conviction is necessary.

Afterwards, when we were alone, I said: I suppose you realise that I have no conviction. 'Yes', he said. I had long ago seen 'the Truth' in my own way and cannot impose upon myself a given mode of thought. All you teach remains outside me, an aspect of human thought that I may one day examine for myself in its Sanskrit sources, for it is certainly of very great interest.

The fact is, my *whole* viewpoint is that of the poet: I cannot see any mode of thought otherwise than artistically, as anything but form, in itself accidental.

21.VI.43.

Pudnal tells me that the man who sold me the Kali image afterwards re-sold it to the wife of the chief Justice. She had a dream similar to mine—of violence and destruction.

26.VI.43.

Everything that is not of the deepest significance must be put aside. The level and quality of my life has been cast by natural loyalty to the essential. The human goodness that gives me others' tasks is weakness, a mask.

Dreams.

Before leaving, tidying the family house where I have been staying for some time. Accumulation of many useless things.

Late twilight. Dark wet stone. Gangs of men, women, children, on steps, hauling something from the sea.

In the empty early-morning streets of a new North Indian town I am half-flying in a kind of imaginative intensity. Approaching, in the road, by the kerb, a sort of Arabian Nights magician in more or less Chinese dress—complex, highly coloured. Strange and slightly sinister.

Temple-front like the low *étalage* of a shop—something rather sordid and commercial about it, as if aimed at tourists. It is divided into several gangways, each facing a god. Glass vessels of yellow-green oil, a wartime substitute, with a slightly unpleasant crude smell. The priests are dropping little black 'candles' of incense into offering-vessels of bronze, as *prasad*.

I enter the 'temple', to the right. The young *pujari* gives me a mass-production copper mask of the god as *prasad*. I ask him confidentially to give me instead something good, however small, trying to make clear that of course I will compensate him for it. I think there is almost certainly at hand in the temple some old and beautiful trifle. He seems to understand me in another sense—very beautiful, intense, rather non-human, with the form and colour of a copper image, he embraces me, pressing urgingly, in spite of the presence of priests in the parallel gangways.

28.VI.43.

[Ekadesi, the darkest digit of the moon and close to the solstice, traditional day of fast in the Hindu lunar month.]

Ella comes with this message noted down from the Jnani's carefully chosen words:

Feeling it profitless to continue an unheard-of anomalous situation of the present type, I withdraw from it entirely, leaving Mr. Thompson free. We need no longer call him Chillilananda.

I need not arrange the *Conversations with the Guru [on which Thompson had been working for a long time from his meticulous notes during daily satsang]*. I will write out nonetheless, arrange under main headings and send it to him. I need not write out the completed version of the Jnani's *Atmaraman*, but will finish it for Ella and P.N.

Later in the day.

Her impression is: the Jnani affirms that I have understood his hints about the necessity of a yogic movement, but go on postponing it or do it for a day or two and then drop it. 'Yet', he says, '*advaita* is poison to him'.

From the first conversation of the sort she heard at Malakkarai, she had an unpleasant, uneasy impression—can't see where this movement can lead. She can only suppose it may work out something in myself.

She does not herself feel the happiness and satisfaction her mother supposes from having found a Master. In practice the inward help perhaps received is not felt (received on levels where we are unconscious of it). Yet to talk with the Jnani every day certainly helps her to keep her thought on the question of 'the Reality'.

Taking the Jnani as what I imagine him—but, if I am consistently sincere, must want to know by experience!—it is, like all his acts, from this point of view, one of perfect love and grace, whose depth, no doubt, I cannot fathom.

I feel as if a veil had been removed: now I can look at him clearly.

He has thought of an excellent way of relieving the tension without changing anything unchangeable. The tension is with himself, yet to work out all that is implicit in me I need freedom. Freedom (as disinterestness) is my first 'position'. What is required is not paralysing *tension* with the guru-problem—either guru or no guru!

As for my 'metaphysical' attitude or 'destiny', he really does not make me feel what he once said, that he understands it. If he had, the deadlock could not have arisen. To a friend I may perhaps at last express it all in my own terms—begin where I really begin, in my aphorisms.

I can now freely pursue my free examination of all the tradition and experience of the 'nature of Reality' on this planet: really, investigation of the Human—free of premature deadlock by short-circuiting imaginative generosity with a man supposed one with that Reality. An act unnecessary to my 'absolute faith'—'Reality' entirely complete and present now—in which our existence and our extinction are equivalent and for which only integral experience can be real.

Love's parallels that meet only in Infinity where they were never separate! Must not their solitude be exhausted if there was ever only One? Yet only by the sleep of understanding or imagination self-circled to its own limits can one seem to become the other: the circle is only symbol. The Sphere once willed contains it unchangeably—as, after all, an abstraction. For the human which in completion of understanding or imagination (love, identity by sympathy) reaches its limit, this Sphere is indeed Terror. And before there is oneness with It the non-human and anti-human, that which was never 'given' and is invented only by perversity and madness, has also to be exhausted.

29.VI.43.

According to Ella, this is what the Jnani told her:

'I have to make this clear for my own sake to myself, to put myself in order: that I have nothing more to do with Thompson.'

Ella understood this to imply that he had felt he had had something to do with me.

'Thompson is to go into *samadhi* to get strength—to do all he wants to do he must establish himself in the centre that supports the mind—otherwise he has nowhere to stand.'

He told Ella long ago that in the *Ashtavakra Gita* and even in the *Gita* itself I isolate the verses that suit my point of view.

'Words in themselves convey nothing, only what is Understood through them: as the disciple progresses he understands more and more with fewer words till he reaches the silence.'

The paradox of *advaita* in little!

30.VI.43.

Letter to the Jnani.

My faith is in that Infinity by which I mysteriously continue to exist.

If you are in any way one with that Truth and that Love your action comes from it and supports me: if not, it is empty and meaningless.

3.VII.43. Draft of letter to the Jnani.

I do not ask for comfort, belief, agreement.

As I explained in my conversation on the 26th. of June, I only point out the inherent paradox of *teaching advaita*—and the Truth. If, as Ella would lead one to think, you really do believe I do not admit, indeed affirm, the truth and inevitability of *advaita*—then how far indeed are you from even the possibility of understanding what I have from the beginning been saying to you.

5.VII.43. Museum Gardens, Trivandrum.

I no longer react against a surface fatigue: deep within is a timeless equanimity for which its transience is as if it never were. I no longer turn my back perversely upon that equanimity—for has not paradox also been the impossibility of really doing so? That everything is simply disinterestedness in itself—bottomless Peace and Love.

The days in the quiet country have favoured (though certainly not caused) this rediscovery.

The garden is rich with extravagant but harmonious forces—suave glooms of shade, the most elegant generosity of form and scent and colour.

13.VII.43.

No-one can know you: in this world there are only appearances. Your relation with others must be governed first of all by perfect objectivity: one must perceive first, mentally and vitally: one's speech and action, one's appearance, must be first of all an act of understanding and sympathy. Here the greatest intelligence and sensibility, the greatest patience, resource and promptitude, may be fulfilled. It is the finest and completest of all arts, which may contain all cosmic and yogic knowledge. All else is egoism—vulgarity, disorder.

Behind this is the innocence, the perfect disinterestedness and freedom of the heart—centred in the human but not of it, for it represents the Perfect Man, Autonomous Spirit.

My former, natural, child-like way of speaking directly to pure Heart or Intelligence is certainly first and last right, but in the world of relativities it amounts almost to perversity: it must be ratified, there, by the perfection of art. This art perfectly resolves relative difference—cancels it by fulfillment.

All this is demanded by non-egoistic realism, for it is impossible to reveal oneself directly.

As for explaining oneself, that is against all laws of form.

And only so is the reality of understanding and sympathy, where it can be reciprocal, in every way safeguarded. And here art itself will have its moments of inspired daring, and its pure felicities. This alone, also, safeguards the pure significance of sleep and solitude, in which one's own nudity, gravity, joy and wisdom develop.

There is absolutely no fear of my ceasing, inwardly, to be a child. Indeed all this is to be the ratification of that fact, its self-completion in the world of nature.

23.VII.43.

A chief point about Krishnamurti is that, like the Buddha, he has "not the closed fist of the teacher" (reported saying of the Buddha): he knows and acts and lives that Absolute Light is here and now: he knows that there are no *degrees* of darkness (*avidya*) to be "unfolded", presumed and exploited by a teacher. All degrees are endlessly and inextricably of darkness: there are no degrees of Light. Krishnamurti does not *compromise* with *jnana*, which cannot be taught. He has real unqualified Love and Generosity—there is really none for him who "does not understand". Where does "the Spiritual" lead but to inextricable darkness, obscuration, confusion even between friends? All in the name of abstract Love and

Truth. Then that Sphinx is my greatest and subtlest enemy, and the greatest enemy of all who have but one faith; to which their very imperfection has been sacrificed.

20

Preparations For Departure

27.VII.43. Dream.

Books about some very special, saturated, elaborate Buddhist cult—Far Eastern, but with a strong North Indian Tantrik flavour. I take down these rich yellow-bound books, published in Asia, from shelves above the tall first-floor windows of a spacious semi-circular room overlooking the drive of a stately house, with something of the atmosphere of the Martin Lings [*the noted Islamicist*] hotel, but more independently withdrawn from cities. Outside, a rather cold, lonely, grey or even rainy park. This has been preceded by long handling of books in another room, and the general atmosphere of all this inside the house is like that of memories of treasures and bibelots found as a child in the perfumed cabinets of the drawing-room or in other seldom-used rooms of 'The Priory'.

The book I look through is an elaborate study of the cult. Photographs of festive scenes, with crowds and complex bronze images about twice human size, distinctly India.

This Buddha originates from a sort of incest between Adi-Buddhas or other primordial Principles. The frontispiece shows a remarkable, simplified, wooden carving, of the highest Chinese strength, subtlety and intimacy, somehow representing this.

The same Buddha appears in other photographs as a powerful, non-human image, greater than life-size, with a face entirely stylised, like a mask—without the usual human features. The effect is very powerful, indescribably special; something normally remote, mysterious, secret, inaccessible, prepotent, has been concretised, and it changes the value of everything, provides an inescapable focus.

This followed my thinking of renting a haunted room on a sort of Butte de Montmartre—the great city below pearly with distance—where I shall live alone. It is bare, upstairs in an abandoned, partly crumbling house, very cold, entirely without furniture or conveniences and I have hardly any money. —Something of the atmosphere of my solitude in rooms in London.

I dreamt this before dawn, but even at 10 o'clock, when I write this out, the non-human Buddha figure, with its extraordinary concentration and prestige, is still present in me. An image that begins to be associated with it, quite outside the context of the dream, is that of the Boar-incarnation of Vishnu (at Udayagiri), perhaps only because of its combination of spiritual prestige with a simplified human face.

There is little doubt that the whole development now, including the Jnani's withdrawal, is towards non-humanistic objectivity and integration of the non-human aspect.

9.VIII.43.

Study as Poetry—as I naturally see it, without unprofitably complicating mental considerations: a real 'new humanism' of the Poetic Genius which is Man—free of provincial limitations like the Jnani's, free of Pharisaism, religiosity and every other sort of stupidity.

13.VIII.43. letter to P.K.R.

The guru idea is false to the Western spirituality. 'Be ye perfect...' and Christ's '...follow me' is of love and tenderness—the Shepherd—not of authority. Authority—the Pharisees—continually opposed. There is no 'authority' but Love.

25.VIII.43. Kodapannakunnu, near Trivandrum.

A fairy-tale landscape, its richness a little facile and unreal, the suave, vivid, elaborate, rampant plant- and tree-forms as if unseizable in the brilliant light.

Everything temporary, plausible, too quickly grown. Walls and houses of bistre or cinnamon earth, thatched roofs overgrown with pumpkin, courtyards and platforms of beaten earth pale with dried cowdung-paste. Cocoa and areca palms soar like rockets and burst complexly without sound. Baked children everywhere, and a rare bent, wind-blown old man with a staff talking to himself along the roads. Hibiscus, jasmin, lotus, flowering tree: jak, pepper, mangoes, tapioca, pineapples, bananas, rice. Small neat black cows; goats, buffaloes; crows, green parrots suddenly launched from the tree-top like a flight of arrows.

A country of kathakali dance-drama and black magic.

29.VIII.43. Sri Padmanabhaswami temple group.

Sri Kanthesvara temple, also a name of Subrahmanyam. After the benignant opulence of the Vishnu temple it has a strange austerity. With the light, rhythmical, electrical ritual touch the *pujari* applies sandalpaste to the moon-crested Head. Incomparable temples in the Himalayas haunted by yogins and tyagins—remote and pure shrines of the Absolute Strangeness of Reality.

My 'tablets' (MSS and money) dropped twice while I was before the shrine for the third time I placed it myself in offering on the ground. An old bearded Brahmin with me said the omen meant I should offer something to the god and I turned out all the small change that would come. Archana was to be made. I thought the Brahmin asked if I knew the name of the god and, having heard several ejaculations, I replied Kantheswara—suddenly realising, when *nakshatra* was also asked for, that it was my own name that was wanted. But having given the god's own name I would not withdraw it and the 108 names were recited.

30.VII.43. Dream.

M. [*a disciple of the Jnani who has become deeply antagonistic to Thompson*] shows me a writing table I have been using and tells me he is tearing everything up. I open the drawer and see all my manuscripts have been destroyed...I have the idea that I must no doubt feel relieved—in a way I am ...or a quiet calm dismay that accepts the fact as something always known to be possible. Feeling that if all were suddenly found restored—or the two ideas came together—how gratefully scrupulous I should be for the truthfulness of all I write—a religious feeling directed towards Shiva.

The acceptance in the dream of the destruction of the record of all my independent thought, certainly the feeling I had about it, is of course completely real. It clarifies my attitude to these aphorisms—the perpetual pull between the highest, classical standard and the sentimentality of the surface ego.

Truthfulness, because it absorbs the whole person, is always impersonal.

[This dream prefigures an incident several years later when Thompson momentarily experienced a feeling of profound relief when all his manuscripts in their entirety were temporarily lost in the state of turmoil, rush and confusion of a big railway junction, and only retrieved 'by chance'.]

1–2.IX.43. Dream. Manthencode.

Dream of climbing a Dantesque poem (sic)—a kind of light-ladder filled in with cane-work. I am accompanied by a faithful dog and cat (or rat or squirrel), very intelligent, almost human. One can see nothing as one climbs but the cane-work with its slight bamboo struts that serve as rungs: the rest is empty space, apparently at a great height. After a time, at an even greater height, the ladder grows more nearly vertical, narrower, a supplementary width of cane-work under the struts disappearing. Many of these struts have fallen away, the ladder is of the flimsiest, it is a question how one can advance. The squirrel (it certainly is, now, of that size and shape) hangs perilously from a hole in the cane-work. Nothing but empty space around and below, at a terrific height. Difficult also to retreat, all is so frail. Deadlock of painful danger. Yet this is the last section before the end, a sort of platform or heaven in space, for the poem has been carried no further.

Without remembering the climb we are somehow there and a feast is being prepared for us. But I ask myself how this 'end' is supported in empty space. I read thin, difficult poems. And wonder how I am to return. There seems something almost foolish in this rare, dangerous isolation, exaltation.

3.IX.43.

The Heart. Certainly one's being demands the perfection of the saint (of love and goodness) as well as of the yogin and the jnani (of psychic knowledge and mastery and of Wisdom). In fact, it is only all these together, with the perfection of action and expression (karma) that can unify the whole being as a vehicle of the Transcendent *Lila*.

August, 1943.

When Rilke or any other sincere and serious man feels that his work is in a sense given him by a kind of grace, he evidently means that his greatest integrity was fulfilled by some resource of which he has no other knowledge than in this fulfilment. *Can* the 'higher ranges' of our being be truly known, indeed, except by experience, and is not Rilke right in insisting that life must be entirely Transformation?—though he saw it rather as the integration of 'this provisional, perishing earth' through our experience of it into the Invisible Whole than as the fulfilment ('redemption') of the transient by that Wholeness (the kingdom of heaven on earth).

August, 1943.

Homeopathic remedy last night. Till I remembered this I could not account this morning for a state of disorder at some depth in the *prana* (subtle breath), as if from emotional disturbance—a kind of subtle perturbation with a very rapid vibration. As if, also, one had overrun oneself—a state of suffocation through having forced beyond one's strength out of fervour, perversity or enthusiasm. —A state I have often known, so if it is now produced by Lycopodium, that has no doubt an affinity with me. The tendency to this sort of self-exceeding is very old, perhaps indeed constitutional.

After a long interval without it, insomnia. Though it began with almost yogic richness—deflected partly by the hellish heat, noise, glaring light and general odious barbarity which in this Hostel continue till one or two in the morning.

November. Yesterday a homeopath gave me an unnamed remedy for myocardial symptoms. After mental emotion and effort over my letter to Ella there was violent phosphaturia this morning (after sleep not always energetic enough to get beyond superficial dreams) my tongue was coated, I felt the peculiar phosphaturia weakness, the slight pain in left lung again, and my stools were streaked with blood. I had a sudden instinct to eat camphor but put it aside. When I went to the doctor he told me he had given a high potency of arsenic iodide which is counteractive by camphor.

[As a consequence of his rupture with the Jnani, Thompson thought it best to inform the chief Minister of Travancore—to set the record straight, since the state, a relatively small territory, was rife with gossip and the last thing he wanted was to be, unwittingly, the cause of malicious rumours which might harm the reputation of the Jnani and the inmates of his ashram.]

4.IX.43. Trivandrum—copy of correspondence:

1. Registered 'Personal' letter from L.T. to the Diwan to the Maharaja of Travancore, dated 15.VIII.43.:
   'Some time ago I had the occasion to write to you that (the Jnani)...was my guru. That is no longer the case. This naturally leads one to doubt if, in spite of my willingness to say so, it ever really was.'
2. The Diwan to L.T., dated 18.VIII.43. *[The envelope apparently addressed by himself.]*
   'I was very glad to receive your letter. At no time had any doubts in the matter, but one of the inevitable handicaps of European and American students of Hindu Philosophy (sic) is the difficulty of meeting the right sort of people and the likelihood of being misled

by appearances. I hope your fellow-aspirants will also awake to a similar realisation.'

3. L.T. to the Diwan, dated 4.IX.45:

'I had occasion, formerly, to tell you, without explanation, that (the Jnani)...was my guru; when, recently, the situation changed, without explanation I wrote to tell you so. This was purely a matter of formal correctness: I could not, in common courtesy, allow you to remain under a false impression.

'At first, therefore, I thought it no concern of mine that in your reply you go so far beyond what is warranted by the purely technical statement in my letter; but on reflection I see that it might be said that by not being more specific I have misled you.

'I must therefore clearly state that if (the Jnani)...ceases to be my guru it is because of metaphysical difficulties raised by me. Presumably in order to help me in the stress of these difficulties, in fact, *he himself withdrew*. It is simply to this withdrawal that my letter referred.

'The last sentence of it was perhaps unnecessary and over-scrupulous: it referred to the fact that the word 'guru' was from the beginning used between us in a special context to which there was no need to refer in my original statement to you, though at the same time it would have been ungenerous and indirect in the circumstances to have said *less* than I did. I may illuminate this by saying that (the Jnani)...was never, for me a *dvaitic* (dualistic, or 'worldly') sense: the 'spiritual dialogue' between us began on both sides by definition beyond that level and I could not have pursued it on any other basis; but on the *dvaitic* plane this relationship could, I thought, be expressed only as I expressed it. From the beginning, however, certain difficulties were latent in the situation and it is these which, coming to the surface, have (for the present, anyway) brought our dialogue to deadlock.

'I do not claim to fathom one to whom is attributed, with every appearance of justice for those who really know him, so complete a spiritual attainment (this refers to advaitic *sahaja*), but it ought not to be necessary for me to have to say that my attitude so far as (I do not say 'knowledge of') his character is concerned remains unchanged. In spite of the technical change (which none but ourselves, certainly, is in a position to understand), there is no personal breach between us.

'I would remark at once, however, that I have told (the Jnani) nothing of either this or my preceding letter to you: in this matter I act entirely of my own accord and I have at no time received any advice from him that could in such a case influence me one way or the other.

'...I can hardly say more in a letter of this kind: I have said enough for the present purpose and if the whole is still not clear, that is because matters of more than ordinary depth and subtlety are involved.

For the rest, I have begun what (if it survives continual editing) may become a long letter to you.

[If ever there was need of proof that the world of decorous bureaucratic and diplomatic exchange does not sit comfortably with high-flown metaphysical subtleties this is it. The hilarious coils of verbosity in which Thompson becomes entangled show how profoundly inimical to each other are the worlds of spiritual gnosis and officialdom. It was not long before Thompson wearied of explaining himself to a baffled Chief Minister and gave up trying to finish his letter.]

10.IX.43.

No doubt instinctively to counter Ella's old tendency to overvalue me—her original idea of my even being greater than the Jnani, I reply: and what about me, am I not left in the air?

17.IX.43. Nanthencode. Dream

My own face long, fine, spare cheeks, freshly coloured but with dark hollows under the eyes as if from strain or lack of sleep.

There is no element of surprise or interest in seeing my own face and it is only accidentally, so to speak, that I remember the dream. It is rather as if my face saw itself.

25.IX.43. Courtallam.

We are seated on grass mats in a big sitting-room typical of Southern India—floor of red tiles, whitewashed walls, beamed ceiling, doors and windows painted dark glossy green. It is early afternoon: outside, the leaves scintillate with heat. No furniture in the room except a broad bench filled with mattresses and pillows. From a cord hang gold-bordered clothes and a heavy silk sari belonging to the Tamil mistress of the house. On the floor boxes and baskets. With nods and wavings of the head to emphasise his fine points an old man is playing the vina—an ancient instrument with metal strings and a carved griffin's head, still one of the most important of Indian instruments. It sounds rather like a harpsichord but more brilliant. The classical music of the South is formal, learned, elaborate, dry and lucid—rather like 18th century European music. But this, purely melodic, is more subtle and has greater rhythmic resource. He plays compositions by a former Maharaja (and is a relation of the present Maharaja of Travancore). They are large and leisurely, with an insistent feudal simplicity.

There is something fresh and clean like creme-de-menthe about music in which melody does not depend on implied harmony, but is purely linear. It is sung, too, in a 'white' head-voice, with the minimum of overtones. Imitating Westerners, the Tamils humorously exaggerate how they sing and speak gruffly or unctuously from the throat. All is in the line, with its delicate and complex 'graces', and in rhythmic pattern.

28.IX.43.

'They threatened me', said the madman gently, 'but I don't want to bathe under the water fall.' He looks this way and that, distracted, like a bird, but all the time docilely following me. Perhaps he feels that I am a kindly man who won't cross him, even that I understand madmen. He sits in my room all day and asks if he may sleep in the corner at night. He sits perfectly still for hours, humble, innocent, very quietly, very gently distraught.

At first he looked at nothing, nobody—overtaken by a formless absence; but now this absence is focussed upon me: from his corner he stares at me continually with eyes that cannot remember.

Last night I dreamed that I was mad, spinning on my heel with an ease and regularity that surprised me, and smiling with a like fixed facility.

I was awake much of the night and all the time he was making busy little noises—like the combing of lank hair (but his is short), like the sifting of sand, like the waving of plumes, like the digging up of treasure.

He spreads finger and thumb across his cheek bones: 'Eyes. If somebody gives a cut...'then from jaw to ear'...Cut with penknife. Thieves...

'My body has got special colours. No-one must touch, must not go outside. That's why I'm private..

'See nobody touching my eyes, my head. Cut, break. Thieves.'

He sits hunched against the wall, hands limp on the floor, thumbs turned in like a corpse. He asks for paper and pencil and writes in a large clear mechanical, puerile script with prolongations as in American handwriting:

'eyes Head all parts of my body special colours—must not touch
by others thieves cut break Head must not hurt eyes—'

One must live entirely from one's own centre with absolutely no criterion but one's own truth.

28–29.IX.43. Dream.

Two burly evil magicians at Tiruvannamalai try to hypnotise me into thinking that a yellow silk kerchief passed through my hands is a snake.

The first who tried it evidently expected to succeed almost at once. Failing, he is reinforced by a second beating with a cymbal relentlessly by my head to help hallucinate me. They go on and on, but I know that so long as I keep my own imagination under control they cannot succeed, and I repeat aloud to all their chanting and effort: 'Silk, silk, silk'. The association is Benares silk. We move about, the two always close at my ear. In the intense combat of imagination, at a little balcony at the head of a stairway I push them from me. They have failed.

30.IX.43.

Setting out for Madras, I stopped to take leave of the gentle Maunaswami (vowed to silence) on the Tenkasi road. I have known him for seven or eight years.

He unlocked his silver bowl and offered me sugar-candy and scraped coconut.

I thought his sweet kindness and simple dignity enough to explain my emotion. But when by a gesture he seemed to ask if I would return to Travancore the tears overflowed.

In his kindness he was dismayed and concerned. Because the heart is bottomless and silent, the mind exhausts every perversity.

For the mind, of course, this is a piece of literature: it has no means of measuring it and can only regard it coldly as something inexplicable.

8.X.43. Letter to Ella Maillart.

I have just received yours of the 6th, so answer it first. Ethel Merston offers just what I wanted and I am so glad it comes through you. I'll write to Rajghat School, Benares today.

I heard this morning of one tutorship obtained for me, but, appropriately, only after I had read your letter, so I have called it off.

Yes it is interesting to find you reviewed in the fairly high-brow *Listener* in company with Freya Stark, who wrote of the Hadramaut, I believe...

Letter to the Principal, Rajghat School, Benares:

Dear Sir:

I hear through Miss Merston that you are willing to have me as teacher at your school. I shall be very happy to come.

I have taught before, both classes and individuals.

Miss Merston asks if I like young people: I certainly do.

I know no Hindi but can in a week or two learn enough here, I think, for immediate needs.

As for salary, I don't know your resources or the cost of living in Benares. But I live simply in the Hindu style. All I need, then (supposing you offer the little house rent-free), is enough for clothes, good simple food, a servant perhaps and a small margin for personal expenses. I should think 60 or 75 rupees a month would cover this, but I leave it to you to decide.

The main point is that I feel attracted by your offer and want to come.

Yours truly,
Lewis Thompson.

17.X.43 Dr. Ranganathan's house, Madras. Dream.

(Bundles of notes on the Jnani re-arranged with other things in trunk yesterday.)

Visiting the Jnani again in a house new to memory—I am seated on a chair in the verandah, he standing talking in open space with a low wall; at some distance a few other undefined persons.

The Jnani is talking as usual freely and variously: 'When I mention Sri Krishna's adulteries, see the dirty heads rise from behind the wall.'—They do—a crowd of disciples' heads, with a coarse sickly laugh.

I am sullen, dissatisfied. (Two or three late nights recently—vina-tabla-violin, dilruba-tabla-song with Chandran, Rajan and his sister.)

In the same bedroom with Father lying down, I thinking of sleeping on the other side of the room. He asks if I'll be free tonight or tomorrow—in his characteristic way, without at first telling my why; but it comes out that he wants me to visit "the padre"—who doesn't understand me—and I feel a certain sadness and scorn for Father's and Mother's inability to deal with me. No good will come of it, I explain. The fact to be faced is that for the last half hour we have been together in the same room without even speaking or looking at one another, so little understanding or sympathy is there between us.

The scene has shifted through a right angle to a narrower and darker room. I tell Father I know what he is dissatisfied about, and begin to say, with some emotion, that of course it's an irony that an old man should have to run hither and thither all day in sun or rain for only three pounds a week (letter from Mother recently about his early jobs), but—it's all part of a situation to which my birth, my existence, also belongs—which I also suffer, but would face and resolve in all its wide implications, not sentimentalise about.

(A certain obstinacy and sincere realism in facing and living out the unsatisfactory—as with the Jnani. Accepting no "Father-Image", but remaining on my own axis, true to my actual suffering—seeking a direct concrete truth, not through the 'mediation' of padres who know and care nothing for the truth of actuality and are resorted to only by weakness and incapacity).

(Sleeping again) With the Jnani, seated in a chair to his right as if at Trivandrum. 'For establishment of the Reality', he says, 'members of the *parampara* have always gone to Benares.' I see him extremely clearly, and remark to myself on this, testing it. Perceiving this, he gives me for a moment a curious, sympathetic, penetrating look. (Once at Trivandrum, sitting very close, I examined his face minutely.)

'Though Benares represents so much that is wrong with the point of view of the Reality, but (smiling) some of which I used.'

Because you could re-absorb it into the Reality, I remark.

He looks at a clock: it is about 5 o'clock in the morning. He remarks that those women (Ella and others) will be coming. A crowd of little girls and boys comes in. He shows pleasure, gets up and goes outside, as if to meet newcomers. Some of the children remark that I wear no garland (an outward sign of 'religiousness').

Even in the dream, I am so interested to record it that I go to the far end of the tent-like, earth-floored ochre-walled room with bright chinks of sunlight showing from outside, and help myself to a coloured pencil some woman is keeping beside her embroidery. I begin to note it on some slips—which I saw before as I came down (in a well-appointed country house, new to me, of Uncle Harry's). He is already up and I know he will approve my getting up so early. I notice with interest and some speculation a lot of old slips (the usual slip envelopes re-used), the top one bearing in pencil "L. Thompson" and a note of my address.

(Yesterday, I took out of my box duplicate copies of the talks of Krishnamurti to give away, and this morning, after this dream, glancing through them, see once more how axiomatic what he says has always been for me. What I thought in the dream is after all essentially what he says in those talks.)

28.X.43. At Ram Gopal's house in Bangalore.

Kunju Kurup, a deep and sweet man, now over sixty, mimed for us, with perfect mastery and discretion, Shiva with Ganga, Parvati, Genesha, Ravana; opening lotus, bees, and lotus dying—in his face the life died away from within. So powerful is this art of kathakali, so beautifully performed, that one entirely forgot the absence of make-up, costume, music.

Ram danced at the Musée Guimet. Hence he met Jean Cocteau. —His green-lighted room with Greek plasters. Talked of herbs and occult secrets from Malabar. Strange small dark eyes like a snake that has swallowed a goat. *(Cocteau's eyes; Ram Gopal's were large.)* Cocteau extraordinarily young, diamond-like intellect.

29.X.43.

Our talk on the roof of course unrecountably like everything that even tries to be true to the real insupportable difficulties...of Reality-Unreality—to the continual insupportable failure of integral truthfulness...For me as usual, it was pitched where his offer of material help with such delicacy is so irrelevant that it can hardly be attended to. 'Look upon me as your brother—more and more I see the simple boy in you, a transparent lake.' This is all so 'prior' to my 'problem' and the struggle with the never satisfied, merely human, need, that I have to behave as if I were absolutely sceptical about all of it.

Does my neglect of his offer come from great humility or great pride!—I believe neither.

30.X.43.

Evening: all is perfectly resolved. Love is of the central being for the central being and organises all: nothing else can do this. Ram can be for me a special *sadhana* to this end, is the divine gift of the perfect love that has always failed me, so that I cannot recognise it when it comes.

1.XI.43.

Interview with Sanjeeva Rao (Principal of Queen's College, Madras) to whom is evidently largely due (and through his influence with the Government) the building up of the Rajghat School, founded by Annie Besant on behalf of Krishnamurti. There are said to be several unexcavated cities on the rise by the Ganges at Kashi. He has now broken away from the Theosophical Society and wishes to retire from his chairmanship of the Rajghat Trust to a position in which he will merely influence, if that is required.

He asks me to come to Benares about the middle of the month, stay at the school and see if it will be possible for me to work there, no doubt on the Hostel side.

4.XI.43. Madras. Letter to Ella.

Since I took leave of you on August 23rd., on paper and in my head I have been composing a letter to you. The whole affair I'm trying to write about is very subtle and complex. Such a letter can, in fact, hardly be organised: I write it out of strong impulsion, certainly with no *motive* of any kind. And besides, I can hardly do more to make things clear now than I could at Trivandrum.

In the circumstances the perfect letter would be too cryptic, would in fact vanish away entirely in a collapsing series of understatements. That might be esthetically satisfying, but would not resolve the personal difficulty.

About ten minutes after I left you in Trivandrum I made this note:

'I went to Ella with the general feeling that because of complicated failure (especially in the inextricable Jnani affair) of clear and simple 'hearty truth' (comment below), it would be goodbye to her too.

Yet, I could not explain this without going into the whole irresoluble question. I saw that even the clarity of parting was not possible.

I thought as the leave-taking drew out (I was paralysed with sadness, hopelessness, dismay)—true if one is to express oneself in emotional terms—that in her voice there began to be a possibility of tears.

Let me know where you are, she said: don't disappear. And with all her sterling goodness, smiling, radiant (I thought) with emotion and restraint (I could only half glance): 'Goodbye, Lewis".

I could not feel or re-act but walked away in an even stiller general impersonal state of death and loss. This indeed, all, a dying to an old, too sanguine and imperfect life.'

Thoreau: 'Between whom there is hearty truth there is love.' I agree with this. By 'hearty' I understand simple, genial, generous, robust.

The impulse in this letter is simply to recover at least recognition that such basic personal truth is a necessity to self-respect and respect of others.

Withdrawal (by the Jnani) recognises something non-advaitic to withdraw from. Yet at the same time it is a refusal of the sort of 'trans-advaitic' relation I proposed... In view of that, was there not a crucial double sense in my complaint in that last conversation with the Jnani that I felt none of the satisfaction, intellectually or otherwise, of having a guru—that I was not satisfied? Why should I not have quietly said this and gone away!

I said that a spiritual dialogue has formally (the level where I was writing to the Diwan) come to deadlock: it is not possible to withdraw from anything real. I have never been concerned with a mere individual and it is only as and from individuals that one can withdraw.

What I have ever said about the guru has been said spiritually, not individually.

If I could accept the only explanation that directly fits the facts—that the Jnani has never understood me (and I mean spiritually)—I might be happy (and if I needed or could accept that kind of happiness); but if such an interpretation could be of any use to me I should never have entered, and kept up, the dialogue with him; for my basic problem was there, and stated, from the start. In other words, I specifically placed the whole thing beyond individualities from the beginning.

Why am I writing all this to a 'disciple' of an admired sage?

Because the very fact that 'Reality' is prior to truth and untruth makes truthfulness crucial in the 'relative sphere', otherwise one is entirely lost.

Repudiate *me* by all means, if you must, and have done; but let not confidence, trust in truth, be undermined.

If you must repudiate me and have any real kindness, or if you think there is any hope for me at all, you will, I am sure, explain all that is dark to me. And this might prevent further dark tangles that are no doubt possible.

...I accepted your left hand by the same token by which I have at every crisis offered the Jnani the 'solution' that I am an *asura* (as Aurobindo claimed)—a solution he has always vehemently refused.

Disinterested imagination is formal, but only those who are attached to their imaginations, for whom Reality is an imaginary ideal, will say it is therefore foolish. The children of this world are only wiser in their generation than the sons of light. But he alone faces Reality, the Self-known who puts aside all preconception. This means he completes imagination as a formal mode—he fulfils his childhood, remains innocent and incorruptible. This innocence makes him in the world the perfect actor—in the end his whole existence becomes a play. The 'worldly', recognising only worldly necessity, think a play cannot be serious. But it is the fulfilment of seriousness.

Intellectually, I am quite sure that no-one who has not been able to raise and tackle in and by himself, spontaneously, the problems various doctrines claim to solve can understand those doctrines; for they can be understood as one understands a work of art, only as more or less perfect expressions: otherwise one *believes* them, one turns them, and their teachers into idols: one becomes subject to them, loses one's Humanity, one's spiritual autonomy.

The gulf between those for whom words *have* meaning—for whom there is therefore Truth, doctrine, *sadhana*—and those who *give* words meaning is evidently unbridgeable.

For one tribe Eckhart's "God is neither good nor true" is the word of a philosopher: it defines the Absolute, which is to be reached, expounded. For the other it is the genial exasperation of a poet. The second kind of man never was within the sphere of discourse—it is within him, and even then only for its own sake. Which is why he alone really knows and obeys the immediate Truth that the Truth can not be told.

The misunderstandings that arise from the speaking together of these two kinds of beings are of a completeness and subtlety strictly unfathomable.

What is *nirvikalpa-samadhi* but the ninny proof of it, and a measure of Reality only for those who began by accepting it and all its logic?

Definition: The guru will either teach you 'the Truth' or tell you it is beyond words.

Puzzle: Define the guru.

Answer: The guru is ignorance idolised. Since nothing but ignorance can idolise ignorance, the guru is ignorance active upon itself.

6.XI.43. Continuation of letter:

I was really touched by your card...Fatigue at its length made me cut out much from the draft of my letter, when I was assembling it from various scraps written under lamp-posts etc.—for the sake of simplification I entirely dehumanised it.

6.II.43

Anyone who teaches puts himself in a sense in the position of a *sadhaka*. I have always said: no *sadhana* and no teaching! But this will be understood only by spiritual geniality. For both teaching and *sadhana* are in the 'relative' world 'unavoidable': this is even the sense and occasion of what I say!

8–9.XI.43.

Useless to go to Benares with more or less frivolous, half-examined motives, continuing failure in half-acceptance of it.

Nothing yet binds you there: nothing must in any way bind or qualify. Your interview with Sanjeeva Rao was plastic, observant, non-committal.

Do not be led in anyway to consider yourself from the outside, as object individual (all such are anyway incomplete and inexplicable: here there is only confusion). Hold fast in every sphere to true inwardness, the only relation with Perfection.

Anguish has no doubt passed, but this means that the way is less easy to distinguish—a smooth and lifeless air, a polished ice in which even intensity cannot be felt, in which one can lose one's way with a dangerously good grace, because there is no way but that most strictly and subtly felt within...All the elements have become one colourless silence: the force that informs it can be sensed and followed only by the deepest core of the heart.

—The heart which, in this suave desert where the air is all unsubstantial mirage is so easily forgotten, for there is nothing, no stress or contrast to remind one of its secret life—hidden by the roaring of the blood, the restless exacerbation of the mind. Nothing to make it ring like an echo—Baudelaire's Angel of peace and tenderness, the soul unveiled by the temporary discharge of obstreperous nature in debauch, vibrating in complement with that unreal degradation.

It is just because experience and thought have sufficiently dealt with lesser objects that perversity can sustain them in a subtle new disguise as real. This is weakness and confusion.

Cultivation of *the will* towards spiritual ends must be assimilated from the Christian mystics—so long as it is entirely technical, not (as for the average Westerner) a necessity, almost an appetite of the individuality.

November 1943

In Scott's *Hermetica*, two Nestorian Christian sayings:

> He who publicly reprimands any one deserves blame and contempt.
>
> The height of magnanimity is to be merciful to fools.

30.XI.43.

Refusal of simplicity: Of course it leads to endless complication, not the happy and vigorous fulfilment of real complexity.

From now on, preparation for the new life in the North.
Nothing pure will happen while the will is not single.

[Some time after Thompson arrived in Benares he wrote a letter to a friend which can be taken for a considered summary of the position he had arrived at after spending eleven years in India.]

As you know, I shall naturally tend to see the choice which, again and again, at different levels, is put to us—the choice between continuing our individual life, the ego's life, still seeking the satisfactions which by itself it can never give up (and which do not depend, though, on itself, but on cosmic conditions—on *karma* dispensed by gods, the cosmic powers)—the choice between that (which can *never* in the end be satisfying and from which we are *bound*, sooner or later, and after clearer and clearer experience, to awake) and conscious recognition that, just and last and always, the only true purpose in life is spiritual—that the satisfaction we seek is the Peace and Perfection of Reality itself, and so then, conscious surrender to it, self-dedication to that aim. This means transposing our whole life to a new centre, it means a complete re-arrangement of our energies; the *giving up inwardly* of the ego's desires, tendencies, purposes, the seeing through them; the *choosing* of a life that carries us a whole new step forward into another world, another dimension, in which all purposes and all perspectives are different—where we have chosen peace, where we are joyfully, with kindliness, affection, sympathy, detached from all worldly purposes, because we see that the world is not its own cause or end and does not explain itself—because we have recognized and seek, Reality, our Self-perfection which is already and always there, *containing* all the dreams of those dream-figures, all the interdependent human egos...(In saying all this I am evidently going far beyond myself, but I believe you will understand it.) All the dreamers must in the end wake up, but we can see, and seize, and choose, and joyously lend ourselves to the wonderful possibility of waking up into that infinite, unchangeable Joy, Certainty, Illumination, Love. We *must* come to it sooner or later, for there is no other true resting-place and what is ever-present cannot be evaded; but when we choose it, if only for an instant, It has chosen us, and that deep destiny that took Radha away from her king and made her do all her worldly duties with detachment will emerge again and again; we shall wake suddenly in the darkest night of bewilderment and suffering and hear, and perhaps doubt if we really hear, that subtle Flute, the sound that our deepest soul has always known, the call of that Joy and Beauty we have always sought because they are the ground of our very being.

21

The City Of Light

8.XII.43. Benares.

The little boy beside me in the train suddenly smiled and pointed. There, the sun westering, a delicate river of light—like that I saw in my dream: "Sweet Mother Ganga, bless me.". And softly silhouetted against the sun, that famous water-front, all simpler, more ancient, less townlike than the photos make one imagine. And a countryside silence; little paths by the water-edge. Along the bank, they say, the Buddha used to walk from Sarnath. And Kashi was an ancient city then.

9.XII.43. Rajghat College, ancient site of Kashi, early name of Benares.
Dream: Shiva of the burning-ground—Shudalai.

A woman shows me her great treasure—a little linga of a pinkish-yellow semi-transparent, probably semi-precious stone, the top a bulbous, slightly flattened cone. It proves the connection between Shaivism and Buddhism. The word *Pashupata* comes as I record—(Vedic Lord of the Beasts). But waking I no longer remember its exact form and name. —Nor that of a black linga, a kind of compact ornament in several strata, to be worn round the neck, a kind of portable *vigraha*. Beneath the squat black *pitha*, three flat objects, one coinlike, the other two small squat dark grey cylinders, one a little bigger than the other. All three, I realise, bear *mantras*. They seem to correspond with the *yantra* beneath a vigraha. If they could be read, a great deal would become clear. Partly out of politeness to the old woman, partly out of reverence for the old paths and teachers, I put it to my forehead.

The second old woman (in a dark, almost black dress) shows me a small secret object. So that none in the temple courtyard may see, she moves behind a small white shrine (Shiva? Buddha?) before which I stand and open. In connection with this object she spills out into her palm from a cloth a few dark-grey metallic-looking discs, irregular as if flattened between finger and thumb. I think they may be preparations of some drug, but perhaps alchemical. Then with naive old-peasant-woman triumph she places on the black lid a little ivory oval bead which I realise is solidified mercury. I am conscious of the honour these *sadhus* do me in showing their treasures. Finally she carefully places a light, yellowish, shell-like object like a worn vertebra of a big fish-bone, upon the top of the little black box.

(Sleeping again.)

We overtake a very long procession of mourners, all in black and white like nuns. My companion, a religious lady, gets down from the car at the entrance to a church or monastery and is in tears to hear of the death. Though I am not a Catholic I accept a little paper in which *water* is done up —to wipe the face, in token of purification or of sorrow.

The body, in a black and white habit (Catherine of Sienna had joined the Dominican sisterhood and wore the white robe and black veil), with legs stretched out and head huddled forward in a half-sitting, half-lying posture, is balanced like a shovel at a single point on the edge of the round top of a sort of plinth more than six feet high, though I see it from above, under cold, rather bare Gothic arches. This seems to be the usual way of disposing the corpse.

All have gone but one or to police or other officials and I am also about to leave, when, looking back over my shoulder, I see the beautiful young Saint Catherine suddenly lift her head and look about: she is not really dead. But she sees that I have seen. —A fresh, delicate, intelligent pink face. Association, while recording, with Blanca Schlamm, who met me when I arrived here last evening. Subconsciously I have evidently perceived what I now recognise is true, that she is in a way like a nun.

10.XII.43.

Deep peace and silence here. Delicate, luminous river scenes.

Hindu music. Psychic learnedness. Perhaps because of Muslim influence, become a little over-subtle and corrupt—inwardly honeycombed into a self-lost, even bottomlessly self-wearied dream. But what strange sweetness and delicate sinisterness inhabits this endless world. —Full of self-existent gods of an almost abysmal refinement—honey tasting honey, perfume dying into perfume.

Suggestion of the peculiar quality of the Northern saints.

The famous Faiyaz Khan. —The same vices as in the South, but in another form: egotism, showmanship, ingenuity, the music—all true musical interest—entirely thrust into the background for the sake of display. Cheap buffoon. Nursery-music: he has found the level of his audience. Poverty-stricken stuff: no true imagination or sensibility.

[This marginal note of caustic criticism of the most famous, even exalted Northern classical singer, was crossed out by Thompson. And within the note, individually scored through were: "mere false and facile wit...Really rather a vain old fool."]

Dream:

In my recording of a dream in dream, *Sabaoth* is taken to mean Matter... I deeply experienced but could not hold and mentalise (too deep and subtle) the powerful feeling of the self-circling, almost nightmare, nature of the endless limited series of attitudes (e.g. the Vaishnava ones) towards the Divine (cp. my note about Indian music yesterday—and thought of SKM). The experience was dense, golden, lucid. —This inevitable circle self-sick. Its weight due to the *truth* at any moment of each attitude, and only such truth, quite apart from the blind inevitability of ... Krishna Self-limited, is liberating. *[SKM has by this time become Thompson's code for the Jnani.]*

This feeling arose after I had as a matter of course been treating with pungent familiarity someone known in another form as 'the Supreme'.

My so-called 'purely negative' acts as positive* just because it is not experienced *disinterestedly in its own sense*, for that is done by what is neither positive nor negative—"neither good nor true"—and which may here be called Innocence.

11.XII.43.

I have not yet seen the centre of the town, the ghats or the lanes leading down to them.

The town. Everything lightly improvised, like a stage-setting—corresponding with a dream-consciousness in which nothing is permanent or real. All is put forth from, and remains in, the subjectivity: the whole town as if created and sustained by enchantment. —Result, perhaps, of centuries of *maya-vada*.

Dream: Bathing in a muddy yellow pool or river, having lost all sense of up and down, feeling that when I turn over I might fall into the sky, rather

* See further elaboration of this cryptic phrase in marginal note added to 12–17.VII.

surprised that somehow I don't, though 'down' is no more real or secure than 'up'.

J. Krishnamurti always axiomatic to me; schoolboy interest in Pythagoras, and in the Buddha, whose anti-metaphysical dialectic is natural to me; special appreciation, in 1933, of Scherbatskvi's translated extracts from the *Madhyamika-sutras*; vision of the Christ. *[In 1942].*

15.XII.43.

When all is perfect there will be nothing to analyse or record, no complication or comparison *within* the subjectivity—all will be one seamless Autonomy, Absolute Poetry, Lila. That is indeed already the truth, it has only to have completely loved, understood and 'absorbed' in its own mode everything that can in any way even seem to be 'untruth' or incompletion: all possible seemings, within, towards or from oneself, must be known and understood as 'That' which is neither seeming nor non-seeming, or both or either (so formal, so beautifully limited is rational language!)

17.XII.43. Dream.

Anxious secret advance into Japanese territory. Long journey by a sort of plane piloted by a sea-captain at the wheel. I am wrapped up asleep almost in his seat (identification symbolised by proximity). Almost vertical flight from the top of a mountain, as high as Everest or higher, reached in some earlier phase. —Flight so excitingly, disorientingly rapid, easy and steep in the great, perfectly controlled machine – so interplanetary in its feeling, that the very motion of the stars shrilly luminous in intense cold arid wideness like a dust of diamonds seems changed by it. Image of the tall, strong stem of a white hyacinth, rich and suave, lucid and exquisite, its complexity viewed, like the mountain-side from above. It is felt as a symbol for the mountain and of the descent.

Unusually cold night. Activation of kidneys also due to nervous effect of afternoon tea.

Tea should be stopped. One is led to use it by a natural intensity—because it helps self-exaltation of the *prana* (breath) to the delicate, lambent richness, volatility, hyper-lucidity, 'presence', which seem the norm of the nature. But this leads to a continual exceeding of the normal base in the physical, whose rhythm must however be accepted and strengthened. —This exceeding has in fact gone on so long that tea is now used rather to correct slowness, fatigue in a nervous system continuously overdriven—vicious circle, in which less and less prompt reactions tend to drive deeper a deficit of the vital force till it affects even liver and heart—deeper, more organic, levels. This must be corrected—true centrality, normality, established.

[Between these entries, 12–17.XII.43. Thompson adds a long marginal note, 'to be filed under Evil (reference under Perversity')]:

Kafka: "What is laid upon us is to accomplish the negative; the positive is already given." Those who still in any way need to believe in the positive can never understand this. One will be giddy and lose one's head completely if one looks from a tightrope over an abyss—in itself pure sterile order and rigidity.

Don't wait till you 'understand': it is literalism that waits, that which will never understand: destroy at once. That is at least a measure of understanding, makes understanding for an instant seem almost possible... Because I could go on like this, it is all literal. I only know that by this measure the heart is utterly empty—more than empty, non-existent. —It is laid on us to accomplish the negative.

(*Ebauche* [rough outline] to Ella, Nov. '43:)

No-one can understand simplicity who doesn't entirely understand complexity and perversity. Real simplicity is at the opposite pole from every possible kind of sentimentality, but nearly everyone has only a sentimental idea of simplicity.

My perversity is a devouring spark struck between my simplicity and a non-existent opposite. That opposite is the Negative to be mastered. (See Kafka above.) As a *person* a man is perfect only as a *saint*, as will, intellect, passion, sensibility it is different. Let those who have tried to conjugate these together judge the resonance of every word and of all the words deliberately, again and again, stifled.

(Ebauche to Ella, 27.XI.43.):

Only Innocence can see *Evil* as the sign of a positive beyond the point of *shastra*, the 'Absolute' that can be pointed to discursively.

My entrance into this field proves the reality of all I have always most deeply intended: here it becomes realistic, here it is *sadhana*.

—Everyone defends his own sanity, I do not want anything that needs defence... These are not the days in which it is understood that the only courtesy, the only natural, unthinking way with others, is to treat them in all respects as equals. Yet, first and last, nothing else is spiritually true. There are gurus, for example, only for those who think something objective, for whom there is still something judgeable... If I clung to this sort of objectivity I should say I do not know for certain one strong or intelligent man: then what would become of my own degree of strength or intelligence? Why should I suffer such pain, esthetically, at the too close view of P's mind and behaviour?: why not dismiss him in 3 words?

... Where did Yeats limit and 'save' himself but in his beautiful arrogant "mask"?: he wanted to be a poet. It is a man's smallness that makes him great. If he could in this life have gone one step further, it would have been into a 'negative'. How many negatives have we not to exhaust, master and take to our love before there is only the 'positive', no longer limited, therefore, by positiveness?

So far as there is in any sense relative existence, it can be organised only as *sadhana*: only so is it whole, lucid, true to itself. And this demands a centre on its own plane... In order to be free you must consent to be wholly committed, now, as you stand. It is freedom itself, alone, which can so consent. "He who would save his soul shall lose it..."

21.XII.43. Dream, 4 a.m. One of many with skeletons of a Tantrik sort.

A being in himself invisible, taken as human in form, who appears as the uniformly black *shadow of a skeleton*, enters several times into my room, where I am lying at ease, awake on my bed. Some thought of Woodford, but the room is bigger, more comfortable, more luminous, more Indian. He sits at what is felt to be a Tantrik, and rather Tibetan, puja and/or magical process.

The skeleton-shadow is very clear, perfect, elegant, in fact distinctly beautiful, with a cool, suave and finished compactness—tall and graceful, seated before its *puja* erect, easily, one knee raised against the body. It is seated at right angles to me opposite the open door by which it enters, facing in the same direction as I lie two good paces away, the head of my bed a little behind it so that I have a three-quarter view from the back.

At first he pays no attention to me, but my interest in him finally attracts him to come to me. He sits on the edge of my bed. I take the slender black hands, which I expect to feel like flesh, but they are not solid and cold like a dead man's, only subtly unsubtantial without being warm.

I cannot remember what was said at this stage, except that 'he' remarked that there was space for a woman to lie beside me (and the impression of her lying). I say there is certainly no woman, but he replies that he can see her *sukshma* presence and says something to the effect that she is necessary to me, part of me. I feel her deeply peaceful, beautiful, harmoniously identified with me, (See following dream of 26.XII.43.)

Then there was some question of my looking into those eyes, which see the state of purity of one's inmost thought, but somehow they were not to be met—again showing that the being was 'myself'—too subtle, deep, *unlocated.*

A little later 'he' is telling me that mine is the "universal", not the "individual" (Arhat, simple *mukta* path)—here memory is blurred: in the dream I wrote down in a sentence what he subtly and exactly said, and that this is why I have various experiences, including various kinds of love and of various kinds of people etc. —the suggestion is of mastering all spheres. I am in tears with impersonal tenderness and ardent self-surrender.

(Marginal note added 4 August:)

This is the clearest direct 'revelation' about myself I have ever had. It seems to come entirely from beyond my individual consciousness.

As I record, it occurs to me: Is the dead supernatural shadow in my boyhood Woodford room my own reputed Tantrik past?

It all has the effect of representing blessing and encouragement, a giving of authority.

This linking of Shiva (Tantra) and Buddhism in its Mahayana aspect (Bodhisattva-theory etc.) again perfectly corresponds with Benares—and with my interest in Chandidas's affirmation of Man—*"Listen, O brother Man—there is no truth higher than Man"*—the *sahajiyas* deriving from Buddhist Tantra.

All this detailed psychic experience during recent years especially is no doubt due to decline of original direct intuitive perception, intellectual passion and imaginative will, which contain and foreknow all this kind of 'proof'; yet in another way it is no doubt necessary for complete knowledge and understanding, for complete realism—to make practice of one's intuition possible and unavoidable.

26.XII.43. Dream, 2.30 a.m. (cp. dream of 21st.)

Just inside the courtyard of an ancient and famous, apparently Southern, Indian temple that I enter, a woman in all the elaborate dress and headdress (tall *kirita mukuta*) of a sculptured goddess stands awaiting me. A very individual woman, young, playful; yet all the time I also feel reverence and would like to touch her feet, she tells me, mostly in Tamil or some other language I do not understand, though she makes an attempt to speak a few child-like words of English. Mellifluous mode of speech. Though perfectly direct, she is very subtle and hard to seize, she will come to me, in a "distant place", it seems for good, as my companion. She would have gone, but I keep in contact with her, talking with her, till a crowd of people enters at the temple gate, and it seems she cannot simply vanish in their presence as she would have done if we had been alone: they see her and she moves among them. —She comes with me *now*, then: hand in hand, we walk through the sanded *prakaram* with a tiresome old man, a brahmin, I feel, in these unorthodox proceedings. I realise, on examination waking, that we were, by the way, moving widdershins, the temple to our left: I am not quite sure of it, but think the old man with his lean, bare, rather dark torso overtook us in the same direction! He advises us as to the proper process for getting married. She is annoyed but I manage to be polite and tell him we have already arranged all that.

She comes to a narrow, simple, first-floor room with a strip of red carpet as my bed which I seem, though, recently to have left. Stooping a little, lightly and quickly so that none shall see, she enters, intending somehow to live with me there in secret. The room broadens at the end and there she finds Gauri, P.K.R.'s wife, on the floor asleep. She would have wakened and seen her, but by her power as a goddess my companion does not allow it: Gauri struggles to and fro in a powerful dream. But Kantham (P.K.R.'s Tantrik partner) (I have sometimes playfully called these two women "the Shaktis".) is there awake—it is day-time—and the girls will make friends.

Throughout, peculiar sweet intimacy with this playful girl with her fair Indian complexion and a very individual rather than formally beautiful face. Some association with Polonnaruwa frescoes. She is tall, erect, well-made, bears herself very well. I feel, so to speak, the weight and quality and perfume of her flesh, so real is she. And all the time, in all her quick lightness and dignified grace of movement, there is the memory in my mind of the tremendous weight of elaborate life-size sculpture.

Visiting the temple, which now seems unfamiliar in style, as if in Northern India. Shrine on a flat roof with view from there of main shrine. I mentally remark on the stolid Egyptian frontality of black Shasta-like images on horseback—a group in the *prakaram*. Beautiful gardens about the temple—something light, cool and lyrical, unlike the South. Some sense of A.K. Coomaraswamy visiting.

Travelling in the train. Suggestion of same strip of red carpet as bedding.

Waking, I feel inclined to meditate, but don't succeed in remaining in contact with the woman of the dream.

30.XII.43. Dream (Before dawn).

Hindu erotic exercises for body and mind. One of them, which I begin to practise, is simply to stand alternately tensing the whole body in alertness, for half a minute or less, then letting it relax in a very easy posture. The rest of the dream seemed to bring over something from Burnier's excellent photos of North Indian sculptures, many from Khajuraho—reduced with the most powerful and learned art to the richest, deepest and most subtle effect with the simplest, most formal, means. One that particularly impressed me for these qualities, which I want to experience deeply, was a *maithuna* (copulation)—the whole work a superb *yantra*.

Having heard I was here, Burnier asked to meet me and came to lunch with Blanca Schlamm on the 28th., though I had told her that from reports of them I could see no point in our meeting and would do everything to avoid it. At once Burnier asked me to help with the English of their articles. David MacIver had some time ago suggested this for Alain Daniélou's *Introduction to the Study of Musical Scales*.

1944, Jan. 2:

Again there arises a moment of that intransigent Passion which cannot tolerate anywhere anything but its own purity—which again and again restores the all-or-nothing perspective in which all men, all action, appear insufferably feeble, craven, knavish, self-indulgent. Rimbaud knew it!

It is Perversity which, at the height of this passion, looks for an old scrap of paper to draft these words upon instead of using what is to hand when paper is scarce in wartime. It is Perversity which tolerates nothing facile, romantic or random: the salamander coldness of artist, lover, magician, Tantrika, for which Reason is perfected as pure Hypocrisy. How well this was known, surely, in ancient and medieval India; Blake too could see it, and Beethoven surely, but what a sickly deliquescence now!

... Is not the contradiction between this intransigence and spontaneous kindness, tenderness, sympathy, simplicity, humility ...the whole substance of the dialogue with SKM and his "Heart"? But how can I love or take seriously or have any joy in a man or woman who lacks passion?

What kind of weakness, incontinence, self-indulgence is it to write this?

What kind of criticality not to write it out till I have re-read it in another mood though for itself there can be no other mood?

What Hypocrisy writes it out in order to stand beyond it—to retain silence, calm and non-attachment? —By which perfect Innocence and perfect Sophistry are one.

O Supreme who art neither good nor true—Love of Love, Joy of Joy, Death of Death, Perfection of Evil!, by Love of whom alone—that intransigent fidelity—Passion, without ceasing to be itself, becomes Humility. For He is Infinite Passion—Passion Itself.

Ethel Merston tells me: You are certainly a passionate man, artistic, emotional, demonstrative, and, what I never knew before, have "very expressive eyes". Ella said that people misunderstand me because they watch my mouth and do not see that my eyes remain cold, aloof, unchanging. But by her context Merston makes it clear that she means particularly that my eyes express the fact that I am, and it is true, by nature "very affectionate".

Gestures of the hands start very quick, decided and direct, then are "frustrated" through evoked or delayed response, failure of speed, losing the point, proportion, scintillation—in what I feel mentally as complexity, paradox, impatience, exasperation with the foreknowledge from experience that one will almost certainly not be understood and that the very occasion of speaking is metaphysically and psychologically false—the conflict of this with much more immediate simplicity, generosity, geniality.

This is how Merston interprets my bodily 'aesthetic' undulations Ella remarked on. These gestures were entirely unconscious until Ella mentioned them two years or less ago and still are, except very rarely, even now. Merston suggests that one should watch them and see exactly *what* is the occasion of exasperation, scepticism etc. "You have a good body, well built", it should be powerful and not at all so lean: it is lean because energy is continually wasted in violent outflow and immediate recoil. This corresponds, of course, with emotional, imaginative and mental expenditure.

Certainly my body, except for transient effects of overstrain, or of years of under-nourishment, though very sensitive is certainly sound and when it is not divided against itself I certainly have endless nervous energy. All the 'strong' people, when it is a question of working or even walking with me, very soon collapse. MacIver thought "almost miraculous" the speed with which, about a year ago, a poisoned finger healed when I was with him at Tiruvanamalai. There is no weakness of the vital force itself, the strain is on the physical transmitting apparatus, which is either scattered or burned out by the volume and intensity of the current. This would not be true, though, unless there were strong *resistance* somewhere: it is by Paradox that one is crucified.

Merston quoted Gurdjieff as agreeing with me, in effect, when he said that everything is spiritual work—except the one friend with whom we go on holiday. A holiday I have only tried, paradoxically, to *invent*, so that such experiments become the most subtle, deep and difficult work of all!

But in general it is in the mechanics of things that there is difficulty. For example, if I could dictate my thought at its own speed on its own occasion, my whole life would enter a much stronger and truer rhythm. As it is, I am poisoned by the slowness of the physical that compels lengthy musing, rehandling every memory! I answer a letter, for example, instantaneously in my mind, and that is my immediate, sufficient answer; yet to write it (and on the margin of more pressing tasks) involves me in the *soil* of it: in all those problems and connections which can only be perfectly resolved with the whole cosmos itself! Everything necessary is formed in an instant with full resonance, but Time makes it a *task* to be true to that directness—and brings in again in ever-new forms the secondary and irrelevant which that directness organised or overpassed—doubt, scepticism, every kind of qualification, complication. Yet that directness, singleness, may be complete —"the kingdom of heaven on earth" —all this has indeed to be commanded. No wonder Blake made Art the type of the work ordained by Christ. —Our only rest is the moment in which we salute, with love and joy, good men and true whose work and words have real virility. When we call upon them the blessing of God they already have, that blessing and their blessing light upon us in tears of sweetness—in that adoration of the Divine Beauty from which our souls have been sold away.

Spiritually, in terms of integrality, I have always known what has to be done: it is at the same time the most simple and most difficult of all things. The difficulty in getting it done is certainly, in practice, from the fact that it involves an immediate clearing up of complication and obstruction on inferior planes where there is the most subtle and ingenious procrastination and betrayal. To tackle external signs of this first, Merston seems to think, would 'give' a base on the earth' and make the work much easier. According to Gurdjieff, only the "physical brain" in man is at all developed—in its way very conscious. It is therefore easier and more profitable to work on than emotion or mind. When I was describing a kind of strain I endured for many years, though a very little of it drove someone she knows mad (SKM once professed himself painfully exhausted after an hour or so of it in sympathy with me), she remarked that my body has extraordinary natural resistance.

(11 Jan.) But my refusal to work from below, from outside, as if the spiritual were a definable object, is precisely my refusal, always, of *sadhana* as of religion and mysticism: the spiritual, if it is anything, is its own end and beginning: one has only to be true to the self-sufficiency of 'Reality'. In the relative sphere, therefore, I am completely sceptical and only the non-metaphysical dialectic of primary Buddhism seems, as dialectic, pure to me —better, the complete 'trans-discursiveness' of Zen Buddhism. It is by this

complete scepticism which *intends and means* nothing but the Autonomy of Reality, that my imagination, however mobile and disinterested, cannot, as soon as I appear on its level, escape becoming passion!

It is only during the last few years that this descent to the psychic has taken place: before that my imagination was purely esthetic. Whereas, now, I see the mind as purely formal, conventional, it was simply impossible, then, for me to make any mental judgment: there was only direct, motiveless, unqualified self-identification, as if infinitely plastic—in this sphere pure Experience, pure consciousness without comparison or memory, pure youth. It was while this still continued that almost all the thoughts on Imagination were written.

(2 Jan.) I pointed out to Merston the littleness and impotence of humanistic, psychological judgment, its confusion of unconscious and super-conscious (the key to this is in the *Mandukyopanishad*), and told her of my experience that while *samskaras* can exist at all, to resolve them in one form or at one level, though completely, as I once seemed to have done with sexual *samskaras*, is only to find them in another form at a subtle level, for a universe is a universe of form! Whereas, by real disinterestedness, all can be known, understood, fulfilled, 'transformed' directly from within: Truthfulness is the *economy* of the nature—which also canalises *bhakti*, *karma*, *jnana*. —It is the logic of Sri Aurobindo's way which so appealed to me and with which I remained so long in tension because the "surrender" he insists on is the first essential, by its very essentiality can be real only as the last achievement: complete surrender is final realisation: this dynamism is, as ever, simply the completeness and clearness of paradox. Yes, it is just paradox, the individuality itself—(cp. my draft of Street Song poem) that has to be surrendered! This is the surrender of everything—of our highest intelligence, deepest sensibility, uttermost perversity, that all may be sincerity—then no longer even sincerity, but Truth Itself, that which in no sense but its own need be 'true'—Autonomy, Infinity.

Ebauche to Ella *[Yet again a marginal addition of a passage from the long letter to Ella summing up his position in the conflict with SKM:]*

My dialogue with SKM had reached a pitch of incandescent imagination. No doubt inwardly—but how can I truly know? I am a creature of wild, reckless emotion and imagination. My coldness, apparent intellectuality, are willed—pure fatigue.

I see that my *nature* is centred in the psychic, in Imagination: it is imaginatively, with the passion, subtlety, recklessness, sophistry, or ever-simplifying dramatisation of imagination, that I conceive, act and re-act. I am evidently, by type, a poet. But a poet who begins in Rimbaud's problem...

My exhaustion is from continually suppressed or qualified passion, rage, perversity, love, extravagance, gaiety or frenzy. I have nowhere, and with no person, any rest or enjoyment, yet I have a great capacity for both. This is, after all, the position of every *sadhaka*, particularly of every *bhakta*!

I must understand, for example, the Venus-Ketu opposition in my supposed horoscope—ease, grace, beauty, richness, gaiety continually overridden by the dark 'non-existent' dragon-tail of criticism, scepticism, choice of the most difficult, of the Impossible. And the powerful contrary of Saturn (seriousness, gravity, patience, rootedness) and Mars (passion, impetuosity, intransigence, intensity—violently expansive). Venus and Mars cannot marry, for each is opposed by its enemy. And both are held by the third force of Jupiter, Wisdom, through whom must be achieved an order, knowledge and harmony deeper than any possible to either, and which their force and grace must serve. Certainly this horoscope can only be understood in terms of *nivritti* (return path toward Godhead).

7.I.44.

Stella Kramrisch (distinguished art historian, later Curator, Philadelphia Museum of Art), educated Vienna, Hungarian husband. Very much as I pictured her from her books to MacIver at Ajmer. But I forgot to mention the strong nose and did not think of the prominence at the top of the high crescent-shaped forehead. When I mentioned that I can only compare her with Cocteau for trained, athletic, psychic sensibility, she told me that she practised tightrope-walking as a girl—even, I understood, as a circus professional. She has very much the determined self-compacted air of a girl in frilled skirts toeing the cord. Habit of rapidly pouting the mouth which expresses the kind of contained re-application of sensibility her work seems to involve. Invites me to visit at 2/1 Bright St., Calcutta–Baliganj tram from Howrah Station.

9.I.44. Dream.

Awoke from a sense of the charm of B.—that quick, intelligent, silver, musical voice; eyes soft and impenetrable like a moth's; that avid, sinuous, cerebrally sensuous mouth; the tender body pale like honey, almond, ivory, the magnolia; its very subtle, hardly perceptible perfume; and in all, that disturbing "strangeness in the proportion" by which beauty is not quite human. As if to Ella!: *Of course* I eliminate the blind and limited individuality: every lover does. *Of course* I complete imperfect signs into their perfection, for it is Perfection alone that we can perfectly love, and therefore love makes every limited form a symbol of the Object of all love.

What movement, re-arrangement, secret charm or correspondence, what return upon themselves of the vital forces, leads to such an impression, such a *presence*, independent of all analysable thought or memory?

Juliette (Ethel Merston) in a letter, 24 Jan.: "How feline your inclinedness..." I replied that tiger and leopard attract me by their union of intensity and elegance.

10.I.44.

Alain Daniélou confirms what is evidently so true in the South, that infinite gentleness, politeness and patience must be used in dealing with Hindus: especially since he is an intruder, the European must behave with the greatest delicacy. And, once more the great importance of etiquette.

He says that servants and workmen often deliberately test a foreigner's patience and that their inefficiency is often assumed. In any case, they resent being forced to do things in an unfamiliar way.

[Long marginal ebauche to Ella which harks back to the very long entry that began as far back as Jan. 2 and ran on for 5 days]:

I was going to say that my exasperation over this letter was due to the fact that you do not understand me well enough to have the right to understand me—but for my being for a moment a little pleased with the phrase, I see it is not quite true—or if it is, I am not interested in its truth. Once more, one has nothing to say *to anyone*...

If I had not so long trained myself not to relate my own impressions with myself, should I not see, in the late night, cold, in which only a dog barks far away, in a world full only of arid tasks and of what is alien, with no satisfaction, with no friend before whom I need not restrain tenderness or passionate foolishness (with whom, therefore, both would find their truth), with no laughter, no beloved in my bed, with an old mother 6000 miles away worn out with suppressed sorrow but obstinate in a brave resource of pride—should I not see where and what I am, what the world is, and return, perhaps, to a simple depth like the earth? But our sincerity must make trial of every falsity, must conquer even God: our intelligence must become our *being*. —And I *write* all this!, as if to a tune: no part of me moves in it, not even my mind. —Even the falsity that has to be conquered becomes fatigue, we fall down into it like men drunken—who can arouse themselves, on the verge of madness, only by extravagant, despairing passion, more sceptical than fatigue.

And your loneliness... the loneliness of everyone, hidden, unconscious, in different ways. The loneliness of God. —That which must be completed, beside which all is endless, joyless folly.

And when strength is in us we are blind with unconscious cruelty, or foolishly forget the cruelty to ourselves by which, once more, we refuse to meet and overcome God—and so to replace Him, to become all Love and Truth, to realise the Void...

The tired life and mind indulge in empty ingenuities; the heart cannot even weep; the eyes are fixed and glazed like a man alone in the desert who has long forgotten even death. Yet how simple is our love, our truthfulness...

Who but Rimbaud has expressed this with its own intensity?: "Innocence, innocence, innocence—fleau!" (scourge)

Yet I know perfectly well that this is all indulgence, sentimentality, hypocrisy—a lowering of level due to fatigue.

11.I.44. Dream

Rich forest scene. Ure is seated opposite at the foot of a hill all thickly covered with trees, practically jungle. Renée *(LT's sister)* beside me on a bench by a path that skirts the dell above, to Ure's right. A tiny insect placed upon a bare patch of a big tree will turn it red. I see a light moisture spreading from it which slightly darkens the exposed barkless patch of cochineal purple-red, rather surprisingly fills it entirely, then dries, leaving the colour much as it was. But after another minute or two, young leafy saplings suddenly burst from the patch and completely cover it: in the breeze they delicately sway their flowering tops. Ure says it is a miracle. (Yesterday I was revising with Danielou his translation of an essay on the World Tree by Coomaraswamy—with lengthy footnotes; there was a question of its shoots and buds—*Gita* XV,2: "Just as the branches put forth buds—we wrote —so bodies, the result of deeds, develop spheres of perception—sound, touch, sight, taste and smell".) But almost as soon, through a gap opposite Ure, where one of the rich, tall trees has a plume of very light, tender-leaved branches, a strong wind begins to blow. The storm increases little by little to such a gale that whole big branches are torn off and hurtle about wildly, dangerously, almost black, in the wind. Its direction is so far constant, so that Renée and I are sheltered, and Ure, though facing it, remains a spectator too. I see no sign of it stopping: it has risen already to a very frightening pitch—the wind may change at any moment, then one may be killed by the flying branches. There is a roaring and tearing of the gale and rain, everything is darkened by the flying green branches. If the trees represent the World Tree, does this correspond with the present World War?

A party of girls picnicking here today, including the one I noticed before who is like a Khajuraho *apsaras*, came and sat in my room and asked me to lunch with them.

Another auspicious sign today (this everyone says) was half an hour of thunder, lightning and rain this afternoon while most of my things had been moved across the Varuna to Sarai Mohana, the little village where I am to live in the fields by the ancient Panchakroshi pilgrim-track.

Sarai Mohana. Night. In this silent, ancient place, in this beautifully simple house, in the midst of a life profoundly based that has not essentially changed for thousands of years, every word seems to recover a rich and fundamental meaning: by this immemorial pilgrim path through the soft, blooming, timeless field, the weight, subtlety and lucidity of "fire", "night", "earth", "river", "guest" is restored in a primordial poetry.

"Purify my speech."

14.I.44. Sorai Mohana. With the children.

It would require the greatest genius to express perfectly even a few moments of the beauty, fantasy, passion these little girls and boys bring to their play. I feel as if, in the delicate wildness of it, I had been immersed in a sparkling element a thousand times more limpid and intense than light. The little Bengali girl, Jayasri, exquisite as a jasmin flower, has an especially pure, original and subtle nature. Blanca, her house warden, tells me that she is related with the Tagores and with Sri Krishna Prem's (Professor Ronald Nixon) guru, a Chakravarti woman.

Here, if it is accepted with perfect disinterestedness, is absolute poetry. How profound the Christ's words "For such is the kingdom of heaven" —Sahaja, the autonomy, the incomparable ever-new intensity of Lila.

The mind, not entirely carried away by this play but foolishly seeking to be quick, subtle, intelligent enough for it, is tired by it; or rather, isolated and immobilised. It must be entirely exhausted or entirely carried away.

> "... and learn in Wonder's schools
> To be, in things past bounds of wit, fools—if ye
> be not fools."

17.I.44. Dream.

From beneath a grey-blue curtain comes out a small, frail form, about four feet high or a little more, but apparently of a man. He is wrapped in an old white cotton cloth or robe. I bow at his feet with deep and sweet emotion, feeling his extraordinary sanctity. He greets me by name

("Thompson") though he can know nothing about me by ordinary means. I am a stranger and only heard of him a few minutes before on a random wandering visit: he says in a moment he will speak with "the English scholar". I tend to associate him with Harihara Baba whom I visited a week or more ago on his boat at Asi Ghat, at night, when only the grave, silent, stooping, immobile seated form could be seen. I felt that something august and remote was focussed there. Women bowed their heads, as I also did, on the cot, touching his feet, crossed under him. He made no movement or response and his features could not be seen. I must visit him again as soon as possible, in daylight, and see if there is, perhaps, anything corresponding with the impression of the dream. *[I know that there was indeed a close similarity. 'Hari Baba' became a familiar figure in Anandamayi Ma's ashrams—a frequent visitor with his devoted entourage who often persented little 'dramas' of an amusing holy sort during satsang. Hari Baba favoured loud chanting of bhajans, standing in his bent posture in the centre of his devotees, banging his brass gong very loudly indeed with a wooden eardrum shattering mallet.]*

[Dream continues:] I am rather surprised at his good English. He asks the others to withdraw for a time: he wants to speak to me alone. He brings me very near him, seated with our faces almost touching, his hands upon my arms; for a moment I feel his balloon-like belly. Speaking very softly and gently he says: Don't you realise that you can't psychically, also spiritually, "protect" yourself? (Does he put his arms about me as if to shield from hostile forces?) Moved, almost in tears for he makes it seem in a way self-evident, I ask: Then help me to see completely and with conviction that this is so; but I immediately feel that even this is unnecessary and, so to speak, selfish, and say so. In a low whisper so that no-one else may hear he gives me advice in obscure terms which I think no-one but myself can understand.

For some time after half-waking I am still so impressed by his presence that I do not realise it is a dream. Yet it by no means ranks, in the power and clarity of its effect, with the most remarkable dreams I have had, such as a recent dream in the South about Ramana Maharishi in a cave and being swallowed by an elephant—unless it is that I am 'getting used' to them.

There is an unfamiliar flavour about him that I associate with the sights, movements, smells, atmosphere of Benares, of the North.

Before trying to meditate a little, afterwards, I realised how complete, apparently, is SKM's psychic withdrawal and thought once more of various aspects of that episode—how little one knows of possibilities in such spheres; on the other hand how strange the development of the kiss episode in the Malakarai experience; and so on.

18.I.44.

On the way to the College, not more than ten minutes walk, depending on whether the ferryboat is in use or the seasonal bamboo bridge has been erected over the little Varuna river, a mood of deep, sweet, happy tenderness became almost a psychic identification with what seems to be SKM's prevailing state of love: it almost seemed, as often before, that my face became his—grave, heavy like honey in this sweetness, the eyes absorbed in that other-than-human depth of the *guru-puja. [Marginal note added later]*: It was only on reading over these entries that I saw how this sensation seems to deny the idea of complete separation from SKM.)

19.I.44. Dream.

SKM comes into the sanded courtyard. I am strained, disturbed, want to find some simple way of going into everything again with him, especially into the fact that in several ways I feel him sinister—I have already mentioned this. (Marginal note:) At one moment I was in tears in his arms, thinking You don't know how difficult, and important all this is for me, but was aware that this might seem weakness, and restrained myself.

Keeping up very ingenious talk, he embraces me, rubs the top of my head round and round for a minute or two, till I begin to wonder if he is perhaps 'abstracting' something from me, undoing something, the talk a patter to distract attention. He repeats that I should not be so overstrained, weak and below weight, that the strain should not affect me "here"—placing his hands at root of throat and upper chest—where in the dream I do in fact feel the 'phthisic' strain, and I am spitting. There was a certain expenditure over my lesson today and I am in general a little strained and tired, have not yet overcome even the most immediate arrears of tasks and letters or established a harmonious rhythm of work.

He says that for the weakness it is good to touch a "bodhi tree" about a mile away. I already know the tree and this makes me realise that in spite of our separation I am living very near him. He will come with me so that I can talk alone about the sinister suggestion in him. He suddenly realises that he will have to walk back (very egoistic note here), but says he will come all the same.

I want to ask SKM if he is not really supremely selfish, entirely directed towards enjoyment of his 'states', even exploiting others in that direction.

[Thompson had only been in Benares a couple of weeks when he had an inner experience of the utmost subtlety. In the process of adapting his style of discontinuous and relatively short 'apercus' from the postcard-size

paper slips—which proved so marvelously appropriate in their restricted dimensions to goad and inspire a degree of luminosity— to the greatly enlarged format of 29 x 23 cms, he seized the opportunity to develop a newly meandering and exploratory style with which to set off on the trail of his elusive and intricate theme. The appearance of the script spread across three pages, with his customary neat and small handwriting, tells us some important things about the kind of experience, and the quality of closely woven reflections upon it. As always, the reader has no idea what the subject of any given journal entry is going to be about, nor what the author's all-important mood is likely to be. There is almost no action or event that each entry will record or describe. His life at Rajghat appears tranquil, slow-moving and remarkably uneventful. Or at least, Thompson hardly ever describes any events which might have occurred on a daily basis. What we get is—well ninety per cent at any rate—reflections on his inner life and his dreams, with just the occasional passing reference to new friends made or very brief and undramatic little accounts of the children in the school. Now in the case of a long entry (these are to become increasingly frequent during the next five years), it is the format and the look of the manuscript layout that is so striking. On the first, left-hand, page the entry on January 20th opens with a long, very neat and very legible paragraph that has an absolute surety of style and expression—it may well have begun as a hastily drafted note to himself—in which the reader shares with the writer the experience of discovery. An entirely fresh theme about an arrestingly special inner train of thought begins to unwind. By the time we reach the second paragraph, still not clear as to where all this is leading, we begin to realise that Thompson is engaged in tracing a particularly labyrinthine course. The second page is an extraordinary contrast to the first. What has happened is that the lengthy second paragraph departs from the relative concision of the first, some fifteen lines are lightly crossed out (though still fully legible), two interpolations get long arrow lines right across the page to the gatefold on the main paragraph's left as a second column fills out every available remaining space still left and the handwriting gets smaller and smaller, so that eventually the reader can no longer grasp the gist of what is being written about. Though the sequence of sentences is very hard to follow, the substance of what is being written is orderly. But the longer the paragraph goes on, the reader's protracted journey towards its conclusion will hopefully correspond to the act of discovery which Thompson is in the process of making. Unless and until the entry is transcribed by myself as editor, its content cannot be grasped. It is like a sequence of action photographs which, until they are spread out in their proper succession, cannot be assessed as a record of instants following one after another to the final denouement: as Thompson said in 'Journal about Journal' "from history through to Potentiality—or 'horoscope' ".]

20.I.44. Benares.

A very clear and subtle perception today, which I must try to describe: —Whatever situation one is in, the consciousness remains the same in quality and extent, like a self-closed sphere in which all is already contained, like a conscious dream, producing no change or re-action: all one says and does, or that happens, is spontaneous, frictionless, automatic, without result or implication, like one's action, appearance, presence here or there in a dream: one is as it were a vision of oneself, an emanation put forth and moving within one's own consciousness, this vision carrying with itself (again as in a dream) its whole world of circumstance, persons and events. The vision-quality of sight has changed: looking at a tree one *sees*, as in conscious dream, that it is real only in and by the mode of being seen: it exists in the closed eye of the 'sleeper' awake beyond, in and through it: it is an accidental vein or light-drift within that Eye, entirely part of It. Like an object seen in dream, therefore, it does not, in being seen, seem tangible: to touch it is a change in the dream, a different tree in a different time, in a slightly different order of 'the world': this act re-arranges the whole dream and may give it an unforeseen direction. Yet, as in conscious dream, one can do whatever one can wish or think and 'the world' corresponds. Yet one's wishing and thinking is all dream—formal, desireless, making no change in knowledge. (The form—of one's thought, activity etc. at a given moment—is, however, complete in itself and so far, at the moment, one is absorbed in it: otherwise there would be no dream-world; yet there *is* one, in this way, just because of the possibility of there not being one—as the obverse involved in that possibility, which does not even 'prove' it, because it is absolute.)

It is quite clear to me that this is a phase only, but if I try to describe to myself exactly what it represents I shall begin to elaborate and formalise with my mind (if I have not begun already): the description will then remain in the dream, not really go deeper and explain *in experience*, not theoretically, how it is that we dream and if there can be any sense in *changing* the dream (the cosmos)—especially since, for perfect geniality, disinterestedness, freedom from preconception, the 'manifestation' is in every way, and in whatever 'evil' (which only our fear of it, or division by it, resists), esthetically perfect—pure causeless Marvel. *[Crossed out:]* Perhaps it is some such thing that Rimbaud saw, for he had so strongly the sense of Poetry, when he said that "la morale est la faiblesse de la cervelle".

(21st Jan.) —the change would be made *yogically*—from the point of view of the transforming esthetic of action; but that can never really be pure and free except when the esthetic of contemplation is perfectly established: only when Marvel is absolute is every other aspect of *Lila* released.

[Interpolated afterthought in the margin eighteen months later, 24.Oct.1945:]

Such 'change' can evidently be nothing but Lila: *all change*, the manifestation itself, is nothing but Lila: it is oneness with the Lila that seems to 'transform' (Samarpana), but the idea of transformation is a metaphor dependent on a side-tracking of *jnana*: it is valid only for those who still effectively find, or (the same thing) wish to sustain, 'forms'.

As far as I have read, Sri Aurobindo nowhere acknowledges more than the Purusha-Prakriti dualism (which Sri S. himself shows is not a sufficient definition of *jnana*): he consistently under-estimates (indeed takes only a popular estimate of) Shankara and primary Buddhism (essentially *jnana*). Sri Aurobindo does not in fact directly acknowledge pure *jnana*, "direct perception", at all (if he did, indeed, there would be nothing else to say: he merely defines what appears instead from his characteristically yogic point of view.) On the plane where he expresses himself mentally, therefore it is impossible for him (as indeed for everyone else!) to demonstrate that, or has realised, he really understands pure *advaita*, for from the *jnani*'s viewpoint the Absolute and the Transcendent *can* only be one: the Spirit-Matter dualism which is the armature of all Sri Aurobindo's *expression*, anyway, cannot exist beyond the mind, and "supermind" is still Mind—"below the Sachchidananda". (In view of what Sri Aurobindo is reported to think of Sri Ramana Maharishi, it is interesting that the latter is reported to have said that Sri Aurobindo has not got beyond the mind!) But I am touching here on a matter far too deep to be dealt with casually. There must be at least two terms for any kind of thought, relative experience or discourse. Call them, in principle, Spirit and Matter, Purusha-Prakriti. So far as *advaita-shastra* exists, the *Ashta-vakra* and *Avadhuta-gita* discourse only around what first existed and proves their occasion; these two terms are acknowledged as the occasion of all teaching and all *sadhana*, though there can be no real occasion for either, both depending entirely upon *avidya*. We may say, then, that Sri Aurobindo would absorb all traditional *jnani* (to the limit of his *discourse*), and would absorb all into Spirit. Yet in experience, for both these can, ultimately, only be "sahaja" or completed (and endless...) transformation. But these are matters far too fundamental to be dealt with thus casually. My interest in both almost obliges me to thresh out the whole question in a treatise on Sri Aurobindo and *advaita*. But though I always find time to write, and have in fact written a certain amount on this question, I have never time to put together any *book*!: I go on being my own unfinished *opus*!

Otherwise one is still *involved* in dream. In other words: for Lila Itself (and Lila is the fact that there never 'was', 'is' or 'can be' anything else), *mukti* (Liberation, which comes through Knowledge of Self) is at the same time meaningless and indispensable: This is the nature of *mukti*. For Sri Aurobindo's purely dynamic (Tantric, yogic) way, this inevitability of *mukti* (because it is absurd to say that the Supreme is *mukta*), is directly represented (for the individuality in which we find ourselves or as which we appear) by absolute *samarpana*. From this point of view the situation with David MacIver (a disciple of SKM who was at loggerheads with Thompson) is rather piquant: though he cannot deny that SKM is *mukta,* "as the transcendent bhakta he remains in a position of uncompleted *sadhana*".

SKM says that in spite of his claim MacIver is not, and really knows he is not, *mukta*. It really looks as if the Jnani is right in saying that; because MacIver does not effectively understand the Absolute he cannot possibly understand the Transcendent—or my concept which I call "Poetry". (In the letter I have quoted, the word 'transcendent' suddenly appears repeatedly, but always in this same vague adjectival way.)

[Thompson may have discovered some precious insight through ploughing into MacIver's verbiage; his reader is left out in the cold. I have had occasion to remark upon the vast amount of turgid abstraction and sterile sophistry that was the inevitable and truly dispiriting side of his daily stint on his journal, the privacy of his 'sadhana', the negative side of his soul-searching. It is also the outward and visible sign of the terrible exhaustion which often overcame him. I have avoided as far as I possibly can the inclusion in these selections from the journal of such inconclusive mental acrobatics. But evidence was needed of Thompson's ability to rise above the pedantry of monotonous routine keep-fit exercises—by revealing the price he paid when he fulfilled his determination to record his 'vacillations and detours'.]

1.II.44

How can I serve You of whom the limited mind can only say You are the Perfection of truth and of the Lie, of love and hate, unless I use with perfect truthfulness every faculty I seem to possess? Does this not demand a purity like Yours—that one should live beyond Tragedy, Evil, Perversity,

Damnation, beyond Enjoyment, Good, Seduction, Beatitude, having completed them by truthfulness? Yet there is disorder, incompleteness, insubordination, impurity, licence, self-indulgence, indulgence of mixture and weakness, of pride and false humility, of the subtlest and most cruel and self-cruel hypocrisy. There is the false, endless crucifixion upon a cross of all fragments, crookedness, not that unwavering patient nameless crisis whose straightness is the axis of the world. Oh, in what humility, in what well of sweetness is it planted! Sweeter than any speech, too pure to know its sweetness (all knowledge ever returned into that sweetness), like the babbling of a child.

3.II.44.

"Nel mezzo del cammin di nostra vita..."

Except Perfection itself, all must be work towards it. There is nothing else but these two things. To fail from the work offered in every occasion, every mode of our existence, is to make Perfection an idol merely—it is to enter into laziness, confusion, doublemindedness, hypocrisy. That is indeed unhappiness; but for him who conceives and wills Perfection, who is devoted to Reality as Self-completion, Its own cause, there is no question of happiness or unhappiness.

Ebauche to Ella:

My objective intelligence knows very well that certain kinds of thought, imagination and experience are unknown to you: I can often even foresee exactly how you must misread what I write. And one cannot without pain, even perversity on its level, go against a disinterested faculty. Yet on the other hand, I accept that you are in some ways more limited than I and act accordingly, contradicts imaginative generosity and would be merely worldly. Between these two my spontaneity is completely broken.

(28 Feb. marginal note:) But this stifling of spontaneity *is* the problem of the world. In asking me not to "smash" my "single, simple, vivid, self, you want me to evade this problem with you also, not to solve it. But one can have no interest in being spontaneous *for one's own sake*: that would in any case deny the whole nature of spontaneity, essentially disinterested. The individual problem is the cosmic problem. *Advaita*-theory may recognise *sahaja* (Sanskrit for spontaneity, amongst other things), it can say nothing of its content. Is this not, perhaps, because it never recognised the cosmic as such, but worked always in terms of the individual? There is the same difference between Hinayana *Arhat* and Mahayana *Bodhisattva*. *Advaita* is unquestionable for the intellect that formulates it: it *is* the intellect's rec-

ognition of the Infinite, (in which the individual intellect may be fulfilled.) But the intellect is also part of that cosmos which is contained in Him who seems even infinite only to the finite. 'Liberation' and 'bondage' are equally part of His Ineffable Lila. By 'liberation' one only knows one is His *bhakta*. (This is in fact what Ramana Maharishi said to me about *Gita* XVIII,54, when he quoted the *sloka* to the effect that it is the *jnani* who is the *bhakta*.) *Advaita* is the end of speech, that is all—the beginning of that truth I first wrote in my teens that "The universe is the only perfect poem", the only Speech—the Concreteness which for all other speech is Silence, and which made Rimbaud pray: "Il nous sera loisible de posseder la verite dans une ame et un corps". For the body as such is formed by and inseparable from the Cosmos. He had written years before: "Le poete... est chargé de humanité, des *animaux* même." (letter to Demeny, 15 May 1871.

This is of course intellectual irritablility, but O I wish you were less naive... so that I could be naif with you.

If the *karma-mukta* competes his realisation in subtle cosmic spheres, does not the *jivanmuka* in reaching *sahaja*, do the same in the body? None fulfils himself in this but Him who is Fulfilment (therefore, not even Fulfilment); *but this*, as Sri Aurobindo sees, is true of the cosmos as such as well, for every 'as such' is for Him not even Nothing. For the man who sees this, *nirvikalpa samadhi* may well be his rest, his *sleep*! (SKM told me to rest in *nirvikalpa samadhi*.) I do not want to rest. *What* does this mean?: that is the question SKM will not clearly answer. Is this not only because he insists on making yoga merely individual?

16.II.44.

It is the old story of obstinately maintaining the rational focus, the point of view of Normality, of the Kingdom of Heaven on earth—which so many, including the typical drug-taker, only want to get away from, because they are helpless and passive there.

My consciousness is *immediately* focussed, *where I find it*, only in another, a 'trans-rational', way. Yet I have always refused to forsake the norm of the most ordinary man: hence my refusal of 'spirituality', of *sadhana*, of *samadhi*, of my insistence on stating myself in terms of poetry etc., common to all men at all periods. The Christ by his direct universality is the Supreme Poet.

It is this fact that the inner consciousness is already established elsewhere that may lead the rational consciousness to use a drug—to make in its own terms, without forsaking its own province, the change to what actually is !

A man who does this will evidently never be *intoxicated* by a drug and this is, of course, the exact opposite of the romantic evasion.

Or, technically, a drug is required to bring the vital force to a state of vibration corresponding with the inner consciousness—which otherwise keeps it under a continual strain. *Bhang* and *ganja*, for example, greatly increase the rate of vibration of the *prana*, so that one is lifted, from the physical point of view, to the plane, and to the speed of one's most intense and subtle thought and experience—tension with the physical and rational resistance is overcome, one uses wings. Of opium Cocteau writes: "J'avis a mon esprit des ailes de fumée", but it is really the body that is lifted to the norm of the mind: no physical drug can give the mind what it does not already possess. The drug is chosen, and works, by an intuition of the mind whose state corresponds with its effect. Merely to think of *bhang* normalises my consciousness. Whereas the romantic chooses his drug mechanically, or sentimentally: he chooses *what he is not*, which, therefore, he will never understand. This adjustment would normally be made by *yoga*. But so many *sadhakas* use *bhang*, and *ganja* is employed in Tantrik ritual—as Peruvian, Greek and other cults made use of drugs to change, stabilise or support the state of consciousness.

Cocteau is certainly, I should say, the opposite of the romantic drug-taker—a serious *sadhaka*, entirely classical in his outlook and intention, as indeed his work shows. The classical is what relates to Normality and to concrete realisation in all domains. Ultimately it means Absolute Realism: "Thy will be done on earth as it is in heaven." The Hermetic process for achieving this, for squaring the circle, for making earth and heaven one, the Sole Reality, also appeared a strange and complex alchemy.

17.II.44. With Alain Daniélou at Asi Ghat.

Barcelona gipsy *canto* (Manuel Villejo) with guitar deriving no doubt from the pure and powerful medieval music lost with the gross and superficial tempered scale—pure passionate intensity, direct as seed or blood, with concentrated rhythmic pattern in the accompaniment.

Then the first movement of Franck's violin sonata in A major, exquisitely played by Yehudi Menuhin and his sister Hephzibah—of extraordinary, of heavenly beauty, so that the very instruments seem to acquire strange sweet and intense harplike overtones or a new poignant, subtilised depth of resonance.

Listening to the second movement when what afterwards turned out to have been a heavy dose of *bhang* was beginning to make all experience purely and directly subjective, I found the real meaning for this effect in the first Western music I have heard for a long time, and which, out of sympathy, I interpreted positively. Every note was in fact flattened, and degraded, half-muted, the vertical column of overtones stifled and distorted, and these mutilated resonances knotting in the air into an ugly, damping, almost sinister tangle. Daniélou says that after his practical and theoretical work on 'traditional' music he normally perceives this now.

27.II.44. Marginal comment:

Listening to the same sonata without *bhang*, I find exactly the same monstrous distortion and impurity.

A pure 5th on Daniélou's perfectly tuned instrument sounds like a single note. I now understand that there is a physiological base for the remark of Hindus about the *confused* nature of Western music.

And when the ears are thus sensitised, as happened to me, also, with peyotl, the music loses all meaning: you see how excessively conventional it is—that we read emotion into it *mentally*. This is what Daniélou means by saying that Western music is entirely intellectual. Perhaps this continual infusion of emotional meaning into forms wrenched and debased from all transparent natural correspondences partly explains the 'sentimentalism' of modern Westerners and their tortured nerves. Because Hindu music is the music of Nature, even at its most intense it is perfectly restful—like an image of Kali or the dancing Shiva.

18.II.44. Dream.

A devotee (? myself) applies *vibhuti* with such devotion to an image (? of Hanuman) that it comes to life and with its stone head glittering with granite crystals applies *kumkuman* between his brows.

20.II.44.

At breakfast the morning after my experiment with *bhang*, Daniélou says it relaxes me, brings out more of the jovial 'Franciscan saint'. He says it is very obvious, from my kind of tenseness, that I have long been living on my own substance, in a self-sustained vacuum. Yet by broadening one's base one may reach a greater height, though it seem less.

22.II.44.

Everything must be done by rhythm, not by force. Not by will but by sensibility and intelligence.

A much slighter dose of *bhang* produces what Daniélou says is the characteristic sensation of heat or pressure at the nape. Under the much heavier dose the other day (the servant who prepared it, an *habitué*, seems surprised I stood it so well). I made a strong effort to resist being entirely immersed in another world: this time, such an effort was hardly necessary. The whole thing seemed more physiological, less intensely subjective.

Asi Ghat, Daniélou sings a setting by Duparc, contemporary of Proust, of Baudelaire's "Mon amie, ma soeur, Songe à la douceur d'aller la-bas vivre ensemble!" I think it was not only sympathetic interpretation that made me feel it an intimate revelation of his sensibility, but afterwards I understood that it is the same spirit that is in his Indian music. If one has never heard Balinese music, one can hardly know that such a world exists; so this was for me an entirely new psychic experience, a new tone, a new possibility in the world of emotion. The poem is exquisitely fulfilled by this music—like one of those tiny, flat Japanese flowers of wood pulp or cotton which swell in water and open out, till every nuance of form and colour has reached the fullest expansion.

The impression was quite different from that of my own reading of Baudelaire's poems, but as Daniélou agrees, a poem that is more than cerebral condenses into seed or *yantra* from almost endless possibilities for whose truth it is the key; and the poet need only have felt *one* of them directly. If he fully knew what worlds or beings fulfil or represent themselves through his work, he would be a yogin, not a poet at all.

Though the Supreme Yogin, as the *Gita* testifies, is also the Supreme Poet. And these two natures seem to have been united in the Christ. Rimbaud experienced to its depth the *conflict* between them in the individual who has to choose the mode of his spiritual fulfilment. And in this he went to the heart of the Western conflict between Christ (the kingdom of heaven on earth—"la verité dans une âme et un corps", the spiritual) and this world (art and science as human invention and experiment, knowledge of good and evil, magic). —The same conflict that Blake dealt with mythologically, and as a man by his virile faith.

I had never thought that so exposed a sensibility exists, a fineness and purity whose passivity, however, flatters it under a beginningless and endless ceiling of dark cloud. But what was so poignant was its extremeness —a world so special (advanced like a blind tunnel into the unknown) that it is in effect lost to all contact with any common centre, any norm. It is true that *bhang* helps one to experience with almost perfect singleness the wonder and desolation of states self-contained and lost like heaven or hell, but in any case the impression was so specific and so deep that it continued hardly diminished for two full days afterwards.

I had also never perfectly understood before that for some souls it is entirely tenderness that expresses itself in sexuality so that the sexual impulse is fused with it, though this explains all that a more intellectual temperament finds almost inexplicable attachment, and which seems to imply a feminine incapacity for analysis. Sexuality for me always seemed to express pure joy, delight in the marvel of charm and beauty so deep that it becomes the most joyous, concentrated worship.

Sexuality may of course become the vehicle and means of expression for almost any psychic possibility; and this is the reason why all mental conclusions about it, such as the new barbarism of the West abounds in are ludicrously shallow or false.

23.II.44.

Letter to David MacIver, otherwise so meaningless, must be deep *sadhana*. —Is reliance on goodness and truthfulness, with the continual failure of even integral *will* to their completion, which is God, a deep blindness, weakness, limitation, sterility, even a deep sentimentality, to be overcome? —Evidently, if "God is neither good nor true". And if the depth of what I mean by Poetry or "Luxury" (Li.la)—the Infinite Joy and Beauty which is also Infinite, Monstrosity and Terror—is to be realised *in every domain*.

25.II.44.

The connection of this affair with the question of SKM and Evil is evidently not accidental.

[There are several of David MacIver's letter in the Washington University archive which provide evidence of this deadeningly useless and sickly meandering stuff that Thompson was left to deal with after his departure from Trivandrum.]

Yet will to completion fails (and 'realisation' is spontaneous) just so far as goodness and truthfulness are real, that is disinterested: then they represent absolute faith in God, the faith that is Knowledge. And it is surely this Knowledge that is expressed in my analysis of Truth and Evil.

In overcoming every *form* of goodness and truthfulness, then, one is overcoming the last *appearance* of the ego—the "saint" that the "demon" has always opposed. It is in some such way, perhaps, that the conflict between disinterested tenderness, sympathy, simplicity and disinterested passion, intransigence, perversity may be resolved in nameless, all-containing Wholeness—the "Presence" and "Spontaneity" both could conceive but neither grasp.

25.II.44. Visit from the boys of the College (In other words, 'senior boys', as distinct from the children in the Junior School who share the campus.):

For the individual, the only immediate (natural) relation with those our equals mentally or in sensibility is vital or physical, whether in attraction or repulsion, and whether these are instinctive or experimental. An imaginative sympathy is still *in itself* only humanistic (artistic or psychological).

In other words: it is just where individual relation is most clearly imperfect, perverse or sentimental that the possibility of true love, the 'activity' of the disinterested wholeness of one's being, is defined as an indubitable reality.

It is only by such love that sympathy is fulfilled as perfect insight and understanding, and nothing short of it can make mental, vital and physical modes entirely means and entirely flawless—entirely modes of Presence, Wholeness, Spontaneity. If this is possible, no change of *mode* is necessary or can have any but a formal (relative) meaning: this fulfilment is the only real 'transformation'.

26.II.44.

Little Chaitanya (8) tells me that at night in their dormitory when the jackals howl outside the boys stop them by closing their fists.

27.II.44.

Daniélou says that a dog will not bark at a naked man, so thieves in India go about at night without clothing. *[An ex-convict thief in England told me the same thing years before I read this remark by Daniélou.]*

3.III.44.

I noticed once again two or three days ago, in partly cerebral fatigue, and also when, as now, I was hungry, that curious 'taste' as of semen in the head* repeated now when tea, which I thought I could safely drink this morning, has subtly over-excited the brain and I have been attentively reading one of Coomaraswamy's closely woven essays (because I felt unfit for direct mental effort). This taste of semen also follows mental exertion after sexual expenditure. It seems quite clear that this effect is to be connected with the "*amrita*" which, yogins say, drops from the brain and is burned up by the fire of the stomach, thus consuming one's life, unless the process is stopped by *kechari-mudra*. Quite clearly, I feel as well as taste the passage of some such "nectar" from high up behind the uvula. Then one senses as if by reflection from there the centre in the middle of the head which is strained by intense thought. During the last few nights I have noticed again, I think for the first time in Benares, the faint burring in the ears which SKM said is a sign of mental strain.

*LT's Footnote: Evans-Wentz refers somewhere to a Tibetan text (no doubt Tantrik) where it is said that the source of semen is in the brain, a fact confirmed by SKM and certainly supported by my own experience.

7.III.44.

I learn from Daniélou that *shukra* (semen) means *teja-svarupa* (brilliance of the self). Shankaracharya says that the root of this world is semen, the white (*shuddha*), the light-substance (*jyotishmat*), the form of the self-brilliance of awareness (*chaitanya*).

The mango-trees are all in flower. Their scent at night is rich and suave like the odour of semen, an impression greatly enhanced if they are taken in the mouth. In the Tamil country the fruit is given to girls to hasten puberty.

5.III.44.

In sunlight the branching spires of yellow-russet blossom, loud with bees, have an apricot sweetness – the scent is lighter, more exalted, almost entirely loses that unradiant moony weight.

This evening, on the broad sands of the Ganges, where the lower structure of a little Shiva and a little Ganesha shrine has crumbled away, among the disordered slabs and rubble I found and carried off a fragment of a reddish stone image of a 4-(?6) armed Ganapati with the trunk turned to the left (*vama-marga*) and with a flying *gana*. The style seems nearer that of the Shiva-Parvati than to the 10th century piece.

[He has not referred to finding that piece of sculpture. In the early days at Rajghat College many fragments of sculpture were found in the woods.]

Sunset. In a little boat on the river, under the glare of a Petromax lamp, five delicate figures with tall crowns of gilded leather-work dressed in bright red, with scarves of cerise silk, with flowers and jewels, their cheeks and forehead painted with designs in silver and gold, even the eyelids silvered. I ask who these children are and a young man in the boat, wearing a garland of dark marigolds, his forehead smeared with vermilion, explains: "They are our gods", Rama, Sita, Lakshmana. They have been acting the

Ramayana at stations of the pilgrim way and are now returning to the town.

Dream.

In a clear starlit sky I see a filmy black parachute drift past. Some distance away, very high up, it becomes still. I watch the figure of a man climb to the top of it, then dexterously open a big, lightly framed oblong mirror (all is silver and delicate in the night-sky). He bends it through a small angle (a bright pane of light passing for a moment across us), till it shows up part of a busy street. Is it perhaps a Japanese device to see where to bomb? Then he sits outside the mirror. People are curious and rather alarmed, not knowing whether he is an enemy or one of our own men practising. After some time a light rain begins to fall and he is seen coming down, far off, like a drifting black thread.

If sleep can be made conscious, one is established in the timeless—the whole of history and one's own individual appearance purely formal.

Love. There is none but the Divine intransigence that is not really blindness, or re-action or incapacity. Divine: that is, Infinite, Self-caused.

[A whole paragraph very sedulously crossed out, followed by this account of another experience with bhang.]

19.15 hrs. One teaspoonful, with anis, cardamon, pepper and milk.

19.30. A certain relaxation in the limbs.

20.00. Unlocalisable intoxication (solar plexus and head are in it) that will evidently soon develop into that peculiar subtle vibration of the nerves, or *praana*, in all the limbs. Handwriting noticeably relaxed. Peculiar glow in intestines. No doubt because I'm tired today (oilbath, and phosphatoria yesterday and this morning), eyes are a little affected—tend to weigh down slightly in a sort of glamorous languor. Later: pupils dilated. Surface of tongue so vibrating already that it suggests the taste of something faintly sour and astringent like iron.

Before 20.15. At the first bite of food, the effect is enhanced. Till thought, imagination, even action, tend to get lost in themselves, each thought an endlessly self-developing world. This naturally tends to interfere with the sense of time, but hardly more than as a deduction, not yet physiologically.

Returned at 23.00. Effect still at full strength. Has never the depth and 'Vedantic' interest of first big dose at Rewa Koti. But no warmth and weight at the nape this time.

Even at this late stage sugar seems to enhance the effect—states of thought tend to be deeper, more self-lost. The sense of time is made to turn on the still axis of each thought-world. Each therefore discrete: no time-continuity between them, only their common spawn-globality of being thoughts. Without *bhang* one might not be able to see the need of "common" with "globality", this represents so subtle, though so necessary, a qualification of the thought at so deep a level.

10.III.44.

But sleep vague, a deep cloud. In the morning, relaxed but faintly tired and debauched—mind, will, sensation less sharply focussed.

Only centrality can find the effective personal truth or use of anything...

While there is any semblance of individual life, how can it be anything but deep, continual prayer? What other true shape or satisfaction can it have: Yet this can be large and genial only if there is greatest realism, the widest and most specific love and wisdom, in one's knowledge of every aspect of life.

And it is only by centrality that one can keep up with and exhaust the present—only then that it is one's true present, the true, nude, weighty, simple, transparent drama. Result of a perfect harmony between mind and will and the deeper, more immediate truth they serve, instead of something always to be overtaken by mind and will as a task. —I must still go to the bottom of the deep *bhang* experience. And re-read *Les Parents Terribles* of Cocteau in the attempt to grasp fully the reactions I had not the strength and inward leisure to express and exhaust on my first reading two days ago.

Re-read it, but of course the impact is not the same, cannot twice produce the same re-arrangement of feelings and ideas, the same new view so unfamiliar, so simple that it needed great energy to seize... Not unfamiliar in itself, only an apparently simpler arrangement of very old material.

How can I know, how can I think out, what is 'really' happening with my mother? When the reality of what I am doing, or not doing, at my own end escapes me? And I think it is at least equally impossible for her, either, to know for herself.

So long as this is so there is pure event, pure 'fate'. The medieval horoscope says: "She being but a bond", and to understand all that one's horoscope represents is to understand the cosmos in its terms. I have expressed to her this mysterious impersonal element. Out of love, goodness, heroism and the cruel *force majeure*...she has appeared resigned. But of course one is never resigned: to appear so only shows almost despair. Is it not the same with my 'spiritual' problem? But there can only be solitude, one can have no duty to anyone—unless one is to accept a mother in that sphere also and merely impotently repeat the nightmare! In her case and mine, in all cases, one has to get beyond the last solitude, the last despair, the last *mystery*. Only then is there nothing but pure Love and absolute Understanding.

I do not mean any of this formally, literally: I am trying to make a note of something very difficult to express.

[This is followed by a resume of lines in French from Cocteau's original play.]

Daniélou told me the other day that Jean Cocteau is as transparent personally as his work and his handwriting would lead one to expect.

Guru. As usual, deep strain brings back the focus of pain in the left lung. One cannot live except for something greater than oneself, yet by this very fact cannot sacrifice oneself to one's own imagination of something greater. Yet all is imagination except direct, complete knowledge and experience —identity.

To live, even to look after one's health with all one's true intelligence and sensibility—to have any reason even to recognise one's needs, demands self-dedication to the Infinite, the Transcendent. Otherwise, our anguish, our ignorance, is conscious as perversity: we ruin ourselves precisely by our purity of soul, because it is disengaged, unrecognised, denied—because it can be recognised and accepted in its own sense only in absolute self-surrender... To be pure for oneself is no purity.

Yet "Tu ne me chercherais pas si tu ne me possedais." "You will not seek me if you don't possess me" *[alternative crossed out]*: "have already found me". All is the mystery of the ego, of individual mind and will, of *avidya* (ignorance), *maya* (illusion). *[Next two sentences lightly crossed out]* And even to be technically 'liberated' from it is not enough, is even only an escape: it has to be understood to the bottom, in all its modes. Only such understanding can be absolute Truth, absolute Love.

Is it really true that Mahayana with its ideal of the Bodhisattva failed to understand the 'pure *jnana* of the Buddha? Can it really be true that Sri Aurobindo understands neither *advaita* nor the Buddha? Can it really be true that the Christ was less than a '*mukta*'? And if not, can one accept the importance of saying (yes, of *saying*!) "It is beyond words"? What is this but a light that does not illuminate? —This is the problem I have in every way, at every level, to solve.

11.III.44.

Dream of Schnabel playing Beethoven in a special room in a train. Close-up of deep, preoccupied smile of pleasure and sensibility at some beauty of the sonata as he leans close to the keys. The piano has about ten pedals: he makes subtle, learned dabs at them. The face leaner, more spare and nervous than Schnabel's as I saw it at concerts, and browned by the sun, the same almost bear-like force, but carried further into a more expressed and so more golden sensibility—more mental, less passionate.

Afterwards I meet him—big, easy, athletic figure, rather debonair, in loose overcoat and slack felt hat: only the sensitive face would make one remark him. We sit down in a sort of roof cafe with various dark-clad, dark aura'd women relations of his. I feel I am disturbing a family habit, so get up and excuse myself.

[Lightly crossed out with carefully ruled diagonal lines:]

But sometimes, under a great vault of blue-grey cloud, the still fields of silvery wheat, the great unmoving trees spread like fans, like domes against the sky, the intimate gathering of pale earth-coloured houses with curving roofs of thatch, all in a deep and delicate stillness, compose a beauty too ancient, too richly simple, too flawless to describe.

Then the gong or bell from a temple not far away—a sound so sweet, so ancient, clear and mellow as gold, so purified a quintessence of all human joy and sorrow, exaltation and melancholy, yet having been so denuded and luminous a shell of sound, so exalted beyond time and space, so other-worldly, and continuous in the mind: you must listen again and again before you can believe it has really stopped. (Wrong method: too analytical, too discursive, much too loud. It needs subtle images—much more difficult.)

13.III.44.

To act and perceive always from the centre of one's being (instead of from some inconclusive, blind, unsatisfying surface, by habit or improvisation), one must be conscious of that centre and remain in it.

14.III.44.

Malati (Principal of the school) told me that not long ago two young men in a troop train crossing the bridge over the Ganges here jumped into the sacred river, preferring to die there than in the jungles of Burma.

15.III.44.

Dream.

David MacIver riddled with every sort of dishonesty and evasion, the eyes not only indirect but tortured. I shall have to give him up. I tell him I am practically convinced he is a devil. Only notice on waking that this was just what Mrs. O. said to me! Even on the question of money he is now rather coarse and quite abandons any attempt at largeness. He is reading an *écrasé* leather edition of the *Gita*, the big hands cramped on this little book more than ever tortured. List of elements in his final 'confession' includes disbelief in honesty and truthfulness, of every sort of crooked passion—all negative.

17.III.44.

I can make no decision in relative matters, because I see that every possible decision is only formal and have therefore as good reason to revise it as I had to make it. No *individual* has a right to decide anything.

There is only one decision that can overcome the necessity and the impossibility of all decisions—self-surrender to the Infinite.

19.III.44.

On the Varna at one in the afternoon, the heat is intense, the grey-green water dazzling. The sunlight on the back of one's hands stings like the touch of a thistle, the sky is bleached with radiance. Frail with Spring leafage, the trees hold their breath, dead still.

In the town, the metalled road is like quicksilver, eyes ache with the glare. The whole town so dry it looks as if it might catch fire at any moment.

20.III.44.

Poetry

'The Manifestation" can in no sense limit or qualify 'Reality', Its own definition, than which there is nothing else and nothing 'different'. The Manifestation *as such* exists only by failure to grasp this Reality—while It is seen only as an abstraction. If one is centred in that Reality, to which everyone unconsciously returns every night in sleep, all is Li.la: nothing can or need be 'changed' except as a poet works for formal perfection and no other can be '*achieved*'. One can do this with perfect intelligence only when one is centred in that 'Reality' which is Its own, and the only, Perfection.

Every other motive to formal perfection is, in the subtlest sense of the word, sentimental mystical, religious, humanistic, esthetic etc.

21.III.44.

Hideous over-tiredness for the last week or more (not to speak of the heat of Benares in late March). Even ten hours sleep doesn't change it.

Of course it is linked with the endless bitter, unprofitable tasks that stand between myself and my true life and work. —The SKM-MacIver-Ella Maillart affair; SKM notes to put in order; study never pursued; struggle to make something real of teaching in an independent school that has almost hopelessly compromised with a pernicious educational system.

1. Undertake no new task, however slight, "If you wish to live with hilarity, be unwilling to do many things."

2. As far as possible, avoid fatigue and especially the habit of over-driving the system from the mind.

3. As far as possible, avoid talk, however slight.

4. As far as possible, never explain yourself.

5. As far as possible, don't write letters.

6. Never make a promise (positive or negative).

7 Get up not later than 4 o'clock (time for self-recollection; *sattvic* effect upon the whole rhythm of one's day).

8. Regular oil-baths, and care with tea. It is most important to avoid accumulation of tension in the system. For it becomes, also, a knot of destructive self-will in the vital nature.

22.III.44.

My idea of a perfect life, as far as my *nature* is concerned, would be that of the Tibetan yogins described by David-Neel and Evans-Wentz, in surroundings of richness and elegance, entirely given up to spiritual exercises. But I cannot believe in the base of it: all that metaphysic, occult knowledge, mythology, ritual, symbolic art could satisfy me only formally (though as nothing else can). Without any of the privileges or satisfactions of such a perfectly ordered, luminous and satisfying life, I have to find out if its base is true. A task without fulcrum. It is my refusal of *sadhana* again. *Sadhana* begs the question. The only true *sadhana*, then, is refusal of *sadhana*. Refusal of sadhana is refusal of one's relative existence. One cannot refuse one's relative existence. This is to begin and end in Anguish. Which is the human state. To cling to it, knowing it is pure paradox, is perversity. Was the Christ perverse? What did Chandidas mean?

"My perversity is a devouring spark struck between my simplicity and the non-existent opposite." One's simplicity is that one is not human. It is this Non-humanity that chooses the human: the human is the Impossible, proof of the Infinity of Reality as Its own Imagination of Itself. That in one who feels this true—that Imagination Itself—can never *believe* this, can never *rest* in itself because it *is* entirely Itself...

To be satisfied with such 'sophistry' would be, not naivety, but incapacity for naivety—damnation.

23.III.44., evening.

Visited Harihara Baba for the second time. As I bowed before him he said a few words. I thought I could catch: "*Bahut japa* (? *tapa*)"

The ruddy darkness of his body exposed to all weathers for years, the lifted shoulders resting on tapering arms, seem to correspond with the dream of the 4-armed Swami.

Afterwards I was told someone had remarked that people nowadays get their knowledge from newspapers and books and do not seek for realisation. In reply Hari Baba simply said "The world is His".

A detailed account of that visit at nightfall on the Ganges would be something incomparable. But such tours-de-force always demand an energy greater than any one has available. The saint on his boat, bowed, naked, with a long white beard, graceful and circumspect women offering garlands, bowing, touching his feet; the crafty-eyed *sadhu*, abysmal hypocrite, leading the *bhajana*, "Ram-Ram–Sita-Ram", with the little sweetly clinking cymbals; the brahmin visitor gratuitously reciting and explaining verses from the holy books; the journey there and back by boat along the *ghats* with their complex piles of building—temples, houses, stairways, palaces, abutting, receding, projecting at all angles.

31.III.44.

The *provincialism* of Ramana Maharshi, Sri Krishna Menon, perhaps of all teachers who are still only Hindu. In a sense they are peasants—peasants who have found the Truth, perhaps, but are incapable of sympathy with un-peasant modes of thought and experience. They can only stab them with the sword of their own kind of understanding, they really do not grant or love or really master them. This is not good enough for the world as a whole. Their admirable simplicity is a limitation: in the end it appears a crudity, a woodenness. And most of their subtlety is self-defence, not a real, free, genial, laughing subtlety. Up to a certain point they still take themselves seriously or are clumsy enough to allow themselves to be taken seriously.

5.IV.44. (These five pages were written out in bed, in hospital, when I was still weak from typhoid fever.)

Last, I think third, visit to Sri Ananda Mayi.

Sri Aurobindo said of a photograph of her: An incarnation of Purity and Beauty. She has realised the Sachidananda, the highest attainment possible.

The devotee who told me this says he had it from a devotee of Sri Aurobindo. Later, Ajit Basu tells me it was Dilip Kumar Roy who asked Sri Aurobindo what was Sri Ananda Mayi's state and that he said: "She is always floating in the Sachidananda consciousness."

The same devotee, who seemed serious, intelligent and well-informed, told me that she doesn't initiate, but some have had visions of her. She does, though, he says, advise certain *sadhakas* and can always help those who find they stagnate in their *sadhana*.

She has never learned to read or write *[Not literally 100% true—only at the most elementary level]* but answers pandits as if she knew *shastra*.

A devotee, Gurupriya Didi, is keeping a diary of her movements and sayings. Three volumes of it have been published in Bengali, 6 eventually, and in English translation. The printing of a fourth is delayed for wartime lack of paper.

"She has been watching you." She never forgets one she has seen. She has said that "When anyone thinks of me his image rises before me."

Ram Thakur, apparently a Tantrika (who has been known to appear in several different places at the same time, etc.) once came and prostrated before her and told his devotee: She is the Bhagavati you worship.

The same devotee confirmed what I have several times been told, that she had no guru. He says that *all sadhanas* "passed over her body". She had awareness of the Self from birth—was not born out of *samskaras*.

While I was sitting only a yard from her at the *sankirtan* at Dasaswamedh Ghat, she looked me in the eyes for several seconds. —An indescribable look that aroused in me tears of deep emotion. In that look, somehow, it came to me, was recognition of the Oneness, of the One, and for a moment it seemed to absorb, to obliterate, my whole consciousness.

A little later she asked that a garland she had worn be given me, and soon after that someone who was fanning her gave me another. Both were of jasmin.

After some time Mother got up and, with the crowd pressing behind her, began to descend the steps to return to the boat on the river by which we had come from the temple near Asi. After descending, with difficulty, perhaps half a dozen of the steep steps, she suddenly turned, re-ascended and was lost in the crowd. She made *pradakshina* about the *murti*, the centre of *sankirtan*, around which so many had been dancing themselves into ecstasy one old man having to be supported but refusing to stop till several times he collapsed and had to be stretched upon the ground. A devotee told me that no doubt she did this as an example.

The ego—an habitual feeling and idea. Other thoughts and feelings hunch about it. But all can be disaggregated, freed, can become freedom itself.

All is within oneself: there is no possibility of thought or of desire as absence from oneself or division within oneself.

... Certainly the presence of such a person uplifts and harmonises the whole consciousness.

6.IV.44.

Journal and action. Yes, and let the physical remain physical, emotional emotional.

As an individual, a man can only be a *bhakta*. Otherwise his existence is anguished or demoniac. It is only by the completion of *bhakti* that the individuality can be dissolved on its own plane, and *bhakti* is possible and real so far as it does so exist.

16.IV.44.

Imaginative plasticity. The more plastic the greater the need of organisation. As with *bhang*, the same force either multiplies scatteredness (profitless, exhausting, inconsistent nightmare) or enhances concentration.

11.IV.44.

The delicacy of the Hindus. This evening on the ferry-boat crossing the Varuna, an old villager greeted me (I have seen him several times before). When we reached the other side, he lifted out a heavy brass *kandal* (vessel) nearly 3 feet high. I naturally took one side of it and we carried it between us. When we came to my cottage, by way of offering to help him the rest of his way, I asked where he was going. But he gracefully declined, hoisted the vessel on the end of his thick staff and laid it over his shoulder. Then I saw that it was much easier for him to carry it that way: he had allowed me to 'help' him purely out of courtesy.

13.IV.44.

Strong sense of the presence of Sri Anandamayi—its peculiar note, the active, saturated richness. A warm perfume, also, as of a physical presence. —It is very powerful and enveloping, but when I try thus to define it, I find myself outside it.

16.IV.44.

The object of my writing things down has been precisely in order *to avoid* memory, to keep the mind free.

30.IV.44.

What cannot so be done must therefore be done as prayer: this possibility of the individuality must be fulfilled and exhausted.

Later: all this remains purely mental.

1.V.44.

Sex: vital-physical means of continuing *samsara*, Pain, Ignorance. *Kundalini*: "She binds the fool and liberates the wise." The basic condition in Sri Aurobindo's yoga.

I am so sceptical, or is it humility, or mere self-knowledge? that I can never even think I may be loved, could be worthy of love. This has always been so absolute that it may perhaps lead me to be strangely blind and cruel... Such strange adventures. It is a fact that I can never believe in another's love of me, find only an impenetrable mystery. I think it is because it sidetracks the absolute equality and disinterestedness with which, axiomatically, I wish to treat another—my respect, itself a mode of love... for their ultimate integrality. And because the question of knowing or finding myself in the world, of *existing*, in myself never arises!

8.V.44.

Remain in a state of virginity—the virginity of yourself as you are, physically, psychically, mentally. Don't force mental form upon it, let it increase and form itself with what distils from within and above.

Plans of work perpetuate Absence: only the present moment is, for action, real. The true demands of the being in that moment put the mind in its proper place: it shrinks, therefore, to a point, a point of pure clarity and brilliance.

Raymond Burnier considers Lizst, Grieg and Tchaikowski major composers.

Because, as their taste in music, literature and other matters shows, Alain Daniélou and Burnier cannot personally rise beyond the emotional—and a decadent, almost morbid psychic world at that—they can conceive the purely intellectual, intuitive and spiritual only in mental terms: hence their incapacity to go beyond mere form in these spheres and their fanatical dependence on it. Their incapacity, therefore, really to understand such forms or discriminate among them.

This comfortable, but, of course, really unhappy as well as ungenial and uncharitable deficiency is very well shown by the fact that the best they can say of Anandamayi is that she has "a magnetic personality": note that this sort of jargon, in such a case, is all these pedants have to fall back upon.

(Almora, 27 July:) Of course they appear in this context pedants only by the limitation I have described: neither is pedantic in his own sphere.

An interesting fact that appeared the other day when Raymond had brought up the subject of dreams, is that both say they never remember them. Alain says he has noticed that people who concern themselves with their dreams are always "unbalanced". Raymond considers only such dreams as can be plausibly explained by physiological causes and says it is as morbid to note one's dreams as to note a rumble in one's stomach.

When I remarked that all the same one does not truly know the waking state unless one knows what is complementary with it and that their attitude would be justified only if they could actually live without dreaming, and when, finally, I refer to the Mandukyopanishad and the at least incidental necessity of fulfilling and surpassing all three states for the sake of the Actual Immediacy of Consciousness, Alain, very characteristically said that "dreams" in that Unpanishad "means something else." Plain texts made innocuous by authority, by the *true* interpretations known only to those who are affiliated with the *right* traditional line, are to hide behind, to stabilise a status quo!

In sleep, strong desire to paint. I decide to use the simplest materials.

The subconscious S. *(probably Samant, a teacher)* asked me to read him some English prose. Because I happened to have casually noticed it mentioned the other in a book by Arnold Bennett, I said I would read the 40th Chapter of Isaiah. Although I must certainly have heard or read it as a boy, I could not remember anything whatever about it. As I came into S's garden

I found myself repeating: "Comfort ye, comfort ye, my people". When I opened the book I found that these are the first words of the chapter.

10.V.44.

This intense dry heat gives the imagination a corresponding vividness, passion, condensation. *[May is the most terribly hot month in the whole year at Benares and L.T. was killed by this heat 5 years later.]* And, as I noticed on the way to Ajmer, it exalts sexuality *psychically* to an extraordinary pitch of vigour and calm perversity. —All the qualities of the fragment of 10th century sculpture, with its lucid, foursquare madness, its concentrated, sensually beautiful violence.

This effect is enhanced by perfumes. In fact it is only now that one understands the more rich or sombre Indian scents.

In the evening, feeling very weak and tired (but, it seemed, with no more than the fatigue I have so often overridden), as I had for some time intended, I visited a homeopath who had been recommended to me—chiefly in order once more to see if anything definitive could be done towards curing or understanding this fatigue. This doctor said that until he had felt my pulse he would not have believed I am so weak.

During the next few days I discovered that I had typhoid fever.

Beautiful song by Sir Thomas More on the transience of human life. (I read his son-in-law's life of him today.) It is in effect an Indian *raga*. Though lucidly clear, somehow impossible to recover. Very delicate, tender, original.

10.V.44. (In fever)

It seemed that all the knowledge and experience of the world (I was still rather sceptical about the possibility of so gathering it) was in my bed, torn to fragments like little ravelled pieces of sheet.

22

Log Upon The River

11.V.44. 17.30: 104° (Throughout the illness no delirium)

12.V.44. 18.00: 104.2°.

[Here LT rails, as he does from time to time, against modern Hindus —and regrets having done so, to the extent of very carefully, but without to the slightest degree obscuring what he has written, crosses it out!]

I have often found, and once again this morning with S., that modern Hindus, including the most selfish or most idealistic and chattersome, sooner or later come out with their fundamental philosophy, direct opposite of what by all the signs seems to have been the original complete Hindu geniality, that capacity for Lila—the philosophy that, as S. openly expressed it, "Nothing matters". In this abysmal slime all, including the most elementary logic, is dissolved: here is something worse than corruption, worse than the worst sentimentality, and which explains the complete, the so to speak *absolute*, unreliability of modern Hindus. Having lost almost every single representative of what is positive in *rajas*, they cannot distinguish between *sattva* and *tamas* and are afraid of *rajas*. Nature being what it is, *tamas* thus reaches, in all spheres, almost an ultimate.

14.V.44.

Causality, Dream: Marvellous songs, of a new *dimension* (here lies, perhaps, what SKM calls the Heart) in which it is shown once and for all that the depth, the richness, the whole unnameable quality of suffering can *in no way* be measured by its cause—all causes are formal. —The cruel puritan abstraction of supposing that the hungry man should be content with dry bread, whereas his suffering has in any case only *for its sign* the lack of bread. This is understood, of course, by all true poetry. —The songs lost, I can only thus analyse. Re-read Rilke's beggar, leper songs.

20.V.44.

Realise that you can trust your body and stand in it—that it gives you a very pure and essential non-mental time and space of perception in which you can turn round, in which you can complete every fact and every vision.

The body seemed perhaps accidental, but not so the flesh knowingly built up again from the long fast of illness—luminous, one's own substance of awareness.

Unfortunately one is not really so conscious as this. The body is an irresolution—false, egoistic self-nourishing, interrupted by fastings towards a purity it could never sustain even if those fasts could be completed. But they could be completed *now* only in death: the body remains as that we need, an expression of the 'problem' to be resolved. When in 1932 I set out for Ceylon and India without money and without plans, driven by an irresistible need to reduce ignorance and mystery of existence to its simplest terms, I could not yet have recognised mentally that if I were to die of starvation it could only be because this body was no longer relevant to the solution of the problem, had been exhausted or overpassed as medium or support of spiritual effort and destiny.

The body is the minimum comfort that I have always tended to refuse, or rather to override. Yet it is *intelligence itself* in its substantial mode of 'comfort', which, unlike the critical mind, does not attend to known factors of obstruction and imperfection, but, recognising them fully and precisely by its intelligence, has by that fact dismissed them and remains at ease in its own awareness. The mind, with its suffering from imperfection, must not invade the body—it can only build, there, a dry and rigid skeleton.

22.V.44.

I think some time before I left Madras, even before I left Travancore, I had the idea that an illness that should oblige complete rest would be good for me. Though I never consciously believed in its likelihood or accepted the idea. Now this mysterious enteric fever, the first certifiable illness I've had since epidemic influenza as a boy *[presumably a reference to the pandemic influenza of 1918]*, seems exactly to fulfil these conditions, and in a very kindly way, with no painful symptoms. The doctors say that though the attack was not mild, I very quickly developed "immunity".

26.V.44. (Exaltation of *prana* from Darjeeling tea.)

Sense of very vivid and buoyant Tantrik ritual, full of intensely genial precision and verve, a lucid richness and exalted dancing power.

[LT usually indicates a dream, but here does not. Yet it surely must be.]

Western intuitives. Novalis, Goethe, Blake ... The darker the night, the more penetrating, lightning-like may revelation be when it occurs. Though at the same time fragile, special, momentary.

4.VI.44.

"At the edge of the town that any proper bomb". Rewritten poem.

Every movement on every plane of consciousness tends continually to complete and perpetuate itself—on its own level can therefore produce deep hypnosis and hallucination (cp. sexuality). It is only 'vertically' and from a centre deeper than individuality that reorganization of consciousness is possible.

The tendency to let minor movements, really exhausted by understanding, repeat themselves is fundamentally due to deadlock over the *advaita*-"trans-*advaita*" problem, the next great matter to be tackled. I am certainly not satisfied with the purely jnanic solution: there must be a completion of *yogin* and *karma-yogin* and *bhakta* too—a completion that will exceed the framework in which these distinctions first appear and their first apparent limits.

5.VI.44.

"When words have come to void, their proper order" poem written.

9.VI.44.

Whether Malakarai experience *[Samadhi etc.]* is true in Sri Krishna Menon's sense or not, it had long been intellectually true as recognition of *jnana*, of *advaita*. What remains necessary is yogic fulfilment, and what can fulfil all the actual necessities and possibilities (psychic—with reputed past-life experience of *bhakti*, of sense of the Transcendent) but yoga in the widest Tantrik sense such as Sri Aurobindo represents?

As soon as I am well such a yoga must be one-pointedly begun, everything else without exception subordinated to it, the whole of life re-interpreted and transformed by it. Here alone lies fundamental satisfaction, and true integration of all my faculties.

(13th) With intellectual resolution of the Sri Aurobindo-*advaita* question, this is also the only way to overpass long preoccupation with him.

[But it was not to be—or at least not in these terms. LT was even preoccupied with Aurobindo during his last three days alive. There is a strong echo in this entry of Krishna Menon's view of what LT would have to do next:]

Mental foreseeing or expectation, a form of calculation and therefore impure, is also an absurd waste, damming, sterilisation of energy. What happens spontaneously, entirely unthought of, is never surprising: it is borne upon the equanimity of that truthfulness to oneself which contains and organises all possibilities.

10.VI.44.

A face free of all fear, irritability, expectation...

11.VI.44.

Indignation, irritation come from the moral side of us, from the will: they express impotence and resentment at a thwarting or deception of the will from the outside. But the outside, all that is beyond the sphere of what we can directly change, on its own level can only be viewed esthetically. Any other attitude is stupid as well as ugly or grotesque.

The Hindu understanding of this. —Anger disgraceful self-betrayal, proof of lack of wisdom and dignity to the point almost of obscenity. Pettiness and ridiculousness from the Hindu point of view of the taut, shallow European excitability and 'self-control', its mere opposite on the same plane.

14.VI.44.

Indian 'esthetics'. *Rasa.* It is obvious that this is the essential—without it, no experience. And the word, applying both to the work and to the enjoyer, exactly represents the relation between subject and object, their essential oneness.

[The word 'Rasa' is virtually untranslatable. The nearest English would be 'esthetic rapture, wonder, even Ecstatic delight in response to a work of art'.]

16.VI.44.

[Entry marked carefully on left margin with a rare ruled double line indicating its importance to LT.]

Delicate forevision of events—in thought or preparing action. (Yet this is not known as forevision, is not subject to time, but rather an act of Presence.) —Perfect dovetailing of events; immediate finding of quotations required, etc. Footnote: Cocteau, *Opium*: "Since the marvellous derives from an order which is easily disturbed, it is understandable that it appears to us always in connection with unimportant matters. This enables us to confuse it with slight coincidences."

Live incessantly self-surrendered, in perfect harmony with the Divine Actuality, before and after time, embracing all possible worlds.

This must give perfect harmony of the whole nature on all its planes and therefore perfect joy and illumination—with the *particular* occult knowledge that one's place and nature in the cosmos determines else by infusion of Grace, by the caresses of Divine Love.

17.VI.44. Dream.

Playing and singing the most exquisite Mozart and other songs—the greatest, most tender beauty, the most subtle and penetrating emotion. Beside the piano, M. is almost swooning with the effect.

In the depth and lyricism of my feeling I also improvise songs.

18.VI.44. Dream.

I pass a Shiva temple, deserted, empty, remote. But in the stony compound there is a little open kiosk (association with the kiosk beside the confluence of Varuna and Ganges two minutes' walk from Rajghat) where a youth has just finished preparing *bhang* for a sadhu I know by sight. While I am wondering if he will offer me any he begins to drink up all the *bhang*. As he has almost finished, a few people come up to the kiosk: following custom rather than his heart he offers them the little that remains.

Down the slope to my left, a bacchantic *sadhu*-throng overtakes me, all excited by the drug. One offers me water in a black roughly oval wooden bowl. I take a little and purify myself, casting over my head, invoking Shiva. Those who follow give me a very big light-brown bolus (*pill*) of which a sector has already been half cut to make it easy to attack with the fingers, for it is almost too big to be put whole into the mouth. It is a sweetmeat containing hemp, I presume. I eat it.

Down the slope past the temple, the sadhus are leaping in the air, on their way, I feel, to some festival in town. I find I can leap with the best.

21.VI.44.

Confucius: Have only friends who are your equals.

Indeed, at the human level, this is essential: anything else leads to dissatisfaction, complication, suffering, misunderstanding. But it is impossible. All that Confucius seeks can only be attained formally, by a formal organization of society: one may have friends who are conventionally one's equals, and friendship itself may be conventional. Any other factual equality can only be the mechanical, finally subhuman, one of democracy, fascism or communism—which do not conventionally protect but simply no longer recognise, are in fact no longer capable of character, personality. Spiritually, there is only one 'equality', the Self-oneness of Essence, the singleness of the Spirit in all men. But here we are at the level of Lao-tzu.

The "excitement" which, Dorothy Wellesley tells us, Yeats valued and which as I know from experience! it is so difficult for Hindus and I suppose Chinese to understand or appreciate is the expression of emotional and intellectual disinterestedness ('pure passion') to which the individuality is sacrificed—their expression in terms of an expansive, rajasic, *kshatriya* temperament. And alas, I am afraid the Hindu calm and dignity, refusal to move or be moved, is nowadays only too often the self-defence, through a timid and armoured, crab-like ego, of a hopelessly debile soul and intellect that only wish to remain undisturbed to die. It is the survival of an outward form and habit after the supporting and justifying reality has collapsed; for in every way these people seem to show, on the whole, nothing but passive fecklessness and unreliability combined with the most unprincipled opportunism.

There is no doubt that modern Hindus, with few exceptions, represent the negation and opposite of that vast and powerful ancient geniality.

It is excellent to know that Hafiz, with his mystical poems, written from experience, also wrote obscene ones. Here, it seems, is an almost Hindu vigour and completeness.

I have little doubt that, normally, the more powerful spirit, soul and intellect the more subtle, rich, intense the Eros.

Contemporary mentalism in this sphere, so complicated and superficial, is of a piece with the general lack of integral vision and experience, of psychic and intellectual geniality, in this age.

To Ethel Merston: re Herrick. ... And that his poems are only, as you say, "subjective or personal" is, of course, the great difference between them and the far more important poetry of vision in Blake, some of Wordsworth, Rimbaud. Yet, for subtle minds! grace, charm and elegance can *symbolise* a still higher value.

... *Nothing* is really wonderful except the Absolute Wonder, the true Present, that we cannot grasp; so whenever we show admiration, identifying ourselves by imaginative or intellectual sympathy with this or that, 'small' or 'great', it is a purely symbolic act of worship. "I talk about literature (women, horses...)", each can say "because at this point I am free—I know exactly *how* I really care nothing for them".

22.VI.44.

Dream of an album of erotic pictures belonging to someone unknown to me before. Dozens of softly grey and white printed postcards of skeletons interlaced in endlessly varied combinations. There is nothing whatever erotic even in their attitudes—which in fact are hardly analysable in the compact abstract patterns.

Then I read a description by a young man of his sexual acts with these skeletons. The whole effect is morbid and macabre.

[There will be a number of other skeleton dreams.]

... There is no doubt, somewhere deep within or above, a real surrender or a real contact; but why not let it be conscious and enjoyed, permeating and transforming the whole nature, leaving no independent, forgetful surface visited only by gleams, or moved only by a pressure unknown to it? Why not live in the full light and power?

I am already *in fact*, by nature, like every other creature, entirely surrendered, *muslim*—entirely contained within the Divine Actuality—the fact that Reality is by definition entirely present here and now—and formed by it; but the truth of this as a factor in spiritual completion must be lived. This is the exhaustion of the individuality on its own plane, in its own sense.

(3 August) In proportion to our inward truth and harmony the divine Actuality is joy for us—joy and illumination greater than that of the angels.

23.VI.44.

Just before fully waking—when light and bird-sounds were increasing—on the table where I had been eating in the dream I was recording it as actual, so real it seemed.

Dream: Father dances and sings in improvised Franck-like verses. Very tall and thin, his hands often held high, 2 or 3 long white fingers outstretched in a gesture of intensity.

The first 'verse' is based on the Christ's saying about idolatry (?) in which Father dramatically brings out the paradox. With each verse he particularly addresses some one of the family group.

I am at the table eating buttered toast. When it comes to my turn he improvises something to the effect that I have a fear that, in war or in some such circumstances, I may be something indecent—that I have, anyway, some sexual difficulty or preoccupation. As he speaks I have a slight erection and I think he is aware of it. (Body heated, need to urinate.) He seems to know what occurred in a dream yesterday or a few nights before, but which I had forgotten, (thus remembering in dream a dream the waking mind has forgotten.) that, in an old Woodford lane, I looked at a sheaf of obscene photos and showed them to others. I am surprised at his clairvoyance, but he is in an inspired, exalted state.

He takes down, apparently from the high kitchen mantelshelf, a slice of toast and tells me that if I eat it the difficulty will pass away. I ask if I may butter it and he replies Yes: I know you want butter on it. This may represent at the same time need of recuperation from illness, and, generally, of increased, or more harmonious, energy, and the possibility in the erotic sphere that would correspond with a Tantrik interpretation of Sri Aurobindo's.

Marginal note: Raymond Burnier at Almora, with whom I stayed during convalescence from 20th July gave me buttered toast every day at breakfast. I have not eaten it regularly—if at all—since I stayed with Margot at "Highlands" years ago. I also stayed with Frank Townsend and Ethel Merston and they too, without my asking, also gave me buttered toast.

A little lizard-like gesture, the kind of coloured miniature dragon with long, fine tail and crested head that live on trees, comes in through a sort of skylight high up, that covers the whole width of one end of the room. Outside, a cold light of late evening in winter. I pick up the little animal though it bites rather sharply, but not maliciously, and give it to Father, who takes it and goes away through the skylight into a sphere that seems to belong to him.

Afterwards the rather charming little dragon returns. I take it up again, Margot *[LT's sister]* looking on with interest, and return it to the skylight so that it may go free. As it hangs on the glass Margot points out that its body is so small it can only eat insects.

Left alone, I go on eating toast. I thought I had finished the slice Father gave me, yet seem only now to butter it liberally and eat. I begin to record this experience. One of the pieces of folded paper seems to contain writing of or somehow from Father and to be equivalent to the toast he gave me.

This dream seems to be a response to some hidden conflict with my father. His exit from the skylight and the state of inspired exaltation that he would never have shown in life no doubt expresses irritation from the dead. Though it corresponds with his nervous irritability and his extravagant, dramatic, yet passive manner sometimes, of developing a grievance with Mother about her eternal soup.

Impossibility of possessing, therefore of giving: all possessions are part of the earth: there can be none but symbolic meaning in transferring them from one hand to another, whether of giver or receiver, not to own but to act: the earth will support it from within so long as its action is necessary. And the hand itself as such is part of the earth and unpossessable. "The earth is the Lord's and the fullness thereof."

[LT's attitude towards the possession of money was a literal application of this.]

24.VI.44. Dream.

Long talk and play with a delightfully charming Indian boy of 5 or 7: his mother, who lives near Woodford station, allows him to wander about all day. After perhaps hours of companionship we part: he will return home by himself.

I find myself in a big draper's shop where a girl asks if I know "Babu", the child, and gives me a note for him from Lin Yutang, whose *My Country and My People* I read not long ago—a visiting card. I did not know the child was so celebrated, but it's no doubt rather that Lin Yutang has seen him by chance, I suppose in this shop, and had the intelligence and sensibility to appreciate his charm.

On the broad granite sill like that of a building in the City of London, abutting the busy street, I find the child curled up, covered with a small light cloth. Though he looks a little depressed, his eyes are so pure and shining that I feel a very keen and specific reverence for him as a sign of the Reality. I feel he corrsponds with Sri Krishna—the first time, I think, He has been represented in my dreams. As we walk away I think of giving Him Lin Yutang's note. I imagine it a line or two in English arranging to meet him, and he will no doubt ask me to translate.

26.VI.44.

My use of tea which, by mobilizing the *prana*, makes it easier to raise it to one's highest working level, has directly corresponded with the effort to raise oneself always to a higher, to an *absolute*, state of transparency—to absolute Presence. In this way one enters into tension with one's *actual* degree of harmony and transparency and even with its physical form and base: its undeniable nature is denied in the sense of its own essential absoluteness. Thus one's highest spiritual attainment presents itself as the paradoxical relation with Sri Krishna Menon.

12th August: It is, in fact, essentially the old conflict between Absolute and Transcendent as aims, or implications, of spiritual effort: —though the whole being be brought in line, it remains only perception. Whereas in SKM's teaching, but not how his apparent action and experience demonstrate it, between *jnana*—even between direct *perception* of the Infinite as the essential way to contain and surpass all other paths—and direct *recognition* from the start of the Transcendent, and in the broadest sense the Tantrik path of Lila corresponding to it, the paths of *jnana* and *mukti* are indeed contained and overpassed.

But any given state perfectly accepted is a perfect transparency: here the way of surrender removes all tension.

[I think the above paragraph is a typical specimen of LT's continual effort to nail his flag to the mast of spiritual aims—at painful cost to himself and an open invitation to ridicule. Despite its formidable difficulty, even so, I think it deserves careful and patient scrutiny.

If the Malakkarai experience had been more complete, or accepted, or repeated and stabilised, it would more clearly have provided the turning-point from one method to the other: the normal *enantiodromia* (Greek term for metamorphosis into the opposite) from the 'ascending' way of effort or Anguish to re-descent towards the world, towards *sahaja-sthiti*.

27.VI.44.

The great thing is not to let the blinding crust of the outer nature with its icicles of activity build itself up again as one grows stronger: must keep steadfastly open to the new possibility.

28.VI.44.

To Julie Merston about writing verse:

"... the subtle, perilous, delicate, prolonged, suspended interplay of the experience, 'state', idea, with the possibilities and the traps, blind alleys, wasteful branchings, indulgences, stupidities, *fausses routes* of expression in words; until at last they have completely interfused and exhausted each other, for good or ill, in the poem.

"It is of course quite arbitrary to present dreams as literature, so to speak: this surface charm or interest of the mental recording is more or less, though it cannot be entirely, accidental. The real felicity in the case of ordinary dreams, as against what may be called visions* is in the way they meet, resolve, explain or comment on a psychological situation. For example, the Angel-rivers-bathing-child dream *[Not included in this edit]* has a detailed, specific meaning no-one but myself could ever possibly guess. In fact, when one looks deeply, a series of meanings, one behind another. In this way every dream is a new illustration of one's fundamental myth.

[This partial obscurity of the Father-and-toast dream is justifiably included here for its obvious retrospective value as biography relating to LT's family, in itself so rare.]

"The way dreams express with perfect economy a meaning that lies on quite another plane from their flawless surface (which produces its own closed effect) may well give one to think about Expression (Manifestation) and its laws in general."

*Marginal comment: (Not sent.) By visions I mean psychic experiences super-individually organised. They have a coherence more intense than that of our ordinary waking experience, so that on emerging from them it is the latter that seems loose and frail like a dream. And they leave an impression far deeper, more vivid and lasting than any dream or waking experience. They often emerge from or lapse into more or less ordinary dream experience, but they may also directly replace the waking state—even in its own terms (certain kinds of 'miracle' belong to this category).

[This is an important clarification of LT's reflections on dream early in the journal. The reader may like to put this to the test by re-reading, for example, the mysterious experience of the strange nocturnal 'apparition' who pierces LT in Ceylon, or the dream about Ramana Maharshi in an underground cave, or the game of snakes and ladders with a young girl.]

1.VII.44. First line of a poem:

"Men think earth solid and earth-shape they know..."

The thunder creaks, widely and elaborately warps, crumbles away, or it is riven, splits, explodes. It hesitates—dense, tense, self-pleasuring, self-delayed like the deepest urges of the body. Its hard relentless shattering is astringent, cruel, like the weight and taste, the tearing jaggedness of iron.

3.VII.44. Dream

Strange town. The day passed in wandering, in talk with children known through chance meetings, in hunger through forgetting to eat. Only at the end do I realise that like a madman I have run away from Rajghat without taking leave of Sanjiva Rao or discussing my work with him. At this point (3 a.m.), I realise that the dream expresses vagabondage—a state of suspense from spiritual life with a central aim ordering everything.

The dream, like the town, was very multifarious; I cannot remember all its elements, shuffled one behind another. Throughout, a strange innocence and lightness like that of a harmless, even illumined, madman. Hazard and planlessness.

Indeed my life is like this—unexpectedly leaving the hospital, tactfully following the wishes of others; new room, temporary like all else, in which I arrange a few books, spread a black and gold Lucknow shawl, an Ajmer cloth, place a Gupta fragment—the portable scenery; people with whom I have affectionate relations but who can never know me, this world is such for all; proposed journey to Almora—yet another temporarily suspended life: all is this various dream, only very slightly interesting. To all of which one is in no way engaged or bound. And behind all is spiritual indecision, complication, drift.

21.VII.44.

This morning at the Brewsters', in their big L-shaped room with rugs of white yak-wool, looking out on to the Himalayas, Alain played the *vina*. Old Hindi song in the profoundly sad Asavari *raga*: a young man living in a palace goes mad from hearing every day on the hidden stair the anklets of the queens in purdah. —Madness expressed as the *perfect acceptance* of hopeless longing—the disinterested perfection of imagination and sensibility.

You can only explain yourself from your own point of view—which cannot and need not be explained. To explain oneself, then, is either vanity or perversity; to believe that such explanation can or need be understood is sentimentality, confusing the possibility of the true 'heartless' Love that no individuality can understand. The integrity of one's existence, if it can only simply be sustained, has already put aside all questions. Whether "taken" or "left"—and it can really neither be left nor taken—it remains unquestionable.

28.VII.44.

To consider how others must interpret one's acts, words, appearances belongs entirely to art, or rather to the criticism of art. (15th August) Intercourse with others as relative existences, and so, needless to say, oneself appears for them only as art—can have no harmony or stability but that of art. And it is no doubt the most subtle art of all, with the most complex, various and changing physical, psychic and mental material. It is only in the soul or Spirit that there is no longer relation but essential unity; and soul and Spirit have never been committed to the world of appearances. Yet soul and Spirit may continually cut across the possibility of art. Saint and sage have absorbed it altogether.

1.VIII.44. Line of poem just written: "Lost like a man long dead..."

Aphorisms can either be finished as first general intuitions and completed and illustrated afterwards by detailed studies, or they may wait till those studies are more or less complete—but that will mean for an indefinite number of years.

There is an advantage individually in having clearly expressed one's essential intuitions, one's level and directions—at the same time as having declared oneself and thereby been released into one's true arena for further development.

On the other hand there is no need for this and it is even a perilous convenience: the advantages of being unmanifest (i.e. 'not expressing oneself') and anonymous are very real. And unless there is very deep and strict criticism allowing only what is perfectly pure in its kind and so far valid from every possible angle, much may in this way be put forward that is temporary or immature and may afterwards have to be denied or revised. August 5th. Line of poem just written: "What stars upon their track..."

7.VIII.44.

Earl Brewster on Padre Pio whom he met in Italy. *[Early 30s, I think.]* His photographed stigmata; levitation, miracles, —the first cure of a hunchback. He told him his crookedness was due to the hatred in his heart, then said "Stand up!" The man at once stood up straight.

Marginal note, 13.I.46: I see that *this* was where I got "hate-crooked beast and back" in "Dionysiac" lines at Almora.

9.VIII.44. Line of the relevant poem just written: "The Dionysiac frenzy.

Attempt at restraint, e.g. the futile SKM-MacIver-Ella Maillart dispute clamps a suffocating and extraneous gag upon my naturally intense and even violent rhythms of mind, vital, nervous system—the natural rhythm, after all, of so deeply pitched and paradoxical a theme! Intellect and artistic sense, and in another way soul, as yet far from being possessed, would keep all static, ordered, calm, restrained like a temple to Apollo; yet this is a dance, resolving through movement—even the most extreme movement possible.

Dionysus and the Vaishnava Decadence. Christ and Dionysus. Western sentimentalism. —Outrance Dionysus! Turned aside from endless attempts to answer Ella Maillart otherwise than with spontaneous passion and intensity, to the poem "The Dionysian frenzy..." *[Crossed out]*: at the worst frantic group agitation, confession, togetherness, and all the little Boyscout-ish Protestant sects with their knowingness and living with the Jesus who has saved them from their sins.

Marginal comment on 22nd July: From memory, W.B. Yeats: *The Unicorn from the Stars*, 1908, Act II. Martin Hearne's tirade goes like this: (I have no copy so extemporise.) I have been beyond the earth. In Paradise, in that happy townland, I have seen the shining people. They were all doing one thing or another, but not one of them was at work. All that they did in their paradisaic Malakarai was but the overflowing of their idleness, and their days were a secret gig of their frenzied hearts, a Celtic *kathekali*. No man can be alive—certainly not an Irish redbeard—for what is Paradise but fulness of life? —if whatever he sets his hand to in the light of day cannot carry him from exaltation to exaltation, from everlasting to everlasting, if he does not rise into a frenzy of contemplation in the night silence?

When mental and psychic urgency is continuous and very great, there's never time to establish an harmonious base in the body. Hence, no doubt, Cocteau's opium and Picasso's misogyny.

12.VIII.44. Dream.

I travel to SKM. Am seated with various devotees on the floor in a room unlike any at Malakarai or Trivandrum. I notice that I am *held* in the situation, of that kind of leisure that might disinterestedly observe the room. SKM seated on a couch. During conversation with others, when someone points out apparent contradictions and paradoxes in his words and actions, he weeps quite openly, loudly, convulsively at this inevitable suffering which can never be explained to disciples, and I think of my own suggestions in this direction. Later, in some other connection, he goes into one of his deep emotional states.

He gives me, through another, a garland from his neck: I am moved to tears. Later I see him looking rather hard at deep magenta and other coloured garlands heaped in my lap, like dahlia, orange flowers from Pondicherry Ashram seed, sunflowers given by Earl Brewster as greeting on this birthday of Krishna. I see that one—no doubt the one I had put round my neck—is broken and tie it together again.

I approach SKM to ask if I may speak to him about *the break* (sic.), its connection with David MacIver's present visit. At first he puts off private conversation, is cold, seems unwilling to take up the question once again.

But I follow him, or find him, in a garden where, drinking milk, he squirts the remainder of it from his mouth at the root of a plant in a sort of open, more or less round greenhouse. SKM is cold in a way I have never known. With anguish and tears I try to explain how important it is for me to make clear what happened last time at Trivandrum, that I am convinced he cannot have understood that it concerns other people. He does not seem disposed to listen and I realise that he may not read a long letter if I write.

Earl Brewster remarks that physically I might be D.H. Lawrence's brother *(Earl was a close friend of Lawrence and his host in Ceylon]* and that I have similar earnestness, intensity, honesty, rapidity of thought: no-one has ever seemed to him so like D.H.L. Achsah, Earl's wife, says: similar clarity of mind and speech.

10.X.44. Benares. *[Condensed list of LT's "Pattern for use of time".]*

If one only keeps deeply tuned, all, including the most trivial action or event, serves a deepening music. The true use of imagination, artistic sense and technical intelligence is to further this.

1. (Sun-time). 4. a. Self-recollection—Observation of one's state in its own terms: immediate trans-mental truthfulness. Re-definition of perfect Leisure: Involves perfect disinterestedness towards all and re-discovers fundamental concentration in all necessary work. —Yogaswami: "Work is rest". (Watching health). Natural Concentration, etc. 4. b. *Samarpana* (to open whole individuality to the Spirit

3. c.7. Weak tea, fruit, *aval*, raisins and milk (Put on water for washing crockery.) Walk if inclined; also read Journal or something to remind of deepest purposes. 4. With deepest intention read yesterday's Journal. Write up any dreams. Brief exercises. Bath—Saturday (or other day free of classes). Oil bath in the sun. c.9.30 Breakfast. Chief work. 5. Dust and sweep room. Clean breakfast things. Wash clothes. Bathe. 6. c.11 Lunch. Relaxation. (Poetry, imaginative literature.) 7. Letters (fewest possible)—aim at eliminating. Classes. 8. Anthology for College. 9. STUDY. 10. Hindi. 11. Walk/Piano. 12. Milk and honey before sunset (eat only if really hungry). 13. Study (sometimes German) 14. Self-recol-

lection. Samarpana. Read day's journal. Until self-recollection is established consider how day has been used in all domains

17.VIII.44.

Language. Speech has its power and beauty from the fact that there are things which, if we are true to them, can never be said in words. The presumption that all (or nothing) can be said, reduces language to sterility: it makes speech and silence equivalent instead of complementary, while yet both, and their occasions, still remain. —That violence against speech, recoiling, makes hollow and powerless even this simplest word.

For speech *as such* does not extend beyond the mind. And it can serve what is above, or deeper, or beyond, only according to its own limits, its own laws: it cannot elevate itself beyond itself. Its perfection is art and it is in its nature to be perfect.

Yet it is the mind that says all this, within language; and if the mind is carried away, speech, as it is, may be used bodily by a power or vision beyond the mind, like Sri SKM speaking "from the Ultimate." This spiritual perfection exceeds and subsumes that perfection of art which the limits of language and its occasions define for themselves. Yet if the intelligence and sensibility that make the beauty of language are entirely integrated into spiritual perfection, there will be a perfection of art so complete and spontaneous that it will have become a perfection of Nature. Such words, in scripture or from the mouth of sages, provide the norm of human speech.

21.VIII.44.

Staying for 4 or 5 days with Frank Townshend, author of books on mysticism.

If immediately on the surface:

Little temple with images of Shiva, Ganesha, Satyanarayana and Lakshmi, the Buddha, Shanmukta. The road winding along a ridge, and little hills with pine-trees and rich grass thrown out against deep valleys; the Himalayas, remote, exalted, pure, unveiled at the horizon. Some mood favoured by all this *made almost visible*, as if a yard away on the road, a lovely boyish form, richly pale like a honeyed flower, dancing perhaps, so graceful His pose, simply stepping up the slope, right knee and perfect thigh put forward, the warm ivory torso a little turned, head and shoulders lifted and thrown back.

Charming, wayward, delicate, lovely yet austere with perfection, the force of His majesty become, in this tender lad, a dense precision of beauty. He seemed to carry in His hand some attribute (could it have been the *vel* of Muruga?) and perhaps, over His shoulder or about His loins, a leopard-skin, or maybe only a soft russet-brown cloth. Perhaps I should have sat down and tried to stabilise this vision, if vision it was.* *(The impression, anyhow, is still strong and clear until now ten days later—evidently it belongs to a deep level of consciousness.) But the next minute, rounding a turn in the road, there came a party of boys and I turned back with them. The most charming, Jagdish (Jagadishwara) Chandra, about 12, sweetly, mischievously laughing, evading my endearments till at last, his hand in mine, he wanted me to walk all the four miles to Almora.

22.VIII.44.

A certain impatience and vehemence come, no doubt, from my being exposed to the whole world of relativities with the Infinite in play! If I could limit or protect myself, avoiding or treating with caution all who are not *sadhakas*—imagine doing the *sadhana* of Subrahmanya! —all would be easier. But intellect and sensibility, naked to all ideas and all experience, naked to all actual confusion, expose the body as well to immediate circumstance. No rights, no role!

Nought but centrality, complete self-dedication to the Beloved, to the One Reality, can guide through all with peace and harmony, with patient wisdom, undeflected power. Yet how difficult that surrender! One's existence is too light, too wayward, ingenious, complicated, casuistical, perfidious for that faithfulness and that humility. How Radha suffers from her coquetry!: it has always arisen and is already working in her before she can even really look at or attend to the Beloved Krishna.

23.VIII.44.

Sleep, in any case a surrender of individual consciousness, could be made the spiritual surrender—to the Chit-Shakti ever, in truth, unqualified. (This would resolve *nirvikalpa-samadhi*—proposed by Sri. K as solution of the immediate deadlock—into the true next step, whether from his point of view or Sri Aurobindo's or mine—the centring in the Heart.

How can anything be enjoyed if I am not at peace with myself? How can even the most favourable circumstances be used if, through the endless iridescent shiftings of the inconstant outer nature, the central work is continually evaded and postponed? How can anything be rightly done or said or understood except as part of this work? —Without it there is no constant skill or resource, no true clarity or measure, wisdom or beauty, no unerring sensibility or intelligence, no strength or peace or joy.

Yet how difficult it is to be steady under the terrible releasing blade!: the unregenerate nature shudders, full of feverish, over-simple or over-subtle excuses and devices to get away.

What constant prayer, humility, watchfulness are necessary!

Yet how perverse the nature is!, for it is only in this work that any part or mode of it can find enlightenment or satisfaction. —The nature always evades the Now of the Infinite that transfixes it, the crucial Present Moment.

I appeal to the deep heart, to that in me which is ever Present, whose being is one with that Infinity: Support me, aid me, make this moment real and irreversible.

Ah, from what a hell you lift us to your Light and Joy!

24.VIII.44.

The mind should not initiate anything: that is pure superficiality. It should remain always the perfectly disinterested and flexible instrument of an integral immediacy entirely prior to it—the deepest knowledge of the heart.

Alain Daniélou on the "conspiracy of silence": Sri Aurobindo and Sri Ramana Maharshi, not visibly affiliated with Vedic tradition, do not mention living traditional masters. Daniélou takes it that every possible *siddhi* must be presented to a man (as a barrier put up by Nature) on his way to *mukti* and uses this to argue that if Sri Aurobindo and Sri Ramana Maharshi really have deep spiritual experiences they cannot, or need not, be *ignorant* of great orthodox illuminated experiences and writings in the past or present; it would seem, then, that their silence is deliberate. He seems to think that Sri Aurobindo and Sri Ramana Maharshi are barriers to the true expansion of Hindu wisdom for the whole world: they baulk and absorb enquirers from the West who thus never come to know of the orthodox India in which such men are but peculiar phenomena.

26.VIII.44. Line from poem just written:

"Could I be mad or rapt away".

Let not sleep be defined, and therefore veiled, by the outer nature: approach it as what it is—absolute strangeness.

Work can be real only as *sadhana*, is otherwise a suffocating imposition;

yet *sadhana* is possible only as a function of surrender. And for this tension, deadlock, suspense, surrender is an abstract possibility, a perfect status, not a living form. What sleep, what diversion, what madness could restore me to myself? Marginal note: I had entirely forgotten this when, in the evening, I wrote the verses beginning "Could I be mad or rapt away".

27.VIII.44. Dream

A lean girl rather like Margot and I find ourselves on the perilously curving massive stone roof of an Indian temple overlooking the lighted pavements. I clamber towards a kind of pavilion with a rectangular opening or shallow recess below, a sort of pool or impluvium. It is elaborately carved in a dull pink stone much in the rather sweet and trivial debased North Indian style. Towards the front there is an image that suggests that the temple is perhaps dedicated to Ganesha. On a little undersunk ledge there are several ex-voto figures, most only a few inches long, placed there by devotees who wish to avoid sexual dreams—obscene doll-like images of naked women in a smooth, almost glossy pinkish material like soapstone or hard wax, one with finger pointing to the vulva. Looking more closely, I notice one nearer me, bigger, in a greyish stone, of a little man licking the vulva of a much bigger woman lying flat on her back; yet somehow at the same time she gives the tongue-kiss or they are sucking each other's tongues. The vulva grows bigger, the little figure puts in its head and makes as if to follow entirely. These figures excite me: though I try to move away, as it were, from the possibility, I am overtaken by orgasm. Later in the night there was another, though not definitive, very lustful dream. This is the second or third since I began to take a phosphate tonic about a week ago (I shall stop it); and I think they are also connected with heatedness and exertion after oil-bath in the sun yesterday.

Another episode: —Juliette Merston and I visit a rather deserted-looking temple. A not very pleasant, dark, curly-haired young man in European dress approaches us, speaking French. We agree that he is tiresome and try to avoid him, though with insensitive officious helpfulness he is inclined to act as guide. The Portugese built the temple perhaps hundreds of years ago; it has been shut in underground by an earthquake. The young man calls to him and, as he does from time to time, the trapped architect, still alive, also calls out and knocks firmly, with a dull wooden sound, as if to attract attention. I wonder if he were to get out and emerge into daylight, perhaps looking rather frighteningly strange, how the more or less stupid man or boy passing at that moment would deal with him: no one makes any attempt to rescue him, partly, no doubt, because it would mean dismantling the temple. I am myself shut in, close to the temple wall by piled stones that become smooth machinery which finally locks me in entirely, much as he is imprisoned—in a kind of huge wheel. I somehow raise myself out, or the whole machine rises out of itself vertically, and I enter or re-enter another part of the house with the pictures.

The will that thinks it can or should resist any power the gods bring to bear arises *on the basis* of this compromise: as Oedipus, as all ancient peoples knew, it is derisory. Only the Supreme Shakti, one with pure Spirit, can master Her own manifested powers. The modern Western 'will' operates at a level *below* that of Tragedy, the nobility of man as man, the natural disinterested heroism of *avidya*—'ignorance'.

The Christian way of ascribing the powers and beauties of Nature (consider the hallucinating life of those strangely dark blue-purple and magenta-red convolvuli by the gate this morning) to an abstract God, though Christians, like other men, are held and bound in nature and know in themselves only natural modes, and the vague kind of nature-worship which in Wordsworth and others developed from this, always walking on the edge of fatuity, makes the mind and will that adopt them a barrier. The gods must be directly recognised on their own plane—all the non-human and non-moral beings that stand behind tiger and storm and rose, in which only the self-sterilised mind sees a merely formal or literary beauty.

The perfection of the Hindu tradition is that it has never lost command over the relation between the psychically-centered consciousness of the ancient world which in the Vedas, in Egypt, in Crete, in Scandinavia, in the Celtic lands, knew the gods directly, and the pure spirit of which all this is the manifestation. It is not blinded by the Ishwara, the Demiurge, that middle term for a given cosmos between the Supreme of all endless possible worlds.

It is true that Faith, Hope and charity are the three modes in which the soul is felt, made tenderly nude by the temporary depletion of blinding and self-blinded natural forces.

30.VII.44.

Long dream. Did not record till getting up, perhaps two or three hours afterwards.

As, or identified with, a rather different person, I come, on a little bluff overlooking the green countryside, to a big roughly rectangular stone, square in section but tall, set upright on a square base of the same or similar stone, the whole taller than a man. The general relationship is that of lingam to yoni. The stones, irregular throughout and very slightly rounded at the edges and there is a certain amount of free play at the bottom. Where it meets the base a fierce shower of sparks bursts out of it. This is the lightning-stone—a thunderbolt, or *vajra*, definitive spiritual energy and illuminating intelligence which had been foretold in a former dream. I set the stone moving a little to and fro, massive, heavy, so that the sparks gradually increase and become flames rising like the corona of a flower round the base: "churning" in yoga and *kundalini*-like as described in Tantra—ascending from the *muladhara* at the base of the *sushumna* to the upturned petals of a chakra. At the base, in a plain hollow chamber which those who guard it consider quite difficult and dangerous to enter, though I manage to set aside all my initial misgivings, I find gold—in the form of small balls heavy like lead shot, only rather dully dark grey and shiny—alchemistic gold and lead: lead not yet transformed. Yet there is no doubt that it is genuine gold.

Afterwards, in a vague warm-earth-yellow Indian room, one of the young men associated with this place talks of his experience of the Goddess. I am sympathetic to him, have told him a little of my own experience of the Goddess, and do not mind him asking for my wallet and even feeling for it in my inner jacket pocket. And I do not mind sacrificing the few aphorisms and 5 rupees the wallet contains, though it is my loose-leaf notebook and file.

For some time I have felt that if the aphorisms remain long enough unread, condensed and arranged, the whole rather autobiographical world of thought of these reflections may be surpassed in some entirely impersonal, traditional, form of expression. But this would, rather, suggest surpassing by completion, possession, of gold (Light, Sun, *Sahaja*) in the heart—apparently by a yogic process. And in one of my recent poems I have used lightning from beyond the sun (of this world, or of the Absolute as final term of thought) as a symbol of the dynamic Transcendent.

31.VIII.44.

Mata Ananda Mayi. Simple, childlike freshness of speech and laughter.

1.IX.44. 122 libs (8 stoen 10.)

There is no true base for relation with this world but surrender to the Supreme. Otherwise there is only the endless impurity and inconclusiveness of one's own ego and the ego of others. This surrender is the only purity, the only light and guide in the darkness of this world. —My mind can see this, but alas, I lack the strength to implement it. —What strength is needed for surrender? Only the strength of our actual weakness, which the ego cannot acknowledge. But also the strength of the intrinsic joy and purity of our being—the only true, perfect, disinterested strength there is.

There can be no question, in the present situation, of changing the form of the outer life. It was entirely foreign to my attitude towards money to have borrowed any, but the simple fact that I owe small sums to various friends is enough to determine that I have no right to leave a situation in which I can earn money until I have repaid them. Quite apart from the fact that my coming to Rajghat may well correspond with and serve the deepest development. —It is only that the ego confuses the pattern of events, for it is no doubt true that I can never again, or at least not again in the same way, live the over-denuded life of the first years in India. Even what still seems necessary *intellectual* work demands a certain minimum security and continuity. The years I spent in Madras to be near the library failed of their purpose in obstinate, prolonged, almost despairing suffering because of a basic contradiction between two modes: all intellectual work was sterilised by the continual attempt to overpass it immediately. This tension was no doubt necessary till inward development (which doubtless it favoured) had reached a certain point. But now things must be done in order. And this at once means that tension must be replaced by surrender, self-dedication and as the basic mode, the organising energy. *This* is the relation with Shakti so long necessary before, but which the acute inward tension of the existence itself replaced and excluded. —Did I not feel strongly at Pondicherry that what I lacked was acknowledgement of the Mother, and was not my relation with Her really a North-to-North antagonism? Was I not really tending continually to over-ride Nature, to attain Immediacy by completion of crisis, of lucid madness (anti-preconception in all fields), by Passion, by Despair, by Denudation, even by Perversity? —Does not Krishnamurti, also, too exclusively emphasise the Purusha aspect? and is not his vehemence too, a result of the fact that his absolute spiritual force has to operate through the *void* of the fact that nothing else can exist, and so, seems to contain its own contradiction? (This is also the tension of Ibn 'Arabi's *Treatise on Singleness.*) Does not this, indeed, reduce everything to paradox?, so that Power can prove Itself only as perfect impotence—or absolute, destructive violence which destroys oneself first yet cannot, for it is really Infinite Power, remain silent and so seems never to get beyond that occasion. The life of the Christ appears to end on the cross; the rest seems apocryphal, and yet Christianity leans on it for 'proof' that he was the Christ. Yet the fact that indeed he was is the fact that no proof is necessary: the resurrection could never have succeeded as proof.

4.IX.44.

It is most important, in relation with others, that the ego should not intervene. There must be perfect economy and perfect sensibility—nothing originated by the ego, and all that arises met with the deepest and truest sincerity and intelligence. The humility and deep attentiveness of this economy is the only true ground of relation with others, the only ground through which real Love of all can flower.

The incontinent ego would betray and confuse everything: in its impotence and in fear of its life, it would knot all into more and more ingenious and sickening perversity.

One's inner life can only remain secret: it must change all, but it can never speak through the ego or be truly spoken of by its impurity, frivolity, ignorance, impatience, sentimentality.

The humility and sincerity of one's inner life is its secrecy—the modesty of the bride in which all the depth and power reside in the dignity of her love.

Nothing can become harmoniously and irreversibly manifest except what is rooted once and for all in His Truth and flowers out from Him by that same Truth and as that Truth.

Only the Perfect Man has perfect Love, and meanwhile precisely the deepest and simplest qualities are to be turned towards 'the Reality' (for their childlike shortsightedness That may certainly seem a pure darkness).

"Wise as serpents and harmless (in this context I would write *simple*) as doves." Discretion is necessary in the world precisely in order to implement true love, love of the essential being of all others, the recognition which is identity and has always existed and always will—Love's equality with Its own Absoluteness. And here one can begin to understand the fundamental pure seriousness, the Realism, of SKM. —And the antinomy involved in the fact that childlike simplicity, affection, spontaneity, though pure, are satisfied, can fulfil their own truth, only in perfect Realism. There must indeed be no capitulation to the Prince of this World and his standards, to the merely grown-up, but the Child must in his own sense become Adult and therefore complete mastery of the grown-up: his disinterested objectivity must know that world without judgement or compromise: only so can Love, Sympathy, Understanding be real, only so can they fulfil their own absoluteness, only so can we really love our neighbour as ourself. This fulfilment can only come by the first essential, faithfulness to God.

The Life of the Christ, "Son of Man", is refusal to admit that there is a particular 'spiritual life' or to accept its privileges: it is Absolute Realism, and so, humanly, complete exposure. There is no *way*. "I am the Way". "This world" is recognised paradoxically only by what refused it in the desert temptations and which, after crucifixion (fulfilment of Exposure and Paradox in all dimensions), arose from death, descended into hell. The Christ must 'come again' only for those who cannot accept or complete this Paradox, who cannot understand Geniality of Spirit which is absolute and can never, therefore, without denying itself, appear as generosity. He appeared of all men the most despised and afflicted. —He "ascended into heaven" only for those who wish to escape the suffering and evil of this world—by those who do not understand His 'descent'—that there was never any other status to descend from and no-one to descend, that Love is immediate, Absolute. "Behold, I am with you always"; and "the Kingdom of heaven is within."

7.IX.44. Dream.

I am to be married. In some sort of light carriage or tonga through streets like those of Madras. In a sort of office the man who is to perform the ceremony is waiting.

In this rather small, dark, low wood-ceilinged panelled room have assembled several relations of my mother's side. Two or three tall old ladies with black veils and dark (I think black) dresses, each with several gold chains of various lengths about the neck. Torsos spare and straight with long and wide skirts. We have never met before, or not for countless years, but they embrace me with solid affection. I don't particularly think of it, but am evidently in European clothes, black or at any rate correct from their point of view. They are dignified, but behind their perfect system of conventional forms very human—robustly sensitive and intelligent, shrewd and witty, with an harmonious salty goodness. —Perfectly poised, with an unquestionable place and lightness, entirely without inner question or conflict, hence genial, understanding, realistic, joyful. I never see any bride. They sit down to what they would perhaps have called a collation—I think sandwiches and wine. One of them, when she removes her headgear, appears quite bald at the back of her head where the hair, though faded in colour, is quite long. Elbow-length black gloves. Or do some of the dresses end in a simple wrist-band, the sleeves puffed above? When I told this dream to Juliette Merston, for I knew it would interest her, she thought that the 'marriage' represents fusion with the innate forces or elements now beginning to become conscious in me as the old ladies. And this, she says, argues a sufficient centre of stability for this kind of "synthesis" to become possible.

She says that a "collation" at about eleven in the morning was a custom of my great-grandparents' generation. The wrist-band dresses (and light white, pearl-grey or black kid gloves) also belong to that period.

With quiet perfunctoriness, Blanca Schlamm *[later Atmananda]* joins a sort of procession. She is in black—elaborate, tasselled clothes. After a moment or two I remember: she is in mourning for her father.

I awoke in the state of deep, subtle, quiet, exposed emotion of the dream—too specific, wide, long-known and fundamental to describe.

I feel I understand why the Buddha, diamond-clear intellect, is seen as the embodiment of fathomless Compassion: he must have seen all relative experience directly as a tissue of the most subtle and intimate sorrow—so specific, delicate, inexpressible, that each life is joined and continues as the very substance of that undischargable, perfect sorrowing, that unacknowledgeable tenderness and state of being lost. There is a keen note of it in the Christian Middle Ages.

> "O the rose, the gentle rose,
> And the fennel that grows so green!
> God give us grace in every place
> To pray for our king and queen."
>
> *The Seven Virgins*

Poignancy, bitter-sweet depth of the sculptures of Chartres.

I can truly say that I have no individual relationship with anyone—no relationship based upon and presuming the passive individuality, and any such could even appear to exist only by falsity. The only relation that, necessarily, represents a bond or a duty is that with my mother, while her attitude towards me can neither be denied nor changed. All others are purely incidental, rootless, transitory, at best can only be symbolic. Even that with SKM must surely, in the last resort, appear more purely and simply symbolic than any other.

As real inward freedom takes to itself level after level, it can less and less seem, even in appearances, to myself or others, that any 'relation' with others is possible, even by the most resourceful perversity, which has also in some way to be exhausted and understood.

The fact that sexuality represents *free*, *plastic* energy (at the physical level it directly represents Eros, the energy of the psychic nature)—a power that can be turned to uses that exceed man as he is, is shown by its almost endless generative capacity and by the fact that it is not dependent upon physical strength as such: the body may gain from it as mind and emotion do, but may also limit it: by harmonious lightness and balance the body must share its mobility. If the nerves are exacerbated or the brain poisoned by too coarse a strong tea, this harmony is destroyed: through dammings, knots and countercurrents the vital energy in the nerves is forced to short-circuit through the sex-centre, or it acts destructively in the brain and nerves themselves.

I see that nothing around me nowadays, mentally either, is of any *organic* interest to me whatever—the old question of non-satisfaction of one's deepest imagination, the basic Sensuality. Some of the books in my dreams stand for that order of rich, trans-mental art and knowledge represented, I feel, by Tantra and by all in Asia akin to it—a mode that is undoubtedly very strong in me. Examination of all I have written should help to find it in its own sense, to free it from the obliqueness and half-unconsciousness imposed upon it by surface Western 'literary' modes. But I must find some way of establishing and sustaining contact with it outwardly. Even in Tantrik ritual? Has not the whole of the past to be brought to the surface to be completely understood and fulfilled?

14.IX.44.

Spontaneous expansiveness must be turned towards the Supreme, its only true justification: all *occasion* must be fulfilled as discipline, purification, *sadhana*: only so can its limits be sincerely and intellectually admitted, understood, used and surpassed. To allow oneself to expand upon occasion is plainly a betrayal of principle, unfaithfulness, drunkenness, incontinence, degradation, licentiousness, immodesty. Think of the modesty, the chastity, of Radha, her faithfulness to Sri Krishna—the *secrecy* of all true love, which is utterly open only in its own pure sense.

Spiritually, in spite of all our willed activity in its own terms, the waking state is just as passive as dream or sleep.

Every waking activity without exception must become *sadhana*—must be directed towards real wakefulness, the pure Self-definition of absolute Consciousness which is both subject and object and neither.

17.IV.44. Dream.

In a dismal, dilapidated kitchen, a girl of perhaps 12 or 14, in very poor clothes is crouching by the fire. Her head and face are covered with an aluminium helmet. Association: when my finger had been poisoned by the rim of an aluminium vessel, V. Ayyar at Tiruvannamalai told me that aluminium is considered the leper among metals. *[Interesting Indian acuteness of perception decades before aluminium is discovered to be a dangerous substance.]*

Among the kitchen rubbish half-arises a fair-skinned, lean, slender, almost completely naked figure that has been rolling there. I realise that this person is a saint in some strange state of consciousness. When the figure, at first seen from the back, turns at once, stands up and looks at me, I realise that it is a tall woman, but still there is a certain sexlessness such as one sees in very pure people or in harmless infantile idiots like Govindaswami, the frail, birdlike avadhuta at Trivandrum who seems to be immersed, even lost, in some delicate non-human state. To my surprise she speaks in good English but I have forgotten what she said, except that it was mostly against me and I felt humility and contrition. The gaze of the round, wide-open eyes—association here and elsewhere: image of Kali bought at Trivandrum which gave me a hideous dream, causing me to return it to the brass shop in Chalai Bazaar)—very wild and piercing, and the smile, as if insane, are rather frightening. But her words are very sane.

I go away with the companion who brought me there. Then I feel that I should return and offer her money. I take some at random from many loose coins as I have at present in a wallet, like the fine-grained black one I bought in France. I refrain from counting them, and go back to her alone though she is in retirement now. She received me seated on a sort of throne, or rather in a kind of high portico-shaped niche of dark stone like those which in temple walls enshrine large images of gods. With tears I prostrate myself on the ground, offering the grubby little bundle of money below the *pitha* (like the loose foot in *lilasana*—so that the Kali was represented): touching a stone foot broken off the rest of an image. My attitude is as if asking Her to be kind to me, and She is in fact much more kindly and intimate than before—though propitiously objective; She says I should get myself examined for "infectious disease". It might seem that this deity represented Kali in one of Her aspects as a goddess of disease. Juliette points out that the goddess is placated by the offering of money which stands for what money represents—means to strength and health and to which, she thinks, I still pay insufficient attention. "Your lungs are dark." I think it is I who mention the spine as a channel of force and it was at this point in recording that I remembered the earlier dream about *muladhara*. I tell her that lately things have been going wrong as far as the vital force is concerned. (Earlier: sexual dream with Renée! Thought the other day of astrologer's saying that she was the wife of my previous life.) Because of this did not get up early to see Anandamayi before Her departure this morning. Reaction against Juliette's "pathological themes" in Cocteau's *Les Enfants Terribles* in which it has never occurred to me to find anything but its rare and difficult perfection. I suppose it's all my own fault. She seems to agree but says that in a way it was unavoidable. I affirm that I can never give up my deepest ambitions, by which all can be turned to good. But, she replies, it may be necessary to use certain Tantrik or yogic techniques. It tell her that I realise this more and more.

Recording this dream, I realise that it is the incalculable, intransigent Kali-aspect of the Pondicherry Mother that chiefly struck me in her.

Stephen Spender on Cecil Collins, aged 35, with reproduction of "The Pilgrim Fool", 1943 and another of his paintings: *Horizon*, London, Feb.44. This painting made a deep impression—by something more than *imaginative* identification. (China, Yeats *A Vision*, Fairy-tales, *Parsifal*, Shakespeare etc. Difference between the Fool and the eccentric.) *[This is LT's first reference to the important inspiration of Collins's Fool which led to writing the series of Fool poems right at the end of his life.]* *Horizon*, p.117. Spender: "The fool is the symbol of a human emotion completely felt by someone indifferent to social appearances. The fool becomes completely that which he feels, and approximates to Keats's idea of poetic being: of the poet becoming that which he sees and which his senses experience... The fool is a figure of wisdom, passion, sensuousness, dandyism in Baudelaire's sense of the word and sometimes he has perverse and unnatural qualities."

Cecil Collins (p. 118): "All real art transcends the image of its creation, because it transforms it."

A.N. Brailsford on C.C. exhibition at the Lefevre Gallery (?Feb.44): Mr. C.C. is a poet who happens to use form and pigment instead of words... The fool is creative innocence."

22.IX.44.

Taking leave of Earl Brewster. He said in effect: I feel a relation with you one seldom feels—a kind of chemical affinity, quite without barriers. Moved, I told him how I value his directness, honesty, simplicity, sincerity; they give a deep and quiet tone of kindness, seriousness and purity. I wrote in the *Aparokshamebhuti* "with love". Scanning it, he said in his beautifully simple, sincere and generous voice: "*I'm glad.*" I was so absorbed that I could not re-act to my perception, half-unconscious therefore, that he seemed to make to embrace me: the moment of hesitation after which

I remained still made him half-totter an inch or two, for his legs are weak from pernicious anaemia.

Yesterday was his 66th birthday and in reply to Pandit Joshi he said he hoped he is still a child.

26.IX.44. poem, *Flower Pollen* written on 13th.

Novalis: "Genius is the power of treating imagined objects as real and...the real as though they are imagined."

And Picasso: "One lets imagined objects dress themselves with real appearances."

The Vedantic Knowledge amounts to this: that the real is the perfection of the imagined (Pure Marvel)—as I have put it: Poetry is the Source and Substance of all that can appear.

27–8.IX.44. Dream

Horrible suffering in a dream in which I beat Margot about the face with a little black wallet that I use for current aphorisms and other notes. This is merciless criticism for not letting me read in peace. As if reading were a sin, I say—conscious all the time of real sin. Margot takes my part... That pitiful, motionless face, bearing all, unable to explain, knotted in its own bitter, helpless problems.

Waking, I remember yesterday's attempted letter—heartlessly conceived chiefly with some sort of literary or pictorial effect...

And thought of SKM—the almost impossibility of keeping one's motives pure, of remaining in the utter sensitiveness and unfathomable selfless intelligence of love...

The Fool is also one who by his innocence bears his own inhumanity—the inhumanity which in others is pure unawareness, limitation, and which only the Saint has surrendered to God.

28.IX.44.

Explained to Sri Rama Rao (Principal of Besant College, Rajghat, and for years the companion of J. Krishnamurti) proposals for helping selected groups of boys to express without qualification their actual thought and experience—with all that is implied about the nature and importance of Language. He leaves me entirely free to do as I wish and will do all he can to help.

29.IX.44. 115 lbs.

1.X.44.

Efforts at getting established in new house at Bharavati, a hamlet of Bharavas, workmen, across the Varuna.

[This is a charming little house, a gauzed-in verandah its full width, with a little avenue of rosemary-like bushes from the gate to the door. Beautiful tall silvery pampas grass grows robustly all around. One could sit on the veranda and look out over the mirror-like Ganga only a few yards away, and watch the fishermen gliding by with their nets in the early morning. Later the house would be occupied by the famous socialist politician Achyut Patwardhan who came there at Krishnamurti's invitation and worked with the community development people.]

The ease with which I let myself be sickened and exhausted at the inertia, deception, carelessness, unreliability, stupidity or weakness of every man one has to deal with in this country only shows on what a surface tension of despair, doubt, suspense I am all the time living—what facile lies, optimism, subjectivity keep me afloat and blind. Can it be that black sorrow, despair and horror, which can never in their purity be expressed to the mind that separates itself from sensibility—that these are the deepest reality, all else evasion, cowardice, pretense, facility, intoxication, heartlessness, a coarse Emersonian optimism? No, I could never believe it; but chronic exhaustion, uncertainty, dissatisfaction on all planes may at moments become poisonous for one's overdriven body, mind and sensibility. Yet of an accident we say "*He broke* his leg": all poisoning is deliberate.

[There is some truth about this as a general observation. But at the same time I can't help recalling Bharavati as one of the most beautiful little hamlets I visited in the rural outskirts of Benares, where the weaving community produce highest quality silk brocades, and always treated me with great courtesy. If I wanted a light switch to be re-positioned or have the walls of my cottage whitewashed then the obverse side came to the fore in the way LT describes.]

10.X.44.

Only for perfect denudation—the purity, singleness, disinterestedness of the desert, can there dawn a light that is eternal, shadowless.

We return to what we think is 'the same' waking state and world because it is in terms of it that we conceive sleep and by its absence that sleep is for us oblivion. The ego of the waking state ascribes sleep to itself. But if sleep becomes conscious, all reality is the "ever-new" of the Vedic text: there is no longer any ego to maintain the *memory* which Sri Shankaracharya says is *maya*, the spell-binding Illusion of this world by which it, and the individuality which we think perceives it, seem real in their own right.

12.X.44.

The life-force in everyone is self-enjoying. Those who do not seek to enjoy it in sexuality may make it their own in rarer, keener, wider and more subtle ways. It is these, often, who will use those drugs that are keys to more subtle levels of enjoyment and help to stabilise them. And conversely, such experience acts like a drug—producing a frail yet tensile concentration, lucid madness, sober frenzy, in which we share the ever unnameable Marvel of that 'Reality' that can never need to be real. —That honey of wonder and delight ever more and more specifically, intimately, openly and secretly self-tasting—that ever-unseizable yet never evadable Infinity of the Supreme's own reflection in Himself—fathomless self-experience of the fathomless.

14.X.44.

As I was thinking of asking one of the guides to get me *kunkumam* from Sri Vishvanatha Temple to fill a little silver box I had bought for the child of one of the school teachers on her naming-day, some College boys met me and said that I might certainly enter. So I bought a garland and sweetmeats and received them back as *prashad* for the child, with a white lotus from the pool about the slightly irregular egg-shaped lingam of fine dark-mauve stone, over which worshippers pour water from little spouted copper vessels.

Then I plunged into the wonderful lanes between the brass-bazaar and the Town Hall. When I had quite lost myself, one of the College boys greeted me through the window of a house and invited me in. He told me that on this day, sacred to Dhanteshwar, Lord of Wealth, people who can afford it buy some vessel of silver. After he had brought me food I found that his name is Annapurna Prashad.

[LT was lucky. Nowadays non-Indians would never be allowed to enter the Sri Vishwanatha Temple. Annapurna is the Giver of Food and Plenty. Her temple is next door.]

15.X.44

Listening to Blanca Schlamm playing Chopin, I realise to what a degree childhood sensibility and imagination can be transfixed and paralysed by the mind. But no doubt their physical support in the adult is the seed; and as Purohit Swami has written, too often spent, it loses the perfume and freshness, the deep resilience of resource, that give light and colour and transforming force to the richest and most resonant experience.

As far as possible never sleep out of physical, nervous or psychic fatigue.

16.X.44. (Divali)

These boys of 10 or 12, in their talk and play, radiate an intense electricity of emotion, imagination, fantasy—something nascent, timeless, frontierless. Light and delicate as foam, it could float armadas, argosies, undermine continents. What would have happened to history if the children's crusade in 1212 had not come to grief?

22.X.44. Bharavati.

This perversity, equivalent with capacity to do all with really perfect tact, discretion, equanimity—with perfect love and joy—arises because it is impossible to accept anywhere a real occasion, occasion of seriousness: by perversity, the ego tries to prolong itself in a mad fastidiousness—in which it is the first not to believe. Perfection, perfect seriousness, could only be disinterested; perversity (and the profitless, deliberate, subtle, ingenious, ridiculous suffering it entails) expresses refusal of that surrender to the Supreme which actual disinterestedness has already made, and it expresses at the same time the fact that nothing else but this surrender could free in the relative world the truth of one's nature. The truth that one's being is essentially one with that 'supreme' is therefore at the same moment undeniable and unacceptable—because pure paradox. This paradox is the abyss of perversity.

Perversity is Innocence impossibly attempting to be other than Innocence. Because this betrayal of Innocence is impossible, perversity is perversity and not despair. Despair is passive, perversity diabolically active. It simulates, even in the physical nature, every weakness, every ingenious complication and indirectioness, because it knows that there is but one Power and Simplicity.

Because that Power is prior to it, perversity is a measure of the richness of love, the capacity for surrender. The Infinity of love would find it perhaps the most intense and subtle mode of Love.

In relation with this essential oneness, perversity is a negative recognition of the Transcendent, a recognition which thus makes Anguish absolute. And this is possible only when Anguish in its true relative sense has been overpassed. It could be overpassed only in Peace and Certainty: Perversity, refusing these, tries to cast doubt upon the reality of the original, pure, undeniable Anguish of the nature. Perversity represents the fact that Anguish never really existed, that the nature is refusal to see this. This means that Perversity is refusal of the fact that Anguish is surpassed as soon as it is recognised.

And so, correspondingly, in its terror of committing itself to relative occasion (of being spiritually serious in the worldly sense), Perversity is the supreme pudor.

[So, it would surely be sheer perversity to publish this entry!]

14.XI.44.

You are a Nothing that is All. And thus the All is not. Why should the Nothing be distressed because this cannot even be called Peace? But if the Nothing would continue here, it can only be an inscrutable Perversity. This Perversity, like the incomprehensible *maya*, can only be a mental concept of all relativities set against the Absolute. This is the never-begun, ever-forgotten sick dream of the Changeless Ocean of Light—not really a dream, then, but a subtle unwitnessed lapsing of those timeless waters, a gleaming musical collapse of wave into wave, in which that boundless sea tastes its own sweetness in an exquisiteness so special and delicate that it is like a bitterness; or as if the self-luminous could cast infinitely subtle and specific shadow upon itself.

This evening I felt that Chopin's Nocturne Op.15 No. 1 in F major, expressed with a directness and exactitude that words can hardly attain with such sweetness and joy of angelic serenity—a self-poised, timeless, inner state like an ocean of light momently lapsing into itself with inexhaustible tenderness and lucidity—with the secret intimacy of the sea in a starlight become one equal suprahuman radiance, an unnameable tensionless exaltation. At one moment it expresses the complementary divine force and abandon of self-caused laughter, extravagant wit of reckless lucidity, that creates, that mocks—as I wish I could do in my lumbering prose—with more than intimate motherly gentleness, and ever re-absorbs every possibility of emotion and of passion.

Whether such experiences are realised and entered as "states", the individuality based in the body depends upon the richness and intensity of the vital force—a purely yogic factor. What perceives them, it seems to me, is more than an intuition: it *is* the inward experience itself but leaves mind and vital not carried away or possessed by it, free to express it. In this sense SKM is justified, I suppose, in taking it that exact expression of understanding or experience is proof of its reality in the person concerned, for though the words in themselves present only a mental form it is organised entirely as a symbol that is beyond mind. Thus when I commented once that though the *form* of certain perceptions remain the same their whole inward quality may alter, he responded: That is exactly it! And again made the remark: You are a yogin. He meant that I could not express this independently as an understanding of what he had put in a different way unless I had experienced the kind of yogic change in question.

The importance of the vital in formal *realisation* of spiritual experience *is* the importance of yogic fulfilment which my natural demand for realisation in terms of each plane in its own sense also makes necessary. The deadlock with Sri K can appear merely doctrinal, and paradoxically irresoluble only because of a hesitation, perversity of inward division that refuses to accept formal work for this fulfilment.

And yet it *is* true that I am not metaphysically satisfied, that in practice SKM offers no base for such work but the concept of the guru, which, in terms of his doctrine, in repeated assertions, he began by removing: "For you there is no guru"—Advaita-vedanta as such, because it is stated for the mind, cannot really recognise or justify in their own sense *immediate trans-mental demands and possibilities*. Hence, no doubt, SKM's "states" (*bhava*, *mahabhava*) for me always the essentially interesting suggestion in him of something 'beyond' ('beyond-advaita'). Yet he does not relate them directly with his critique of *bhava* and *samadhi* as "only states": he distinguishes between his teaching self and these states and says he knows nothing about them! In the same way he denies the reality of the guru for me yet acts as one. Yet this denial he also attributed to a "state", whereas one would think that it must be from the point of view of his "states" that he remain a guru—that the guru is the direct sign of the Transcendent.

Nirvikalpa-samadhi is merely a measure of this failure of direct recognition. Even SKM's "Direct perception" can only be *perception* of the 'Absolute', for all perception is relative. The transcendent (represented by *sahaja*) is not perceived: for the relative it is pure *Dynamis*, and whoever directly wills it is yogin or Tantrika. That is why, in practice, *jnana* must recognise *sahaja-sthiti* for which there can be no place in a purely intellectual theory: in *mukti* the intellect is exhausted. Yet this is not even the 'beginning' —simply the state described directly and without self-elaboration in the *Ashtavakra-Gita*, where all intellectual apparatus and eidolons can do no more than deny themselves. Yet merely to say that this returns us to what is "beyond words", beyond expression, is still to have failed to understand the Manifestation, the Word Itself. —*Than which there is nothing else*, yet this is not true of it as 'manifestation' ('*of*' an 'Absolute'). Realisation of this *Than which there is nothing else* is *sahaja*, but it cannot in any sense be 'approached' by intellectual means: the intellect can only exhaust itself; yet for *sahaja* this is senseless: the intellect can have no real occasion for doing so. It is strange that SKM cannot also *state* this in such a way as to 'prove' that he understands it! but on the contrary refuses to meet my formulations of it and in the end "withdraws". He could offer no 'solution' but to enter *nirvikalpa-samadhi* or to use my "will" to put the problem aside! —though both will and *samadhi*, even at a lower level, he quite logically analyses away. C.K. has every excuse, externally, for having told Q.S.: "His *[i.e. LT's]* guru does not understand him". Yet of course I can never accept this, for it falls far below the level of the problem, or at least below my interest and of my approach to SKM.

Of course I feel that I am to blame, yet I must understand exactly how. This *is* the guru-problem. The whole concept of the guru is an insuperable obstacle, for the Transcendent also can be approached directly—indeed, even 'more' than the Absolute, it can only be approached directly and is *everywhere* the only effective directness; this (as SKM seems to have granted from the start—way back when we first met) has been my movement ever since I became mentally conscious; more I cannot mentally know or say.

What is normal for a 'nature' like mine, is immediate experience not abstractly direct recognition, for all "perception" falls at the Absolute: Chit 'perceives' Itself: only so can I be true to myself *even in the mind*; my criticism of the mind and what I have written about "Poetry" and the "Transcendent" bear this out in my aphorisms. But though SKM says (in what "State" ???) "We are One" he can present the Transcendent only as the Guru. Is this not by the same token by which 'he' is passive to his "states" and, he says, knows no more of them than we do?

If I am to formulate all this correctly in a letter to SKM—without confusion, weakness or impurity, I must live a life perfect in all respects: the attitude to work, to children, to the body, to aquaintances, must be absolutely serious, economical and transparent. Only so can there be really true and deep feeling and intuition.

[This, after two years of deep reflection, is probably the most definitive statement Thompson ever wrote on his dispute with Sri Krishna Menon. It is remarkable that, difficult as it no doubt is to follow, it is barely more than two pages long and for so complex a problem surprisingly succinct. I have heard many people pronounce their view of the conflict, for the most part loftily and unfavorably, with virtually no respect or sympathy for Thompson, revealing themselves as having a very superficial grasp of the issues or any appreciation of the profundity of what was at stake, or the depth of his insight as to what happened and why.]

3.XI.44.

Treat the canteen food here and the whole environment with the pure disinterested imaginative identification, entirely without preconception, with which you would experience it in dream. This will make it, as in yogic meditation, a means of enrichment. It was thus that everything Indian was experienced, in 1933 and for long afterwards.

All in itself is formal, but through the intense one-pointedness of perfect imaginative leisure becomes a channel of energy.

Let not the grey sands of Reason, the law of the god of this world, drift over the living fire.

4.XI.44. Dream

Rapidly, by a decisive event, the pearly water-mists are withdrawn from the horizons, from the hills. All is released, becomes intensely, marvellously clear. Distance is open, living, beautiful; the rocks of a nearby ridge in the new joyous light have a cubic clarity like jewels. It is early morning. I remark to my companion that Brewster, seeing all this from his verandah, will be delighted.

9.XI.44.

This evening, as we walked along the ghats to visit Harihara Baba, Ranganathan told me that in 1935 or 6 Swayam-prakasha Swami or Sundamangalam told him: I could admit Thompson where you, though a brahmir, could not enter. It is by the effect of his *purya-janma* (which evidently he could see). This apparently refers to his having invited me to enter the actual shrine of Sri Dattatreya where I made *pradakshina*.

24.XI.44.

Blanca says that my prose fragments very evidently correspond with something that is always to be felt in me—express me much more recognisably than verses. It is this element that made her say that the atmosphere of my room at Rama Rao's, after I had been there only a few days, was indescribably strange, as if magic or alchemy were practised there. I had never 'meditated' there.

None of this is necessarily false but none of it can be integrally true while I am still not serious in the most elementary physical things—food, use of time and energy.

Night. I don't take myself seriously in the only way that would truly free me from that necessity, so am continually brought down, like an animal tied by a cord. The cord must be wound up, the stake pulled out. Then alone can there be real freedom from "thought or thing". *[Reference to his poem with that title.]*

26.XI.44.

Simplicity and truthfulness, perfect integrity, like Blake's, is all that is required; then at once, in every matter, there is guidance and help from the deepest truth, the deepest law of all things.

27.XI.44.

In the period of youthful spontaneity, before I began to analyse my intuitions or my nature and my action, I *lived* my natural metaphysic, only directly *suffering* all that contradicts it: I was the problem, the paradox. Hence the ringing, weightless intensity and brilliance of that period. It would have been inconceivable for me to have kept a journal in those days, and I remember nothing of them but a haze of moments of brilliance. Since then, I have entered, psychically and mentally, a period of self-consciousness and complication, no doubt necessary to complete awareness, command an understanding not only of myself but also of the world...

Dream. Vague memory of other subtly strange dreams earlier in the night. Returning to a dreamed Almora just in time to find the hills rise in great overhanging snowy peaks and escarpments, much closer than at Almora itself. They are blue, the snow only flecked in the granite surface. We have climbed to a kind of roofed platform. Association, more or less: top of Adam's Peak in Ceylon; but here, of course, the mountains are far above us, filling almost all the sky. All colours and forms near at hand marvellous in tone and quality—softer and richer in the delicate mistiness of the air than in any sunset, and the feeling here, anyway, is rather of sunrise. There are several vague members of the party, all feel like Europeans, in long overcoats. Anyone standing near in this wonderful atmosphere appears a rich, soft amethyst.

Chirico mentioned last evening when I was explaining to Blanca how I thought a *Danse* should be played—repeating much that I had said before in connection with the strong and delicate psychic truth of Chopin's music, and about the wayward intensity of the psychic world, so unlike human passion and seeing it cold, dangerous, fascinating and unreliable, as faery things do to the human in all folklore and legend. I used this, also, to explain the 'sexlessness' in the human sense, of the psychic world and even though it and they be most subtly and intensely erotic—that for example I find even certain children of 11 and 12 here much more 'human' than I in this respect, partly of course, because of their precociousness through life in joint families, servants, oriental temperament. —This throws a new light on my relation with physical sexuality: you never see the ground your feet are standing on. M., after I had gone though the whole act, said: "you are really beyond sex".

30.XI.44.

I should learn the fundamentals of Indian music. There is an important element that would be directly expressed, released, completed by *bhakta* songs: this would give form, presence and consciousness to something in my *nature*, too, a psychic sonority, which already, sometimes, is inclined to sing and dance, the element, perhaps, that made Daniélou say I look like a minstrel, but which at present only, so to speak, floats around me and remains oblique. The gulf between 'psychic' prose fragments and 'intellectual' verses very well marks a failure of perfect indivisible wholeness—the adamant presence which is then subtle, immediate, all-suffusing like a perfume—such inexhaustibly rich, sweet and powerful presence as SKM has.

1.XII.44. Line of poem recently written:

"At noon beneath the taut and splendid towers"

Exquisitely beautiful *pink* parrots, 6 or 7 of them, on the paved path of a rich and sunny garden, its borders softened and overhung with tufted or trellised flowers and perfumed like the apricot. I call these birds parrots, for that is their suggestion, but they are more keenly graceful than ordinary parrots, raised beyond the blindness of numb clenched head—the parrot in the world of the gods. Yet they keep some tone of peculiar wise, condensed realism which in the ordinary parrot is expressed in the powerful beak and the lifting, prehensile claw and which make him such a comical, but not innocuous, busybody. At this point, recording, I remembered that I have thought that Juliette looks like a parrot. She once told me, with enjoyment, a story of a parrot, a cat and an early Victorian lady. They dance in a most charming way, with tentative zest and curiosity daring a strange insect, yellow and black, like an immense hunched butterfly, but at once forgetting it, pacing, prancing, preening, hustling, bowing, opening in the lovely light their arched and spreading fans, intense like rose, or shell-pink with the purest light of yellow. Their colour has at moments something of the almost supernatural richness and subtlety of the blue and amethyst in the mountain dream (28 Nov.)—at a certain angle, as a bird bows with half-open wings, it fuses with the singing light in a soft intangible dazzle that brings in a very subtle purple or mauve.

Blanca is walking beside me down the path. So that she may see them before they are disturbed, I stop her with my palm for a moment against her breast.

A little later Prem Chand and another lad come up and make to turn off to the right. Prem Chand is charmed and he caresses one of the parrots with his characteristic smile and the warm, direct, good-hearted delight in his lion eyes. Thought of parrots is associated with Rangadevi, I mean Ratidevi, and with the Mother in general. Their being pink and so beautiful suggests Lakshmi. And of course I remember that Goddess Minakshi at Madura bears a parrot in Her hand.

(Attempted poem on Madura Minakshi.)

The least vanity vitiates truth in spiritual things. For example in demonstrating that dreams are related with our waking life by more than mere past impressions—that dream contains and *changes* future as well as past, interpenetrates and guides the threads of our waking existence.

The humility required is simply the pride and reserve and strength of a lover.

2nd. Dec: Lines of recently written poem: "Let me with words come close."

The true base of equanimity can be found only when all paradox, madness and the weakness and folly of this world are completed and accepted in the mind—when there is no longer any traffic or tension with them. The base of *absolute* equanimity is necessarily secret to all that is human. In the end it is inevitable to enter this state—of pure luminosity and pure darkness. An absolute continence of the whole existence is pre-human.

Reality is not mental, though it needs a clear, indeed a pure, mind to see this. Great importance of the non-mental: *here* is real substance, real expression—in the way you walk, open an envelope, a knife—in the immediate texture and rhythm and resonance of every mode...

Tues. 5th. Still rather liverish. Weight dropped back to 110 lbs., 53 kilos approx. c.23.cc hrs. After walk to Sarnath (4 miles across open fields in bright sunlight.) This means that sensuality is not *integral*:

Dream in 4th–5th night:

Structures of bamboo with stretched cloth on which people lie on little screened sections the size of a bed. I think of dropping my feet to the ground, look down and find it is far below. The bamboos are very insecure: in trying to find a safe perch I can only move with difficulty and risk.

These bamboo erections seem to be tenanted by vagabonds or people like the Russians at the edge of Marseilles (refugees from Stalin around 1930). I come to them barefoot, through dirty streets like a mixture of India and the quarter round, say, the Old Vic (theatre in London famous for Shakespeare plays). Theatre entrance, pavements with red betel-gobs, crouched children selling *pan*, marigold garlands, playing-cards. Association: the town of tents by the Ganges that grew up for the great *yajna* a month or two ago. And there was a roofed platform of bamboo for musicians, very high, approached by a rough bamboo ladder. —I place this dream with others of height and insecurity and with those of directionlessness.

The horrible unsatsfactoriness of this life – of my life always, in one way or another. —The attempt, in every sphere, always against the grain, to make something of nothing. When all I really need, perhaps, is the first period of real rest and relaxation since childhood... —The simplest, most native, psychic and intellectual satisfactions out of reach. Barbarism all around. Living always on one's own substance, always *beyond* dryness... Always acting, giving, filling up defects and voids: no-one joyous, genial, subtle, intelligent, energetic, for years and years around. Even the children cannot really play, or if you begin really to play everyone gets frightened. And one has to *see*, in the end, that this is the miserable folly, emptiness, despair, pure profitless task that one is living in.

[One has to view this in contextual perspective. With a shock I realise that British rule is still, just, in place and the Nationalist leadership, including the future Prime Minister, Pandit Nehru, are about to be released from prison, with the war and the discovery of Auschwitz only a few months away from reaching their climax. Krishnamurti is confined to America, away from his aids at Rajghat. Half-Jewish Thompson is aware of what is going on in the larger world. His new colleague at Rajghat, Blanca Schlamm awaits news of relatives in still-occupied Vienna. Thompson, for the first time, has board and lodging free and a steady job, but on a salary that of the peons (male servants). He is recovering from enteric fever—this 'white sahib' whose fellow countrymen very visibly rule the roost.]

Only one solution: Live one's own life at all costs, then with utter secrecy: treat all else with perfect hypocrisy. Strip at all costs to the poetic essential. Leave no-one any semblance of inroad into anything but the pure flat cardboard of Jack and Ace, the perfectly empty sleeve. —Well, there isn't anyway. But O the endless goodwill that sincerely pretends, that cannot measure the bottomless ocean and therefore floats on it—with a lightness heavier than the heaviest stone and which the body continually feels.

6.XII.44.

It has always been obvious: energy cannot be defined in physical terms, but only psychically, through imagination. If the natural flexibility of the psychic is allowed, there is continual renewal. —A matter of elementary intelligence, avoidance of mental obstinacy— the mind far too gross and slow. The little imaginative holiday I took with the Introduction to a Buddhist Tantra (Gaekwar Series, Baroda)—it affirmed, with exalted metaphysics, that realisation is impossible without a Shakti, that realisation is through fulfilment of desires—that the incestuous have the best chance of it, with the seller of peacock-feathers, in an unfamiliar part of the town—is enough. Why close oneself to the Infinite, virginal, iridescent, laughing in the whole scintillating Manifestation? —Bar of the mind, absurd self-starved formality. —By which habit even pleasures become forced, become vice.

10.XII.44.

Pagan beauties again. When love cannot be integral, so that erotic and sexual, by being completed in full and joyful acceptance, become purely symbolic, the great thing is to avoid distraction, which upsets rhythm and therefore energy: there must always be sustained the direct, vivid, mobile disinterestedness and freedom from preconception which perceive and enjoy in art—which are concerned with *truth*, and only the more subtly, richly and keenly because through the imaginative, emotional and sensuous mode.

13.XII.44.

Sensation which in childhood was a kind of nightmare, but now I remain outside it—of a minute point, as if the apex of a funnel, infinitely nearing, that reduces all to more and more extreme minuteness—an inward space in which, for childhood, all, including myself, would be absorbed. Hence a kind of terror of strangeness. This occurred waking. I see now that this point nears from without, but is never one with some centre in the head. It seems to be another way of feeling the centre activated by tendency to intense thought when brain and nerves are tired.

The subtle tension continued and sought to work itself out—formal although so keenly delicate and sweet—no organic connection with any memory or *samskara*.

Dream: My hand, but smaller, wrapped in a glove and bandages—or is it merely the thickened ash-grey flesh and skin in a wastepaper basket. When I lift it I find that it is decayed like a dead hand—in the hollow glove-like skin, reduced almost all to a grey dust with a little red powder—the dried iron oxide, I suppose, of the blood. And the other hand too, small, plump and elegant like those of medieval Tamil bronzes or Chola paintings. I wonder how new bones have grown in my living hands.

This relates in my mind with a very subtle and simple sensation, dreamed a night or two ago, of the spatial temporiness of the body, particularly of the skull, whose impermanence and 'exchangeability' one's existence contains as it were in another time and space remote, perilous, even terrible from the first. I am simply drawing very approximate and wayward mental lines around something very specific and special and never so perceived before. *[This relates to other skeleton dreams.]*

15.XII.44.

Letters, after so many years, from Renée and Margot.

[Mail connections between Britain and India were less restricted by this time, particularly in the run up to Christmas.]

It is at such moments that we feel it quite clearly—that all strength and wisdom have but one flower, Love: that love is the only activity and the only understanding that is both immediate and final; that all our effort, weakness, experience, sensibility, can lead only to this first and last Realism. Here the great saying of Chandidas is made true, that there is nothing beyond Man. This is the justification of the Bodhisattva ideal, though metaphysically it falls short of the 'ultimate': Love is beyond even the perfection of metaphysics.

The greatest strength and the greatest delicacy are required only in order that we may be capable of love—supreme union of Beauty and Wisdom, Rapture and Sobriety.

17.XII.44.

This morning, when the sky cleared after rain, the river under wind and sun looked just like the water in my latest dream:

On a marvellously clear day, every building of Algiers is clearly visible across a strait no wider, apparently, than a river: the net of little waves* (Footnote: *Purely literary metaphor in attempt to express the criss-cross cone-surface of the sea with its pointed quilt of waves, like concave facets of cut glass) is woven of joyous light, like liquid gold. People even wade a good way out, the water is so shallow. I am surprised and delighted —with my companion think of crossing at once. We are in a town opposite, as if perhaps Marseilles. 'Algiers' is partly built upon a little ridge and I tell my companion that there is the 'native quarter'. Nearer must be the long street with big shops where we shall be able to find French books. The buildings, one with Doric columns of dark blue-grey and capitals of red, are like models.

The whole of life must become the art of faithful concentration upon the One Perfection. But to accept this bondage unto freedom I still lack simplicity, purity, resolution... Though I gain nothing otherwise but disorder; unresolved, unformulated doubt; suspense, delay, confusion, folly, despite unhappiness—still picking over like an idiot the shredded rope of the ego that can no longer bind any two things together.

(18th.) Yet it is the mental will which, at first anyway, would have to sustain surrender in the outward nature, and the mind cannot act consistently without complete conviction: what is needed is metaphysical certainty and clarity—an intellectual form perfectly corresponding with the deepest vision and intention of the soul and with every potentiality of the nature.

Thus the first need really is, as indeed I continually feel it, to resolve all that is represented in the Sri Aurobindo and Sri Krishna Menon deadlock, and in completion of aphorisms and of study.

(19th.) Still it is precisely the ignorance or imperfection we first find that has to surrender: only this faithfulness can open to a higher knowledge. "He who is not faithful in little, who will give him much?" The senses, sensibility and every kind of perceptiveness, the mind, reason, will and thought, must first be perfectly loyal to the prior Condition by which they incomprehensibly find themselves: this is the only immediate honesty, goodwill, intelligence: all else is frivolity*, licentiousness, perversity or mere self-closed Anguish, helpless paradox, refusal to acknowledge what is prior to the human.

[LT's footnote] *In fact there is no other serious occasion for seriousness—for the best use we are capable of, all the time, of every faculty, every mode and means of perception and expression. Our frivolity, licentiousness, perversity, anguish are nothing but signs of this fact—that we can be serious (and therefore surpass the limitation of seriousness) only towards the Transcendent.

...The Christ's dramatic method, "Let this cup pass from me, yet not as I will, but as Thou wilt", corresponding with the ancient Mysteries—a method of self-induced crisis, in which the Here is also Seer and Poet, Oedipus and Sophocles, Achilles and Homer, oracle and history, bringing all cosmic and human connections—all language, to their consummation.

19.XII.44.

Visit to "the blind Sadhu", Sarananda Swami (his guru was called Shankarananda). Tall, grey-bearded, robust, and very well preserved, in spite of winter wearing only a loin-cloth. The strong mouth and teeth one so often sees in the genial sadhu-type, good nose with long sensitive nostrils, eyes widely placed, forehead rounded in front, rather higher than broad, sensitive hands, strong spontaneous laughter. Air of authority, deep kindness, calm, dignity, illumination.

When his host asked if I wished to meet him alone, I said that I had no question to ask; but now when I was seated with others before him upstairs, people again asked if I really had no question. I replied that the only spiritual matter in my mind was one beyond words. This was translated to the Swami and he asked: "Because you cannot formulate it?" —No: it could be stated in words but I doubt if it could be answered so.

"It could be answered to the same degree in which it could be stated..."

"Is there any one experience that is the highest of all?"

"One I am told is the highest."

"Then if it is not permanent, is one not restless without it like a fish out of water and does one not desire it?"

"No, one does not desire it."

I soon had to explain that what I might express to him alone (yet there is no real reason to and it might even not be proper to) cannot be dealt with in general terms, is a matter of specific experience in which I seem to have reached a deadlock. Taking up what I thus vaguely explained, the Swami said that when every resort of heart and intellect has become useless, there is a stage of "pure want" (he uses a few English words, like "*kevala* want", in which the whole being is absorbed—something beyond the "personal" mind and heart. This is a stage beyond all effort (cp. SKM) in which One is borne like a log upon the river. Only two things are necessary then: not to despair, and not to suppose that this want applies to the future instead of to the present.

It was time for the Swami to leave for Calcutta. People garlanded him, touched his feet. He was brought fruit (I saw only guavas), asked where I was, came and gave me an orange (of the same kind I offered him yesterday). In the situation produced by the conversation, I was moved and had difficulty not to weep; in gratitude for his kindness touched his feet; he murmured, would have prevented me; placed his palm upon the centre of my chest; for a minute or two we stood grasping each other's arms, I would almost have embraced him.

Again, after two or three days, I notice it: this state of subtle, exposed emotion, in which all is paradox and deadlock, is, in its physical effects, almost exactly like acute love sickness. It affects the nerves to some extent, but rather by reflection, the solar plexus, and especially "the rhythmic system"—heart and lungs. There is an extreme exposed tenderness; thought is intense, rapid, extravagant, exhausting; tendency to feverishness, no appetite. And it could easily symbolise itself in the most subtle and hopeless erotic longing—it seems indeed the real meaning of all longing. It is the motive of our imaginative completion of the unnameable, sweet, cruel charm and wonder of the beloved. Is there, with corresponding depth and subtlety, a perversity, obstinate scrupulousness, here like that which made me suffer so with K. at Courtalam ?

25.XII.44.

The tidiness of my room is in a way a subtle, 'subconscious' defence, anonymity, neutrality: no one enters it, practically, who is not blind, insensitive, mediocre or barbarous: if my own rhythm and interests leave their natural traces in it, they are directly trampled by the gross, idle, frivolous hoofs of morons; but when every book and paper, every smallest object, is returned immediately after use to a formal 'place', if they are disturbed by animal curiosity it is only as if they were objects in a museum, in a sterile laboratory. But the true way is to keep the room closed and have two chairs on the verandah for visitors, then to live with one's own unrestricted rhythms—the only *organic* economy.

A room, if you have one at all, should be the true shape of your solitude.

Reading Cocteau again with the right freshness in spite of sickness and fatigue—helped by fresh recognition of emotional and intellectual isolation. "Man does not live by read alone": imaginative food is indispensable. Otherwise one dries up, becomes a skeleton, a ghost. All energy, and the clear and strong organisation of energy—a certainty clearer than all fate, the superior fate of Herakles, Ulysees, Cuchulain, is through imagination —psychic opening and influx. Not to put this first, where (as one's life) it is experienced, is to descend into the cold dust of a meaningless tomb. O, the endless fatigue of courtesy in which one is kind to the dead, to ghosts, to the impotent, to insects—false, poisonous, treacherous 'saintliness'. Indeed the virtue of poetry is intense, real virtue.

26–7.XII.44.

At first, outwardly linked with deep state of sorrow—
SKM
Fauré's "Diane, Seléné"
Renée's announcement of approaching marriage...

But this marginal short-circuiting of the real sorrow only makes matters worse—brings even physical energy to hopeless, sickening inconclusiveness. Though by itself, indeed, it would only circuit round a wider and more complicated arena: it was acute awareness of my inward crisis which so long refused every outward circle.

The only truthfulness, humility and purity in this sorrow is to surrender the will to the primacy of Joy which I have always affirmed. After first hearing Duparc's exquisite songs—and Fauré's—Debussy too, in a way—all the music of that peculiar and special epoch, I told Alain and Raymond that I had never directly realised before that erotic emotion may express subtle and hopeless sorrow, had always myself looked upon it, in itself, as an impulse of pure joy and delight. Yet now indeed I see how subtle and perfect an emotional wilderness cries out and shudders in this way—with what desperate economy like that of the pains of hell. Looking last night at the Trivandrum photos of myself, taken in 1941 and 1943, I saw for the first time the fastidious fineness and tenderness of the lips, their extreme quick sensitive expressiveness and exposedness—yet the straight line of truthfulness between them, the uncompromising spirit and intellect in eyes and brow above! What a crucifixion is this body! What a superabundance of life it defines, must resurrect into!

The only solution for the deepest as well as the most superficial difficulties—the only possible consistency—is ardent and sustained surrender of the will to what is felt truest, most beautiful, most real.

It is useless to return again and again to this recognition, one's life spiritually and in all other ways in the meantime left in disorder, complication, profitless anguish and delay.

This moment must be made real by what follows it. Only a crucial change, held in spite of every initial confusion, obstruction and slipperiness, can set up a new all-resolving, illuminating rhythm.

The truth of this moment can be protected and sustained only by recollection. Do not monks, sufis, sadhakas spend the first and greater part of their day in such ardent recollection, arranging all to help it? Yet a mind open to the fact that spirituality is not necessarily religious nevertheless has no formal physical or psychic basis of support. I begin from the ebb of light and strength.

30.XII.44.

I dream that Rimbaud is one of the few poets who have set one of their own poems, like a pool of ultramarine, expressing precisely through music his own feeling and intention in it.

The inexplicable strangeness of one's life. One must become conscious of one's life in as many ways as possible—to complete and dissolve that 'objectivity' by consciousness.

30.XII.44.

Sanjiva Rao affirms what the Principal Rama Rao has also told me: it is certainly literally meant that I need not take classes or do any kind of work here. "You are too valuable a person to help boys to pass examinations". There cannot possibly be an obligation because the College provides the minimum needs that everyone here has a right to. He invited me here because he thought the place would benefit by my presence if I go on with my own work. He also explained the difficulties here and that he cannot interfere in domestic or economic arrangements. After earning a good deal as Principal in a big college in Madras he retired on a small pension and does his work at Rajghat with some difficulty, meeting his own travel and expenses, getting an overcoat from his brother, but no new clothes for years etc.

He says that he did all the difficult work setting up the place because Krishnamurti *speaking as the Christ* begged him to and promised to "ask the *devas* to make the place nice for us"—it was "wild" and there had been hunting in the woods. Though later, when this was referred to, Krishnamurti brushed it aside and said, Never mind that, only try to understand what I say now. He had always taken the attitude that the devas, the angels and the fairies do exist, but the physical world is no less wonderful.

Nevertheless, I told him I shall still see what can be done with some of the more eligible boys to deal fundamentally with Language.

1.XII.44.

Evening walk along the ghats and through the narrow lanes. How strange and powerful, Benares. Must I not paint, dance, sing, write poems of a new vividness, intensity, perversity? to express this singular, this subtly pungent and deep-rooted world. O sombre, brilliant wine, musky, suavely maddening, matured through how many thousands of years.

And how all creativity—even all strangeness! deeply and subtly stirs the Eros! O Lalita! And if to You I turn this sweetness, ardour and pain, how terrible indeed, how dangerous, Your simple, so omniscient charm! At one smile of Yours, so long ago, the sea and all the stars still shudder—unable to cast out the terrible sweet poison!

(Lalita is an affectionate name of Krishna in the hymns of devotional poets.)

Hard is devotion—
Like a pit of fire,
A deadly whirlpool:
Who can enter it?
Hard like a cup of poison,
Like a sharpened sword
That no-one can endure:
How can the soul
Not feel despair?
Hard is devotion,
So has Jani proved it;
Yet through devotion and
The Company of saints
We gain the one true end.

Jana Bai, Marathi, 14th century or earlier—a foundling adopted by the poet Namdev. Slightly re-worded by LT from *Poems by Indian Women*, OUP. 1923.

Additional Commentary

Vedanta: Jnana Yoga

Need for anchorage in some kind of training led Thompson to spend most of the first decade of his life in India involved in the austere routine of ashram life under Sri Ramana Maharshi and the jnani, Sri Krishna Menon. Both were exponents of jnana, the yoga of the mind, and both were highly proficient modern representatives of Advaita Vedanta—'unified awareness'—an elaboration by Shankara of the teachings first propounded in the ancient classical texts known as the *Upanishads*. The first injunction, and sole focus, of this difficult path is *Atmanam viddhi*: 'Know the Self'. The subtle paradoxes and sheer force of rigorous exposition in Vedanta are of immeasurable importance to the whole of Indian spirituality, and still very much a living influence on the outlook of the modern Indian.

While millions now see themselves as committed to modern scientific and technological development, nevertheless this constellation of Upanishadic ideas, Vedantin gnosis and their poetic synthesis in the Bhagavad Gita, remain at the very root of all Indian attitudes toward the nature of reality. Though many Indians nowadays might be reluctant to admit it openly, inquiry into the nature of the Self still retains its prestige as the final option in a full life, the ultimate responsibility without which an individual's existence is somehow incomplete, abbreviated. Thus, classical Indian thought holds that the Self, or Atman, or consciousness, subsists beneath all levels of awareness, awake or asleep. The crux of the matter is contained in the simple answer of the Upanishads to the question 'Who am I?': 'I am That'—*Tat Tvam Asi.*

Central to any such inquiry is the necessity to penetrate the veil of the ceaselessly self-deluding ego to clear perception of the individual quintessence, the Atman, and to final realisation that the Self is identical with the All, the Divine Ground, or Brahman. Vedanta focuses on the paradoxical interplay between the whirling diversity of the atomistic ego and the eternal existence of this imperishable nucleus prior to individuality.

However, Thompson's own preference was to attend closely to the simpler teachings of Krishna in the great spiritual poem—bedrock of Hinduism, the *Bhagavad Gita*. Like Vedanta, the *Bhagavad Gita* is a flower of the exultant, world-affirming spirit of the Upanishads. But Vedanta, with its emphasis on a self-annihilating conception of the Atman as the essentially passive, aloof spectator of the life-process, was too life-denying in its tone for a temperament like Thompson's. Admire it though he did as in its own way prefect, he could not respond to the emphasis on renunciation and retreat from the world which runs through Vedanta.

From the point of view of Vedanta, the Christian notion of God as ordinarily understood is the first stumbling-block for the Western seeker. This presented no problem for Thompson; nevertheless it is important for those who wish to understand the Indian perspective on this matter to take it into account. The classical view of Advaita Vedanta is well summarised by Heinrich Zimmer: 'It is...merely to the unenlightened mind that God appears to be real, endowed with such attributes as omniscience, omnipotence, and universal rule, and disposed to the attitudes of benignity and wrath. The pious preoccupations centering around God, the rites of the various religious communities, and the cogitations of their theologians belong to and support an atmosphere of the most subtle and respectable kind of self-deceit. They have, of course, their priceless value as preliminary means. They supply a kind of ladder by which the utterly selfish individual may climb from the dim dungeon of his own ego.' (*Philosophies of India*, New York, 1951, p. 427)

As is well known, all Indian traditions posit a state of enlightenment variously called *nirvana*, *moksha*, *mukti*, *turiya*, *samadhi*, where the individual attains final liberation from the veil of ignorance. It is customary to speak of this ultimate attainable goal as *realisation*. Thompson always objected strongly to any suggestion from others that his goal was 'realisation'. '*Samadhi*, ecstasy, etc. is a technical fact like others, meaningless in itself. Whoever seeks *this* is superficial, superstitious, evasive or self-indulgent.' 'Realisation cannot be an experience in the illusion. Any *state* is defined by the illusion and can never be eternal. *Nirvikalpa samadhi* is consciousness complete as a state of balance beyond expression, it is defined by the terms of the balance and otherwise irrelevant.' He also noted a remark of Ramana Maharshi concerning the tendency of neophytes to attach too much importance to states of rapture: 'Trance and unconsciousness are only for the mind and they do not affect the Self.' True, Thompson's teachers would explain that 'realisation' is a necessary invention of the imagination, but as a poet who believed in the power of the Word to incarnate Truth, such double-think, however well-intentioned, was a source of aggravation, an unendurable twist to the screw of paradox.

In the tradition of the Vedanta school, the texts and teachings of the individual's own guru, the *shastras* (sacred texts) and the Vedanta texts, prepare the novice by reiterative refutation of erroneous views. By scrupulous study of texts—reading them again and again, even memorising them —those new to the path gradually become steeped in the imagery and mode of awareness attained at higher levels by adepts, preceptors, masters. By emulation, concentration, discussion, meditation, and above all, through love of the guru, the ego becomes less insistent and the disciple begins to listen to the silence of the Self. In his own way, Thompson submitted to such a course, and crucial to this, indeed what made it bearable, was the spiritual grace and realisation 'at the Heart' of the two very remarkable men, the Maharshi and the Jnani, for both of whom Thompson felt the deepest reverence. These two men had attained, in Thompson's view, a pure state of *sahaja*, perfect synthesis of *advaita jnana* and the Presence, Head and Heart. This synthesis is the predominant theme which runs through all Thompson's poetry.

Equivalent antitheses are Word and Void, another level at which fundamental duality is played out. A reluctant dialectician, in so far as Thompson mistrusts philosophy, he is constantly engaged in resolving pairs of opposites, whether of Truthfulness and Hypocrisy, Absence and Presence, Innocence and Perversity. In his poetry, the sovereign pair of symbols is Sun and Moon; noticeable towards the end of his residence in South India is a conscious recognition of the need to give greater attention to the Moon-aspect of his inner nature, to come to grips with the darker side of himself and the world, reach 'exhaustion' of perversity and achieve integration of the non-human in what he envisaged as a trans-humanistic integrity.

Thompson's character, which veered from predominantly austere, sober studiousness to one that was passionate, reckless, lyrical, was both *vedantin* and *sahajin*. For Vedanta, the presiding deity is the dark god Shiva, austere, yogic, ascetic; for Sahaja, the presiding deity is the wayward, erotic, lilaic Krishna, playful deity who, like Orpheus, enchants the world with music. 'I am not naturally "an advaitin"', Thompson writes, 'in the usual sense, for I am not, in my essence, it seems, really "thinker" at all, but (according to this mode of discourse) rather poet, and my natural method and outlook is no doubt completely in the broadest possible sense yogic rather than jnanic—or it is only my *daimon* that is yogic. What I am really trying to say (as poet) refers to a level beyond yoga and jnana as sadhanas.'

This does not prevent the imagery of Thompson's verse from being, almost invariably, yogic; its symbolism and images drawn from the concrete, sensuous world, is meant to be understood as referring to the psychic landscape rather than to Nature. Though yogic, it does not fit the schema and scenarios of conventional sadhana. The poet seeks to make his life one that is consistently participative activity, a vortex of intense feeling, devoid of compulsive necessity, of conformism—a life of non-attachment. He wants to approach as closely as possible the ideal of *lila*: the passionate masquerade of sacred play—a mercurial plasticity, an elan and dance of endlessly buoyant celebration.

THE JNANI—SRI KRISHNA MENON

From time to time, Thompson used to stay at the comfortable house of his friend, S.N. Ure, tutor to the son of the Maharaja of Travancore. One of the advantages of this arrangement was that Ure possessed a piano and Thompson liked to practice on it; he stored his sheet-music here. In 1936 he heard through Ure of Sri Krishna Menon, a remarkable Nambudri Brahmin *jnani* who had done a full service in the Maharaja's police force for twenty-five years, attaining the rank of deputy superintendent before retiring to spend all his time practising his *sadhana*. In the latter part of his service he went through a profound and radical spiritual development that completely transformed him, and he eventually began to accept disciples for initiation and instruction after attaining realization. Thompson visited him at Quilon, north of Trivandrum, and was deeply impressed. In those days, the Jnani had few disciples. Subsequently, he became famous and after the death of the incomparable Ramana Maharshi was widely regarded as the most important guru in South India, attracting a great many disciples, many of them foreigners.

Ramana Maharshi was a man of few words and for long periods remained absorbed in silence. On the other hand, the *Jnani* was a talker; moreover he spoke English fluently. These were important considerations for the loquacious Thompson.

Photographs of the Jnani show him in a rather stern light, brooding, somewhat forbidding, even arrogant and authoritarian, with a piercingly steady gaze, keen intelligence and strength of character. However, from Thompson's account, there was a much less intimidating aspect to his character, charm of manner and gracious smile. Certainly, he could unbend in the privacy of his long talks with Thompson in the years before the ashram became a busy and crowded place; at such times he revealed a richly emotional side which won Thompson's heart.

One feature of the Jnani's career is particularly revealing: he was practising his *sadhana* while concurrently fulfilling his duties as a senior police officer; this became so intense that he went through his duties in a kind of trance. There was no outward indication of this—he followed a strict routine and maintained his function as a police officer with full competence while in a state of total detachment, almost a state of *samadhi*, walking to and from work at the high court without regard for oncoming traffic and pedestrians in the bustling thoroughfare of Trivandrum. It is a striking feature of the Indian spiritual life that the individual appears to manage without any severe signs of strain to function on two distinct planes of awareness between which there is no connection at all, untroubled by what to an occidental would be contradictory modes. In the West, we would probably conclude that an individual who behaved thus did not have his heart in his work and that its quality would suffer accordingly. I believe this aspect of the Jnani's formative years when he was preparing to take early retirement in order to practise his *sadhana* full-time, may have been a significant factor in the establishment of mutual misunderstanding between the two men, at least at a very basic level of difference in temperament. For Thompson, the poet, life was indivisible (whatever Yeats says of Phase 17), his work inseparable from his spiritual life—one more reason why he could not conceive the idea of demarcating between *sadhana* and creative activity, still less draw a distinction between the 'spiritual' and the 'worldly'. 'We all live in the world', he would say with a shrug. This division of consciousness in the *Jnani*'s spiritual development may relate to an observation by the Jnani's personal physician, a yogin of keen insight, to the effect that the Jnani might have understood Thompson's spiritual situation and level of attainment but not his nature. I also think this apparent split between a trance-like superconsciousness and ordinary perception in the Jnani while still in the police force may relate to his admission of one standard for his disciples and another for Thompson.

It was Thompson (as a non-beneficiary) who introduced a millionaire Englishman to the Jnani. As an ardent devotee he placed considerable sums at the disposal of the ashram for its development and expansion into a place with an international focus. I regard this highly advantageous introduction of a wealthy patron as a factor to take into account when anyone considers the matter of Thompson's banishment from the Jnani's establishment, particularly since it was the clique associated with this benefactor who connived at Thompson's dismissal. Some time after Thompson departed, a financial dispute, which did not involve the Jnani, between the benefactor and ashram personnel erupted on such a scale of bitterness that the Prime Minister, Pandit Jawaharlal Nehru, felt called upon to intervene. Thompson, of course, had long since left, and had never been entangled in any financial complications whatsoever.

Before we look at the relationship between the two men more closely, it is first necessary to grasp what is meant by the much-abused word, *guru*. In recent years, due to vulgarisation of the guru's role in the Western world, the term has been brought into general usage and, like the misspelled term *pundit*, has acquired pejorative connotations, to the effect that it can mean an authoritarian teacher of dubious credentials with whom the credulous are infatuated. In its pristine original meaning 'guru' is simply a teacher or master. But in a more technical sense, upon the relationship between guru and disciple—the guru-shishya relationship—the entire structure for imparting knowledge in traditional Indian civilisation has, for millennia, solidly rested.

To maintain the highest standards of learning in a culture where traditionally transmission by word of mouth has absolute priority and enjoys the highest prestige, exceptionally able and patient teachers are a prime necessity. Through this method, continuity in the transmission of oral tradition has been ensured over immense spans of time. Rote-learning, aided by the chant, is the root of such training techniques. This impersonal formality is mitigated by close contact between master and pupil, often for many years. The guru would take on no more than five or ten pupils, who often lived under his own roof and were considered members of the family, who shared duties of the household (if the guru was still a householder and had not renounced his family to take the vows of the *sannyasin*) and imbibed as much from intuitional learning and observation as from the lengthy course of formal instruction. These households of learning, or forest hermitages in the case of the guru-renouncer, were the original Indian ashrams.

The *guru-shishya-parampara*—continuity of tradition through master to disciple—was something altogether more demanding than most Western systems of instruction, such as apprenticeship and university, but not far removed from that which existed in medieval monasteries. The guru-shishya relationship is of an initiatory character. Whatever the branch of learning or craft, it is sealed at the outset with a ceremony of initiation—*diksha*. Initiation is a 'death to the old', a shedding of the past and the formation of a 'new man'. Hence the significance of the name-giving which customarily accompanies all monastic induction.

The pupil must have *vinaya*, humility: this means the complete surrender of the individuality on the part of the pupil to his guru, and he must accept without demur whatever he is told. The system ensures purity of mind and body, humility, a sense of service, a devotional attitude of reverence for the supra-individual master and, ideally, freedom from economic worries for the pupil. It also protects the pupil from loneliness and, in the outside world (where the institution used to be universally respected) provides a high degree of security. The sovereign integrity of the *parampara* is absolute. Because the pupil develops *vinaya* tempered with a feeling of love and worship for his master, his vanity and pretension are gradually worn away. Initiation is always into an ordered system, deeper and wider than the mere subjective restrictions of the individual, his idiosyncrasies and ill-judged initiatives. The system is seen as a joint enterprise of the gods and the ancestors, and hence participates in being. It is a model of perfection, a frame of reference based on centuries of experience, a centralisation that tolerates coexistence with a diversity of similar institutions. The *parampara* is woven of and into the social fabric. In other words, the more the pupil participates in this system, the more does he enter into the *real* and the less likely is he to be diverted into self-deluding, alienated, or isolated egoistic actions which, having no model, are arbitrary, wayward, without sanctuary.

The uniquely specific individual bond between the *guru* and each *shishya* is of such impenetrable subtlety that, it is said, even to the outside scrutiny of a perfected yogin it remains impenetrable. In one sense it is a totally impersonal relationship, or rather it is supra-personal. In another sense it would be fair to say that, in India, it is the deepest, closest, most intimately personal relationship which an individual can establish. Without love and devotion not even the most rigorously austere and analytical *jnana* can progress. Little wonder that there is a saying: 'gurus there are in hundreds: the real disciple is one in a million.

Thompson's attitude towards the role of guru is ambivalent, as indeed it remains for most Indians too. To begin with he was attracted by the course of the Buddha's formative years prior to attainment of Nirvana. As he bluntly put it: 'Gautama—no guru; he was able for himself to say "I do not know" without working out the superstition of knowledge at the feet of a teacher.' An enormous amount of time was devoted to discussion of the matter in the Jnani's ashram. Early in their relationship, Thompson woke one night around two in the morning and wrote: 'The guru provides a short-range focus onto the Divine, something within our constant capacity. Next (and the two things are inseparable) he makes possible the full concretisation of our relations with the Divine, he gives them immediately their full all-or-nothing Realism and Practicality at all levels of our being. Our relation with him immediately transcendentalises our life as it is, interprets it entirely as our spiritual path and destiny.'

His chief stumbling-block was the act of surrender to the will of the guru—that preeminently un-Western but crucial gesture. 'The pure soul can accept nothing', he wrote some time later, 'until it has acknowledged God...Without this first and last simplicity the greatest richness or subtlety of the nature becomes poisonous, the greatest simplicity Terror or Anguish. Till at last there is either disintegration, or the saturation in which one sees that the poison was never anything but refusal of one's purity. And then one may wake from the tortuous, exasperating and fragmentary dream to find in complete light all smiling, self-determined, timeless, tangible.'

By 1942, the year of Thompson's greatest closeness to the Jnani and perhaps spiritually one of the richest in his life, there was nonetheless a perceptible tension in the relationship. So marked was Thompson's progress that he was regarded as the most advanced pupil in the ashram; but by the same token, the Jnani exerted the greater pressure on him to follow a strict path of instruction, including a general outlook, conduct—'path' would be the appropriate word—of *bhakti* (devotion). But Thompson did not consider himself a *bhakta*, and wrote in his journal 'From the point of view of *advaita* or *yoga*, certainly, the guru is real only so far as he is inwardly one with us, our own real essence or resource. There seems to be no absolute reason why a man whose way is not that of *bhakti* in other respects should be a *bhakta* only in relation with the guru: if the guru is not one with a man's way, the very force and light of that way, he is not a guru but merely a superstition. In the guru we recognise more immediately than elsewhere our own Self or our own deepest spiritual will: the guru is real to us only if we have found him where he is established within ourselves. Only so can he lead beyond *avidya* (spiritual ignorance).'

In his usual direct way, Thompson wrote to the Jnani about the mounting tension between them:

> 'As a conception, a dogma, a *considered* possibility, a *proposed* means, or something separately sought the guru can only be a superstition.
> What then is my attitude to those who seem to me realised men and why am I not indifferent to them? Of course one feels love and respect for, and delight in, anyone or thing that for one's consciousness is a convincing expression of the Fullness one would realise.
> But otherwise I question men who appear realised in order to find out why I question them. —Because they can by definition offer the spiritual *resistance* that one can nowhere else find.'

Apart from this resistance—which the Jnani repeatedly shrugged off as Thompson's own way of dealing with him and not in any way reprehensible—relations between them were often extremely warm. On a number of occasions, the Jnani was so carried away by their private talks that he would fall into an exalted state, swoon, or *bhava* altogether different from his behaviour in public. It seems that Thompson's reckless intensity in discussion elicited a like response. At such moments the Jnani reiterated with strong conviction and emphasis that while no formal initiation had been given, a bond had been established between them that nothing could break. But he was equally emphatic that, for Thompson, there was no necessity for a formalized *guru-shishya* tie, and no *sadhana* need be prescribed. For example, these private talks were conducted at a level which exceeded the normal terms of the Jnani's public discourse and went 'beyond *advaita*', as he put it, in response to Thompson's free-flowing 'lila' style. 'The jnani says that he entirely agrees with the "beyond *advaita*" view that the *guru-shishya* relationship can be given meaning only in the sphere of *Lila*. This is the real *advaita* which he has always meant. "No guru necessary", at the advaitic level was not at all a concession, but said from the bottom of his heart.'

It is perfectly clear from Thompson's obviously meticulous care in transcribing his talks with the Jnani (the transcriptions he made of public discourse were circulated in the ashram with the full approval of the Jnani) that, long before any friction developed between them, the Jnani was giving instruction to him which was not for the ears of other disciples. 'This is true for you and nobody else', he said. This was not merely the guru's customary acknowledgement of the uniqueness of each and every disciple, but that his teaching, in Thompson's case, did not fall within the strict terms of Advaita Vedanta, to which he otherwise adhered closely. Had he not seen the matter this way, the Jnani would, no doubt, have formalised the relationship, initiated Thompson and become his guru. Discussion between the two men was complex enough as it was without this split in levels, since each stuck to his own terminology and much time was spent in elucidation of each other's point of view in language which by no means coincided. In his published writings and statements, the Jnani is precise when using Sanskrit terminology, but his English is full of vague generalisations and metaphors which Thompson found confusing. It is a fact that as long as Thompson remained with the Jnani these confusions of language were tidied up prior to publication, and in this respect his constructive role was recognised by all.

If nothing else, the record of this relationship in Thompson's journal is fascinating for the skill with which he puts into words the delicate balancing act of the *guru-shishya* interplay, its fundamentally paradoxical nature. And as Thompson says, 'Paradox: the positive aspect of duality. Masters address themselves to those who are in the ordinary sense unworthy, because for them there is no ordinary sense and because they do not need to address themselves. Their innocence and their command of sincerity—the perfection of their hypocrisy—is that they do not know this latter fact, or if they do (that is, if they *know* at all) it is a laughter.'

In the ordinary course, public exposition of Vedanta is conducted in a detached and impersonal style; the Jnani's discourse was no exception.

But the sheer lilaic emotionality of the private talks between himself and Thompson was another matter altogether, with their swoons, embraces and tempestuously dramatic endings in the heat of soaring delight. Thompson's fellow disciples would suggest that he was so carried away by all this that he was committing the cardinal error of the personality cult. But he was adamant that he avoided misperception of the Jnani, discriminating carefully between adulation of a mere individual and reverent impersonality towards the supra-individual. 'If we are influenced by individualities (i.e. the personality of the guru) in our recognition of the Truth, it is still not recognition of the Truth, it can at best be only provisional. Then only if the individual concerned (i.e. the man only) is one with the Truth (which he cannot be as individual) can such provisionality not be obstruction. And then our belief in what he says or willingness to allow it must, by the irreversible relation it sets up with him, lead to the Truth as quickly as possible for us. But if all this is seen from the start, this relation becomes the putting aside of his individuality, the individuality called the guru: the apparent individual in question becomes, as such, one with the anguish, the paradox, of our own individuality: we oppose him in opposing ourselves, for in our essence, Truth, we are one with him.' The Jnani always insisted 'I am one with Thompson'.

Moreover, the Jnani also recognised that Thompson's *resistance* was positive and necessary. The oppositional Western approach had met its match. Thompson claimed that the only man he ever knew who could meet his resistance perfectly was the Jnani. The fierce intensity with which he engaged the Jnani in public discussion was deeply shocking to the ashram inmates, accustomed as they were to treat their guru with traditional reverence. Tensions within the circle also exacerbated the friction between the two men. Rajeshwar Dayal, who visited the ashram in those days—he was later appointed U.N. Secretary General's Representative in Africa—says that the conflict was primarily the result of Thompson's inability to surrender gracefully to the will of the Jnani. Had he done so, from Thompson's own point of view this would have been less than perfect hypocrisy; it would also mean that he would lose the very resistance he most ardently sought. Whatever the ultimate cause of the rupture which came with suddenness in 1943, the most charitable interpretation we can put upon the Jnani's startlingly abrupt manner of terminating the relationship was that the time had come for Thompson to fend for himself as he had always insisted. This was to be the most crucial moment of all in his life and the mode in which he faced the challenge would remain ever in his mind until his death.

Later he would write the poem, *One Head*—on the following page—in which he tried to put into words the 'anguish' of his paradox, and its opening line might be said to constitute his motto:

One Head

Let me with words come close,
Closer than blood and bone,
To present self-existence—
Death of words
Because the Word Itself—
No word
Because with none to hear,
Because with nought to say.

The silence of this Word
Is all that's disexplained,
Is all that only words
Can and can not explain.
Words measure none
But their own void:
They have no other nothing,
None but word-things;
And this too is word-thing.

Do not mistake me if you hear;
Do not mistake me if you say I speak.
I say you hear
Because I do not speak;
You say I speak
Because I do not hear.
Hearing hears only speech,
Speech speaks to hearing;
Ear listens to no ear,
Tongue speaks no tongue:
Tongue seeking tongue
In dumb despair
Cannot beget the Word;
The phone's ear at my ear
Cables the tongue-lie back.

Undo the coiled
Concupiscence,
This world-equator,
Knot of ignorance:
Hear your own ear,
Speak your own tongue;
Speak not because you hear,
Hear not because you speak:
One head is all.

It was the Jnani who had the last word. Indeed, he wrote on this matter of parting company with Thompson, including the following to Ella Maillart, written six months after Thompson's death:

> 'As regards Thompson's Torment and your depression etc., I have only to repeat what I have often told you. Understanding Truth and clinging to it helps one to establish one's Real Centre. Until that is accomplished misery will not cease as the false identification with body and mind is there. It is this false identification that is the root of all misery. It must therefore be the sadhaka's endeavour always to put emphasis upon the Real I-principle, and rise above this false identification. It is this subjective transformation, so to say, that cuts at the root of all misery. The objective world can well be there. It does not do any harm provided it is seen in the right perspective as taught by the Guru. To seek to solve the problem in the objective world itself can never be crowned with success. Only by your concession can it have a reality. Thompson has been fighting against this position all through his life. Hence his Torment. When the Truth that had gone deep into him in spite of himself began to dawn, his Torment ceased and the rebellious mind dissolved...

The last observation refers to a vision in which the Jnani saw Thompson's posthumous resolution of his problems, so that he would not need to be born again in any further incarnations.

At a meeting with the great Bengali sage, Sri Anandamayi, some years after Thompson had parted from the Jnani, he heard her speak to someone else about the problem of surrender, using the Yeats metaphor of the bursting pod:

> Question: God has given us the sense of 'I'. He will remove it again. What need is there for self-surrender?
>
> Answer: Why do you ask? Just keep still and do nothing!

Question: How can I possibly keep still?
Answer: This is why self-surrender is necessary!

A heated discussion then ensued, one argument following another, without its leading to any feasible solution; someone who was getting tired of this endless controversy said, 'there is a saying that when a lemon is squeezed too much it becomes bitter. To which Sri Anandamayi replied:

> 'When a fire is raked it burns brighter. Similarly, by discussing philosophy one's interest in these subjects grows. Of course, it is also true that a lemon becomes bitter if squeezed too much. But when an earnest seeker discusses with a sincere desire to find Truth, his eyes will be opened. Some people's confusion is cleared up by reasoning, while others become only more perplexed by discussion. Everyone has his own way. When one's problems are made more acute one feels disturbed and thereby one's Search will be intensified. Before thread can be spun and woven into cloth the pod in which the cotton was enclosed has first to burst open and be entirely destroyed. To prepare oneself really means to uproot completely the sense of 'I'.'

Thompson was not afraid to admit his faults. Thus he would say that to concede when there is nothing to concede only adds a further twist to the spiral of perversity which refuses to concede! He expressed his feelings in a poem he wrote for the Jnani after their parting and to whom it is dedicated. This is one of the only two poems that he published during his lifetime:

Bitterness All

Bitterness all, and yet all bitterness
Is but our zeal, our prowess, our desert
For the unceasing nectar of the heart.
It is not pride, then, that will not confess,
Play out and profit by, not even observe,
That all our life is tragic innocence,
But counters pain with its own violence:
It is not pride and not despair, but love.

Resistance and Receptivity

It is often said that, at least in the West, art is born of conflict and that creative thought is born of failure. I once had a head-on conflict with Jiddu

Krishnamurti in a staff meeting at Rajghat School, Benares, where I countered his (as I thought) sentimental notion that art can only be created when the mind is serene and disinterested, by stating this contrary, albeit typically Western way, of creativity. In one of his aphorisms, Thompson writes: 'It was Goethe who said that his disquiet is the best of the man.' No doubt this is true in Thompson's case, but by no means rules out his very evident capacity for joyous radiance. His suffering, as he records it, is real enough —Blanca Schlamn confirmed that for me convincingly—but we must also take him at his word when he writes:

> '...happiness means nothing to me, so nothing makes me really unhappy, for my 'anguish' is really the substance of pure joy and all below is shadow; in the world I am a ghost—whom it seems no responsibility can bind; all ordinary logic, even of spiritual ambition, is dust to me.'

In a letter to Earl Brewster he also says he is only 'interested in *real* Reality, and this passion...will endure any hell rather than accept or delude itself with any less than Absolute Enjoyment, Oneness.' *This* is the best of the man. And in a letter to the Jnani he sounds a distinctively modern note when he says he 'questions men who appear realised in order *to find out why I question them*, because they can by definition offer the spiritual *resistance* that one can nowhere else find'. By the same token, though he has no need to tell this to the Jnani, it follows that the man who *appears* realised will respond with equanimity to the resistance of a man like Thompson, as revealed by the vehemence of his investigative questioning. Resistance of this order is *yogic*, but it also corresponds to the modern Western determination to be unillusioned. Resistance is an intrinsic feature of perfectibility and hence a threat only to the immature and the sentimental. Coupled with critical scrutiny, it is the most distinctive tool in Thompson's kit and gives his work its cutting edge. He uses it daily, applies it to each and every experience. He deploys resistance in his journal, in his scrutiny of 'anyone or thing that for one's consciousness is a convincing expression of the Fullness one would realise'. But this yogic poet, having tested the evidence through resistance—but only then—'feels love and respect for, and delight in' that Fullness. His tension is neither with the supra-individual he names Jnani nor with a particular Brahmin called Atmananda, but with his own ego. His journal is a running commentary on the struggle between the egoic Jacob and the non-egoic doppelganger Angel.

Thompson's fiercely spiritual intellect in relation to the Jnani is the opposite side to the same coin: heads resistance—tails receptivity. Resistance saves him from falling into the trap of gullible ego-centred rapture—that sentimentality so prevalent among the spiritually immature. He dismisses his *nirvikalpa-samadhi* as inconclusive. Exactly right! 'Everything is yet to be done'. But so also does he continue to exercise resistance when he experiences samadhi in dream and hence fails to respond at that moment to the dreamed Jnani's kiss. It is innate poetic integrity. Without it—a little detached, a little too inclined, perhaps, to observe rather than participate —we would never have his journal. Bearing in mind that it is written in tension with the ego, 'it represents precisely what is not well-organised...lapses and vacillations from ...the perfect economy, sensual, mental, active with its own satisfaction.' He sees his journal as a means to 'discourage relapsings and build up a habit and fortification against them.' 'A journal can be free of egoism or sentimentality only if it *tests* and extricates the Potential, the new, the unknown.'

It obviously takes a mature person to handle such a task effectively. He was just that by the time he developed his closest rapport with the Jnani, and engaged in his most intense 'hypercriticism' of him in 1942–3. Critical interventions during public meetings of master and pupils was obviously a big risk. It is often thought that the critical spirit is destructive of the creative spirit, but this is simply not true. The painter, Francis Bacon, states in an interview with David Sylvester how 'very often I think probably what makes one artist better than another is that his critical sense is more acute. It may not be that he is more gifted in any way but just that he has a better critical sense'. Thompson's critical sense was the least appreciated and most feared side of his personality, but certainly a crucial aspect of his work which he exercised with great openness, fearlessness and freedom. Since he did not stop being a writer when he stepped into the ashram circle his critical zeal tended to be unstoppable. 'If only', ran the argument, 'he would stop writing and concentrate on dissolution of the ego first!' Apart from the fact that writing was his yoga, his sadhana, had he abandoned it and, at some hypothetical time later on attained perfect egolessness (were such curtailment of his natural metier conducive to any kind of attainment), how then would we obtain this vivid dramatisation against which to measure our own lapses and vacillations, and to build up a habit and fortification against them? Thompson's exhausting detours, his patient concentration on their detail, his love of exactitude and clarity where all was disorder and perplexity— these are *how it really is*. From such truthfulness we distil the Potential.

His close examination of experiences not readily accessible to the rationality we associate with the critical spirit annoyed academics. Frequent attention to paranormal experience, to ineffable mystical states, to spiritual persons whose behaviour borders on lunacy, to the non-material and to the phenomenology of the Transcendent is uncommon in a 'literary' context. But this, of course, begs the vexed question of whether this is indeed a literary context. Does it not rise above that rather dispiriting category, 'alternative culture and occultism'? Until very recently—I would guess not until the great decade of breakthrough in quantum physics prior to World War Two—it has been the overwhelmingly predominant tendency of scientists, of course, to ignore, or actively discount or pooh-pooh non-material phenomena. Admission by the likes of Nils Bohr, Eddington and Whitehead during Thompson's lifetime that the ultimate nature of matter rests upon non-material causes is consonant with Thompson's disinterestedly cool outlook. Where he does diverge is in the area where intuitive wisdom, ancient and modern, fuses direct perception of phenomena with spiritual perfectibility. Nils Bohr put forward the view that in the absence of an observing mind atoms are not properly real, while Wheeler proposes that the Universe attains to self-awareness through mind. Both approaches reflect the cosmological view of ancient Indian intuitive insight. Thompson's researches have something of a 'scientific' temper about them—not in the technical sense of verification by repeatable experiment, but certainly kindred to the dispassionate, even-handed coolness of observation which led Leonardo da Vinci to such an advanced mental outlook several centuries ahead of his time. Scientists and mathematicians can also be poets, as Thompson learned from Parmenides.

The dialogue between the Jnani and Thompson (recorded on 8.IX.41.) is evidence of his stature, keenness of mind and, unexpected as it might seem from what he elsewhere calls the 'provincialism of the guru'—the sophistication of both these men. Any spiritual master would be glad to have so dynamic and poised an interlocutor. Why then did Thompson not make even more substantial progress towards that *Fullness* he so passionately sought? One side of his personality clearly shows that he was inclined to respect genuine authority. Though he had the very qualities which one could imagine capable of 'surrender to the guru's will', he made no move in the direction of wanting the Jnani to become his own guru. The clue may lie in the word 'Fullness': that it was simply a matter of Thompson practising addition while the Jnani demanded subtraction. This Fullness implies a path at loggerheads with the reductive path to Self-Realisation. Here, I think, lies the innate intransigence of the committed poet: the fiery genius who knows wherein lies his true usefulness— to the Kingdom of Heaven on Earth, as he would say with Blake. (It should not be forgotten that one of the key texts for Thompson was the fierce intransigence of Blake's *Marriage of Heaven and Hell*, which sets everything upside down!) He also knows how to work within his limitations—an artist's secret—in order to surmount those limitations. His role is formative, not assimilative (Picasso's 'I do not seek—I find'), he wants to *create* something, which sets him light years apart from the discipular.

He knows perfectly well that this calls for a degree of humility, patience and receptive passivity (in a Rilkean sense of the poet as vehicle). But he also sees that his creativity is not particularly relevant in his immediate environment. The longer he lives the more he directs his communication in an entirely different direction—towards people of his own kind, which has nothing to do with class, nationality, race, but spiritually kindred fellow visionaries and toilers in various creative fields. He belongs in the Resistance—in other words, the truly anarchist fraternity opposed to all kinds of conformity. The signs are unmistakable, for the journals eventually become full of references to the more radical shining lights he heard about. By the end of his life Thompson is as much a practising and professional member of this cosmopolitan vanguard as any of his Western contemporaries, but also in a kindred secretive tradition in the style of Sufis, who to all outward appearances are engaged in conventional employment. His frame of reference radically enlarges beyond his original band of intransigents: Villon, Blake, Rimbaud and joins issue with Chandidas, Mann, Malraux, Jung, Genet, Cocteau, Chaplin, Graves, Giacometti, Coomaraswamy, and to some extent his own generation whose work he reads in *Horizon*, *New Writing* and *La Nouvelle Revue Francaise*. His late and lyrical sympathy with Blake, Chandidas and Baul minstrelsy, his fascination with Chaplin's street wise Jewish perversity in *The Great Dictator*, his delight in the songs of Gracie Fields heard when at Devlali Barracks, and his discovery of drawings by the visionary Cecil Collins, celebrating the Holy Fool—all these show his turning away from orthodox Hindu social hierarchies to the poetic expression of a cooperative, folkloric, community-based society where he might be able to develop that receptive passivity he withheld in his idiosyncratic relationship with the Jnani. He was profoundly true to himself, to his simplicity, by pointing out that since the Jnani himself said there was no need for him to enter the guru-shishya relationship, his 'surrender to the guru' could only be a superstition. One of the most extraordinary features of their actual relationship was the way the Jnani, so carried away by what passed between them in private, 'surrendered' to Thompson's magic charm, fell into a swoon for minutes at a time, or rushed from the room in a gust of emotional rapture, his *mahabhava*.

One has to ask the question no one dared to pose: had the tables been turned? The fact that an advaitin went 'beyond advaita' by his own admission while imparting advice to Thompson is not in itself exceptional—for Indian gurus in our day display a remarkably indoctrinaire outlook. Nevertheless, careful records of these private discussions with the Jnani indicate that the latter shifted ground to the point of confusion. In addition to the needed resistance, a positive and energetic flexibility was what Thompson desperately needed. I am not the first observer of the Indian ashram scene to see signs that as time goes by a guru—the very essence of freedom—can become entrapped within the norms and boundaries of the 'institution' (if so uninstitutional a role assumed by a spiritual master might possibly become). When I suggested that this might indeed be so to Kathleen Raine and Phillip Sherard they reacted as if I had uttered an unpardonable solecism. Thompson had been extremely fortunate to find so magnetic and tolerant a teacher; it is a tragedy that the relatively free and easy days were followed by a very different kind of regime.

Sahaja, Poetry (Chandidas) and Relationships

'Ever keeping present the divine Reality in unbroken continuity of awareness': such is the simplest description of one who seeks *sahaja*.

Although Thompson's (26.VI.44) entry is an awkward comparison of the conflict between the aims of the Head—Absolute *jnana,* and of the Heart —Transcendent *sahaja,* nevertheless it expresses his sense of their realized perceptions; *jnana*—Absolute descent encompasses *sahaja,* and all movement ceases in the ineffable unity of Atman and Brahman; *sahaja*—Transcendental ascent is unceasing for the liberated soul of the devotee (there is no final unity with God), who becomes *like* God in a 'lila' or 'divine play' of Transcendent love.

Although Thompson's Transcendent experience of *nirvikalpa-samadhi* expressed the liberation of the *sahajin*, he resisted its inconclusiveness— 'there was still work to be done.' He also resisted Absolute aim which, acknowledging *sahaja* as an important step in realization—'Knowing the Self' or Atman—demands a further step—'Knowing the Truth'; Absolute *gnana* absorbs Transcendental *sahaja.*

Thompson felt that the absorbing aim in Absolute perception was too all-levelling. It was also misleading, since it depended on the mind, and *bhava* was beyond the mind.

Thompson's greatness lies in the dedicated effort of his great spiritual intellect to steer a 'trans-humanistic', 'trans-discursive' and 'trans-advaitic' course beyond *vedantin* unity and *sahajin* 'lila'. His Integral aim of real mastery, 'seamless Autonomy, Absolute Poetry, Lila'—may be called Innocence, which is entirely disinterested, spontaneous and dynamic.

Before leaving Europe, Thompson read with keen interest a recently published essay on this aspect of *sahaja* by the great scholar Ananda Coomaraswamy. Years ahead of its time, daring in its focus on sexual enlightenment—which seemed impossibly idealistic in the prevailing Western climate of opinion—kindred with the spirit in which D.H. Lawrence at the same date was proposing a more liberal outlook, Coomaraswamy's essay focusses on the ideas and beliefs of the major fifteenth century Bengali poet-saint, Chandidas. This essay was to have a lasting influence on Thompson, and he always carried a typed copy with him wherever he went.

In the poetry of Chandidas the metaphor of 'earthly lovers locked in each other's arms', where "each is both", is made to stand not only for literal fact—a reference to the controversial relationship between the Brahmin Chandidas and the low-caste washerwoman, Rami—but also for the relationship of the soul and God, Atman and Brahman. Coomaraswamy explains how, in the case of Chandidas (as in that of certain other Indian mystics), the experience of profoundest and passionate sexual rapture becomes one with the deepest and most rigorously astringent spirituality, a state of ecstasy which is the perfect analogy of that between the divine Krishna and Radha. 'Here', writes Coomaraswamy, 'illicit love becomes the very type of salvation.'

Only in India's spiritual climate, where he had no ties to kin and caste, could Thompson breathe freely; in such a society, where social convention is so strict, such a love involves a surrender of all that the world values, and sometimes even of life itself. In Bengal, the Sahajiya cult—ritual worship and adoration of young and beautiful girls—'was made the path of spiritual evolution and ultimate emancipation.... The love songs of Chandidas were more like hymns of devotion....' At once, Thompson could see a connection here between Chandidas and Rimbaud. In both, poetry tends to spill over into action. Not only does their poetry provoke new psychological states and liberate people from restrictive custom; 'it also has its mission the invention of a new eroticism and the transformation of passional relationships between men and women. Rimbaud proclaims the need to "reinvent love"... Poetry is the bridge between utopian thought and reality, the moment when the idea becomes incarnate.' (Octavio Paz) In the poetry of Chandidas, Thompson finds a close correspondence with Rimbaud's celebrated call: 'to possess the truth in one *soul* and *one* body'. It is this mystical context of the great Bengali's poetry which Coomaraswamy outlines:

> 'He has explained in his songs what he means by sahaja. The lovers must refuse each-other nothing, yet never fall. Inwardly, he says of the woman, she will sacrifice all for love, but outwardly she will appear indifferent. This secret love must find expression in secret; but she must not yield to desire. She must cast herself freely into the sea of contempt, and yet she must never actually drink of forbidden waters: she must not be shaken by pleasure or pain. Of the man he says that to be a true lover he must be able to make a frog dance in the mouth of a snake, or to bind an elephant with a spider's web. That is to say, that although he plays with the most dangerous passions, he must not be carried away. In this restraint, or rather, in the temper that makes it possible, lies his salvation. "Hear me", says Chandidas, "to attain salvation through the love of woman, make your body like a dry stick—for He that pervades the universe seen of none, can only be found by one who knows the secret of love." It is not surprising if he adds that one such is hardly to be found in a million.'

This passage is the key to understanding Thompson's approach to personal relationships and the extremist passion with which he took issue against those who had no stomach for the logical consequences of such a stance in worldly terms. It should be obvious, also, that if the path of sahaja be undertaken with consistent seriousness its implications for relationship with others are inclusive; that is to say, wider than those merely between the sexes. This line of thought is clearly apparent in everything Thompson wrote in *Mirror to the Light* on human relationships. The principal challenge of his views rests in that one word of Coomarawamy—*restraint.* On restraint in India—an outlook much wider based than just on sexuality —Thompson's rigour as thinker and his ethics are based. It is also an indication of the extent of his debt to the root sensibility of restraint underlying so much of Indian spirituality and the *tendresse* of its human intimacy. Ardent years of yogic training and *tapas* implicit in the attainment of such restraint are not only too obviously beyond the reach of so-called permissive society. A persistent theme in Thompson's journal are his successes and failures at making his body 'like a dry stick'—a modality of *tapas* which most Westerners mistake for asceticism, or even puritanism. This *tapas* has nothing to do with Protestant morality, any more than has Thompson's 'truthfulness'. The concept of sahaja, as put forward by Chandidas and Coomaraswamy, affected his life root and branch, notably in his emphasis on an *impersonal*, disinterested trans-humanism, or 'new humanism', that goes beyond morality. The revolutionary temper of the sahaja proposed by Chandidas—which challenges some of the most basic assumptions of Brahminical spirituality and codes of ethics—is epitomised in the stirring assertion of Chandidas translated by Thompson thus:

> Listen, O brother man,
> Above all else, Man is the Truth:
> Beyond that, there is nothing.

For Thompson, then, the ultimate purpose—the highest good and perfection of our nature—'must be one without desire', as Coomaraswamy phrases it, 'because desire implies a lack....' The entire being of the spiritual freeman 'will be in all he does, and it is this which makes the virtue of his action. This is the innocence of desires'. The incandescent spontaneity of the *sahajin* is indeed a fount of inspiration for Thompson; in his own copy he underlined as personally significant these words of Coomaraswamy:

> 'It is only by pursuing what is already ours by divine right that we go astray and bring upon ourselves and upon others infinite suffering —to those who do not pursue, all things will offer themselves. What we truly need, we need not strive for.'

Once again, here lies the source of Thompson's problems in relation to orthodox Hindu tradition—its insistence on the gradualness of spiritual progress—and why he remained in such deep tension with the laborious step-by-step progress of the *sadhaka*, the daily programme regulated by the clock, the injunctions of a master to progress by degrees, even the very notion of the seeker and the implication that there is anything to seek. Though he could not avoid the inevitability of gradualness, he rejoiced, as poet, in a witticism of Picasso that bespeaks another order of discipline and restraint: 'Je ne cherche pas, je trouve.' The Jnani conceded that Thompson did indeed *find*, but implied that this also conferred on him the privilege to seek. Thompson rebelled, prompting an astute observer to state that whereas the Jnani understood Thompson spiritually, he did not understand his *nature*.

To live the life of a sahajin is to live dangerously; even in India it has always been too scandalous a breaking of powerful tabus to be practised other than in secret. For this reason the poetry of Chandidas has not lost its revolutionary edge so many centuries after his death. Coomaraswany again:

> 'We are now, perhaps, in a better position to know what is meant by Chandidas when he speaks of the difficulties and the meaning of sahaja. What he intends by 'never falling' is a perpetually uncalculat-

> ed life in the present, and the maintenance, not of deliberate control, but of unsought, unshaken serenity in moments of greatest intimacy: he means that under circumstances of temptation none should be felt —not that temptation should be merely overcome. And to achieve this he does not pray to be delivered from temptation, but courts it.'

Thompson would call this a state of Presence, demanding perfect disinterestedness in all dealings with the world in every domain, both inner and outer. But as Coomaraswamy makes plain: 'those who are capable of this spontaneous control will have been already accustomed to willed control under other circumstances: and a control of this kind implies a certain training'. That is to say, in common with a diversity of disciplines, paths and schools, sahaja is inconceivable without the prior discipline and practicality of yoga. In his own curious way, Thompson submitted himself to such training, though in a form that, it seems, the Jnani regarded as inadequate. But Thompson was adamant: 'It is not by non-participation but by non-attachment that we live the spiritual life'.

If we keep in mind Thompson's own, albeit idiosyncratic, yoga, it is possible to understand the few occasions when he did reverence to boys and young men as the *vigraha*—embodiment of the divine in earthly form. He discussed with the Jnani such instances when he attempted to attain true sajaha. The Jnani acknowledged the validity of this approach in Thompson's case, on the grounds that no mere sexual motive lay behind such action.

Part of the difficulty Thompson experienced in Europe had been his inability to find a culturally supportive social environment in which to resolve the conflict between spiritual and physical love. The Jnani, on the other hand, could draw on traditional Hindu ideas, yoga, Tantra and ritual sympathetic to this issue. After listening carefully to Thompson's account of an encounter involving sexual intercourse he told the young English poet that he had achieved reconciliation between the two aspects of love in a state of *mahabhava*, a Sanskrit term for a state of high spiritual rapture—a 'trance of delight'. Thereafter, but only in passing, and casually, Thompson mentions other incidents of a similar nature.

To be specific, we should consider an incident (whether it could be called *mahabhava* is not the issue here) related to me by Ella Maillart, which demonstrates the unforced naturalness with which Thompson could spontaneously make a gesture of reverence towards living people without it seeming melodramatic or pretentious. On a visit to the great temple at Srirangam, he and Ella were debarred entry to the precincts because they were regarded, as is the custom, as ritually impure Europeans. In the ensuing ripple of public embarrassment, she said, a little girl, who had been an attentive bystander, spotted some spiritual quality behind the crestfallen expression on Thompson's face. Unprompted, she approached him without a trace of self-consciousness, gazed intently at him and, in a solemn gesture, placed a garland round his neck. Transported by the rapture of the moment, Thompson prostrated in the street before the child, addressing her as the deity from whose presence within the temple he had seemingly been excluded.

On other occasions, so his distinguished Brahmin friend, Dr. Ranganathan, told me, in the days of strict orthodox decorum, when an Englishman in a cotton *lungi* was a very rare sight, Thompson often conspicuously disregarded conventional behaviour, particularly with regard to touching high-caste Brahmins. On a visit to the temple of Kanya Kumari at Cape Comorin, he and Ranganathan were walking down a lane in front of the temple gateway. The street was thronged with devout orthodox Brahmins coming to and from worship at the temple. They were thus in a state of ritual purity. Thompson caught sight of a young brahmin boy of radiant beauty, a tonsured temple *brahmachari* conditioned to disregard all strangers and most particularly to avoid physical proximity with cast-less Europeans. But Thompson at once recognised in him a *vigraha* of the deity. In full view of a potentially hostile crowd, he crossed the street, approached the youth, gracefully offered *namaskaram* with folded hands and defying both custom and propriety—with a slow, deliberate gesture plain for all to see, caressed the boy's arm and addressed him as the deity in human form. All movement in the busy street instantly ceased and silence fell. Watching with alarm from the other side of the street, Ranganathan expected that Thompson's rash move would provoke violent hostility. The boy responded, however, with imperturbable dignity and the disdain of the priestly bystanders evaporated. The Englishman was hailed as a man of God who had acted from spontaneous feelings of *prema*—spiritual love.

Drawing on precedents in the Sufi, sahajin and medieval Christian traditions, Thompson hesitantly, with great trepidation, felt his way along a razor's edge of obvious risk towards a mode of relationship towards young Hindus and Muslims which, though he saw it all as quite simple and natural, goes by the rather pompous name of theophanism. According to Sufi tradition, the Spirit manifests itself in a physical form which the 'Active Imagination' transmutes into a theophanic figure. A real individual person then becomes, like the Beloved of the Christian *Fedeli d'amore*, like Beatrice for Dante, the real Beloved who manifests himself or herself. Had it not been for the advice of the Jnani, Thompson's wide reading on such matters would probably have earned him no more than the unconscious recasting of his sexual desires into something merely religious, a sentimental and ethically worthless pose.

A group of Sufis had attached themselves to the circle round the Jnani and through them Thompson became acquainted with texts by one of the supreme geniuses of Sufism, Ibn 'Arabi, on the 'dialectic of love': 'It is He who in every beloved is manifested to the gaze of each lover...and none other than He is adored, for it is impossible to adore a being without conceiving the Godhead in that being... So it is with love: a being does not truly love anyone other than his Creator.' So Thompson came to view his most intense and intimate relationships almost literally "in the light of another world". Neither literalism nor allegory, he considered this way of seeing personal relationships—a function of Imagination—as kindred to those of both the Sufis and William Blake. For example, it is through the organ of trans-sensory perception—Active Imagination—that the Sufi perceives the dullness of the ego and how it may be polished until it becomes a mirror of the attributes and actions of the Beloved. This Imagination transmutes sensory objects and living creatures into symbols. The Active Imagination simultaneously retains the reality of the person and of the symbol. It depends not on fidelity to the laws of logic, but on fidelity to the service of love. A distinguished contemporary Sufi scholar, Henry Corbin, has explained Ibn 'Arabi's subtle and elusive dialectic of love with the most delicate sympathy: "In the nature of mystic love this dialectic discovers the encounter between sensory, physical love and spiritual love. Beauty is the supreme theophany, but it reveals itself as such only to a love which transfigures it. Mystic love is the religion of Beauty, because Beauty is the secret of theophanies and because as such it is the power which transfigures. Mystic love is as far from negative asceticism as it is from the aestheticism or libertinism of the possessive instinct.' (Henry Corbin, *Creative Imagination in the Sufism of Ibn 'Arabi*, Princeton, 1969, p. 98.) Corbin draws a clear distinction between mystic love and 'simple natural love which, since it is interested only in itself, strives only for the possession of what it looks upon in a given object.' It is this crucial distinction which gave Thompson cause to examine his conscience most rigorously, giving rise to much agonised self-scrutiny in his journal when, at the end of 1943, he began to focus on the true nature of his own feelings—particularly in the wake of his *nirvikalpa samadhi*. 'The divine lover', says Ibn 'Arabi, 'is spirit without body; the purely physical lover is body without spirit; the spiritual lover That is, the mystic lover, possesses spirit and body.' Once again—an echo of Rimbaud's credo. As we shall see, Thompson's aphoristic reflections bear a close resemblance to this view of Ibn 'Arabi. Incidentally, but not relating to the foregoing matters here, Thompson did some very difficult translation from French of an important Ibn 'Arabi text originating from the Guénon circle in Cairo while he was at the Jnani's ashram.

Ultimately, Thompson recognised that sexual relationship, as distinct from rapture and reverence towards the beloved, was unsatisfactory for him. He would say that he'd gone beyond all that, so could only play mental games of cold, lilaic playfulness, a kind of mental over-emphasis that he recognised as damaging both to himself and his partner. But he was far too scrupulous and sensitive to relapse into mere sensual indulgence and libertinism. He could only break this vicious circle at the level of poetic imagination, as in his major long poem, *Black Angel.*

Humanism, Dharma, Tapas

During the early years in India, Thompson began to face a challenge which every Western individual who is a sincere spiritual seeker has to deal with sooner or later. The same problem arises in all spiritual and mystical traditions, but in India, due to an integral holistic system of social ethics woven together into a single tapestry with social and psychological consequences, a Westerner finds it particularly intractable—and likewise his or her teachers in India will find it to be the most obstructive feature of their pupils' spiritual development.

A Westerner usually experiences it first as a certain felt indifference on the part of Indians towards his or her singularity as a person, an impersonality, a form of disconcertingly detached realism. It can easily be mistaken for a sudden break in the customary courteous manner of the Indian, a callousness, and is experienced as a direct threat to the *ego*, a feeling that what is being disregarded is precisely that which the individual from the west holds most dear: who one IS. At issue here is what Thompson called 'the fulcrum of all problems'—more precisely the Western humanistic ego. This is the stumbling block against which so many have fruitlessly vented all their futile rage and frustration. It is even the point of no return in the very area of modern Western psychological exploration that is commonly regarded as most sympathetic to Indian forms of spirituality, Jungian psychoanalysis. Jung, and all 'Jungians', insist on acceptance of the Ego as the fundamental basis of psychoanalytical investigation. Nothing, either of Indian life or of Thompson's struggles with it can be understood if we do not take into account acute and deep-seated cross-cultural differences in the perspective on this very problem. It is also made more acute by the Western prior assumption that the particular strength and excellence of Western approaches to other cultures than their own is *intellectual mastery*. Sooner or later, the Westerner, confronted by this alterity of Indian modalities, and the difficulties attendant upon any study of another culture, will fall back upon the ultimate redoubt of certainty: intellectual mastery of a problem is the best way to solve it. This is why centuries of conditioning have ensured that the Western position is so formidably well-defended. In the final analysis, this is rooted in the Western ego structure.

It is an inescapable fact that the attitude towards the ego is, within the Indian context, related to all human conduct both collective and individual, with ramifications extending into every cultural and spiritual manifestation. It lies at the root of all human motivation. It is the very antithesis of all that the West has come to associate with the precious tissue of humanistic culture, with its concomitant compassion, aesthetic sensitivity and anguish in the face of the Human Tragedy. This Indian antithesis to humanism—in its prime—Thompson located, for the most part, in the past. He regarded it as positive, calling now for a fresh surge of development, or repossession. He gives it the Nietzschean name *trans-humanism*, and occasionally, looking into the future, foresees the advent beyond that too, of a *new* humanism.

Strictly speaking, the term *Hindu realism* is a wholly Western concept. Ask a well-educated Hindu what he calls his 'faith' and he will answer: the Sanatana Dharma. The rock upon which transhumanism rests in India is the Dharma, the divine moral order. It is by *dharma* that the social structure is knitted together; and it is the same *dharma*, in a secondary, role, which gives continuity and structure to the lives (the plural is important) of the individual. At the level of the social collective (a complex system involving many caste communities) every individual is a member of a caste, the latter determined by the natural consequences of *karma*—the residual effects of former lives. Within the implacable tissue of the universal *dharma* the life of the individual is viewed as participation, in a distinctly formal manner, in a vast interplay of roles, of assumed masks. From a certain lofty perspective, this interplay is seen as the *lila* of God, enjoyment of global play within phenomenal reality—maya—the magic phantasmagoria which is essentially illusory—in the sense that what flickers on the movie screen is illusory.

According to the divine law of *dharma* one is not free to choose to which caste one belongs or to diverge from the code of conduct proper to one's caste, and one's particular stage in life proper to one's age (or life stage). *Dharma* is not so much a prison or a strait jacket as the structural framework within which considerable latitude is afforded—so long as one rightly perceives the ultimate destiny of individuality: perception of the ego as an illusion; and of the nature of the true Self, the *Atman* as identical with the Divine Ground, the Brahman. In a fine exposition of *dharma* Heinrich Zimmer writes:

> 'And since this circumstance not only determines to the last detail the regulations for one's public and private conduct, but also represents (according to this all-inclusive and pervasive, unyielding pattern of integration) the real ideal of one's present natural character, one's concern as a judging and acting entity must be only to meet every life problem in a manner befitting the role one plays. Whereupon the two aspects of the temporal event—the subjective and the objective—will be joined exactly, and the individual eliminated as a third, intrusive factor. He will then bring into manifestation not the temporal accident of his own personality, but the vast, impersonal, cosmic law, and so will be, not faulty, but a perfect glass: anonymous and self-effacing. For by the rigorous practice of prescribed virtues one actually can efface oneself, dissolving eventually the last quirk of impulse and personal resistance—thus gaining release from the little boundary of the personality and absorption in the boundlessness of universal being. Dharma is ...the way through which to pass into the transcendental consciousness and bliss of the purest spiritual Self-existence.' (*Philosophies of India*, p. 153, New York, 1951.)

The idea of *dharma* is definitely one Indian concept to have had a profoundly challenging impact on Thompson's thinking, particularly in regard to the manner in which he saw his own role as poet, as writer, and particularly as writer of his journal. This was the razor's edge, no doubt about it. Poetry and religion are a revelation. But the poetic world dispenses with divine authority, at least in the Western world. This is why the Jnani ordered the total destruction of everything Thompson had written. Poetry, aphorisms and journals are the revelation of himself that man makes to himself. The religious word, on the contrary, aims to reveal a mystery that is, by definition, *other*. That is why Rimbaud said of the source whence his poetry came: 'Je est un autre'—I is an other. Thompson is on safer ground when he reminds himself in his journal that it would be a deviation from his path if he were to embroil himself in what he calls 'the human pathos': acceding to the illusory function of the ego as determining all individual activity. By 'pathos' Thompson means the false sentimentalism of the humanistic ego. He writes on humanism in *Mirror to the Light*:

> 'All humanistic sensibility depends for its perfect intelligence on a

> certain capacity for resourceful self-pathos, a continual self-dramatisation in terms of it, a capacity for *volte-faces*, quick-change, which continually exploit and renew it, by a kind of usury, *exchanging* the ego for this particular kind of experience. Hence the drama of friends and lovers, the mise-en-scene of complex mental-emotional reactions. The transhumanistic existence, in its solitude, is free from sentimentality or the perverse indulgence of inhumanity only first of all in perfect humility, and in the end in perfect love, towards all. In other words, its sensibility is completely disinterested and for humanism this is a scandal; it does not obey the rules, it settles for nothing it does not want to gain, nor aim to give, enjoyment.
> —*Mirror to the Light, London*, 1984, p. 79.

It should be clear from this that Thompson by no means rejects what we feel to be an essential feature of human existence and of everything which has the pulse of human feeling and concern for others: the warmth of love. But to gauge the temper of his particular kind of warmth we should make a brief excursion away from ethical issues to yoga and consider what is called *tapas*. This is a strange archaic and important word of ancient usage, sometimes translated as 'austerities', which literally means 'heat', to designate the ardour of self-discipline, the annealing fire of inner sacrifice. *Tapas* is to all spiritual effort (*sadhana*) what fire is to the metal-worker. Its most archaic layer of meaning relates to the idea of creative energy attained through the magic power of heat by deliberate resort to sweating, and not so dissimilar from the thinking behind the Native American practice of the sweat bath. In alchemy, *tapas* is the heat of the inner furnace for the transmutation of the human soul. In yoga, *tapas* becomes a technique of holding the breath to achieve transmutation of physical energy. In the more conventional context, it is *tapas* which gives Thompson's aphoristic style of writing its ardent vertical thrust. By *tapas* he seeks to 'overpass' humanism and the human pathos to attain 'love towards all'. The astringency so characteristic of Thompson's whole demeanor is visible evidence of *tapas*. His fiery 'tapasic' temperament helped him to inject into his equivalent to *sadhana* a psychologically and emotionally intense form of *tapasya*. This was polarised by its extreme opposite: 'the hell of pure cold madness and self-punishment which our refusing or incapacity for surrender makes itself endure...I have somehow exhausted or remain outside (on the level where at present I am, at least) the possibility of a human (individual) love-affair that this can only be another *contrivance*—ritual, *tantra*, cold, scientific, inhuman, yet without real faith, even, in the inhuman Object symbolised, —Or faith so real it continually burns the means, the ritual, away?'

Consider the acrimonious nature of the discussions between Thompson and the Jnani. On the one hand, the two of them had always had a kind of mutual understanding that, for Thompson, poetry is its own authority. It simply could not be otherwise, considering that he viewed Poetry to be the archetype of perfect action, and therefore not merely a literary issue (as Hackett recognises was also the case for Rimbaud). On the other, it was to do with the 'Thompson package deal'—that what he did, or attempted to do, with his pen, since it aspired to deal only with the divine, did not conflict with his relationship to the Jnani. But as the Jnani repeatedly affirmed, this meant that there was never any question of his becoming a guru to Thompson in the same strict sense as he was guru to all his other disciples. One gets the impression from accounts of the later private talks with the Jnani in his journal, that the bond of deep mutual love and respect between the two men was manifest at a level of *trance* more than at a level of *discourse* with devotees. This was a source of confusion—I believe for both men, not just Thompson—and that the Jnani gave him a unique and extraordinary Sanskrit name, also in a trance, in an effort to resolve the contradiction. But when the contradiction itself conflicted with what the Jnani expounded in public, Thompson challenged him in such a way that, to put it crudely, he 'gave the game away'—namely, revealed that he was treated differently by the Jnani to the annoyance, and eventually the inflamed jealousy, of those who held the purse-strings. They too felt they had just as much right to special treatment as Thompson.

I think that here we come up against a fundamental problem of all mystical teachers, which is summarised by the Buddha as : 'The Truth can not be told'. And as Thompson himself said, anything less from the lips of the fully Illuminated has to go by the positively-meant term, Pure Hypocrisy. There is a whole field of speculative Buddhist study which addresses the Wittgensteinian problem: Of What the Buddha Could Not Speak. Thompson spends a good deal of time on the brink of literally ineffable experience. He would have had a fine old time talking to Wittgenstein, a man to whom he bears, in several respects, a close and revealing resemblance. I like to imagine them both meeting in their next life to chant mantras and falling about in helpless laughter.

It was never Thompson's intention to live in India in order to 'study Hinduism', certainly not to 'become a Hindu'—both aspirations being common amongst foreigner 'Indophiles' of his acquaintance. Hinduism was solely instrumental in furthering his needs as a seeker. He wrote more about the Christ than he ever wrote about Shiva or Krishna. His principal teachers, besides the Jnani, Ramana Maharshi and Sri Aurobindo, were

Pascal, Blake, Yeats, Meister Eckhart and Nietzsche. He was proud of his Western heritage and never tried to conceal it by wearing a mask of Hinduism. His non-technical vocabulary, developed prior to his arrival in India, was a kind of basic *lingua franca*, universal in its unpretentious simplicity. So by resorting to such terms as 'Western Identity', or by confining the man to a Hindu context, we loose sight of the real core of the problem. For the matter to which he devotes so intense a scrutiny, finally and precisely, rests upon a single issue: What exactly is the status of his writing? Particularly since there is no language with which to overleap the gulf between the positions in which the two impassioned men were entrenched.

Surely it would have been more sensible for all concerned had the Jnani got a grip on the situation, particularly in view of Thompson's true worth —instead of petulant refusal 'to have anything more to do with him', as he put it to Ella— simply to send him away for a period of some years' *tapasya*, to work upon himself alone, as he always had done with unswerving concentration throughout the seven years of their association. As it was, the Jnani had so contrived this peremptory dismissal that it would continue to fester in Thompson's mind until the last months before he died, when he at last freed himself, characteristically, in a series of dreams.

Conversation with Raja Rao on Lewis Thompson

Raja Rao was a celebrated Indian novelist. He was a disciple of the Jnani and came to know Thompson quite well, mostly by watching him closely at the ashram. Like everybody else there, R.R. adopted a very patronising attitude to what he termed 'Thompson's spiritual problem', which he grandly proposed to explain to me one day. He never did, considering me to be without any insight in such matters. In a letter to R.R. c. 1943, Thompson wrote the following:

> 'In spite of your atavistic Brahmanhood we seem to be moving, intellectually, in opposite directions. My whole work since I came to India has been to analyse away, in and for myself, on all planes, in all its ramifications, the Western romantic humanism, that sentimentalism of the ego for which the given individuality is something central. This might be seen as a completion and fulfilment of the transhumanistic objectivity which Rimbaud could only deny but not transcend, which within the humanist limits brought him to despair. And this is why I have not yet reached the stage of dealing with the Indian tradition, have not read the Upanishads even in translation (have in this sphere only perhaps a certain direct intuition) nor

learned any Indian language, but am neither here nor in Europe. Yet it is more and more evidently into a transhumanistic realism that I am to emerge.'

The following notes were taken immediately after a meeting I had with Raja Rao in New Delhi, 1983. The frequent "he" in these notes refers througout to Lewis Thompson.

He would tremble with intensity of emotion. An extremely emotional man. He would talk in a very quick-moving way.

He could be extremely short tempered but also very warm and gentle. When he lost his temper he would withdraw.

In 1938-9 he would sleep on the streets of Madras.

He carried a pack of his bedroll on his back. Only two pairs of clothing, always immaculately white and spotless. He carried only two books with him as he moved around South India—Rimbaud and Valery.

He was very interested in the psychology and sexuality of women, and also interested in Tantra.

He was highly intellectual and this definitely obscured, or obtruded on, his spiritual luminosity.

He looked like a sannyasi.

He would ask questions in an extremely oblique and subtle way.

Sri Krishna Menon (Sri Atmananda Guru) was absolutely devoted to him. The row was over the whole issue of acceptance of the guru.

His translations of Valery were very beautiful. Rilke said that the most difficult thing to do is to write good prose.

He was a genius in the deepest, most essential way.

When I last saw him (at our last meeting) I said "I am going where you ought to go, Trivandrum", and he said, "Oh well, I'm going to Benares" (implying that he was going there to die).

[Raja Rao said this was 1948, but he may be mistaken and the date was probably 1949 and the place Bombay. There may be an entry in his journal which can be checked.]

Ella Maillart and Thompson went to consult a palmist and astrologer, who said that Thompson would marry. The palmist ignored Ella, but then she held out her hand. I remember this moment as being extremely touching—and she asked if she would marry. It was like a cry of desparation from the soul. For she was ugly, predominantly masculine, had short cropped hair. And of course he replied in the negative.

A Poet's India

Man's most ancient belief, like the earliest memories of the individual, is his identity with the world—the indivisibility of thought and life, consciousness and being, being and existence, object and name—the primordial unity. Poetry is a means of inner liberation from alienated consciousness; it invites us to be that which we are. Through poetry we discover once again the way back to this unity of consciousness and existence. Poetry is both a revelation of our condition and the creation of an image which 'opens up to us the possibility of being that is intrinsic in every birth; it recreates man and makes him assume his true condition....' (Octavio Paz). Though poetry and religion have a common origin, for Thompson it is the divergence of religion into belief, system, interpretation, where he experiences tension in his attitude towards all traditions of wisdom. The first signs of it are to be found in his boyhood, when he first turned towards Eastern modalities to free himself of false religion. Later, he found in Blake the precursor of that modernist tendency which was to reach its crisis in poets like Rimbaud —the striving of poetry to become pure, spontaneous action, the poetic society a kingdom of heaven on earth. Blake's contemporary, Novalis, for example, proclaimed that poetry is the original religion of mankind, religion merely practical poetry. This movement for the conversion of society into a community based on the poetic word had a formative influence on the young Thompson.

But poets draw strength, in the first place, from themselves; to sustain their individual vision they are involved in the kind of inner search which calls for a special kind of energy or inner force qualitatively distinct from both active will and passive receptivity. Thompson sees these inspirational resources as best commanded through yoga, in the broadest sense of the word, irrespective of any direct and conscious exploitation of specific techniques which we associate with the Indian body of tradition known by that name. In Eastern tradition, intrinsic to this harkening of the poet to being, is the deeply held conviction that the reality of things is to be found in their utter nothingness. In India, tradition holds that experience of Nothingness, the Void, *sunyata*, or absolute emptiness is not threatening but, on the contrary, a benediction. To anyone for whom the teaching of Christ is as significant as for Thompson there is likely to be at least a residual attachment to some notion of the substantiality of being, and with it the concomitant notions of the ego's reality and the power of individual will. A poet from the West who admires Heidegger and who tries, in India, to affirm the identity of absolute emptiness with the being of things in the world will encounter a good deal of resistance from both Europeans and Indians. He must steer a course between passionate activity and patient surrender, and plumb the enigma contained in such cryptic sayings as this: "What is here is nowhere. What is not here is everywhere.' Thompson's attempt through his 'integral yoga' to find being in existence is not, fundamentally, in opposition to all classical Indian thought, but it is contrary to the spirit of Vedanta and, I think it would be correct to say, contrary to Indian common sense if the attempt is made to translate it into a philosophy of action. However, it *is* the attitude of the sahajin and whenever Thompson was challenged on the issue it roused him to passionate argument. For here he took his last stand as poet and refused to surrender an inch of his ground, not only to the teaching of his master, but to the very notion that 'surrender' is the sole condition for perception of being's Nothingness. I think it possible, for all the storms which blew hot and blew cold, that Thompson cared not one jot for these redoubtable abstractions; what did matter was the heat of emotion that experience of the paradox provoked in him—and impelled him ever forward to perfect Presence, perfect Poetry. The Christ is his Supreme Poet and so too does the *Gita* name Krishna.

He felt called upon to justify his stance as poet and writer on numerous occasions:

> 'As Shakespeare says, the poet "is of imagination all compact". When I say I am *by nature* a poet, I am not indulging in a fancy theory, I am simply stating the very evident fact that for me imagination is the central mode which intellect must *serve*. (In saying 'He is really a yogin', the Jnani was pointing out the same thing, for yoga uses the same medium as imagination does—the psychic). The Jnani relates poetry, emotion and *bhakti*; I relate poetry with imagination and yoga: my emotion, being in this context dynamic, is passion; the psychic vehicle is the same, but it must be clear enough by now that the Jnani's explanation of me as a man of the heart in his sense does not cover all the facts. My intellectual justification of this primacy of Poetry is in essence and in writing, complete—has only to be worked out more fully in experience: this justification is not only my 'intellectual', but, in all spheres, my personal ('spiritual') work. If the 'Heart' is the organ of something beyond the 'head', Imagination in

my sense can represent what is beyond intellect; but in the one case imagination is passive, receptive, feminine and appears as emotion, in the other it is active, expansive, masculine and appears as passion. The bhakti is not concerned with transformation as such: he grows big with the god.

When I say I do not *believe* in anything, it is because in me Imagination is prior to the need of belief and so powerful that it entirely exceeds it. But such Imagination continues, is sustained, as passion, as belief sustains itself as faith.

And who without profound Imagination can understand the infinite subtlety of passion?—its daring, delicate modesty, its capacity to stand with endless ingenuity at its own opposite—the mad generosity by which it overleaps and has forestalled every kind of understanding.

Yet, from the opposite side, whenever force arises I have to damp it. All stamina is spent in remaining weak because otherwise I can only be strong for myself and that does not interest me. I have to speak with *au's* and *um's*, with crow-cries, not with words, for all my words are too direct, too passionate, too extravagant. I put myself in the wrong, in dullness and feebleness, because I know none values, but all fear, a passion that does not respect the human. If Shakespeare had not respected the human, would he not have been more mad and terrible and full of love than the lovely Beethoven, whose trumpet, in the end, became too intense for hearing?

Nothing is more impersonal than passion. Because I thwart and cover it, I am left with this sickliness of *eloquence*.'

It is the phrase 'passion that does not respect the human' which offers a clue to the peculiar incandescent temper of Thompson as poetic writer. Poetry in this broad sense is the prime resource whereby he goes beyond himself to find out who and what he is. This *furor poeticus* is full of perils and exaltations, the vertiginous course towards the unilluminated abyss to discover that which was hidden by alienated consciousness. The poet looks into the entrails of experience and discovers the unknown lost half of existence in the night of life and death. In the passionate storm of this search the poet seems possessed by violent and excessive forces, uncertain whether it is he himself or some ineluctible power of the supernatural that sways him. 'If we let ourselves fall into the abyss', says Heidegger, 'we do not go tumbling into emptiness. We fall upward, to a height. We must learn to hear and to attend more closely to that language which makes of it an abode for the being of mortals'. The rules of good and evil do not prevail in the sacred realm, and Thompson likes to quote Meister Eckhart to this effect: 'God is neither good nor true.' It is useless to seek reasons for this breaking and entering, to psychologise, to moralise, for such precipitate ascents and descents carry the seeker into that other world—treasure-house of redemptive images which show us the abyss translucent.

Perhaps Indians held Thompson in respect because they favoured a certain *quality of concentration* that is indeed yogic:

> 'By yoga I mean what is entirely non-religious, non-metaphysical and non-mystical, which is rather the completion of Art wherever it can be completed. My word for it has been Technique. Thus yoga is "spiritual" only as will be the complete Actuality of the Spirit. Yoga is thus Transformation into the "Divine" and of the "Divine" into everything.'

One can readily agree with Thompson's claim that writing is his own form of yoga. He invents a personal form of yoga for himself, and this includes the attempt to command, with complete realism, his own physical state at any time, its vitality or its fatigue. Exhaustion, shattered nerves, just as much as moments of heightened tone, are deliberately used as leverage—imprinting the sheer density of his prose with immediate traces of his physical condition and sensuous response to the environment in his 'will to the Spirit':

> 'The sole effective presence of the "Absolute" is concentration—perfect sensuality. Thus concentration may be defined as the application of perfect inner leisure or of perfect devotion to God. But all definition is metaphysical and concentration is magical, not metaphysical.'

During the first three or four years after his arrival in India, Thompson was hard at work on two research projects which entailed periods of intensive reading, as well as 'feeling his way' into India's living spiritual culture. His friend the library scientist, Dr. Ranganathan, recalls how he became intrigued by the young Englishman who would always be first into the library in Madras, and last out at night, never taking a break, even for a midday meal. The fruit of this period were two fairly massive bundles of notes on 'Art and Expression' and on philosophy. This was apprentice work and never completed. But it provided a form of anchorage while he explored, both outwardly and inwardly, the effects of a powerful way of life; this entailed journeys that carried him far from the beaten track—again, both into an inner world and out to the major sacred places and ashrams of South India. He moved around a great deal, but destroyed almost everything he wrote by way of description, the remaining content, by 1937, retaining no more than a bare outline of his movements up till the time when he first met the Jnani. This section of the present volume opens with this itinerary, exactly as noted down, and it reveals only the bare gist of the experiences he went through at the time. The sheer intensity of his inner states, the heightening of consciousness in dream, vision and reverie—the direct consequence of the extraordinary people and places encountered during his periodic wanderings—made him an astringent critic of what he wrote.

It was Rimbaud who had taught him to hold back, for he was only too well aware that the language in which he recorded his experiences was contradictory to the living quick. At most, he wrote verse of a stark and taut kind, but felt most at ease in the aphoristic form, which was at least congruent with the extreme fugitive nature of his insight, as much as he could handle in the white heat of a moment's inspiration.

However, he did preserve a number of important fragments of prose, all of which are included here: short lyrical descriptions of landscape that mirror some inner state, accounts of several experiments with drugs, some encounters with remarkable people, and the development of a way to record his more memorable dreams. The latter is of some importance to his later work in his journal, as I have examined above at greater length. But this set of fragments from the early Indian years is really a prelude to keeping a journal.

A characteristic of Thompson's prose is its unexpected rhythm, avoidance of the obvious, and extreme density—all calculated to retard the pace of reading and ensure adequate reflection on each completed thought. He springs surprises round every corner, contrives to postpone one's sense of the direction in which a thought is heading until the very last possible moment. Like a game of hide-and-seek with somebody else doing the concealment, we get 'warmer' or 'colder' with each opened cupboard, depending on our attention to his cryptic signals.

Dross

As Thompson admitted, description of one's life in a journal is *dross*. At first sight, this may sound like a huge and blundering contradiction. There is, of course, a marvellous acrobatic energy to the rigorous exclusion of irrelevant verbiage which courses through the abundant wordage of Thompson's copious literary papers. But this is no more than a matter of literary style—something in which, again and again, he emphatically declares he has no interest. 'A journal', he says, and for that matter, aphoristic reflections, a poem, and especially letters with their convention of descriptive expression between friends, 'can be sustained only for the sake of, or in tension with, the ego. Otherwise, there is transformation.' There lies the central challenge he poses to himself, both in relation to others and to his very existence itself. Writing is nothing to Thompson if it is not instrumental: his means to Action—*marga*. If writing 'is not a means of absolute sincerity produced by the need of it, it is inevitably complacent, egotistic, and therefore incompletely intelligent. At best, he regards his journal as a method of recording lapses and vacillations from his prime objective, 'the magic of Transformation'. It is but a fractional shift in emphasis that he then explains further what direction this Transformation takes: 'the satisfaction of the most organically direct and continuous will to growth towards the fullness of Reality'. And synonyms of 'fullness', used even more often, are Wholeness, Completeness.

"Intelligence is complete only in freedom from the ego'. Even so, 'it may entirely exhaust egoism as a scepticism', and 'shows the ego as *what a man is not*, shows its complete accidentality'.

Thompson is tireless in his effort to drill into his own consciousness the fact that the ego is a loose cog, it drifts around in helpless and complacent passivity, it misses the point of what life is all about. He is disarmingly straightforward as to why he bothers to write a journal at all:

> Rereading of this journal in the sense of the will to Reality can more and more discourage relapsings and build up a habit of fortification against them. The sole justifiable object of the journal is such a full acknowledgement of mistakes and failures and conscious progressive integration of their lesson.

Given that writing is Thompson's yoga of transformation, *description*, which panders to and flatters the ego 'is external, partial, perpetuates some division of consciousness, represents something incompletely possessed and understood that cannot be symbolised or commanded by consciousness as a whole. Description confuses the symbol.' He knows that there is no saying anything in description but the picturesque, no saying something about something and getting it exactly right. There's more to description than sentences. It overflows thought and eventually proves uncontainable, as he realises when he tries to describe the multilayered intricacy of Benares. But when he describes barrack room life during his brief conscription, he turns a relatively lighthearted account into a lilaic and humorous moment of magical luminosity: 'O, Man is indestructible, Ancient, Marvellous.'

Now, some of the most affectingly pellucid and simple passages in the Journal are to be found in those letters he wrote expressly for his mother which he copied into the journal. Mrs. Thompson wanted *description* most of all. Everything *else* was dross! So he tries to imbue such passages with a sensuous metaphorical imagism.

Similarly, there was a phase in his poetic output when he gave the *Word* an iconic function directly related to his yogic experiences. On the face of it, these poems are extremely dry, taut and abstract. But *Word* plays a role in his imagination as do the idols, vigrahas and ritual bronzes in many of his dreams: for *Word* read *Murti*, the Sanskrit for a temple image of a deity. In the months following his experience of nirvikalpa samadhi at Malakkarai, many entries in his journal acquire an almost hallucinatory aura of psychic concussion.

I see a connection between the dismay and distress which momentarily overcame his family when, at my prompting, they recalled with difficulty memories of Lewis where his behaviour, or his writing, seemed to arise from his spontaneous tendency to imbue whatever he said to them with mystifying *en-strangement* (as in "enthrallment"). This term derives from a modern Russian scholar, Viktor Shklovsky, who demonstrates a certain ability amongst writers to give words breathtaking immediacy. Thompson's brand of en-strangement in letters to his family was definitely not appreciated. Somewhere in its collective psyche, perhaps the culture, the society and its religious faith, the unfamiliar style and alien cast of thought were shocking; they did not feel comfortable with a certain kind of words—Lewis' kind.

Perhaps there was nameless grievance for what their Prodigal Son did by leaving home and going far away to write down words that were so strange, so inexplicable, so unlike anything ever said at home, and so unlike any words they so desperately hoped he would write.

When I read all the tender and beautiful things Lewis wrote to his mother that seemed to go unnoticed, I see a dramatisation of the very thing which makes the writer Lewis Thompson so extraordinary and unexpected. Indeed he is completely unexpectable. He confounds all likelihood. And he knows this with every word he writes, with ineffable sorrow. It seems the only way he can obtain forgiveness—from God, from mother, family and friends, is to endow words with the alchemy of magic Transformation. He simply could not allow his words to fool around in the back yard, or to go careening off to dance a merry-go-round in the meadow, but to tell tales in the firelight.

'Let me with words come close.'

Thompson, L. and Bhattacharya, Deben, "Songs from Chandidas," *New India Annual 1948.*, Government of India Publications, New Delhi, 1948. 3 pp.

Thompson, L., "Benaras,""Bitterness All," two poems from *Penguin New Writing 35.* pp. 79–80, Harmondsworth, Middlesex, 1948.

Thompson, L. and Bhattacharya, Deben, translations of Chandidas, *Two Themes in Indian Poetry*, Encounter 6, London, March 1954. pp. 42 –47.

Thompson, L., "Black Angel," "Rose," two poems from *Atlantic Book of British and American Poetry*, Edith Sitwell, Ed., 2 Vols., pp 869–872, Little Brown, New York, 1958; Gollancz, London, 1959.

Thompson, L., *Mirror to the Light: Reflections on Consciouness and Experience*, edited with an introduction by Richard Lannoy, Coventure, 1984, Shaftsbury, Dorset, Sigo in USA.

Thompson, L., *Black Sun: The Collected Poems of Lewis Thompson*, edited with an afterword by Richard Lannoy, foreword by Andrew Harvey, Hohm Press, Prescott AZ, 2001.

About the Editor

Born in 1928, Richard Lannoy is one of those Englishmen who lost his heart to India and has communicated extensively about it's people, language and customs since 1953. A visual artist and writer, he is the author of the following titles, *The Speaking Tree: A Study of Indian Culture and Society*, 1971 (in print today from the Oxford University Press); *India: People and Places*, 1955; *Eye of Love: Erotic Indian Sculpture*, 1975; *Anandamayi: Her Life and Wisdom*, 2000; *Benares Seen from Within*, 1999, a photo-journalist record of one of the great spiritual cities of the world.

Lannoy's 1953 finding in Benares of Lewis Thompson's handwritten literary archive opened to Lannoy, and to the world through Lannoy's work, a unique account of a young Englishman's intense spiritual and artistic life abroad in India.

> "The experience of dipping into manuscripts meticulously dated day by day and indexed, without knowing the barest details of Thompson's wandering life for seventeen years in India prior to his untimely death at the age of forty, was one of the most extraordinary experiences of my life."

From this archive, Lannoy has edited *Mirror to the Light: Reflections on Consciousness and Experience*, by Lewis Thompson and *Black Sun, The Collected Poems of Lewis Thompson*, 2001. He continues his work with this archive as he edits Volume II of the Thompson journals.

Trained as a painter, Richard Lannoy was a founding staff member of the Institute of Contemporary Art (ICA) in London. He founded the Independent Group of the ICA. He was a curator of the first great London retrospective exhibition of Henri Cartier-Bresson. As an artist he exhibited at the Bath International Festival and the John Moore Exhibition at the Walker Art Gallery in Liverpool.

As a freelance photographer he served on assignment for the United Nations photographing the Palestine refugee camps. He married the Indian novelist and UNESCO official, Violeta Dias, and was for many years director of the European branch of Friends World College (Long Island) in Norfolk, England.

Richard Lannoy lives in Lymington on the South Coast of England and has just completed the first volume of his autobiography.

Lightning Source UK Ltd.
Milton Keynes UK
06 April 2010

152377UK00001B/41/A

9 780971 78061